Michael Jackson:

For The Record

2nd Edition – Revised & Expanded

Chris Cadman & Craig Halstead

Bright Pen

Visit us online at www.authorsonline.co.uk

A Bright Pen Book

Second Edition

ISBN 978-07552-04778-6

Authors OnLine Ltd
19 The Cinques
Gamlingay, Sandy
Bedfordshire SG19 3NU
England

This book is also available in e-book format, details of which are available at www.authorsonline.co.uk

MICHAEL JACKSON
29th August 1958 ~ 25th June 2009

*'My brother, the legendary King of Pop, Michael Jackson,
passed away onThursday June 25th 2009 at 2.26pm.
It is believed he suffered cardiac arrest in his home.'*

Jermaine Jackson

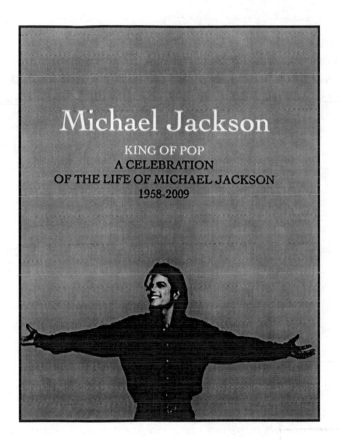

Here are just a few of the hundreds of tributes paid to Michael, in the hours and days following his sudden and tragic death:

*'To you, Michael is an icon.
To us, Michael is family,
and he will forever live in our hearts.'*

Janet Jackson

'I am shocked beyond words.
It's like a dream – a bad dream.
This cannot be. How can Michael Jackson not be here?
As a kid, Michael was always beyond his years. He had a knowingness
about him that was incredible. Michael was, and will remain,
one of the greatest entertainers that ever lived. He was exceptional, artistic
and original. He gave the world his heart and soul through his music.'

Berry Gordy

'I'm totally devastated.
I just don't have the words. Divinity brought our souls together and allowed
us to do what we could through the 80s. To this day that music is played
in every corner of the world, and the reason is because he had it all: talent,
grace and professionalism. I've lost a little brother today
and part of my soul has gone with him.'

Quincy Jones

'I can't stop crying, this is too sudden and shocking.
I am unable to imagine this. My heart is hurting.
I am in prayer for his kids and the family.'

Diana Ross

'My heart... my mind... are broken.
I loved Michael with all my soul and I can't imagine life without him.
We had so much in common and we had such loving fun together.'

Elizabeth Taylor

'I am so very sad and confused with every possible emotion.
I am heartbroken for his children, who I know were everything to him,
and for his family. This is such a massive loss on so
many levels, words fail me.'

Lisa Marie Presley

'It's so sad and shocking.
I feel privileged to have hung out and worked with Michael.
He was a massively talented boy-man with a gentle soul.
His music will be remembered forever and my memories
of our time together will be happy ones.'

Sir Paul McCartney

'I can't stop crying over the sad news.
I've always admired Michael Jackson – the world has lost
one of its greats, but his music will live on forever.
My heart goes out to his three children and other members.'
of his family. God bless.'

Madonna

'I am devastated. He was a dear, dear friend...
he was a wonderful man, a really nice, wonderful man.
He was a genius talent and I will miss him until the day I go.'

Liza Minnelli

'I was lucky enough to know and work with Michael Jackson
in his prime. Michael was an extraordinary talent
and a truly great international star.'

John Landis

'The incomparable Michael Jackson has made a bigger impact
on music than any other artist in the history of music.
He was magic. He was what we all strive to be... I love you, Michael.'

Beyonce Knowles

'Just as there will never be another Fred Astaire or
Chuck Berry or Elvis Presley, there will never be anyone
comparable to Michael Jackson. His talent, his wonderment
and his mystery make him legend.'

Steven Spielberg

'We have lost a genius and a true ambassador of not only pop music,
but all music. I can't find the words right now to express how
deeply saddened I am by Michael's passing.'

Justin Timberlake

'Michael Jackson was extraordinary.
When we worked together on Bad, I was in awe of his absolute
mastery of movement on the one hand, and of music on the other.
Every step he took was absolutely precise and fluid at the same time.
It was like watching quicksilver in motion.'

Martin Scorsese

'I'm having a million different reactions I didn't expect I would fell.
He was a great singer – God gives you certain gifts, and this
child was just an extraordinary child touched by this ability.
He could sing like nobody else and he was able to connect with people.'

Cher

'Michael had a great voice and millions of people yet to be born
will hear his songs. This tragedy should teach us a lesson to value and praise
those gifts while we still have them in the world. If even a
small portion of the praise that is bestowed on Michael Jackson
now in death was given to him last year in life, he might well still be
with us. That is the sad truth. One consolation is that
he will triumph by his legacy.'

Robin Gibb

About the authors:

Chris and Craig's writing partnership began in 1990, when they compiled 'The Complete Michael Jackson Solo Discography 1972-90' for Adrian Grant's official fan magazine, *Off the Wall*. Chris also did much of the research for the first edition of Adrian's best selling book, *Michael Jackson – The Visual Documentary*.

Chris launched his own fanzine *Jackson* in 1995, with Craig as contributor, proof reader and eventual co-editor (*Jackson* is no longer published). Chris and Craig's first two books, *Michael Jackson – The Early Years* and *Michael Jackson – The Solo Years*, were published in 2002 and 2003, respectively. *Jacksons Number Ones* followed later in 2003, and their first non-Jackson book, *ABBA Gold Hits*, was published in 2004. The first edition of *Michael Jackson: For The Record*, was published in March 2007.

Chris was born in July 1961 in West Bromwich, England. A Karate Black Belt First Dan by the age of 15 years, he joined the family business on leaving school, a business he still helps to run today, supplying and servicing saws for companies across the West Midlands, where he still lives. He is married to the love of his life, wife Lynne, and has two daughters, Samantha and Stephanie.

Craig was born in June 1959 in Rochdale, England. He studied Applied Chemistry and Biochemistry at Huddersfield, gaining a B.Sc. (honours), but since November 1986 he has worked as a Community Worker at a small, multi-cultural Community Centre. He also writes fiction and is the author of one novel, which he has published under a pen-name. He lives in the North West with his young son, Aaron.

for
Prince Michael,
Paris Katherine Michael
&
Prince 'Blanket' Michael II Jackson

ACKNOWLEDGEMENTS

This has been a difficult book for us to complete, for obvious reasons, and we couldn't have done it without the help, support and encouragement of our families and friends.

Firstly, we would like single out Christina 'Scoop' Chaffin (mjjvault.us), Richard Lecocq (mjdatabank.com), Jay 'MJ Brainace' Leggett, Alex 'Korg/nex' & Paul Voth (jacksonvillage.org), for special thanks. Christina, your enthusiastic support and encouragement has been an inspiration, and we have you to thank for finding the great cover photograph for us, as well. Richard & Alex, many thanks for helping us to verify entries in this edition and for additional research, your help and dedication was invaluable.

Several other people have been with us from our first book to this one, so we would like to say a huge thank you to Damiano (mjfanclub.net), DjHot7 (mjtunes.com), Justin (*aka* Waldo), Christopher Kimberley, Big Kev ('The Shadow'), Yoann Galiotto & Philippe (mjcollectorland.com). Many thanks, too, to jackson5abc & the old J5-collector site, for help with Jackson 5 tour dates.

Once again, we have incredibly talented Jamie Martin (jamiemartinart.co.uk) to thank for designing our cover – another stunning piece of work, and one we are very proud to be associated with. Your drawing of Michael is pretty awesome, too. Thanks, as well, to Christina & Jay, for having a go at designing a few sample covers for us – you can see their excellent work on our Cadman-Halstead Music Books website.

Along our journey, a host of people have joined our internet family and marched either side of us, always keen to help us out in one way or another. We thank (in no particular order): Raisa Carmen, Giuseppe Mazzola, Paul Akinbanjo, Kathlenn Horning, Antonio Taliaferro, Jayne Ross (mjworld.net), Martin Logan (mjtkop.com), Nikki Harris, Ludovic 'Foulcamp' Guyot, Maximillian 'Mistermaxxx' Muhammad, Katie 'Gumbo54' Doty, James ('Bottle of Smoke'), Francois ('Franeck'), L.K. Forney, Corey Sheppard, Mark ('thespecialone'), Yannick, Marco A. Viejo Manga, Matt East, Manu, Deborah Dannelly, Tanja Kovac, Mike Eder, Justin Ostoforoff, Gabriele Prandini, Can Koymen, Jamie 'Jimmy Mack' McCormick, Jason Makris, James Whitney, Janice Murphy, Sonia Chandler, Robert Schmidt, Phil Chamberlain, Jasmin Woitek, Elizabeth Defries, Robert (UK) & Robert Johnson.

We would like to say thank you everyone who contrinutes to the numerous online forums devoted to Michael Jackson and/or music in general – the information you freely share is greatly appreciated, and makes our job a lot easier than it might otherwise be.

We must also acknowledge the support, encouragement and wise words of our editor at Authors OnLine, Richard Fitt. Grateful thanks, Richard, for everything you and your team have done for us over the years.

Chris would like to pay tribute to his wonderful parents, Ron and Brenda. Love to his brother Dean, sister-in-law Louise and nephews Oliver and Jake, sister-in-law Sue and family, and all other family members. To his best friend, Allan, his wife Pearl and father Ray. Last but not least, the three most important girls in my life, my wife Lynne and our daughters, Samantha and Stephanie, and my baby Alfie, our Golden Retriever.

Craig would like to congratulate his son Aaron on passing his karate brown belt grading ~ carry on training hard, and your dream of becoming a black belt will become reality soon. Lots of love to Aaron, mum Jean and Alf, Zoe and Garry, Kathy and Neil, and John. Not forgetting other family, friends and colleagues too numerous to mention – thanks for everything.

By the same authors:

Michael Jackson: For The Record
ABBA Gold Hits
Jacksons Number Ones
Michael Jackson – The Early Years
Michael Jackson – The Solo Years

www.cadman-halstead-musicbooks.com
www.mjjcharts.com
www.the-michael-jackson-archives.com

x

CONTENTS

*'Michael, your artistry is a timeless gift the world will always treasure.
Thank you for being my ultimate inspiration.'*

Christina Chaffin

*'Your love lives on in all your fans, Michael.
We miss you endlessly.'*

Tanja Kovac

*'You gave me a world of sunshine, you made
me feel special. I'm going to miss you,'*

Waldo

INTRODUCTION

Michael Jackson's sudden and tragic death on 25th June 2009 shocked the world, and it has taken a long time for the truth to sink in: the King of Pop is gone, but his music will live forever.

Michael first entered a recording studio in November 1967, just three months after his ninth birthday. Two years later he and his older brothers scored their first hit, *I Want You Back* – and, to the day he died and beyond, Michael's legion of fans have remained incredibly loyal.

The aim of the first edition of *Michael Jackson: For The Record*, was to document the many songs Michael has been involved with over the years – as singer, as writer, as producer, or simply as the inspiration or subject. This original listing has been up-dated, with some minor errors corrected, and now forms Part 1 of the book: The Songs.

At the time of Michael's passing, we had already completed much of 'FTR2', as we called it, and the revised and expanded version also includes:

- Part 2: The Albums – a complete, chronological listing of albums released by Michael (solo and with his brothers) in the USA and/or UK, together with details of selected compilations issued outside the USA/UK.

- Part 3: The Films – full length films and short films/music videos.

- Part 4: The Home Videos.

- Part 5: The Books – written by Michael.

- Part 6: Chartography – chart action, with trivia, from seven diverse countries, namely Australia, Canada, Holland, Germany, New Zealand, the United Kingdom & the United States (Pop & R&B charts).

- Part 7: USA Discography – complete discography for the Jackson 5/Jacksons and Michael solo, including albums, box-sets, home videos, 7" singles, 12" singles, cassette singles & CD singles.

- Part 8: UK Discography (as USA).

Following the publication of the first edition, we received many positive comments, and a number of suggestions as to how we might improve the book – some of which we have taken on board, but others we have not.

Everyone, ourselves included, would love to replace the black/white illustrations in the book with full colour, but current print-on-demand technology simply doesn't make this possible, at least not at an affordable price.

We have, to try to keep the book affordable, gone for a larger format than the first edition, and we have sacrificed hard covers for soft covers. The new format allows two columns per page for much of the book and this, we believe, is much more suited to the book's content.

Two other common suggestions we received were to re-vamp the A-Z listing of songs, as a chronological listing, and to add an index of songs.

We have thought long and hard about the best format for the songs listing in the book, and ultimately we agreed to stick with the A-Z format, as re-arranging the songs chronologically would have involved far too much guesswork – especially with regards to unreleased songs. And, since specific songs are easily located with an A-Z listing, an index of songs is superfluous.

The A-Z listing includes a wealth of information on medleys, performances, samples, cover versions, etc. – however, the inclusions are not and are not intended to be exhaustive, rather we have included snippets we think will interest readers.

The first edition of the book took us nearly three years to research and write, and we have spent the best part of two years on this edition – once again, we hope you enjoy reading our book as much as we have enjoyed researching and writing it.

Craig Halstead & Chris Cadman.

PART 1: THE SONGS

Over the years, Michael was involved with numerous songs – as singer, as writer, as producer, or simply as the inspiration or subject. These songs are listed numerically and alphabetically, and each listing includes the artist, release date and connection to Michael, together with other interesting information.

We have used a number of sources in compiling this listing. The starting point, naturally, was the officially released singles and albums by Michael and his brothers, not forgetting the numerous collaborations he was involved with over the years.

Many unreleased songs Michael wrote or co-wrote have been registered – most commonly by his music company Mijac Music – with one or more professional bodies, including:

- The United States Copyright Office.
- The Songwriters Hall of Fame.
- The American performing rights organisation, BMI.
- The American Society of Composers, Authors & Publishers.
- The Canadian Musical Reproduction Rights Agency Ltd.
- EMI Music Publishing.

Michael name-checked numerous songs he had written or co-written in copyright court cases – most notably, in Mexico in 1993. All these titles are detailed, as are the poems – but not the reflections – featured in Michael's 1992 book of poems and reflections, *Dancing The Dream*. We have also included and detailed:

- Official remixes.
- Notable demo versions.
- Cover versions & other hit versions.
- Notable adaptations and tracks, especially hits, which have sampled a Jackson or Jackson-related song.

We recognise we have not included every demo version or every cover version or every song to sample one of Michael's recordings – to do so would be impossible.

Every song Michael has ever been involved with recording surely exists – or once existed – in at least one, and probably numerous, demo versions. The vast majority of these will never be heard and it would serve no purpose to simply mention 'demo version exists', for every title listed. Therefore, we have only detailed demos that have been officially or unofficially released, or where interesting facts about the demo are known.

Numerous unofficial remixes also exist – again, for the most part, we have made no attempt to detail these.

We are indebted to a number of contacts, who shall remain nameless, who have confirmed the existence of numerous unreleased songs – for example, one contact has in his possession some rare, unreleased Motown demo tracks, and a list of unreleased cover versions recorded by the Jackson 5.

It was inevitable, in compiling a list like this from scratch, we would come across songs Michael was rumoured to have written, or recorded, or been involved with, but which we didn't feel comfortable including in the main list, due to a lack of hard evidence they actually exist.

At the same time, we didn't simply want to ignore such songs or omit them completely – hence, following the main listing, we have compiled a 'Rumour Has It' section. This features a list of titles that might exist and might be Michael-related, but equally might not.

We don't doubt some people will feel certain songs in the main list should be in the rumour section, or not be in the book at all, or visa-versa. It's equally certain we have left out songs other people would have included and, while we have striven for 100% accuracy, we wouldn't be human if we didn't make the occasional error.

1-2-3

Early, rejected title for the Jackson 5's second hit single, *ABC*.

Chorus included the alternate lyrics, '1-2-3, easy as A-B-C, or simple as do-re-me. 1-2-3, A-B-C, baby you and me.' Bootleg recording known to exist – no official release.

2 BAD

Written by Michael with Bruce Swedien, Ivan Moore and Dallas Austin.

Featured on the album HIS*TORY PAST, PRESENT AND FUTURE BOOK 1* (hereinafter shortened to HIS*TORY*), released in June 1995, and in Michael's mini-movie, *Ghosts* – it was the only song in the mega-rare first version of the short film, with *Ghosts* and *Is It Scary* added later. The original version also had different effects, colours and sounds, other incidental music, plus a different transformation of the Mayor.

Official Versions:
Album Version.
Refugee Camp Mix.

Refugee Camp Mix featured on the 1997 album, *BLOOD ON THE DANCE FLOOR* – featured alternate vocals and a sample of Michael's own *Beat It*.

2-4-6-8

Song the Jackson 5 recorded for their second album, *ABC*, issued in May 1970 in the States and August 1970 in the UK.

Released as a single in the Philippines with *La La (Means I Love You)* on the B-side.

Featured in the 'Drafted' episode of the Jackson 5 cartoon series in 1971.

Snippet featured in the opening montage of clips from Michael's film, *Moonwalker*.

7 ROOMS OF GLOOM

Four Tops hit the Jackson 5 recorded a version of – remains unreleased.

The Four Tops took the song to no.10 on the R&B singles chart and no.14 on the Hot 100 in the States, and to no.12 in the UK, in 1967.

9 *FRAGMENTEN UIT NIEUWE ELPEE BAD*

Flexi disc issued free on the cover of the Dutch magazine *Top 10* in 1987, featured excerpts from all the tracks on the album *BAD* (excluding *Just Good Friends* and the CD-only bonus track, *Leave Me Alone*).

Later issued in Holland as a 7" vinyl promotional single with picture sleeve.

16 CANDLES

Song the Jackson 5 recorded for their album, *MAYBE TOMORROW*, issued in April 1971 in the States and October 1971 in the UK.

Featured in the 'Mistaken Identity' episode of the Jackson 5 cartoon series in 1971.

B-side of *How Funky Is Your Chicken* in Holland and Sweden.

Originally recorded by the Crests, for their album, *THE CRESTS SING ALL BIGGIES* – they took the song to no.2 on the Hot 100 and no.4 on the R&B singles chart in the States in 1959.

2000 WATTS

Written by Michael with Teddy Riley, Tyrese Gibson and J. Henson, and recorded by Michael for his album, *INVINCIBLE*, issued in October 2001 – featured background vocals by Riley.

Originally scheduled to appear on a Tyrese album in 2001, but Michael fell in love with the track and recorded it himself. Tyrese, although he decided against recording the song as well, nevertheless titled his new album *2000 WATTS*.

2300 JACKSON STREET

Written by Jermaine, Jackie, Tito and Randy Jackson with Gene Griffin and Aaron Hall.

Title track of a Jacksons album recorded by Jermaine, Jackie, Tito and Randy (but not Michael and Marlon), issued in June 1989.

Featured backing vocals by 'The Jackson Family and Children', including Michael, Janet, Rebbie and Tito's sons, 3T.

Charted at no.9 on the R&B singles chart, but failed to make the Hot 100, in the States – peaked at no.76 in the UK.

Promo short film, directed by Greg Gold, featured members of the Jackson family, including Michael.

Official Versions:
Album Version.
Single Edit.

A BABY SMILES

Song Michael considered for his album, *DANGEROUS*, and cited he had written in his Mexican court deposition in November 1993 – remains unreleased.

Lyrics featured as a poem, titled 'When Babies Smile', in Michael's book of poems and reflections, *Dancing The Dream*.

Titled *Baby Smiles*, one of five songs hand-written by Michael circa 1979 – lyrics included in a personal notebook, with young actor Mark Lester on the cover, which formed part of a 10,000+ piece collection of Jackson memorabilia purchased by Universal Express and some of its entertainment partners, in November 2006.

A BRAND NEW DAY

Song featured in Michael's first movie, *The Wiz*, an all-black remake of *The Wizard Of Oz* with Diana Ross in the starring role, as Dorothy. Michael played the part of the scarecrow, and among his co-stars were: Lena Horne (Glinda, the good witch), Richard Pryor (the Wiz), Ted Ross (the cowardly lion) and Nipsey Russell (the tin man).

Movie premiered in 1978, and was accompanied by a double soundtrack album that achieved no.17 on the R&B albums chart in the USA, and no.40 on the pop albums chart.

Album version has Diana Ross singing the lines Michael sang in the film.

Credited to 'The Wiz Stars', released as a single in several continental European countries (but not the UK or USA), going all the way to no.1 in Holland and Belgium – where it kept Michael's *Don't Stop 'Til You Get Enough* out of the top slot.

A CHANGE IS GONNA COME

Pre-Motown recording by the Jackson 5 first heard in 1993, when it featured on a Japanese release, *BIG BOY*; later the same year, included on *THE JACKSON*

FIVE FEATURING MICHAEL JACKSON, issued on the Stardust label in the UK/Europe.

Two versions released, an over-dubbed extended remix and the track as it was originally recorded, way back in 1965-7.

Longer version appeared on *SOUL MASTERS*.

Written and originally recorded by Sam Cooke, for his album *AIN'T THAT GOOD NEWS*, as a response to Bob Dylan's *Blowin' In The Wind*. Cooke's version achieved no.9 on the R&B singles chart in the States in early 1965. It peaked at no.31 on the Hot 100 but failed to chart in the UK.

A FOOL FOR YOU

One of 19 rare and previously unreleased tracks on the Jackson 5's *SOULSATION!* 4CD box set, released in 1995.

Penned by Ray Charles, the Jackson 5 originally recorded the song on 12th February 1970, with producer Bobby Taylor.

Ray's original version featured on the 1958 album, *RAY CHARLES AT NEWPORT*.

A PLACE IN THE SUN

Stevie Wonder song the Jackson 5 recorded a version of – remains unreleased.

Stevie took the song to no.3 on the R&B singles chart and no.9 on the Hot 100 in the States, and to no.20 in the UK, in 1966. Stevie's version featured on his album, *DOWN TO EARTH*.

A PLACE WITH NO NAME

Song based on America's 1971 hit, *A Horse With No Name*, recorded by Michael in 1998, but failed to appear on his *INVINCIBLE* album three years later.

Original song written by Dewey Bunnell, new lyrics by Michael & Dr Freeze, who also produced Michael's version, with CJ de Villar, who used to work with Quincy Jones and P. Diddy.

'The band was honoured that Michael chose to do their song,' said Jim Morey, America's current manager and Michael's manager in the late 1980s and early 1990s, 'and they hope it becomes available for all Michael's fans to hear.'

'It was a song I worked on not only as a recording engineer, but as a bass player as well,' said CJ de Villar. 'It was what I call a muse track for Michael and producer Dr Freeze... I'm not certain if it was Freeze or Michael who kicked off the idea first, but I know Michael loved the America song, though he did work out lots of other music explorations for the fun of it, or at least with no specific outcome in mind, other than finding a surprise in the process.'

Short, 25 second snippet leaked on the internet site TMZ.com in July 2009, just three weeks after Michael's passing – no official release.

'That sound clip is definitely a session rough mix,' said de Villar, 'since it doesn't have a mix and master polished sound on it. For those unfamiliar with what a session rough mix is, it's from the session multi-track tape that was up on the recording console that day, for whatever work was being done to it, which was quickly or roughly mixed, and recorded to a recordable CD or DAT tape as Michael liked it... what was most fun was playing bass on the track, and how it showed me Michael's relentless musical energy so vividly... Michael certainly inspired me, and brought out the best energy I had by him getting into it as only Michael can. And then I realised – he's all about the music.'

CD de Villar stated he believed, at the time of his passing, Michael could have close to 1,000 pieces of material in some form, with at least a few hundred in post production stage, at least.

A PRETTY FACE IS

Song written by Stevie Wonder circa 1974 (some sources say as far back as 1968), possibly intended for the Jackson 5 or as a duet by Stevie with Michael.

Stevie confirmed the song's existence in an interview in Japan in 1988, and he stated he envisioned the song as a duet with Michael. Michael and Stevie are reported to have recorded the song for Stevie's 1988 album, *CHARACTERS*, but it remains unreleased.

Other unreleased songs Stevie worked on around the time he wrote *A Pretty Face Is*, which may or may not have been written for Michael and his brothers, include: *No News Is Good News, Bumble-Bee Of Love, Sky Blue Afternoon, The Future, If Your Mama Could See You Now* and *Would I Live For You, Would I Die For You.*

Also known by the title, *A Pretty Face*.

ABC

Title track of the Jackson 5's second album, issued in May 1970 in the States and August 1970 in the UK.

Originally titled '1-2-3' and 'ABCD' – demo versions have leaked on the internet.

Premiered on the *American Bandstand* TV show in the States, on which Michael also revealed he was a big Beatles fan.

Appeared on a promotional film sent to concert promoters in 1970, to let them know who the Jackson 5 were – performance filmed at the group's first Motown concert in Philadelphia.

Released as a single in February 1970 in the USA and May 1970 in the UK. Achieved no.1 in the States on both the Hot 100 (for two weeks), where it toppled *Let It Be* by the Beatles, and the R&B chart (for four weeks). Charted at no.8 in the UK.

Outsold the Jackson 5's debut hit, *I Want You Back*, and was the no.8 best selling single of 1970 in the States.

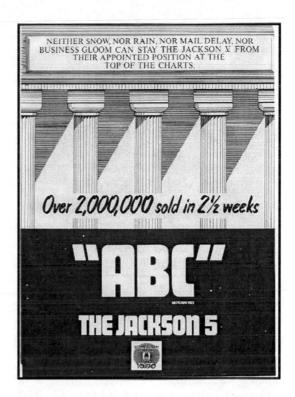

NEITHER SNOW, NOR RAIN, NOR MAIL DELAY, NOR BUSINESS GLOOM CAN STAY THE JACKSON 5 FROM THEIR APPOINTED POSITION AT THE TOP OF THE CHARTS.

Over 2,000,000 sold in 2½ weeks

"ABC"

THE JACKSON 5

Motown celebrated the success of *ABC* by pressing gold (yellow) vinyl copies, with an accompanying press release that stated: 'Because of all the million selling records we've had in the past, none soared beyond the million mark faster than *ABC* by the Jackson 5. It did it in less than 12 days!'

Grammy Award nomination: Best Contemporary Vocal Performance by a Duo, Group or Chorus (the Carpenters took the award, for *(They Long To Be) Close To You*).

Featured in 'It All Started With', an episode of the Jackson 5 cartoon series, in 1971.

Following its success, co-writer Freddie Perren confessed the music of *ABC* is the chorus of *I Want You Back*. 'All we did was take that music and keep playing it, adding a couple of steps to it,' he admitted. 'We cut the track for *ABC* before *I Want You Back* was really a big hit!'

Cited by Michael, in the early 1970s, as one of his three favourite songs he had recorded for Motown, along with *I'll Be There* and *Never Can Say Goodbye*. Also named by Michael named as one of his three personal Motown favourites in his autobiography, *Moonwalk*, published in April 1988.

Previously unreleased live medley of *I Want You Back* and *ABC*, recorded at the Jackson 5's Los Angeles concert on 26th August 1972, featured on the TV soundtrack album, *THE JACKSONS: AMERICAN DREAM*, issued in October 1992 in the States and July 1993 in the UK.

Performed by the Jackson 5 on the *Carol Burnett Show* in 1974.

Original mono version included on the 4CD box-set, *HITSVILLE USA: THE MOTOWN SINGLES 1959-1971*, issued in the States in 1992.

Salaam Remi's Krunk-A-Delic Party Mix, on the album *MOTOWN REMIXED* in 2005, featured alternate vocals.

Other remixes:
Love Stream Mix – from the album, *SOUL SOURCE – JACKSON 5 REMIXES*, released in Japan in 2000.
Kubota, Takeshi Remix – from the same album as above.
Readymade Super 524 Mix – from the album, *SOUL SOURCE – JACKSON 5 REMIXES 2*, released in Japan in 2001.
Justa Roots Rock Mix – from the same album as above; also included on the Jackson 5 album, *SOUL LEGENDS*.
DJ Friction Remix.

Vocal and instrumental version featured on the karaoke compilation, *MOTOWN*

ORIGINAL ARTISTS, VOL.2: MY GIRL, released in September 2003.

Remix version made available on Tito's website in February 2008.

Sampled by:
Vanilla Ice on *Dancin'*, from his 1990 album, *TO THE EXTREME*.
Naughty By Nature on *O.P.P. (Other People's Property)* – charted at no.5 on the R&B singles chart and no.6 on the Hot 100 in the States, and no.35 in the UK, in 1991.
will.i.am on *Fantastic*, from his 2007 album, *SONGS ABOUT GIRLS*.

Posthumous hit: no.34 in the USA (Hot Digital Songs) and no.50 in UK.

ABC – I'LL BE THERE – THE LOVE YOU SAVE

Medley of hits the Jackson 5 performed on their own TV special in the States in 1972.

ABC – THE LOVE YOU SAVE

Medley performed by the Jacksons during the *Michael Jackson: 30th Anniversary Celebration, The Solo Years* concerts, staged at New York's Madison Square Garden on 7th and 10th September 2001.

ABCD

Early, rejected title for the Jackson 5's second hit single, *ABC*.

AFTER THE STORM (THE SUN WILL SHINE)

Unreleased track from the Jackson 5's Motown era – written by Willie Hutch.

AIN'T NO MOUNTAIN HIGH ENOUGH

Classic song the Jackson 5 recorded two versions of, one mid-tempo with a spoken intro (as per the Diana Ross recording), and the other up-tempo – both remain unreleased.

It's also a song Michael used to sing to British singer/actress, Patti Boulaye, whenever he met her, as he thought she looked like Diana Ross.

Hit versions:
Marvin Gaye & Tammi Terrell – no.3 on the R&B singles chart and no.19 on the Hot 100 in the States in 1967.
Diana Ross – no.1 on the Hot 100 and R&B singles chart in the States, and no.6 in the UK, in 1970.
Boys Town Gang (medley) – no.46 in the UK in 1981.

Jocelyn Brown – no.35 in the UK in 1998.
Whitehouse – no.60 in the UK in 1998.

Marvin & Tammi's original version featured on their album, *UNITED*.

AIN'T NO SUNSHINE

Track on Michael's debut solo album, *GOT TO BE THERE*, released in January 1972 in the States and May 1972 in the UK.

Issued as Michael's third solo single in the UK in July 1970 (*I Wanna Be Where You Are* having been chosen as the third release in the States), peaking at no.8.

Alternate version remixed by Dean Burt included on the 1987 album, *THE ORIGINAL SOUL OF MICHAEL JACKSON*. SSY Remix featured on the album, *SOUL SOURCE – JACKSON 5 REMIXES 2*, released in Japan in 2001.

Original version by writer Bill Withers featured on his 1971 album, *JUST AS I AM*.

Title track of a budget compilation of Michael's Motown output, released in 1982 by the Pickwick label in the UK.

Other hit versions:
Bill Withers – no.3 on the Hot 100 and no.6 on the R&B singles chart in the States in 1971.
Sivuca – no.56 in the UK in 1984.
Sydney Youngblood – no.51 on the R&B singles chart in 1991.
Kid Frost – no.95 on the Hot 100 in the USA in 1995.

Ladysmith Black Mambazo featuring Des'Ree – no.42 in the UK in 1999.
Bill Withers – no.40 in the UK in 2009.
Kris Allen – no.37 on the Hot 100 in 2009.

AIN'T NOBODY

Song written by Rufus keyboard player, David 'Hawk' Wolinski, which Quincy Jones requested Wolinski give to Michael, for the album that would become *THRILLER*. Having already promised the song to producer Russ Titelman, Wolinski decined – subsequently recorded by Rufus, with lead vocals by Chaka Khan.

Hit Versions:
Rufus & Chaka Khan – no.1 on the R&B singles chart and no.22 on the Hot 100 in the States in 1983, and no.8 in the UK in 1984.
Rufus & Chaka Khan – no.6 in the UK in 1989.
Jaki Graham – no.44 in the UK in 1994.
KWS & Gwen Dickey – no.21 in the UK in 1994.
Diana King – no.13 in the UK in 1995, and no.63 on the R&B singles chart in the States in 1996.
LL Cool J – no.46 on the Hot 100 in 1996 and no.27 on the R&B chart in 1997, and no.1 in the UK in 1997.
Course – no.8 in the UK in 1997.

AIN'T NOTHING LIKE THE REAL THING

Opening track on the Jackson 5's album, *LOOKIN' THROUGH THE WINDOWS*, issued in May 1972 in the States and October 1972 in the UK.

Released as the B-side of *Skywriter*, a single released in the UK (but not USA) in 1973, peaked at no.25.

Performed by the Jackson 5 on *The Flip Wilson Show* in the States in 1972.

Original version, by Marvin Gaye & Tammi Terrell, featured on their 1968 duets album, *YOU'RE ALL I NEED*. Single topped the R&B charts in the States for three weeks in 1968; also charted at no.8 on Billboard's Hot 100 and no.34 in the UK.

AIN'T THAT PECULIAR

One of several cover versions the Jackson 5 often performed in the early, pre-Motown days – co-written by Smokey Robinson.

Recorded by Jermaine for his debut solo album, *JERMAINE*, released in 1972.

Live recording with Jermaine singing lead, originally featured on an album released in Japan, titled simply *IN JAPAN!* Later featured on the album, *LIVE!*, credited to Michael Jackson with the Jackson 5, released in the UK (but not USA) in 1988. Recorded at the Osaka Koseinenkin Hall, Japan, on 30th April 1973.

Included on the limited edition CD, *IN JAPAN!*, released by Hip-O Select in 2004 – only 5,000 copies pressed.

Marvin Gaye's original version – from the album *MOODS OF MARVIN GAYE* – hit no.1 for a single week on the R&B singles chart in the USA in 1965. It also achieved no.8 on the Hot 100 but wasn't a hit in the UK.

AIN'T TOO PROUD TO BEG

Temptations hit the Jackson 5 recorded a version of – remains unreleased.

One of several songs the Jackson 5 performed at their Motown audition – filmed by Johnny Bristol, but this part of the audition has never been publicly released.

'At the very first audition,' said Berry Gordy, 'Michael sang his songs like he had experienced everything he was singing about – and he was only nine years old. When they jumped into the Temptations' *Ain't Too Proud To Beg*, Michael sang it like it was his song alone – and all of them moving together like little David Ruffins.'

Hit versions:
Temptations – no.1 on the R&B singles chart and no.13 on the Hot 100 in the States, and no.21 in the UK, in 1966.
Rolling Stones – no.17 on the Hot 100 in 1974.
Rick Astley – no.89 on the Hot 100 in 1989.

The Temptations' original appeared on their album, *GETTING READY*.

AL CAPONE

Song Michael cited he had written in his court deposition in November 1993 – failed to make his album, *BAD*. Demo version recorded at the Bee Gees' studio exists, but remains unreleased.

Evolved into *Smooth Criminal*.

'I recorded the demo for *Smooth Criminal* at the Bee Gees studio in the 1980s,' said Bruce Swedien. 'It was called 'Al Capone' at the time.'

See also: *Smooth Criminal*.

ALL I DO

Track on Stevie Wonder's 1982 Grammy winning album, *HOTTER THAN JULY*, featuring Michael on backing vocals – album released in 1980.

Official Versions:
Album Version.
7" Edit.
Full Unedited Version.

B-side of Stevie's single, *That Girl*.

ALL I DO IS THINK OF YOU

Track on the Jackson 5's album, *MOVING VIOLATION*, released in May 1975 in the States and July 1975 in the UK.

B-side of the last Jackson 5 single, *Forever Came Today*, issued while they were still a Motown act. Charted in its own right on the R&B singles chart in the States, peaking at no.50, after it became known the group were leaving Motown for CBS/Epic.

Performed by the Jackson 5 on *Soul Train* in the States in 1975, and live from Las Vegas, on the *Mike Douglas In Hollywood* TV show.

Cover version by Pasadena quintet, Troop (standing for 'Total Respect Of Other People'), hit no.1 on the R&B singles chart in the States in 1990.

Version by teen group B5 released in 2005.

Sampled by the Roots, on the track *Can't Stop This*, from their 2006 album, *GAMES THEORY*.

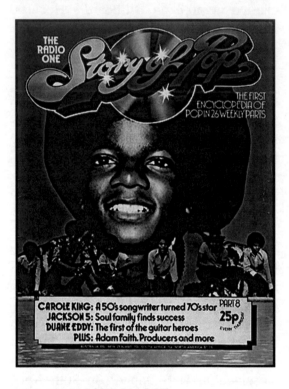

ALL IN YOUR NAME

Anti-war song Barry Gibb of the Bees Gees confirmed, in October 2005, he worked on with Michael in the summer of 2002 – the song was a protest against the United States government's plan to invade Iraq (which took place in March 2003).

Originally believed to be titled *Prayer For Peace* – slated to appear on an album Michael was working on in 2003.

Demo version by Barry and Michael known to exist – remains unreleased.

ALL NIGHT DANCIN'

Song written by Michael and brother Randy, featured on the Jacksons' album, *DESTINY*, released in December 1978.

B-side of the single *Shake Your Body (Down To The Ground)* in the UK (but not USA).

Performed by the Jacksons during their Destiny Tour – featured in a concert screened on BBC2 in the UK, and later released as a home video in Japan.

ALL THE THINGS YOU ARE

Track on Michael's third solo album, *MUSIC & ME*, released in April 1973 in the States and July 1973 in the UK.

B-side of *Too Young*, issued as a single in Italy in 1973.

Included on the tribute album *MOTOWN CELEBRATES SINATRA*, released in 1998, which also featured a shot of Michael dressed as Frank Sinatra on the sleeve (taken from the 1971 TV special, *Diana!*). Same photo used on the sleeve of Michael's Swedish single, *Rockin' Robin*.

ALL THE WORLD

Song American actor/singer Kevin Bacon revealed in an article in Billboard magazine he wrote in the early 1970's, when he was in his teens. 'I wrote it for Michael Jackson,' he confirmed, 'of course, he never heard it!'

ALRIGHT NOW

Song written by Michael with John Barnes in 1989.

Recorded by Ralph Tresvant, for his 1990 album, *RALPH TRESVANT* – only featured on the CD version.

ALRIGHT WITH ME

Track on the Jacksons' album, *2300 JACKSON STREET*, released in June 1989.

B-side of the Jacksons single, *Nothin (Compares 2 U)*.

Michael wasn't one of the Jacksons who recorded this song.

AM I BLUE

Song the Jacksons performed on their TV series in 1976, with their special guest star, Sonny Bono (of Sonny & Cher), as part of a medley with *More Than You Know*, *For Once In My Life* and *Try A Little Tenderness*.

AMERICA THE BEAUTIFUL

Patriotic American song – words by Katharine Lee Bates and music composed by church organist/choirmaster Samuel A. Ward.

Sang by Michael, as part of a celebrity choir backing Ray Charles, on the steps of the Lincoln Memorial in Washington, D.C., on 18th January 1993.

ANGEL

Song written by Babyface, who described it as 'simply fantastic', and recorded around 1998 by Michael for a greatest hits compilation that didn't happen – remains unreleased.

ANOTHER DAY

Song Lenny Kravitz confirmed in 2001, in an interview in *Blender* magazine, he had been working on with Michael – failed to make the final track listing of Michael's album, *INVINCIBLE*.

'Working with Michael Jackson was probably the best recording experience of my life,' said Kravitz. 'He was totally cool, absolutely professional and a beautiful, beautiful guy – and let's not forget, Michael is a musical genius.' Remains unreleased.

ANOTHER PART OF ME

Song written and recorded by Michael.

Originally featured in the short film *Captain EO*, a 17 minute 3D space fantasy shot for Disney, and premiered at the Epcot Center in Orlando, Florida, on 12th September 1986. Costing $30 million, *Captain EO* was billed as 'a celebration of triumph over evil', and was directed by Francis Ford Coppola and produced by George Lucas. The final screening was at Disneyland, Paris, on 16th August 1998.

Included on Michael's album, *BAD*, released in September 1987, ahead of another of Michael's compositions, *Streetwalker* (which was finally issued in 2001, as one of the bonus tracks on the special edition of the same album).

Sixth single lifted from *BAD*, hitting no.1 (for one week) on the R&B singles chart in the States. As the fifth R&B chart topper from *BAD* (*Dirty Diana* stalled at no.5), it equalled a record held by Janet Jackson, for the most no.1 singles from one album (in her case, from *CONTROL*).

The first five singles from *BAD* topped the Hot 100 (another record), but *Another Part Of Me* only made no.11, and peaked at no.15 in the UK.

Official Versions:
Album Version.
Extended Dance Mix.
A Cappella.
Instrumental.
Radio Edit.
Dub Version.
7" Version.

Extended Dance Mix featured alternate vocals.

Promoted with a 'live' video, filmed at various cities, including Michael's Wembley Stadium concert, on 15th July 1988, and Paris – directed by Patrick T. Kelly. Premiered on 30th July 1988, during the 90 minute TV special, *Michael*

Jackson: Around The World. HRH Princess Diana, Elizabeth Taylor, Sophia Loren and Tina Turner all attended the concert.

Part of a lawsuit heard in Mexico in 1993, when Robert Smith (*aka* Robert Austin), Reynard Jones and Clifford Rubin claimed it infringed the song, *Send Your Love* – the judgement was in Michael's favour.

Featured in the film, *Rush Hour* (1998).

ANTHOLOGY MIX

17 minute medley of Michael's solo hits, featured on one of seven 12" singles from the rare promo box-set *Twelves*, released in the UK in 2003, to promote Michael's greatest hits compilation, *NUMBER ONES*. Placed together, the seven exclusive picture sleeves formed a large *Off The Wall* era picture of Michael.

ANYONE NAMED JACKSON IS A FRIEND OF MINE

Song performed by the Jackson 5 on *The Carol Burnett Show* in the States, on 21st January 1974.

ARE YOU LISTENING?

Poem written by Michael – included in his book of poems and reflections, *Dancing The Dream*, published in 1992.

ART OF MADNESS

Track on the Jacksons' album, *2300 JACKSON STREET*, released in June 1989. Issued as a single in several continental European countries, but not in the UK or USA.

Michael wasn't one of the Jacksons who recorded this song.

ASHES TO ASHES

Incidental piece of music Michael composed with Nicholas Pike, for his *Ghosts* short film, premiered in October 1996.

ASK THE LONELY

Song originally recorded by the Jackson 5 in 1970, but that remained unreleased until 1983, when a remixed version appeared on the Motown compilation, *MOTOWN SUPERSTARS SING MOTOWN SUPERSTARS*.

Album also included a version of Michael's *I Wanna Be Where You Are*, performed by Thelma Houston. Liner notes incorrectly stated 'originally released by the Jackson 5'.

Original version – with the same lead vocal but slightly different backing vocals – included as one of 19 'Rare & Unreleased' tracks of the fourth CD of the Michael/Jackson 5 box-set, *SOULSATION!*, issued in June 1995 in the States and July 1995 in the UK – demo version also known to exist.

Song originally recorded by the Four Tops, for their eponymous 1964 album. They took the song to no.9 on the R&B singles chart, and no.24 on the Hot 100, in the States in 1965.

ATTITUDE

Song Michael co-wrote with Kathy Wakefield and Michel Pierre Colombier, and registered with EMI Music Publishing – remains unreleased.

AVE MARIA

Song the Jackson 5 recorded for their *CHRISTMAS ALBUM* circa 1970, but which failed to make the final track listing – remains unreleased.

For many years, Motown asserted no out-takes from the *CHRISTMAS ALBUM* sessions existed – however, an ex-employee has recently named 15 songs Michael and his brothers did record but which weren't used, of which this is one.

Hit versions:
Shirley Bassey – no.31 in the UK in 1962.

Lesley Garrett & Amanda Thompson – no.16 in the UK in 1993.
Andrea Bocelli – no.65 in the UK in 1999.

BABY BE MINE

Written by Rod Temperton, and recorded by Michael for his solo album, *THRILLER*, released in December 1982.

B-side of *Human Nature* in the States (not issued in the UK), and of *I Just Can't Stop Loving You* in both the USA and UK.

Demo version leaked on the internet, with *Starlight*, in 2008 – no official release.

BABY I NEED YOUR LOVIN'

Four Tops hit the Jackson 5 recorded a version of – remains unreleased.

Hit versions:
Four Tops – no.11 on both the Hot 100 and R&B singles chart in the States in 1964.
Fourmost – no.24 in the UK in 1964.
Johnny Rivers – no.3 on the Hot 100 in 1967.
O.C. Smith – no.30 on the R&B singles chart and no.52 on the Hot 100 in 1970.
Eric Carmen – no.62 on the Hot 100 in 1979.

Song heard in the TV mini-series, *The Jacksons: An American Dream*, but not performed by the Jackson 5.

BABY IT'S LOVE

One of two songs allegedly penned for, and maybe recorded by, the Jackson 5 and Diana Ross in 1970, but unconfirmed by Motown.

BABY, YOU DON'T HAVE TO GO

Pre-Motown recording by the Jackson 5 first heard in 1993, when it featured on a Japanese release, *BIG BOY*; later the same year, included on *THE JACKSON FIVE FEATURING MICHAEL JACKSON*, issued on the Stardust label in the UK/Europe.

Extended four minute version made available in 2005, on the Jackson 5's download compilation, *SOUL MASTERS*.

BABY'S FIRE

Song co-written by Michael with Ryan D, Groves, and registered with the BMI in January 2009.

Alternate titles: *Baby's On Fire*, *Higher Baby's Fire*.

BACK IN MY ARMS AGAIN

Supremes hit the Jackson 5 recorded a version of – remains unreleased.

Hit versions:
Supremes – no.1 on the Hot 100 and R&B singles chart in the States, and no.40 in the UK, in 1965.
Genya Ravan – no.92 on the Hot 100 in 1978.

BACK TO THE PAST MEDLEY

One of two promo medleys, released on 12" and CD as *The Medleys*, in Brazil in 1994:

Featured: *Rock With You, Burn This Disco Out, Off The Wall, Don't Stop 'Til You Get Enough, Shake Your Body (Down To The Ground), Blame It On The Boogie, Thriller* and *Billie Jean*.

BAD

Written and recorded by Michael, for his solo album of the same name, released in September 1987.

Working title, before Michael penned the lyrics: 'Pee'.

Originally intended as a duet with one of Michael's main rivals in the 1980s, Prince. 'Prince was excited to have been asked,' said Susan Rogers, 'but he said to me, "I just don't do that stuff", and I think he felt Michael was going to make himself look better.'

In an interview with Chris Rock in 1997, Prince further explained: 'The first part of the song is, "Your butt is mine." Now, I was goin'… who is singing that to who? 'Cos you sure ain't singing that to me, and I sure ain't singing it to you – so right there, you know, right there we gotta problem.'

Michael's idea was to have him and Prince square off in the short film, taking turns to sing and dance, in order to determine who was the 'baddest'. Although Prince turned Michael down, he did submit *Wouldn't You Love To Love Me*, a song he had originally demoed in 1976, for *BAD*. Michael passed, so Prince gave the song to Taja Sevelle, for her self-titled 1987 album (released on Prince's Paisley Park Records).

'I was there for a couple of meetings with Prince and Michael, Quincy and all,' said Bruce Swedien. 'Personally, I think that after meeting with Michael, Quincy, Freddy DeMann and his team, Prince realised that he couldn't win this duet/duel with MJ, artistically or otherwise – and he pulled out. He left the building, so to speak…'

Second single lifted from *BAD*, hit no.1 on the Hot 100 for two weeks and the R&B singles chart for three weeks, in the States. Charted at no.3 in the UK, where a limited edition red vinyl 12" single was issued.

American Music Award: Favourite Soul/R&B Single, Male.

Soul Train Awards: Best Single of the Year, Male.

Clip of Michael's performance from one of his Bad World Tour concerts at Wembley, UK, in 1988 screened at the MTV Video Music Awards. Different performance screened as part of a Bad concert shown on Nippon TV in Japan.

Official Versions:
Album Version.
Dub Version.
A Cappella.
7" Single Mix.
Dance Remix Radio Edit.
Extended Dance Mix (incl. False Fade).
Short Film End Credits Version (featured additional vocals).

The Music.
The Moves.
The Magic.
And the World Premiere of "Bad"...the Video.

MICHAEL JACKSON "THE MAGIC RETURNS!"

AN ALL-NEW CBS SPECIAL!
7PM CBS ○●WCCO TV ○

Short promo film directed by Martin Scorsese, recruited at producer Quincy Jones's suggestion, loosely based on the

20

true story of Edmund Perry, a young black man shot dead when he returned home to Harlem, New York, from a private college. Around 17 minutes long, with a lengthy opening shot in black/white, in which Michael took on a 'serious' acting role for the first time – gang members included a young, and at the time unknown, Wesley Snipes. The musical, technicolor segment of the short film was filmed at a subway station in Brooklyn.

Short film premiered on 31st August 1987, on the TV special, *Michael Jackson: The Magic Returns*.

Alternate version can be heard during the rarely broadcast short film's end credits.

Bad: Pepsi Commercial – with new lyrics written by Michael in 1986 – registered with the United States Copyright Office in March 1987. Series of commercials, also featuring *Billie Jean*, ran as follows:

- *The Jacksons*
- *The Jacksons & Kids*
- *The Magic Begins*
- *The Dressing Room*
- *The Chase*
- *The Chopper*
- *The Museum*
- *The Finale*
- *Looking For Me?*

In late 1988, Sammy Davis, Jr. performed a comedy version of *Bad* during one of his concerts. Before his performance, he said of Michael: 'I've seen him grow from a small boy to this huge star, and it's frightening to see where else he'll take it to.' Michael and choreographer Michael Peters helped out Sammy, on some break dancing steps for the film, *Cry Of The City*.

Featured as a sample in *I Got The Money*, from the stage musical *Sisterella*, which Michael supported financially.

Sampled in 2000 by rapper Trina on *Da Baddest Bitch*, and by Italian ska group Roy Paci & Aretuska – the words 'who's bad?' – on the song *What You See Is What You Get*, from their 2005 album, *PAROLA D'ONORE*.

Sixth of Michael's 20 *'Visionary – The Video Singles'* reissues, with the music on one side of a Dual Disc and the accompanying short film on the other side. Issued in March 2006 in the UK – charted at no.16.

Posthumous hit: no.15 in Switzerland, no.20 in Spain, no.23 in USA (Hot Digital Songs), no.25 in Sweden, no.27 in Australia, no.40 in UK and no.44 in Germany.

BAD – BILLIE JEAN – BLACK OR WHITE

Medley performed live by Michael's nephews, 3T, with some of the contestant's on France's talent show, *Star Academy*.

BAD COMPANY

Written by Tito Jackson for the Jacksons' 1984 album, *VICTORY* – remains unreleased.

Described as an uptemo fun song with a beackbeat and guitar solo by Tito.

BAD GIRL

Song Michael cited he had written in his court deposition in November 1993 – remains unreleased.

BADDER

Entertaining re-make of Michael's *Bad* short film, as featured in his 'movie like no other', *Moonwalker*, premiered in 1989. Nine year old Brandon Adams played Michael, lip-synching to Michael's original recording. Michael's nephew, Jermaine Jackson, Jr., was among the *Badder* dancers.

BANANA BOAT SONG, THE

Traditional Jamaican folk song first recorded – as *Day De Light* – by Trinidadian Edric Connor & The Caribbeans in 1952. Best known, however, for Harry Belafonte's 1957 recording.

Started by Stevie Wonder, sang to Belafonte by the USA For Africa stars – including Michael – assembled at the A&M studios in Los Angeles on the evening of 28th January 1985, to record the charity single, *We Are The World*.

'It's not everyday,' quipped Belafonte, 'you get *The Banana Boat Song* sung to you by Michael Jackson!'

Hit versions:
Harry Belefonte – no.5 on the Hot 100 and no.7 on the R&B singles chart in the States, and no.2 in the UK, in 1957.
Tarriers – no.4 on the Hot 100 and no.14 on the R&B singles chart, and no.15 in the UK, in 1957.
Shirley Bassey – no.8 in the UK in 1957.

Alternate titles: *Day-O (The Banana Boat Song, Banana Boat (Day-O)*.

BAREFOOTIN'

Song the Jackson 5 performed regularly in the early days, initially in and around their home town, Gary, Indiana. Whilst singing, young Michael often used to kick off his shoes, and dance around the stage.

The Jackson 5 won Gary's city wide Talent Search with *Barefootin'* in 1965, and earned their first press write-up in the *Gary Post-Tribune*.

A hit for Robert Parker in the States in 1966, making no.2 on the R&B singles chart and no.7 on the Hot 100.

BASSOUILLE

Song written by Michael with Bruce Swedien in 1994, but failed to make Michael's HIS*TORY* album, and remains unreleased.

BE A LION

Song featured in Michael's first movie, *The Wiz*, and on the accompanying double soundtrack album. Lead vocals by Diana Ross, who played Dorothy in the film, with Michael and his co-stars singing a few lines each.

BE A PEPPER II

Two short radio jingles (30 seconds and 60 seconds) recorded by the Jacksons, including Michael, for Dr Pepper's 'Be A Pepper II 1979 Campaign' in the States.

BE ME 4 A DAY

Song written by Michael with Grey Calix Days (who also worked with Michael's nephews, 3T), and registered with the BMI – remains unreleased.

Known by several alternative titles: *Be Me For A Day*, *Just For One Day Be Michael*, *Just For A Day*, *Me 4 A Day* and *Be Michael*.

BE MY GIRL

Song mentioned in the January 1973 issue of *Rock & Soul* magazine, as having been performed in concert by the Jackson 5 in mid-to-late 1972 – cited as the group's latest single, with Jermaine on lead.

Recorded by the Jackson 5 for Motown – remains unreleased.

Known among fans, mistakenly, by the title *Paper Doll*.

BE NOT ALWAYS

Song written and produced by Michael, with additional lyrics by brother Marlon – originally written in 1979.

'Michael and I have co-written a song about children,' revealed Marlon in March 1984. 'We wrote a song called *Be Not Always* and it's about children.'

Although effectively a solo cut by Michael, featured on the Jacksons' album *VICTORY*, released in July 1984.

Titled *Always, Be Not Always*, one of five songs hand-written by Michael circa 1979 – lyrics included in a personal notebook, with young actor Mark Lester on the cover, that formed part of a 10,000+ piece collection of Jackson memorabilia purchased by Universal Express and some of its entertainment partners, in November 2006.

BE WHAT YOU ARE

One of five songs the Jackson 5 performed as a medley at the Grammy Awards on 2nd March 1974, to introduce the nominees for Best Rhythm & Blues Vocal Performance by a Group, Duo or Chorus.
A hit in 1973 for the Staple Singers, achieving no.18 on the R&B singles chart and no.66 on the Hot 100, in the States.

BEAT IT

Track written and co-produced, with Quincy Jones, by Michael.

Featured a soaring guitar solo – inspired by the song *Eruption* – by Eddie Van Halen, who was invited to guest on the track by Quincy Jones. Van Halen initially believed he was receiving crank calls, before establishing proper communication with Jones – and recorded his contribution completely free of any charge, so keen was he to be involved.

'I did it as a favour,' said Van Halen. 'I was a complete fool, according to the rest of the band, our manager and everyone else. I was not used. I knew what I was doing – I don't do something unless I want to do it.'

'Quincy Jones and Michael took a skeleton version of *Beat It* up to Eddie's place, as they wanted him to solo over the verse section,' explained Steve Lukather, who also worked on the song. 'Initially, we rocked it out as Eddie had played a good solo – but Quincy thought it was too tough. So I had to reduce the distorted guitar sound and that is what was released.'

A technician, unaware Van Halen was beginning a take, knocked on the studio door and entered, quickly closing the door when he realised his mistake. Afterwards, it was agreed to leave this in, and the knock on the door can be heard on the final version of the song.

One of the last four songs Michael completed for *THRILLER*; the other three were *Human Nature*, *The Lady In My Life* and *P.Y.T. (Pretty Young Thing)*; Michael is rumoured to have written an early version of the song in 1979.

Third single from Michael's solo album, *THRILLER*, following *The Girl Is Mine* and *Billie Jean*. In the States, Frank DiLeo (Vice President of Epic Records, and later Michael's manager) convinced everyone *Beat It* should be released

whilst *Billie Jean* was still heading towards no.1, and predicted both singles would be in the Top 10 at the same time.

On the Hot 100, *Billie Jean* was replaced at no.1 by Dexy Midnight Runners' *Come On Eileen*, which spent a solitary week at the top, before Michael reclaimed the no.1 slot with *Beat It*. Both singles occupied Top 5 positions at the same time, a feat only matched by the Bee Gees, Olivia Newton-John, Linda Ronstadt and Donna Summer in the 1970s.

Beat It topped the Hot 100 for three weeks and R&B singles chart for one week, and peaked at no.3 in the UK.

RIAA Platinum Record Award (USA million seller).

Promo video, directed by Bob Giraldi, financed to the tune of $140,000 by Michael himself after CBS got cold feet. Inspired by *West Side Story*. Cast included 18 professional dancers and four break dancers, choreographed by Michael Peters, and real life members of two rival Los Angeles street gangs.

Billboard Video Awards: Best Overall Video Clip, Best Performance by a Male Artist, Best Use of Video to Enhance a Song, Best Use of Video to Enhance an Artist's Image, Best Choreography.

American Music Awards: Favourite Pop/Rock Video, Favourite Soul Video.

Grammy Awards: Record of the Year, Best Rock Vocal Performance, Male.

Billboard Video Awards: Best Overall Video, Best Dance/Disco 12" (joint with *Billie Jean*).

Rolling Stone: No.1 Video in both the Critics Poll and Reader's Poll.

Black Gold Awards: Best Video Performance.

Inducted into the Music Video Producer's Hall of Fame.

Official Versions:
Album Version.
Edit.
Moby's Sub Mix.

Featured in the National Highway Safety Commission's anti-drunk driving campaign in the States, with the slogan, 'Drinking and Driving can Kill a Friendship', and included on the accompanying NHSC promo album. Michael collected a special award from President Ronald Reagan at the White House, for his support of the campaign.

Eddie Van Halen joined Michael and his brothers on stage, to perform *Beat It* with them during the Jacksons' Victory Tour, on 4th July 1984.

Live performance by Michael, at his Dangerous Tour concert in Bucharest, Romania, on 1st October 1992, featured on the DVD released as part of his box-set, *THE ULTIMATE COLLECTION*, issued in November 2004.

Different concert performances screened by Nippon TV in Japan (from the Bad World Tour), and several countries from the *His*tory World Tour, including Australia, Denmark, Germany, New Zealand, Romania & Sweden.

Performed by Michael and Slash during the *Michael Jackson: 30th Anniversary Celebration, The Solo Years* concerts, staged at New York's Madison Square Garden on 7th and 10th September 2001.

Performed by the Chipmunks in a 1983 episode of *Alvin & The Chipmunks*, where the Chipmunks and Chipettes faced-off against bullies at an ice skating rink.

Sampled on the Refugee Camp Mix of Michael's own *2 Bad*, from his 1997 remix album, *BLOOD ON THE DANCE FLOOR*.

Featured in several films, including: *Back To The Future II* (1989), *Zoolander* (2001) and *Undercover Brother* (2002).

Performed by Metallica at the 2003 MTV Video Music Awards.

Latin influenced cover version by Señor Coconut released as a single in the UK in 2004.

Ranked no.4 'World's Favourite Song' by UK voters in Sony Ericsson's global poll in 2005, behind Michael's *Billie Jean*, *Thriller* and Queen's *Bohemian Rhapsody*.

Fifth of Michael's 20 *'Visionary – The Video Singles'* reissues, with the music on one side of a Dual Disc and the accompanying short film on the other side. Issued in March 2006 in the UK – charted at no.15.

Two cover versions by Fall Out Boy, a live version and a studio version, featured on the album and accompanying DVD, both titled *LIVE IN PHOENIX*, released in 2008. Live version recorded in June 2007 at the Cricket Pavilion, Phoenix. Studio version, featuring guitar solo by John Mayer, achieved no.19 in the States and no.21 in the UK.

Posthumous hit: no.5 in Switzerland, no.7 in Holland & USA (Hot Digital Songs), no.8 in Norway, no.12 in Finland, no.14 in Germany, no.15 in Ireland & Spain, no.16 in Denmark, no.19 in UK and no.24 in New Zealand.

BEAT IT 2008

Re-working of the above song for the album, *THRILLER 25*, released in February 2008.

Mixed Michael's original album vocals with new vocals by Fergie (real name Stacy Ann Ferguson), effectively turning the song into a duet.

Charted on the strength of downloads alone in several countries, achieving no.31 in Denmark, no.41 in Switzerland, no.43 in Sweden, no.77 in Canada and no.177 in the UK.

Released as a promo CD single, with the original album version of *Beat It*, in Japan.

Posthumous hit: no.8 in Sweden and no.14 in Austria.

BEAT IT – MUSCLES

Medley performed by Diana Ross at her second concert in Central Park in 1983.

BEAUTIFUL GIRL

Written by Michael, and recorded by him, between 1998 and 2004.

Demo version featured on Michael's box-set, *THE ULTIMATE COLLECTION*, issued in November 2004.

BECAUSE OF YOU

Title track of Ne-Yo's second album, released in 2007, of which Ne-Yo (real name Shaffer Chimere Smith) said: 'If people didn't notice, I'm thinking everybody did, but it's very Michael Jackson. Michael Jackson is a huge part of why it is I do what I do – so that is kind of my ode to him, this song.'

Single achieved no.2 on the Hot 100 and no.7 of the R&B/Hip Hop singles chart in the States, and no.4 in the UK.

BEHIND CLOSED DOORS

Performed by the Jacksons on *The Tonight Show* in the States in 1977, as part of a medley with *Without A Song, You've Got A Friend, Make It With You, You've Made Me So Very Happy, You Are The Sunshine Of My Life, You And Me Against The World*.

No.1 hit for Charlie Rich on the Country chart in the States in 1973; also achieved no.15 on the Pop chart, and no.16 in the UK the following year.

BEHIND THE MASK

Song written by Chris Mosdell and Ryuichi Sakamoto, with additional lyrics by Michael.

Original instrumental version, with choral backing, recorded by the Yellow Magic Orchestra, for their 1979 album, *SOLID STATE SURVIVOR*. Quincy Jones heard Yellow Magic Orchestra's version during the *Thriller* sessions, and brought it to Michael's attention.

'I didn't know who Michael Jackson was – I wasn't into that whole soul disco stuff,' confessed Chris Mosdell. 'When Michael Jackson recorded it, he also added an extra melody line and a few extra lyrics, so they wanted to split the royalties – which is quite impossible. You can't take a Beatles song and add a melody line, a few more lyrics, and ask for fifty percent.'

Legal battles meant Michael's version didn't make his *THRILLER* album and remains unreleased.

Michael's keyboardist, Greg Phillinganes, did record a version for his album, *PULSE*, issued in 1985. Released as a single, it achieved no.77 on the R&B singles chart in the States, but failed to make the Hot 100 and wasn't a hit in the UK.

Phillinganes first met Michael and his brothers during the sessions for the Jacksons' *DESTINY* album in 1978, and went on to serve as musical director for Michael's Bad World Tour.

Phillinganes, who also played with his band, brought the song to Eric Clapton's attention. Clapton's cover version, on which Phillinganes played keyboards and sang backing vocals, hit no.15 in the UK in 1987. This version, curiously, failed to credit Michael as one of the song's co-writers – but Chris Mosdell has confirmed Michael did take 50% of the song-writing royalties.

Coming full circle, Sakamoto – after hearing Clapton's version – recorded a vocal version of the song.

BEI MIR BIST DU SCHON

Old standard the Jackson 5 sang as part of a 'Salute to the Vocal Groups' medley with *Opus One*, *Yakety Yak*, *Stop! In The Name Of Love*, an untitled Jackson 5 ditty and *Dancing Machine*, on *The Carol Burnett Show* in the States in January 1975 – clip included on the Vol.31 DVD of the show.

Originally written in Yiddish – translates as 'To me, you are beautiful'. English lyrics by Sammy Cahn and Saul Chaplin, and first recorded in English by the Andrew Sisters in 1937. Recorded by numerous other artists, including Cab Calloway and Benny Goodman.

Performed by Michael and his brothers during their *The Jacksons* TV series.

BELONG 2

Song written by Michael with Teddy Riley in 1999, for Michael's *INVINCIBLE* album, but failed to make the final cut and remains unreleased.

BEN

Title track of Michael's second solo album, released in August 1972 in the States and December 1972 in the UK.

Initially intended for Michael's teen rival Donny Osmond, until lyricist Don Black suggested Michael might make a better job of it.

Title song for a tame horror movie, the sequel to *Willard*, in which youngster, David Garrison (played by Lee Montgomery), has a rat as his best friend. In the film, Montgomery sings the song whilst sat at a piano. Michael's version of *Ben* played at the end of the movie, when the rat reappears, after Garrison believes it has been killed – Michael confirmed in 1980 he recorded two versions of the song, and this was almost certainly the second, unreleased take of the song. 14 year old Michael wasn't old enough to go see the film when it was first released. Movie version of the song remains unreleased.

Gave Michael his first no.1 on the Hot 100 in the States, where it also achieved no.5 on the R&B singles chart. In the UK it peaked at no.7.

28

Michael promoted *Ben* with several TV appearances in the States, including *American Bandstand* (alternate version), *The Sonny & Cher Comedy Hour*, *Soul Train* and the Jackson 5's own TV special in November 1972 – also performed by Michael on *The Jacksons* TV series in 1976. Golden Globe Award and Academy Award nomination for Song of the Year – Michael performed the song at the latter, but the song failed to pick up an Oscar. Also honoured with an ASCAP Award.

Rare one-sided 7" promo, on the Cinerama label, featured an excerpt of *Ben*, accompanied in the background by the sound of screaming rats.

Live version featured on the Michael/Jackson 5's *LIVE!* album, issued in September 1988 in the UK (no USA release). All songs on the album were recorded at a concert on 30th April 1973, at the Osaka Koseinenkin Hall in Japan. Also included on the limited edition CD, *IN JAPAN!*, released by Hip-O Select in 2004 – only 5,000 copies pressed.

Second live version, recorded at a concert at Madison Square Garden in September 1981, featured on the Jacksons album, *LIVE*, issued in November 1981.

Live performance by the Jacksons, at a concert in Mexico in 1976, included on the home video, *The Jacksons In Concert*, released in 1981 in the UK (no USA release). Michael also performed the song during the Jacksons' Destiny Tour, screened on BBC2 in the UK.

Short version featured in the 'Stark Raving Dad' episode of *The Simpsons*, in which Michael guested – however, contractual obligations meant a sound-a-like performed *Ben* and *Billie Jean*.

Remixed version titled HF Remix #2 featured on the album, *SOUL SOURCE – JACKSON 5 REMIXES 2*, released in Japan in 2001.

Vocal and instrumental versions featured on the karaoke album, *MOTOWN ORIGINAL ARTISTS, VOL.6: STOP! IN THE NAME OF LOVE*, released in September 2003.

Used as the theme song for the Japanese soap, *Aikurshi*, in 2005 – reissued in Japan in May 2005 as a 3-track CD single, featuring the original recording and two new mixes (*HF Remix* and *Orchestral*). Charted at no.48, a four place improvement on the song's original placing in 1972.

Cover version recorded by Marti Webb in 1985, in aid of the Ben Hardwick Appeal, peaked at no.5 in the UK. Ben Hardwick was a terminally ill little boy whose story touched hearts across the country when it was told on the popular TV show, *That's Life!* Michael's version of *Ben* was played at Ben Hardwick's funeral.

Also in the UK, talent show *Opportunity Knocks* winner Toni Warne recorded a version of *Ben*, which charted at no.50 in 1987.

Covered by Crispin Glover, to coincide with a re-make of *Willard*, the prequel to the film, *Ben*.

Other cover versions include:
Boyzone – on their 1996 album, *A DIFFERENT BEAT*.

Eoghan Quigg – on the X-Factor finalist's self-titled debut album in 2009.

Performed by Billy Gilman during the *Michael Jackson: 30th Anniversary Celebration, The Solo Years* concerts, staged at New York's Madison Square Garden on 7th and 10th September 2001.

Posthumous hit: no.6 in Holland, no.14 in Australia, no.24 in Ireland, no.46 in UK and no.75 in USA (Hot Digital Songs).

BETTER ON THE OTHER SIDE

Tribute song, recorded within a couple of days of Michael's death on 25th June 2009, by The Game, Chris Brown, P. Diddy, Polow The Don, Mario Winans, Usher and Boyz II Men.

BIG BOY

Believed to have been written by Jesse Reese, but officially credited to Gordon Keith, released as the Jackson 5's first ever single by Steel-Town Records in January 1968 (USA only).

Demo recorded circa November 1967. Initially hand-sold by Michael and his brothers, at the many gigs they played. Picked up for national distribution by Atco, a subsidiary of Atlantic Records, who pressed 10,000 copies. Sold well locally, but failed to register on any of Billboard's charts.

Re-issued as a limited edition CD single, backed with *You've Changed*, in the States on the Inverted record label, in June 1995.

An ex-engineer, who engineered on all the sessions, has confirmed the Jackson 5 recorded eight songs for Steel-Town, only six of which have been released, including:

- *Big Boy.*
- *You've Changed.*
- *We Don't Have To Be Over 21 (To Fall In Love).*
- *Jam Session* (the version on the B-side of *Big Boy*).

Two of the six released songs are unconfirmed, but are probably:

- *Some Girls Want Me For Their Lover* (aka *Michael The Lover*).
- *I Found A Love.*

The remaining two recordings were believed to be *Take My Heart* and *Jackson Man* – however, the founder and owner of Steel-Town, Gordon Keith, has refuted this.

All the other 'lost Steel-Town recordings', it's speculated, were actually taped by Shirley Cartman, possibly in her own living room. According to Cartman, only one copy of the tape ever existed. Many years after the recordings were made (by which time she had moved to Atlanta), a friend recommended she have the recordings transferred to professional archival tape, to preserve them for historical purposes. This she did, using a local Atlanta company – then, just a year or so later, the first of many compilations of 'lost' recordings surfaced, released by S.D.E.G., a small Atlanta record label.

When she learned of the commercial release of her recordings, Cartman was understandably angry – more so, because some songs she had written especially for the Jackson 5 (including *Lonely Heart*), were credited to Gordon Keith (founder and owner of Steel-Town).

Gordon Keith has denied *Take My Heart* and *Jackson Man* were recorded while the Jackson 5 were with Steel-Town, and claims they must be early Motown recordings.

See also: *Take My Heart*, *Jackson Man*.

BILLIE JEAN

Track written and co-produced, with Quincy Jones, by Michael.

Originally titled 'Not My Lover' (to avoid any confusion with the tennis player, Billie Jean King), and inspired by an obsessive young women who accused Michael and his brothers of fathering their sons. Michael's mother, Katherine, expressed surprise at the song's lyrics, especially where Michael vehemently proclaimed, 'the kid is *not* my son!'

Producer Quincy Jones wasn't too impressed with the demo of *Billie Jean* – he didn't much care for the bass. Original demo version included on the special edition of *THRILLER*, issued in 2001.

Second demo version, over six minutes with alternate vocals and ad-libs, is known to exist – remains unreleased.

Mixed by Bruce Swedien, who usually did just one mix of a song – but he did 91 of *Billie Jean*, before the second mix was eventually chosen.

'Quincy said, okay, this song has to have the most incredible drum sound that anybody has ever done, but it also has to have one element that's different, and that's sonic personality,' said Swedien, admitting he lost a lot of sleep over what exactly Quincy meant. 'What I ended up doing was building a drum platform and designing some special little things, like a bass drum cover and a flat piece of wood that goes between the snare and the hi-hat... the bottom line is that there aren't many pieces of music where you can hear the first three or four notes of the drums, and immediately tell what the piece of music is. But I think that is the case with *Billie Jean* – and that I attribute to sonic personality.'

'That fantastic guitar solo is actually the David Williams guitar solo from the demo of *Billie Jean*,' said Swedien. 'We recorded the *Billie Jean* demo in Michael's studio at his home... it was just after Michael wrote the song, I think. When we did the finished track on Billie Jean, we tried many times to have David replay that solo, and it never was just right.'

Original album sleeve credits guitar solo to Dean Parks.

Spelling on original vinyl acetate of the *THRILLER* album: 'Billy Jean'.

Second single from Michael's 1982 solo album, *THRILLER*, following his light-weight duet with Paul McCartney, *The Girl Is Mine*.

Conquered the R&B singles chart in just three weeks – the fastest rising no.1 since 1970, when the Jackson 5 scored a hat-trick of equally quick chart toppers with *ABC*, *The Love You Save* and *I'll Be There*. Hit the top just one week after *The Girl Is Mine* was toppled by the Gap Band's *Outstanding*, and stayed at no.1 for an impressive nine weeks.

Also no.1 on the Hot 100 in the States for seven weeks, and no.1 in the UK for a single week. *Billie Jean* and *THRILLER* topped the singles charts and the albums charts on both sides of the Atlantic in the same week – a feat very few acts have ever achieved.

Short film directed by Steve Barron – premiered on MTV on 2nd March 1983, becoming the first music video screened that told a story, and resulted in Michael becoming one of the first black artists to be added to the MTV playlist.

No.3 best selling single of 1983 in the States, and no.9 best selling single of the same year in the UK.

RIAA Platinum Record Award (USA million seller).

American Music Award: Favourite Pop/Rock Single.

Grammy Awards: Best New R&B Song, Best R&B Vocal Performance, Male.

Cashbox Awards: Top Pop Single, Top Black Single.

Billboard Video Awards: Best Overall Video, Best Dance/Disco 12" (joint with *Beat It*).

NARM Awards: Best Selling Single.

Black Gold Awards: Best Single of the Year.

Canadian Black Music Awards: Top International Single.

Michael's third best selling single in the UK, after *Earth Song* and *One Day In Your Life*.

Inducted into the Music Video Producers Hall of Fame in 1992.

Official Versions:
Album Version.
Instrumental Version.
12" Extended Remix.
Original Demo Recording.
Four On The Floor Radio Mix.
Pepsi Version.

Tony Moran Remix scheduled to be included on Australian CD maxi-single in 2003, to celebrate the 20th anniversary of *THRILLER*, but cancelled; later featured on the MJ Megaremix, but not in its entirety.

Performed by Michael – to massive critical and popular acclaim – at *Motown 25: Yesterday, Today, Forever*, staged in the Pasadena Civic Auditorium on 25th March 1983. He 'moonwalked' in public for the first time, and went on to earn an Emmy nomination, for Best Individual Performance on a Variety or Music Program.

Victory Tour 'Live' Promo, directed by Patrick T. Kelly, used to promote the Jacksons tour of the same name – full version shown on *Night Flight Profile* in the States, and on *The Tube* in the UK.

Live performance by Michael, at his Dangerous Tour concert in Bucharest, Romania, on 1st October 1992, featured on the DVD released as part of his box-set, *THE ULTIMATE COLLECTION*, issued in November 2004.

Live performances also aired as part of concerts screened in Japan, Germany and New Zealand.

Cited by Michael as his favourite song to perform live: 'but only when I don't have to do it the same way,' he said. 'The audience wants a certain thing – I have to do the moonwalk in that spot. I'd like to do a different version.'

Coupled with Steely Dan's *Do It Again* in 1983, titled *Do It Again/ Billie Jean*. Italian group Club House's version charted at no.11 in the UK and no.75 on the Hot 100 in the States. Slingshot – studio musicians from Detroit – took their version to no.25 on the R&B singles chart in the States.

Medley of *Billie Jean* and Junior Giscombe's hit, *Mama Used To Say*, released as a single by Shinehead in 1984.

Sampled by numerous artists, including:
LL Cool J's *Who's Afraid Of The Big Bad Wolf*, which he contributed to the 1991 Disney tribute album, *SIMPLY MAD ABOUT THE MOUSE*.

BLACKstreet's *Billie Jean Remix* of *No Diggity* in 1996 – hit no.1 for four weeks in the States on both the Hot 100 and R&B singles chart, and peaked at no.9 in the UK.

Bar-Kays (a parody) on *Dirty Dancers* – featured of the group's 1996 album, *THE BEST OF – VOLUME 2*.

Chanté Moore on *I Started Crying*, a track included on her 1999 album, *THIS MOMENT IS MINE*.

Pras on *Avenues*, from his 2001 album, *GHETTO SUPERSTAR*.

Babyface on the *Jammin' G-Clef Billie Jean Remix* of *There She Goes*, in 2001.

Featured in the film, *Charlie's Angels* (2000), and in the video game, *Grand Auto Theft: Vice City*.

Ranked no.16 'Best Song' on the UK's Channel 4 TV/HMV's 'Music of the Millennium Poll' in early 2000, in which over 600,000 votes were cast.

Ranked no.7 on MTV Europe's 'All-Time Top Ten R&B Songs' millennium poll.

Ranked no.35 on MTV USA/TV Guide's '100 Greatest Videos Ever Made' millennium poll.

Performed by Michael and Slash during the *Michael Jackson: 30th Anniversary Celebration, The Solo Years* concerts, staged at New York's Madison Square Garden on 7th and 10th September 2001. Also performed by Destiny's Child, wearing fedora hats and white gloves, as a medley with their own hit, *Bootylicious*. Beyonce Knowles, of Destiny's Child, said, 'When I wrote and produced that song (*Bootylicious*), I totally had Michael Jackson in mind. I was just feeling Michael – he taught us so much.' At his first meeing with the trio, Michael sang a few lines from *Bootylicious*, which achieved no.1 on the Hot 100 and no.2 on the R&B singles chart in the States, and no.2 in the UK, in 2001.

Ranked no.3 'World's Favourite Song' on Sony Ericsson's global poll in 2005, in which over 700,000 people in more than 60 countries voted. UK voters placed *Billie Jean* at no.1, ahead of *Thriller*, with a further five of the Top 10 being solo recordings by Michael.

Fourth of Michael's 20 *'Visionary – The Video Singles'* reissues, with the music on one side of a Dual Disc and the accompanying short film on the other side. Issued in March 2006 in the UK – charted at no.11, and spent over 40 weeks on the Top 200, making it the most successful reissue by some distance.

Cover versions include:
Miki Asakura – on his 1984 Japanese album, *DANCIN' M*.
The Bates – no.67 in the UK in 1996.
Linx – as *Billie Jean Got Soul*, in 1997.
Ian Brown (flip-side of *Dolphins Were Monkeys*) – no.5 in the UK in 2000.
Sound Bluntz – no.32 in the UK in 2002.
Chris Cornell (former Soundgarden frontman) – performed live during an acoustic set in Stockholm, Sweden, in September 2006, and recorded for his 2007 album, *CARRY ON*.
Sly & Robbie – included on the 2009 compilation, *UNCOVERED*.

Ian Brown commented: 'I love Jackson … I want to do a Jackson EP, with *Thriller*, *Beat It*, *Billie Jean* and *Rockin' Robin* or *ABC* on it. Hopefully I'll get it done.'

Voted the Greatest Dance Record of All Time in 2008 by listeners to BBC Radio 2 in the UK, ahead of Donna Summer's *I Feel Love*.

Posthumous hit: no.2 in Switzerland, no.3 in Holland & Sweden, no.4 in Spain & USA (Hot Digital Songs), no.5 in Norway, no.7 in Australia, no.8 in Denmark, no.10 in the UK, no.11 in Finland & Ireland, no.14 in Austria, no.15 in New Zealand and no.18 in Germany.

Michael's passing inspired LL Cool J to re-envision the song as *Billie Jean Dream*. 'After hearing the tragic news of Michael Jackson's death,' said LL Cool J, 'the lyrics for the *Billie Jean* remix came to me in a dream. Michael was one of my childhood idols and has always been a great inspiration to me.'

Michael look-a-like danced to Billie Jean & Wanna Be Startin' Somethin', as a tribute to Michael, at Madonna's concert at the O2 Arena, London, on 4th July 2009. Madonna told the audience Michael was 'one of the greatest artists the world has ever known, Michael Jackson – long live the King!'

BILLIE JEAN 2008

Re-working of the above song with Kanye West, recorded for *THRILLER 25*, released in February 2008.

This version used the original album version of the song, with the vocals time-stretched and slowed down.

Charted as an album track, on the strength of downloads, for a solitary week at no.183 in the UK.

BLACK OR WHITE

Written by Michael, with rap lyrics by Bill Bottrell.

Opening guitar first recorded at Michael's Encino home. 'That piece of music, the beginning part that Slash plays on, was recorded at Michael's house,' confirmed Bottrell. 'Michael asked me to dig it out of the vault in August of 1989. He had in mind to use it as the intro to *Black Or White* – it took a long time before we got Slash on it.'

'For me, the best thing about *Black Or White*,' said Bottrell, 'was that his (Michael's) scratch vocal remained untouched throughout the next year (of work on *DANGEROUS*), and ended up being used on the finished song.'

'I didn't produce this but, again, I added percussion to the track,' said Teddy Riley. 'I used wood percussion – cow bells, shakers and thisngs like that.'

Lead single from Michael's album *DANGEROUS*, single and album both released in November 1991.

Fastest no.1 on Billboard's Hot 100 in the States since 1969, when *Get Back* by the Beatles also conquered the chart in just three weeks. No.1 for seven weeks, but stalled at no.3 on the R&B singles chart.

RIAA Platinum Record Award (USA million seller).

No.8 best selling single of 1991 in the States.

First single by an American to enter the UK singles chart at no.1 since Elvis Presley's *It's Now Or Never* in 1960. Spent two weeks in pole position.

Also no.1 in Australia, Austria, Belgium, Cuba, Denmark, Finland, France, Israel, Italy, Mexico, Norway, Spain, Sweden, Switzerland and Zimbabwe.

Series of remixes by Richard Clivilles and David Cole of the C&C Music Factory. Issued in January 1992, charted in their own right in the UK, achieving no.14.

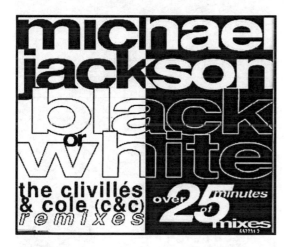

Official Versions:
Album Version.
Instrumental.
Radio Edit.
Tribal Beats.
Clivilles & Cole House/Club Mix.
Clivilles & Cole House/Dub Mix.
Clivilles & Cole Radio Mix.
Underground Club Mix.
House with Guitar Radio Mix.
Pepsi Version.
Grammy nomination: Best Pop Vocal Performance, Male.

Promo 11 minute short film, directed by John Landis, premiered on 14th November 1991. Estimated global audience in 27 countries of 500+ million – the highest ever for a music video. Co-starred: Macauley Culkin (*Home Alone*), George 'Norm' Wendt (*Cheers*), cartoon characters Bart and Homer Simpson, brother Jackie's daughter Brandi, and a cameo appearance from director Landis.

Final, non-musical segment of promo – in which Michael interpreted the black panther's wild and animalistic behavior – was highly controversial, with complaints flooding in from many shocked viewers. Michael issued a press statement that read:

It upsets me to think Black Or White *could influence any child or adult to destructive behavior, either sexual or violent. I've always tried to be a good role model and, therefore, have made these changes to avoid any possibility of adversely affecting any individual's behavior. I deeply regret any pain or hurt that the final segment of* Black Or White *has caused children, their parents or other viewers.*

Final segment edited out of most future screenings, but made available on the home video *Dangerous – The Short Films*, issued in 1993, with swastikas and Klu Klux Klan graffiti added to give focus to Michael's uncharacteristically violent outbursts.

International Monitor Awards: Music Video with the Best Special Effects.

NAACP Image Awards: Outstanding Music Video.

Michael performed *Black Or White* for the first time at MTV's 10th Anniversary Special in November 1991. Joined on stage by Slash, former Guns 'N Roses guitarist, who also played guitar on the recorded track. Slash also joined Michael on stage in Tokyo, Japan, at his Dangerous World Tour concerts on 30th and 31st December 1992.

Live segment, from Michael's Dangerous World Tour, screened at the Billboard Awards in December 1992.

Live performance by Michael, at his Dangerous Tour concert in Bucharest, Romania, on 1st October 1992, featured on the DVD released as part of his box-set, *THE ULTIMATE COLLECTION*, issued in November 2004.

Live performances from Michael's *History* World Tour shown as part of televised concerts in Germany and New Zealand.

Also in 1992, song used in Michael's Japanese advert for *Kirara Basso*.

Performed by Michael and Slash during the *Michael Jackson: 30th Anniversary Celebration, The Solo Years* concerts, staged at New York's Madison Square Garden on 7th and 10th September 2001.

Remixed version included on the first acetate version of the special, expanded edition of *DANGEROUS* – bonus disc later shelved.

Eleventh of Michael's 20 *'Visionary – The Video Singles'* reissues, with the music on one side of a Dual Disc and the accompanying short film on the other side. Issued in April 2006 in the UK – charted at no.18.

Posthumous hit: no.6 in Australia, no.7 in Switzerland, no.11 in Sweden, no.13 in USA (Hot Digital Songs), no.16 in New Zealand, no.17 in Austria, no.22 in Ireland & Spain, no.25 in UK, no.28 in Holland and no.31 in Germany.

BLAME IT ON THE BOOGIE

Written by Mick Jackson – no relation – with Stevie Wonder in mind.

First brought to the attention of the Jacksons, after one of their representatives heard it, at the Midem Music Festival in 1978.

Lead single, and the only track the brothers didn't write themselves, from the Jacksons' album *DESTINY*, issued in December 1978.

Charted in the States at no.3 on the R&B singles chart and a lowly no.54 on the Hot 100, and peaked at no.8 in the UK.

Special 7 Minute Extended Disco Remix featured slight alternate vocals.

Accompanied by the Jacksons' first proper promo video, featuring Michael and his brothers in an entertaining, toe-tapping feature with – for the time – advanced special effects. Peter Conn directed the promo.

Official Versions:
Album Version.
Mono Version.
Special 7 Minute Extended Disco Remix.
John Luongo Disco Mix.

Mick Jackson's original version rush-released, once it became known the Jacksons' cover was being issued as a single. Two versions by similarly named artists understandably led to confusion among record buyers, especially in the UK, where Mick's version charted at no.15.

Mick Jackson has confirmed he loves the Jacksons version of his song, and Jay Kay's 2003 cover as well. Michael and Mick Jackson have met several times. 'The first time was in a lift in the Montcalm Hotel in London, and we just said hi,' Mick recalls. 'Later, at the *Top Of The Pops* TV show in London, he asked me to sell him my jump suit I was wearing for the show and I declined… MJ was performing *Destiny* with his brothers.'

Performed by the Jacksons, when they guested on *The ABBA Special: Disco In The Snow Part II*, filmed in Switzerland in February 1979 (and screened on BBC1 in the UK in April), and on Germany's *Musik Laden* the same year. Also featured in a Destiny Tour concert screened on BBC2 in the UK.

Other hit versions:
Big Fun – no.4 in the UK in 1989.
Clock – no.16 in the UK in 1998.

Cover version by Nouvelle Star, from the French version of *American Idol,* hit no.1 in France in 2005.

Posthumous hit: no.55 in the UK.

BLESS HIS SOUL

Written and produced by Michael with brothers Jackie, Marlon, Randy & Tito, also featured on the Jacksons' album *DESTINY*.

According to Marlon, the song is about 'this person who's doing these things in the world, and people aren't paying all that much attention to him, so he tries harder and harder until he gets across.'

B-side of Michael's solo single *Girlfriend* in the UK, and of the Jacksons' single *Lovely One* in the States, both released in 1980.

BLOOD ON THE DANCE FLOOR

Written by Michael with Teddy Riley, who came up with the evocative title.

Title track of Michael's solo album, sub-titled 'His*tory In The Mix*', issued in May 1997. Album opened with five previously unreleased songs, followed by eight remixed songs from Michael's HIS*TORY* album.

Originally recorded for Michael's *DANGEROUS* album in 1991, but failed to make the final track listing. Teddy Riley, reportedly, was angry Michael didn't call him to 'vacuum clean this old master' – that is, to give the song a more current sound, before its inclusion on *BLOOD ON THE DANCE FLOOR*.

Finalised in January 1997 in Montreux, Switzerland – Michael played it to some fans who were outside the recording studio.

Some formats of the single release carried the dedication: 'Dedicated to Elton John. Thank you for everything. I love you' – an acknowledgement to Elton from Michael, for putting him up and supporting him, following his troubles in late 1993.

Michael Jackson on tour - July '97

Promo short film, directed by Michael and Vincent Paterson, premiered in the UK on *Top Of The Pops* on 28th March 1997 – several weeks ahead of its release as a single. Ploy generated enough interest to shift 85,000 copies in its first week, good enough to take the no.1 spot from R. Kelly's *I Believe I Can Fly*. Michael's seventh UK chart topper as a soloist, but tumbled from no.1 to no.8 in its second week on the chart.

Unreleased short film shot – revealed to exist by Vincent Paterson during a tribute to him, 'Master Of All media', at New York's Walter Reade Theater on 13th January 2008. 'Michael loved it,' said Paterson, 'but Sony hated it and refused to release it, which is where all the trouble might have started.' Posted on YouTube in June 2009, but no official release.

Disappointed in the States, peaking at no.19 on the R&B singles chart and no.42 on the Hot 100.

Official Versions:
Album Version.
Refugee Camp Edit.
A Cappella.
Refugee Camp Mix.
Fire Island Dub.
Fire Island Radio Edit.
TM's O-Positive Dub.
Switchblade Edit.
Fire Island Vocal Mix.
TM's Refugee Camp Dub.
TM's Switchblade Mix.
T & G Pool Of Blood Dub.

The Refugee Camp Mix, rather than the original mix, featured on Michael's home video, His*tory On Film Volume II*.

Michael, interviewed in 1998 about the remixes on *BLOOD ON THE DANCE FLOOR*, confirmed he didn't really like remixes, as he didn't appreciate other producers altering his work – his record company, however, asserted 'kids love remixes.'

Live performance, from Michael's *His*tory World Tour, screened as part of a concert by Sat 1 TV in Germany.

Twentieth and last of Michael's 20 *'Visionary – The Video Singles'* reissues, with the music on one side of a Dual Disc and the accompanying short film on the other side. Issued in June 2006 in the UK – charted at no.19.

Master tapes from Teddy Riley's Future Records studio surfaced on eBay, featured unreleased mixes:

Blood On The Dance Floor Mix 6 #24 (6:14)
Blood On The Dance Floor Mix 6 #24 (7:40)

BLOWIN' IN THE WIND

Bob Dylan song the Jackson 5 recorded a version of – remains unreleased.

Hit versions:
Peter, Paul & Mary – no.2 on the Hot 100 in the States, and no.13 in the UK, in 1963.
Stevie Wonder – no.1 on the R&B singles chart and no.9 on the Hot 100 in the States, and no.36 in the UK, in 1966.

BLUE JEAN (SAFE SEX)

Track by Jeru The Damaja that refers to Michael and *Billie Jean*, from the 2000 album, *HEROZ4HIRE*.

BLUES AWAY

Written by Michael about a man coming out of depression, and featured on the Jacksons' eponymous debut album, released in November 1976.

B-side of *Show You The Way To Go* – the first time one of Michael's own songs was issued on a single.

Performed solo by Michael on *The Jacksons* TV series in 1976.

BODY

Written by, and essentially a solo recording by, Marlon Jackson, featured on the Jacksons' album *VICTORY*, issued in July 1984.

Third single lifted from *VICTORY*, but failed to match the success of the first two, *State Of Shock* and *Torture*.

Charted at no.39 on the R&B singles chart, and no.47 on the Hot 100, in the States. In the UK, failed to make the Top 75, but spent a solitary week at no.94 on 'The Next 25' section of the chart.

Official Versions:
Album Version.
7" Mix.
7" Instrumental.
Extended 12" Remix.
Extended 12" Instrumental.

Although credited to all six Jackson brothers, Michael and Jermaine declined to appear in the promo video.

BODY LANGUAGE (DO THE LOVE DANCE)

Song featured on the Jackson 5's album *MOVING VIOLATION*, issued in May 1975 in the States and July 1975 in the UK.

Scheduled to be released as the follow-up to *Forever Came Today/All I Do Is Think Of You* in the States on 18th September 1975. Promo single issued, but full release cancelled, when it became known Michael and his brothers (Jermaine apart) were leaving Motown for CBS/Epic.

Performed by the Jackson 5, with Vicki Lawrence, on *The Carol Burnett Show* in January 1976, and on their own TV series the following year.

Live performance by the Jacksons, at a concert in Mexico in 1976, included on the home video, *The Jacksons In Concert*, released in 1981 in the UK (no USA release).

Remix – Fat's Camp Lovedance Mix – released in 2005 on Universal Music's DJ WhistleBump label.

BOOGIE MAN, THE

Song featured on the Jackson 5's album *SKYWRITER*, issued in March 1973 in the States and July 1973 in the UK.

Scheduled for release as a single in the States in March 1974, but withdrawn. Promo copies with a picture sleeve were issued – today, a great rarity.

Released as a single in the UK in April 1974. Failed to make the Top 50, but registered at no.58 on the 'breakers' section of the chart.

BORN TO LOVE YOU

Song featured on the Jackson 5's debut album, *DIANA ROSS PRESENTS THE JACKSON 5*, released in December 1969 in the States and March 1970 in the UK.

Originally recorded by the Temptations, for their 1965 album, *THE TEMPTIN' TEMPTATIONS*.

BOTTLE OF SMOKE

Song written by, and possibly recorded by, Michael circa 1989.

Considered for Michael's *DANGEROUS* album, but failed to make the final track listing, and remains unreleased.

BOYS AND GIRLS, WE ARE THE JACKSON FIVE

Originally released in 1989, titled 'Monologue', on the pre-Motown compilation *THE BEGINNING YEARS 1965-1967*.

First titled *Boys And Girls, We Are The Jackson Five* on a Japanese release, *BIG BOY*; later the same year, included on *THE JACKSON FIVE FEATURING MICHAEL JACKSON*, issued on the Stardust label in the UK/Europe.

BOZO INTRODUCTORY SONG

Medley of the biggest Bozo songs of the past, performed to introduce the Bozo Awards on the *Sonny & Cher Show*, in 1976 – the entire cast, including the Jacksons and Sonny & Cher, sang the medley. The Jacksons also performed *Enjoy Yourself*.

BRACE YOURSELF

Promotional clip, accompanied by Orff's *Carmina Burana*, which featured excerpts from Michael's concerts, music videos, album and magazine covers, etc. – sub-titled 'A Kaleidoscope of Michael Jackson'. Originally, the term was used by Michael to introduce his *Black Or White* short film.

Clip, directed and edited by Bob Jenkins, included on Michael's home videos, *Video Greatest Hits – History* and *History On Film Volume II*.

BRAND NEW THING

Song written by Michael with brothers Jackie, Jermaine, Marlon and Tito, and performed by the Jackson 5 in concert in the 1970s, to introduce young Randy on to the stage – never recorded.

Registered with the United States Copyright Office in April 1972.

Performed by the Jackson 5 on the American TV show, *Hellzapoppin*, in 1972.

BREAK OF DAWN

Written by Michael with Dr. Freeze.

Featured on Michael's solo album *INVINCIBLE*, released in October 2001.

Originally conceived as a Jacksons project; it's rumoured Dr. Freeze cut a demo where he sang lead with Michael's brothers on backing vocals.

Following the success of *You Rock My World* and *Butterflies*, cited by many critics as the track most likely to give Michael a sizeable hit in the States, but never released to radio or as a commercial single – it's release, at the beginning of 2002, was reputedly blocked by Sony's Tommy Motolla.

Demo surfaced on the internet in 2005 – authenticity unconfirmed.

BREAKING FREE

Short poem written by Michael – included in his book of poems and reflections, *Dancing The Dream*, published in 1992.

BREEZY

Song that appeared on the Jackson 5's album *MOVING VIOLATION*, issued in July 1975.

BRIDGE OVER TROUBLED WATER

Cover version recorded, with Jermaine singing lead, by the Jackson 5 for *THIRD ALBUM*, released in September 1970 in the States and February 1971 in the UK.

Originally recorded by Simon & Garfunkel in early 1970, for an album of the same title – their version hit no.1 on both sides of the Atlantic, and in many other countries as well.

BUFFALO BILL

Written by Michael, and first mentioned just prior to the release of the Jacksons' album *VICTORY* in 1984, by Michael's manager at the time, Frank DiLeo. Also considered by Michael for his solo album, *BAD*, but failed to make the final track listing.

Engineer Bruce Swedien has commented the song had a more vocal sound, with Michael's brothers singing more than in the past, and that it had a 'big symphonic opening and a charming melody'.

Inspired by James 'Wild Bill' Hickok (*aka* Buffalo Bill) and the way he died: shot in the back by Jack McCall during a poker game in Deadwood, Dakota Territory, in August 1876.

Name-checked on the unofficial *Michael Jackson: Unauthorised* home video, released in 1992 in the UK.

Cited by Michael in his court deposition in November 1993, and mentioned by him on *THE MICHAEL JACKSON INTERVIEW* CD, released by Baktabak in the same year – remains unreleased.

BUMPER SNIPPET

Unreleased snippets that surfaced on the internet, from a recording session where Michael is awaiting the go ahead, and sings a few lines including, 'Give me a little more keyboard! Give me a little more bass! Girl, I wanna groove!'

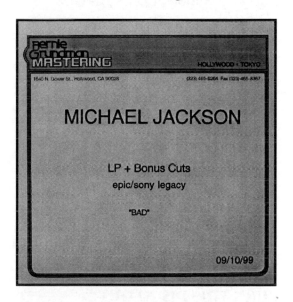

Included on the first acetate version of the special, expanded edition of *BAD*, but later withdrawn – no official release.

```
Bernie Grundman Mastering Date: 9/9/99
----------------------------------------
Label: EPIC/LEGACY/ Cat. No.:
----------------------------------------
MICHAEL JACKSON
"BAD"
----------------------------------------
Track Title                  Duration Pause
----------------------------------------
   1   BAD                     4:07   0
   2   THE WAY YOU MAKE ME F    4:58   1
   3   SPEED DEMON             4:01   0
   4   LIBERIAN GIRL           3:53   0
   5   JUST GOOD FRIENDS       4:06   2
   6   ANOTHER PART OF ME      3:54  14
   7   MAN IN THE MIRROR       5:20   0
   8   I JUST CAN'T STOP LOV   4:11   2
   9   DIRTY DIANA             4:41   0
  10   SMOOTH CRIMINAL         4:17   5
  11   LEAVE ME ALONE          4:39   2
  12   BUMPER SNIPPET          0:13   0
  13   STREETWALKER            5:51   0
  14   SOMEONE PUT YOUR HAND   4:33   0
  15   I JUST CAN'T STOP LOV   4:06   0
  16   FLY AWAY                2:46

----------------------------------------
   Total duration including pauses:  66:02
```

Another snippet featured a child screaming into the microphone. This was one of the Bonus Cuts included on the first acetate version of the special, expanded edition of *DANGEROUS*:

1. *Bumper Snippet (Kid).*
2. *Monkey Business.*
3. *Work That Body.*
4. *If You Don't Love Me.*
5. *Serious Effect.*
6. *Happy Birthday, Lisa.*
7. *She Got It.*
8. *Black Or White (Remix).*
9. *Dangerous (Alt. Version).*
10. *Who Is It (Remix).*

Bonus Cuts CD cancelled – no official release.

BURN THIS DISCO OUT

One of three song's Heatwave's Rod Temperton wrote for Michael, around the same time as *Rock With You*, for his first solo album for CBS/Epic, *OFF THE WALL*, released in August 1979.

Initially, Temperton was invited to deliver just one song, and was surprised when all three of his songs made the final selection. Michael recorded vocals for all three songs in one weekend, having already mastered the lyrics – professionalism that impressed Temperton.

B-side of Michael's single *Beat It* in the UK (but not USA).

BUTTERCUP

Song written circa 1974-75 by Stevie Wonder, at a time he said he was working on songs for a Jackson 5 album (that never happened). Article in the Spring 1975 issue of *Rock & Soul Songs* mentioned the collaboration, and cited *Buttercup* as a future single.

Recorded by Carl Anderson for his 1982 album, *ABSENCE WITHOUT LOVE* – released as a single three years later. Included on *THE WONDER OF STEVIE*, a two disc tribute to Stevie, featuring other artists singing his songs. Anderson died of leukaemia in February 2004 – Stevie played at his funeral service.

BUTTERFLIES

Song Michael recorded and co-produced with Andre Harris, for his solo album *INVINCIBLE*, issued in October 2001.

Backing vocals by Marsha Ambrosius, who co-wrote the song with Harris. Ambrosius and Natalie Stewart, of the UK duo Floetry, were invited by Michael to visit the studio while he was recording the track.

'It was incredible because he asked,' said Ambrosius, 'he continually asked, "Marsh, what's the next harmony? Girls, does this sound right? What do you think? Is this what you were looking for?" He was so open.'

Released to American radio stations in October 2001, and became the second of Michael's singles to chart on the strength of airplay alone. Achieved no.2 on the R&B singles chart and no.14 on the Hot 100 – however, the lack of a commercial single almost certainly cost Michael a chart topper (no UK release).

BMI Urban Awards: Best Song.

Official Versions:
Album Version.
Michael A Cappella.
Eve A Cappella.
Master Mix Instrumental.
Track Masters Master Mix feat. Eve.

Outland Remix featured on a promo only 12" single – no official release.

Original demo version recorded by Floetry was included on the duo's debut 2002 album, *FLOETRY*, as a bonus track.

BY THE TIME I GET TO PHOENIX

Song performed by the Jackson 5 as part of a medley – with *Danny Boy* and *Killing Me Softly With His Song* – during their Las Vegas shows in 1974. Also performed on *The Tonight Show* – hosted by Bill Cosby – in America in March 1974.

Hit versions:
Glen Campbell – no.26 in the States in 1967.
Isaac Hayes – no.37 in the States in1969.
Mad Lads – no.84 in the States in 1969.
Glen Campbell & Anne Murray – no.81 in the States in 1971.

CALIFORNIA GRASS

Song Michael cited he had written in his court deposition in November 1993 – remains unreleased.

CALL OF THE WILD

Song featured on the Jackson 5's album *MOVING VIOLATION*, released in May 1975 in the States and July 1975 in the UK.

Scheduled as the B-side of the cancelled single, *Body Language (Do The Love Dance)*, in the States.

CALL ON ME

Song recorded by Michael on 4th September 1973 and included, with added overdubs and remixed, on the solo compilation *FAREWELL MY SUMMER LOVE*, issued in May 1984 in the States and June 1984 in the UK.

B-side of *Farewell My Summer Love*.

Original 1973 recording released in the States in March 1995, on Michael's anthology series compilation *THE BEST OF...* (no UK release).

CALLING MICHAEL (UNITED FANS FOR MICHAEL)

Fans tribute to Michael, recorded by United Fans For Michael during his court appearances in 2005.

CAN I GET A WITNESS

Marvin Gaye hit the Jackson 5 recorded a version of – remains unreleased.

Hit versions:
Marvin Gaye – no.15 on the R&B singles chart and no.22 on the Hot 100 in the States in 1963.
Lee Michaels – no.39 on the Hot 100 in 1971.

CAN I LIVE

Song co-written by Sisqó and Teddy Riley.
Originally intended for Michael's album *INVINCIBLE*, until Sisqó recorded it for his second album, *RETURN OF DRAGON*, in 2001.

CAN I SEE YOU IN THE MORNING

Song included on the Jackson 5's album, *THIRD ALBUM*, issued in September 1970 in the States and February 1971 in the UK.

Also featured on a rare, six track EP of songs from the same album, issued with a picture sleeve in the States.

B-side of *Goin' Back To Indiana* in several continental European countries, including Denmark, France, Holland, Germany, Norway and Sweden.

Heard in the 'CinderJackson' episode of the Jackson 5's cartoon series in 1971.

Electric Sheep Mix featured on the album, *SOUL SOURCE – JACKSON 5 REMIXES 2*, released in Japan in 2001.

CAN YOU...

Song Michael worked on with will.i.am in early 2007 – could be unfinished, but Michael's vocals were recorded.

Remains unreleased.

CAN YOU FEEL IT

Co-written by Michael with brother Jackie, opening track on the Jacksons' album, *TRIUMPH*, released in October 1980.

Third single lifted from the album, fared much better in Europe than in the States. Charted at no. 6 in the UK, but only achieved no.30 on the R&B singles chart and no.77 on the Hot 100, in the States.

Promoted with innovative short film 'Triumph – Can You Feel It', directed by Bruce Gowers and Robert Abel, and costing around $140,000. Michael and his brothers were cast as larger-than-life, demi-God figures, who cast stardust on the world, as children gazed up with smiling faces – featured an alternate version of the song.

Song chosen to open the Jacksons' Triumph Tour concerts.

Live version, recorded at a concert at Madison Square Garden in September

1981, featured as the opening track on the Jacksons album, *LIVE*, issued in November 1981.

Performed by the Jacksons during the *Michael Jackson: 30th Anniversary Celebration, The Solo Years* concerts, staged at New York's Madison Square Garden on 7th and 10th September 2001.

Hit cover versions:
Raze & Champion Legend (two versions on different sides of one single) – no.62 in the UK in 1990.
V (double A-side with *Hip To Hip*) – no.5 in the UK in 2004.

Hip hop version, titled *Can U Feel Me*, featured on BLACKstreet's 1999 album, *FINALLY*.

Adaption – with new lyrics by Jim Dyke and Steven Gittleman about a woman with a chimney pot on her head – titled *Feel It*, recorded by the Italian combo, the Tamperer featuring Maya in 1998. Gave Michael his eighth chart topper as a song-writer in the UK – also hit no.1 in

Ireland, but only registered at no.103 on the 'bubbling under' section of the Hot 100 in the States.

Sampled by:
Parkride on a 1998 track, also titled *Can You Feel It*.
Steps on their version of *My Best Friend's Girl*, featured on their 1999 album, *STEPACULAR*.
Female rapper, Charli Baltimore on her song, *Feel It*.
Swedish rap group, Snook, on their track, *Superfitta*.

Sorry, the second single lifted from Madonna's 2005 album, *CONFESSIONS ON A DANCE FLOOR*, was originally reported to sample *Can You Feel It*. However, although something very similar to the bass-line from *Can You Feel It* could be heard, *Sorry* didn't credit Michael and brother Jackie among the song-writers – charted at no.1 in the UK and no.58 on the Hot 100 in the States.

Posthumous hit: no.44 in Holland and no.59 in UK.

CAN YOU REMEMBER

Song recorded by the Jackson 5 on the 10th and 15th July 1969, and featured on the group's debut album, *DIANA ROSS PRESENTS THE JACKSON 5*, released in December 1969 in the States and March 1970 in the UK.

Performed live – as a medley with *Sing A Simple Song* – by the Jackson 5 during their first national TV appearance in the States, on ABC-TV's *The Hollywood Palace Special*, aired on 18th October

1969. Michael and his brothers were introduced by Diana Ross. Album titled *MOTOWN AT THE HOLLYWOOD PALACE*, including *Can You Remember*, followed in March 1970 (no UK release).

Originally recorded by the Delfonics, for their 1968 album, *LA LA MEANS I LOVE YOU*.

Michael and his brothers first met the Delfonics in the pre-Motown days. 'We used to do a lot of shows at the Regal Theater in Chicago, and at the Capitol Theater there,' recalled William Hart, of the Delfonics. 'I remember they (the Jackson 5) didn't have a place to change clothes, and we had a big trailer and all… and they thought that was nice of me, to let them come in and change. I remember Michael saying, "Thank you! Thank you! Thank you!"'

CAN'T GET OUTTA THE RAIN

Written by Michael with Quincy Jones, and recorded by Michael – developed from the ending of *You Can't Win*, his only solo offering from his first movie *The Wiz*, with a slight lyric change from 'game' to 'rain'.

B-side of Michael's first duet with Paul McCartney, *The Girl Is Mine*, issued in 1982.

Made its CD debut in 2007, on the USA-only 'ringle' release of Thriller – a CD single that also included a downloadable ringtone and wallpaper. However, the ringle was quickly withdrawn from sale, as it was found to be defective.

Also released on CD in Japan in early 2008, on the first CD (with *The Girl Is Mine*) in a limited edition 7CD box-set of the seven singles lifted from *THRILLER*.

CAN'T GET READY FOR LOSING YOU

One of 19 'Rare & Unreleased' tracks on the fourth CD of the Michael/Jackson 5 box-set, *SOULSATION!*, issued in June 1995 in the States and July 1995 in the UK.

Recorded by Motown song-writer Willie Hutch for his 1973 album, *FULLY EXPOSED*.

CAN'T LET HER GET AWAY

Written and produced by Michael with Teddy Riley, for his solo album *DANGEROUS*, released in November 1991.

'This was mostly from a sample CD that I just put together myself,' revealed Riley, 'and it kind of reminded me of the James Brown sound. I could feel it. I thought I'd bring a shadow of some of the greatness of the James Brown production sound to this.'

Released as a promo 12" single in Costa Rica.

Featured in the film, *The Meteor Man* (1993).

Master tapes from Teddy Riley's Future Records studio surfaced on eBay, featured several unreleased mixes:

Can't Let Her Get Away Drum Beats 6
  Tracks
Can't Let Her Get Away Cassette
  Remix #5
Can't Let Her Get Away New
  Overdubs #19
Can't Let Her Get Away Mix 3 #22
Can't Let Her Get Away #24
Can't Let Her Get Away Mix 1 #33
Can't Let Her Get Away #56
  Instrumental With Backups

CARAVAN

Song performed by the Jacksons, with special guest Caroll O'Connor, on their TV series in 1976, as a medley with *Don't Get Around Much Anymore* and *Take The 'A' Train*.

CARMINA BURANA

Instantly recognisable piece of classical music written by Carl Orff. Michael used *Oh Fortuna – Carmina Burana* to great effect, during his Dangerous World Tour; the version used was as performed by the Prague Festival Orchestra & Chorus.

Featured on Michael's home video, *Dangerous – The Short Films*.

CAROL'S THEME

Short song written by Joe Hamilton – used on *The Carol Burnett Show* as the show's theme song.

Performed by Michael onstage at his 'MJ & Friends' concert in Munich, Germany, on 27th June 1999.

CAROUSEL

Song Michael originally recorded for his 1982 album, *THRILLER*, but failed to make the final track listing when *Human Nature* was chosen instead.

Also known as 'Circus Girl'.

Unreleased until October 2001, when an edited version was added to the expanded, special edition of *THRILLER* as one of three bonus tracks.

Full length version by Michael posted on writer Michael Sembello's official website; Sembello's version can also be heard on the site.

Full length version – with a shorter instrumental bridge section than the version on Sembello's site – officially released in 2008, when it was included on the Italian and French editions of the compilation, *KING OF POP*.

CEILING DANCE

Part of the score for Michael's *Ghosts* short film, composed by Nicholas Pike – made partially available by Pike on his website in August 2009.

CENTIPEDE

Song written and produced by Michael, for eldest sister Rebbie's debut album of the same name, released in 1984. Michael also sang backing vocals on the track.

Issued as Rebbie's debut single, achieving no.4 on the R&B singles chart and no.24 on the Hot 100, in the States. Failed to chart in the UK, despite being released twice.

RIAA Gold Record (USA million seller).

Official Versions:
Album Version.
Extended Mix.
Single Edit.
Instrumental Edit.
Instrumental Extended Mix.

Although she was the last Jackson sibling to enter the recording studio, Rebbie did tour with her brothers, and along with Janet and La Toya she joined them for their TV series. 'The first date I did with them,' she recalls, 'was in Vegas at The Grand hotel, which was nice… I sang on several number like *Midnight At the Oasis*, when we did a TV series in 1976, which Michael coached for me.'

Sampled by:
Kurupt on *Who Do U Be*, a track on their 1998 album, *KURUPTION*.
Brand Nubian on *Let's Dance*, released for their 1990 album, *FOUNDATION* – also featured Rebbie's vocals.

CHAINED

Song recorded by the Jackson 5 with producer Bobby Taylor, for their debut album, *DIANA ROSS PRESENTS THE JACKSON 5*, released in December 1969 in the States and March 1970 in the UK.

CHATTANOOGIE SHOE SHINE BOY

Song the Jacksons performed on the TV series in 1976, with special guest, Johnny Dark.

CHEATER

Song written by Michael with Greg Phillinganes, recorded in 1987 and originally slated to appear on Michael's album, *BAD* – failed to make the final track listing, despite being one of Michael's favourites at the time, as the track list was already too long.

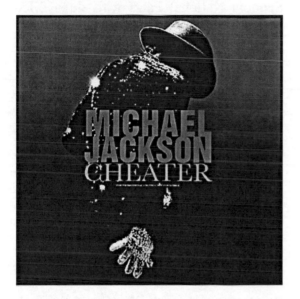

Re-worked in 2000 with Rodney Jerkins and Fred Jerkins III, but failed to make the final tracl listing of Michael's *INVINCIBLE* album.

Demo version included on Michael's box-set, *THE ULTIMATE COLLECTION*, issued in November 2004.

One track promos released in 2005, to promote the box-set and as a potential single – full release cancelled.

CHICAGO 1945

Song written by Michael with Toto's Steve Pocaro.

'Years ago, Michael and I wrote a song called *Chicago 1945* – I did the music and Michael the lyrics,' Pocaro confirmed on Toto's web-site. 'He recorded the song twice, but never put it on an album... the instruments were played in a constant rhythm in the 16th note, which was called 'yada'. When I explained this to Michael, he liked it so much he gave me that nickname!'

In the film, *Moonwalker*, in an outdoor shot of Michael with Brandon Adams and Sean Lennon, a clapper-board with 'Chicago Nights' on it can be seen – possibly an alternate title.

Cited by Michael in his court deposition in November 1993.

Worked on again by Michael with Rodney Jerkins, Fred Jerkins III and Norman Gregg, with a view to recording it for *INVINCIBLE*, but didn't make the album – all versions remain unreleased.

CHILD OF INNOCENCE

Poem written by Michael – included in his book of poems and reflections, *Dancing The Dream*, published in 1992.

CHILDHOOD
(Theme From 'Free Willy 2')

Written by Michael, and recorded at the Hit Factory Studios, New York, on 29th

March 1995; featured on his solo album HIS*TORY*, released in June 1995.

One of a small number of songs Michael recorded live (*Smile* was another; both songs were recorded on the same day).

Theme song from the film, *Free Willy 2: The Adventure Home*.

Michael has described *Childhood* as a reflection of his life:

'Our personal history begins in childhood and the song 'Childhood' is a reflection of my life . . . it's about the pain, some of the joys, some of the dreaming, some of the mental adventures that I took because of the different lifestyle I had, in being a child performer. I was born on stage and 'Childhood', it's my mirror – it's my story.'

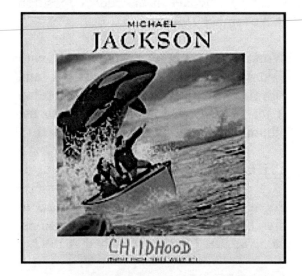

B-side of Michael's duet with sister Janet, *Scream*, but listed alongside *Scream* on the Hot 100 in the States, where it debuted and peaked at no.5 – the highest ever new entry on the chart at the time (previous record holder, *Let It Be* by the Beatles, entered at no.6).

Instrumental version featured on the soundtrack album, *FREE WILLY 2: THE ADVENTURE HOME*.

Promo short film directed by Nick Brandt, shot in a fantasy forest. Filmed in Sequoia National Park, with ships filled with children (including the young star of the *Free Willy* films, Jason James Richter) floating over the treetops – paid homage to *Peter Pan*.

Official Versions:
Album Version.
Instrumental.

Scheduled performance by Michael, during his HBO special in December 1995, was cancelled.

CHILDREN OF THE LIGHT

Song recorded by the Jackson 5 for their album *LOOKIN' THROUGH THE WINDOWS*, released in May 1972 in the States and October 1972 in the UK.

Title track of a Jackson 5 compilation issued on the Spectrum record label in the UK in 1993.

CHILDREN OF THE WORLD

Poem written by Michael – included in his book of poems and reflections, *Dancing The Dream*, published in 1992.

CHILDREN'S CHRISTMAS SONG

Song the Jackson 5 recorded for their *CHRISTMAS ALBUM* circa 1970, but which failed to make the final track listing – remains unreleased.

The Supremes took the song to no.7 on Billboard's Christmas Singles chart in the States in 1965.

CHILDREN'S HOLIDAY

Written and produced by Michael, and recorded by Japanese children's choir, J-Friends.

Issued as a single in Japan – entered the singles chart at no.1. Instrumental version and limited edition of 10,000 box-set mini CDs also released, with pin badge and J-Friends card.

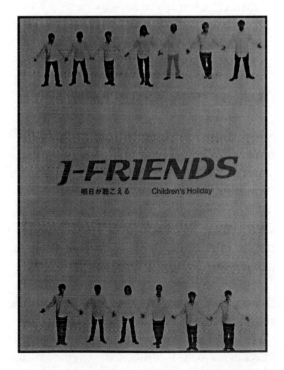

All proceeds donated to a charity set up to aid the victims/families of the devastating earthquake that hit Kobe City, Japan, in January 1995.

CHILDREN'S HOUR, THE

Song Michael cited he had written in his court deposition in November 1993 – remains unreleased.

CHRISTMAS EVERYDAY

Song the Jackson 5 recorded for their *CHRISTMAS ALBUM* circa 1970, but which failed to make the final track listing – remains unreleased.

CHRISTMAS GREETINGS FROM
   MICHAEL JACKSON

Eight second greeting from Michael, originally included on a promo 7" single titled *Seasons Greetings From Motown Records*, sent to radio stations in the States circa 1973, so festive messages could be aired between the songs – also featured greetings from Jackie, Jermaine and Tito (but not Marlon), and other Motown artists.

Included on the 1995 festive compilation, *MOTOWN CHRISTMAS CAROL* – also featured the Jackson 5's *Santa Claus Is Coming To Town*, *I Saw Mommy Kissing Santa Claus*, *Frosty The Snowman* and *Have Yourself A Merry Little Christmas*.

See also: *Seasons Greetings From Motown Records*.

CHRISTMAS SONG, THE

Ever popular festive song recorded by the Jackson 5 – with Jermaine on lead vocals – for their *CHRISTMAS ALBUM*, issued in October 1970 in the States and December 1970 in the UK.

Released as a single in the Philippines.

Hit versions:
Nat 'King' Cole – no.80 in 1960, and no.65 in 1962, in the States; no.69 in the UK in 1991.
James Brown – no.12 on the Christmas Singles chart in the States in 1965.
Herb Alpert – no.1 on the Christmas Singles chart in the States in 1968.
Alexander O'Neal – no.30 in the UK in 1988.
Christina Aguilera – no.18 in the States in 2000.

CHRISTMAS WON'T BE THE SAME THIS YEAR

Another festive song the Jackson 5 recorded for *CHRISTMAS ALBUM*.

B-side of *Santa Claus Is Comin' To Town*, released in December 1970 in the States and two years later in the UK. Listed alongside *Santa Claus Is Comin' To Town* for one week only on Billboard's Christmas Singles chart.

CINDERELLA STAY AWHILE

Song Michael recorded for his fourth solo album, *FOREVER, MICHAEL*, released in January 1975 in the States and March 1975 in the UK.

CIRCUS GIRL

Alternate title for Michael's solo recording, *Carousel* – one of the bonus tracks added to the special edition of his *THRILLER* album, released in October 2001.

See also: *Carousel*.

CISCO KID, THE

One of five songs the Jackson 5 performed a medley of at the Grammy Awards ceremony on 2nd March 1974, to introduce the nominees for Best Rhythm & Blues Vocal Performance by a Group, Duo or Chorus.

Latin group War took the song to no.2 on the Hot 100 and no.5 on the R&B singles chart in the States. RIAA Gold Record Award (USA million seller).

The Jacksons performed *The Cisco Kid* on an episode of their TV series in 1976.

CLIMB E'VRY MOUNTAIN

Song from Rodgers & Hammerstein's musical *The Sound Of Music*, which starred Julie Andrews and Christopher Plummer.

First song Michael ever performed in public in August 1963, aged five years, at his school, Garnett Elementary.

'I was five years old and it was a public school recital,' recalled Michael in 2001. 'We had to wear white shirts and short knickers. And I remember them saying, "Little Michael Jackson is coming up to sing *Climb Ev'ry Mountain*". I got the biggest applause. When I went to my seat, my grandfather and mother were crying. They said, "We can't believe how beautiful you sound". That's the first one I remember.'

In his autobiography *Moonwalk*, Michael recalled, 'the reaction in the auditorium overwhelmed me. The applause was thunderous and people were smiling; some of them were standing... It was such a great feeling.'

Performed by Alex Burrall, who played the part of young Michael, in the TV mini-series, *The Jacksons: An American Dream*.

Hit versions:
Tony Bennett – no.74 on the Hot 100 in the States in 1960.
Shirley Bassey – no.1 in the UK in 1961.
Hesitations – no.90 on the Hot 100 in 1968.

CLOUD NINE

Temptations classic the Jackson 5 performed in concert in the early days.

Hit versions:
Temptations – no.2 on the R&B singles chart and no.6 on the Hot 100 in the States in 1968-69, and no.15 in the UK in 1969.
Mongo Santamaria – no.32 on the Hot 100 and no.33 on the R&B singles chart in 1968-69.

COLOUR OF MY SOUL

Song known to have been recorded by Michael; date uncertain – remains unreleased.

Michael's brother, Randy, is known to have recorded a demo – with an unidentified female singer – titled *Color Of Love*.

COME ALIVE IT'S SATURDAY NIGHT

Song Rebbie Jackson recorded for her 1984 album, *CENTIPEDE* – written by her brothers Jackie, Marlon, Randy and Tito – but not, as is often cited, Michael.

COME AND GET IT

Song the Jackson 5 recorded for Motown – remains unreleased.

(COME 'ROUND HERE) I'M THE ONE YOU NEED

Song the Jackson 5 recorded for their second album, *ABC*, issued in May 1970 in the States and August 1970 in the UK.

Featured in the 'Ray & Charles Superstars' episode of the Jackson 5 cartoon series in 1971.

Originally recorded by the Miracles for their 1966 album, *AWAY WE A GO-GO*. Single achieved no.4 on the R&B singles chart and no.17 on the Hot 100 in the States, and no.45 in the UK. Reissue hit no.13 in the UK in 1971.

COME TOGETHER

Lennon/McCartney cover Michael recorded, soon after his engineer was messing around with the song, and Michael realised it was his favourite Beatles song.

'During the *Bad* sessions, Michael asked me to drive him home to Westwood one night,' said Bill Bottrell. 'During the drive, we played lots of Beatles songs he had compiled on a tape; he was pretty interested in my opinion, and I told him we should pick *Come Together*. Within a couple of days, I had thrown a track together, playing guitars and using some crude midi stuff. I never intended that track to be released that way – they put it out without informing me, and I still don't know what the credits say.'

Filmed as the finale of Michael's 'movie like no other', *Moonwalker*, premiered in 1989 – co-starred, as one of the three children, Sean Lennon (son of John), and directed by Jerry Kramer.

Originally scheduled to get its first commercial release in 1990, on the *DAYS OF THUNDER* soundtrack, but Michael's record company refused to grant permission. Also scheduled to appear on Michael's cancelled greatest hits compilation, *DECADE 1980-1990*.

B-side of Michael's 1992 single *Remember The Time* in the UK (but not USA), where the full length version was featured. Listed alongside *Remember The Time* on the singles chart from the fourth week, peaking at no.10.

Made its album debut in June 1995, in an edited version, on Michael's HIS*TORY*.

Official Versions:
Album Edit.
Full Extended Version.

Live performance in Auckland, New Zealand, screened in that country as part of a *His*tory World Tour concert.

Other hit versions:
Beatles – no.1 in the States and no.4 in the UK in 1969 (double A-side with *Something* in the UK).
Ike & Tina Turner – no.57 in the States in 1970.
Aerosmith – no.23 in the States in 1978.

COMING HOME

One of 19 'rare & unreleased' tracks released on the Michael/Jackson 5 4CD box set *SOULSATION!,* issued in June 1995 in the States and July 1995 in the UK – demo version also known to exist.

(COMING) OUT OF THE CLOSET

Original title for Michael's hit, *In The Closet*, which he wanted to record with Madonna.

Demo version, featuring Michael and Madonna, may exist.

See also: *In The Closet*.

CONVOY

Song guest C.W. McCall performed on *The Jacksons* TV series in 1976, with Michael and his brothers singing backing.

C.W. McCall took *Convoy* to no.1 on the Hot 100 in the States and to no.2 in the UK. RIAA Gold Record (USA million seller).

CORNER OF THE SKY

Song originally written for Frankie Valli and the 4 Seasons, until his persistent no shows led to the Jackson 5 recording it for their album *SKYWRITER*, released in March 1973 in the States and July 1973 in the UK.

From the Berry Gordy financed musical *Pippin* – as well as a version by John Rubinstein, the Jackson 5's version of the song featured on the original cast album as a bonus track.

Performed by the Jackson 5 on *Soul Train* in 1972.

First single from *SKYWRITER* in the States (no UK release), charting at no.9 on the R&B singles chart and no.18 on the Hot 100.

COTTON FIELDS

One of many songs Michael recalled singing, with his mother and family, as a young boy in Gary, Indiana.

'We started out singing at home. I was five years old in the beginning,' said Michael. 'My father had a group called the Falcons. They were three brothers, and they played guitars and sang, so there was always a guitar lying around. My brother Tito would pick up the guitar and play, and eventually we would start singing to the playing. We would sing old songs like *Cotton Fields Back Home*, and some old Ray Charles and James Brown stuff.'

COULD IT BE I'M FALLING IN LOVE

One of five songs the Jackson 5 performed a medley of at the Grammy Awards ceremony on 2nd March 1974, to introduce the nominees for Best Rhythm & Blues Vocal Performance by a Group, Duo or Chorus.

The Spinners (known as the Detroit Spinners in the UK) took *Could It Be I'm Falling In Love* to no.1 on the R&B singles chart and no.4 on the Hot 100 in the States in 1973. RIAA Gold Record Award (USA million seller). Charted at no.11 in the UK.

Hit cover versions:
David Grant & Jaki Graham – no.5 in the UK in 1985, no.60 on the R&B singles chart in the States in 1986.
Worlds Apart – no.15 in the UK in 1994.

CRACK / CRACK KILLS

Song Michael planned to record with rappers Run-DMC in the period 1986-87, for his album, *BAD*, but shelved as Michael didn't like Run-DMC's negative attitude towards him.

Cited (as *Crack Kills*) by Michael in his court deposition in November 1993 – remains unreleased.

Rough demo version *Crack (Demo For Michael Jackson)* was one of four bonus tracks added to the 2005 deluxe edition of Run DMC's album, *TOUGHER THAN LEATHER*, originally released in 1988.

Unfinished lyrics, consisting of two verses and a drawing of a face in pencil, put up for auction in November 2005, and again on the internet auction site eBay, a year later.

CRY

Song Michael cited he had written in his court deposition in November 1993 – remains unreleased.

CRY

Song composed by R. Kelly, and recorded by Michael for his solo album, *INVINCIBLE*, issued in October 2001.

Officially premiered on Michael's website on 20th September 2001, and dedicated to the thousands of people who lost their lives in the 9/11 terrorist attacks in the States.

Initially released in the States at the same time as Michael's *You Rock My World*, as a jukebox single. Briefly released to radio, but proved unpopular, so was quickly withdrawn and *Butterflies* distributed instead.

Promo short film, directed by Nick Brandt, was shot in six different locations (five in California and one in Nevada) – but didn't feature Michael at all, as he was in dispute with Sony over the promo's budget. Premiered in the UK on *Top Of The Pops* on 2nd November 2001.

Released as a single in the UK on the same day as sister Janet's *Son Of A Gun (I Betcha Think This Song Is About You)* – the first time Michael and Janet had gone head-to-head. Janet's single charted at no.13, Michael's at no.25 – his worse showing on the UK chart since 1993, when *Gone Too Soon* – the ninth single from *DANGEROUS* – stalled at no.33.

CRY

Song Marsha Ambrosius – who co-wrote *Butterflies* – confirmed she and Michael were working on, before his passing in June 2009.

Ambrosius performed a snippet of the song at the Jazz Café, London, during her UK Soul Jam appearance in July 2009. 'Before I sing (*Butterflies*),' Ambrosius told the audience, 'I'd like to perform a song we were working on, but never got to finish.'

CRY OUT OF JOY

Tribute to Michael recorded by Akon – premiered a month's after Michael's passing, in late July 2009.

DADDY'S HOME

Solo single Jermaine Jackson promoted on *Soul Train* in 1972, with the rest of the Jackson 5 on backing vocals.

Featured on Jermaine's eponymous 1972 debut album. Released as a single – hit no.3 on the R&B singles chart and no.9 on the Hot 100 in the States, but wasn't a hit in the UK.

Live version featured on the Michael/Jackson 5's *LIVE!* album, issued in September 1988 in the UK (no USA release). All songs on the album were recorded at a concert on 30th April 1973, at the Osaka Koseinenkin Hall in Japan. Also included on the limited edition CD, *IN JAPAN!*, released by Hip-O Select in 2004 – only 5,000 copies pressed.

Other hit versions:
Shep & The Limelites – no.2 on the Hot 100 and no.4 on the R&B singles chart in the States in 1961.
Chuck Jackson & Maxine Brown – no.46 on the R&B singles chart and no.91 on the Hot 100 in the States in 1967.
Cliff Richard – no.2 in the UK in 1981, no.23 on the Hot 100 in the States in 1982.

D.A.N.C.E.

Track recorded by Paris-based production duo Justice, for their 2007 album, *CROSS* – referenced *P.Y.T.*, *Black Or White* and *ABC*, and dedicated to Michael.

DANCE MIX 1

Megamix of Motown recordings by Michael and his brothers featured on the double CD, *THE MICHAEL JACKSON MIX*, issued in the UK in December 1987.

Featured songs: *ABC*, *I Want You Back*, *Get It Together*, *The Boogie Man*, *Just A Little Bit Of You*, *The Love You Save*, *Farewell My Summer Love*, *Love Is Here And Now You're Gone*, *Hallelujah Day*, *Skywriter* and *Lookin' Through The Windows*.

Promo edit featured: *ABC*, *I Want You Back*, *Get It Together* and *The Boogie Man*.

See also: *Dance Mix 2, Love Mix 1 & 2*.

DANCE MIX 2

Megamix of Motown recordings by Michael and his brothers featured on the double CD, *THE MICHAEL JACKSON MIX*, issued in the UK in December 1987.

Featured songs: *Sugar Daddy, Don't Let It Get You Down, Girl You're So Together, Mama's Pearl, My Girl, Dancing Machine, Shoo-Be-Doo-Be-Doo-Da-Day, Doctor My Eyes, Rockin' Robin* and *Little Bitty Pretty One*.

See also: *Dance Mix 1, Love Mix 1 & 2*.

DANCE ON THE CEILING

Incidental piece of music Michael composed with Nicholas Pike, for his short film, *Ghosts*, premiered in October 1996.

DANCING MACHINE

Song featured on the Jackson 5's album *GET IT TOGETHER*, released in September 1973 in the States and November 1973 in the UK.

Second single lifted from the album, following the title cut, and became the groups most successful single since *I'll Be There* in 1970.

No.1 for one week on the R&B singles chart in the States, but held at no.2 on the Hot 100 by Ray Stevens and his novelty smash, *The Streak*.

Sold over two million copies in the USA.

Promoted in the States by a host of TV appearances, including:

- *American Bandstand*.
- *The Bob Hope Special*.
- *The Tonight Show* (in April and November 1974 with host Johnny Carson, and in August 1974 with host Bill Cosby).
- *The Carol Burnett Show*.
- *The Jerry Lewis Telethon*.
- *The Merv Griffin Show* (in April 1974 and again in September 1974).
- *The Mike Douglas Show*.
- *The Sonny & Cher Comedy Hour*.
- *Soul Train*.
- *The Jacksons* TV series.

Small earthquake struck Los Angeles on 16th March 1974, as the cameras were rolling during the filming of *The Carol Burnett Show* – the film studio shook, but neither Michael or the show's host went out of character.

Failed to make the Top 50 singles chart in the UK, but registered at no.53 on the 'breakers' section of the chart.

Grammy Award nominations: Best R&B Song and Best R&B Vocal Performance by a Duo, Group or Chorus (it didn't win either).

Edited version with opening cut featured on, and used as the title track of, the Jackson 5 album that followed *GET IT TOGETHER*.

Live performance by the Jacksons, at a concert in Mexico in 1976, included on the home video, *The Jacksons In Concert*, released in 1981 in the UK (no USA release); released in France in 1984. Also performed during the group's Destiny Tour – one concert was screened on BBC2 in the UK.

Song chosen to open the Jacksons' Destiny Tour concerts.

Remix by Nigel Martinez and Derek Marcil, with alternate vocals, featured on Michael's 1987 album, *THE ORIGINAL SOUL OF MICHAEL JACKSON*.

Second remix, with different alternate vocals, included on the 1992 TV soundtrack album, *THE JACKSONS: AN AMERICAN DREAM*.

Topless In Action Remixxx, as included on the Japanese album *SOUL SOURCE – JACKSON 5 REMIXES 2* in 2001, featured alternate vocals.

Other Remixes:
Dub Mix.
Extended Dance Mix.
Radio Remix.

Performed by the Jacksons and 'N Sync during the *Michael Jackson: 30th Anniversary Celebration, The Solo Years* concert, staged at New York's Madison Square Garden on 7th September 2001.

Sampled on the B-side of M.C. Hammer's hit *U Can't Touch This* in 1990, which rose to no.1 on both the Hot 100 and R&B singles charts in the States, and achieved no.3 in the UK.

Also sampled on:
The Street Mix by Mag 7 – no.56 on the R&B singles chart and no.93 on the Hot 100 in 1998.
Dance Wit Me by Antuan & Ray Ray – no.66 on the R&B singles chart and no.125 on the 'bubbling under' section of the Hot 100 in 1998.
Dancin' by Vanilla Ice, from his 1990 album, *TO THE EXTREME*.

Appeared on the *INKWELL* movie soundtrack album, released on Warner Brothers in 1994.

DANGEROUS

Written by Michael with Bill Bottrell and Teddy Riley.

Developed from a song titled *Streetwalker*, which Michael wrote for his album *BAD*, and featured on the expanded special edition CD issued in October 2001.

Title track of Michael's solo album, released in November 1991.

'The genesis of the songs we co-wrote (for *DANGEROUS*),' said Bottrell, 'consisted of Michael humming melodies and grooves, and him then leaving the studio while I developed these ideas with a bunch of drum machines and samplers.'

'*Dangerous* was about a woman who was just so beyond, you know, beyond the best girl he's ever been with,' said Teddy Riley. 'That was the name of the album, so we thought about doing a song called *Dangerous*, and Michael came up with the hook. So I said, "Let me get into the music." I went to my lab and put the song together.'

'The track evolved; Michael came in with the hook,' revealed Riley. 'I did the music and then we finalised the song. We used a drum machine, the Akai MPC-60, and a lot of the sounds from that and samples I had on my samples CD. There's no science to it, I just feel my way through the production. I always feel my way – I never do anything the same.'

Planned as an unprecedented 10th single release from *DANGEROUS*, but cancelled, after allegations of child molestation were made against Michael in August 1993.

Official Versions:
Album Version.
Roger's Dangerous Edit.
Roger's Dangerous Club Mix.
Roger's Rough Dub.
Early Version.

Radio Spanish.
Radio English.

Radio Spanish and Radio English versions included on a Sony sampler CD released in 1992.

First performed by Michael when he opened the 20th annual American Music Awards ceremony, staged in Los Angeles on 25th January 1993. He went on to perform the song twice at the Soul Train 25th Anniversary Hall Of Fame show on 31s October 1995 (aired on 22nd November), the MTV Video music Awards, on the popular German TV show, *Wetten Dass?*, and twice on the *American Bandstand* 50th anniversary special in Pasadena in April 2002.

Live performance in Auckland, New Zealand, screened in that country as part of a *His*tory World Tour concert. Different live performance from the same tour screened by Sat 1 TV in Germany.

Short promo *Dangerous* teaser directed by David Lynch.

Dangerous Tour montage, directed by Joe Wilcots, featured on Michael's home video, *Dangerous – The Short Films* in 1993.

Subject of a court hearing in Colorado in February 1994, after songwriter Crystal Cartier accused Michael of stealing the song from her, claiming she had written, copyrighted and recorded the song in 1985, as part of another song, *Player*.

Michael testified how *Dangerous* grew out of a song titled *Streetwalker*, which he co-wrote with William 'Bill' Bottrell in 1985. His original demo version was played in court; Michael also gave *a cappella* performances of *Dangerous* and *Billie Jean*, and provided the court with a rare insight into his songwriting habits.

At the trial, Michael also spoke of similarities between *Dangerous* and *Another Part Of Me*, as far the melody at the end of the choruses sounds: 'You're no damn lover friend of mine' and 'You're just another part of me'. As Cartier was unable to supply any original tapes to back up her claim, the judge found in Michael's favour, and his accuser was denied the chance to appeal.

Remix featured on Michael's *Blood On The Dance Floor* single in 1997.

Performed by Michael at his *Michael & Friends* concert in Munich, Germany, on 27th June 1999 – screened by ZDF TV.

Alternate version, plus a remix titled 'Roger's Rough Dub', both included on the first acetate version of the special, expanded edition of *DANGEROUS* – bonus disc later cancelled.

Early edited demo version featured on Michael's box-set, *THE ULTIMATE COLLECTION*, issued in November 2004. A different, longer version also exists, with Michael heard screaming at the beginning – after a sound protection wall fell on him as he was about to record.

Master tapes from Teddy Riley's Future Records studio surfaced on eBay, featured several unreleased mixes:

Dangerous II #1
Dangerous II #3 (Non-Mix)
Dangerous Long Version Ending Version Mix I #15
Dangerous Original Version Before Teddy Mix 14 #23 (Bill Bottrell Version)
Dangerous II Instrumental With Piano Solo #45
Dangerous Original Instrumental #57

Epic/Sony DAT (Digital Audio Tape) sold on eBay in August 2009 featured 10 unreleased remixes by Roger Sanchez:

Roger's Funky Jeep Mix.
Funky Jeep Radio.
Bad Boy Beats.
Jeep instrumental.
Roger's Dangerous Club.
Club Radio Mix.

Roger's Rough Dub.
Roger's Tribal Treatment.
Subterranean Dub 1.
Subterranean Dub 2.

DANGEROUS MEDLEY

Exclusive six minute medley of seven songs featured on Michael's *DANGEROUS* album: *Black Or White/Can't Let Her Get Away/Dangerous/Who Is It/Remember The Time/Give In To Me/Heal The World*.

Released in May 1992 in the UK and continental Europe (but not the USA), as a Pepsi promo-only cassette single, with the previously unreleased solo recording, *Someone Put Your Hand Out*.

500,000 copies distributed as freebies, competition prizes, etc.

Released as a CD single in Japan only.

DANGEROUS NEW JACK MEDLEY

One of two promo medleys, released on 12" and CD as *The Medleys*, in Brazil in 1994.

Featured: *Remember The Time*, *In The Closet*, *Jam* and *Black Or White*.

DANNY BOY

Song performed by the Jackson 5 as part of a medley – with *By The Time I Get To Phoenix* and *Killing Me Softly With His Song* – during their Las Vegas shows in 1974.

Also performed on *The Tonight Show*, hosted by Bill Cosby, in America in March 1974.

DAPPER-DAN

Song featured on Michael's fourth solo album, *FOREVER, MICHAEL*, released in January 1975 in the States and March 1975 in the UK.

DARLING DEAR

Written by George Gordy (Berry's brother) and his wife Rosemary.

Featured on the Jackson 5's *THIRD ALBUM*, issued in September 1970 in the States and February 1971 in the UK – recorded on 24th May 1970.

B-side of *Mama's Pearl* in both the USA and UK (mono version).

Appeared on the promo *Third Album EP*, along with five further tracks, released with a picture sleeve in the States in 1970.

Heard on 'The Michael Look' episode of the Jackson 5's cartoon series in 1971.

Rejuvenated By MURO Mix, as included on the Japanese album *SOUL SOURCE – JACKSON 5 REMIXES* in 2000, featured slightly extended vocals.

Sampled by Mic Little featuring Ne-Yo, on their 2006 American R&B hit, *Put It In A Letter*.

Originally recorded by Smokey Robinson & The Miracles for their 1970 album, *A*

POCKET FULL OF MIRACLES. As the B-side of *Point It Out*, listed for a solitary week at no.100 on the Hot 100 in the States.

DAY BASKETBALL WAS SAVED, THE

Previously unreleased track – with an introduction by Rosey Grier – featured in the *Goin' Back To Indiana* TV special in July 1971. Later included on the Jackson 5's album, *GOIN' BACK TO INDIANA*, released in September 1971 in the States (no UK release).

DAYDREAMER

Song written for, and performed by, the Jackson 5 on their TV special that aired in the States on 5th November 1972 – no official release.

DEAR MICHAEL

Song Michael recorded for his solo album, *FOREVER, MICHAEL*, issued in January 1975 in the States and March 1975 in the UK.

B-side of *Just A Little Bit Of You* in both the States and UK/Europe.

American TV actress, Kim Fields, recorded a cover version in 1984. Fields, who appeared in NBC's *Facts Of Life*, was a good friend of Michael's sister, Janet. She also picked up Michael's *Ebony* American Music Award in 1984, when he couldn't make the show, to collect it in person.

DESCENDING ANGELS

Incidental piece of music Michael composed with Nicholas Pike, for his short film, *Ghosts*, premiered in October 1996.

DESTINY

Song written by Michael with brothers Jackie, Marlon, Randy and Tito – Michael is on record as saying the song was written about him.

According to Marlon, he and his brothers were aiming for a country sound. 'That's what we wanted to go for,' he said. 'We just laid down this track and tried to go for a country feel with the acoustic guitar at the beginning, then going into something nice and mellow. The lyrics are about the world today and what we want – some place where there's not a bunch of cars and smog.'

Title track of the Jacksons' third album, issued in December 1978.

Released as a single in the UK (but not USA), where it achieved a lowly no.39.

Promoted, during the group's European visit, on *Top Of The Pops*, and on the Jacksons' own *Midnight Special* in the States in 1979 (where Jermaine re-joined his brothers for this song). Also featured on a Destiny Tour concert screened on BBC2 in the UK.

DIDN'T I (BLOW YOUR MIND THIS TIME)

Song Jackie Jackson recorded for his 1973 eponymous, debut solo album, with his brothers including Michael on backing vocals.

Hit versions:
Delfonics – no.3 on the R&B singles chart and no.10 on the Hot 100 in the States in 1970, and no.22 in the UK in 1971.
Millie Jackson – no.49 on the R&B singles chart in 1980.
New Kids On The Block – no.8 on the Hot 100 and no.34 on the R&B singles chart in 1989, and no.8 in the UK in 1990.

DIFFERENT KIND OF LADY

Written by Michael with brothers Jackie, Marlon, Randy and Tito, for the Jacksons' album, *GOIN' PLACES*, released in October 1977.

Opening horns missing from the version included on the *GOIN' PLACES* picture disc released in the States.

B-side of *Find Me A Girl* in the States, and of *Even Though Your Gone* and *Heartbreak Hotel* in the UK.

DIRTY DIANA

Song originally written by Michael in 1983; a second version Michael completed the following year was discarded, and he returned to the first version, which he recorded for his solo album, *BAD*, released in September 1987.

Inspired by rock groupies, who follow musicians and artists around the tour circuit. Guest guitarist, Steve Stevens, was Billy Idol's lead guitarist.

'I got a call from Quincy Jones to do that,' said Stevens. 'I had an experience where I had worked with Diana Ross, where she wasn't in the studio. My prerequisite to him (Quincy) was that

Michael had to be present when I was recording. He (Michael) was very receptive, and he made some sensible suggestions.'

Fifth single lifted from *BAD* – and the fifth single to hit no.1 on the Hot 100 in the States, a record breaking achievement. Also charted at no.5 on the R&B singles chart, and no.4 in the UK.

B-side featured an Instrumental version.

7" single version replaced the original on later pressings of *BAD*.

Official Versions:
Album Version.
Single Version.
Instrumental.

Performed at a Wembley concert attended by Diana, Princess of Wales – at her insistence. 'I took it out of the show in honour of Her Royal Highness,' Michael said. 'She took me away and said, "Are you gonna do *Dirty Diana*?" So I said, "No, I took it out of the show because of you". She said, "No! I want you to do it. Do it – do the song!"'

Promoted by Michael's first 'live' video, filmed at Long Beach, California – directed by Joe Pytka. Premiered on MTV on 14th April 1988. Alternate short film featured live footage from Michael's Bad World Tour.

World Music Award: Number One Video In The World (Michael accepted the award via a live satellite link).

Used by Diana Ross to open her 1989 concerts – snippet opened her *GREATEST HITS LIVE* album, released in 1989. Album also featured a live version of *Muscles*, which Michael wrote.

Cover version recorded by Lucy Diamonds – who named herself after the Beatles' classic, *Lucy In The Sky With Diamonds*. 'I always loved MJ's intensity in that song, and how he really works his vocals to portray this sort of fierceness from the lyrics,' said Diamonds. 'I wanted to portray the song from Diana's point of view, so my version is more mellow, with only slight changes to the lyrics… it actually wasn't supposed to get out, because it's only completed in the demo form, but it's gotten a great response just the same.' Leaked on the internet, and posted by Diamonds on her MySpace page.

Eighth of Michael's 20 *'Visionary – The Video Singles'* reissues, with the music on one side of a Dual Disc and the accompanying short film on the other side. Issued in April 2006 in the UK – charted at no.17.

Posthumous hit: no.5 in Denmark, no.13 in Switzerland, no.17 in Norway, no.22 in Germany, no.23 in Holland, no.26 in UK, no.27 in Ireland, no.29 in Sweden and no.32 in USA (Hot Digital Songs).

DISCO KIDS

One of three songs James Whitney has confirmed he wrote for Michael between 1976-79 – recorded by Michael but remains unreleased.

See also: *Goodness Knows*, *Sweet Music*.

DMC MEGAMIX

Fifteen minutes 40 seconds megamix of some of Michael's solo hits, released in various guises – including some formats of *Earth Song* – in 1995.

Songs featured: *Billie Jean, Rock With You, Bad, Thriller, Don't Stop 'Til You Get Enough, Black Or White, Remember The Time, Scream* and *Wanna Be Startin' Somethin'*.

Eleven minutes 18 seconds edit featured: *Billie Jean, Rock With You, Bad, Thriller, Don't Stop 'Til You Get Enough, Black Or White, Scream* and *Wanna Be Startin' Somethin'*.

DO I OWE

Song recorded by Jackie Jackson, with the Jackson 5 on backing vocals, for his only solo album for Motown, *JACKIE JACKSON*, issued in 1973.

Promo 7" single distributed to radio stations in the States.

DO THE BARTMAN

Song featured on the album *THE SIMPSONS SING THE BLUES*, issued in 1991.

Includes the lyrics: 'If you can do the bart, you're bad like Michael Jackson' and 'Eat your heart out, Michael'.

Much speculation surrounded Michael's involvement in the song, before Simpsons' creator Matt Groening finally confessed at the second annual World Animation Celebration in Pasadena, USA, in February 1998, that Michael did in fact sing on the song – Michael and Bryan Loren also contributed backing vocals.

'The background vocals in the bridge are just me,' stated Loren, 'but the harmonies in the chorus are performed by the two of us… we did them simultaneously. It was a quick and painless process.'

Loren further confirmed he wrote and produced the track alone.

Nancy Cartwright, the voice of Bart Simpson, worked on *THE SIMPSONS SING THE BLUES*, with producer John Boylan. 'We were jammin' to the sample of *Do The Bartman* when John leans over and says, "I won't be directing you on this one." Oh, bummer! I replied.

"Yeah," he went on, "some guy named Michael's gonna lead you." It took a few seconds for the penny to drop – and my jaw quickly followed.'

Cartwright felt she must buy Michael a present, but what? 'Little Lucy, all of nine months,' said Cartwright, 'got her finger in the string of a taking Bart doll and I heard my own altered voice saying, "Eat my shorts!" Problem solved… I had the doll behind my back because I wanted to surprise him. I had signed the doll's belly and written "Bart loves Michael" on the front of his T-shirt. Just as we finished our greetings, I pulled the doll out from behind my back and handed it to him, saying, "This is from me to you."

He just about had a heart attack! His eyes lit up like a six year olds, and he took it and hugged it… he thanked me profusely and, from that moment on, I knew we were going to have a great time.'

'We went into the studio and began rehearsal for *Do The Bartman*,' said Cartwright. 'Michael was absolutely incredible. We had so much fun. It didn't take us very long at all because he knew exactly what he was doing. We started at the top and just ran through it a couple of times, and he couldn't stop laughing. He absolutely loved Bart and when I spoke like him, Michael was delighted – like a kid at Christmas. At one point in the song, there was plenty of room for ad-libbing. I went nuts. I added this one towards the end, "Eat your heart out, Michael!" and he loved that!'

Released as a single in the UK (but not USA), hitting no.1 for three weeks in February 1991.

Registered on the Hot 100 Airplay chart in the States, achieving no.11 during a nine week run.

Official Versions:
Album Version.
LP Edit.
7" House Mix – Edit.
Bad Bart House Mix.
A Cappella.
Swingin' In The House Mix.

DO THE FONZ

Song performed by the Jacksons on their CBS TV series in 1976.

DO WHAT YOU WANNA

Song Michael wrote with brothers Jackie, Marlon, Randy and Tito, for the Jacksons' album *GOIN' PLACES*, released in October 1977.

B-side of *Goin' Places* and *Blame It On The Boogie* in the States and UK.

DO YOU KNOW WHERE YOUR CHILDREN ARE

Song Michael cited he had written in his court deposition in November 1993 – remains unreleased.

DO YOU LOVE ME

Contours hit the Jackson 5 recorded a version of – remains unreleased.

Hit versions:
Contours – no.1 on the R&B singles chart and no.3 on the Hot 100 in the States in 1962.
Brian Poole & The Tremeloes – no.1 in the UK in 1963.
Dave Clark Five – no.11 on the Hot 100, and no.30 in the UK, in 1964.

Deep Feeling – no.34 in the UK in 1970.
Andy Fraser – no.82 on the Hot 100 in
1984.
Contours (reissue) – no.11 on the Hot
100 in 1988.
Duke Baysee – no.46 in the UK in 1995.

DO YOU LOVE ME

One of two songs Babyface revealed he
had completed with Michael in late 1998,
for a solo album by Michael scheduled
for 1999, where they were aiming for a
'streeter' sound – remains unreleased.

DO YOU WANT ME

Song written by Sisqó and Dru Hill circa
1999, as a contender for Michael's
album, *INVINCIBLE* – remains
unreleased.

'I was driving when Michael Jackson
called me on my cell phone,' said Sisqó.
'He wanted me to know how much he
loved the record. We wanted to do a duet
together. Next thing I did was to put my
girlfriend on the phone, so she could also
talk to Michael.'

DOCTOR MY EYES

Song the Jackson 5 recorded for their
album, *LOOKIN' THROUGH THE
WINDOWS* released in May 1972 in the
States and October 1972 in the UK.

Released as a single in the UK – achieved
no.9. No American release, as Jackson
Browne's original version hit no.8 on the
Hot 100 in early 1972.

DOES YOUR MAMA KNOW
ABOUT ME

Track recorded by Jermaine Jackson,
with the Jackson 5 on backing vocals, for
his 1973 album, *COME INTO MY LIFE*.

A hit in the States in 1968 for Bobby
Taylor & The Vancouvers, peaking at
no.5 on the R&B singles chart and no.29
on the Hot 100.

DOGGIN' AROUND

Song Michael recorded for his solo
album *MUSIC AND ME*, released in
April 1973 in the States and July 1973 in
the UK.

Scheduled to be issued as a single in the USA in February 1974, but cancelled – test pressings do exist.

Released as a single in Holland.

Alternate version featured on the 1987 album, *THE ORIGINAL SOUL OF MICHAEL JACKSON*.

Hit versions:
Jackie Wilson (original version) – no.1 on the R&B singles chart and no.15 on the Hot 100 in the States in 1960.
Klique – no.2 on the R&B singles chart and no.50 on the Hot 100 in the States in1983.

DOIN' IT IN A HAUNTED HOUSE

Parody of Michael's *Thriller* by Yvonne Cage.

'I hope Michael won't be offended, I'm his number one fan and would love to meet him' said Cage. 'A lot of people have interpreted the song as being about sex, but I prefer to think about it as togetherness. I don't think it's vulgar – I think it's rather discreet.'

DOIN' THE JERK

Song the Jackson 5 performed regularly in the pre-Motown days, with Jermaine on lead vocals.

Performances included a department store at Glen Park, Chicago, in 1964, where Katherine Jackson hand-made the costumes her sons wore.

A hit in the States in early 1965 for the Larks (titled simply *The Jerk*), charting at no.7 on the Hot 100 and no.9 on the R&B singles chart.

DOING DIRTY

Song written by Michael with brother Marlon circa 1982 – remains unreleased.

DON'T BE MESSIN' AROUND

Powerful ballad Bruce Swedien revealed, around the time *THRILLER 25* was released, Michael had completed.

'Michael plays piano on it,' said Swedien, 'and it's just beautiful.'

Remains unreleased.

DON'T GET AROUND MUCH ANYMORE

Jazz standard written by Duke Ellington & Bob Russell in 1940 – originally titled Never No Lament.

Song performed by the Jacksons, with special guest Caroll O'Connor, on their TV series in 1976, as a medley with *Caravan* and *Take The 'A' Train*.

Recorded by numerous artists, including Duke Ellington, Ink Spots, Willie Nelson, Harry Connick, Jr., B.B. King, Paul McCartney and Rod Stewart.

DON'T KNOW WHY I LOVE YOU

Song featured on the Jackson 5's second album, *ABC*, released in May 1970 in the States and August 1970 in the UK.

Featured in the 'The Michael Look' episode of the Jackson 5 cartoon series in 1971.

Originally recorded by Stevie Wonder.

DON'T LET A WOMAN MAKE A FOOL OUT OF YOU

Song recorded by Joe 'King' Carrusco for his album, *SYNAPSE GAP (MUNDO TOTAL)*, issued in 1982.

Michael was standing in the corridor outside Studio 55 in Los Angeles, when Carrusco invited him in to sing backing on *Don't Let A Woman Make A Fool Out Of You*, and Michael readily agreed.

'He (Michael) was in the studio next door to where we were recording,' said Carrusco, 'and I was just thinking, "Goddammm, here's the best f*** singer in the world, man – I gotta get him on my record"… one day, man, I saw him sitting out in this office, staring into space. I just said, "Hey, Mike, why don't you come sing on my record, man?" And I just kinda made off with him. When his managers got back and found him in the studio with us, they flipped. But the track was down, man – it was too late!'

Issued as a single, with picture sleeve, in France and Spain.

DON'T LET IT GET YOU DOWN

Song Michael originally recorded on 31st August 1973 – the same day he also recorded *Farewell My Summer Love* and *Girl You're So Together*.

Remained unreleased until May 1984, when an over-dubbed and remixed version was included on *FAREWELL MY SUMMER LOVE*.

Original recording featured on Michael's *THE BEST OF…* anthology series compilation, released in March 1995 in the States (no UK release).

DON'T LET YOUR BABY CATCH YOU

Song the Jackson 5 recorded for their album, *LOOKIN' THROUGH THE WINDOWS*, released in May 1972 in the States and October 1972 in the UK.

B-side of *The Boogie Man* in the UK (USA release cancelled, though promo copies with a picture sleeve were issued).

DON'T SAY GOODBYE AGAIN

Song featured on the Jackson 5's album, *GET IT TOGETHER*, released in September 1973 in the States and December 1973 in the UK.

Performed by the Jackson 5 on *Soul Train* in 1973.

DON'T STAND ANOTHER CHANCE

Song written by Marlon Jackson, for sister Janet's second solo album *DREAM STREET*, issued in 1984.

Backing vocals by Michael, Jackie, Marlon and Tito Jackson.

Released as a single in the USA (but not UK), achieving no.9 on the R&B singles chart and no.101 on the 'bubbling under' section of the Hot 100.

Official Versions:
Album Version.
Remixed Version.
Dub Version.

DON'T STOP

Fleetwood Mac hit Michael performed on stage at President Bill Clinton's Inaugural Gala on 19th January 1993, as part of an all-star choir.

Achieved no.3 on the Hot 100 in the States and no.32 in the UK for Fleetwood Mac in 1977.

DON'T STOP 'TIL YOU GET ENOUGH

Song written and recorded by Michael, for his first solo album after leaving Motown, *OFF THE WALL*, released in August 1979.

'We had little arguments, nothing very serious, during the first record we made, which was *Don't Stop 'Til You Get Enough*,' said Quincy Jones. 'Most people at Motown didn't sing low and I needed him to sing low. I wanted him to do a very sexy kind of sound at the bottom. At first, he was a little reluctant, but that's okay. It was never contentious, and that's where the trust comes in.'

Lyrical content shocked his mother, Katherine, who pointed out the title could easily be misinterpreted – Michael asserted it wasn't a reference to sex, but

that it could mean whatever people wanted it to mean.

Lead single from the album – heralded Michael's arrival as an adult solo performer, and paved the way for a new beginning to his musical career.

Promo short film, directed by Nick Saxton, premiered in October 1979.

Hit no.1 on the Hot 100 in the States, giving Michael his first chart topper since *Ben*, and gave him his first no.1 on the R&B singles chart. Also no.1 in Australia, New Zealand, Norway and South Africa, and no.3 in the UK.

Michael's first solo hit in Germany – it peaked at no.13.

Official Versions:
Album Version.
Masters At Work Remix.
7" Edit.
7" Edit w/Intro.
12" Version.
Original Demo Recording.
Roger's Underground Club Solution.

1992 Masters At Work Remix and Roger's Underground Club Solution featured unreleased vocals and ad-libs, as the remixers were given access to the master tapes, which included vocals that didn't make the final album version of the song.

Rare 12" acetate, from Allen Zentz Studios, titled *Don't Stop* – featured a high quality, unreleased version of the song.

Live version, recorded at a concert at Madison Square Garden in September 1981, featured on the Jacksons album, *LIVE*, issued in November 1981. This version was included on the 12" single of Michael's *Beat It* in the UK.

Inpromptu performance by Michael at New York's Peppermint Lounge on 25th March 1983 when, following a set by Grandmaster Flash & The Furious Five, he took to the stage and surprised everyone by lip-synching to *Don't Stop 'Til You Get Enough* and (10 minutes later) *Wanna Be Startin' Somethin'*.

Introduction re-recorded for Michael's performance at the MTV Video Music Awards in 1995.

Sampled by Baby Bump on *I Got This Feeling*, a no.22 hit in the UK in 2000.

Spliced with Q-Tip's *Breathe And Stop* by Mr On vs. Jungle Brothers, on *Breathe, Don't Stop* – registered with the BMI, but unofficial.

Michael recorded a version with Chris Tucker for the latter's movie, *Rush Hour 2*, in which Tucker was seen singing the song – remains unreleased.

Second of Michael's 20 *'Visionary – The Video Singles'* reissues, with the music on one side of a Dual Disc and the accompanying short film on the other side. Issued in February 2006 in the UK – charted at no.17.

Posthumous Hit: no.9 in the USA (Hot Digital Songs), no.10 in Holland, no.20 in Switzerland, no.21 in Australia, no.38 in UK, and no.50 in Sweden.

DON'T STOP 'TIL YOU GET ENOUGH

Alternate title of Ashaye's 1983 hit, *Michael Jackson Medley*.

See also: *Michael Jackson Medley*.

DON'T WALK AWAY

Song written by Michael with Teddy Riley, Richard Stites and Reed Vertelney.

Featured on Michael's album *INVINCIBLE*, issued in October 2001.

DON'T WANT TO SEE TOMORROW

Song the Jackson 5 recorded for their album, *LOOKIN' THROUGH THE WINDOWS*, released in May 1972 in the States and October 1972 in the UK.

DOWN BY THE OLD MILL STREAM

Song the Jacksons performed on their TV series in 1976, with their special guest star, Joey Bishop.

DOWN IN THE VALLEY

American folk song, also known as 'Birmingham Jail', Michael and his brothers often sang in the pre-Motown days, with their mother Katherine.

DREAM GOES ON, THE

Solo recording by Jermaine Jackson, included on the Jacksons TV soundtrack album, *THE JACKSONS: AN AMERICAN DREAM*, issued in October 1992 in the States and July 1993 in the UK.

Michael wasn't involved with the recording of this song, which was a tribute to the Jacksons.

DREAMER

Song the Jacksons recorded, with Michael on lead vocals, for their eponymous debut album, released in November 1976.

Cited by Michael in an interview in 1977 as one of his favourite tracks from the album to sing. 'I felt they (Kenneth Gamble & Leon Huff) could have written it with me in mind,' said Michael. 'I have always been a dreamer. I set goals for myself. I look at things and try to imagine what is possible, and then hope to surpass those boundaries.'

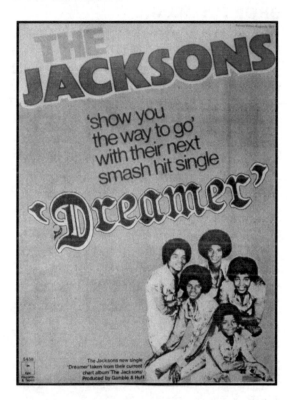

Issued as a single in the UK (but not USA), as a follow-up to the chart topping *Show You The Way To Go* – disappointingly peaked at no.22. Single version longer than the album version, with an extended instrumental bridge section.

Promoted on the UK's premier TV music show, *Top Of The Pops*, with a rarely seen promotional film clip (as very early music videos were called) filmed by the

Jacksons, and performed by the group on *The Mike Douglas In Hollywood Show* and their own TV series in 1977.

DREAMS

Song written by Michael and registered with the BMI – remains unreleased.

DROP THE MASK

Song written by Diana Ross with Tim Tickner and Christopher Ward, and recorded by Diana as a bonus track on her 1999 album, *EVERY DAY IS A NEW DAY*.

Clearly aimed at Michael, the song opened with the lyrics:

> *Look in the mirror, who do you see?*
> *Where is the man that you used to be?*

Diana goes on to urge: 'Drop the mask – be yourself.'

D.S.

Song written by Michael, and featured on his album HIS*TORY*, issued in June 1995.

According to the lyric, 'Dom Sheldon is a cold man' – however, 'D.S.' is widely acknowledged to be a verbal attack on the State District Attorney, Thomas Sneddon, the man who led the criminal investigation against Michael in 1993 (and, indeed, the more recent failed investigation in 2004-05).

Live performance in Auckland, New Zealand, screened in that country as part of a *His*tory World Tour concert.

DUDE, THE

Song Quincy Jones recorded, with Michael on backing vocals, for his 1981 album of the same title. Other backing vocalists: Quincy Jones, Patti Austin, Syretta Wright, Jim Gilstrap & LaLomie Washburn.

EARTH SONG

Song written by Michael in a hotel room in Austria – evolved from a song titled, *What About Us*, which Michael wrote circa 1989-90.

'I was feeling so much pain and so much suffering at the plight of the planet Earth,' said Michael. 'And for me, this is *Earth Song*, because I think nature is trying so hard to compensate for man's mismanagement of the Earth… and that's what inspired it. And it just suddenly dropped into my lap, when I was on tour in Austria.'

Included on Michael's album HIS*TORY*, released in June 1995, and issued as the follow-up to *You Are Not Alone* in most countries (but not the USA).

Shirley Caesar, of the Caesar Sisters, has confirmed Michael originally wanted her to be involved with the song. 'The studio technicians played the tape of the song Michael wanted me to consider,' she wrote in her book, *The Lady, The Melody & The Word*, 'but it didn't sound like something I'd sing. The name of it was

'Earth', and it dealt with environmental issues. I guess I felt that way because he had only rough taping of the song, but the finished product was awesome.' Caesar withdrew from the project when the Church world became critical of her involvement with Michael. 'Let the record show, however,' she stated, 'that I love Michael Jackson, and I don't allow anyone to discuss him negatively in my presence.'

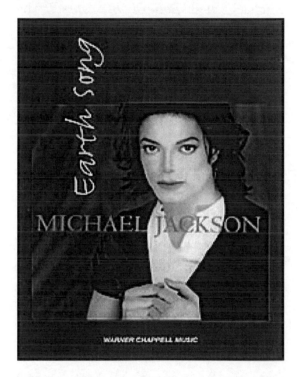

Michael's most successful single in both the UK and Germany – it topped the chart for six weeks in both countries. In the UK, it captured the coveted Christmas no.1 slot, and went on to shift over one million copies. In Germany, it gave Michael his first no.1 (for six weeks), and went on to become his only million seller.

Official Versions:
Album Version.
Hani's Club Experience.
Hani's Around The World Experience.
Hani's Radio Experience.
Hani's Extended Radio Experience.
Radio Edit.

Promo short film shot by Nicholas Brandt was filmed on four different continents: South America (Amazon Rainforest), Africa (Tanzania), Europe (Croatia) and North America (New York).

Grammy nomination: Best Music Video, Short Form (the award went to the Beatles, for *Free As Bird* – one of the songs *Earth Song* kept out of the no.1 slot in the UK).

Genesis Awards: Doris Day Music Award (given for an animal sensitive music work).

French Film Awards: Best Video Award.

Promoted with three unusually high profile TV appearances: the German TV show, *Wetten Dass?* in 1995, The Brits awards ceremony in February 1996, and the World Music Awards in May 1996.

Michael, in his first British TV appearance since 1979, was named Artist Of A Generation at The Brits – Sir Bob Geldof presented him with the award. Michael's 'quasi-religious' performance upset some, including the lead singer of Britpop group Pulp, Jarvis Cocker, who invaded the stage halfway through the song, causing mayhem. Later, in a statement, Michael said: 'I am sickened, saddened, shocked, upset, cheated and angry, but was proud with how the cast remained professional.'

Live performance in Auckland, New Zealand, screened in that country as part of a *His*tory World Tour concert. Different live performance from the same tour screened by Sat 1 TV in Germany.

Opening piano bars used in the 'I bring you the future' advertisement, for the Esconic Video CD Player, in 1997.

Live performance at the *Michael Jackson & Friends* concerts, staged in Seoul, South Korea, on 25th June 1999, and in Munich, Germany, two days later.

Seventeenth of Michael's 20 *'Visionary – The Video Singles'* reissues, with the music on one side of a Dual Disc and the accompanying short film on the other side. Issued in June 2006 in the UK – charted at no.34, making it the least successful of all the reissues.

Posthumous hit: no.4 in Switzerland, no.12 in Germany, no.13 in Austria & Holland, no.25 in Ireland and no.33 in UK.

EASE ON DOWN THE ROAD

Song from Michael's first film, *The Wiz*, which he performed with Diana Ross and his co-stars. Featured on the accompanying soundtrack album, issued in September 1978 in the States and October 1978 in the UK.

Included in the original Broadway musical, on which the film *The Wiz* was based – the musical, which starred Stephanie Mills as Dorothy, scooped seven Tony Awards, including Best Musical and Best Score.

'I think the stage and MGM version (*The Wizard Of Oz*) kind of missed the point,' said Michael, comparing them to L. Fred Baum's original story; he felt the film *The Wiz* was much closer. 'The message (of the book) is that these people are looking for something they already have. It's inside them already, but they don't know it because they don't have that belief in themselves to realise it.'

Michael cited *Believe In Yourself*, by Lena Horne and Diana Ross, as his favourite song from the film. 'It's my favourite,' he said, 'because of what it says – I like what it says.'

Released as a single, credited to Diana Ross & Michael Jackson, achieved no.17 on the R&B singles chart and no.41 on the Hot 100 in the States, and no.45 in the UK.

Versions & Mixes:
Album Version #1.
Single Version.
Album Version #2.
12" Extended Mix.
Album Version #3.
French Promo Mix.

One of three songs Michael sang a medley of, when he appeared on the *Kraft Salutes Disneyland's 25th Anniversary Show* TV special in 1981. The other two songs were *Follow The Yellow Brick Road* and *When You Wish Upon A Star*.

Performed by Michael and Diana Ross on her TV special, *diana!* in 1981.

Performed by Al Jarreau, Jill Scott, Monica and Deborah Cox during the

Michael Jackson: 30th Anniversary Celebration, The Solo Years concerts, staged at New York's Madison Square Garden on 7th and 10th September 2001.

EAT IT

Parody of Michael's *Beat It*, written and recorded by Weird Al Yankovic, with Michael's blessing.

A no.1 smash in Australia; charted at no.12 in the States and no.36 in the UK.

'The only reason he (Michael) let me is that he has a sense of humour,' said Weird Al. 'It is heartening to find somebody that popular, talented and powerful, who can really take a joke.'

Grammy Award: Best Comedy Recording.

EATEN ALIVE

Song written by Michael with Barry and Maurice Gibb – two of the Bee Gees.

Originally written, and registered in March 1985, by Barry and Maurice Gibb. Michael heard their demo and felt it needed something else; Barry offered to share credit with Michael, if he wanted to supply what he thought was missing. Michael agreed and a second demo – recorded by Michael – was registered in July, with the note, 'words and music in the choruses have been completely rewritten'.

Both demo versions, recorded in Los Angeles, remain unreleased.

Recorded by Diana Ross in mid 1985 in Los Angeles, with Michael and the Gibb brothers on backing vocals, for her album of the same title, issued in September 1985.

Produced by Michael with Barry Gibb, Karl Richardson and Albhy Galuten. Michael was present during the recording of the instrumental tracks, and judged whether they were suitable by dancing to them in the studio. He also supervised the mixing, settling on one that Galuten wasn't too happy with.

Performed by Diana at the American Music Awards in 1986.

Issued as a single: charted at no.10 on the R&B singles chart and no.77 on the Hot 100 in the States, and no.71 in the UK.

Official Versions:
Album Version.
Instrumental.
Extended Remix.
Single Version Edited.

ECSTASY

Poem written by Michael – included in his book of poems and reflections, *Dancing The Dream*, published in 1992.

EKAM SATYAM (THE ONE TRUTH)

Song composed by popular Indian singer A.R. Rahman, with lyrics originally written by A.R. Parthasarathy in Sanskrit, with an English translation by Kanika Myer Bharat.

Rahman has confirmed the song, 'was penned especially for the *Michael Jackson & Friends* concert, which was held in Munich in June 1999.'

Michael (singing in English) and Rahman (singing in Sanskrit) recorded the song as a duet around September 1999. However, it failed to make Michael's *INVINCIBLE* album, and talk of the song being released as a single proved unfounded – remains unreleased.

ELIZABETH, I LOVE YOU

Song specially written by Michael for his close friend Elizabeth Taylor, and performed for her at her 65th birthday celebration, on 16th February 1997.

Birthday celebration, including Michael's performance, aired on ABC-TV in the States on 25th February 1997.

No official release, but bootleg recordings (taken from the TV special) are known to exist; an edited version of the song was included on a rare, promo broadcast CD.

Known Versions:
Live Version.
Edited Studio Version.

ELUSIVE SHADOW, THE

Poem written by Michael – included in his book of poems and reflections, *Dancing The Dream*, published in 1992.

E-NE-ME-NE-MI-NE-MOE
(THE CHOICE IS YOURS TO PULL)

Song included on the Jackson 5's *LOOKIN' THROUGH THE WINDOWS* album, issued in May 1972 in the States and October 1972 in the UK.

ENJOY YOURSELF

Song featured on the Jacksons debut, self-titled album, released in November 1976.

Issued as the Jacksons' debut single, hitting no.2 on the R&B singles chart and no.6 on the Hot 100 in the States, and achieving no.42 in the UK.

Promoted in the States by the Jacksons on *The Mike Douglas In Hollywood Show*, *Sonny & Cher Show*, *Wonderama* and on their own TV series, and in Germany on *Muzik Laden*. Also featured on a Destiny Tour concert screened on BBC2 in the UK.

Official Versions:
Album Version.
Extended Version.

Promotional film clip (as very early music videos were called) filmed by the Jacksons.

RIAA Gold Record (USA million seller) – Michael and his brothers' first (Motown at this time wasn't affiliated to the RIAA, so the mega-sales of several Jackson 5 singles went unrecognised).

Alternate version featured on the 2004 compilations, *THE ESSENTIAL JACKSONS* (USA) and *THE VERY BEST OF THE JACKSONS* (UK).

Sampled by:
A+ on *Enjoy Yourself* – no.5 in the UK in 1999.
Backstreet Boys on *Let's Have A Party*, from their eponymous 1996 album.

ESCAPE

Song written by Rodney Jerkins, Fred Jerkins III, LaShawn Daniels and Harvey Jay Mason, and recorded by Michael during the *INVINCIBLE* sessions.

Surfaced on the internet in 2002 – known to fans by the title *Xscape*; Michael's attorneys immediately threatened legal action, if sites didn't remove access to download the track.

Possibly re-worked by Michael in 2003, for an album that was ultimately shelved – no official release.

ESCAPE FROM THE PLANET OF THE ANT MEN

Song recorded by Jermaine, with his brothers excluding Michael on backing vocals, for his solo album *JERMAINE JACKSON* (titled *DYNAMITE* in some countries, including the UK), released in May 1984.

One of three songs from the album featured on *Three Sides Of Jermaine Jackson*, a rare promo EP issued in the States.

Featured on the 12" release of Jermaine's duet with Pia Zadora, *When The Rain Begins To Fall*, in several countries.

ETERNAL LIGHT, THE

Song featured on the Jackson 5 album, *JOYFUL JUKEBOX MUSIC*, issued in October 1976 in the States and December 1976 in the UK.

First album released by Motown after Michael and his brothers (Jermaine apart) left for CBS/Epic, and credited to 'The Jackson 5 featuring Michael Jackson'.

EUPHORIA

Song Michael recorded for his solo album *MUSIC & ME*, released in April 1973 in the States and July 1973 in the UK.

EVEN THOUGH YOU'RE GONE

Song featured on the second Jacksons album, *GOIN' PLACES*, issued in October 1977.

Released as a single in the UK (but not USA, where *Find Me A Girl* was preferred) – charted at no.31.

Promotional film clip filmed by the Jacksons.

Performed by the Jacksons on *Calendar Kid* TV show in the States.

Official Versions:
Album Version.
Single Edit.

EVERYBODY

Written by Michael with brother Tito and Mike McKinney.

Recorded and produced by the Jacksons for their album *TRIUMPH*, released in October 1980.

EVERYBODY IS A STAR

One of 19 'Rare & Unreleased' tracks on the fourth CD of the Michael/Jackson 5 box-set, *SOULSATION!*, issued in June 1995 in the States and a month later in the UK – demo version also known to exist.
Lead vocal shared between Tito, Jackie, Jermaine and Michael.

Originally recorded by Sly & The Family Stone, and included on their *GREATEST HITS* compilation in 1970.

EVERYBODY'S SOMEBODY'S FOOL

Song Michael recorded for his second solo album, *BEN*, issued in August 1972 in the States and December 1972 in the UK.

Scheduled to be released as a single in the States in early 1973, but cancelled – test pressings known to exist.

FACE

Song Michael considered including on his 1995 album, HIS*TORY*, but ultimately rejected – remains unreleased.

FALL AGAIN

Song Michael planned to complete and include on his 2001 album, *INVINCIBLE*, but when his son Prince was taken ill he didn't have time to finish it and it didn't make the album.

'We worked to the point that we were three-fourths of the way finished,' confirmed Walter Afanasieff in January 2000, 'then the incident happened when his son got very sick. We're going to have to reserve a little spot to finish the song.'

Demo version, recorded in 1999, released in November 2004 as one of the previously unreleased tracks on *THE ULTIMATE COLLECTION* box-set.

Recorded by Glenn Lewis – his version featured on the soundtrack album, *MAID IN MANHATTEN*, issued in late 2002.

Fake duet version by Michael and Glenn Lewis surfaced on the internet in 2005.

FAN LETTER TO MICHAEL JACKSON

Tribute song recorded by Rheostatics, for their 1995 album, *INTRODUCING HAPPINESS*.

FANFARE TRANSITION

Song written by Michael in 1992, and registered with the United States Copyright Office in August of the same year – remains unreleased.

Also known by the title, *Fanfare 1992*.

FANTASY

Song Michael cited he had written with brother Jermaine at his copyright hearing in 1993 – remains unreleased.

FAR, FAR AWAY

Song written by Michael, and cited by him at his copyright hearing in 1993; he couldn't originally recall whether he had written the song or not, but later confirmed he did – remains unreleased.

FAREWELL MY SUMMER LOVE

Song originally recorded by Michael on 31st August 1973 – the same day he also recorded *Don't Let It Get You Down* and *Girl You're So Together*.

Remained unreleased until May 1984, when it was one of nine previously unheard songs remixed and included on a 'new' Motown album, *FAREWELL MY SUMMER LOVE 1984* (the '1984' was quickly dropped).

Title track preceded the album as a single, and surpassed all expectations, charting at no.7 in the UK, no.37 on the R&B chart and no.38 on the Hot 100 in the States.

Official Versions:
Album version.
Single Version.
Extended version.

Cover version by Chaos peaked at no.55 in the UK in 1992.

Original mix included as a bonus track on Michael's posthumous *HELLO WORLD* compilation, issued in July 2009.

FAT

Second parody of one of Michael's hits – this time *Bad* – by Weird Al Yankovic, released in 1988.

Failed to match the success of *Eat It*, struggling to no.80 in the UK and no.99 in the States.

Grammy Award: Best Concept Recording.

FEAR

Song written by Michael circa 1993, and considered for his album, HIS*TORY* – remains unreleased.

FEELIN' ALRIGHT

Song performed by the Jackson 5 with Diana Ross, for her 1971 TV special, *Diana!*, and included on the accompanying soundtrack album.

Serviced to DJs in the States as a promo 7" single with picture sleeve – today a great rarity, as disappointing airplay meant the planned single was cancelled.

Snippet of the Jackson 5 rehearsing the song included on the promo film the quintet shot, to be played at concert venues during their 1970 dates.

Live version recorded at the Jackson 5's homecoming concert in Gary, Indiana, on 29th May 1971, included on their album, *GOIN' BACK TO INDIANA*, issued in September 1971 in the States (no UK release). Footage from the concert featured on the *Goin' Back To Indiana* TV special aired in the States on 19th September 1971.

Recorded by Dave Mason, for his 1972 album, *HEAD-KEEPER*.

FERRY 'CROSS THE MERSEY

Written by Gerry Marsden, and originally recorded by Gerry & The Pacemakers.

Michael was shown, on a DVD showing the recording of *I Have This Dream*, played during a court disposition in London in 2008, singing the song circa 2005 – led to speculation Michael was planning to cover some old rock'n'roll songs on his new album.

Hit Versions:
Gerry & The Pacemakers – no.8 in the UK in 1964.
Christians, Holly Johnson, Paul McCartney, Gerry Marsden & Stock Aitken Waterman – no.1 in the UK in 1989 (charity recording).

FEVER

Classic song Rebbie Jackson performed on *The Jacksons* TV series in 1976, accompanied by brothers Michael and Marlon, who danced in the background.

Hit versions:
Little Willie John – no.24 in the States in 1956.
Peggy Lee – no.5 in the UK, no.8 in the States in 1958.
Helen Shapiro – no.38 in the UK in 1964.
McCoys – no.7 in the States, no.44 in the UK in 1965.
Rita Coolidge – no.76 in the States in 1973.
Peggy Lee – no.75 in the UK in 1992 (re-issue).
Madonna – no.6 in the UK in 1993.

FIND ME A GIRL

Song featured on the Jacksons album, *GOIN' PLACES*, released in October 1977.

Issued as a single in the States (but not UK) – failed to enter the Hot 100, but charted at no.38 on the R&B singles chart.

Official Versions:
Album Version.
Single Edit.

FINGERTIPS

Stevie Wonder song the Jackson 5 recorded a version of – remains unreleased.

Stevie – as Little Stevie Wonder – took the song to no.1 on the Hot 100 and R&B singles chart in the States in 1963.

FIRE IS THE FEELING

Original title of La Toya's debut hit, *Night Time Lover*, which Michael co-wrote with her – written with Donna Summer in mind.

See also: *Night Time Lover*.

FLAT FOOT FLOOGIE, THE

Song performed by Michael with siblings La Toya, Rebbie and Marlon, on *The Jacksons* TV series in 1976.

FLY AWAY

Song Michael cited he had written at his copyright hearing in 1994.

Recorded by Michael's sister Rebbie, for her 1998 album, *YOURS FAITHFULLY*, with Michael co-producing (with

StoneBridge and Nick Nice) and singing backing vocals.

'That's simply a beautiful song,' said Rebbie, speaking about *Fly Away*. 'After he (Michael) wrote it, he said he could hear me singing it. It's about not wanting to lose a relationship".

Michael's own version of the song was finally heard in October 2001, when it was one of the bonus track added to the expanded, special edition reissue of his album *BAD*. Rebbie's version, compared to this version, has extra background vocals by Michael.

FOLLOW THE YELLOW BRICK ROAD

Originally from the Judy Garland film *The Wizard Of Oz*, one of three songs Michael sang a medley of, when he appeared on the *Kraft Salutes Disneyland's 25th Anniversary Show* TV special in 1980. The other two songs were *Ease On Down The Road* and *When You Wish Upon A Star*.

FONZ, THE

See: *Do The Fonz*.

FOR ALL TIME

Song originally written by Michael Sherwood, David Paich and Steve Porcaro during the *Thriller* sessions; later, a contender for Michael's album *DANGEROUS*, but it wasn't released at the time.

Version surfaced on the internet towards the end of 2002.

Finally officially released in February 2008, as one of the bonus tracks on *THRILLER 25* – this version appeared to mix old and new vocals – possibly from the *BAD* era – by Michael.

FOR ONCE IN MY LIFE

Stevie Wonder classic the Jackson 5 recorded a version of – remains unreleased.

Song the Jacksons sang the chorus of, as guest Sonny Bono performed a medley of *More Than You Know*, *Am I Blue*, *For Once In My Life* and *Try A Little Tenderness*, during their TV series in 1976.

Hit versions:
Tony Bennett – no.91 on the Hot 100 in the States in 1967.
Stevie Wonder – no.2 on the Hot 100 and R&B singles chart in the States, and no.3 in the UK, in 1968.
Jackie Wilson – no.70 on the Hot 100 in 1968.
Dorothy Squires – no.24 in the UK in 1969.

FOR THE GOOD TIMES

One of Katherine Jackson's favourite songs, which son Michael sang to her at her birthday party on 4th May 1984, staged at the Bistro Garden Restaurant in Beverley Hills – Michael also flew in his mother's favourite pianist, Floyd Cramer, from Nashville for the occasion.

Hit Versions:
Ray Price – no.11 on the Hot 100 in the States in 1970.
Perry Como – no.7 in the UK in 1973.

FOR THE REST OF MY LIFE

Track rumoured to have been recorded in late 1970 by the Jackson 5 with Diana Ross – never officially acknowledged by Motown.

FOREVER CAME TODAY

Supremes hit covered by the Jackson 5 on their album *MOVING VIOLATION*, released in May 1975 in the States and July 1975 in the UK.

Last Jackson 5 single issued whilst the group were still a Motown act, achieved no.6 on the R&B singles chart and no.60 on the Hot 100 in the States, but failed to chart in the UK.

Promo 7" singles on blue and red vinyl released in the States – now rare collectors items.

Promoted on *Soul Train*, *The Rich Little Show* and *The Carol Burnett Show* in 1976 – the latter was the group's first performance without Jermaine (Marlon and Randy lip-synched his vocals). Also performed by the Jacksons on their own TV series in 1976.

Live performance by the Jacksons, at a concert in Mexico in 1976, included on the home video, *The Jacksons In Concert*, released in 1981 in the UK (no USA release).

Alternate mix featured on the 1993 Jackson 5 compilation, *MOTOWN LEGENDS*.

Remixed 'Disc-O-Tech #3 Version' appeared on the album *DISC-O-TECH* in 1976 – this version was added to the '2 Classic Albums on 1 CD' re-issue of *DANCING MACHINE & MOVING VIOLATION*, released in the States in August 2001.

Original version by the Supremes, issued in 1968 on their album *REFLECTIONS*, achieved no.17 on the R&B singles chart and no.28 on the Hot 100 in the States, and no.28 in the UK.

FREE

Song Michael cited he had written at his copyright hearing in Mexico in 1993 – remains unreleased.

FROM THE BOTTOM OF MY HEART

Original title of Michael's charity recording, in aid of victims of Hurricane

Katrina, in 2005 – title may have been changed because Stevie Wonder's new album featured a song with the same title.

Official press release named artists who would have participated: Babyface, Mariah Carey, R. Kelly, Jay-Z, James Brown, Missy Elliot, Snoop Dog, O'Jays, Yolanda Adams, Ciara, Mary J. Blige, Lenny Kravitz, Wyclef Jean & Lauryn Hill.

Remains unreleased.

FROSTY THE SNOWMAN

Perennial Christmas favourite the Jackson 5 recorded for their *CHRISTMAS ALBUM*, released in October 1970 in the States and December 1970 in the UK.

B-side of *Mama's Pearl* in Turkey.

One of four songs from the album on the *Michael Jackson & The Jackson 5 Christmas EP*, issued in November 1987 in the UK.

FUTURE, THE

Song will.i.am confirmed, at a Black Eyed Peas press conference in South Korea in August 2007, he had recorded with Michael – remains unreleased.

GET AROUND

Song Michael cited he had written in his court deposition in November 1993 – remains unreleased.

Re-worked 2000 version crediting Rodney Jerkins, Fred Jerkins III and

LaShawn Daniels considered for Michael's *INVINCIBLE* album – failed to make the final track listing and remains unreleased.

GET HAPPY

Song the Jacksons performed on their TV series in 1976.

GET IT

Michael's second duet with Stevie Wonder.

Michael completed the recording of his vocals whilst touring in Japan, the tapes of the songs having been personally delivered to him by Barry Betts, a fan who was hand-picked from the audience at one of Stevie's concerts.

'I was on tour in England by that time, and I had to record my vocals for that song in a studio, in London.' said Stevie. 'Quincy and Michael needed those tapes urgently or we wouldn't meet the deadline, but when I came out of the studio that day, it was too late to send the tapes with those express carriers. That same night, I was doing a show in London and I asked the audience if someone was willing to go to Los Angeles right away, all expenses paid, to deliver the tapes. There was one guy that was ready to do it and he left right away, took the plane and gave the tapes to Michael and Quincy – that's how they got them on time. Finally, Michael finished the song in Tokyo a few days later, he recorded his vocals there and we got the track on time to put it on the album.'

Featured on Stevie's album *CHARACTERS*, released in 1988.

Disappointed as a single, peaking at no.4 on the R&B singles chart and no.80 on the Hot 100 in the States, and no.37 in the UK.

Official Versions:
Album Version.
Single Edit.
12" Extended Mix.
12" Extended Mix Instrumental.
Single Instrumental.

GET IT TOGETHER

Title track of an album the Jackson 5 released in September 1973 in the States and November 1973 in the UK.

Sold a respectable 700,000 copies as a single in the States, achieving no.2 on the R&B singles chart but a lowly no.28 on the Hot 100 – better than the UK, where it failed to chart at all.

Promo 7" red vinyl single released in the States with two alternate record labels.

Performed by the Jackson 5 in the States on *The Bob Hope Special* (an alternate version), which aired on NBC TV in the States on 26th September 1973, *Soul Train* and *The Mills Brothers Special* in 1974, and by the Jacksons on their TV series in 1977.

Alternate vocals version featured on the Jackson 5's 1980 compilation, *MOTOWN SUPERSTAR SERIES Vol.12* and the 1986 compilation, *ANTHOLOGY*; another alternate version included on the 1993 compilation, *MOTOWN LEGENDS*; a rare mix, with Michael humming, is also known to exist.

4Hereo Remix, as included on the Japanese album *SOUL SOURCE – JACKSON 5 REMIXES 2* in 2001, featured extended vocals. Same remix made available on Tito's website in February 2008.

GET ON THE FLOOR

Song written by Michael with Louis Johnson of the Brothers Johnson.

Developed from a song the Brothers Johnson were working on, for their *LIGHT UP THE NIGHT* album. Michael heard the incomplete song, put a melody to it, and recorded it himself.

Featured on Michael's first solo album for CBS/Epic, *OFF THE WALL*, released in August 1979.

Re-arranged by Michael in early 1980 – this newer version – with a more prominent guitar sound – was included on new pressings of *OFF THE WALL*, in place of the original recording.

Original version appeared on the CD single, *Liberian Girl*, and a variety of Japanese pressings of *OFF THE WALL*, including the original CD pressing.

Newer version featured as the B-side of *Rock With You* in the UK and *Off The Wall* in the States.

GET READY

Temptations hit written and produced by Smokey Robinson, which the Jackson 5 often performed on the Chiltin' Circuit in the mid-to-late 1960s.

Performed by the Jackson 5, with the Temptations, in 1971 at the PUSH – Expo concert in Chicago.

Comedy version performed by the Jacksons on their TV series in 1976 – dressed in inflated, heavyweight suits, and billed as 'The Ton-Tations'.

The Temptations took the song to no.1 on the R&B singles chart, and achieved no.29 on the Hot 100, in the States in 1966. The single hit no.10 in the UK.

GHOSTS

Song written by Michael with Teddy Riley, developed after Michael was asked to write the theme to a new Addams Family film. He ultimately declined, and instead wrote his own short film (which became *Ghosts*), including the song he originally wrote for the film, *Is It Scary*.

Failed to make the final selection for Michael's HIS*TORY* album, and first heard in Michael's mini-movie *Ghosts*, which cost an estimated $7-9 million and premiered in Beverly Hills on 24th October 1996.

One of five previously unreleased songs featured on Michael's remix album, *BLOOD ON THE DANCE FLOOR*, issued in April 1997.

Double A-side single with His*tory* in most countries (but not the USA), charting at no.5 in the UK – Michael's eighth consecutive Top 5 single.

Official Versions:
Album Version.
Radio Edit.
Remix.
Mousse T's Radio Edit.
Mousse T's Radio Rock.
Mousse T's Club Mix.
Mousse T's Radio Rock Singalong.
Mousse T's Club Mix TV.

Alternate version, with different backing vocals, sound effects and bass, leaked after they were used during the production of the final credits of the *Ghosts* short film (the final version of the song wasn't ready in time).

Title of a critically acclaimed 40 minute short film directed by Stan Winston, in which Michael played all the lead characters – written by Michael with Stephen King.

'We wrote it on the telephone, Stephen and I,' said Michael. 'He's a lovely guy – he's amazing. We wrote it on the phone, just talking together.'

Bob Fosse Award: Best Choreography in a Music Video.

GHOSTS – MEDLEY OF HIGHLIGHTS FROM 'BLOOD ON THE DANCE FLOOR – *HISTORY* IN THE MIX'

Medley given away on promo cassette, as part of the *Ghosts* promotional pack, at the UK premiere of the short film in London in May 1997.

Tracks featured: *Stranger In Moscow (Tee's In-House Club Mix), Blood On The Dance Floor, Scream Louder (Flyte Tyme Remix), Ghosts, Earth Song (Hani's Club Experience), You Are Not Alone (Classic Club Mix)* and His*tory (Tony Moran's History Lesson)*.

GIRL DON'T TAKE YOUR LOVE FROM ME

Song included on Michael's first solo album, *GOT TO BE THERE*, released in January 1972 in the States and May 1972 in the UK.

Featured in the 'Jackson And The Beanstalk' episode of the new Jackson 5 cartoon series in 1971.

GIRL IS MINE, THE

Written by Michael and recorded as a duet with Paul McCartney, for Michael's album *THRILLER*, issued in December 1982.

McCartney spent three days at Westlake Studios, Los Angeles, working on the song with Michael from 14th-16th April 1982 – the year after the pair first worked on *Say Say Say* and *The Man*, although it was the first Jackson/McCartney duet to gain a release.

Michael is on record as saying the duet is one of his most enjoyable recording moments:

'One of my favourite songs to record, of all my recordings as a solo artist, is probably *The Girl Is Mine*, because working with Paul McCartney was pretty exciting and we just literally had fun… it was like lots of kibitzing and playing and throwing stuff at each other and making jokes… and we actually recorded the track and the vocals pretty much live at the same time, and we do have footage of it, but it's never been shown – maybe one day we'll give you a sneak preview of it.'

Footage of Michael and Paul in the studio was screened at some venues during Paul's world tour in 1990.

Several demo versions known to exist, including a solo version by Michael, and others of him working on different keys for the melody of the song – some of these were played at the court deposition hearing in Mexico in 1993. Solo demo version released in some countries, including the UK, on *The Girl Is Mine 2008* CD single.

Lead single from *THRILLER*, hitting no.1 on the R&B singles chart and no.2 on the Hot 100 in the States, and no.8 in the UK. Cover photograph of Michael and Paul by the latter's late wife, Linda.

RIAA Gold Record (USA million seller).

Subject of two lawsuits, firstly Michael testified in a Chicago court on 6th December 1984, when Fred Sandford claimed it was the same as his song, *Please Love Me Now*. Secondly, in Mexico in 1993, after Robert Smith (*aka* Robert Austin), Reynaud Jones and Clifford Rubin claimed it infringed two of their songs, *Don't Let The Sunshine Catch You Crying* and *Happy Go Lucky Girl*. In both cases, the judgement found in favour of Michael and his record company.

In the Sanford case, Michael stated in court: 'It started with Quincy Jones asking me to write a song about two guys quarreling over the same girl, and I thought about it and I came up with *The Girl Is Mine*.'

'I woke up from my sleep and I had this song,' said Michael, explaining his inspiration for writing the song, 'and I went over to the tape recorder and I sang it into the tape recorder, and I sang exactly what I heard in my head, starting with the melody and the keyboard and the strings and everything. So I just orally put it on tape.'

The rap in the song, Michael explained, was Quincy Jones's idea. Asked about his other songs, and if any of them were similar to *The Girl Is Mine*, Michael replied, 'Oh, yes, lots of other songs… they are mainly the same chords that I use in so many… *That's What You Get (For Being Polite)* is one. Others would be *Why Can't I Be*, *Thank You For Life* – all have the same main, the same type of chords as *The Girl Is Mine*.'

To prove his point, Michael sang *The Girl Is Mine* to an instrumental version of *That's What You Get (For Being Polite)*.

Sampled by Stevie Wonder – without credit – on *Fun Day*, from his 1991 album, *MUSIC FROM THE MOVIE JUNGLE FEVER*.

Cover version recorded by Yellowman.

'New edited version' – the original version minus rap by Michael and Paul – was released as a promo 7" single.

GIRL IS MINE 2008, THE

Re-working of the above song, for Michael's album *THRILLER 25*, released in February 2008.

This version had McCartney's vocals removed, and vocals by William 'will.i.am' Adams added; Michael's vocals on the track were taken from the original demo version of the song, which was included on the CD single released in the UK.

First single lifted from the album in many countries, including the UK where it charted at no.32. Also achieved no.12 in Holland, no.21 in Germany and no.22 in France.

Released as a 12" single in France.

Posthumous hit: no.45 in France.

GIRL YOU'RE SO TOGETHER

Song Michael originally recorded on 31st August 1973 – the same day he recorded *Don't Let It Get You Down* and *Farewell My Summer Love*.

Remained unreleased until an up-dated version featured on Michael's solo album, *FAREWELL MY SUMMER LOVE*, issued in May 1984 in the States and June 1984 in the States.

Second and last single lifted from the album in many countries, including the UK (but not USA), where it charted at no.33.

B-side of *Touch The One You Love* in the States.

Original mix included as a bonus track on Michael's posthumous *HELLO WORLD* compilation, issued in July 2009.

GIRLFRIEND

Written by Paul McCartney, and mentioned to Michael at a Hollywood party in 1978, as a song he might like to record. Nothing happened, so Paul recorded the song himself, for the Wings album, *LONDON TOWN*.

Brought to Michael's attention again by producer Quincy Jones, when they were looking for songs for Michael's first solo album as an adult. This time Michael did record the song, and included it on *OFF THE WALL*, released in August 1979.

Fifth single from the album in the UK (but not USA), where it gave Michael a then record fifth hit from one album, peaking at no.41.

GIRLS GIRLS GIRLS

Track Jay-Z recorded, with Kanye West producing, for his 2001 album, *THE BLUEPRINT* – one planned remix was to feature Michael singing a hook, but if recorded it remains unreleased.

'My Mom likes it,' commented Jay-Z, around the time of the planned remix, 'because she gets to see how successful her son is – you're working with Michael Jackson, you must be all right; you must be pretty good!'

GIVE IN TO ME

Written by Michael with Bill Bottrell, and recorded by Michael with special guest Slash – from Guns N' Roses – on guitar.

'He sent me a tape of the song that had no guitars other than some slow picking,' said Slash. 'I called him and sang over the phone what I wanted to do.'

Slash, at the time, was just leaving for Africa, so he and Michael managed to work it out so they could record Slash's contribution when he returned from Africa. 'I basically went in and started to play – that was it,' said Slash. 'Michael just wanted whatever was in my style. He just wanted me to do that – no pressure. He was really in synch with me.'

'Slash come over for a couple of tracks,' said Bottrell. 'Interestingly, there was no alcohol, drugs or cigarettes on the session at all. Only one crew member smoked and he had to go outside to do it. But when Slash cam, MJ knew it was part of his thing. He said, "let him have his alcohol, cigarettes, whatever it takes", so we set up another room at the Hit Factory, and Slash had his people send over the list... the drink of the day was Jack (Daniels) and coffee, if I recall correctly.'

Featured on Michael's solo album, *DANGEROUS*, issued in November 1991.

One demo version is known to fans as *Love Is A Donut* – no official release.

Seventh single released from the album in the UK, where it charted at no.2. American release cancelled, and *Who Is It* issued instead, following Michael's *a cappella* rendition of the song during his televised interview with Oprah Winfrey.

Official Versions:
Album Version.
7" Vocal Version.
Instrumental.

No.1 in New Zealand and Zimbabwe.

Promo 'live in concert' short film, also featuring Slash, shot in just two hours in Munich, Germany. Directed by Andy Moharan, and premiered on 10th February 1993, on *Michael Jackson Talks… To Oprah* – an interview that attracted around 100 million viewers.

Posthumous hit: no.74 in the UK.

GIVE IT UP

Written by Michael with brother Randy, and recorded by the Jacksons for their album *TRIUMPH*, released in October 1980.

B-side of *Time Waits For No One* in the UK (no USA release).

GIVE LOVE ON CHRISTMAS DAY

Song recorded by the Jackson 5 for *CHRISTMAS ALBUM*, issued in October 1970 in the States and December 1970 in the UK.

Released as a single in the Philippines.

Promo CD single released in the States in 1986, to promote the release of *CHRISTMAS ALBUM* on CD for the first time.

GIVE ME HALF A CHANCE

Song originally recorded – but not released – by the Jackson 5 between 1970-73.

One of the 'Never-Before-Released Masters' included on *LOOKING BACK TO YESTERDAY*, an album credited to Michael solo, released in February 1986 in the States and May 1986 in the UK.

GLOVED ONE, THE

Song written circa 2000-01 by Sisqó, for Michael's *INVINCIBLE* album – remains unreleased.

GOD REST YE MERRY GENTLEMEN

Well known festive song the Jackson 5 recorded for their *CHRISTMAS ALBUM* circa 1970, but which failed to make the final track listing – remains unreleased.

GOIN' BACK TO ALABAMA

Song written by Lionel Richie and recorded by Kenny Rogers, with Michael and Richie on backing vocals, for his 1981 album, *SHARE YOUR LOVE*.

Collaboration came about when Rogers asked Richie, who was producing his album, whether it would be possible for him to work with Michael, as he was a big fan. Michael, in turn, was a fan of Rogers and so was eager to work with him.

GOIN' BACK TO INDIANA

Song originally featured on the Jackson 5's *THIRD ALBUM*, issued in September 1970 in the States and February 1971 in the UK.

Released as a single in several European countries, excluding the UK, hitting no.1 in Sweden.

One of six tracks featured on *Third Album EP*, released with a picture sleeve in the States in 1970.

Live version recorded at the Jackson 5's homecoming concert in Gary, Indiana, on 29th May 1971, included on their album, *GOIN' BACK TO INDIANA*, issued in September 1971 in the States (no UK release).

Goin' Back To Indiana TV special recorded in the States on 9th and 10th July 1971, and included concert footage of the Jackson 5's success homecoming on 29th May, aired on ABC-TV on 19th September 1971.

Featured in the first episode – titled 'It All Started With' – of the Jackson 5 cartoon series, which aired weekly in the States, starting 11th September 1971. Version featured was an alternate mix, with a slower tempo, and minus the horns and strings.

Performed by the Jackson children at The Jacksons Family Honors concert, staged at the MGM Grand Garden, Las Vegas, on 19th February 1994.

GOIN' PLACES

Title track of the Jacksons second album, issued in October 1977.

Charted at no.8 on the R&B singles chart and no.52 on the Hot 100 in the States, and no.26 in the UK.

Promotional film clip filmed by the Jacksons.

Official Versions:
Album Version.
Single Edit.

GOIN' TO RIO

Song written by Michael with Carole Bayer Sager circa 1976, and considered for his album, *OFF THE WALL*. Cited by Michael in his court deposition in November 1993 – remains unreleased.

GOING TO A GO-GO

Smokey Robinson song the Jackson 5 sometimes performed live on the Chitlin' Circuit, prior so signing for Motown in 1969.

Hit Versions:
Miracles – no.2 on the R&B singles chart and no.11 on the Pop chart in the States, and no.44 in the UK, in 1966.
Sharonettes – no.46 in the UK in 1975.
Rolling Stones – no.25 on the Pop chart in the States, and no.26 in the UK, in 1982.
New Situation – no.92 on the R&B chart in the States in 1989.

GONE TOO SOON

Song Michael recorded for his solo album, *DANGEROUS*, released in November 1991. Demo version featured different vocals and 'perfect sunflower' lyric – no official release.

Prelude composed, arranged and conducted by Marty Paich.

'I think he (Michael) was trying to re-invent himself and become more credible, more commercial, and he achieves that here,' said Teddy Riley. 'It reminds me of a more wordly versions of *She's Out Of My Life*. With this album, he's hinting at his past songs, as well as trying to re-invent himself.'

Written for and dedicated to the memory of Ryan White, a haemophiliac who was diagnosed with the AIDS virus aged eleven years, and who died just after turning eighteen in April 1990.

Ninth single lifted from the album in numerous countries, excluding the USA but including the UK, where it achieved no.33 – Michael's ninth Top 40 hit from the one album, thus equalling his own record, set with *BAD*.

B-side featured an Instrumental version.

Promo short film – directed by Bill DiCicco – featured footage of Michael with Ryan White, as well as brief coverage of Ryan's funeral, which Michael, Elton John and Barbara Bush attended. Footage of Ryan and Michael was used with Ryan's mother's permission; Michael had promised Ryan he could appear in his next short film, but Ryan died before that happened.

Performed by Michael on 19th January 1993, at *An American Reunion: The 52nd Presidential Inaugural Gala*, for the incoming President, Bill Clinton. Michael, as well as dedicating the song to his late friend Ryan, used the occasion to speak out in favour of funding AIDS-related research:

'He is gone, but I want his life to have meaning beyond his passing. It is my hope President-elect Clinton, that you and your administration commit the resources needed to eliminate this awful disease that took my friend, and ended so many promising lives before their time.'

Following the tragic death of Diana, Princess of Wales on 31st August 1997, Michael permitted the inclusion of *Gone Too Soon* on an album titled *TRIBUTE*, with all proceeds from the sale of the album going to the Diana, Princess of Wales Memorial Fund. Michael also dedicated his Ostend concert to the memory of Diana and, speaking via Kingdom International, took a swipe at the world's paparazzi:

'As one who has been under scrutiny the majority of my life, I speak with authority when I say that I am horrified that the paparazzi, supported by the tabloids' animalistic behaviour, may be acceptable to the public. The world's acceptance of this practice, if continued, will accelerate tragedies of this magnitude.'

Performed, with guest Stevie Wonder, by Babyface during his MTV Unplugged in New York City show, which aired in the States on 21st November 1997. Subsequently included on Babyface's album, *MTV UNPLUGGED NYC 1997*.

Performed by Usher at the 'A Celebration of the Life of Michael Jackson 1958-2009' memorial concert at the Staples Center on 7th July 2009.

Posthumous hit: no.24 in Holland and no.67 in USA (Hot Digital Songs).

GOOD TIMES

Song the Jacksons recorded for their debut, self-titled album, released in November 1976.

B-side of *Dreamer* in the UK.

Promotional film clip (as very early music videos were called) filmed by the Jacksons.

Performed at the American Music Awards in 1977, where Michael also presented an award with Lola Falana to

Chicago, for Favourite Rock/Pop Group. Also performed on *The Jacksons* TV series in 1977.

GOODNESS KNOWS

One of three songs James Whitney has confirmed he wrote for Michael between 1976-79 – recorded by Michael but disagreements around publishing rights mean it remains unreleased.

Whitney's association with Michael was through producer Bobby Taylor, and he met Michael at Crystal Sound Studios and at their homes.

Recorded by Whitney for his 2007 album, *LET'S FALL IN LOVE*.

See also: *Disco Kids*, *Sweet Music*.

GOT THE HOTS

Song written by Michael with Quincy Jones, and cited by Michael in his court deposition in November 1993.

Included on the first acetate of the expanded, special edition reissue of *THRILLER* in 2001 – later withdrawn.

Finally released in February 2008, on the Japanese only version of *THRILLER 25*; later featured on some editions of Michael's *KING OF POP* compilation.

Lyrics re-written by Rod Temperton, and recorded as *Baby's Got It Bad* by Siedah Garrett, for her 1988 album, *KISS OF LIFE*.

GOT TO BE THERE

Title track of Michael's debut solo album, released in January 1972 in the States and May 1972 in the UK.

Originally intended for the Supremes, then the Jackson 5 – indeed, Michael's brothers did feature on backing vocals, as they did on many early songs credited to Michael alone.

Michael's debut solo single, and in releasing it he broke a Motown tradition, as he became the first Motown artist to go solo whilst still an active member of a group (Diana Ross, Smokey Robinson and David Ruffin all had to leave their respective groups before becoming solo artists).

Sold around 1.6 million copies in the States alone, where it achieved no.4 on both the Hot 100 and R&B singles chart, and charted at no.5 in the UK.

Promoted in the States on the *Hellzapoppin* TV show in 1972.

Featured in the 'Michael In Wonderland' episode of the new Jackson 5 cartoon series in 1971.

Live version featured on the Michael/Jackson 5's *LIVE!* album, issued in September 1988 in the UK (no USA release). All songs on the album were recorded at a concert on 30th April 1973, at the Osaka Koseinenkin Hall in Japan. Also included on the limited edition CD, *IN JAPAN!*, released by Hip-O Select in 2004 – only 5,000 copies pressed.

Title given to a cassette-only budget compilation released in 1989.

Cover versions include one by Chaka Khan, which she recorded for her eponymous 1982 album. 'I actually didn't like the original much,' she admitted, 'but Arif Mardin (her producer) was adamant

I cover it. It turned out fantastic, and gave me a new respect for Michael's version.'

Other cover versions by:
The Boys (featuring Stokley of Mint Condition) – from their 1990 album of the same name.
The Lovelites – from their 1990 album, *THE LOVELIGHT YEARS*.
Smokey Robinson & The Miracles – from their 2004 album, *THE LIVE COLLECTION*.
Boyz II Men – from their 2007 album, *MOTOWN: A JOURNEY THROUGH HITSVILLE USA*.

Alternate take with extra and different background vocals released in July 2009 on the compilation, *THE STRIPPED MIXES*.

GOT TO FIND A WAY SOMEHOW

Song written by Michael in 1979, and registered with the United States Copyright Office in November 1984 – remains unreleased.

GOTTA DANCE

Snippet of a song Michael performed as part of a three song medley – also including *Putting On the Ritz* and *They Can't Take That Away From Me* – on *The Jacksons* TV series in 1976.

GRAMMY NOMINATIONS MEDLEY

Brief medley performed by Michael and his brothers (minus Jermaine), at the Grammy Awards ceremony on 2nd March 1974, to introduce the nominees for the Best Rhythm & Blues Performance, Duo or Group: *Could It Be I'm Falling In Love*, *The Cisco Kid*, *Midnight Train To Georgia*, *Love Train* and *Be What You Are*.

GRAMMY NOMINATIONS RAP

Short ditty performed by the Jacksons at the Grammy Awards ceremony, staged in the Hollywood Palladium on 19th February 1977, to introduce the nominees for Best Rhythm & Blues Performance, Female – Natalie Cole won the award for *Sophisticated Woman (She's A Different Lady)*.

GREAT SPECKLED BIRD, THE

One of numerous songs Michael recalls singing, with his mother and siblings, as a young boy – mentioned in Katherine Jackson's autobiography, *My Family, The Jacksons*.

GREATEST HITS CLASSIC MEGAMIX

Medley of Michael's hits: *Bad*, *Rock With You*, *Don't Stop 'Til You Get Enough*, *Thriller*, *Rock With You*, *Remember The Time*, *Billie Jean*, *Black Or White*, *Thriller*, *The Way You Make Me Feel*, *Wanna Be Startin' Somethin'* and *Thriller*.

GREATEST SHOW ON EARTH

Song featured on Michael's second solo album, *BEN*, issued in August 1972 in the States and December 1972 in the UK.

GROOVE OF MIDNIGHT

Written by Rod Temperton, and dating from the *BAD* era. Short demo version by Michael surfaced on the internet in 2003, which also featured a snippet of Michael talking about why his hair looked longer: 'I've rolled it up. I use what's called Sebastian gel, which tightens it up. I didn't put it in today, I do it every other day, then it gets too hard – like a brick.'

No official release.

Recorded by Siedah Garrett for her 1988 album, *KISS OF LIFE*.

GUESS WHO'S MAKING WHOOPEE WITH YOUR GIRLFRIEND

Song recorded by the Jackson 5, that evolved into *Mama's Pearl*, as Berry Gordy felt the lyrics of the original song were unsuitable for the group's wholesome image.

Remains unreleased, but has leaked on the internet.

HALLELUJAH DAY

Song included on the Jackson 5's album, *SKYWRITER*, released in March 1973 in the States and July 1973 in the UK.

Lyrics celebrated the end of the Vietnam War.

First single on which Michael's voice could be heard to be breaking; promo USA single featured a mono version.

Sold a disappointing 250,000 copies in the States, achieving no.10 on the R&B singles chart and no.28 on the Hot 100. Charted at no.20 in the UK.

HAPPY BIRTHDAY

Song written and originally recorded by Stevie Wonder, for his album *HOTTER THAN JULY*, issued in 1980.

Hit cover version:
David Parton – no.4 in the UK in 1977.

Michael joined Stevie on stage on 17th July 1998, to sing the song to Nelson Mandela, at his 80th birthday celebration.

HAPPY BIRTHDAY, LISA

Track featured on the Simpsons album, *SONGS IN THE KEY OF SPRINGFIELD*, issued in 1997.

Featured in the Simpsons episode titled 'Stark Raving Dad', in which Michael guested.

For many years mystery surrounded Michael's involvement with the song, however, the albums sleeve credited copyright ownership of the song to Mijac Music – Michael's publishing company, which registered the song with the United States Copyright Office in September 1991.

It has been confirmed Michael – under the pseudonym John Jay Smith – voiced his character, but *Happy Birthday, Lisa* was sung by sound-a-like, Kipp Lennon – a member of the family band, Venice. Michael was present when Lennon recorded his vocal: 'This is kind of weird,' said Lennon at the time, 'he's right next to me and I have to do him in front of everyone, on command!'

Michael's version included on the first acetate version of the special, expanded edition of his album, *DANGEROUS* – bonus disc subsequently cancelled. Michael's version (1:36) leaked on the internet in 2007 – no official release.

HAPPY (LOVE THEME FROM 'LADY SINGS THE BLUES')

Song written by Smokey Robinson and Michael Legrand, originally included on Michael's album *MUSIC & ME*, released in April 1973 in the States and July 1973 in the UK.

Didn't feature in the movie *Lady Sings The Blues*, in which Diana Ross gave an Oscar-nominated performance as the blues singer, Billie Holiday.

Live performance by the Jacksons, at a concert in Mexico in 1976, omitted from the home video, *The Jacksons In Concert*, released in 1981 in the UK (no USA release).

Issued as a single in 1983 in many countries (no USA release), to promote the TV advertised compilation *18 GREATEST HITS*, credited to Michael Jackson Plus The Jackson 5 – the album spent three weeks at no.1 in the UK.

Picture disc single and wrap-around poster sleeve helped the single to no.52 in the UK.

Smokey Robinson's version featured on his 1975 album, *A QUIET STORM*, along with *The Wedding Song* – which Smokey wrote especially for the wedding of Jermaine Jackson and Hazel Gordy.

HARLEY

Written by Jackie, Jermaine, Randy & Tito Jackson with Attala Zane Giles, and recorded by the Jacksons for their 1989 album, *2300 JACKSON STREET*.

Michael wasn't one of the Jacksons who recorded this song.

HAVE YOURSELF A MERRY LITTLE CHRISTMAS

Song featured on the Jackson 5's *CHRISTMAS ALBUM*, issued in October 1970 in the States and December 1970 in the UK.

Released as a single in the Philippines.

B-side of Michael's Dutch release of *Little Christmas Tree* in 1973.

HE WHO MAKES THE SKY GREY

Written by Jermaine Jackson with Sheik Abdullah of Bahrain, with vocals by Michael – no official release.

'The track was done a while ago now and was called *He Who Makes The Sky Grey*, but has not been released to date and I don't know if it ever will be,' said backing vocalist, Kim Chandler. 'Michael's vocals were already down, so we didn't get to meet him, unfortunately. However, he did ring up during the session, to speak to the session conductor – she was pretty excited!'

HEAL THE WORLD

Song written and recorded by Michael for his solo album *DANGEROUS*, released in November 1991.

Prelude composed, arranged and conducted by Marty Paich.

'*Heal The World* is one of my favourite of anything I have ever recorded,' said Michael in 1996, 'because it is a public awareness song. It is something that I think will live in the hearts of people for a long time, because it is about something that is very special, and something that is very innocent and something that is very important.'

'This has strong global issues – it was a big song,' said Teddy Riley. 'I didn't produce it though, all I did to that song was complement it… I did quite a lot of the percussion on there, I did that on there to bring something extra to the mix.'

Fifth single lifted from the album in the States, sixth in the UK and elsewhere. Fared poorly in the States, peaking at no.27 on the Hot 100 and no.62 on the R&B singles chart, but hit no.2 in the UK – kept out of the top spot by Whitney Houston's mega-hit, *I Will Always Love You*.

Official Versions:
Album Version.
Album Version – with special message from Michael.
7" Edit.
7" Edit With Intro.

Anti-war promo short film, directed by Joe Pytka, didn't feature Michael, but instead focussed on impoverished children playing around armed soldiers and tanks.

Lyrics included in Michael's book of poems and reflections, *Dancing The Dream*, published in 1992.

Gave its name to Michael's Heal The World Foundation, which was officially launched on 30th September 1992 in Burcharest, Romania. A playground at an orphanage, and a medical mission to Romania by 12 qualified doctors/medical staff, were among the first projects the Foundation funded.

Live performance by Michael, at his Dangerous Tour concert in Bucharest, Romania, on 1st October 1992, featured on the DVD released as part of his box-set, *THE ULTIMATE COLLECTION*, issued in November 2004.

Version including a special message from Michael featured on the rare promo Cd single, *Signature Series*, released in the States in 1993.

Cited by Michael in his 1993 Mexican deposition, where he explained unusually for him, when he created the song he wrote both the lyrics and music at the same time.

Performed by Michael on 19th January 1993, at *An American Reunion: The 52nd Presidential Inaugural Gala*, for the incoming President, Bill Clinton, and during the half time interval at the

American Super Bowl Final twelve days later.

Live performances, as part of concerts staged during Michael's *History* World Tour, screened in Germany and New Zealand.

Short, impromptu live performance on 16th December 1998, when Michael attended the grand opening of The Royal Towers of Atlantis Resort in the Bahamas – Michael was handed a microphone and asked to sing which, somewhat reluctantly, he did.

Performed by Monica, Deborah Cox, Mya, Rah Digga and Tamia during the *Michael Jackson: 30th Anniversary Celebration, The Solo Years* concerts, staged at New York's Madison Square Garden on 7th and 10th September 2001.

Fifteenth of Michael's 20 *'Visionary The Video Singles'* reissues, with the music on one side of a Dual Disc and the accompanying short film on the other side. Issued in May 2006 in the UK – charted at no.27.

Performed by invited guests and Michael's 'This Is It' dancers at the finale of the 'A Celebration of the Life of Michael Jackson 1958-2009' memorial concert at the Staples Center on 7th July 2009.

Posthumous hit: no.3 in Norway, no.7 in Denmark, no.9 in Switzerland, no.16 in Holland, no.18 in Germany & Sweden, no.19 in New Zealand, no.26 in Australia, no.39 in USA (Hot Digital Songs) and no.44 in Spain & UK.

HEAL THE WORLD – WE ARE THE WORLD

Medley performed by Boyz II Men at the VH1 Honors Awards in 1995 – Michael joined in with *We Are The World*, and was presented with a Special Award for his charitable works by Boyz II Men .

HEARTBREAK HOTEL

Written by Michael and recorded by the Jacksons for their album, *TRIUMPH*, released in October 1980.

Nightmarish opening scream courtesy of Michael's sister, La Toya.

Most successful Jacksons single on the R&B chart in the States, where it spent five weeks at no.2. Also charted at no.22 on the Hot 100 and no.44 in the UK.

Promo footage, of the Jacksons dancing around a swimming pool, remains unreleased.

Official Versions:
Album Version.
Single Edit.
John Luongo Disco Mix.

Single edit on USA 7" single and Japanese 3" CD single remixed, with a slightly different synthesizer sound.

Re-titled *This Place Hotel* on later releases, to avoid any confusion with the Elvis Presley classic with the same title (this didn't stop Whitney Houston from recording yet another song titled *Heartbreak Hotel* in 1998, and turning it into a smash hit).

Live version, titled *This Place Hotel* and recorded at a concert at Madison Square Garden in September 1981, featured on the Jacksons album, *LIVE*, issued in November 1981. This version appeared on the B-side of Michael's single, *P.Y.T. (Pretty Young Thing)*, in the UK.

Live version, recorded at one of Michael's Bad World Tour concerts in Australia, included on the home video, *A Legend Continues...*, released in 1988 (1989 in the States). Another live version, from the same tour, was screened on Nippon TV in Japan.

Samples include:
Quo's *Quo Funk* (released on Michael's MJJ Music label in 1996).
Ideal's *Creepin' Inn*, from their eponymous 1999 album.
Ma$e's *Cheat On You*, from his 1997 album, *HARLEM WORLD*.
Heavy D & the Boyz's *Peaceful Journey*, the title track of their 1991 album.
Kik Franklin & God's Property's *You Are The Only Ones*.
Lil' Kim's *The Games In Trouble*, from the 2006 reissue of her album, *THE NAKED TRUTH*.

HEARTBREAKER

Song written by Michael with Rodney Jerkins, Fred Jerkins III, LaShawn Daniels, Mischke Butler and Norman Gregg, and recorded for his solo album *INVINCIBLE*, issued in October 2001.

HEAVEN CAN WAIT

Written by Michael with Teddy Riley, Andra Heard, Nate Smith, Teron Beal,

Eritza Laues and K. Quiller, and featured on his album *INVINCIBLE*, issued in October 2001.

Featured additional background vocals by Dr Freeze and 'Que'.

'When I did that song with him (Michael),' said Riley, he held his heart and he said, "Teddy, is this mine?" I said, it's yours if you want it, Michael. He's like, "I want it! Let's go get it!" He was so excited.'

Included on the Sony 'an epic valentine' 8-track multi-artist promo CD, along with Ginuwine, Glenn Lewis, Ruff Endz, Muet, Collin, Best Man & B2H. Scheduled for release to radio stations across the States, but cancelled. Many R&B stations started playing it anyway, resulting in a no.72 placing on the R&B singles chart during a lengthy 16 week run.

Originally lined up to feature on BLACKstreet's 1999 album, *FINALLY* – Riley stated in 2006 he was planning to

re-make the song, for a new BLACKstreet album.

'The one thing that I wanted to do, which I told him, and I got a chance to tell him, that I wanted to make *Heaven Can Wait* over with BLACKstreet,' said Riley, following Michael's passing. 'That's the only thing that I asked to do, and I will reiterate that with the family, because I want that on the new BLACKstreet record, and whether a part of the proceeds go for his Foundation or whatever, I don't care. I want to do the song because that song never came out as a single, and that was one of our favourites.'

HEAVEN HELP US ALL

Stevie Wonder song the Jackson 5 recorded a version of – remains unreleased.

Stevie took the song to no.2 on the R&B singles chart and no.9 on the Hot 100, and to no.29 in the UK, in 1970.

HEAVEN IS HERE

Poem written by Michael – included in his book of poems and reflections, *Dancing The Dream*, published in 1992.

HEAVEN KNOWS I LOVE YOU, GIRL

Song included on the Jacksons album, *GOIN' PLACES*, released in October 1977.

HEAVEN'S GIRL

Song written by R. Kelly, originally intended for Michael's *HISTORY* album, but eventually was recorded by R. Kelly himself in 1995, for the Quincy Jones album, *Q'S JOOK JOINT*.

HERE I AM (COME AND TAKE ME)

Song recorded on 6th June 1973, and released for the first time – in an up-dated version – on Michael's *FAREWELL MY SUMMER LOVE* album, issued in May 1984 in the States and July 1984 in the UK.

Title given to a reissue of *FAREWELL MY SUMMER LOVE*, originating from Germany.

Original mix included as a bonus track on Michael's posthumous *HELLO WORLD* compilation, issued in July 2009.

Originally recorded by Al Green, and featured on his 1973 album, *CALL ME*. Single achieved no.2 on the R&B singles chart and no.10 on the Hot 100 in the States.

HE'S MY BROTHER

Song La Toya Jackson recorded for her 1995 album, *BAD GIRL*, as a tribute to brother Michael – the song sampled a snippet of his hit, *Bad*.

B-side of La Toya's Italian single, *You And Me*.

HE'S MY SUNNY BOY

Supremes cover, re-titled *I'm Your Sunny Boy* as Michael could hardly sing 'He's my sunny boy', the Jackson 5 are known to have recorded – remains unreleased.

Original version featured on the 1968 Supremes album, *LOVE CHILD*.

HISTORY

Written by Michael with James Harris III and Terry Lewis, and recorded for the album, HIS*TORY*, released in June 1995.

Backing vocals by Boyz II Men.

New pressings of HIS*TORY* in 1996 saw a slight modification to the opening of *History*, which used parts of Mussorgsky's *The Great Gates Of Kiev*.

Released as a double A-side single, with *Ghosts*, in many countries (no USA release). Charted at no.5 in the UK, where radio stations favoured *History* over *Ghosts*.

Official Versions:
Album Version.
Album Version – different intro.
The Ummah DJ Mix.
The Ummah Main Acappella.
The Ummah Radio Mix.
The Ummah Urban Mix.
MARK!'s Future Dub.
MARK!'s Keep Movin' Dub.
MARK!'s Phly Vocal.
MARK!'s Radio Edit.
MARK!'s Vocal Club Mix.
MARK!'s Vocal Dub Mix.
Tony Moran's History Lesson.

Tony Moran's History Lesson Edit.
Tony Moran's Historical Dub.

Numerous other remixes exist (some released as promos), including:

MARK!'s Full On Bonus Beat.
MARK!'s Full On Vocal Remix.
MARK!'s Radio Edit (shorter).
Tony Moran's Fountain Of Life Dub.
Tony Moran's Journey Of Life Dub.
Tony Moran's Time Machine Anthem.

Promoted with live footage filmed during Michael's *His*tory World Tour – directed by Jim Gable. Featured the Tony Moran Remix. Screened on *Top Of The Pops* and the Lottery show in the UK.

Short His*tory Teaser* directed by Rupert Wainright – filmed in Hungary.

Featured in an advert for Michael's isotonic drink, *Mystery*.

HISTORY (album message)

Special message Michael recorded for inclusion on some pressings of his HIS*TORY* album, distributed in France, Germany and Holland. Michael said:

'Hi, this is Michael Jackson. I want to thank all my fans in (country) for their continuing support over all the years. I hope to come and visit you very, very soon and perform for you all. I look forward to seeing you. Until then I'd like to say goodbye. I love you. Take care. 'Bye.'

*HIS*TORY BEGINS MEDLEY

Short (2 minutes 38 seconds) promo CD with a medley of hits featured on the first CD – titled '*His*tory Begins' – from Michael's album, HIS*TORY*, released in 1995.

Songs featured: *Thriller (Intro)*, *Billie Jean*, *Black Or White*, *Rock With You*, *Bad*, *Beat It*, *Remember The Time*, *The Way You Make Me Feel*, *Man In The Mirror*, *Don't Stop 'Til You Get Enough* and *Thriller*.

H.M.S. PINAFORE

Spoof performed by the Jackson 5 on the *Sandy In Disneyland* TV special in the States in April 1974, where they also performed a medley of their hits.

HOLD MY HAND

Song Michael recorded with Akon – first surfaced on the internet in June 2008, and written by New York singer-songwriter, Claude Kelly.

'I wrote the song and gave it to Akon, with the intention of it going to maybe Whitney Houston,' said Kelly. 'Akon said he wanted to cut it himself – I thought, "It doesn't get any bigger than this". A few months after, Akon plays the song for me and all of a sudden I hear Michael Jackson's voice – I was literally shaking by the time the song was over!'

Slated to appear on forthcoming albums by both Michael and Akon, but left off Akon's 2008 release, *FREEDOM*, following its premature leak.

'Musically we were on the same level,' said Akon, 'and we wanted it to be special. We wanted it so that when people got my album, it was something that was never heard. But the leak stopped those plans. We will be doing more things together in the future, though.'

No official release.

HOLD ON! I'M A COMIN'

Sam & Dave hit the Jackson 5 often performed on the Chitli' Circuit in the mid-to-late 1960s, as confirmed by their father Joseph, in an interview with *Blues & Soul* magazine in 1978.

Sam & Dave took the song to no.1 on the R&B singles chart and no.21 on the Hot 100 in the States in 1966 – not a hit in the UK.

HOLIDAY INN

Song written by Michael in 1976, and registered with the United States Copyright Office in November 1984 – remains unreleased.

HOME

Song La Toya Jackson recorded for her shelved 2002 album, *STARTIN' OVER* – whole album leaked on the internet in 2006.

Released as a digital single on 28th July 2009, as a tribute to Michael – all proceeds to the charity, Aids Project L.A.

HONEY CHILE

Song recorded by the Jackson 5 for their album, *MAYBE TOMORROW*, issued in April 1971 in the States and October 1971 in the UK.

Featured in the 'Farmer Jackson' episode of the Jackson 5's cartoon series in 1971.

Originally recorded by Martha Reeves & The Vandellas, and featured on their 1968 album, *RIDIN' HIGH*. Single charted at no.5 on the R&B singles chart and no.11 on the Hot 100 in the States, and no.30 in the UK.

HONEY LOVE

Song on the Jackson 5's *MOVING VIOLATION* album, released in May 1975 in the States and July 1975 in the UK.

HOT FEVER

Michael's original title for his hit, *The Way You Make Me Feel*, written in 1985 and registered with the United States Copyright Office in October that year – remains unreleased.

Promo pressings from 2001 carried the title: *The Way You Make Me Feel (Hot Fever)*.

See also: *Way You Make Me Feel, The*.

HOT STREET

Song written by Rod Temperton that failed to make Michael's album, *THRILLER*, as Temperton and Quincy Jones didn't feel it was strong enough. Michael, however, said at his Mexican deposition hearing that he liked the song – remains unreleased.

Early demo version titled *Slapstick*.

HOW CAN YOU MEND A BROKEN HEART

Song recorded by the Bee Gees for their 1971 album, *TRAFALGAR*, which Michael sang a few lines from during an interview in 2004.

'And "How can you stop the rain from falling down?" sang Michael. 'I love that. "How can you stop the sun from shining? What makes the world go 'round?"' sang Michael, joined by film/music video director, Brett Ratner. 'I love that stuff! And when they (the Bee Gees) did *Saturday Night Fever*, that did it for me. I said, "I gotta do this – I know I can do this"… And I just started writing songs. I wrote *Billie Jean*, I wrote *Beat It, (Wanna Be) Startin' Somethin'*. Just writing – it was fun.'

HOW FUNKY IS YOUR CHICKEN

Song included on the Jackson 5's *THIRD ALBUM*, issued in September 1970 in the States and February 1971 in the UK.

Released as a single in France, Holland and Sweden.

Featured in 'The Winners Circle' episode of the Jackson 5's cartoon series in 1971.

HOW MUCH DO YOU GET FOR YOUR SOUL

Song recorded by the Pretenders, for their 1986 album, *GET CLOSE* – allegedly written as a swipe at Michael, following his massive sponsorship deal with Pepsi.

HOW SWEET IT IS (TO BE LOVED BY YOU)

Marvin Gaye hit the Jackson 5 recorded a version of – remains unreleased.

Hit versions:
Marvin Gaye – no.49 in the UK in 1964; no.4 on the R&B singles chart and no.6 on the Hot 100 in the States in 1965.
Jr. Walker & The All Stars – no.3 on the R&B singles chart and no.18 on the Hot 100, and no.22 in the UK, in 1966.
James Taylor – no.5 on the Hot 100 in 1975.
Tyrone Davis – no.36 on the R&B singles chart in 1980.

HUM ALONG AND DANCE

Song the Jackson 5 recorded for their album, *GET IT TOGETHER*, released in September 1973 in the States and November 1973 in the UK. Lead vocals – such as they were – by Jackie and Tito Jackson.

Originally recorded by the Temptations, for their 1970 album, *PSYCHEDELIC SHACK* – also recorded by another Motown act, Rare Earth, for their 1973 album, *MA*.

All three versions – including the Jackson 5's – produced by Norman Whitfield.

Rare Earth's version charted at no.95 on the R&B singles chart, and at no.110 on the 'bubbling under' section of the Hot 100, in the States in 1973.

Essentially an instrumental track, with scatting and improvised vocals – the song's chorus states, 'ain't no words to this song, you just dance and hum along.' Michael, in the Jackson 5 version, on hearing the song's chorus can be heard saying: 'Ain't no words? What you mean?' – to which Tito responds, 'we ain't had time to write none!'

Performed by the Jacksons on their TV series in 1976.

United Future Organization Mix issued to dance clubs in Japan in 1999, with release on the album, *SOUL SOURCE – JACKSON 5 REMIXES*, the following year.

Uncut version, clocking in at nearly 15 minutes, featured as a bonus track on the two albums on one CD reissue of *JOYFUL JUKEBOX MUSIC & BOOGIE*, issued in 2004 in the States (no UK release).

HUMAN NATURE

Written by Steve Porcaro and John Bettis. Porcaro recorded a rough demo on a cassette, which fellow Toto band David Paitch put three songs on for Quincy Jones to listen to, as possibles for *THRILLER*. Quincy didn't like Paitch's songs, but he did like the rough demo of *Human Nature* at the end of the tape, and asked if he could use it.

'I had written the song for my daughter Heather,' said Pocaro. 'Something had happened at school and it just inspired me. I wrote the song while we (Toto) were mixing *Africa*, and I was just tinkering with it on the piano. I had written the lyrics, which were the same verse, I was singing over and over again – I had the "why, why" chorus, with the slap echo.'

Full demo version by Porcaro is more haunting, moody and darker than Michael's version.

Last song selected for *THRILLER*, issued in December 1982 – it ousted *Carousel* from the final track listing.

Released as a single in most countries, but not the UK, where it was the B-side of *Leave Me Alone*. Charted at no.7 on the Hot 100 and no.27 on the R&B singles chart in the States.

Alternate version, with a slight difference in the short instrumental segment mid-

way through the song, featured on the Japanese 3" CD single, *Thriller*.

Official Versions:
Album Version.
Single Edit #1.
Alternate Version.
Single Edit #2.

Single Edit recreated for inclusion on the 2005 compilation, *THE ESSENTIAL*, as the original either wasn't remastered or available for some reason.

Live performance by Michael, at his Dangerous Tour concert in Bucharest, Romania, on 1st October 1992, featured on the DVD released as part of his box-set, *THE ULTIMATE COLLECTION*, issued in November 2004.

Different live performance screened on Nippon TV in Japan, as part of one of Michael's concerts.

Sampled on a remixed version of *Right Here*, by SWV: Sisters With Voices. Logged seven weeks at no.1 on the R&B singles chart in the States, and achieved no.2 on the Hot 100, in 1993 – charted at no.3 in the UK. RIAA Gold Record (USA half-million seller). Featured on the original soundtrack album, *FREE WILLY*.

Other samples include:
The Power Of Human Nature – a popular 1989 bootleg recording also featuring Snap's *The Power*.
It Ain't Hard To Tell by Nas, on his 1997 album, *ILLMATIC*.

Thug Nature by Tupac '2Pac' Shakur, featured on his 2001 album, *TOO GANSTA FOR RADIO* (samples SWV's *Right Here/Human Nature*).

Why Why, a track on BLACKstreet's 2003 album, *LEVEL II*.

A remix of the 2006 no.1 hit *So Sick*, by Ne-Yo featuring LL Cool J – featured on the latter's 2006 album, *TODD SMITH*.

Cover versions recorded by Boyz II Men, with Claudette Ortiz, for their 2004 album, *THROWBACK*, and by David Mead for his 2004 album, *INDIANA*.

Performed by John Mayer at the 'A Celebration of the Life of Michael Jackson 1958-2009' memorial concert at the Staples Center on 7th July 2009.

Posthumous hit: no.21 in the USA (Hot Digital Songs), no.38 in Sweden and no.62 in UK.

HURT, THE

Song written by Michael with brother Randy in collaboration with Toto's David Paich and Steve Porcaro.

'I'd been playing one concept for days on the keyboard at David Paich's house, with the drum machine going,' said Randy. 'One day Michael started singing to it. Jackie joined in, and we worked it until it became a song.'

Recorded by the Jacksons for their *VICTORY* album, issued in July 1984.

HYPERACTIVE

Song Thomas Dolby was inspired to write by his memories of Michael as a child.

'You know, back when he was really cute and actually had a fabulous voice,' said Dolby. 'The song was called *Hyperactive*. But I didn't get far into it before I realised it was really all about me, so I kept it for myself, and it became my only substantial UK singles chart hit.'

Charted at no.17 in the UK in 1984.

See also: *Interference*.

I AIN'T GONNA EAT OUT MY HEART ANYMORE

One of seven previously unheard songs included on the Jackson 5's album, *BOOGIE*, released on the Natural Resources label in January 1979 in North America only.

Album quickly withdrawn, and not made available again until 2004, when it and *JOYFUL JUKEBOX MUSIC* were released on one CD (no UK release).

Original version by the Young Rascals featured on their eponymous 1966 album.

I AM LOVE

Longish song recorded by the Jackson 5 for their album *DANCING MACHINE*, issued in September 1974 in the States and November 1974 in the UK.

Lead vocals by Jermaine (later Marlon, after four of the Jackson 5 left Motown). Split into two halves for single release, with Parts 1 & 2 appearing on either side of the 7" single. Charted at no.3 on the R&B singles chart and no.15 on the Hot 100 in the States, but wasn't a hit in the UK.

Performed by the Jackson 5 on *The Cher Show* in 1975, and by the Jacksons on their TV series in 1977.

Live performance by the Jacksons, at a concert in Mexico in 1976, included on the home video, *The Jacksons In Concert*, released in 1981 in the UK (no USA release).

I CAN ONLY GIVE YOU LOVE

Song included on the Jackson 5's album, *LOOKIN' THROUGH THE WINDOWS*, issued in May 1972 in the States and October 1972 in the UK.

I CAN'T GET YOU OFF MY MIND

Song Michael worked on in the early 1970s, demo version/mono acetate known to exist – no official release.

I CAN'T HELP IT

Song written by Stevie Wonder and Susaye Greene, and recorded by Michael for his album *OFF THE WALL*, issued in August 1979.

B-side of the album's lead single, *Don't Stop 'Til You Get Enough*.

Sampled on:
De La Soul's *Breakadawn* in 1993 – no.30 on the R&B singles chart and no.76 on the Hot 100, and no.39 in the UK.
Mary J. Blige's *Sexy*, a track on her 1999 album, *MARY*.
Baby by Fabulous, from the 2004 album, *REAL TALK*.

Also recorded by Kashief Lindo, Peebles and Dashhamer.

Stevie Wonder, although he has performed the song many times in concert, including the UNCF Gala in January 2005, has never released a version of the song.

Performed as a tribute to Michael by Beyoncé at a concert during her 'I Am Tour', staged in Philadelphia, Pennsylvania, on 26th June 2009. On the opening day of the Essence Musical Festival in New Orleans, Louisiana, on 3rd July 2009, Beyoncé changed the lyrics to her hit, *Halo*, to pay further tribute to Michael ('Michael, I can see your halo…').

I CAN'T HELP MYSELF (SUGAR PIE, HONEY BUNCH)

Four Tops classic the Jackson 5 recorded a version of – remains unreleased.

Hit versions:
Four Tops – no.1 on the Hot 100 and R&B singles chart in the States, and no.23 in the UK, in 1965.
Four Tops (reissue) – no.10 in the UK in 1970.

Donny Elbert – no.11 in the UK, and no.14 on the R&B singles chart and no.22 on the Hot 100, in 1972.

Bonnie Pointer – no.40 on the Hot 100 and no.42 on the R&B singles chart in 1980.

Performed by the actors portraying the Jackson 5 in the TV mini-series, *The Jacksons: An American Dream*.

I CAN'T QUIT YOUR LOVE

Song featured on the Jackson 5's album, *SKYWRITER*, issued in March 1973 in the States and July 1973 in the UK.

B-side of *Whatever You Got, I Want* in the States, and of *Forever Came Today* in the UK.

Performed by the Jacksons on their TV series in 1977.

Originally recorded by the Four Tops, and featured on their 1972 album, *NATURE PLANNED IT*.

I DON'T KNOW

One of two songs written for Michael by Pharrell Williams, and recorded by Usher for his 2001 album, *8701*.

See also: *U Don't Have To Call*.

I DON'T LIVE HERE ANYMORE

Song written by Michael circa 2001, but failed to make the final selection for his *INVINCIBLE* album – remains unreleased.

Also known by the title, *I Don't Live Anymore*.

I FORGIVE YOU

Song Michael cited he had written in his court deposition in November 1993 – remains unreleased.

I FOUND A LOVE

Previously unheard demo from the pre-Motown days, that surfaced on the download only Jackson 5 compilation, *SOUL MASTERS*, made available in 2005.

No physical release.

I FOUND THAT GIRL

Song featured on the Jackson 5's *ABC* album, issued in May 1970 in the States and August 1970 in the UK. Lead vocals by Jermaine.

B-side of *The Love You Save* but, largely thanks to Jermaine's popularity with girls, listed alongside the A-side on many Billboard charts, including the Hot 100 and R&B singles chart – it hit no.1 on both charts. Achieved no.7 in the UK.

Featured in the 'Rasho Jackson' episode of the Jackson 5 cartoon series in 1971.

Promo red vinyl, double-sided 7" single released in the States.

Opening edited on *DIANA ROSS PRESENTS.../ABC* and the Jackson 5 compilation, *LOVE SONGS* – unedited version can be found on the Jackson 5's *GOLD*.

I GOT A FEELING

Four Tops track the Jackson 5 recorded a version of – remains unreleased.

The Four Tops recorded the song for their 1966 album, *4 TOPS ON TOP*.

I GOT RHYTHM

Song Michael danced to on the Jacksons TV series in 1977, as female backing singers sang, 'He's got rhythm' – Michael sang the title only at the end of the song.

Written by George & Ira Gershwin, and performed by Gene Kelly in the 1951 film, *An American In Paris*.

I GOT THE FEELIN'

James Brown hit performed by the Jackson 5 during their pre-Motown days, and one of the songs performed at their Motown audition in 1968 – remains unreleased.

No.1 for James Brown in 1968 on the R&B singles chart in the States, and no.6 on the Hot 100, but failed to chart in the UK.

I GOT YOU (I FEEL GOOD)

James Brown hit Michael and brothers performed on the Chitli' Circuit, in the pre-Motown days.

Brown's recording, from the 1966 album of the same title, hit no.1 on the R&B singles chart and no.3 on the pop singles chart in the States, and achieved no. 29 in the UK.

I HAVE THIS DREAM

Song Michael wrote with Carole Bayer Sager and David Foster – subject of a song-writing contest organised by Tonos Entertainment and AOL Music. A statement released by Tonos read:

'Music serves as a salve for what ails the human spirit and a remedy to the soul during troubled times. Now, these three musical icons have created an inspiring musical landscape entitled 'I Have This Dream', and they're asking AOL members to come up with an optimistic and uplifting lyric, to complete this anthemic song.'

The contest attracted over 1,000 entries and was won by Ric Kipp, whose lyric 'best reflected our vision for the song'.

Widely expected to be included on Michael's album, *INVINCIBLE*, but didn't feature. Speaking to *TV Guide* in November 1999, Michael said: 'There's a song on the album called *I Have This Dream*. It's a millennium song about the world and the environment, that I wrote with Carole Bayer Sager and David Foster.'

Version, with numerous guest vocalists including R. Kelly, Snoop Dog, James Ingram, Shanice, the O'Jays and Michael's brother, Jermaine, slated for release in early 2006, in aid of the victims of Hurricane Katrina.

Played during a court disposition in London in 2008 – remains unreleased.

I HAVE THIS LOVE OF ME

Song Michael cited he had written in his court deposition in November 1993 – remains unreleased.

I HEAR A SYMPHONY

Supremes cover recorded, when Michael suggested singing a male version of the song, by the Jackson 5 between 1970-73.

Remained unreleased until it was included on Michael's solo album, *LOOKING BACK TO YESTERDAY*, issued in February 1986 in the States and May 1986 in the UK – demo version also known to exist.

B-side of the promo 7" single *Love's Gone Bad*, issued in Canada only.

Version with alternate vocal take featured on the 1995 box-set, *SOULSATION!*.

The Supremes took the song to no.1 on the Hot 100 and no.2 on the R&B singles charts in the States, and no.39 in the UK, in 1965.

I HEARD IT THROUGH THE GRAPEVINE

Motown classic the Jackson 5 recorded a version of – remains unreleased.

Hit versions:
Gladys Knight & The Pips – no.1 on the R&B singles chart and no.2 on the Hot 100 in the States, and no.47 in the UK, in 1967.
Marvin Gaye (original version) – no.1 on both American charts in 1968, and no.1 in the UK in 1969.
King Curtis – no.83 on the Hot 100 in 1968.
Creedence Clearwater Revival – no.43 on the Hot 100 in 1976.
Roger – no.1 on the R&B singles chart and no.79 on the Hot 100 in 1981.
Slits – no.60 in the UK in 1979.
Marvin Gaye (reissue) – no.8 in the UK in 1986.
California Raisins – no.84 on the Hot 100 in 1988.

I JUST CAN'T STOP LOVING YOU

Song written by Michael for his album, *BAD*, released in September 1987.

Recorded as a duet with virtual unknown Siedah Garrett, after Whitney Houston and Barbra Streisand both turned down the opportunity to record the song with Michael – Streisand simply never showed, on the day she was scheduled to record the song with Michael. Siedah was unaware Quincy Jones wanted her to record the song as a duet with Michael, until she turned up for the actual recording session.

Lead single from the album, topping the Hot 100 and R&B singles chart in the States, where it was the no.3 best selling single of 1987.

RIAA Gold Record (USA million seller).

Also no.1 in Belgium, Ireland, Holland, Norway and the UK.

Spoken introduction edited from later pressings of *BAD*, plus greatest hits compilations, from HIS*TORY* onwards.

Official Versions:
Album Version (with spoken intro).
Album Version (minus spoken intro).
Spanish Version.
Anglo-Spanish Version.
French Version (unreleased).

Performed live by Michael with Sheryl Crow during his Bad World Tour, and with Siedah Garrett during his Dangerous World Tour.

Live performance by Michael, at his Dangerous Tour concert in Bucharest, Romania, on 1st October 1992, featured on the DVD released as part of his box-set, *THE ULTIMATE COLLECTION*, issued in November 2004.

Different live performance aired as part of a concert screened by Nippon TV in Japan.

Performed by James Ingram and Gloria Estefan during the *Michael Jackson: 30th*

Anniversary Celebration, The Solo Years concerts, staged at New York's Madison Square Garden on 7th and 10th September 2001.

Spanish and French language versions recorded by Michael and Siedah, titled *Todo Mi Amor Eres Tu* and *Je Ne Veux Pas La Fin De Nous*, respectively.

Spoken intro sampled by Sweetback, featuring Maxwell, on the track *Softly, Softly*, from Sweetback's eponymous debut album, released in 1996.

Sampled by Jason Phats on his 2007 track, *Can't Stop*.

See also: *Je Ne Veux Pas La Fin De Nous, Todo Mi Amor Eres Tu*.

(I KNOW) I'M LOSING YOU

Song recorded by the Jackson 5 for their debut album, *DIANA ROSS PRESENTS THE JACKSON 5*, issued in December 1969 in the States and March 1970 in the UK.

Included on the *ABC* EP released in Portugal.

Originally recorded by the Temptations, and included on their 1967 album, *WITH A LOT 'O SOUL*. Single hit no.1 on the R&B singles chart and no.8 on the Hot 100 in the States, and no.19 in the UK.

I LIKE YOU THE WAY YOU ARE (DON'T CHANGE YOUR LOVE ON ME)

Song written by Willie Hutch and recorded by the Jackson 5 in 1970.

Remained unreleased until included on Michael's album, *LOOKING BACK TO YESTERDAY*, issued in February 1986 in the States and May 1986 in the UK.

I LOVE YOU

Words Michael sang when James Brown, the Godfather of Soul, called him up on stage at a concert staged at the Beverly Theater, Los Angeles, in September 1983. Brown, at Michael's insistence, then called Prince on stage, to introduce him to the crowd.

At the 3rd annual BET Awards in June 2003, Michael presented Brown with a long silver cloak, as he was given a Lifetime Achievement Award.

'I am extremely shocked and saddened by the death of my mentor and friend,' said Michael in an official statement, issued following James Brown's death on Christmas Day 2006. 'Words cannot adequately express the love and respect that I will always have for Mr. Brown. There has not been, and will never be, another like him. He is irreplaceable. I send my love and heartfelt condolences to his family.'

Michael attended the funeral in Augusta, Georgia. 'I don't care what the media says tonight, James Brown wanted Michael Jackson here with him today,' the Rev. Al Sharpton, who led the ceremony, told the 9,000 mourners. '(James Brown) said, "I love Michael… tell him, don't worry about coming home. They always scandalise those that have talent".'

I LOVE YOU, ALPHA BITS

Advertising jingles the Jackson 5 performed in 1971, to promote breakfast cereals – several different were shot, including:

- Airship No.1 – featured the Jackson 5 floating away in a balloon, while singing and talking about the breakfast cereal.

- Airship No.2 – featured the group singing *ABC*, with Michael saying, 'Can you dig it? Well, you got it – that's our smash hit, *ABC*!'

- Bunk Beds – featured Michael waking up, sliding down a fire pole, and joining his brothers at the breakfast table, singing, 'Give me a U, give me a P, getting up with Alpha Bits is E-Z!'

- Convertible Car & Park – featured the Jackson 5 running around in fast motion, with Michael singing, 'Give me an A, give me a B, gotta have my Alpha Bits with *ABC*!'

- Over The Fence – featured the Jackson 5 looking over a fence, as three kids learn letters from their cereal; free magic trick also mentioned.

- Sugar Smacks – featured the Jackson 5 singing *I'll Be There*, with a cartoon character talking about the free records on the back of Super Sugar Crisp and Super Orange Crisp breakfast cereals.

A couple of other commercials are rumoured to have been made, but were probably not released: one with the Jackson 5 in a clubhouse, and the second with the group sitting around a piano and eating cereal. The latter also shows Michael's brothers rolling him around inside a giant cheerio (stills from this commercial are known to exist).

Three breakfast cereal packet designs featured the Jackson 5:

- Alpha Bits – version A: with song titles on cartoon flowers, no mention on the Jackson 5. Played one of three songs: 1. *Sugar Daddy*. 2. *Goin' Back To Indiana*. 3. *Who's Lovin' You*.

- Alpha Bits – version B: similar to version A. Played one of three songs: 1. *I'll Be There*. 2. *Never Can Say Goodbye*. 3. *Mama's Pearl*.

- Rice Krinkles – with a photo of the Jackson 5 standing off to the left. Played one of five songs: 1. *ABC*. 2. *I Want You Back*. 3. *I'll Bet You*. 4. *Darling Dear*. 5. *Maybe Tomorrow*.

I NEED YOU

One of 19 'Rare & Unreleased' tracks on the fourth CD of the Michael/Jackson 5 box-set, *SOULSATION!*, issued in June 1995 in the States and July 1995 in the UK. Credited to Jermaine Jackson.

I NEED YOU

Song recorded by Michael's nephews (brother Tito's three sons), 3T, for their debut album, *BROTHERHOOD*, issued in 1995.

Featured Michael on backing vocals.

Charted at no.3 in the UK (no USA release).

Official Versions:
Album Version.
Linslee Campbell Remix.
Christmas Mix.
Singalong Version.
Linslee Campbell Breakdown Mix.

I NEVER HAD A GIRL

B-side of *Let Me Carry Your Schoolbooks*, a single issued by Steel-Town Records in the States in 1971, credited to 'The Ripples & Waves + Michael' – a name the Jackson 5 reputedly used in the early days.

Nearly 20 years later Gordon Keith, founder and owner of Steel-Town Records, stated: 'The fine vocals were provided by another Gary, Indiana talent, Michael Rodgers' – not Michael Jackson.

Both songs featured on the Jackson 5 album, *PRE-HISTORY – THE LOST STEELTOWN RECORDINGS*, released in the States in June 1996 (no UK release). The sleeve notes implied, without actually saying, the Jackson 5 and the Ripples & Waves + Michael were one and the same group.

I NEVER HEARD

Written by Michael with Paul Anka circa 1980, and recorded by Safire for her album, *I WASN'T BORN YESTERDAY*, issued in 1991 in the States (no UK release).

I ONLY HAVE EYES FOR YOU

Song Jermaine recorded, with the Jackson 5 on backing vocals, for his debut solo album, *JERMAINE*, released in 1972.

No.1 for Art Garfunkel in the UK, and no.18 on the Hot 100 in the States, in 1975.

I SAVED MY LOVE FOR YOU

Song the Jackson 5 performed in concert in the summer of 1972, with Jermaine on lead vocals – recorded by Jermaine for his debut solo album, but failed to make the final track listing and remains unreleased.

I SAW MOMMY KISSING SANTA CLAUS

Song the Jackson 5 recorded for their *CHRISTMAS ALBUM*, issued in October 1970 in the States and December 1970 in the UK.

Released as a single in a limited number of countries (excluding the USA and UK), including New Zealand, where it charted at no.3, and the Philippines.

Lead song from a four track EP, *Merry Christmas From Michael Jackson With The Jackson 5*, released in the UK in 1987 – it charted at a lowly no.91.

Other hit versions:
Jimmy Boyd – no.1 in the States and no.3 in the UK in 1953.
Beverley Sisters – no.6 in the UK in 1953.
Billy Cotton & His Band – no.11 in the UK in 1953.

4 Seasons – no.19 on the Christmas singles chart in the States in 1964.

I SHOT THE SHERIFF

Eric Clapton hit the Jacksons performed on their TV series in 1976, along with War's *The Cisco Kid*.

Clapton took the song to no.1 on the Hot 100 in the States, and no.9 in the UK, in 1974.

I WANNA BE WHERE YOU ARE

Song Michael recorded for his debut solo album, *GOT TO BE THERE*, released in January 1972 in the States and May 1972 in the UK.

Written by Leon Ware and Arthur 'T-Boy' Ross – Diana's younger brother.

Issued as a single in the USA (but not UK), where it achieved no.2 on the R&B singles chart and no.16 on the Hot 100.

B-side of *Ain't No Sunshine* in the UK.

Featured in the 'Michael White' episode of the new Jackson 5 cartoon series in 1971.

Promoted by Michael on *American Bandstand*, and at a five day Black Expo – Save The Children concert, in Chicago, in 1972.

Live version by the Jackson 5, recorded at the 'Black Expo' event, included on the double *SAVE THE CHILDREN* album issued in 1974.

Second live version featured on the Michael/Jackson 5's *LIVE!* album, issued in September 1988 in the UK (no USA release). All songs on the album were recorded at a concert on 30th April 1973, at the Osaka Koseinenkin Hall in Japan. Also included on the limited edition CD, *IN JAPAN!*, released by Hip-O Select in 2004 – only 5,000 copies pressed.

Performed by Monday Michiru remix featured on the album, *SOUL SOURCE – JACKSON 5 REMIXES*, released in Japan in 2000.

Recorded by Motown song-writer Willie Hutch for his 1973 album, *FULLY EXPOSED*.

Cover version by Jason Weaver featured on the album, *THE JACKSONS: AN AMERICAN DREAM*, issued in October 1992 in the States and July 1993 in the UK. Included on a three track promo CD single circulated to American radio stations, but no commercial release followed.

Numerous other covers versions recorded, including those by Marvin Gaye and the Fugees.

Song's hook used by the Fugees on a song unofficially titled *Wannabe*, which leaked in 2006.

Sampled by Jennifer Lopez on *Gotta Be There*, a track on her 2007 album, *BRAVE*.

I WANT TO BE FREE

Original title of the Jackson 5's debut hit, *I Want You Back*.

I WANT TO TAKE YOU HIGHER

Live recording by the Jackson 5, from their concert in Gary, Indiana, on 29th May 1971, included on the album *GOIN' BACK TO INDIANA*, issued in the States in September 1971 (no UK release). Footage featured on the group's *Goin' Back To Indiana* TV special, which aired on 19th September 1971.

I WANT YOU BACK

Song originally titled *I Want To Be Free*, and written for Gladys Knight & The Pips.

Recorded by the Jackson 5, as their debut Motown single and for their debut album, *DIANA ROSS PRESENTS THE JACKSON 5*, released in December 1969 in the States and March 1970 in the UK. Actually recorded by Michael, Jackie and Jermaine only, as their brothers Marlon and Tito were still in Gary, Indiana, at the time.

Test pressing played to Stevie Wonder by Deke Richards, 'because this was a guy I really respected. We were friends. Everyone else was too influenced by Berry (Gordy) to give me an objective opinion. He listened to it carefully, and said: "Now, man – I don't like the drums!" I had to laugh!'

Hit no.1 on both the Hot 100 and R&B singles chart in the USA, and achieved no.2 in the UK.

Promo 7" red vinyl single with printed sleeve released in the States.

Promoted in the States on numerous TV shows, including: *Hollywood Palace Special*, *Ed Sullivan Show*, *Joey Bishop Show*, *American Bandstand*, *Andy Williams Show*, *Soul Train*, the *Goin' Back To Indiana* TV special and the group's own TV special.

Deke Richards has confirmed a different mix was used for the Hollywood Palace Special: 'I purposely pushed the strings up a little, especially in the intro... if you listen closely, you will hear the difference... those parts near the end are not in the released mix. In fact, those parts were not even sung by the J5, it was actually Freddie, Fonce and myself – the Corp 3!'

Featured in the 'Drafted' episode of the Jackson 5's cartoon series in 1971 – alternate mix had Jackie ad-libbing rather than Jermaine.

Newly recorded version, with an introduction by Bill Cosby and Tommy Smothers, included on the Jackson 5's album, *GOIN' BACK TO INDIANA*, issued in September 1971 in the States (no UK release).

Previously unreleased live medley of *I Want You Back* and *ABC*, recorded at the Jackson 5's Los Angeles concert on 26th August 1972, featured on the TV soundtrack album, *THE JACKSONS: AMERICAN DREAM*, issued in October 1992 in the States and July 1993 in the UK.

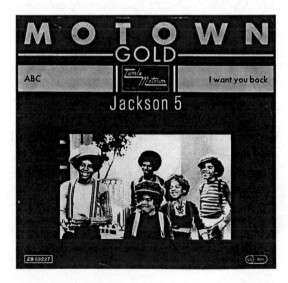

Remixed in 1988 by Phil Harding, and credited to Michael Jackson with the Jackson 5. Promoted with the clip from the 'Drafted' cartoon episode. Achieved no.8 in the UK (no USA release).

Original mono version included on the 4CD box-set, *HITSVILLE USA: THE MOTOWN SINGLES 1959-1971*, issued in the States in 1992.

Covered by numerous artists, including: the Newtrons (co-produced by Michael's eldest brother Jackie in 1990), Human Nature, Diana Ross, Graham Parker, David Ruffin, Martha Reeves, Incubus, Lauryn Hill, Red Hot Chilli Peppers and Jive Bunny & The Mastermixers.

Sampled by numerous artists, including:
Jermaine Jackson in 1991, on his *Word To The Badd!!* – charted at no.78 on the Hot 100 and no.88 on the R&B singles chart in the USA.
Kris Kross in 1992, on their global hit, *Jump* – no.1 on both American charts, and no.2 in the UK.

Nadanuf in 1997, on the track, *The Breaks Featuring Kurtis Blow*.
Tamia on her 1998 hit, *Imagination* – charted at no.12 on the R&B singles chart and no.37 on the Hot 100 in the States.
BLACKstreet & Maya's 'Want U Back Mix' of their 1998 hit, *Take Me There* – peaked at no.10 on the R&B singles chart and no.14 on the Hot 100 in the States, and no.7 in the UK.
Jay-Z on *Izzo (H.O.V.A.)* – peaked at no.4 on the Hot 100 and no.8 on the R&B singles chart in the States, and no.21 in the UK, in 2001.

Cover version by Cleopatra in 1998 – charted at no.4 in the UK.

Original Jackson 5 recording remixed by Sean 'Puffy' Combs in 1998, for the album *MOTOWN 40 – THE MUSIC IS FOREVER*. Featured added rap by Black Rob, with additional lyrics heard on the fade. Scheduled release as a single in the UK cancelled, following the success of Cleopatra's cover version – promo CD single issued.

Adaptation, featuring a studio recreated loop of *I Want You Back*, titled *My Baby* by Lil' Romeo (11 year old son of hip-hop artist Percy 'Master P' Miller) in 2001 – hit no.1 on the R&B singles chart and no.3 on the Hot 100 in the States, but only achieved no.67 in the UK.

Kei's Routine Jazz Party Mix, with alternate vocals, included on the Japanese album *SOUL SOURCE – JACKSON 5 REMIXES* in 2000, and the album *SOUL LEGENDS*. The former album also included the Readymade 524 Mix.

Z-Trip Remix, on the album *MOTOWN REMIXED* in 2005, featured alternate vocals. The Australian version of the album featured alternate vocals on the Suffa 'Hilltop Hoods' Remix. A promo 12" featured the Z-Trip Bonus Beats remix.

Other Official Versions:
Album Version.
Mono Version.
Live Version.
12" Remix.
Extended Version ('76).
Remix Edit ('88).
PWL Remix ('88).
PWL Remix ('88) Single Version.
You Know We Got Soul Dub Mix.
Black Rob Club Mix ('98).
Black Rob Acappela w/rap ('98).
Black Rob TV Track ('98).
Black Rob Instrumental ('98).
Clean Radio Edit w/rap ('98).
Black Rob Radio Edit w/out rap ('98).
Readymade 524 Mix.
Kel's Routine Jazz Party Mix.
A Cappella.
Instrumental Version.

Another remix was made available on Tito's website in February 2008.

Featured on an unreleased remix of 3T's *Sex Appeal*, which also featured Dealz – Jackie Jackson's son, Siggy.

Ranked no.9 on MTV and *Rolling Stone* magazine's poll in November 2000, to find the '100 Greatest Pop Songs' of all time.

Performed by the Jacksons during the *Michael Jackson: 30th Anniversary Celebration, The Solo Years* concerts, staged at New York's Madison Square Garden on 7th and 10th September 2001. *My Baby* performed by Lil' Romeo & Master P during the same concerts.

Performed live by Stevie Wonder in 1989, at a concert at Wembley, London.

Performed live by Jermaine and four other contestants on the UK's 2007 *Big Brother* TV show, as part of a 'Battle Of The Tribute Bands' competition.

Alternate version, with extra/different ad libs and a cute little giggle at the end, featured on the compilation, *THE STRIPPED MIXES*, released in July 2009.

Posthumous hit: no.31 in the USA (Hot Digital Songs), no.40 in Spain, no.42 in Holland, no.43 in UK and no.76 in Germany.

I WANT YOU BACK – ABC

Medley the Jackson 5 performed on the *Ed Sullivan Show* in 1970, at the Black Expo – Save The Children concert in 1972, on *Sandy In Disneyland* in 1974, and on their own TV series in 1976.

Previously unreleased live medley recorded at the Jackson 5's Los Angeles concert on 26th August 1972, featured on the TV soundtrack album, *THE JACKSONS: AMERICAN DREAM*, issued in October 1992 in the States and July 1993 in the UK.

I WANT YOU BACK – ABC – I'LL BE THERE – BEN – DADDY'S HOME – NEVER CAN SAY GOODBYE – THE LOVE YOU SAVE

Medley Michael and his brothers performed when they guested on the Mills Brothers' TV show in 1974.

I WANT YOU BACK – ABC – THE LOVE YOU SAVE

Medley the Jackson 5 performed on *The Flip Wilson Show* in 1971.

Live version featured on the Michael/Jackson 5's *LIVE!* album, issued in September 1988 in the UK (no USA release). All songs on the album were recorded at a concert on 30th April 1973, at the Osaka Koseinenkin Hall in Japan. Also included on the limited edition CD, *IN JAPAN!*, released by Hip-O Select in 2004 – only 5,000 copies pressed.

Performed live by the Jackson 5, during their 1972 European Tour, at the Royal Command Performance in the UK – attended by HM The Queen Mother.

Second live performance by the Jacksons, at a concert in Mexico in 1976, included on the home video, *The Jacksons In Concert*, released in 1981 in the UK (no USA release).

Third live version, recorded at a concert at Madison Square Garden in September 1981, featured on the Jacksons album, *LIVE*, issued in November 1981.

Performed live in concert by N'Sync, with Justin Timberlake amongst the line-up.

I WANT YOU BACK – I'LL BE THERE – NEVER CAN SAY GOODBYE – THE LOVE YOU SAVE – DANCING MACHINE

Medley the Jackson 5 performed when they guested on Cher's TV show in 1974.

I WANT YOU BACK – THE LOVE YOU SAVE

Medley performed live by the Jacksons at *Motown 25: Yesterday, Today, Forever,* staged in the Pasadena Civic Auditorium on 25th March 1983.

Jermaine rejoined his brothers, to reform the Jackson 5, for the start of the medley, before young Randy came on stage as well – the six brothers also performed versions of *Never Can Say Goodbye* and *I'll Be There*.

I WANT YOU BACK – THE LOVE YOU SAVE – I'LL BE THERE

Medley Michael has performed live on numerous occasions, and screened on TV in the following countries:

- Japan (Nippon TV) – from the Bad World Tour.
- New Zealand – *His*tory World Tour.
- Germany (Sat 1) – *His*tory World Tour.

Live performance by Michael, at his Dangerous Tour concert in Bucharest, Romania, on 1st October 1992, featured on the DVD released as part of his box-set, *THE ULTIMATE COLLECTION*, issued in November 2004 – here, *I'll Be There* was listed as a separate song.

Known among fans as the 'Motown Medley'.

I WANT YOU TO COME HOME FOR CHRISTMAS

Song the Jackson 5 recorded for their *CHRISTMAS ALBUM* circa 1970, but which failed to make the final track listing – remains unreleased.

I WAS MADE TO LOVE HER

Stevie Wonder cover originally recorded between 1970-73 for a solo album by Michael, but remained unreleased until January 1979, when it was included on the Jackson 5's *BOOGIE* – issued in North America only, and quickly withdrawn.

Made available again, as a shorter edit with alternate vocal, on Michael's 1986 album, *LOOKING BACK TO YESTERDAY* – the same version was included on the Jackson 5's 1986 compilation, *ANTHOLOGY*.

Stevie took the song to no.1 on the R&B singles chart and no.2 on the 100 in the States in 1967, and no.5 in the UK.

I WILL FIND A WAY

Song the Jackson 5 recorded for the album, *MAYBE TOMORROW*, issued in April 1971 in the States and October 1971 in the UK.

B-side of *Maybe Tomorrow* in the States.

Featured in 'The Tiny Five' episode of the Jackson 5 cartoon series in 1971.

I WILL MISS YOU

Song will.i.am confirmed, in July 2009, he and had worked on with Michael.

'When James Brown passed away,' said will.i.am, 'he (Michael) and I went into the studio to record a song that was called *I Will Miss You*. And that was never complete… and for that song to come out now, you know, that would be something.'

The music, will.i.am revealed, was on his PC's hard drive – but he didn't have the vocals Michael recorded, as Michael kept them on his own hard drive.

Asked if he could work with the Jackson family, to bring the music and vocals together, and complete the track, will.i.am replied, 'That would be wonderful. I didn't want to be about money or profit earlier, and I don't wanna do that now so – if they come to me and wanna do it, I'd be thrilled… if I could marry the two hard drives, with his vocals and my music – that would be great.'

I WISH

Song Stevie Wonder wrote and recorded for his 1976 Grammy winning album, *SONGS IN THE KEY OF LIFE*.

Cover version recorded by Donny Osmond, which he played to Stevie and later Michael, when Stevie told him, 'he (Michael) really needs a friend right now.'

'And he (Michael) said, "I love it, let's do it",' said Donny. 'We were going to do a duet, and then he called me up as soon as that thing (the trial) hit, and said, "I've got to pull out".'

Stevie's original version hit no.1 on both the Hot 100 and R&B singles charts in the States, and achieved no.5 in the UK.

I WISH IT WOULD RAIN

Temptations hit – one of the songs the Jackson 5 performed at their Motown audition, and at gigs in clubs in Arizona, Boston, Chicago and New York.

No.1 on the R&B singles chart for the Temptations in 1968, also no.4 on the Hot 100 and no.45 in the UK.

I YOU WE

Poem written by Michael – included in his book of poems and reflections, *Dancing The Dream*, published in 1992.

(IF I CAN'T) NOBODY CAN

Song known to have been recorded by Michael and his brothers for Motown – remains unreleased.

IF I DON'T LOVE YOU THIS WAY

Song featured on the Jackson 5's *DANCING MACHINE* album, issued in September 1974 in the States and November 1974 in the UK.

Michael, in an interview with Don Cornelius in 1974, stated he originally recorded the song for a solo album, but that it was included on *DANCING MACHINE* instead.

Performed solo by Michael on *Soul Train* in the States in 1974.

Originally recorded by the Temptations, and included on their album, *HOUSE PARTY*, released in 1974.

IF I HAVE TO MOVE A MOUNTAIN

Song the Jackson 5 recorded for *LOOKIN' THROUGH THE WINDOWS*, released in May 1972 in the States and October 1972 in the UK.

B-side of *Little Bitty Pretty One* in the USA (but not UK).

Featured on 'The Opening Act' episode of the new Jackson 5 cartoon series in 1971.

IF I TOLD YOU THAT

Song written by Rodney Jerkins, originally intended for Michael and Whitney Houston:

'That song was meant for Whitney and Michael,' Jerkins confirmed in 1998. 'We didn't make it happen and the next person was George Michael.' It's likely news of Michael's involvement leaked too soon, hence he cancelled the project.

Solo version recorded by Whitney, for her 1998 album, *MY LOVE IS YOUR LOVE*.

Duet version by Whitney and George Michael released as a single – achieved no.9 in the UK, and subsequently included on Whitney's compilation, *THE GREATEST HITS*, issued in 2000.

IF WE STILL LOVE

Song Michael worked on with will.i.am in early 2007 – could be unfinished, but Michael's vocals were recorded.

Remains unreleased.

IF YOU DON'T LOVE ME

Previously unreleased recording by Michael, scheduled to be included on the expanded, special edition of *DANGEROUS* in 2001 – bonus CD shelved, so remains unreleased.

IF YOU REALLY LOVE ME

Stevie Wonder song the Jackson 5 recorded a version of – remains unreleased.

Stevie took the song to no.4 on the R&B singles chart and no.8 on the Hot 100 in the States, and to no.20 in the UK, in 1971.

IF YOU WANT HEAVEN

Song recorded by Michael and his brothers for Motown – remains unreleased.

IF YOU'D ONLY BELIEVE

Song featured on the Jackson album, *2300 JACKSON STREET*, issued in June 1989.

Michael wasn't involved with recording this track, however, he did join his family and other guests on stage, to sing it at the Jacksons Family Honours show in 1994.

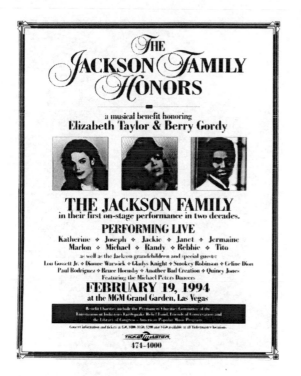

IF'N I WAS GOD

Song recorded by Michael in the early-to-mid 1970s, unreleased until it appeared on his *LOOKING BACK TO YESTERDAY* album, issued in February 1986 in the States and May 1986 in the UK.

Longer version (a full minute longer), with alternate vocals, included on *THE BEST OF MICHAEL JACKSON*, released in the States in March 1995 as part of Motown's Anthology series (no UK release). On one version Michael sings, 'everyone needs...everyone', and on the other he sings, 'everyone...needs everyone'.

Originally recorded by Bobby Goldsboro, for his 1973 album, *SUMMER (THE FIRST TIME)*.

IGNITION (REMIX)

One of Michael's favourite R. Kelly songs – a short snippet of Michael dancing to the song in a car featured in the documentary, *Michael Jackson's Private Home Movies*, which first aired in April 2003.

R. Kelly took the song to no.2 on both American charts in 2002, and all the way to no.1 in the UK in 2003.

I'LL BE THERE

Song featured on the Jackson 5's *THIRD ALBUM*, released in September 1970 in the States and February 1971 in the UK.

Hastily re-worked by Willie Hutch, after Motown producer Hal Davis contacted him in the middle of the night: Motown boss Berry Gordy liked the title but not the song, and he wanted it finished for a recording session the following morning. Hutch stayed up all night, working on the song, before presenting it to Gordy at 8.00am; pleased with the new song, Gordy ordered Hutch into the studio, to arrange the vocals for the Jackson 5.

Featured on the promo film Michael and his brothers shot, to be played at concert venues during their 1970 dates.

Issued as a single ahead of *Mama's Pearl*, when Berry Gordy decided a change of pace was called for.

Fourth no.1 from as many Motown releases on both charts in the States – a new record at the time. Achieved no.4 in the UK.

No.1 best selling single of 1970 in the States, ahead of Simon & Garfunkel's classic, *Bridge Over Troubled Water*.

Estimated global sales: 6 million – good enough, at the time, to make it the no.2 best selling Motown single of all time, after Marvin Gaye's *I Heard It through The Grapevine*.

Featured in the 'Pinestock USA' episode of the Jackson 5 cartoon series in 1971.

Cited by Michael, in the early 1970s, as one of his three favourite songs he had recorded for Motown, along with *ABC* and *Never Can Say Goodbye*.

Performed by the Jackson 5 on the *Jim Nabors Hour* in September 1970, and for a TV advertisement for Sugar Crisp breakfast cereal in the States.

Used as the closing song for *The Jacksons* TV series in the States in 1976 and 1977.

Live version, recorded at a concert at Madison Square Garden in September 1981, featured on the Jacksons album, *LIVE*, issued in November 1981.

Live performance by the Jacksons, at a concert in Mexico in 1976, included on the home video, *The Jacksons In Concert*, released in 1981 in the UK (no USA release). Another performance, part of a Destiny tour concert, screened on BBC2 in the UK.

Performed live by the Jacksons at *Motown 25: Yesterday, Today, Forever*, staged in the Pasadena Civic Auditorium on 25th March 1983.

Title given to a budget cassette compilation released in the States in 1989.

Edited adult version featured in the Pepsi 'Now & Then' commercial – scheduled to appear on the cancelled compilation, *DECADE 1980-1990*, so remains unreleased.

Original mono version included on the 4CD box-set, *HITSVILLE USA: THE MOTOWN SINGLES 1959-1971*, issued in the States in 1992.

Small Circle Of Friends Remix, as included on the Japanese album, *SOUL SOURCE – JACKSON 5 REMIXES* in 2000, featured alternate vocals.

Vocal and instrumental version featured on the karaoke album, *MOTOWN MASTER RECORDINGS – ORIGINAL ARTIST KARAOKE: DANCING IN THE STREETS*, released in September 2003.

Recorded by Willie Hutch for his 1973 album, *FULLY EXPOSED*.

Cover version by Mariah Carey, from a MTV Unplugged session and featuring uncredited vocals by Trey Lorenz, went all the way to no.1 on the Hot 100 in 1992 – also achieved no.11 on the R&B singles chart and no.2 in the UK. Featured on Mariah's third album, *MTV UNPLUGGED*, and was her sixth no.1 on the Hot 100.

Covered by numerous other artists, including La Toya Jackson (for her 1995 album, *STOP IN THE NAME OF LOVE*), Gloria Gaynor, Westlife, Temptations and Dane Bowers. La Toya's album, a collection of dance-style Motown covers, was reputedly recorded in just one hour, and the album's original cover featured an un-censored topless photograph from her infamous *Playboy* shoot.

A cappella version recorded by Michael in 1993, for a Pepsi Cola commercial.

'Previously unreleased version', with alternate lyrics and a longer, unfaded close, included on Michael's *LOVE SONGS* album, issued in the UK in January 2002 (no USA release) – this version was actually officially released in Japan in 1971, on a Jackson 5 greatest hits compilation.

Performed by Mariah Carey & Trey Lorenz at the 'A Celebration of the Life of Michael Jackson 1958-2009' memorial concert at the Staples Center on 7th July 2009.

Posthumous hit: no.29 in the USA (Hot Digital Songs) and no.49 in UK.

I'LL BE THERE – FEELIN' ALRIGHT

Medley the Jackson 5 performed the *Diana!* TV special, first aired in the States on 18th April 1971.

Featured on the TV soundtrack album of the same title, released in March 1971 in the States and October 1971 in the UK.

See also: *Feelin' Alright*.

I'LL BET YOU

Song featured on the Jackson 5's *ABC* album, issued in May 1970 in the States and August 1970 in the UK.

Featured in the 'Mistaken Identity' episode of the Jackson 5 cartoon series in 1971.

Official Versions:
Album Version.
Edit.

An edited version featured on later vinyl copies of *ABC*, and on 1990s onwards CD compilations.

Originally recorded by Funkadelic for their debut, eponymous album, issued in 1970.

I'LL COME HOME TO YOU

Song Michael recorded for his solo album, *FOREVER, MICHAEL*, released in January 1975 in the States and March 1975 in the UK.

I'LL TURN TO STONE

Four Tops hit the Jackson 5 recorded a version of – remains unreleased.

The Four Tops took the song to no.50 on the R&B singles chart and no.76 on the Hot 100 in the States in 1967.

I'M DREAMIN'

Song named by will.i.am, in an interview with *Rolling Stone* magazine in February 2007, as one of eight he and Michael were working on, for Michael's new album – remains unreleased.

The other seven songs will.i.am and Michael were working on were not named.

I'M GLAD IT RAINED

One of 19 'Rare & Unreleased' tracks on the fourth CD of the Michael/Jackson 5 box-set, *SOULSATION!*, issued in June 1995 in the States and July 1995 in the UK.

I'M IN LOVE AGAIN

Song recorded by Minnie Riperton, with Michael on backing vocals – released in 1980, after her death, on her album *LOVE LIVES FOREVER*.

Michael paid tribute to Minnie on the back of the album sleeve: 'She was phenomenal – she did things with her voice that were incredible.'

I'M IN LOVE WITH MICHAEL JACKSON'S ANSWERPHONE

Novelty single recorded by Julie, released in the UK in October 1984 – not a hit.

Name-checked several of Michael's hits, including *Beat It* and *Billie Jean*.

I'M INTO SOMETHING GOOD

Written by Gerry Goffin & Carole King.

Michael was shown, on a DVD of the recording of *I Have This Dream*, played during a court disposition in London in 2008, singing the song circa 2005 – speculation Michael was planning to cover some old rock'n'roll songs on his new album remains unconfirmed.

Hit Versions:
Herman's Hermits – no.1 in the UK, and no.13 in the USA, in 1964.

I'M MY BROTHER'S KEEPER

Song recorded by Jermaine Jackson, for his 1982 album, *I LIKE YOUR STYLE*.

Prevented from joining his brothers on their Triumph Tour, Jermaine instead went into the studio, to record a new album for Motown – including this song about Michael:

'When they went on the road,' said Jermaine, 'I went into the studio and did

that song – I wanted to show how much I care about Michael.'

I'M SO HAPPY

Non-album recording by the Jackson 5.

B-side of *Sugar Daddy*, issued in November 1971 in the States and March 1972 in the UK.

Featured in the 'Groove To The Chief' episode of the new Jackson 5 cartoon series in 1971.

Made its first album appearance in October 2000, on the Jackson 5's double CD, *ANTHOLOGY* (no UK release).

Original mono version included on the 2-for-1 CD, *THIRD ALBUM & MAYBE TOMORROW*, issued in the States in 2001; also, on the Jackson 5 compilation, *LOVE SONGS*.

I'M STILL THE KING

Song will.i.am confirmed Michael had written, when he was interviewed in 2007 by the magazine, *XL Repubblica*.

'He wrote a song called *I'm Still The King*,' said will.i.am. 'I really don't know if the track will make it on the album – I shall say we are used to that with Michael, aren't we?'

IN OUR SMALL WAY

Song Michael recorded for his debut solo album, *GOT TO BE THERE*, issued in January 1972 in the States and May 1972 in the UK. Also included on Michael's second solo album, *BEN*, released in 1972.

Featured in the 'Groove To The Chief' episode of the new Jackson 5 cartoon series in 1971.

Released as a single in the Philippines b/w *You Can Cry On My Shoulder*.

Included on the *Ben* EP released in Brazil.

Version with countdown introduction included on Michael's 2009 box-set, *HELLO WORLD*.

IN THE ARMS OF GOD

Song composed by Stevie Wonder which, following Michael's passing, may be turned into a tribute song.

Breaking his silence on his death, Stevie described Michael as 'someone very, very special to the world', and he said that 'if he wasn't at peace, he is in the arms of God.'

Stevie urged people to celebrate Michael's legacy, rather than focusing on the 'swirling rumours, speculation and negativity' that has been discussed following Michael's passing.

IN THE BACK

Written by Michael and first registered in 1989; Michael also worked on the song between 1994-2004. Recorded by Michael in 1997 at Mountain Studios in Montreux, Switzerland.

Scheduled to feature on Michael's 1997 album, *BLOOD ON THE DANCE FLOOR*, until *Superfly Sister* replaced it – early press releases listed it as one of the tracks on the album.

Remained unreleased until it was included on his box-set, *THE ULTIMATE COLLECTION*, issued in November 2004.

IN THE CLOSET

Written by Michael with Teddy Riley, and recorded by Michael for his album, *DANGEROUS*, issued in November 1991.

Originally titled *(Coming) Out Of the Closet*, and intended as a duet by Michael and Madonna. Demo version believed to exist – no official release.

Demo version also recorded by Michael solo, which has leaked on the internet – no official release. Other demo versions also known to exist.

'He (Michael) did a demonstration record for me,' said Riley, 'and he was the one who actually came up with the structure of how the song should come out. He would work out these string lines on the synthesiser, then he came up with these mouth sounds that were very percussive – sort of like a drum machine, but different. And it all worked.'

Credited to Michael and 'Mystery Girl' – whose identity was rumoured to be Madonna or Paula Abdul, but proved to be Princess Stephanie of Monaco.

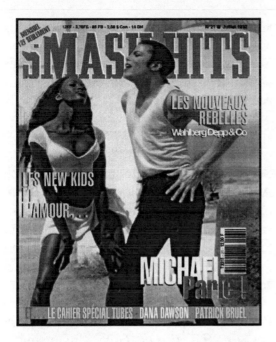

Third single from *DANGEROUS*, released ahead of *Who Is It*, when Michael heard director Herb Ritts' ideas for the promo short film.

Promo premiered on 23rd April 1992. Co-starred supermodel Naomi Campbell – banned in South Africa because of its 'very sensual nature which could offend viewers.'

Hit no.1 on the R&B singles chart in the States, and charted at no.6 on the Hot 100 and no.8 in the UK.

RIAA Gold Record (USA million seller).

Official Versions:
Album Version.
The Newark Mix.
Club Edit.
The Promise.
Club Mix.
The Reprise.
Freestyle Mix.

The Vow.
KI's 12".
Touch Me Dub.
Mix Of Life.
Underground Dub.
Radio Edit.
Underground Mix.
The Mission.
7" Edit.
The Mission Radio Edit.

Instrumental version known to exist – no official release.

KI's 12" and The Newark Mix featured additional vocals not found on the album version of the song.

Master tapes from Teddy Riley's Future Records studio surfaced on eBay, featured several unreleased mixes:

In The Closet Mix 3 #30
In The Closet Vocal & Instrumental 2 Tracks
In The Closet VSO .02 #54
In The Closet Teddy's New #49
In The Closet Mix 4

10" acetate featuring 'Radio Edit 4:36 Full' known to exist – mastered in the UK at Abbey Road Studios. Somewhere between an alternate version and a remix, this is an unreleased version of the song.

Live performances, as part of *His*tory World Tour concerts, televised in Germany and New Zealand.

Thirteenth of Michael's 20 *'Visionary – The Video Singles'* reissues, with the music on one side of a Dual Disc and the accompanying short film on the other side. Issued in May 2006 in the UK – charted at no.20.

IN THE LIFE OF CHICO

One of five songs hand-written by Michael circa 1979 – lyrics included in a personal notebook, with young actor Mark Lester on the cover, that formed part of a 10,000+ piece collection of Jackson memorabilia purchased by Universal Express and some of its entertainment partners, in November 2006.

IN THE STILL OF THE NITE (I'LL REMEMBER)

Boyz II Men recording featured in the TV mini-series, *The Jacksons: An American Dream*, and included on the accompanying soundtrack album, issued in October 1992 in the States and July 1993 in the UK.

Single release included *Snippets From The Jacksons: An American Dream*, and a live Jackson 5 medley of *I Want You Back* and *ABC*, lifted from the album.

Charted at no.3 on the Hot 100 and no.4 on the R&B singles chart in the States, and no.27 in the UK.

Other hits versions:
Five Satins – no.3 on the R&B singles
  chart and no.24 on the Hot 100
  in the States in 1956.

See also: *Snippets From The Jacksons: An American Dream, Medley: I Want You Back – ABC (Live)*

IN THE VALLEY

Song Michael cited he had written in his court deposition in November 1993 – remains unreleased.

INCOMPLETE

Song written by Montell Jordan with Anthony Crawford, with Michael in mind. 'In terms of recording that song,' said Jordan, 'I thought Michael Jackson, Sisqo or Ginuwine. I gave it to God, but even God couldn't get it to Michael Jackson!'

Recorded by Sisqo for his 1999 album, *UNLEASH THE DRAGON* – as a single, topped both the Hot 100 & R&B singles chart in the States, and achieved no.13 in the UK.

INTERFERENCE

Song Thomas Dolby has confirmed he wrote for Michael. 'Initially, I just had the bass and drum groove,' said Dolby. 'I sent him the demo and he said he liked it and would try to add a melody. Then I didn't hear any more, and next thing I knew a Jacksons album called 'Victory' came out – and there was my groove! So like a sucker, I started writing another one for him, inspired by memories of him as a kid.'

Title of the second song: *Hyperactive*.

See also: *Hyperactive*.

INVINCIBLE

Written by Michael with Rodney Jerkins, Fred Jerkins III, LaShawn Daniels and Norman Gregg.

Title track of Michael's album *INVINCIBLE*, issued in October 2001 – featured a rap by Fats.

A lot of songs Michael worked on with Rodney Jerkins during the *INVINCIBLE* sessions remain unreleased, as Jerkins told *Cut* magazine:

'I really want people to hear some of the stuff we did together which never made the cut,' he said. 'There's a whole lot of stuff, just as good, maybe better. People have gotta hear it... Michael records hundreds of songs for an album, so we cut it down to thirty-five of the best tracks, and picked from there. It's not always about picking the hottest tracks,

it's gotta have a flow, so there's a good album's worth of material that could blow your mind.'

IOWA

Piece of classical music written by Michael, as confirmed by his sister Janet, in an interview with *Q* magazine in 1993 – remains unreleased.

'He (Michael) has a song called *Iowa*, that he wrote – people will never hear that song,' said Janet. 'Just before he left to film *The Wiz*, he put all the songs he had written on to tape in the studio in our parents' house. Not one of them has been heard and those were songs to cry for. These are the things that he's written for orchestras, that are classical music – like something by Bach or Beethoven.'

IS IT SCARY

Written by Michael with James Harris III and Terry Lewis, and originally for the movie, *Addams Family Values* and a greatest hits compilation scheduled for late 1993 – cancelled.

First heard in Michael's mini-movie, *Ghosts* – originally, it was heard throughout the film, before Michael wrote and added the title song. One of five previously unreleased songs included on his album *BLOOD ON THE DANCE FLOOR*, issued in April 1997.

Promo CD and vinyl singles released in many countries.

Official Versions:
Album Version.

Downtempo Groove Mix.
Deep Dish Dark & Scary Remix.
Eddie's Love Mix.
Deep Dish Dark & Scary Remix
Eddie's Love Mix Radio Edit.
Radio Edit.
Eddie's Rub-A-Dub Mix.
Deep Dish Double-O-Jazz Dub.
DJ Greek's Scary Mix.

Downtown Groove Mix by Jam & Lewis featured on the rare promo vinyl of the cancelled single, *Smile* – it has been alleged this is the original version written for Addams Family Values, but that it was deemed 'too urban'.

IT ALL BEGINS AND ENDS WITH LOVE

Song featured on the Jackson 5's *DANCING MACHINE* album, issued in September 1974 in the States and November 1974 in the UK.

IT WAS A VERY GOOD YEAR

Song Michael performed, dressed as Frank Sinatra, on the *Diana!* TV special, broadcast in the States on 18th April 1971. Not included on the accompanying soundtrack album – remains unreleased.

Originally recorded in 1961 by the Kingston Trio. Sinatra's version charted at no.28 on the Hot 100 in the States in 1965, but wasn't a hit in the UK.

IT'S CHRISTMAS TIME

Song the Jackson 5 recorded for their *CHRISTMAS ALBUM* circa 1970, but which failed to make the final track listing – remains unreleased.

IT'S GREAT TO BE HERE

Song featured on the Jackson 5 album, *MAYBE TOMORROW*, released in April 1971 in the States and October 1971 in the UK.

Featured in the 'Bongo, Baby Bongo' episode of the Jackson 5 cartoon series in 1971.

Kenny Dope Remix, as included on the Japanese album *SOUL SOURCE – JACKSON 5 REMIXES* in 2000, featured alternate vocals. A second remix, the Jungle Brothers Remix, was included on *SOUL SOUCE – JACKSON 5 REMIXES 2*, released in Japan in 2001.

Other remixes:
Remix.
Extended Remix.

Remix and Extended Remix versions released as a 12" single in the UK in 2003 by Disco Juice Records.

Sampled by:
702 on their single, *All I Want* – charted at no.33 on the R&B singles chart and no.35 on the Hot 100 in the States in 1997.
Mariah Carey on the 'So So Def Mix' of *Honey* – hit no.1 on the Hot 100 and no.2 on the R&B singles chart in the States, and no.3 in the UK, in 1997.
Puff Daddy & The Family on *It's All About The Benjamins*, from the 1997 album, *NO WAY OUT*.

IT'S NOT WORTH IT

Song written by Rodney Jerkins, Fred Jerkins III and LaShawn Daniels in 2001 – offered to Michael for *INVINCIBLE*, but he soon rejected it.

Recorded by Brandy, with a loop of Michael's vocals used as backing, for her 2002 album, *FULL MOON*.

IT'S THE FALLING IN LOVE

Song Michael recorded for his *OFF THE WALL* album, released in August 1979 – featured guest vocals by Patti Austin.

B-side of *Billie Jean* in the UK.

Reportedly, performed by Michael when he made a cameo appearance at the Rose Bowl in Los Angeles, California, during the nine hour Budweiser Superfest on 1st August 1982 – unconfirmed.

Original version by co-writer Carole Bayer Sager featured on her 1978 album, *TOO*.

Also covered by Dionne Warwick and Dee Dee Bridewater.

IT'S THE SAME OLD SONG

Four Tops classic the Jackson 5 recorded a version of, with Jermaine singing lead – remains unreleased.

Hit versions:
Four Tops – no.2 on the R&B singles chart and no.5 on the Hot 100 in the States, and no.34 in the UK, in 1965.
Weathermen (*aka* Jonathan King) – no.19 in the UK in 1971.
KC & The Sunshine Band – no.30 on the R&B singles chart and no.35 on the Hot 100, and no.47 in the UK, in 1978.
Third World – no.77 on the R&B singles chart in 1989

IT'S TOO LATE TO CHANGE THE TIME

Song the Jackson 5 recorded for their *GET IT TOGETHER* album, issued in September 1973 in the States and November 1973 in the UK.

Performed on several TV shows in the States in 1974, including *The Merv Griffin Show*, *Mike Douglas In Hollywood* and *The Tonight Show* (hosted by Johnny Carson).

B-side of *Dancing Machine* in Italy.

Live performance by the Jacksons, at a concert in Mexico in 1976, omitted from the home video, *The Jacksons In Concert*, released in 1981 in the UK (no USA release).

Version with an extended introduction featured on the 1995 box-set, *SOULSATION!*

IT'S YOUR THING

Song the Jackson 5 performed during their first ever TV appearance on the Miss Black America Pageant, staged at Madison Square Garden in New York, on 22nd August 1969 – clip included on Michael's home video, *The Legend Continues...*, released in 1988 (1989 in the States).

Recorded by the Jackson 5 for Motown on 7th August 1969.

Remained unreleased until June 1995, when it was one of 19 'Rare & Unreleased' tracks on the fourth CD of the Michael/Jackson 5 box-set, *SOULSATION!*

Box-set promoted in the States by the release of a seven track promo 12" single, featuring *It's Your Thing*.

Official Versions:
Album Version.
J5 In '95 Extended Remix.
A Cappella ('95)
J5 In '95 House Remix.
Instrumental ('95).

Hit versions:
Isley Brothers – no.1 on the R&B singles chart and no.2 on the Hot 100 in the States in 1969, no.30 in the UK.
Señor Soul – no.39 on the R&B singles chart in 1969.
Salt-N-Pepa – no.4 on the R&B singles chart in 1988.

I'VE GOTTA BE ME

Sammy Davis, Jr. cover the Jackson 5 recorded for Motown – remains unreleased. Sammy's version appeared on his 1968 album of the same title.

Originally penned for the Broadway production, *Golden Rainbow*, as a vehicle for the husband-wife team of Steve Lawrence and Eydie Gorme.

J5 TALK & SING PERSONALLY TO VALENTINE READERS

Flexi disc given away on the front of the October 1972 issue of the British teen magazine, *Valentine*.

As well as Michael and his brothers talking, featured snippets of *I Wanna Be Where You Are*, *I'll Be There*, *ABC* and *Never Can Say Goodbye*.

JACKSON 5

Lead track on Once Around The Park's album, *THIS IS THE SOUND OF MUSIC*, released in 2002.

JACKSON 5 CARTOON THEME

Theme to the Jackson 5's cartoon series, which first aired on ABC-TV in the States on 11th September 1971, featuring the hits, *I Want You Back*, *ABC*, *The Love You Save* and *Mama's Pearl* – specially recorded, rather than an edited medley of the songs, used to open and close the show.

Cartoon series aired in the UK from 8th April 1972 onwards.

JACKSON 5 MOTOWN MEDLEY, THE

Medley of *I Want You Back*, *The Love You Save*, *Dancing Machine*, *ABC* and *I'll Be There*.

B-side of the 12" promo of *Farewell My Summer Love*, issued in the States in June 1984, to coincide with the Jacksons Victory Tour.

JACKSON MAN

One of two unreleased Jackson 5 recordings – said to be 'somewhat of a tribute to their father', Joseph Jackson – featured on a 6.5" metal acetate, with *Take My Heart* on Side 1 and *Jackson Man* on Side 2 – title credits hand-written in green wax crayon.

Acetate discovered by Adey Pierce in Indiana in 2000 – he purchased it from an ex-engineer who engineered the Jackson 5 recordings for Steel-Town.

Originally believed both songs were Steel-Town Recordings – however, this was refuted by the label's founder and owner, Gordon Keith.

'The test record that embodies *Jackson Man* and *Take My Heart* does sound like Michael Jackson and the Jackosn Five,' said Keith. 'It sounds like the beginning stage with Motown in 1968 – kind of like a practice tape or demo which was later changed to *ABC*.'

Keith further stated that he owns all the original Steel-Town master tapes for Michael/Jackson 5, so that others – such as those included in the Henry Vaccaro auction – cannot be what they claim to be.

Acetate value at £3,000 by *Record Collector* magazine, and sold on the internet auction site, eBay, for £4,200 in October 2006.

See also: *Take My Heart, Big Boy*.

JACKSONS OPENING THEME SONG

Written by Michael with brothers Jackie, Marlon, Randy and Tito, as the opening theme for the group's TV series in the

States in 1976 – registered with the BMI, but no official release.

JAM

Written by Michael with Teddy Riley, Bruce Swedien and Ivan Moore, and recorded for his *DANGEROUS* album, issued in November 1991.

Featured rap by Heavy D.

'*Jam* was a track Michael had the idea for,' said Riley. 'He told me to see what I could do with it… it was just a stripped tune until Michael did his vocals and I came in with the icing. I actually added most of the keyboard parts, all of the percussion elements, all of the horn parts, and all of the guitar parts, to make the tune what it is today… that's the way it worked a lot of the time. He'd come in with an idea and I'd flesh it out in the studio… it was my idea to get the rapper Heavy D to perform on there as well – he was Michael's favourite rapper at the time.'

Charted at no.3 on the R&B singles chart and no.26 on the Hot 100 in the States, and no.13 in the UK – hit no.1 in Zimbabwe.

Official Versions:
Album Version.
Roger's Club Mix.
Acappella Mix.
Roger's Club Radio Mix.
Atlanta Techno Dub.
Roger's Jeep Dub.
Atlanta Techno Mix.
Roger's Jeep Mix.
Roger's Club Dub.
Roger's Jeep Radio Mix.
MJ Raw Mix.
Silky Dub!
Silky 7".
Silky 12".
Percapella.
Teddy's Jam.
Radio Edit.
Teddy's 12" Mix.
Radio Edit w/out Rap.
Video Mix.
7" Edit.
7" Edit w/out Rap.
E-Smoove's Jazzy Jam.
Roger's Slam Jam Mix.
Maurice's Jammin' Dub Mix.Roger's Underground Mix.
More Than Enuff Dub.
More Than Enuff Mix.

'Jam' is a basketball term in the States, a theme Michael explored in the promo short film, which was directed by Michael and David Kellogg. Co-starred Michael Jordan of the Chicago Bulls basketball team, Heavy D and young rap duo, Kris Kross.

Song chosen to open Michael's Dangerous World Tour concerts.

Live performance by Michael, at his Dangerous Tour concert in Bucharest, Romania, on 1st October 1992, featured on the DVD released as part of his box-set, *THE ULTIMATE COLLECTION*, issued in November 2004.

Fourteenth of Michael's 20 *'Visionary – The Video Singles'* reissues, with the music on one side of a Dual Disc and the accompanying short film on the other side. Issued in May 2006 in the UK – charted at no.22.

Master tapes from Teddy Riley's Future Records studio surfaced on eBay, featured several unreleased mixes:

Jam 2 Tracks (More Lead Vocals / Less Lead Vocals)
Jam Mix 14
Jam Final DAT Ruff 3 Tracks #8
Jam Mix 12 #10
Jam Mix 18 #14
Jam Mix 11 #20
Jam New Teddy Mixes 3 Mixes #27
Jam Remix 3 Mixes #36
Jam With Comp Mix 22 #38
Jam No Comp Mix 22 #39
Jam Mix 20 #40
Jam Mix 13 #41
Jam Mix 14 #42
Jam Ruff With New Drums #52
Jam Remix Mix #55
Jam Mix 10
Jam Vocal Incomplete Lyrics
Jam Propaganda Films 'Teaser' Sound EFX
Just Jammin' #37 (10 tracks)

JAM – BILLIE JEAN – BLACK OR WHITE

Medley Michael performed live during the half-time interval, at Superbowl XXVII, on 31st January 1993. Michael gave a short speech, before he performed *Heal The World*.

JAM SESSION

B-side of the Jackson 5's second single, *We Don't Have To Be Over 21 (To Fall In Love)*, released on Steel-Town Records circa mid-1968 (no UK release).

Finally released – titled Jam Session (Part 1) – on album in June 1996, on the pre-Motown compilation, *PRE-HISTORY – THE LOST STEELTOWN RECORDINGS* (no UK release).

Title of a pre-Motown compilation released on the Mastertone label in 1998.

JAM SESSION

Pre-Motown recording by the Jackson 5 – different to above – featured on the album, *BEGINNING YEARS 1967-1968*, issued in 1989 in the States and 1990 in the UK.

Album credit: The Jackson 5 And Johnny featuring Michael Jackson.

JAM SESSION (PART 1)

Re-titled version of song that originally appeared on the B-side of *We Don't Have To Be Over 21 (To Fall In Love)*.

Included on the pre-Motown compilation, *PRE-HISTORY – THE LOST STEELTOWN RECORDINGS* (no UK release).

JAM SESSION (PART 2)

Song previously titled, *Boys And Girls, We Are The Jackson Five (Jam Session)* – originally included on the pre-Motown compilation, *THE JACKSON FIVE FEATURING MICHAEL JACKSON*, released in the UK in September 1993 (no USA release).

Included on the pre-Motown compilation, *PRE-HISTORY – THE LOST STEELTOWN RECORDINGS* (no UK release).

JAMIE

One of 19 'Rare & Unreleased' tracks on the fourth CD of the Michael/ Jackson 5 box-set, *SOULSATION!*, issued in June 1995 in the States and July 1995 in the UK.

Originally recorded by Eddie Holland, for his eponymous 1962 album.

JASON NEVINS KING OF POP MEGAMIXES

See: *Thriller Megamix*.

JE NE VEUX PAS LA FIN DE NOUS

French language version of Michael's *I Just Can't Stop Loving You*, recorded as a duet with Siedah Garrett – remains unreleased.

French lyrics written by Christine 'Coconut' Decriox. 'I met Quincy (Jones) in Los Angeles by friends of friends,' said Decriox. 'When I heard *I Just Can't Stop Loving You*, I said to Michael that he should sing it in French, because it is a harmonious language which is appropriate for this kind of romantic melodies. Quincy proposed to me to write the text – I did and Michael recorded it.'

Translation of French title: *I Do Not Want The End Of Us*.

Featured on the 10" acetate version of *Leave Me Alone*, and surfaced on the youtube web-site in 2007.

See also: *I Just Can't Stop Loving You*.

JESUS IS LOVE

Performed by Lionel Richie at the 'A Celebration of the Life of Michael Jackson 1958-2009' memorial concert at the Staples Center on 7th July 2009.

JINGLE BELLS

Festive favourite the Jackson 5 performed at the close of a benefit concert for the Foundation Of The Junior Blind in Los Angeles on Christmas Day in 1970, attended by 400 blind and partially sighted children aged 13-16 years old.

Recorded by Michael and his brothers for their *CHRISTMAS ALBUM* circa 1970, but which failed to make the final track listing – remains unreleased.

Hit versions:

Perry Como – no.74 on the Hot 100 in the States in 1957.

Ramsey Lewis – no.21 on the Christmas Singles chart in the States in 1965.

Booker T & The MG's – no.20 on the Christmas Singles chart in 1966.

Singing Dogs – no.1 on the Christmas Singles chart in 1971.

Judge Dread (medley) – no.64 in the UK in 1978.

Hysterics – no.44 in the UK in 1981.

Crazy Frog – no.5 in the UK in 2005.

JOHNNY RAVEN

Song Michael recorded for his *MUSIC & ME* album, issued in April 1973 in the States and July 1973 in the UK.

B-side of *Music And Me* in the UK.

Version with extended opening included on Michael's 2009 box-set, *HELLO WORLD*.

JOY

Song Michael wrote the melody to, with a view to including it on his album, *DANGEROUS*. Tammy Lucas added lyrics but, ultimately, Michael wasn't happy with the song and didn't record it.

Recorded by Teddy Riley's BLACKstreet, for the group's eponymous debut album in 1994. Released as a single in 1995 – charted at no.12 on the R&B singles chart and no.43 on the Hot 100 in the States, and no.56 in the UK.

Official Versions:
Album Version.
Album Version – No Rap.
Uptown Joy.
Uptown Joy (Long).
Cool Joy.
New Carnegie Mix.
Latin Combo.
Quiet Storm.
Extended Violon Mix.

'Uptown Joy' remix sampled Michael's *I Can't Help It*.

JOY TO THE WORLD

Song the Jackson 5 recorded for their *CHRISTMAS ALBUM* circa 1970, but which failed to make the final track listing – remains unreleased.

JOYFUL JUKEBOX MUSIC

Title track of an album credited to 'The Jackson 5, Featuring Michael Jackson', issued by Motown in October 1976 in the States and December 1976 in the UK –

after Michael and his brothers (minus Jermaine) had signed for CBS/Epic.

JUMBO SAM

Mel Larson, Don Fenceton & Jerry Marcellino composition the Jackson 5 recorded for Motown circa 1973, possibly during the *SKYWRITER* sessions – remains unreleased.

Instrumental version featured on the 1975 compilation album, *THE MAGIC DISCO MACHINE*.

Also known by the title, *Jungle Sam*.

JUMP FOR JOY

Song the Jacksons recorded for their album, *GOIN' PLACES*, released in October 1977.

Alternate version featured on some later editions of the album.

Performed live by Patti Austin on 19th August 1978 – featured on her live album, *LIVE AT THE BOTTOM LINE*.

JUNK FOOD JUNKIE

Song the Jacksons performed, with special guest Mackenzie Phillips, on their TV series in 1976.

JUST A LITTLE BIT OF YOU

Song Michael recorded for his album, *FOREVER, MICHAEL*, issued in January 1975 in the States and March 1975 in the UK.

Achieved no.4 on the R&B singles chart and no.23 on the Hot 100 in the States, but failed to chart in the UK.

Performed by the Jackson 5 on *American Bandstand* and *Soul Train* in 1975, and by the Jacksons on their TV series in 1977.

JUST A LITTLE MISUNDERSTANDING

One of 19 'Rare & Unreleased' tracks featured on the fourth CD of the Michael/Jackson 5 box-set, *SOULSATION!*, issued in June 1995 in the States and July 1995 in the UK – demo version also known to exist.

Originally recorded by the Contours, and featured on their 1962 album, *DO YOU LOVE ME?*

150

JUST BECAUSE I LOVE YOU

Previously unreleased Jackson 5 recording included on the album, *BOOGIE*, released in North America only in January 1979 and quickly withdrawn.

JUST FRIENDS

Song written by Carole Bayer Sager and Burt Bachrach, and produced by Michael with Burt Bacharach, for Sager's 1981 album, *SOMETIMES LATE AT NIGHT* – Michael also contributed backing vocals.

JUST GOOD FRIENDS

Song Michael recorded as a duet with Stevie Wonder, for his album, *BAD*, released in September 1987.

Michael is a huge admirer of Stevie: 'Stevie Wonder is, you know – God, I've learnt so much from him by just sitting in on his sessions, and talking to him and listening... he's phenomenal... I had an interview with George Harrison in England, we did it together, and we were speaking of Stevie and he said, and these are his exact words, he said, Stevie Wonder makes him wanna retire. He said Paul (McCartney) feels the same way.'

Short film, suggesting there may have been plans to release the song as a single, believed to exist – remains unreleased.

JUST SAY NO

Alternate title to Michael's *Morphine*, one of five new songs featured on his album, *BLOOD ON THE DANCE FLOOR*, issued in April 1997 – re-titled in some Far Eastern countries.

See also: *Morphine*.

KANSAS CITY

Song recorded in 1992 by Jason Weaver for the TV mini-series, *The Jacksons: An American Dream*, where it posed as the Jackson 5's debut single.

Featured on the soundtrack album of the same title, issued in October 1992 in the States and July 1993 in the UK.

KEEP HER

Previously unreleased bonus track included on the CD single of the Jacksons' *2300 Jackson Street*, issued in July 1989 in the States and August 1989 in the UK.

Michael had no involvement in recording this track.

KEEP OFF THE GRASS

Song recorded by the Jackson 5 for Motown in the early 1970s – remains unreleased.

KEEP ON DANCING

Song recorded by the Jacksons for their self-titled debut album, issued in November 1976.

Special Disco mix released as a single in Holland.

Promotional film clip (as very early music videos were called) filmed by the Jacksons.

Performed by the Jacksons on their TV series in 1976, on Joe Dassin's *Numero Un* TV special in France in 1977, and featured in the Destiny Tour concert screened on BBC2 in the UK.

KEEP THE FAITH

Song written by Michael with Siedah Garrett and Glen Ballard, and recorded for his *DANGEROUS* album, released in November 1991.

Initially, Michael tried singing the first and second verses in the wrong key – then disappeared. 'I found him standing in the corner of his office, crying his eyes out,' recalls Bruce Swedien. 'He was absolutely heartbroken – cut to the quick.' Michael pulled himself together. 'We went in the studio,' said Swedien, 'cut a whole new demo and recorded a scratch vocal all the way through... we didn't leave the studio until dawn.'

Demo version featured completely different lyrics in some parts – no official release.

'I think he's an incredible singer,' said co-writer Ballard. 'He'll spend two years making a record, then go out and sing all the lead vocals in a week. He's got such confidence and ability. I've worked with him sitting at a piano and having him sing, and it's just a religious experience – the guy is amazing... he's expressive, has great pitch, does incredible backgrounds. His backgrounds are probably as good as anybody I've ever heard – they're textures unto themselves.'

'I really admire the work that went into this track,' said Teddy Riley. 'It doesn't really remind you of any of his other songs, this one's a bit different to his usual tracks, but it stands out. Michael's always innovative. With this track, I just think he went another way due to the structure of the track and the instruments used.'

KENTUCKY

Song Michael cited he had written in the mid-1970s in his court deposition in November 1993 – remains unreleased.

KENTUCKY ROAD

Song the Jackson 5 recorded for Motown – remains unreleased.

KICK IT

Song Michael worked on with Rodney Jerkins, Fred Jerkins III, LaShawn Daniels and Norman Gregg during the

INVINCIBLE sessions, but failed to make the album – remains unreleased.

KILLING ME SOFTLY WITH HIS SONG

Song performed by the Jackson 5 as part of a medley – with *By The Time I Get To Phoenix* and *Danny Boy* – during their Las Vegas shows in 1974.

Also performed on *The Tonight Show*, hosted by Bill Cosby, in March 1974.

Hit versions:
Roberta Flack – no.1 on the Hot 100 and no.2 on the R&B singles chart in the States in 1973, no.6 in the UK.
Al B. Sure! – no.14 on the R&B singles chart and no.80 on the Hot 100 in 1988.
Fugees – no.1 in the UK in 1996.

K.I.S.S.I.N.G.

Song Siedah Garrett recorded for her 1988 album, *KISS OF LIFE* – although not credited, the vocal arrangement was reportedly by Michael.

KREETON OVERTURE

Song written by Michael with Marty Paich, Jai Winding and Pat Leonard in 1984, for the opening of the Jacksons Victory Tour.

Registered with the United States Copyright Office in October 1984 – remains unreleased.

L.A. IS MY LADY

Title track of an album Frank Sinatra released in 1984 – promo video included a brief appearance by Michael and his sister, La Toya.

LA ISLA BONITA

Song penned by Patrick Leonard, who worked with the Jacksons on their Victory Tour in 1984, with Michael in mind.

Michael passed, but Madonna wrote some lyrics for the song and recorded it for her 1986 album, *TRUE BLUE*. Issued as a single, it hit no.1 in the UK and charted at no.4 on the Hot 100 in the States.

LA LA (MEANS I LOVE YOU)

Delfonics cover the Jackson 5 recorded for their album, *ABC*, issued in May 1970 in the States and August 1970 in the UK.

Featured in the 'Jackson Island' episode of the Jackson 5 cartoon series in 1971.

Official versions:
Album Version.
Edit.

An edited version, with the beginning cut, featured on later vinyl/1990s CD releases.

The Delfonics took the song – from their album of the same title – to no.2 on the R&B singles chart and no.4 on the Hot 100 in the States in 1968, and to no.19 in the UK in 1971.

LADIES NIGHT

Song Kool & The Gang recorded for their 1979 album of the same title.

Performed by Kool & The Gang at the the American Music Awards staged on 15th January 1980 – Michael, in the audience, sang along.

Nominated in the Favourite Soul/R&B Single category – beaten by Michael's *Don't Stop 'Til You Get Enough*.

Achieved no.1 on the R&B singles chart and no.8 on the Hot 100 in the States, and no.9 in the UK.

LADY IN MY LIFE, THE

Rod Temperton song Michael recorded for his album, *THRILLER*, released in December 1982.

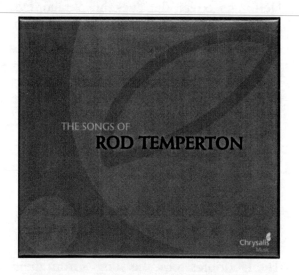

Lyrics to an extra, unreleased verse appeared on the sleeve of original pressings of *THRILLER*. Full version (6:10), with extra verse, included on *THE SONGS OF ROD TEMPERTON*, a promo

only 2 CD box set, issued in the States – it should also have featured on the 3.0 limited edition version of *THE ESSENTIAL* in 2008, but didn't appear.

Cited by Michael as one of the most difficult tracks to cut for the album. 'We were used to doing a lot of takes, in order to get a vocal as nearly perfect as possible, but Quincy wasn't satisfied with my work on that song, even after literally dozens of takes,' said Michael. 'Finally, he took me aside late one session, and told me he wanted me to beg. That's what he said – he wanted me to go back to the studio and literally beg for it. So I went back in and had them turn off the studio lights, and close the curtain between the studio and the control room, so I wouldn't feel self-conscious. Q started the tape and I begged – the result is what you hear in the grooves.'

Included on a single for the first time when it featured on the UK release of *Liberian Girl*.

Sampled by LL Cool J, with Boyz II Men on backing vocals, on his single *Hey Lover*, issued in October 1995 in the States and January 1996 in the UK. Charted at no.3 on both American charts and at no.17 in the UK.

Also sampled by Trae featuring Hawk & Fat Pat, on the song *Swang*.

Cover versions include:
Marc Nelson – on his album
  CHOCOLATE MOODS in 1999.
Mya (re-titled *Man In My Life*) –
  included on her album *FEAR OF FLYING*, in 2000.

Silk – for their 2006 album, *ALWAYS & FOREVER*.

Versions also recorded by Lou Rawls and Diversiti.

LADY MARMALADE

Song recorded by LaBelle for their 1974 album, *NIGHTBIRDS*.

'I was at the Cannes Film Festival (in May 2001) doing a show,' said LaBelle's lead singer, Patti. 'There were only about sixty people, and Mike surprised me – he came on stage and said he wanted to sing *Lady Marmalade*. He lifted my spirit.'

Hit Versions:
LaBelle – no.1 on the Hot 100 and R&B Singles chart in the States, and no.17 in the UK, in 1975.
All Saints (double A-side with *Under The Bridge*) – no.1 in the UK in 1998.
Christina Aguilera, Lil' Kim, Mya & Pink – no.1 on the Hot 100 and no.43 on the R&B singles chart in the States, and no.1 in the UK, in 2001.

LAST NIGHT

One of several songs written by Pharrell Williams and submitted for Michael's HIS*TORY* and *INVINCIBLE* albums, which were later recorded by Justin Timberlake, for his debut album *JUSTIFIED*, released in 2002.

LAVENDAR BLUE

Disney song recorded by the Jackson 5, exists as a bootleg – no official release.

Recording of the song by Burl Ives featured in the 1948 Disney film, *So Dear To My Heart*.

LEARNED MY LESSON

Song written by Michael in 1981, two versions of which were registered with the United States Copyright Office in January 1985 – both remain unreleased.

LEAVE ME ALONE

Song written by Michael, and included as a bonus track on the CD release of his album, *BAD*, issued in September 1987.

'I worked hard on the song, stacking vocals on top of each other like layers of clouds,' said Michael. 'I'm sending a simple message here: Leave me alone! The song is about a relationship between a guy and a girl, but what I'm really saying to people who are bothering me is: Leave me alone!'

Released as the eighth single from *BAD* in many countries, charting at no.2 in the UK (no USA release).

Promoted with a humorous, animated short film, directed by Jim Blashfield and Paul Diener – featured in Michael's 'movie like no other', *Moonwalker*. Included, a clip of Elizabeth Taylor's movie, *Cat On A Hot Tin Roof*, plus footage of Michael's chimp, Bubbles, and his llama, Louise.

Grammy Award: Best Music Video, Short Form. *Moonwalker* also picked up a Grammy nomination, for Best Music Video, Long Form, but Michael's sister

Janet took that award, for her *Rhythm Nation 1814*.

MTV Video Music Award: Best Special Effects in a Video.

Official Versions:
Album Version.
Extended Dance Mix.
Extended Dance Mix Radio Edit.
Dub Version.
Instrumental.
A Cappella.

Tenth of Michael's 20 *'Visionary – The Video Singles'* reissues, with the music on one side of a Dual Disc and the accompanying short film on the other side. Issued in April 2006 in the UK – charted at no.15.

Posthumous hit: no.66 in the UK.

LET IT BE

Beatles classic the Jackson 5 performed *a cappella* on *The Tonight Show*, hosted by Johnny Carson, in April 1974.

The Jackson 5's *ABC* deposed the Beatles single *Let It Be* from top spot on the Hot 100 on 25th April 1970.

Part of the Lennon-McCartney catalogue Michael bought from ATV Music in 1985, for a reputed $47.5 million – now valued at over $500 million.

Michael granted permission for a charity version of the song to be recorded, by Ferry Aid, to aid families of the victims of the Zeebrugge ferry tragedy in 1987. Ferry Aid included Paul McCartney. The project was promoted by *The Sun* newspaper, who publicly thanked Michael for his support.

Hits versions:
Beatles – no.1 on the Hot 100 in the States and no.2 in the UK in 1970.
Joan Baez – no.49 on the Hot 100 in 1971.
Ferry Aid – no.1 in the UK in 1987.

LET IT BE – SHORTNIN' BREAD

Medley the Jackson 5 performed on *The Jim Nabors Show* in the States in September 1970; *Let It Be* they sang *a cappella*, and they were joined by their host on *Shortnin' Bread*.

LET ME CARRY YOUR SCHOOLBOOKS

Single issued by Steel-Town Records in the States in 1971, credited to 'The Ripples & Waves + Michael' – a name the Jackson 5 reputedly used in the early days.

Nearly 20 years later Gordon Keith, founder and owner of Steel-Town Records, stated: 'The fine vocals were provided by another Gary, Indiana talent, Michael Rodgers' – not Michael Jackson.

Featured on the Jackson 5 album, *PRE-HISTORY – THE LOST STEELTOWN RECORDINGS*, released in the States in June 1996 (no UK release). The sleeve notes implied, without actually saying, the Jackson 5 and the Ripples & Waves + Michael were one and the same group.

LET'S DO THE MICHAEL JACKSON

Song recorded by the Broadway Thrillers – released as a 2-track 12" singles in the States (Thriller Records 203) in 2008; single also featured a Dub version.

LET'S GO TO MICHAEL JACKSON'S HOUSE

Track recorded by American folk singer-songwriter, Tom Paxton, for his 1996 album, *LIVE: FOR THE RECORD*.

See also: *Michael And Lisa Marie*.

LET'S HAVE A PARTY

One of 19 'Rare & Unreleased' tracks on the fourth CD of the Michael/Jackson 5 box-set, *SOULSATION!*, issued in June 1995 in the States and July 1995 in the UK.

LET'S TAKE A RIDE

One of several songs written by Pharrell Williams and submitted for Michael's *HISTORY* and *INVINCIBLE* albums, which were later recorded by Justin Timberlake, for his debut album *JUSTIFIED*, released in 2002.

LETTER TO MICHAEL

Song about Michael by Leslie, released in early 1984 on the Stonehenge label.

LIBERIAN GIRL

Song originally titled 'Pyramid Girl', written circa 1983 by Michael, for the Jacksons' *VICTORY* album – re-titled and recorded for his album, *BAD*, issued in September 1987.

'Liberian Girl is one of my absolute favourites of all the music I've done with Michael,' stated Bruce Swedien. 'I love the intro... Quincy had Leta M'Bulu say *"naka panda piya – nake taka piya – mpenziwe"* in Zulu (Swahili), in the intro and in every turn-around. I think that sexy, little speaking line gave the 'Liberian Girl' an identity in this wonderful song... Michael's vocals on *Liberian Girl* are absolutely stellar! The lead, and the big, block background harmonies. Wow!'

Promo video, directed by Jim Yukich, featured a host of stars, including: Brigitte Nielsen, Paula Abdul, Carl Weathers, Whoopi Goldberg, Quincy Jones, Jackie Collins, Rosanna Arquette, Olivia Newton-John, John Travolta, Steven Spielberg, Debbie Gibson, Weird Al Yankovic, Suzanna Somers, Don

King, David Copperfield, Danny Glover, Dan Aykroyd, plus Michael himself and his chimp, Bubbles. Michael dedicated the promo to Elizabeth Taylor.

Ninth and last single lifted from *BAD*, charted at no.13 in the UK – set a new record of nine Top 30 singles from one album.

Official Versions:
Album Version.
Edit.
Instrumental.

Acetate surfaced internet auction site eBay in 2002, including an unreleased instrumental version of the song.

Sampled by:
MC Lyte featuring Xscape's *Keep On, Keepin' On* – no.3 on the R&B singles chart and no.10 on the Hot 100, and no.39 in the UK, in 1996. Reissued in the UK a year later, when it charted at no.27.
'Darkchild' remix of Jennifer Lopez's *If You Had My Love* – no.1 on the Hot 100 and no.6 on the R&B singles chart, and no.4 in the UK, in 1999.
2Pac's *Letter 2 My Unborn* – no.21 in the UK, and no.64 on the R&B singles chart in the States, in 2001.

Posthumous hit: no.35 in Holland.

LIFE

Song written by R. Kelly that Michael wanted to record for his HIS*TORY* album, but Kelly persuaded him to record *You Are Not Alone* instead – which became the first single in Billboard's 55 year history to enter the Hot 100 at no.1.

Recorded by K-Ci & Jo-Jo – featured on their album, *IT'S REAL*, in 1999. Also appeared on the original soundtrack album *LIFE* in the same year.

LIFE OF THE PARTY, THE

Song the Jackson 5 recorded for their album, *DANCING MACHINE*, issued in September 1974 in the States and November 1974 in the UK.

Released as a single in the UK in November 1974 but failed to chart (no USA release).

Promoted on *The Sonny Comedy Revue* in 1974, on the *Carol Burnett Show* in 1975, and performed by the Jacksons on their TV series in 1977.

Live performance by the Jacksons, at a concert in Mexico in 1976, included on the home video, *The Jacksons In Concert*, released in 1981 in the UK (no USA release).

LIGHT THE WAY

Song written by Michael with Prince Sheik Abdullah of Bahrain in 2005, mentioned during a court disposition in London in 2008 – remains unreleased.

LIKE A VIRGIN – BILLIE JEAN

Medley performed by Madonna during her 1985 concert tour – featured on her first live home video, *Live – The Virgin Tour*, filmed in Detroit, Michigan.

LIKE I LOVE YOU

One of six songs written for Michael by the Pharrell Williams of the Neptunes, for his *INVINCIBLE* album, but he didn't like the hook so rejected it.

Recorded by Justin Timberlake for his debut album, *JUSTIFIED* – single charted at no.2 in the UK and no.11 on the Hot 100 in the States in 2002.

'Six of the seven songs we did for Justin were written for Michael like four years ago,' said Williams. 'I want to work with R. Kelly, but I definitely, definitely want to work with Michael. We came so close to working with him so many times, me and him talk about it all the time... and every time something just happens and it just doesn't happen, but we have some amazing songs.'

LIME IN THE COCONUT

Song the Jacksons performed in their TV series in 1976, while dancing the 'limbo rock'.

LITTLE BITTY PRETTY ONE

Song the Jackson 5 recorded for their album, *LOOKIN' THROUGH THE WINDOWS*, issued in May 1972 in the States and October 1972 in the UK.

Charted at no.8 on the R&B singles chart and no.13 on the Hot 100 in the States, but wasn't a hit in the UK.

Featured in 'The Opening Act' episode of the Jackson 5 cartoon series in 1971.

Other hit versions:
Thurston Harris – no.2 on the R&B singles chart and no.6 on the Hot 100 in the States in 1957.
Bobby Day – no.57 on the Hot 100 in 1957.
Frankie Lymon – no.58 on the Hot 100 in 1960.
Clyde McPhatter – no.25 on the Hot in 1962.

LITTLE CHRISTMAS TREE

Festive offering written especially for Michael by Funkadelic's George Clinton.

Originally featured on the album, *A MOTOWN CHRISTMAS*, issued in September 1973 in the States and November 1976 in the UK.

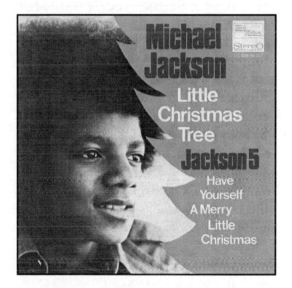

Released as a single in Holland in 1973.

Added, as a bonus track, to the 2003 reissue of the Jackson 5's *CHRISTMAS ALBUM* – re-titled *20th CENTURY MASTERS: THE BEST OF – THE CHRISTMAS COLLECTION*.

LITTLE DRUMMER BOY, THE

Song recorded by the Jackson 5 for their *CHRISTMAS ALBUM*, issued in October 1970 in the States and December 1970 in the UK.

Released as a single in the Philippines and Venezuela.

Hit versions:
Harry Simeone Chorale – no.13 on the Hot 100 in the States, and no.13 in the UK, in 1959.
Beverley Sisters – no.6 in the UK in 1959.
Michael Flanders – no.20 in the UK in 1959.
Johnny Cash – no.63 on the Hot 100 in 1959.
Jack Holloran Singers – no.96 on the Hot 100 in 1962.
Johnny Mathis – no.11 on the Christmas Singles chart in the States in 1963.
Joan Baez – no.16 on the Christmas Singles chart in 1966.
Kenny Burrell – no.21 on the Christmas Singles chart in 1967.
Lou Rawls – no.2 on the Christmas Singles chart in 1967.
Royal Scots Dragoon Guards – no.13 in the UK in 1972.
Moonlion – no.95 on the Hot 100 in 1976.
David Bowie & Bing Crosby (medley) – no.3 in the UK in 1982.
RuPaul – no.61 in the UK in 1994.

LITTLE GIRLS

Song Michael cited he had written in his court deposition in November 1993 – remains unreleased.

LITTLE SUSIE

Song written and recorded by Michael for his album, HIS*TORY*, released in June 1995.

Opens with the *Pie Jesu* segment of Maurice Durufle's *Requiem OP.9*, conducted by Robert Shaw and performed by the Atlanta Symphony Orchestra & Chorus.

Little girl's voice at the beginning belonged to Markita Prescott.

Michael cited he had written *Little Suzy* in his court deposition in November 1993 – this may or may not be the same song Michael later released as *Little Susie*.

One of five songs hand-written by Michael circa 1979 – lyrics included in a personal notebook, with young actor Mark Lester on the cover, that formed part of a 10,000+ piece collection of Jackson memorabilia purchased by Universal Express and some of its entertainment partners, in November 2006. Items also included two sheets with typed lyrics to 'Little Suzie', with changes and edits in pen – these items were included in The Fabulous Jackson Auction, staged at the Hard Rock Hotel & Casino, Los Angeles, at the end of May 2007.

LIVING TOGETHER

Song the Jacksons recorded for their self-titled debut album, issued in November 1976.

Performed by the Jacksons on the TV series in 1977.

LLAMA LOLA

Song Michael mentioned he had written during his copyright hearing in Mexico in 1993 – remains unreleased.

(LONELINESS HAS MADE ME REALISE) IT'S YOU THAT I NEED

Temptations hit the Jackson 5 recorded a version of – remains unreleased.

The Temptations took the song to no.3 on the R&B singles chart and no.14 on the Hot 100 in the States in 1967.

LONELY BIRD

Song Michael cited he had written in his court deposition in November 1993 – remains unreleased.

LONELY HEART

Pre-Motown recording by the Jackson 5, first heard in 1989, when it was included on the album, *BEGINNING YEARS 1967-1968.*

Believed to originate from a demo tape recorded in the living room of 2300 Jackson Street or Tito's music teacher Shirley Cartman, which Cartman planned to pass on to Gordon Keith, founder and owner of Steel-Town Records – however, instead Keith accepted an invitation to hear the Jackson 5 play, and signed them soon after.

Cartman, after moving to Atlanta, had the demo tape transferred to more durable audiotape to preserve the recordings – it appears someone at the taping facility made an illegal copy of the tape, which led to its eventual release without Cartman's knowledge or permission.

Despite crediting Gordon Keith as song-writer, Cartman has confirmed she wrote *Lonely Heart*, as she felt the songs the Jackson 5 were performing at the time were a little too mature for them.

LONELY MAN

Song Michael cited he had written in his court deposition in November 1993 – remains unreleased.

LONELY TEARDROPS

Song written by Berry Gordy for one of Michael's idols, Jackie Wilson, who took it to no.1 on the R&B singles chart and no.7 on the Hot 100 in the States (not a hit in the UK).

Recorded between 1970-73 by Michael as a favour to Gordy, finally released on Michael's *LOOKING BACK TO YESTERDAY* album, issued in February 1986 in the States and May 1986 in the UK.

LOOK WHAT YOU'VE DONE

Tribute song recorded by a group of fans in Nottingham, England, on 4th May 1991 – coincidentally, the day Jackie Jackson and mother Katherine celebrated their birthdays.

LOOKIN' THROUGH THE WINDOWS

Title track of a Jackson 5 album released in May 1972 in the States and October 1972 in the UK.

Charted at no.5 on the R&B singles chart and no.16 on the Hot 100 in the States, and no.9 in the UK.

Promoted on several American TV shows, including *American Bandstand*, *Soul Train* and *The Sonny & Cher Comedy Hour*.

Performed on *Top Of The Pops*, whilst the Jackson 5 were in the UK, as part of their European concert tour.

Live version featured on the Michael/Jackson 5's *LIVE!* album, issued in September 1988 in the UK (no USA release). All songs on the album were recorded at a concert on 30th April 1973, at the Osaka Koseinenkin Hall in Japan. Also included on the limited edition CD, *IN JAPAN!*, released by Hip-O Select in 2004 – only 5,000 copies pressed.

LOST CHILDREN, THE

Song written and recorded by Michael for his album, *INVINCIBLE*, issued in October 2001.

Featured Michael's four year old son, Prince, on narration with Baby Rubba – also contained audio snippets from *The Twilight Zone*.

Home movies snippet of Michael singing the song, at his son Prince's second birthday, screened by 20/20 in the States.

One of three tracks on the album Michael chose as his personal favourites, during his Online Audio Chat appearance on 26th October 2001.

LOVE CALL

Song recorded by the Jackson 5 for Motown on 12th October 1971 – test pressings known to exist, but remains unreleased.

LOVE DON'T WANT TO LEAVE

Jackie Jackson solo recording featured on the Jackson 5's album, *ANTHOLOGY*, issued in June 1976 in the States (not included on UK release).

LOVE FEELS LIKE FIRE

Four Tops track the Jackson 5 recorded a version of – remains unreleased.

The Four Tops recording featured on their 1965 album, *FOUR TOPS SECOND ALBUM*.

LOVE GO AWAY

Song the Jackson 5 recorded for Motown.

Lyrics written by Bob Pappalardo in 1963 – appeared in the Winter 1984 issue, a Michael Jackson special, of *Rock & Soul* magazine.

Remains unreleased.

LOVE I SAW IN YOU WAS JUST A MIRAGE, THE

Song the Jackson 5 recorded for their *THIRD ALBUM*, released in September 1970 in the States and February 1971 in the UK.

Featured on the 'Wizard Of Soul' episode of the Jackson 5 cartoon series in 1971.

Original version by Smokey Robinson & The Miracles – from the album *MAKE IT HAPPEN* – charted at no.10 on the R&B singles chart and no.20 on the Hot 100 in the States in 1967.

LOVE IS HERE AND NOW YOU'RE GONE

Supremes cover Michael recorded for his debut solo album, *GOT TO BE THERE*, issued in January 1972 in the States and May 1972 in the UK.

B-side of *Rockin' Robin*.

Featured on the 'Jackson And The Beanstalk' episode of the new Jackson 5 cartoon series in 1971.

The Supremes original – lifted from the album *THE SUPREMES SING HOLLAND-DOZIER-HOLLAND* – charted at no.1 on both American charts, and no.17 in the UK, in 1967.

LOVE IS THE THING YOU NEED

Song featured on the Jackson 5's album, *JOYFUL JUKEBOX MUSIC*, issued in October 1976 in the States and December 1976 in the UK – originally recorded during the *SKYWRITER* sessions.

LOVE MIX 1

Megamix of Motown recordings by Michael and his brothers featured on the double CD, *THE MICHAEL JACKSON*

MIX, issued in the UK in December 1987.

Featured songs: *Ben, Ain't No Sunshine, One Day In Your Life, Never Can Say Goodbye, Got To Be There, Happy (Love Theme From 'Lady Sings The Blues'), I'll Be There, We're Almost There* and *People Make The World Go Round.*

Promo edit featured: *Ben, Ain't No Sunshine* and *One Day In Your Life.*

See also: *Dance Mix 1 & 2, Love Mix 2.*

LOVE MIX 2

Megamix of Motown recordings by Michael and his brothers featured on the double CD, *THE MICHAEL JACKSON MIX*, issued in the UK in December 1987.

Featured songs: *Who's Lovin' You, I Was Made To Love Her, You've Really Got A Hold On Me, Music And Me, Call On Me, Lonely Teardrops, You've Got A Friend, Girl, Don't Take Your Love From Me, We've Got A Good Thing Going* and *I'll Come Home To You.*

See also: *Dance Mix 1 & 2, Love Mix 1.*

LOVE NEVER FELT SO GOOD

Song written by Michael, with Paul Anka and Kathy Wakefield, in 1980.

Recorded by Johnny Mathis for his 1984 album, *A SPECIAL PART OF ME.*

Demo version by Michael leaked on the internet in 2006 – no official release.

LOVE SCENES

One of 19 'Rare & Unreleased' tracks on the fourth CD of the Michael/ Jackson 5 box-set, *SOULSATION!*, issued in June 1995 in the States and July 1995 in the UK.

LOVE SONG

Non-album Jackson 5 recording.

B-side of *Lookin' Through The Windows*, released in June 1972 in the States and October 1972 in the UK.

Included of the Jackson 5's *ANTHOLOGY* collection, released in the States in October 2000 (no UK release).

LOVE TRAIN

One of five songs the Jackson 5 performed a medley of at the Grammy Awards ceremony in 1974, to introduce the nominees for Best Rhythm & Blues Performance by a Group, Duo or Chorus.

The O'Jays took the song to no.1 on both American charts, and to no.9 in the UK.

LOVE YOU SAVE, THE

Song the Jackson 5 recorded for their second album, *ABC*, issued in May 1970 in the States and August 1970 in the UK.

Hit no.1 on both American charts, and peaked at no.7 in the UK. Promo 7" red vinyl single released in the States.
Featured on the 'Winner's Circle' episode of the Jackson 5 cartoon series in 1971.

Performed by the Jackson 5 on the *Ed Sullivan Show* and *Jim Nabors Show* in 1970, and on their own TV series in 1976.

Title given to a budget cassette compilation released in the States in 1989.

Original mono version included on the 4CD box-set, *HITSVILLE USA: THE MOTOWN SINGLES 1959-1971*, issued in the States in 1992.

Asakusa S.C. '01 Mix, as included on the Japanese album *SOUL SOURCE – JACKSON 5 REMIXES 2* in 2001, featured alternate vocals with two lines not included on the original album version.

Same extra two lines included on the vocal version featured on the karaoke compilation, *MOTOWN MASTER RECORDINGS – ORIGINAL ARTISTS KARAOKE: LET'S GET IT ON*, released in September 2003 – album also included an instrumental version.

LOVELY ONE

Written by Michael with brother Randy, and recorded by the Jacksons for the album, *TRIUMPH*, released in October 1980.

Lead single from the album – charted at no.2 on the R&B singles chart and no.12 on the Hot 100 in the States, and no.29 in the UK.

Official Versions:
Album Version.

Mono Version.
Single Edit.

Live version, recorded at a concert at Madison Square Garden in September 1981, featured on the Jacksons album, *LIVE*, issued in November 1981.

Performed solo by Michael during his Bad World Tour – one performance screened on Nippon TV in Japan.

LOVE'S GONE BAD

Song the Jackson 5 recorded at least three versions of, one in 1972 and two in 1973 – possibly for the album, *SKYWRITER*.

First version originally included on the album, *BOOGIE*, issued in North America in January 1979 and quickly withdrawn. This version also featured as a bonus track on the '2 Classic Albums on 1 CD' reissue of *SKYWRITER & GET IT TOGETHER*.

Alternate version included on Michael's *LOOKING BACK TO YESTERDAY* album, issued in 1986, and released as a promo 7" single in Canada only – a great rarity. This version was credited to Michael solo, but used the same vocal take as the first version, with some backing vocals omitted from the first verse.

Alternate take featured on Michael's 1995 Anthology series compilation, *THE BEST OF...* (no UK release). This take, by a much younger Michael and completely different, is much less polished than the other two versions.

LOVING YOU IS SWEETER THAN EVER

Four Tops hit the Jackson 5 recorded a version of – remains unreleased.

Hit versions:
Four Tops – no.12 on the R&B singles chart and no.45 on the Hot 100,
 and no.21 in the UK, in 1966.
Nick Kamen – no.16 in the UK in 1987.

LUCY IS IN LOVE WITH LINUS

Song Michael cited he had written in his court deposition in November 1993 – remains unreleased.

LULU

One of 19 'Rare & Unreleased' tracks on the fourth CD of the Michael/ Jackson 5 box-set, *SOULSATION!*, issued in June 1995 in the States and July 1995 in the UK.

LULU'S BACK IN TOWN

Song Michael performed a few bars of on a home-made video, filmed circa 1975 by brother Randy – remains unreleased.

Originally written for *Broadway Gondolier* in 1935.

MAGIC MICHAEL JACKSON MIX

Medley released on the Dutch *You Are Not Alone* CD in 1995.

Featured the songs: *Childhood, Jam, Off The Wall, Billie Jean, Wanna Be Startin' Somethin', Black Or White, Jam, Beat It, They Don't Care About Us, Scream* and *Ease On Down The Road.*

The medley rounded off with a special message from Michael.

MAGICAL CHILD / MAGICAL CHILD PART 2

Two part poem written by Michael – included in his book of poems and reflections, *Dancing The Dream*, published in 1992.

MAKE A WISH

Song Michael cited in his court deposition in November 1993, however, he admitted he couldn't recall if he had written it or not – remains unreleased.

MAKE IT WITH YOU

Performed by the Jacksons on *The Tonight Show* in the States in 1977, as part of a medley with *Without A Song,*

You've Got A Friend, Behind Closed Doors, You've Made Me So Very Happy, You Are The Sunshine Of My Life, You And Me Against The World.

Hit Versions:

Bread – no.1 on the Pop chart in the States, and no.5 in the UK, in 1970.

Ralfi Pagan – no.32 on the R&B singles chart and no.104 on the Pop chart in the States in 1971.

Whispers – no.10 on the R&B chart and no.94 on the Pop chart in the States in 1977.

Teddy Pendergrass – no.23 on the R&B chart in the States in 1990.

Pasadenas – no.20 in the UK in 1992.

Let Loose – no.7 in the UK in 1996.

MAKE OR BREAK

Song Michael cited he had written with John Barnes in his court deposition in November 1993 – remains unreleased.

Also known by the alternate titles, *For God's Sake/Make Or Break* and *Make A Break*.

MAKE TONIGHT ALL MINE

Jackson 5 recording included on the album, *JOYFUL JUKEBOX MUSIC*, released in October 1976 in the States and December 1976 in the UK.

Alternate version included on Michael's 1995 Anthology series compilation, *THE BEST OF...* (no UK release).

MAMA I GOTTA BRAND NEW THING (DON'T SAY NO)

Song featured on the Jackson 5's album, *GET IT TOGETHER*, issued in September 1973 in the States and November 1973 in the UK.

Included on the *Get It Together* EP released in Brazil.

Originally recorded by the Undisputed Truth, and included on their eponymous 1970 album.

MAMA'S PEARL

Song the Jackson 5 recorded for their *THIRD ALBUM*, issued in September 1970 in the States and February 1971 in the UK.

Rarer single mix slightly different to album version, most noticeable on Tito's opening backing vocal – this mix would have been included on the album, had it been completed in time.

Broke the group's run of no.1s in the States; peaked at no.2 on both charts, prevented from topping the Hot 100 by *One Bad Apple* – performed in classic Jackson 5 style by the Osmonds.

No.1 on the sales-oriented Cashbox singles chart in the States, and achieved no.25 in the UK. Picture sleeve single and promo 7" red vinyl single released in the States.

Single alternate version featured in 'The Rare Pearl' episode of the new Jackson 5 cartoon series in 1971.

Mono mix included on the Jackson 5's 1971 compilation, *GREATEST HITS*.

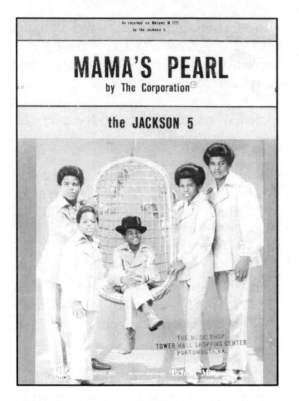

Versions with alternate vocal takes featured on the Jackson 5's 1986 compilation, *ANTHOLOGY*, and on *THE JACKSONS STORY* compilation in 2004 (no UK release) – the latter featured the mono version 'folded' back into the stereo version.

Title given to a budget cassette compilation released in the States in 1989.

Vocal and instrumental version included on the karaoke album, *MOTOWN ORIGINAL ARTISTS, VOL.4: AIN'T NOTHIN' LIKE THE REAL THING*, released in September 2003.

MAMA'S PEARL – WALK ON – THE LOVE YOU SAVE

Medley the Jackson 5 performed the *Diana!* TV special, first aired in the States on 18th April 1971. Featured on the TV soundtrack album of the same title, released in March 1971 in the States and October 1971 in the UK.

Included on the accompanying album, *DIANA!* – where *Walk On* was incorrectly credited to song-writers Burt Bacharach and Hal David (who did co-write Dionne Warwick's hit, *Walk On By*).

MAN, THE

Written by Michael with Paul McCartney, and recorded as a duet for Paul's album *PIPES OF PEACE*, released in November 1983. Background vocals by Paul's wife, Linda.

Planned as a follow-up to Michael and Paul's second collaboration, *Say Say Say*, until Michael's record company blocked its planned February 1984 release, fearing it would compete with releases from *THRILLER*; the 12" single was scheduled to feature an extended remix.

Officially released as a single in Peru, and made available as a promo only single in several other countries.

Acetate featured an unreleased instrumental version.

Official Versions:
Album Version.
Instrumental.

Also known by the title, *This Is The Man.*

MAN IN THE MIRROR

Song written by Siedah Garrett and Glen Ballard, and recorded by Michael for his album, *BAD*, issued in September 1987.

Hit no.1 on both American charts, but surprisingly struggled to no.21 in the UK.

Official Versions:
Album Version.
Single Mix.
Instrumental.

Single Mix recreated for inclusion on the 2003 compilation, *NUMBER ONES*, as the original either wasn't remastered or available for some reason.

Promo short film, which didn't feature Michael, spliced footage of people who have endeavoured to 'make that change' with notorious figures – people like Martin Luther King, John F. Kennedy and Mother Teresa, plus Adolf Hitler and Idi Amin. Directed by Don Wilson.

Performed by Michael at the Grammy Awards ceremony at Radio City Hall, New York, in March 1988.

Grammy nomination: Record Of The Year (Bobby McFerrin's *Don't Worry, Be Happy* took the award).

Soul Trains Awards: Best R&B/Urban Contemporary Single, Male and Best R&B/Urban Contemporary Music Video.

Performed live – along with *What More Can I Give* – by Michael on 21st October 2001, at the 'United We Stand – What More Can I Give' concert, staged at Washington DC's RFK Stadium. Michael dedicated the song to the victims of the 9/11 terrorist attack and their families, saying: 'You are not alone. You are in our hearts, you are in our thoughts, and you are in our prayers.'
Montage of live performances opened Michael's 'movie like no other', *Moonwalker*.

Live performance by Michael, at his Dangerous Tour concert in Bucharest, Romania, on 1st October 1992, featured on the DVD released as part of his box-set, *THE ULTIMATE COLLECTION*, issued in November 2004.

Cover version by Italian singer, Giorgia, featured on her live 1995 album, *NATURAL WOMAN*.

Performed by 98°, Usher and Luther Vandross during the *Michael Jackson: 30th Anniversary Celebration, The Solo Years* concerts, staged at New York's Madison Square Garden on 7th and 10th September 2001.

Recorded by co-writer Siedah Garrett in 2003, for her solo album, *SIEDAH!*. 'This song is very special to me,' said Siedah. 'We (her and Glen Ballard) sat down and almost instantly, we came up with the music, lyric and melody for the first verse and chorus… we knew that afternoon that we had something special.'

Sampled by Rhythme Digital, featuring Redd Angel on vocals, on the track, *All Around The World*.

Posthumous hit: no.2 in the UK & USA (Hot Digital Songs), no.3 in Ireland, no.8 in Australia, no.9 in New Zealand, no.12 in Denmark, no.15 in Norway, no.17 in Austria & no.22 in Holland.

Performed as a tribute to Michael by U2, with *Angel Of Harlem* and a few lines of Michael's *Don't Stop 'Til You Get Enough*, at their concert in Barcelona, Spain, on 30th June 2009.

MAN OF WAR

Song featured on the Jacksons album, *GOIN' PLACES*, issued in October 1977.

B-side of *Music's Takin' Over* in the UK.

MARIA

Song the Jacksons recorded for their album, *2300 JACKSON STREET*, released in June 1989.

Michael wasn't involved in the recording of this track.

MARIA (YOU WERE THE ONLY ONE)

Song Michael recorded for his solo album, *GOT TO BE THERE*, issued in January 1972 in the States and May 1972 in the UK.

B-side of *Got To Be There*.

Featured on the 'Michael In Wonderland' episode of the Jackson 5 cartoon series in 1971.

MAYBE TOMORROW

Originally written for Sammy Davis, Jr. (who had just signed for Motown), recorded by the Jackson 5 for their album of the same title, released in April 1971 in the States and October 1971 in the UK. Two different promo version issued in the States, one over a minute longer than the other; the shorter version is the rarer. Album version also shorter, with some verses edited, while the single featured the original, uncut version.

Charted at no.3 on the R&B singles chart and no.20 on the Hot 100 in the States (no UK release).

B-side of *Little Bitty Pretty One* in the UK.

Featured in the 'Groovatron' episode of the Jackson 5 cartoon series in 1971.

Newly recorded version, with an introduction by Tommy Smothers, performed on the *Goin' Back To Indiana* TV special included on the Jackson 5's album, *GOIN' BACK TO INDIANA*, issued in September 1971 in the States (no UK release).

Cover version by UB40 peaked at no.15 in the UK in 1987.

Sampled by Ghostface Killah on the track *All That I Got Is You*, from the 1996 album, *IRONMAN*.

MAYBE WE CAN DO IT

Song Michael co-wrote with Rodney Jerkins and Sean 'P. Diddy' Combs, and recorded – featuring a rap by P. Diddy – during the *INVINCIBLE* sessions, but failed to make the album – remains unreleased.

In confirming his involvement, P. Diddy said: 'He (Michael) takes an insane amount of time to record a track, but that's just him, it's the way he works. I am, like, the norm and prefer to get the vocal arrangement, then work later on the production side. I got some harsh looks from Michael when I was in the studio,

you can tell when he's not happy because he pulls these funny faces.'

MEDLEY OF HITS

11 minute medley of hits featured on Side 1 of the Jackson 5 compilation, *MOTOWN SUPERSTAR SERIES VOL.12*, released in the States in September 1980.

Featured: *I Want You Back*, *ABC*, *The Love You Save*, *Never Can Say Goodbye*, *Dancing Machine* and *I'll Be There*.

B-side of a Four Tops/Temptations *Medley Of Hits*, released as a 12" single in the States in 1983.

MEDLEYS, THE

Two promo medleys released on 12" and CD in Brazil in 1994:

Back To The Past Medley: *Rock With You, Burn This Disco Out, Off The Wall, Don't Stop 'Til You Get Enough, Shake Your Body (Down To The Ground), Blame It On The Boogie, Thriller* and *Billie Jean*.

Dangerous New Jack Medley: *Remember The Time, In The Closet, Jam* and *Black Or White*.

THE MEDLEYS

MELODIE

Song recorded on 15th January 1973, but remained unreleased until it appeared – newly mixed – on Michael's album, *FAREWELL MY SUMMER LOVE*, issued in May 1984 in the States and June 1984 in the UK.

Remix included on Michael's 1987 album, *THE ORIGINAL SOUL OF MICHAEL JACKSON* – scheduled release as a single in the States in October 1987 cancelled, and the album's one previously unheard recording, *Twenty-Five Miles*, issued instead.

Original 1973 version featured on Michael's *THE BEST OF...* compilation – part of Motown's Anthology series, released in March 1995 in the States (no UK release).

MEN IN BLACK

Song written by Michael with Bryan Loren, who also produced the recording.

Recorded by Michael and included on an ultra rare promo titled 'Promo Flight Only', of which only ten copies exist, given to Sony Executives on their way to Neverland from Europe in 1991, as a teaser for tracks under consideration for Michael's album, *DANGEROUS* – the promo also featured and early version of *Black Or White* and the unreleased *Monkey Business*.

Remains unreleased.

MEPHISTO AND KEVIN

Song, with lyrical reference to Michael, recorded by Primus for the 1998 album, *CHEF AID: THE SOUTH PARK ALBUM*.

MICHAEL

Tribute song recorded by Back 2 Back, to show their support for Michael, following allegations of child molestation in 1993.

MICHAEL AND LISA MARIE

Track recorded by American folk singer-songwriter, Tom Paxton, for his 1996 album, *LIVE: FOR THE RECORD*.

See also: *Let's Go To Michael Jackson's House*.

MICHAEL JACKSON

Track featured on Negativland's 1987 album, *ESCAPE FROM NOISE*.

MICHAEL JACKSON

Dance track echoing Michael's name, and sampling fans singing his name, recorded by Fat Boy Slim (*aka* Norman Cook) for his 1996 album, *BETTER LIVING THROUGH CHEMISTRY*.

MICHAEL JACKSON

Track recorded by the Mitchell Brothers, produced by Calvin Harris, for the 2007 album, *DRESSED FOR THE OCCASION*.

Released as a single in the UK – peaked at no.65.

MICHAEL JACKSON & FRIENDS MEDLEY

Medley Michael performed, with some of his friends including Slash (who came on stage for *Black Or White*), at his concerts in Munich and Seoul in June 1999.

Featured songs: *Don't Stop 'Til You Get Enough*, *The Way You Make Me Feel*, *Scream*, *Beat It* and *Black Or White*.

Alternative titles: *MTV Video Music Awards Medley*, *Greatest Hits Medley*.

MICHAEL JACKSON MEDLEY

Medley of Michael's hits – solo and with the Jacksons – by Ashaye (*aka* Trevor Ashaye), featuring: *Don't Stop 'Til You Get Enough*, *Wanna Be Startin' Somethin'*, *Shake Your Body (Down To The Ground)* and *Blame It On The Boogie*.

Extended 12" version also featured: *Rock With You*, *Billie Jean* and *Get On The Floor*.

Charted at no.45 in the UK in 1983.

Also known by the title: *Don't Stop 'Til You Get Enough*.

MICHAEL JACKSON MEDLEY

Five minute medley of some of Michael's hits, mixed by Wettbewerb von Andreas and Claus Friedrich, released exclusively on a six track limited edition (7,000 copies) CD single of *You Are Not Alone*, in Austria in 1995 – marked VIVA TV's Michael Jackson competition.

Tracks featured: *Beat It, P.Y.T. (Pretty Young Thing), Don't Stop 'Til You Get Enough, Working Day And Night, Man In The Mirror, Heal The World, Remember The Time, Black Or White, Billie Jean, In The Closet, Thriller, Bad, Smooth Criminal, Bad, Scream, Dangerous, Jam* and *Black Or White*.

MICHAEL JACKSON MEDLEY

Medley of Michael's hits by Unlimited Beat, featured: *You Are Not Alone, Don't Stop 'Til You Get Enough, Billie Jean, Thriller, Beat It, Bad, They Don't Care About Us, Black Or White* and *Earth Song*.

Released in 1998 but failed to chart; also featured on Unlimited Beat's album, *THE MEDLEYS VOL.1*.

MICHAEL JACKSON MEDLEY

Medley of *Thriller, Beat It* and *Smooth Criminal* performed by British boy band, Blue. Featured on their 2004 DVD, *Guilty – Live From London* and *THE PLATINUM COLLECTION*, released in 2006.

MICHAEL JACKSON MONOLOGUE

22 second monologue – followed by *I Want You Back* – by Michael, talking about how Diana Ross 'discovered' the Jackson 5 and took them to Motown. Featured on *THE MOTOWN STORY* 10th anniversary box set, issued in the States in March 1971.

MICHAEL MANIA MEDLEY

Medley of Michael's hits – solo and with his brothers – by Replay, with the extended 12" single featuring: *Don't Stop 'Til You Get Enough* (twice), *Another Part Of Me* (twice), *Billie Jean, Working Day And Night, Bad, Blame It On The Boogie, Rock With You, I Want You Back, Shake Your Body (Down To The Ground), The Way You Make Me Feel, Can You Feel It, Wanna Be Startin' Somethin'* and *Thriller*.

Released in 1988 but failed to chart.

MICHAEL McKELLAR

Song Michael cited he had written in his court deposition in November 1993 – remains unreleased.

MICHAEL THE LOVER

Pre-Motown recording by the Jackson 5, originally titled *Some Girls Want Me For Their Lover* and issued as the B-side of *You Don't Have To Be Over Twenty One To Fall In Love* (itself a reissue of *We Don't Have To Be Over 21 (To Fall In Love)*), released in March 1971 in the States (no UK release).

First appeared as *Michael The Lover* on the 1989 release, *BEGINNING YEARS 1967-1968*.

Title of a pre-Motown compilation released on the K-Point label in 1999.

MICHAEL'S IN A JAM

Michael inspired single by the Knight Crew, featuring Monica and Contrelle, released as a single in the States in 2004. Extended version included original material not on the single release.

MICHAEL'S MEDLEY

Instrumental medley of Jackson hits released by Patrick Adams on a 12" single in 1984 in the States. Songs featured: *I Want You Back, Got To Be There, ABC, Wanna Be Startin' Somethin', I'll Be There, Billie Jean, Ben, Beat It, Say Say Say* and *Thriller*.

B-side featured instrumental dub version: *I Want You Back, ABC, Billie Jean, Say Say Say* and *Thriller*.

MIDNIGHT MAN

One of the titles Rod Temperton came up with, when asked by producer Quincy Jones to come up with a title for Michael's follow-up to *OFF THE WALL*.

'Originally, when I did my thriller demo, I called it 'Starlight',' said Temperton. 'Quincy said to me, "You managed to come up with a title for the last album, see what you can do for this album"... so I went back to the hotel, wrote two or three hundred titles, and came up with 'Midnight Man'. The next morning, I woke up and I just said this word – something in my head just said, this is the title. You could visualise it on top of the Billboard charts. You could see the merchandising for this one word, how it jumped off the page as *Thriller*.'

MIDNIGHT RENDEZVOUS

Song featured on the Jacksons album, *2300 JACKSON STREET*, issued in June 1989.

Michael wasn't involved with the recording of this song.

MIDNIGHT TRAIN TO GEORGIA

One of five songs the Jackson 5 performed a medley of at the Grammy Awards ceremony in 1974, to introduce the nominees for Best Rhythm & Blues Vocal Performance by a Group, Duo or Chorus – this song, by Gladys Knight & The Pips, took the Grammy.

Charted at no.1 on both American charts, and achieved no.10 in the UK.

MIND IS THE MAGIC

Song written by Michael with Bryan Loren in 1989 – re-worked for German illusionists Siegfried & Roy, who had worked with Michael on his Bad World Tour, as the theme song for their 'Beyond Belief Show, staged in Las Vegas.
Remained unreleased until 1995, when Michael gave his permission for the song's inclusion on Siegfried & Roy's German album, *DREAMS & ILLUSIONS* (no USA or UK release), which featured music from their show and a TV special.

Featured on the Siegried & Roy compilation, *'MIND IS THE MAGIC' ANTHEM FOR THE LAST VEGAS SHOW*, released in the UK in 2009 (ZYX Music ZYX20881-2).

See also: *Siegfried & Roy*.

MINUTE BY MINUTE

Song the Doobie Brothers recorded for their 1978 album of the same name.

Home movie screened by Entertainment Tonight in July 2009 showed Michael singing a snippet of the song, while on the phone to Elizabeth Taylor – Michael stated he had sung backing vocals on this and another Dobbie Brothers track, *What A Fool Believes*.

No independent confirmation.

The Doobie Brothers took the song to no.14 on the Hot 100 in the States, and to no.47 in the UK.

MIRRORS OF MY MIND, THE

Song the Jackson 5 recorded for their album, *DANICNG MACHINE*, issued in September 1974 in the States and November 1974 in the UK.

MISS LUCKY DAY

Song the Jackson 5 recorded for Motown circa 1973, possibly during the *SKYWRITER* sessions – remains unreleased.

MJ MEGAMIX

Four minutes 58 seconds megamix of some of Michael's solo hits released on various formats in 1995, featured: *Thriller, Billie Jean, Bad, Don't Stop 'Til You Get Enough, Black Or White, Remember The Time, The Way You Make Me Feel, Wanna Be Startin' Somethin', Rock With You* and *Beat It*.

MJ MEGAREMIX

Ten minutes 33 seconds megaremix of some of Michael's solo hits released on various formats in 1995, featured: *Rock With You (Remix by Frankie Knuckles), Remember The Time (Remix by Steve 'Silk' Hurley), Don't Stop 'Til You Get Enough (Original Remix by Tony Moran & Ronnie Ventura), Billie Jean (Remix by Ronnie Ventura), Wanna Be Startin' Somethin' (Remix by Brothers In Rhythm), Black Or White (Remix by Clivilles & Cole)* and *Thriller (Remix by David Morales & Frankie Knuckles)*.

Featured on Michael's home video, *History On Film Volume II*, accompanied by a montage of video clips.

MJ MELODY

Song written by Michael in 1982, and registered with the United States

Copyright Office in November 1984 – remains unreleased.

MJ URBAN MEGAMIX

Four minutes 58 seconds urban megamix of some of Michael's solo hits, released on various formats in 1995, featured: *Rock With You, Billie Jean, Don't Stop 'Til You Get Enough, Remember The Time, The Way You Make Me Feel* and *Wanna Be Startin' Somethin'*.

MONEY

Written by Michael, and recorded for his HIS*TORY* album, issued in June 1995.

Track Sony wanted to issue as a single, ahead of *They Don't Care About Us* – Michael's choice.

Official Versions:
Album Version.
Fire Island Radio Edit.
Fire Island Radio Edit (different Intro).

Fire Island Radio Edit, which featured alternate vocals, appeared on the 1997 compilation, *THE GREATEST DANCE ALBUM IN THE WORLD*.

MONEY HONEY

One of 19 'Rare & Unreleased' tracks on the fourth CD of the Michael/ Jackson 5 box-set, *SOULSATION!*, issued in June 1995 in the States and July 1995 in the UK – demo version also known to exist.

Bobby Taylor was producing the song when Berry Gordy fired him – and had Hal Davis complete the recording.

Originally recorded in the mid 1950s by Clyde McPhatter & The Drifters.

MONEY (THAT'S WHAT I WANT)

Song heard in the TV mini-series, *The Jacksons: An American Dream* – it's possible the Jackson 5 performed this song in concert in the pre-Motown era

Hit versions:
Barrett Strong – no.2 on the R&B chart, and no.23 on the Hot 100, in the States in 1960.
Jennell Hawkins – no.17 on the R&B chart in 1962.
Bern Elliott & The Fenmen – no.14 in the UK in 1963.
Kingsmen – no.16 on the Hot 100 in 1964.
Jr. Walker & The All Stars – no.35 on the R&B chart, and no.52 on the Hot 100, in 1966.
Flying Lizards – no.5 in the UK in 1979, and no.50 on the Hot 100 in 1980.
Backbeat Band – no.48 in the UK in 1994.

MONKEY BUSINESS

Written by Michael with Bill Bottrell, and originally titled *Too Much Monkey Business*, recorded by Michael at Record One Studios and Westlake Studios in 1989.

First mentioned in 1991 in the British magazine *Revolution*, and cited by Michael in his court deposition in November 1993.

'Michael talked like it (*Monkey Business*) was purely fictional, a feeling, really, of poor southern country folk doing mischief to each other,' said Bottrell. 'I can't know if there was anything autobiographical about it, but I believe the title didn't help it get released, after not making the *DANGEROUS* album.'

Included on an ultra rare promo titled 'Promo Flight Only', of which only ten copies exist, given to Sony Executives on their way to Neverland from Europe in 1991, as a teaser for tracks under consideration for Michael's album, *DANGEROUS* – the promo also featured the still unreleased *Men In Black*.

Scheduled to be included on the expanded, special edition of *DANGEROUS*, issued in 2001, before the bonus CD was cancelled.

Surfaced on the internet in 2002 – no official release until it was included on Michael's box-set, *THE ULTIMATE COLLECTION*, issued in November 2004.

MOON IS WALKING, THE

Closing theme song to Michael's 1988 film, *Moonwalker*, performed by Ladysmith Black Mambazo.

MOONWALKER MEDLEY

Medley of 'retrospective' hits and clips featured as a montage in Michael's film, *Moonwalker*.

Songs featured: *Music And Me, I Want You Back, ABC, The Love You Save, 2-4-6-8, Who's Lovin' You, Ben, Dancing Machine, Blame It On The Boogie, Shake*

Your Body (Down To The Ground), Rock With You, Don't Stop 'Til You Get Enough, Can You Feel It, Human Nature, Beat It, Thriller, Billie Jean, State Of Shock, We Are The World, The Way You Make Me Feel, Dirty Diana and *Bad*.

Directed by Jerry Kramer, who also directed the *Man In The Mirror, Badder, Speed Demon, Leave Me Alone, Come Together* and *The Moon Is Walking* parts of the film.

MOOSE SONG, THE

Song Michael is reported to have sang while on a day trip with Lisa Marie Presley and her daughter Danielle, during lunch at a Moose Burger Café.

First four verses of the song written by Tom Payton around 1977, while he was involved in Revolutionary War Re-Enacting – as the song spread, numerous other verses were written and added, with Payton stating the song is in the public domain now.

MORE THAN YOU KNOW – AM I BLUE – FOR ONCE IN MY LIFE – TRY A LITTLE TENDERNESS

Medley of songs performed by guest, Sonny Bono, on the Jacksons' TV series in 1976 – Michael and his brothers sang the chorus.

MORNING GLOW

Song from the Broadway musical, *Pippin* – as well as a version by John Rubinstein & Chorus, Michael's version was included on the 1972 original cast recording album as a bonus track.

Included on Michael's album, *MUSIC & ME*, issued in April 1973 in the States and July 1973 in the UK.

Released as a single in the UK but failed to chart.

B-side of *With A Child's Heart* in the States.

MORPHINE

Written by Michael during the sessions for his HIS*TORY* album, but failed to make the final cut. First released as one of five new songs featured on his album, *BLOOD ON THE DANCE FLOOR*, issued in April 1997.

Sampled an audio clip from the 1980 film, *The Elephant Man*.

Re-titled *Just Say No* in some Far Eastern countries, which are especially strict when it comes to drugs and the law – the song, almost certainly, was inspired by Michael's dependency/addiction to prescribed drugs, around the time he wrote it.

MOTHER

Poem written by Michael – included in his book of poems and reflections, *Dancing The Dream*, published in 1992.

Edited version of the poem included in Katherine Jackson's autobiography, *My Family, The Jacksons*, published in 1990.

Registered with the US Copyright Office in June 1990, as *Mother Dear*.

MOVIE AND RAP

Excerpts of the Jackson 5's *I Want You Back* and *Never Can Say Goodbye*, and

Michael's *Got To Be There*, featured on the Jacksons album, *LIVE*, issued in November 1981.

MOVING VIOLATION

Title track of the last album released by the Jackson 5, whilst they were still a Motown act, issued in May 1975 in the States and July 1975 in the UK.

Performed by the Jackson 5 on the TV shows, *Dinah* and *American Bandstand*, in the States in 1975, and by the Jacksons on their own TV series in 1977. The *American Bandstand* show, on 28th June, was the last time Jermaine performed with the Jackson 5.

Also known by the title, *It's A Moving Violation*.

Sampled by a young Motown artist, Corey, on *All I Do* – featured on his debut album, *I'M JUST COREY*, issued in the States in 2002.

MTV MUSIC VIDEO AWARDS MEDLEY

Medley of hits Michael performed at the MTV Music Video Music Awards, staged at New York's Radio City Music Hall on 7th September 1995.

Featured songs: *Don't Stop 'Til You Get Enough*, *The Way You Make Me Feel*, *Jam*, *Scream*, *Beat It*, *Black Or White*, *Billie Jean*, *Dangerous* and *Smooth Criminal*.

Accompanied by Slash.

Michael also performed *Dangerous* and *You Are Not Alone*.

MUCH TOO SOON

Song Michael wrote circa 1981, and cited by him in his court deposition in November 1993 – remains unreleased.

Believed by some fans to be an early version of *Gone Too Soon* – however, as Michael didn't write *Gone Too Soon* this is unlikely.

MUSCLES

Song Michael wrote and produced for his long time friend, Diana Ross, and featured on her 1982 album, *SILK ELECTRIC*.

'I was coming back from England, after working on Paul McCartney's album, zooming along on Concorde,' said Michael, explaining how he wrote the song, 'and this song popped into my head. I said – hey, that's perfect for Diana! I didn't have a tape recorded or anything, so I had to suffer for like three hours. Soon as I got home, I whipped that baby on tape.'

Issued as a single in September 1982 in the States, and the following month in the UK – charted at no.4 on the R&B singles chart and no.10 on the Hot 100 in the States, and achieved no.15 in the UK.

Official Versions:
Album Version.
Edit.
Extended Mix.

Live version included on Diana's 1989 album, *GREATEST HITS LIVE*.

Cover versions recorded by the Weather Girls, for their 2005 album, *TOTALLY WILD*, and by Club 69 for their 1997 album, *STYLE*.

Sampled by Young Jeezy on *The Inspiration (Follow Me)*, a track on his 2006 album, *THE INSPIRATION*.

MUSIC AND ME

Song Michael recorded for his solo album, *MUSIC & ME*, issued in April 1973 in the States and July 1973 in the UK.

Released as a single in May 1974 in the UK – failed to chart (no USA release).

Live performance by the Jacksons, at a concert in Mexico in 1976, omitted from the home video, *The Jacksons In Concert*, released in 1981 in the UK (no USA release).

Album re-packaged, minus *Doggin' Around*, and reissued in the UK in 1993 – this album was originally issued in the States in 1985, as *MOTOWN LEGENDS*.

MUSIC'S TAKIN' OVER

Song the Jacksons recorded for their album, *GOIN' PLACES*, issued in October 1977.

Released as a single in March 1978 in the UK – failed to chart (no USA release).

MY CHERIE AMOUR

Stevie Wonder cover featured on the Jackson 5's debut album, *DIANA ROSS PRESENTS THE JACKSON 5*, issued in December 1969 in the States and March 1970 in the UK – lead vocals by Jermaine.

Featured on the 'Farmer Jackson' episode of the Jackson 5 cartoon series in 1971.

Stevie Wonder's original recording peaked at no.4 on both American charts and in the UK in 1969.

MY FAVOURITE THINGS

Song from *The Sound Of Music* the Jackson 5 recorded a version of for their *CHRISTMAS ALBUM* circa 1970, but which failed to make the final track listing – remains unreleased.

Hit version:
Herb Alpert – no.45 on the Hot 100 in the States in 1969.

MY GIRL

Temptations classic, written by Smokey Robinson, the Jackson 5 performed to win the City Wide Talent Show at Roosevelt High School in 1965.

Performed, in the early days, with Jermaine singing lead – before Michael took over as the Jackson 5's lead vocalist.

Pre-Motown recording by the Jackson 5 first heard in 1993, when it featured on a Japanese release, *BIG BOY*; later the same year, included on *THE JACKSON*

FIVE FEATURING MICHAEL JACKSON, issued on the Stardust label in the UK/Europe.

Recorded by Michael for his solo album, *BEN*, issued in August 1972 in the States and December 1972 in the UK.

B-side of *Morning Glow* in the UK.

Title of a cassette-only compilation released in the States in 1989.

Hit versions:
Temptations – no.1 on both American charts, and no.43 in the UK, in 1965.
Otis Redding – no.11 in the UK in 1965.
Bobby Vee (medley) – no.35 on the Hot 100 in the States in 1968.
Eddie Floyd – no.43 on the R&B singles chart in the States in 1970.
Amii Stewart & Johnny Bristol (medley) – no.76 on the R&B singles chart in 1980.
Whispers – no.26 in the UK in 1980.
Daryl Hall & John Oates with David Ruffin & Eddie Kendrick (medley) – no.20 on the Hot 100 and no.40 on the R&B singles chart in 1985.
Suave – no.3 on the R&B singles chart and no.20 on the Hot 100 in 1988.
Temptations (reissue) – no.2 in the UK in 1992.

MY LITTLE BABY

Song the Jackson 5 recorded for their album, *MAYBE TOMORROW*, issued in April 1971 in the States and October 1971 in the UK.

B-side of *Doctor My Eyes* in the UK.

Featured in the 'Bongo, Baby Bongo' episode of the Jackson 5 cartoon series in 1971.

MYSTERY

Track written by Rod Temperton – turned down by Michael, then later recorded by Manhattan Transfer, for their 1983 album, *BODIES AND SOULS*. Released as a single in the States – peaked at no.80 on the R&B singles chart, but failed to make the Hot 100.

Cover version by Anita Baker for her 1986 album, *RAPTURE*.

Also the name of a peach flavoured isotonic drink Michael launched in 1996, and of a fan magazine dedicated to Michael.

NEITHER ONE OF US (WANTS TO BE THE FIRST TO SAY GOODBYE)

Gladys Knight & the Pips hit the Jackson 5 recorded a version of – remains unreleased.

Hit versions:
Gladys Knight & the Pips – no.1 on the R&B singles chart and no.2 on the Hot 100 in the States, and no.31 in the UK, in 1973.
David Sanborn – no.56 on the R&B singles chart in 1983.

NELSON MANDELA SONG, THE

Song – title unknown – Michael revealed he was writing for the then President Nelson Mandela, when he attended the

South Africa leader's 78th birthday party in 1996.

'I was working on it last night,' Michael told reporters. 'This is a wonderful, lovely man – I love Nelson Mandela very much.'

In 1987, it was reported Michael was working on a similar song with George Michael, as a proposed duet – however, it was shelved after the idea leaked.

NEVER CAN SAY GOODBYE

Song written by Clifton Davis originally intended for the Supremes, recorded by the Jackson 5 for their album, *MAYBE TOMORROW*, issued in April 1971 in the States and October 1971 in the UK.

Hit no.1 on the R&B singles chart and no.2 on the Hot 100 in the States, but stalled at no.33 in the UK.

Early American copies released with special picture sleeve carrying the inscription: 'See The Jackson 5 on ABC-TV Special *Diana!* April 18th 1971'.

Promoted on the group's TV special and *The Flip Wilson Show* in the States in 1971, and performed by the Jackson 5 on *The Tonight Show* (hosted by Johnny Carson) in April 1974, and by the Jacksons on their own TV series in 1976.

Featured in 'The Rare Pearl' episode of the new Jackson 5 cartoon series in 1971.

Cited by Michael, in the early 1970s, as one of his three favourite songs he had recorded for Motown, along with *ABC* and *I'll Be There*.

Live version featured on the Michael/Jackson 5's *LIVE!* album, issued in September 1988 in the UK (no USA release). All songs on the album were recorded at a concert on 30th April 1973, at the Osaka Koseinenkin Hall in Japan. Also included on the limited edition CD, *IN JAPAN!*, released by Hip-O Select in 2004 – only 5,000 copies pressed.

Live performance by the Jacksons, at a concert in Mexico in 1976, included on the home video, *The Jacksons In Concert*, released in 1981 in the UK (no USA release).

Performed live by the Jacksons at *Motown 25: Yesterday, Today, Forever*, staged in the Pasadena Civic Auditorium on 25th March 1983.

Original mono version included on the 4CD box-set, *HITSVILLE USA: THE MOTOWN SINGLES 1959-1971*, issued in the States in 1992.

Adult solo version by Michael scheduled to feature on the shelved compilation, *DECADE 1980-1990* – remains unreleased.

Sub-title of the Jackson 5 compilation, *MOTOWN LEGENDS*, released in 1993.

Osawa 3000 Remix, as included on the Japanese album, *SOUL SOURCE – JACKSON 5 REMIXES* in 2000, featured extended vocals.

Vocal and instrumental version featured on the karaoke album, *MOTOWN ORIGINAL ARTISTS, VOL.3: MY GIRL*, released in September 2003.

Other hit versions:

Isaac Hayes – no.5 on the R&B singles chart and no.22 on the Hot 100 in the States in 1971.

Gloria Gaynor – no.2 in the UK, and no.9 on the Hot 100 and no.34 on the R&B singles chart in the States, in 1974.

Communards – no.4 in the UK, and no.51 on the Hot 100 in the States, in 1987.

Yazz – no.61 in the UK in 1997.

Numerous other versions, including:

Johnny Mathis – for his album, *YOU'VE GOT A FRIEND*, in 1971.

Dennis Coffey & The Detroit Guitar Band – for the album, *GOIN' FOR MYSELF*, in 1972.

California Raisins – for the album, *SWEET, DELICIOUS & MARVELLOUS*, in 1990.

Dennis Brown – for his album, *MILK & HONEY*, in 1996.

Sheena Easton – for her album, *FABULOUS*, in 2001.

Andy Williams – for his album, *I THINK I LOVE THE 70s*, in 2001.

Supremes – for their album, *70s ANTHOLOGY*, in 2002.

Vanessa Williams – for her album, *EVER LASTING LOVE*, in 2005.

Temptations – for their album, *REFLECTIONS*, in 2006.

Sampled by Lil' J. Xavier on the track *I Love My Music*, from his 2006 album, *YOUNG PRINCE OF THA SOUTH*.

Posthumous hit: no.72 in the USA (Hot Digital Songs).

NEVER DREAMED YOU'D LEAVE IN SUMMER

Performed by Stevie Wonder at the 'A Celebration of the Life of Michael Jackson 1958-2009' memorial concert at the Staples Center on 7th July 2009.

NEVER HAD A DREAM COME TRUE

Stevie Wonder hit, recorded by the Jackson 5 for their *ABC* album, issued in May 1970 in the States and August 1970 in the UK.

Stevie's original – from his album *SIGNED, SEALED & DELIVERED* – charted at no.11 on the R&B singles chart and no.26 on the Hot 100 in the States, and no.6 in the UK, in 1970.

NEVERLAND LANDING

Song Michael cited he had written in his court deposition in November 1993 – remains unreleased.

Version, supposedly by Michael, surfaced on the internet – this was actually a song titled *Wayfaring Stranger*, performed live by Tom Fox.

NIGHT TIME LOVER

Written by Michael with sister La Toya, and recorded by La Toya for her debut, self-titled album in 1980, with Michael producing and singing backing vocals.

Originally titled *Fire Is The Feeling*, and written with Donna Summer in mind.

Issued as a single in the States in August 1980 – peaked at no.59 on the R&B singles chart, but failed to make the Hot 100 (no UK release).

Hit version wasn't the original version, which Michael and La Toya's mother preferred.

La Toya was shocked by Michael's professionalism in the studio. 'I expected we'd joke around,' she said, and he addressed her, 'over the studio intercom, as if talking to a complete stranger.'

Original recording remains unreleased.

NIGHTLINE / NITE-LINE

Originally written by Glen Ballard circa 1982, for Michael's *THRILLER* album, but failed to make the final track listing.

'When I found out it wasn't going to be on there, I just said, I'll be on the next one,' said Ballard in 1999. 'And the truth is, I got on the next two, which cumulatively sold over 50 million. It turned out to be good karma. I feel that if *Nite-Line* had been on *THRILLER*, I would never have written *Man In The Mirror*, which is an infinitely better song, and one of the best in my catalogue.'

Recorded as *Nightline* by the Pointer Sisters, for the original 1983 version of their album, *BREAK OUT* (on the second pressing *Nightline* was replaced by *I'm So Excited*); B-side of the group's hit single, *Automatic*.

Recorded by Ellen Foley for her album, *ANOTHER BREATH*, and by Randy Crawford for her album of the same title, both in 1983.

Known to have been recorded by Michael – no official release.

NIGHTMARE OF EDGAR ALAN POE, THE

Song believed to be written by Michael Jackson with Walter Afanasieff, circa 2000, for the shelved independently financed movie, *The Nightmare Of Edgar Alan Poe*, that Michael was slated to star in – remains unreleased.

Also known by the title, *Edgar Alan Poe*.

NO FRIEND OF MINE

Song by rapper Tempamental, featuring prominent backing vocals by Michael, made available in late 2006 on Tempamental's 'myspace' web page – originally titled, *Gangsta*.

NO NEWS IS GOOD NEWS

Song the Jackson 5 worked on with Stevie Wonder circa 1974 – remains unreleased.

NOBODY

Song the Jackson 5 recorded for their debut album, *DIANA ROSS PRESENTS THE JACKSON 5*, issued in December 1969 in the States and March 1970 in the UK.

Featured on the 'Groovatron' episode of the Jackson 5 cartoon series in 1971.

NOBODY

Track Ne-Yo (real name Shaffer Chimere Smith) recorded for his 2008 album, *YEAR OF THE GENTLEMAN*, as a tribute to Michael.

Ne-Yo played the track, and the album's lead single *Closer*, for Michael and got a positive response. 'He told me that he likes the way I do Michael Jackson,' said Ne-Yo. 'I asked him what he meant by that, and he said, "When you do that, it doesn't feel like you're trying to copy me or trying to be me – it feels like you're complimenting me." And that's what I'm doing. It means the workd that he liked it.'

Ne-Yo confirmed he'd been working with Michael on his long awaited follow-up to *INVINCIBLE*, but declined to elaborate, or name song titles. 'I thought they were kidding!' he admitted, when Michael called him. 'I don't really do the starstruck thing, but when I met him and stood in front of the man, I was shaking like a leaf!'

NONA

Song written by Jackie Jackson, for the Jacksons *VICTORY* album – failed to make the final selection.

Written about Sophia Loren, who was one of Jackie's favourite actresses. 'Her vibes are sexy,' he said. 'She is like a perfect dream – the song is about her, and the feeling she gives off.'

NOT MY LOVER

Michael's original title for *Billie Jean*.

See also: *Billie Jean*.

NOTHIN' ELSE

One of several songs written by Pharrell Williams and submitted for Michael's HIS*TORY* and *INVINCIBLE* albums, which were later recorded by Justin Timberlake, for his debut album *JUSTIFIED*, released in 2002.

NOTHIN (THAT COMPARES 2 U)

Song featured on the Jacksons album, *2300 JACKSON STREET*, issued in June 1989.

Michael wasn't involved with recording this song.

NYMPHETTE LOVER

Song written by Michael in 1981, and registered with the United States Copyright Office in November 1984 – remains unreleased.

ODE TO SORROW

Song written by Michael in 1977, and registered with the United States Copyright Office in November 1984 – remains unreleased.

OFF THE WALL

Title track of Michael's first solo album for CBS/Epic, released in August 1979.

Written by Rod Temperton in 1978, who submitted three songs for the album. 'The one I thought would be their choice was *Off The Wall*,' he said. 'I tried to find out about Michael's character. I knew he liked Charlie Chaplin, and I thought *Off The Wall* would be a nice thing for Michael.'

Charted at no.5 on the R&B singles chart and no.10 on the Hot 100 in the States, and no.7 in the UK.

Official Versions:
Album Version.
7" Remix
Remix
Junior Vasquez Mix.

Remixed for the 7" single released in the States in 1980 – this version also appeared on the Japanese 3" CD single (b/w *She's Out Of My Life*), 1992's *TOUR SOUVENIR* singles pack issued in the UK, and the 2005 compilation, *THE ESSENTIAL*.

Junior Vasquez Mix featured additional vocals not found on the original album version.

Live concert performance screened by Nippon TV in Japan.

Live version, recorded at a concert at Madison Square Garden in September 1981, featured on the Jacksons album, *LIVE*, issued in November 1981.

Sampled by:
Wisdome on *Off The Wall (Enjoy Yourself)* – charted at no.33 in the UK in 2000.
Mariah Carey on *I'm That Chick*, from her 2008 album, *E=MC²*.

Posthumous hit: no.20 in Holland, no.51 in USA (Hot Digital Songs) and no.73 in UK.

OFF THE WALL MEDLEY

Medley of *Rock With You*, *Off The Wall* and *Don't Stop 'Til You Get Enough*, from Michael's *OFF THE WALL* album.

Performed by Michael on his *History World Tour* – Auckland concert screened on TV in New Zealand.

OH, HOW HAPPY

Song the Jackson 5 recorded for their *THIRD ALBUM*, issued in September 1970 in the States and February 1971 in the UK.

Featured on the promo film Michael and his brothers shot, to be played at concert venues during their 1970 dates.

One of six tracks from the album included on *Third Album EP*, released with a picture sleeve in the States in 1970.

Featured in the 'Wizard Of Soul' episode of the Jackson 5 cartoon series in 1971.

OH, I'VE BEEN BLESS'D

Song the Jackson 5 originally recorded for their debut album, *DIANA ROSS PRESENTS THE JACKSON 5*, but that failed to make the final cut.

Remained unreleased until it was included on *BOOGIE*, issued in North America only in January 1979, then quickly withdrawn.

ON THE LINE

Written by Babyface, and originally recorded by Michael for the Spike Lee movie, *Get On The Bus*, but not featured on the soundtrack album.

Lead track of a 3-track 'minimax' CD single, released as part of the 'Deluxe Collector Box Set' of *Ghosts* in December 1997 in the UK (no USA release). Box set also included Michael's *Ghosts* mini-movie on home video and his *BLOOD ON THE DANCE FLOOR* album on CD.

Full length version included on Michael's *THE ULTIMATE COLLECTION* box-set, issued in November 2004.

Featured on a Columbia Pictures *Get On The Bus* promo CD, along with *Over A Million Strong* by the Neville Brothers, as a potential Oscar nominee, for Best Original Song.

Official Versions:
Minimax Version.
Full Length Version.
Film Version.

ON THE WALL

Ditty performed by the Jacksons at the beginning of each episode of their *The Jacksons* TV series in 1976, to introduce their sisters, Rebbie, La Toya and Janet, as well as their special guest star, who would sign their name 'on the wall'.

ONCE WE WERE THERE

Poem written by Michael – included in his book of poems and reflections, *Dancing The Dream*, published in 1992.

ONE BAD APPLE

Song Berry Gordy rejected for the Jackson 5, only for it to be recorded in classic Jackson 5 style by the Osmonds – who held the no.1 spot on the Hot 100 in the States while the Jackson 5's own *Mama's Pearl* stalled at no.2.

'Did you know that record was ours at first?' Michael once asked. 'But Motown turned it down. George Jackson is the producer, and he came to Motown with it, and Motown turned it down because we were in a funky, strong track-type bag, with good melody. George's song was good, but too easy going – we were striving for something much stronger. So he went and gave it to the Osmonds. They sang it, and it was a smash – number one!'

ONE DAY I'LL MARRY YOU

Song recorded by the Jackson 5 between 1970-73, but unreleased until it was included on the album *BOOGIE*, issued in North America in January 1979 then quickly withdrawn.

ONE DAY IN YOUR LIFE

Song Michael recorded for his *FOREVER, MICHAEL* album, issued in January 1975 in the States and March 1975 in the UK.

Released as a single in the UK in April 1975 – failed to chart (no USA release).

Performed by Michael on *Dinah* and *Soul Train* in the States.

Live performance by the Jacksons, at a concert in Mexico in 1976, omitted from the home video, *The Jacksons In Concert*, released in 1981 in the UK (no USA release).

Re-activated by Motown in 1981, to cash-in on the success of Michael's *OFF THE WALL* album – stormed to no.1 in Australia, Belgium, Holland, Ireland, South Africa, the UK and Zimbabwe.

BPI Gold Disc.

Achieved at no.42 on the R&B singles chart and no.55 on the Hot 100 in the States, where oldies rarely chart at all.

Green vinyl 7" single released in Ireland.

Album of the same title also released in 1981, credited to Michael, despite including tracks from two Jackson 5 albums, *GET IT TOGETHER* and *JOYFUL JUKEBOX MUSIC*.

Planned performance, as a duet with Whitney Houston, at Michael's first 30th Anniversary concert at Madison Square Garden, New York, on 7th September 2001, cancelled at the last minute as Whitney was sick backstage.

ONE AND ONLY

Medley of Jackson hits by Mainline released in 2008, featured: *Billie Jean, Thriller (Intro), Don't Stop 'Til You Get Enough, Shake Your Body (Down To The Ground), Blame It On The Boogie, Rock With You, Off The Wall, Thriller & Billie Jean.*

ONE (FINALE)

Song the Jacksons performed on their TV series in 1976, with their special guest, Georgia Engel.

Originally featured in the 1975 Broadway musical, *A Chorus Line*.

ONE MORE CHANCE

Track featured on the Jackson 5's *ABC* album, issued in May 1970 in the States and August 1970 in the UK.

B-side of *I'll Be There*.

Released as a single, with picture sleeve, in Japan only.

Featured in the 'Rasho Jackson' episode of the Jackson 5 cartoon series in 1971.

Cover version by The One charted at no.31 in the UK in 1997.

ONE MORE CHANCE

Written by Randy Jackson, and recorded by the Jacksons *VICTORY* album, issued in July 1984 – Randy also played every instrument on the track, except the fairlight.

One of sister Janet's favourite songs of all time – she even recorded a cover version, which featured on various formats of her 1993 single, *If*.

ONE MORE CHANCE

Only new song – written by R. Kelly in 2001 – featured on Michael's compilation album, *NUMBER ONES*, issued in November 2003. Initially considered for Michael's *INVINCIBLE* album, but failed to make the final track listing.

Charted at no.5 in the UK, and at no.40 on the R&B singles chart and no.83 on the Hot 100 in the States, in 2003.

Official Versions:
Album Version.
Paul Oakenfold Urban Mix.
Ford Remix.
R. Kelly Remix.
Metro Remix.
Ron G. Club Mix.
Night & Day Remix.
Ron G. Rhythmic Mix.
Night & Day R&B Remix.
Slang Remix.
Paul Oakenfold Mix.
Slang Electro Remix.
Paul Oakenfold Pop Mix.

Promo short film shot in Las Vagas and edited, but not completed or released by Sony, as a result of fresh allegations made against Michael (he was, of course, acquitted on all charges). A promo featuring a montage of concert footage was used to promote the song.

OOH BABY, BABY

Smokey Robinson & The Miracles cover the Jackson 5 recorded – remains unreleased.

Also know by the title, *Ooo (Oooh) Baby Baby*.

Hit versions:
Miracles – no.4 on the R&B singles chart and no.16 on the Hot 100 in the States in 1965.
Five Stairsteps – no. 34 on the R&B singles chart and no.63 on the Hot 100 in 1967.
Shalamar – no.59 on the R&B singles chart in 1977.

Linda Ronstadt – no.7 on the Hot 100 and no.77 on the R&B singles chart in 1979.

Romeo – no.67 on the R&B singles chart in 1987.

Zapp – no.18 on the R&B singles chart in 1989.

OOH, I'D LOVE TO BE WITH YOU

Song the Jackson 5 recorded for their *SKYWRITER* album, issued in March 1973 in the States and July 1973 in the UK.

Mistakenly included on the Michael/Jackson 5 box set, *SOULSATION!*, in place of the 'Rare & Unreleased' track *You're The Only One* – which remains unreleased.

OPENING SHORT

Part of the score for Michael's *Ghosts* short film, composed by Nicholas Pike – made partially available by Pike on his website in August 2009.

OPUS ONE

Song the Jackson 5 performed, along with *Up The Lazy River*, with the Mills Brothers, on the *One More Time* TV special in the States in January 1974.
Also performed, as part of a 'Salute to the Vocal Groups' medley with *Bei Mir Bist Du Schon*, *Yakety Yak*, *Stop! In The Name Of Love*, an untitled Jackson 5 ditty and *Dancing Machine*, on *The Carol Burnett Show* in the States in January 1975.

Performed by the Jacksons on their TV series in 1977.

PAIN, THE

Song written by Rodney Jerkins, Jay Harvey Mason and Shawn Stockman in 2000, for Michael's album, *INVINCIBLE* – left off the album and remains unreleased.

PAPA WAS A ROLLIN' STONE

Temptations hit the Jackson 5 often performed live in the early days, and are known to have recorded a studio version of – remains unreleased.

Live recording featured on Michael & The Jackson 5's *LIVE!* album, issued in the UK in September 1988 (no USA release). Recorded at the Jackson 5's concert at Osaka Koseinenkin Hall, Japan, on 30th April 1973, with Jermaine singing lead. Album also known by the title, *IN JAPAN!* – included on the limited edition CD, *IN JAPAN!*, released by Hip-O Select in 2004 – only 5,000 copies pressed.

Comedy skit performed by Michael and his brothers, dressed in inflated costumes as the 'Ton-Tations', on their TV series in 1976.

Live performance by the Jacksons at a concert in Mexico in 1976, with Marlon singing lead, included on the home video, *The Jacksons In Concert*, released in 1981 in the UK (no USA release).

Other covers versions include one by Bill Wolfer (who appeared on *THRILLER*), with backing vocals by Michael, Oren, Julia & Maxine Waters, featured on Bill's 1980 album, *WOLF*.

Hit versions:
Temptations – no.1 on the Hot 100 and no.5 on the R&B singles chart in the States in 1972, and no.14 in the UK in 1973.
Undisputed Truth – no.24 on the R&B singles chart and no.63 on the Hot 100 in 1972.
Bill 'Wolf' Wolfer – no.47 on the R&B singles chart and no.55 on the Hot 100 in 1983.
Temptations (remix) – no.31 in the UK in 1987.
Was (Not Was) – no.12 in the UK and no.60 on the R&B singles chart in the States in1990.
George Michael (medley) – no.1 in the UK (as part of the *Five Live EP*), no.69 on the Hot 100 and no.88 on the R&B singles chart in 1993.

PENNY ARCADE

Song recorded by the Jackson 5 between 1970-73, but unreleased until it featured on the album *BOOGIE*, issued in North America in January 1979 but quickly withdrawn.

PEOPLE GOT TO BE FREE

One of seven demos Michael and his brothers are known to have recorded at their Encino home circa 1975-76, with Bobby Taylor, prior to signing with CBS/Epic.

Originally recorded by the Rascals for their 1969 album, *FREEDOM SUITE* –

as a single, hit no.1 on the Hot 100 and no.14 on the R&B singles chart in the States.

See also: *Piece Of The Pie, Rock In A Hard Place, We're All Alone*.

PEOPLE HAVE TO MAKE SOME KIND OF JOKE

Song Michael cited he had written, probably with one of his brothers, in his court deposition in November 1993 – remains unreleased.

PEOPLE MAKE THE WORLD GO 'ROUND

Stylistics cover Michael recorded for his solo album, *BEN*, issued in August 1972 in the States and December 1972 in the UK.

The Stylistics took the song to no.6 on the R&B singles chart and no.25 on the Hot 100 in the States in 1972.

Version by the Ramsey Lewis Trio included on Motown's various artist album, *SAVE THE CHILDREN*, released in 1974 in the States.

PEOPLE OF THE WORLD

Second song written and produced by Michael in 1998, for the Japanese children's choir, J-Friends – Japanese lyrics by Yasushi Okimoto.

Issued as a single in Japan (no USA or UK release); instrumental version also issued.

PEPSI GENERATION

Jingle based on *Billie Jean*, which accompanied Michael's first sponsorship deal with Pepsi Cola in 1984.

Pepsi campaign 'The Choice of a New Generation' launched at the Lincoln Center, New York, on 26th February 1984. Launch attended by 1,600 people; the programme for the evening came with a 7" promo of Michael's re-working of *Billie Jean*, for the advertising campaign.

Released as a promo 7" single, with 20 page booklet, in the States in 1984.

Included on the album, *GREAT COLA COMMERCIALS VOLUME 2*, issued in the States in September 1998 – short and long versions featured.

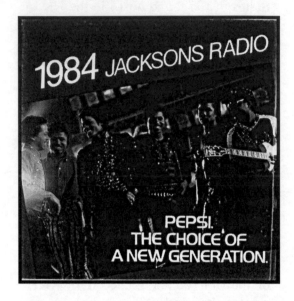

Spoof of Michael's commercial by Bryan Stoller, titled 'The Shadow of Michael Jackson', released in 1984.

PETALS

Song featured on the Jackson 5's *MAYBE TOMORROW* album, released in April 1971 in the States and October 1971 in the UK.
Featured in the 'Jackson Street USA' episode of the Jackson 5 cartoon series in 1971.

PETER PAN

Michael's favourite fictional character – he could be seen singing 'I'm Peter Pan' on the *Michael Jackson – Unauthorised* home video, released in the UK in 1992.

Song mentioned by Michael in the home video *UNAUTHORISED*, released in the early 1990s, and also on *THE MICHAEL JACKSON INTERVIEW* CD released by Baktabak in 1993 – remains unreleased.

Speaking to *Life* magazine in 1997, Michael said he was planning a film version of *Peter Pan*, after he claimed he had been misled by Steven Spielberg, who he believed had reneged on an offer to cast him in the film *Hook* six years ago.

'I worked on the script, writing songs, for six months,' said Michael, 'and they let me down. I was so heartbroken. Steven Spielberg admitted later it was a mistake. I was torn. He put me through a lot. We're friends now, though.'

PHONE MESSAGES

Track recorded in 2000 by girl group, So Plush – produced by Rodney 'Darkchild' Jerkins.

As well as name-checking him, Michael was one of a number of artists – others included Brandy, Tyrese and Toni Braxton – whose voice was sampled, leaving a message on Jerkins's answerphone, to ask about the new So Plush album.

The album has never been officially released, but *Phone Messages* was included on a So Plush promo sampler (Sony ESK 16166).

PICK UP THE PIECES

Song the Jacksons performed on their TV series in 1976, as a medley with *That's The Way (I Like It)*, with special guest, Dom DeLuise.

No.1 on the Hot 100 in the States, and no.6 in the UK, for the Average White Band in 1975.

PIECE OF THE PIE

One of seven demos Michael and his brothers are known to have recorded at their Encino home circa 1975-76, with Bobby Taylor, prior to signing with CBS/Epic.

See also: *People Got To Be Free, Rock In A Hard Place, We're All Alone*.

PLANET EARTH / PLANET EARTH, I LOVE YOU

Song considered by Michael for his album, *DANGEROUS* – remains unreleased.

Lyrics published as a poem in the booklet that accompanied *DANGEROUS*, and featured in Michael's 1992 book of poems and reflections, *Dancing The Dream*. According to the book, this was 'recorded on album, *DANGEROUS*'.

Copyright registered as *Planet Earth, I Love You*.

PLAY IT UP

Written by Jackie, Jermaine, Randy & Tito Jackson with Attala Zane Giles, and recorded by the Jacksons for their 1989 album, *2300 JACKSON STREET*.

Michael wasn't one of the Jacksons who recorded this song.

PLEASE COME BACK TO ME

Song recorded by the Jacksons, and included as a bonus track on one of the 12" singles of *2300 Jackson Street*, issued in August 1989.

Michael wasn't involved with the recording of this song.

POLITICAL SONG FOR MICHAEL JACKSON TO SING

Song recorded by Minutemen, for their 1984 album, *DOUBLE NICKELS ON THE DIME*.

'To sing, to sing – that's the most important part,' said the Minutemen's Mike Watt, 'because I did want him (Michael) to sing it. He never called.'

POP

Hit song featured on N'Sync's album, *CELEBRITY*, released in 2001.

Performed by N'Sync at the MTV Video Awards in September 2001, where they were joined on stage by Michael, who body-popped along to the song's beat.

POWER

Song written by Jackie Jackson, and recorded by the Jacksons for their 1984

album, *VICTORY* – failed to make the final selection and remains unreleased.

'It's about people coming together,' said Jackie, 'to make the world a better place.'

Version recorded by Tramaine Hawkins for her 1987 album, *FREEDOM*.

PRESSURE

Song written by Rodney Jerkins, LaShawn Daniels, Fred Jerkins III and Jay Harvey Mason, for Michael's album, *INVINCIBLE* – didn't make the final track listing and remains unreleased.

Song with the same titled listed as featuring on Riley's unreleased 2001 album, *BLACK ROCK* – may or may not be a recording of the same song.

PRICE OF FAME

Song slated to appear on Michael's 1987 album *BAD*, and to be the theme for his new Pepsi Cola commercial, but it failed to make the album and was replaced by *Bad* on the commercial – remains unreleased.

Price Of Fame: Pepsi registered with the United States Copyright Office in March 1987.

PRIDE AND JOY

Song included on the Jackson 5 album, *JOYFUL JUKEBOX MUSIC*, issued in October 1976 in the States and December 1976 in the UK – originally recorded during the *GET IT TOGETHER* sessions.

Made its CD bow in 1995, on the 4CD box-set, *SOULSATION!*

Originally recorded by Marvin Gaye – he took the song to no.2 on the R&B singles chart and no.10 on the Hot 100 in the States in 1963.

PRIVACY

Written by Michael with Rodney Jerkins, Fred Jerkins III, LaShawn Daniels and Bernard Bell.

Featuring on Michael's album, *INVINCIBLE*, issued in October 2001.

PRIVATE AFFAIR

Song included on the Jackson album, *2300 JACKSON STREET*, issued in June 1989. Promo singles known to exist, but full release cancelled.

Michael wasn't involved with recording this song.

PURPLE SNOWFLAKES

Song the Jackson 5 recorded for their *CHRISTMAS ALBUM* circa 1970, but which failed to make the final track listing – remains unreleased.

Originally recorded by Marvin Gaye for his festive Motown album.

PUSH ME AWAY

Written by Michael with brothers Jackie, Marlon, Randy and Tito, and recorded and produced by the Jackson for their album, *DESTINY*, issued in December 1978.

Performed solo by Michael on *American Bandstand*, and with his brothers on *Soul Train*, in the States in 1979.

B-side of Michael's *She's Out Of My Life* in the UK.

PUTTING ON THE RITZ

Snippet of a song Michael performed as part of a three song medley – also including *Gotta Dance* and *They Can't Take That Away From Me* – on *The Jacksons* TV series in 1976.

P.Y.T. (PRETTY YOUNG THING)

Song originally written by Michael with Greg Phillinganes, but totally re-done to a more up-tempo beat by Quincy Jones and James Ingram. Recorded by Michael for his album, *THRILLER*, issued in December 1982.

Sisters Janet and La Toya were the 'pretty young things' singing 'na na na' back at Michael.

Charted at no.10 on the Hot 100 and no.46 on the R&B singles chart in the States, and no.11 in the UK.

Michael's sixth Top 10 hit on the Hot 100 from six releases from *THRILLER* – a new record from one album.

Official Versions:
Album Version.
Demo Version.

Replayed sample of the album version by Michael sampled by Monica on her single, *All Eyez On Me*, with the original aad-libs by Michael at the end – charted at no.32 on the R&B singles chart and no.69 on the Hot 100 in the States in 2002. 'We used vocals from the song that didn't make the *THRILLER* album,' said Rodney Jerkins. 'He (Michael) had more vocals and ad-libs that were never heard, and we used the ones that were not heard.'

New vocals ('get it on, get it on'), recorded by Michael circa 2000, included on the track featured on the Japanese version of Monica's album, which was cancelled in the States/Europe.

Chorus sampled by rapper Memphis Bleek, on *I Wanna Love U* – sung by Donell Jones. Featured on Bleek's 2003 album, *M.A.D.E.*.

Demo, recorded between April and October 1982, included on Michael's box-set, *THE ULTIMATE COLLECTION*, issued in November 2004.

Sampled by Kanye West featuring T-Pain on *Good Life*, a track on West's 2007 album, *GRADUATION* – peaked at no.3 on the R&B singles chart and no.7 on the Hot 100 in the States, and no.23 in the UK.

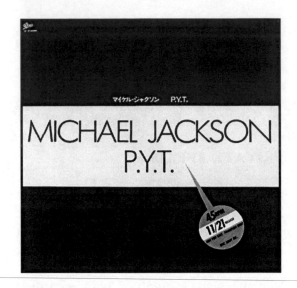

Posthumous hit: no.14 in the USA (Hot Digital Songs) and no.98 in UK.

P.Y.T. (PRETTY YOUNG THING) 2008

Re-working of the above song included on the album, *THRILLER 25*, released in February 2008.

This new remix featured old vocals by Michael, taken from the original demo, as released on *THE ULTIMATE COLLECTION* box-set.

QUANTUM LEAP

Poem written by Michael – included in

his book of poems and reflections, *Dancing The Dream*, published in 1992.

QUICKSAND

Martha Reeves & the Vandellas hit the Jackson 5 recorded a version of – remains unreleased.

Martha & the Vandellas took the song to no.8 on both the Hot 100 and R&B singles chart in the States in 1964.

RAPPIN' WITH THE JACKSON 5

Question and answer interview with the Jackson 5, released on a 7" single in 1971 – available to buy via *TcB!* magazine in the States only.

During the interview, Michael revealed:

- His favourite Jackson 5 songs were *Can I See You In The Morning* and *I'll Be There*. 'I like *I'll Be There* because it's slow,' he said, 'and it's our first time

doing a slow song, and I like slow songs.'

- His favourite groups were the Supremes and Four Tops, and he liked Diana Ross.

- While staying in hotels, he liked to order hamburgers, bacon sandwiches, barbeque – soul food!

- He liked James Bond.

- His first helicopter trip scared him.

- He loved swimming.

- He liked girls with 'pretty big eyes'.

Longer version (15:55) featured on Episode 15: *The Jackson 5 – Brotherly Love*, one of a series of Motown 50 podcasts – no official release. Tracks featured on the podcast: *ABC/The Love You Save/I'll Be There/I Want You Back/Never Can Say Goodbye/Mama's Pearl/I'll Bet You*.

REACH IN

Song the Jackson 5 recorded for their *THIRD ALBUM*, issued in September 1970 in the States and February 1971 in the States.

One of six songs from the album included on *Third Album EP*, released with a picture sleeve in the States in 1970.

Featured in the 'CinderJackson' episode of the Jackson 5 cartoon series in 1971.

REACH OUT AND TOUCH (SOMEBODY'S HAND)

Song included in a book of Jackson 5 sheet music, published by Motown in 1970 – if the group recorded the song it remains unreleased.

Debut solo hit for Diana Ross, charting in 1970 at no.7 on the R&B singles chart and no.20 on the Hot 100 in the States, and no.33 in the UK.

Performed by Michael, his brothers and a host of Motown artists (past and present) performed, with *Someday We'll Be Together*, to welcome Motown founder, Berry Gordy, on stage at *Motown 25: Yesterday, Today, Forever* – celebration held at the Pasadena Civic Auditorium on 25th March 1983.

Performed by Jason Weaver and Holly Robinson in the TV mini-series, *The Jacksons: An American Dream*, in 1992 – failed to make the accompanying soundtrack album.

Last hit for Diana Ross & the Supremes, before Diana went solo – hit no.1 on both the Hot 100 and R&B singles chart in the States, and no.13 in the UK, in 1969.

REACH OUT I'LL BE THERE

Four Tops classic recorded by the Jackson 5 for their debut album, *DIANA ROSS PRESENTS THE JACKSON 5*, in 1970 – listed as the final track on early copies of the album released in the States, but didn't actually appear on the album.

Remained unreleased until it was one of 19 'Rare & Unreleased' tracks on the fourth CD of the Michael/Jackson 5 box-set, *SOULSATION!*, issued in June 1995 in the States and July 1995 in the UK.

Hit versions:
Four Tops – no.1 on both American charts, and in the UK, in 1966.
Merrilee Rush – no.79 on the Hot 100 in 1968.
Diana Ross – no.17 on the R&B singles chart and no.29 on the Hot 100 in 1971.
Gloria Gaynor – no.56 on the R&B singles chart and no.60 on the Hot 100, and no.14 in the UK, in 1975.
Four Tops (remix) – no.11 in the UK in 1988.
Michael Bolton – no.37 in the UK in 1993.

READY OR NOT (HERE I COME)

Originally titled: *Ready Or Not Here I Come (Can't Hide From Your Love)*.

Song featured on the Jackson 5's *THIRD ALBUM*, issued in September 1970 in the States and February 1971 in the UK.

Featured on the promo film Michael and his brothers shot, to be played at concert venues during their 1970 dates.

One of six tracks from the album included on *Third Album EP*, released with a picture sleeve in the States in 1970.

Featured in the 'Jackson Island' episode of the Jackson 5 cartoon series in 1971.

Originally recorded by the Delfonics, for their 1969 album, *SOUND OF SEXY SOUL*.

Hit versions:
Delfonics – no.14 on the R&B singles chart and no.35 on the Hot 100 in the States in 1969, and no.41 in the UK in 1971.
Fugees – no.1 in the UK in 1996.
Course – no.5 in the UK in 1997.

'What I picked up on Michael Jackson, because I study people when I watch them,' observed Wyclef Jean of the Fugees, 'is the way that he counts his rhythm with his feet and his neck at the same time is crazy… so he's hearing multiple things at once – and I don't know anybody who does that.'

RED EYE

Song Michael cited he had written in his court deposition in November 1993 – remains unreleased.

REFLECTIONS

Diana Ross & Supremes cover the Jackson 5 recorded for their album, *GET IT TOGETHER*, issued in September 1973 and November 1993 in the UK.

Original recording achieved no.2 on the Hot 100 and no.4 on the R&B singles chart in the States, and no.5 in the UK, in 1967.

REMEMBER THE TIME

Written by Michael with Teddy Riley and Bernard Bell, and recorded for his album, *DANGEROUS*, issued in November 1991.

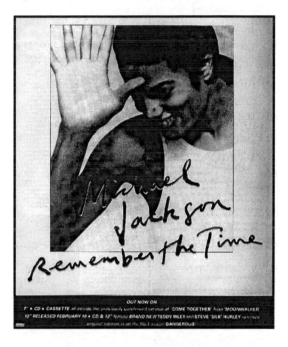

Riley told the *Los Angeles Times* in November 1996, he wrote the song after Michael told him about falling in love with Debbie Rowe: 'I don't know why he didn't marry her the first time around.'

'One of the biggest things Michael really surprised me with on *DANGEROUS* was his vocal delivery on *Remember The Time*,' said Riley. 'That really blew me away… that was the sound I was thinking of for the album… I'd describe that sound as, really, like the New Jack Swing sound,'

Several demo versions known to exist – no official release.

Second single lifted from the album – dedicated to Diana Ross.

Hit no.1 on the R&B singles chart and no.3 on the Hot 100 in the States, and no.3 in the UK. Also achieved no.1 in New Zealand.

RIAA Gold Record (USA million seller).

Official Versions:
Album Version.
New Jack Main Mix.
A Cappella.
New Jack Mix.
Bonus Beats.
New Jack Radio Mix.
Silky Soul Dub.
Silky Soul 7".
Silky Soul 12"
12" Main Mix.
Mo-Mo's Instrumental.
E-Smoove's Late Nite Mix.
Maurice's Underground Mix.
New Jack Main Jazz.
E-Smoove's Late Nite Dub.
7" Main Mix.

Promo 9 minutes short film, directed by John Singleton, had an Egyptian theme. Co-starred Eddie Murphy as Pharaoh Ramses, supermodel Iman as Queen Nefertiti and pro-basketball star Magic Johnson as a slave. Michael shared his first on-screen kiss with Iman (Mrs David Bowie).

American Music Award: Favourite Soul/R&B Single, Male.

Performed by Michael at the *Soul Train* Awards in March 1993 – Michael twisted

his ankle during rehearsals the day before, so sang from a wheelchair.

Twelfth of Michael's 20 *'Visionary – The Video Singles'* reissues, with the music on one side of a Dual Disc and the accompanying short film on the other side. Issued in May 2006 in the UK – charted at no.22.

Performed in October 2007, as a tribute to Teddy Riley, at the VH1 Hip Hop Honours in New York by Doug E. Fresh, Kool Moe Dee, Ne-Yo, Keyshia Cole and T-Pain.

Master tapes from Teddy Riley's Future Records studio surfaced on eBay, featured several unreleased mixes:

Remember The Time Vocal Runs #3
  (3 tracks)
Remember The Time Remix #4

Remember The Time Vocal Runs #6
  (5 tracks)
Remember The Time 2 Tracks Ruff Before
  Tape #43
Remember The Time #9 (6 Tracks)
  (7" Mix/12" Mix/Acapella/Bonus
  Beats/Club Mix/New Jack Mix)
Remember The Time Quiet Store
  2 Tracks #18
Remember The Time Mix 1 #29
Remember The Time Mix 6 #37
Remember The Time #50 (4 Tracks)
  (New Jack Radio Mix/New Jack
  Jazz/Bonus Beats 2/Bonus Beats 3)
Remember The Time Mix 7
Remember The Time Michael Jackson
  Goofing on Remix with T.R. (Teddy
  Riley) & B.B. (Bernard Belle)
Remember The Time M.J. Runs #34
  (8 tracks)
Remember The Time #43 Reff Before
  Tape (2 tracks)

Performed live by Teddy Riley in New York in December 2008; snippet screened during a 'Meet, Great & Speak' with Riley.

Posthumous hit: no.35 in the USA (Hot Digital Songs), no.40 in Australia and no.67 in Germany.

RESCUE SPACE MICHAEL

Space Channel 5 game related track featured on the Japanese release, *SPACE CHANNEL 5 PART 2* – sleeve artwork also featured a drawing of Michael.

RIDE WITH ME (IT'S NOT WORTH IT)

Largely instrumental track Rodney Jerkins included on his 2006 album, *VERSATILITY* – aimed at up-and-coming artists, to help them create their own songs by adding lyrics.

Contained a sample of Michael on backing vocals, as did Brandy's *It's Not Worth It*, but not a new Michael Jackson song as some fans believe.

RIVER RIPPLE

Song about unconditional love Michael was in the process of writing, with the help of his three children, at the time of his passing – inspired by his children, who moved him to tears by singing like 'Earth Angels'.

Michael had wanted to perform the ballad, with an African choir, during his final dates at London's O2 Arena.

ROCK IN A HARD PLACE

One of seven demos Michael and his brothers are known to have recorded at their Encino home circa 1975-76, with Bobby Taylor, prior to signing with CBS/Epic.

See also: *People Got To Be Free*, *Piece Of The Pie*, *We're All Alone*.

ROCK MY WORLD

Original title of Michael's hit, *You Rock My World*.

See also: *You Rock My World*.

ROCK WITH YOU

Song Michael recorded for his album, *OFF THE WALL*, issued in August 1979 – written by Rod Temperton.

'*Rock With You* was a rhythm section I'd had before,' said Temperton. 'I thought I'd go with this one because he's (Michael's) good at handling very melodic things.'

Hit no.1 on both American charts, and achieved no.7 in the UK.

RIAA Gold Record (USA million seller).

No.9 best selling single of 1980 in the States.

Promo short film, directed by Bruce Gowers, premiered in November 1979.

Re-arranged version, slightly jazzed-up (jazzy guitar and added handclaps),

dating from early 1980, was included on new pressings of *OFF THE WALL*, replacing the original recording. Original version featured on the original CD pressing issued in Japan, and on some later Japanese pressings.

Official Versions:
Album Version.
Single Version.
Frankie's Favourite Club Mix.
Frankie's Favourite Club Mix Radio Edit.
Masters At Work Remix.

Masters At Work Remix and Frankie's Favourite Club Mix featured unreleased vocals and ad-libs not heard on the album version, as the remixers were given access to the master tapes of the song, which included additional vocals.

Performed by Michael on two TV specials in the States in 1980, the charity event *Because We Care* and *diana!* – on the latter, he sang the song twice, solo and as a duet with Diana Ross.

Live version, recorded at a concert at Madison Square Garden in September 1981, featured on the Jacksons album, *LIVE*, issued in November 1981. This version was released on the B-side of Michael's UK single, *Wanna Be Startin' Somethin'*.

Live performance part of a concert screened by Nippon TV in Japan.

Sampled by De La Soul, along with numerous other songs, on a 37 second track, *Cool Breeze On The Rocks*, for their 1989 album, *3 FEET HIGH AND RISING*.

Sampled by So Plush on *He Loves Me*, from their 2000 album, *ADVANCE* – the album, produced by Rodney Jerkins, was never officially released, but a snippet of *He Loves Me* (which has similarities to *You Rock My World*) was included on a So Plush promo sampler.

Cover version recorded by Brandy, for Quincy Jones's 1995 album, *Q'S JOOK JOINT*.

Cover version by D'Influence charted at no.30 in the UK in 1998. Versions also recorded by Chuck Loeb and Dashhamer.

Demo version included on the second acetate version of the expanded, special edition of Michael's *OFF THE WALL* album in 2001 – later withdrawn.

Third of Michael's 20 *'Visionary – The Video Singles'* reissues, with the music on one side of a Dual Disc and the accompanying short film on the other side. Issued in February 2006 in the UK – charted at no.15.

Original album version included on the French Collector's Edition of the 2008 compilation, *KING OF POP*.
Posthumous hit: no.17 in the USA (Hot Digital Songs), no.25 in Holland, no.36 in Australia and no.54 in UK.

ROCKIN' ROBIN

Song Michael recorded for his debut album, *GOT TO BE THERE*, issued in January 1972 in the States and May 1972 in the UK.

Not intended to be released as a single, until DJs across the States began playing it – prompting Motown to issue it as the follow-up to *Got To Be There*.

Charted at no.2 on both American charts, and just one place lower in the UK.

Featured on the 'Who's Hoozis' episode of the new Jackson 5 cartoon series in 1971.

Promoted in the States by Michael on *American Bandstand* and *The Dating Game*, where Michael's chosen date was Latany Simmons.

Performed, during the group's European Tour in November 1972, by the Jackson 5 in the UK, on *Top Of The Pops* and at the Royal Command Performance – the latter was attended by HM The Queen Mother.

Performed by the Jacksons on their own TV series in 1977.

Live performance by the Jacksons, at a concert in Mexico in 1976, included on the home video, *The Jacksons In Concert*, released in 1981 in the UK (no USA release).

Sub-title of Michael's solo compilation, *MOTOWN LEGENDS*, released in 1993.

Hit versions:
Bobby Day (original version) – no.1 on the R&B singles chart and no.2 on the Hot 100 in the States, and no.29 in the UK, in 1958.
Rivieras – no.96 on the Hot 100 in 1964.
Lolly – no.10 in the UK in 1999.

ROLL THE DICE

Song written by Rod Temperton, which Michael worked on with Temperton and Quincy Jones during the *THRILLER* sessions – registered with ASCAP.

Cited as *Rolling The Dice* by Michael in his court deposition in November 1993 – remains unreleased.

RUDOLF THE RED-NOSED REINDEER

Festive favourite the Jackson 5 recorded for their *CHRISTMAS ALBUM*, issued in October 1970 in the States and December 1970 in the UK.

Hit versions:
Cadillacs – no.11 on the R&B singles chart in the States in 1956.
Gene Autry – no.70 on the Hot 100 in the States in 1957.
David Seville & The Chipmonks – no.21 on the Hot 100 in 1960.
Melodeers – no.71 on the Hot 100 in 1960.
Temptations – no.3 on the Christmas singles chart in the States in 1968.

RUNAROUND SUE

Dion hit Michael performed, with a whole host of other artists, as the finale

for the Grammy Awards in early 1988 –
he could be seen at the back, dancing and
fooling around with Whitney Houston.

Michael owns the copyright to many of
Dion's recordings, including *Runaround
Sue*.

Dion took the song to no.1 in the States,
and to no.11 in the UK, in 1961.

RYAN WHITE

Poem written by Michael – included in
his book of poems and reflections,
Dancing The Dream, published in 1992.

See also: *Gone Too Soon*.

SAD SOUVENIRS

Four Tops track the Jackson 5 recorded a
version of – remains unreleased.

The Four Tops recording featured on
their eponymous debut album, released in
1965.

SALUTE TO THE VOCAL GROUPS MEDLEY

Medley the Jackson 5 performed on *The
Carol Burnett Show* in the States in
January 1975, featuring: *Opus One*, *Bei
Mir Bist Du Schon*, *Yakety Yak*, *Stop! In
The Name Of Love*, *Dancing Machine*
and *The Beat Goes On*.

Jackie, Jermaine and Randy performed
Bei Mir Bist Du Schon, while Michael,
Marlon and Tito did likewise on *Stop! In
The Name Of Love*. Between *Stop! In The
Name Of Love* and *Dancing Machine*,

Michael and his brothers sang a short,
untitled ditty about themselves.

Sonny & Cher's hit *The Beat Goes On*
was performed by young Randy and even
younger Janet Jackson; the Jackson 5 and
hostess Carol Burnett joined their siblings
on stage towards the end of their
performance.

SANTA CLAUS IS COMIN' TO TOWN

Another festive favourite the Jackson 5
recorded for their *CHRISTMAS ALBUM*,
issued in October 1970 in the States and
December 1970 in the UK.

Released as a single in the States in 1970
– at this time, Christmas singles were
excluded from the mainstream Billboard
charts. Hit no.1 on the special Christmas
Singles chart in 1970 and 1971, and
peaked at no.9 in 1973.

Charted at no.43 in the UK in December
1972.

One of four tracks from *CHRISTMAS
ALBUM* featured on the *Merry Christmas
From Michael Jackson With the Jackson
5 EP*, issued in the UK in 1987 – charted
at no.91.

Other hit versions:
4 Seasons – no.23 on the Hot 100 in the
  States in 1962.
Carpenters – no.37 in the UK in 1975.
Bruce Springsteen – no.1 on the
  Christmas singles chart in the States,
  and no.9 in the UK, in 1985.
Bjorn Again – no.55 in the UK in 1992.

SATISFY

Written by James Harris III and Terry Lewis, and recorded by Mariah Carey – with Michael singing backing vocals – for her album, *CHARMBRACELET*, issued in 2002. Failed to make the final track listing and remains unreleased.

SATURDAY NITE AT THE MOVIES

Song the Jackson 5 often performed in concert in the pre-Motown days.

Remained unreleased until it appeared on the album, *BEGINNING YEARS 1967-1968*, issued in 1989.

Charted at no.18 on both the Hot 100 and R&B singles chart in the States in 1964, and at no.3 in the UK in 1972, for the Drifters.

SAVE ME

Song recorded by ex-Traffic guitarist Dave Mason, with Michael on backing vocals, for his solo album, *OLD CREST ON A NEW WAVE*, issued in June 1980 in the UK and July 1980 in the States.

'I was in one studio and he (Michael) was across the hall,' said Mason. 'I had that song (*Save Me*), and thought it would be cool if someone could sing that really high part, so I thought I'd just go over there and ask him. I thought he'd just do this harmony part and he ended up doing this whole great thing and putting his own spin on it.'

Charted at no.70 on the R&B singles chart and no.71 on the Hot 100 in the States – not a hit in the UK.

SAVE THE BONES FOR HENRY JONES

Songs, from the mid-1940s, performed by Janet, La Toya and Rebbie Jackson, with their brothers on backing vocals/instrumentation, on *The Jacksons* TV series in 1976.

SAVED BY THE BELL

Song Michael cited he had written with brother Jermaine in his court deposition in November 1993 – remains unreleased.

SAY SAY SAY

Written by Michael with Paul McCartney, and recorded as a duet for Paul's album, *PIPES OF PEACE*, issued in November 1983.

Michael and Paul first worked on the song, and their second duet on the Paul's album, *The Man*, during McCartney's 'War' sessions between May and September 1981. Song completed at Abbey Road studios in February 1983.

Produced by Beatles producer, George Martin, who said of Michael: 'He actually does radiate an aura when he comes into the studio, there's no question about it. He's not a musician in the sense that Paul is... but he does know what he wants in music and he has very firm ideas.'

Hit no.1 on the Hot 100, and no.2 on the R&B singles chart, in the States – achieved no.2 in the UK. Also no.1 in Canada, Finland, Italy and Norway.

Owed its success in the UK to *Top Of The Pops*, as it was outside the Top 10 and slipping down the chart, when a snippet of the promo video was featured as part of the American chart count down. Full length screenings on Noel Edmond's popular *Late, Late Breakfast Show* and Channel 4's cult music show *The Tube* followed, catapulting the single to no.2.

Official Versions:
Album Version.
Instrumental.
Jellybean Remix.
Jellybean Remix Instrumental.

Michael's third single of 1983 to top the Hot 100, following *Billie Jean* and *Beat It*

– together, they logged 16 weeks in pole position.

RIAA Platinum Record (USA two million seller).

Humorous short firm directed by Bob Giraldi, featured 'Mac & Jack' as travelling salesmen-cum-vaudeville artists, and co-starred Paul's wife Linda, Michael's sister La Toya, and Mr T (from *The A Team*). Filmed in Los Alamos, California, between 4th and 7th October 1983 – premiered in the UK on Channel 4's *The Tube* music programme on 28th October.

Short film given its first commercial release in November 2007, when it was included as the second track on the first DVD of Paul McCartney's 3-DVD set, *THE McCARTNEY YEARS*.

Cover version by Dutch group Hi-Tack, titled *Say Say Say (Waiting For U)*, hit no.4 in the UK in early 2006. Hi-Tack were also involved with BeatFreakz's hit remake of Rockwell's *Somebody's Watching Me*, also in 2006.

SCARED OF THE MOON

Song written by Michael with B. Kohan circa 1985, which Michael re-worked as a contender for what became his *BAD* album, and cited in his court deposition in November 1993.

Demo version released on Michael's *THE ULTIMATE COLLECTION* box-set, issued in November 2004

SCREAM

Song written by Michael with sister Janet, James Harris III and Terry Lewis, and recorded as a duet with Janet for his album, HIS*TORY*, issued in June 1995.

'Sometimes, the only thing you can do is scream,' said Michael. 'You just wanna let it all out! People should listen, and decide for themselves.'

Lead single from the album, debuted at no.5 on the Hot 100 in the States – the highest ever new entry (the previous record holder, *Let It Be* by the Beatles, made its bow at no.6). Also achieved no.2 on the R&B singles chart and no.3 in the UK.

UK chart rules, which stated only three formats could be counted towards a chart placing, meant one 7" and two 12" singles charted independently, achieving no.43.

No.1 in Finland, Hungary, Italy, New Zealand, Spain and Zimbabwe.

Official Versions:
Album Version.
Naughty Main Mix No Rap.
Clean Album Version.
Naughty Radio Edit w/Rap.
Classic Club Mix.
Naughty Radio No Rap.
Dave 'Jam' Hall's Extended Urban
  Remix.
Naughty Pretty-Pella.
Dave 'Jam' Hall's Urban Remix Edit.
Pressurized Dub Pt.1.
Def Radio Mix.
Pressurized Dub Pt.2.

D.M. R&B Extended Mix.
Naughty Acappella.
Scream Louder – Flyte Tyme Remix.
Naughty Main Mix.
Single Edit.
Single Edit #2.
Scream Louder – Flyte Tyme
  Instrumental.

Futuristic short film, filmed in black and white, directed by Mark Romanek and cost $6 million – the most expensive music video ever. Premiered on 14th June 1995 on ABC-TV in the States.

'My favourite thing about doing the *Scream* video,' said Michael, 'was it was really an excuse to work with my sister, Janet.'

Grammy Award: Best Music Video, Short Form.

Billboard Music Video Award: Video of the Year – Pop/Rock.

Short film nominated for 11 MTV Music Video Awards, but won only three: Best Dance Video, Best Choreography and Best Art Direction.

Song chosen to open Michael's *His*tory World Tour concerts.

Live performances screened in Germany and New Zealand, as part of concerts in Michael's *His*tory World Tour.

Posthumous hit: no.70 in the USA (Hot Digital Songs) & UK.

SCRUB, THE

Song written by Tito's music teacher, Shirley Cartman, who confirmed in her book, *A Teacher Remembers The Jacksons*, the Jackson 5 recorded it and other songs before they signed for Steel-Town Records – all remain unreleased.

SEASONS GREETING FROM MOTOWN RECORDS

Green label promo 7" single, sent by Motown to American radio stations and record distributors in 1973. Featured short messages from 14 Motown artists, including Michael, Jackie, Jermaine and Tito Jackson (but not Marlon).

Re-titled *Christmas Greetings From Michael Jackson*, when included on the 1995 festive compilation, *MOTOWN CHRISTMAS CAROL*.

SEDUCTION

Song written by Michael with Shelby Lee Myrick III in 2000, originally for his album, *INVINCIBLE* – failed to make the album and remains unreleased.

SEEING VOICES

Song written about 'signing' by Michael with veterans Ray Charles and Sidney Fine (who wrote *Lady* for Disney's *Lady & The Tramp* in 1955) in 2000, and recorded by Michael and Ray Charles, with Ray's choir on backing vocals. Mentioned during the recording of Michael's *INVINCIBLE* album, but failed to make the final track listing – remains unreleased.

SEÑORITA

One of several songs written by Pharrell Williams and submitted for Michael's *HISTORY* and *INVINCIBLE* albums, which were later recorded by Justin Timberlake, for his debut album *JUSTIFIED*, released in 2002.

SERIOUS EFFECT

Song written by Michael with Bryan Loren, and recorded by Michael, with rap by LL Cool J.

Scheduled to be included on the cancelled bonus CD of the expanded, special edition reissue of *DANGEROUS* in 2001. Demo version by Michael solo known to exist.

Surfaced on the internet in 2002 – no official release.

SEVEN BRIGHT NEW STARS

Song co-written by Michael with sister La Toya, father Joseph, Lionel Richie and Danny de Pree Brack – registered with the BMI but remains unreleased.

SEVEN DIGITS

Song written by Michael with Bryan Loren – one of 20-25 songs they worked on together, for a new album, but ultimately not one of them appeared on *DANGEROUS* – remains unreleased.

SHAKE ME, WAKE ME (WHEN IT'S OVER)

Four Tops hit the Jackson 5 recorded a version of – remains unreleased.

The Four Tops took the song to no.5 on the R&B singles chart and no.18 on the Hot 100 in the States in 1966.

SHAKE THAT MONEY MAKER

Performed by the Jackson 5 on *American Bandstand* in February 1970, as part of a medley, with *Zip-A-Dee Doo-Dah* and *There Was A Time*.

SHAKE YOUR BODY (DOWN TO THE GROUND)

Written by Michael with brother Randy, and recorded by the Jacksons for their album, *DESTINY*, issued in December 1978.

Started life as a piano piece Randy came up with – he wrote the original melody and lyrics.

Early demo, recorded in 1978 and titled *Shake A Body*, included on Michael's box-set, *THE ULTIMATE COLLECTION*, issued in November 2004.

Song the Jacksons wanted to release as the lead single from *DESTINY*, but their record company insisted on issuing *Blame It On The Boogie* first instead.

Second single from the album – charted at no.3 on the R&B singles chart and no.7 on the Hot 100 in the States, and no.4 in the UK. Single version only half the length of the album version – extended Special Disco Remix also released.

RIAA Platinum Record (2 million copies in USA).

Performed by the Jacksons on *American Bandstand, Soul Train, The ABBA Special: Disco In The Snow Part II* (filmed in Switzerland), and their own *Midnight Special* – estranged brother Jermaine re-joined his brothers for the latter. *Soul Train* performance included on the home video, *Soul Searching*,

released by Video Gems in the States in 1984 – also included *Think Happy* and Jermaine's *Let's Get Serious*.

Special Disco Version released on the 1979 Japanese promo album, *THE LEADER OF 80'S POP*, credited to Michael Jackson & The Jacksons.

Transluscent peach/yellow 12" maxi single released in Colombia.

Official Versions:
Album Version.
Single Edit.
Special Disco Version (*aka* John Luongo Disco Mix.
Demo Version (*Shake A Body*).

40 minute version performed by the Jacksons at the Doobie Brothers 10th Anniversary Celebration, staged at the Friars Club in Beverley Hills, in early 1980 – Michael and his brothers were joined on stage by Michael McDonald, Lenny Loggins, Pablo Cruise and Bonnie Raitt.

Live version, recorded at a concert at Madison Square Garden in September 1981, featured on the Jacksons album, *LIVE*, issued in November 1981.

Performed by Michael during his Bad World Tour – one such concert screened on Nippon TV in Japan.

Performed by the Jacksons during the *Michael Jackson: 30th Anniversary Celebration, The Solo Years* concerts, staged at New York's Madison Square Garden on 7th and 10th September 2001.

John Luongo Disco Mix included as a bonus track on the remastered version of *DESTINY*, released in 2008.

Hit cover versions:
Full Intention – no.34 in the UK in 1997.
N-Trance (adaptation) – no.37 in the UK in 2000.

Sampled by Shaggy on *Dance & Shout* – no.19 in the UK in 2001, and registered at no.104 on the 'bubbling under' section of the Hot 100 in the States in 2000.

'Michael was really great in giving me the sample,' said Shaggy, 'because a lot of people tried to obtain a sample and couldn't get it... there were people that I've used sample with that just wanted everything. He basically was, like – hey, go ahead, man!'

Sampled by N-Trance on *Shake Ya Body* – charted at no.37 in the UK in 2000.

Posthumous hit: no.50 in the USA (Hot Digital Songs).

SHE

Song featured on the Jacksons album, *2300 JACKSON STREET*, issued in June 1989.

Michael wasn't involved with recording this track.

SHE DRIVES ME WILD

Written by Michael with Teddy Riley, and recorded for his album, *DANGEROUS*, issued in November 1991.

Percussion used on the track included motor sounds, trucks, cars screeching, motor bikes revving, car horns – and samples of Michael's tiger! Rap by Wrecks-N-Effect (*a.k.a.* Aqil Davidson & Markell Riley).

'My biggest memory from that recording was that we used all car sounds as drum sounds and it came out perfectly,' said Riley. 'I didn't go out into the field and record actual car sounds and take it back to the studio, I had a sample CD that was really cool. It wasn't something I'd done before; it was the first time I went for unusual sounds in the place of drums.'

B-side of *Heal The World*.

Master tapes from Teddy Riley's Future Records studio surfaced on eBay, featured several unreleased mixes:

She Drives Me Wild New Vocoder Part #11
She Drives Me Wild Teddy's New Stuff #12

She Drives Me Wild New Parts #25
She Drives Me Wild No lead Vocals #33
She Drives Me Wild #51

SHE GOT IT

Song written by Michael with bryan Loren – slated to appear on the bonus CD of the expanded, special edition reissue of *DANGEROUS* in 2001, before it was cancelled.

Snippets leaked on the internet in 2005, and some fans are known to have the full version of the song – no official release.

SHE SAY 'WANT'

Song the Jackson 5 recorded for Motown – remains unreleased.

Also known to fans by the title, 'She Say What'.

SHE WAS LOVING ME

Song Michael wrote circa 2000 with Mark C. Rooney for his album, *INVINCIBLE*, but failed to make the final track listing – remains unreleased.

SHE'LL BE COMING ROUND THE MOUNTAIN

Song Michael's mother Katherine has confirmed in her autobiography, *My Family, The Jacksons*, she used to sing with her young children in the late 1950s/early 1960s, in Gary, Indiana,

SHE'S A RHYTHM CHILD

Song featured on the Jackson 5's *DANCING MACHINE* album, issued in September 1974 in the States and November 1974 in the UK.

SHE'S GOOD

Song the Jackson 5 recorded for their album, *MAYBE TOMORROW*, issued in April 1971 in the States and October 1971 in the UK.

B-side of *Never Can Say Goodbye* – this version featured Jermaine singing solo, while the album version saw Jermaine backed by the Jackson 5.

Featured in the 'Jackson Street USA' episode of the Jackson 5 cartoon series in 1971.

SHE'S NOT A GIRL

Song Michael cited he had written in his court deposition in November 1993 – remains unreleased.

SHE'S OUT OF MY LIFE

Song Michael recorded for his solo album, *OFF THE WALL*, issued in August 1979.

Written by Tom Bahler – originally in E Flat, whereas Michael sang the song in E. Bahler couldn't play the song in E, 'so, Quincy recorded me playing it in my key and we made a tape for the pianist who was going to record it for the album. He took it home and studied it, in order to grasp whatever magic there was in my performance. When I listen to the record, I think – God, it sounds just like me!'

Inspired by Karen Carpenter, who broke up with Bahler, after she discovered he had fathered a child with another woman.

SHE'S OUT OF MY LIFE

Words and Music by TOM BAHLER

Michael Jackson

'How Michael could do such a sincere interpretation of the lyric has always puzzled me, because I know it was an experience he had never even thought about,' said Bruce Swedien. 'It's a very mature emotion, and Michael was only nineteen years old at the time... When we were recording Michael's vocal, he broke down and cried at the end of every take. We recorded about six or seven takes. At the end of each take Michael was sobbing, actually crying. I know he was sincere, because when we finished the last take, Michael was too embarrassed to come in the control room. He just tippy-

toed out the back door of the studio, got in his car, and left the studio building. Quincy said to me, "Hey – that's supposed to be, leave it on there, leave it there".'

Promo short film directed by Bruce Gowers – a simple affair with Michael sitting on a stool and singing, ended in tears as well.

Fourth single from the album – charted at no.3 in the UK, and no.10 on the Hot 100 and no.42 on the R&B singles chart in the States, making *OFF THE WALL* the first solo album to produce four Top 10 singles on both sides of the Atlantic.

RIAA Gold Record (USA million seller).

Performed by Michael during his Bad World Tour – at each concert, one lucky girl was allowed up on stage, to dance with Michael as he sang the song to her.

Live version, recorded at a concert at Madison Square Garden in September 1981, featured on the Jacksons album, *LIVE*, issued in November 1981. This version appeared on the B-side of the Jacksons single, *Wait*, in the UK.

Live performance by Michael, at his Dangerous Tour concert in Bucharest, Romania, on 1st October 1992, featured on the DVD released as part of his box-set, *THE ULTIMATE COLLECTION*, issued in November 2004.

Different live performance screened as part of a concert televised by Nippon TV in Japan.

Cover versions include:
Willie Nelson, for his 1984 album, *CITY OF NEW ORLEANS*.
98°, for their 1998 album, *98° AND RISING*.
Ginuwine, for his 1999 album, *100% GINUWINE*.
Mya (re-titled *Man Of My Life*), for her 2000 album, *FEAR OF FLYING*.
Josh Groban, as a bonus track for his 2003 album, *CLOSER*.
Patti LaBelle (re-titled *He's Out Of My Life*), for her 2005 album, *CLASSIC MOMENTS*.

Planned performance, with Mariah Carey, at Michael's 'What More Can I Give?' concert in Seoul, South Korea on 25th June 1999, cancelled as Mariah arrived too late.

Performed by Marc Anthony during the *Michael Jackson: 30th Anniversary Celebration, The Solo Years* concerts, staged at New York's Madison Square Garden on 7th and 10th September 2001.

SHE'S TROUBLE

Song – known to many fans by the title *Trouble* – written by Terry Britten, Bill Livsey and Sue Shifrin, originally intended for Michael's album, *THRILLER*, but didn't make the final track listing.

Bootleg version known to exist, and a snippet leaked on the internet in 2008 as a part of compilation of *THRILLER* demos, which also featured *Slapstick*, *Starlight*, *Nightline*, *The Girl Is Mine* and *Baby Be Mine* – no official release.

Alternate demo featuring Michael, with different and incomplete lyrics, also exists.

Versions recorded by Scott Baio, for his 1983 album, *THE BOYS ARE OUT TONIGHT*, and by Musical Youth, for their 1983 album, *DIFFERENT STYLE*. Musical Youth's version was a hit in the States, peaking at no.25 on the R&B chart and no.65 on the Hot 100.

SHOO-BE-DOO-BE-DOO-DA-DAY

Stevie Wonder cover Michael recorded for his album, *BEN*, issued in August 1972 in the States and December 1972 in the UK.
Scheduled as the B-side of the planned follow-up to *Ben*, *Everybody's Somebody's Fool*, before it was surprisingly cancelled.

Sampled by Scanty Sandwich on *Because of You*, which rose to no.3 in the UK in January 2000.

Stevie Wonder's original version – from his 1968 album, *FOR ONCE IN MY LIFE* – topped the R&B singles chart, and achieved no.9 on the Hot 100, in 1968 – charted at no.46 in the UK.

SHORTNIN' BREAD

Song the Jackson 5 performed, as part of a medley with *Let It Be*, on the *Jim Nabors Show* in the States in September 1970.

Originally an Afro-American plantation song titled *La Manière Nègre*. Enjoyed a revival during the golden days of radio – made famous by Lawrence Tibbett, and later by Nelson Eddy. Shortnin' refers to all types of fat used in baking, e.g. butter, lard, margarine.

See also: *Let It Be – Shortnin' Bread*.

SHOUT

Written by Michael with Edward Riley, Claude Forbes, Roy Hamilton, Samuel Hoskins and Carmen Lampson, song originally scheduled to feature on the vinyl release of Michael's *INVINCIBLE* album in 2001 – cancelled at the last minute.

B-side of *Cry*, released in December 2001 in the UK (no USA release), and listed ahead of *Cry* and *Streetwalker* on the 12" single.

Version recorded by Backstreet boy, Nick Carter, for his debut solo album *NOW OR NEVER* in 2002, but failed to make the final selection. Bootleg versions of the Backstreet Boys performing the song in concert in 2002 have appeared on the internet.

Sampled by independent artist, Kameko, on *Down And Out* – a track featured on his debut album, issued in 2006.

SHOW YOU THE WAY TO GO

Song the Jackson recorded for their eponymous debut album, issued in November 1976.

First Jackson single to hit no.1 in the UK, where it was promoted twice on *Top Of The Pops*, with one performance taken from *The Jacksons* TV series. Also performed on the *Mike In Hollywood* show in the States, and during a Destiny Tour concert screened on BBC2 in the UK.

Single version featured slight alternate vocals. Charted at no.6 on the R&B singles chart and no.28 on the Hot 100 in the States.

Official Versions:
Album Version.
Single Edit.

Cover version by Danii Minogue (Kylie's sister) peaked at no.30 in the UK in 1992 – recorded for the charity album, *RUBY TRAX*.

Also covered by Men Of Vizion, for the *MONEY TRAIN* soundtrack and their debut album, *PERSONAL*, both released in 1996.

Sampled on the track *Party 2 Nite* by Ladae featuring Chubb Rock, from the 1996 album, *LADAE*.

SIEGFRIED & ROY

Written by Michael for illusionists Siegfried & Roy in 1989, two versions – vocal and instrumental – registered with the United States Copyright Office in January 1990 – remains unreleased.

Likely to be Michael's original title for *Mind Is The Magic*.

See also: *Mind Is The Magic*.

SIGNED, SEALED, DELIVERED I'M YOURS

Stevie Wonder classic the Jackson 5 recorded a version of – remains unreleased.

Hit versions:
Stevie Wonder – no.1 on the R&B singles chart and no.3 on the Hot 100 in the States, and no.15 in the UK, in 1970.

Peter Frampton – no.18 on the Hot 100 in 1977.
Boys Town Gang – no.50 in the UK in 1982.
Blue featuring Stevie Wonder & Angie Stone – no.11 in the UK in 2003.

Recorded by Jermaine Jackson for his 1981 album, *I LIKE YOUR STYLE*.

SILENT NIGHT

Festive favourite the Jackson 5 recorded for their *CHRISTMAS ALBUM* circa 1970, but which failed to make the final track listing – remains unreleased.

The song was written on Christmas Eve, 1818, by Father Joseph Mohr, the priest at a small church in Hallein, Austria – originally titled 'Song From Heaven'.

Best selling version recorded by Bing Crosby on 8th June 1942 (just ten days after he recorded *White Christmas*).

Other hit versions:
Mahalia Jackson – no.99 on the Hot 100 in the States in 1962.
Barbra Streisand – no.1 on the Christmas Singles chart in the States in 1966.
Temptations – no.7 on the Christmas Singles chart in 1969.
Dickies – no.47 in the UK in 1978.
Bros – no.2 in the UK in 1988.
Sinead O'Conner – no.60 in the UK in 1991.
Simon & Garfunkel (medley) – no.30 in the UK in 1991.

SILVER BELLS

Song the Jackson 5 recorded for their *CHRISTMAS ALBUM* circa 1970, but which failed to make the final track listing – remains unreleased.

Hit versions:
Bing Crosby & Carol Richards – no.78 on the Hot 100 in the States in 1957.
Al Martino – no.6 on the Christmas Singles chart in the States in 1964.
Earl Grant – no.3 on the Christmas Singles chart in 1966.

SINCE I LOST MY BABY

Temptations hit the Jackson 5 recorded a version of – remains unreleased.

Song also featured in the TV mini-series, *The Jacksons: An American Dream*, but not as performed by the Jackson 5.

Hit versions:
Temptations – no.4 on the R&B singles chart and no.17 on the Hot 100 in the States in 1965.
Luther Vandross – no.17 on the R&B singles chart in 1983.

SINCE YOU'VE BEEN GONE

Four Tops track the Jackson 5 recorded a version of – remains unreleased. The Four Tops recording featured on their 1965 album, *FOUR TOPS SECOND ALBUM*.

SING A SIMPLE SONG – CAN YOU REMEMBER

Medley the Jackson 5 performed on their first national TV appearance in the States, on 18th October 1969, on ABC-TV's *The Hollywood Palace Special*.

Included on the album, *MOTOWN AT THE HOLLYWOOD PALACE*, issued in the States in March 1970 (no UK release). The opening bar of the song was later used again on the Jackson 5's version of *Zip-A-Dee Doo-Dah*.

Sing A Simple Song, from their 1969 album *STAND!*, was a minor hit for Sly & The Family Stone on the Hot 100 in the States – it peaked at no.89 (as the flipside of the chart topping *Everyday People*).

See also: *Can You Remember*.

SINGLES DISCO MIX

Rare, and very early, megamix of some of Michael's tracks (solo and with the Jacksons), released as a promo 12" single in 1983 in the UK – changed hands among avid collectors for up to £500 in 1983-84.

Featured hits: *Billie Jean (Intro), Rock With You, Burn This Disco Out, Off The Wall, Don't Stop 'Til You Get Enough, Shake Your Body (Down To The Ground), Blame It On The Boogie, Thriller* and *Billie Jean*.

SISTER SUE

Song Michael cited he had written in his court deposition in November 1993 – remains unreleased.

SKINNY LEGS AND ALL

Song the Jackson 5 performed in the mid-to-late 1960s, on the Chitlin' Circuit. Young Michael used to slide under tables, and mischievously lift the ladies skirts, before scurrying away – the audience invariably reacted by throwing money on stage, resulting in Michael and his brothers having pockets brimming with cash by the end of the gig.

SKY IS THE LIMIT, THE

Song Michael cited he had written with brother Jermaine in his court deposition in November 1993 – remains unreleased.

SKYWRITER

Title track of a Jackson 5 album issued in March 1973 in the States and July 1973 in the UK.

Second single, released with a rare picture sleeve, lifted from the album in the UK (no USA release) – charted at no.25. Also released as a single in several continental European countries, including France, Germany and Portugal.

Special advertisement shot by the Jackson 5, to promote the *SKYWRITER* album.

Song used by the Jackson 5, to open their Las Vegas Shows in April 1974.

Reissued in the UK in August 1977, as the lead track on the 3-track EP, *Jukebox Gem*.

SLAPSTICK

Song written by Rod Temperton, which Michael worked on during the *THRILLER* sessions – an early demo version of *Hot Street*.

Snippet of demo version surfaced on the internet in 2008 – remains unreleased.

See also: *Hot Street*.

SLIPPED AWAY

Song Michael wrote with brother Marlon circa 1980 – failed to make the Jacksons album, *TRIUMPH*, and remains unreleased.

SMILE

Song recorded at the Hit Factory Studios, New York, by Michael on 29th March 1995, for his album, HIS*TORY*, issued in June 1995.

One of a small number of songs Michael recorded live (*Childhood* was another; both songs were recorded on the same day).

During recording, engineer Bruce Swedien thought it would be great if Michael sang live, with the orchestra. 'But of course, we didn't tell the players that,' said Swedien. 'We set him (Michael) up in a vocal booth off to the side. They (the orchestra) rehearsed a bit without vocals in, then during the first take Michael sang, and just about knocked them out of their chairs.'

Scheduled for release as a single in the UK/Europe and other countries (not including the USA), as the last single from *DANGEROUS*, in December 1997 – release cancelled, against Michael's wishes.

Promo copies with shortened version issued, some featuring a rare and highly sought after picture sleeve depicting Michael dressed as Charlie Chaplin.

Promo short film, including footage of Charlie Chaplin, believed to have been shot – remains unreleased.

Planned performance, on the German TV show *Wetten, Dass...?*, cancelled.

A Cappella snippet by Michael heard in his infamous interview with Martin Bashir, *Living With Michael Jackson*, first screened in the UK by ITV1 in February 2003.

Hit versions include:
Nat 'King' Cole – no.2 in the UK in 1954.
Tony Bennett – no.73 on the Hot 100 in the States in 1959.
Betty Everett & Jerry Butler – no.42 on both American charts in 1965.
Robert Downey, Jr. – no.68 in the UK in 1993.

Performed by Jermaine Jackson at the 'A Celebration of the Life of Michael Jackson 1958-2009' memorial concert at the Staples Center on 7th July 2009.

Posthumous hit: no.56 in Australia & USA (Hot Digital Songs), no.71 in Germany and no.74 in UK.

SMOOTH CRIMINAL

Song written by Michael, and recorded for his *BAD* album, issued in September 1987 – evolved from another of Michael's songs, *Chicago 1945*.

Opening heartbeat heard on the song was Michael's, recorded by Dr Eric Chevlan, and digitally processed in a synclavier.

Voice of the police chief who says, 'Everybody please leave the are right now!' by Bruce Swedien.

Seventh single lifted from the album – charted at no.2 on the R&B singles chart and no.7 on the Hot 100 in the States, and no.8 in the UK (where it gave Michael a record seventh Top 30 hit from one album).

No.1 in Belgium and Holland.

Official Versions:
Album Version.
Single Version.
Extended Dance Mix.
Extended Dance Mix Radio Edit.
Dance Mix Dub Version.
'Annie' Mix.
A Cappella.
Instrumental.

Featured in Michael's 'movie like no other', *Moonwalker*, which cost him an estimated $27 million, and premiered at the Cannes Film Festival in France on 18th May 1988.

Michael sang extra lines in the film version, compared with the album and single versions – it's believed these were part of the original studio version, but were taken out prior to the album's release (possibly to reduce the running time).

45 degree 'lean' in the short film achieved by using wires; in concert, Michael used an 'Anti-Gravity Illusion' device, to achieve the same effect.

Brit Award: Best Music Video of 1988.

People's Choice Awards: Favourite Music Video.

There are currently four alternate versions of the short film:

- Original *Moonwalker* version, as seen in the film.

- Edited *Moonwalker* version, as included on Michael's home video, Hist*ory On Film Volume II.*

- The Sped Up Video – as seen during the *Moonwalker* closing credits; this version was included on the *Visionary* reissue of *Smooth Criminal*.

- The Album Version – most commonly shown by music video stations; a version edited to be in-sync with the album version of the song.

Live performance by Michael, at his Dangerous Tour concert in Bucharest, Romania, on 1st October 1992, featured on the DVD released as part of his box-set, *THE ULTIMATE COLLECTION*, issued in November 2004.

Different live performances screened in Germany and New Zealand, as part of televised concerts.

Featured in the film, *American Pie 2* (2001).

Highly successful cover version by Los Angeles rockers, Alien Ant Farm, in 2001 which Michael approved: 'I fell in love with it,' he said. 'I heard it and gave it a triple A.' Promo video parodied several of Michael's short films. Single hit no.1 in Australia (for nine weeks), and charted at no.3 in the UK and no.23 on the Hot 100 in the States.

Dryden Mitchell, Alien Ant Farm's frontman, explained how the cover came about: 'We were playing a hometown show and Tye (Zamora, bassist) and Mike (Cosgrove, drummer) started playing it for three seconds, and a bunch of people in the crowd knew what it was. The next day, Mike went out and got the *BAD* tape, so I could figure out the lyrics and they could figure out the music. When we played it, we weren't proud of ourselves or anything, we were just like – this song is good, we like it!'

Opening sampled by Ashanti on the track, *Rescue*, from her eponymous album issued in 2002.

Ninth of Michael's 20 *'Visionary – The Video Singles'* reissues, with the music on one side of a Dual Disc and the accompanying short film on the other

side. Issued in April 2006 in the UK – charted at no.19.

Posthumous hit: no.12 in Sweden, Switzerland & USA (Hot Digital Songs), no.13 in UK, no.14 in Ireland, no.16 in Australia, no.22 in Holland, no.33 in Spain and no.38 in Germany.

SNIPPETS FROM 'THE JACKSONS: AN AMERICAN DREAM'

Snippets of songs featured on *THE JACKSONS: AN AMERICAN DREAM* TV soundtrack album, issued on the Boyz II Men CD single, *In The Still Of The Nite (I'll Remember)*.

Featured snippets: *Who's Lovin' You (Live)*, *Kansas City* (by Jason Weaver), *I'll Be There*, *I Wanna Be Where You Are* (by Jason Weaver), *Dancing Machine (Remix)*, *Jackson 5 Medley (I Want You Back/ABC (Live))*.

In The Still Of The Nite (I'll Remember) charted at no.3 on the Hot 100 and no.4 on the R&B singles chart in the States in 1992, and peaked at no.27 early the following year in the UK.

SO IN LOVE

Song Jermaine Jackson recorded, with the rest of the Jackson 5 on backing vocals, for his 1973 album, *COME INTO MY LIFE*.

SO SHY

Song Bill 'Wolf' Wolfer recorded, with Michael and the Waters Sisters (Oren,

Julia & Maxine) on backing vocals, for his 1982 album, *WOLF*.

SOLDIER'S ENTRANCE

Song Michael worked on circa 1999, with a view to recording it for his album, *INVINCIBLE* – remains unreleased.

SOME GIRLS WANT ME FOR THEIR LOVER

B-side of the Jackson 5's pre-Motown single *You Don't Have To Be Over Twenty One To Fall In Love*, issued in March 1971 in the States (no UK release) – A-side originally titled *We Don't Have To Be Over 21 (To Fall In Love)*.

Featured on the album, *GETTING TOGETHER WITH THE JACKSON 5*, also released in the States in 1971 (no UK release). Despite the title, the album only featured two songs by the Jackson 5.

Re-titled *Michael The Lover*, when included on the Jackson 5's album, *BEGINNING YEARS 1967-1968*, released in 1989.

It has been speculated *Some Girls Want Me For Their Lover* was actually recorded by Michael Rodgers, of the 'Ripples & Waves' fame, and not by Michael Jackson and his brothers – unconfirmed.

SOMEBODY'S WATCHING ME

Song Michael first heard at the Jackson family's Encino home in California, when Rockwell (*aka* Kennedy Gordy –

son of Motown founder and owner, Berry Gordy) played him the demo.

'I played him the tape and the single stuck out in his mind,' said Rockwell. 'He asked if he and Jermaine could do the backing vocals. Michael really wanted to do the song because he identified so much with its message. He often feels like a fish in a bowl – always being watched by people wanting a piece of him.'

Rockwell often used to stand in the wings when the Jackson 5 were on stage, and was seen as a young boy in the 1971 TV special, *Diana!*

Michael missed the first recording session – he was at a theme park with one-time teen rival, Donny Osmond. The following evening, Michael recorded his vocals in just over an hour.

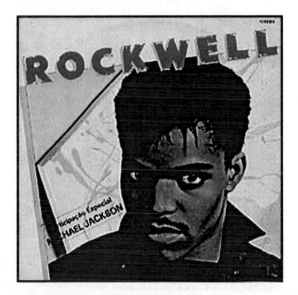

Rockwell used an alias to keep his identity secret from his father, and Michael's contribution went uncredited, as he was under contract to CBS/Epic and the single was issued by his previous record company, Motown.

Released in January 1984 – hit no.1 on the R&B singles chart and no.2 on the Hot 100 in the States, and no.6 in the UK. Also achieved no.1 in Belgium.

RIAA Gold Record (USA million seller).

Official Versions:
Album Version.
Instrumental.
Edit.
Extended Instrumental.

Cover version by Tru, titled *I Always Feel Like (Somebody's Watching Me)*, charted at no.42 on the R&B singles chart and no.71 on the Hot 100 in the States in 1997.

Sampled by the American trio, DC Talk, on *Somebody's Watching*, a track on their 2001 album, *SOLO*. In this instance, the song referred to God, who Christian rapper Toby McKeehan of DC Talk believed was constantly looking out for him.

Cover version by Dutch trio BeatFreakz, featuring a Michael Jackson sound-a-like, hit no.3 in the UK in 2006 – video, starring a pint-sized Michael, parodied Michael's *Thriller* short film. BeatFreakz also recorded a version of Michael's hit, *P.Y.T. (Pretty Young Thing)*.

SOMEDAY AT CHRISTMAS

Song the Jackson 5 recorded for their *CHRISTMAS ALBUM*, issued in October 1970 in the States and December 1970 in the UK.

Originally recorded by Stevie Wonder, for his festive album of the same title, released in 1967.

SOMEDAY WE'LL BE TOGETHER

Diana Ross & the Supremes hit Michael, his brothers and a host of Motown artists (past and present) performed, with *Reach Out And Touch (Somebody's Hand)*, to welcome Motown founder, Berry Gordy, on stage at *Motown 25: Yesterday, Today, Forever* – celebration held at the Pasadena Civic Auditorium on 25th March 1983.

Last hit for Diana Ross & the Supremes, before Diana went solo – hit no.1 on both the Hot 100 and R&B singles chart in the States, and no.13 in the UK, in 1969.

SOMEONE IN THE DARK

Song Michael recorded for the storybook album, *E.T. THE EXTRA-TERRESTRIAL*, issued in November 1982 in the States and January 1983 in the UK.

Michael's record company, CBS/Epic, allowed him to record the storybook album – including one new song, *Someone In The Dark* – for MCA, on two conditions:

One: MCA must hold back the album until after Christmas 1982, so it wouldn't complete with Michael's new album, *THRILLER*.

Two: MCA must not release *Someone In The Dark* as a single.

MCA breached both conditions in the States, by releasing the album in November 1982, and by servicing radio stations with promo copies of *Someone In The Dark*.

Court action resulted in MCA having to withdraw the album, and being prohibited from releasing *Someone In The Dark* as a single – thus creating, arguably, Michael's rarest and most sought after promo single, with copies changing hands for £1,000+.

Official Versions:
Opening Version.
Closing Version.
Long Version.
Short Version.

Extra verse featured on the storybook album, at the end of the second part of the song.

Scheduled to feature on Michael's cancelled compilation, *DECADE 1980-1990*.

Made its CD debut on the special, expanded version of *THRILLER*, released in 2001.

SOMEONE PUT YOUR HAND OUT

Written by Michael with Teddy Riley (who helped to change a verse in Michael's original composition), and recorded in April 1992, having failed to make it on to Michael's *DANGEROUS* album.

Released in the UK/Europe (but not USA) in May 1992, as a Pepsi exclusive, promo cassette single, to promote Michael's up-and-coming world tour. 500,000 copies made available by collecting Pepsi tokens, as competition prizes, etc.

Also released as a special Pepsi promo pack in June 1992, in the UK/Europe – the package included a poster, giant sticker, press file about Michael's world tour and the cassette single.

Issued as a promo CD single in Japan only.

Featured on the first acetate version of the special, expanded edition of Michael's *BAD* – later withdrawn.

Included on Michael's box-set, *THE ULTIMATE COLLECTION*, released in November 2004.

Master tapes from Teddy Riley's Future Records studio surfaced on eBay, featured unreleased mix:

Someone Put Your Hand Out
  Backups/Instrumental Mix 2 #44

Sampled by Ludacris co-starring T-Pain on the track, *One More Drink*, from Ludacris's 2008 album, *THEATER OF THE MIND*.

SOMEWHERE IN TIME

Song written by Michael in 1980, and registered with the United States Copyright Office in November 1984 – remains unreleased.

SONG FOR MICHAEL JACKSON TO $ELL

Song sub-titled *Magical Mystery Tour* – which it's a cover version of, with Beatles samples incorporated into the rave-up at the end. Recorded by Das Damen (German for 'The Ladies'), for their 1988 album, *MARSHMELLOW CONSPIRACY*.

Michael's representatives objected to the song, and forced its withdrawal – Das Damen therefore reissued their album minus this track.

SONIC 3

Michael originally composed the music for the Sega game, Sonic 3 – however, this was pulled due to the child molestation accusations at the time. However, many observers have pointed out similarities between some of the

music that did make Sonic 3 and some of Michael's songs:

- Part of *Carnival Night* appears to be based on *Jam*.

- The chord progression of *Ice Cap* appears to be based on either *Who Is It* or *Smooth Criminal*.

- The Sonic 3 Credits sound like a sped-up version of *Stranger In Moscow*.

SOUL JERK

Pre-Motown recording by the Jackson 5, first released in 1989 on the album, *BEGINNING YEARS 1967-1968*.

SOUL MAN

Song Sam & Dave – Sam Moore & David Prater – recorded for their 1967 album, *SOUL MEN*.

Michael joined Sam & Dave, Michael McDonald, Carla Thomas & Eddie Floyd on stage at the Friars Club in Beverley Hill, to sing the song at the Doobie Brothers' 10th Anniversary Celebration, in early 1980.

Sam & Dave took the song to no.1 on the R&B singles chart and no.2 on the Hot 100 in the States, and to no.24 in the UK.

SOUND, THE

Ten and a half minute medley of hits featured on an official promo 12" single issued in France in 1988, including: *Don't Stop 'Til You Get Enough, Thriller,*

Bad, The Way You Make Me Feel, Beat It, Billie Jean and *Rock With You.*

SPACE DANCE

Not a song as such, but part of the soundtrack of the videogame *Space Channel 5*, which was originally released for Sega Dreamcast in 2000 (and later for Playstation 2 in 2003). Michael featured in the last level of the game, as the character 'Space Michael'.

Michael's voice also featured on the Sega Dreamcast game, *Space Channel 5 Part 2*, released in Japan in 2002 and worldwide the following year – a computer generated, dancing Michael featured in a commercial for the game.

SPECIAL NONSTOP VERSION

Medley featuring *Blame It On The Boogie* and *Shake Your Body (Down To The Ground)*, released on the 1979 Japanese promo album, *THE LEADER OF 80'S POP*, credited to Michael Jackson & The Jacksons.

SPECIAL NONSTOP VERSION
PART 1

Medley featuring *Rock With You, Off The Wall* and *Don't Stop 'Til You Get Enough*, released on the 1979 Japanese promo album, *THE LEADER OF 80'S POP*, credited to Michael Jackson & The Jacksons.

SPECIAL NONSTOP VERSION
PART II

Medley featuring *Don't Stop 'Til You Get Enough, Rock With You* and *Working Day And Night*, released on the 1979 Japanese promo album, *THE LEADER OF 80'S POP*, credited to Michael Jackson & The Jacksons.

SPEECHLESS

Written by Michael, and recorded for his album, *INVINCIBLE*, issued in October 2001 – featured Andrac Crouch and the Andrae Crouch Singers.

'Everything with Michael is a stand-out moment,' said engineer Bruce Swedien, prior to the release of *INVINCIBLE*, 'but an absolutely gorgeous piece of music called *Speechless* was really an event. Michael sings the first eight bars *a cappella*. At the end, he closes it off *a cappella* – it was Michael's idea to add the *a cappella* parts.'

One of three tracks Michael chose as his personal favourites from the album, during his on-line chat with fans on 26th October 2001.

'I was with these kids in Germany, and we had a big water balloon fight,' said Michael, 'and I was so happy after the fight that I ran upstairs in their house and wrote *Speechless*. Fun inspires me. I hate to say that, because it's such a romantic song, but it was the fight that did it. I was happy, and I wrote it in its entirety right there. I felt it would be good enough for the album. Out of the bliss comes magic, wonderment, and creativity.'

Cover version by Ghost featured on the 2002 album, *UNDER THE MOONLIGHT*.

SPEED DEMON

Written – reputedly after he picked up a speeding ticket – by Michael, and recorded for his *BAD* album, issued in September 1987.

Short film, mixing claymation with real life footage, included in Michael's film, *Moonwalker*.

Pencilled in for release as a single in 1989, before *Leave Me Alone* was chosen instead. Promo copies with a picture sleeve, featuring an edited version, issued in France.

SPLASH WE CAN GET WET BABE

Song co-written by Michael with his father Joseph, Danny de Pree Brack and Danny Brack, Jr. – registered with the BMI but remains unreleased.

STAND

Sly & The Family Stone cover the Jackson 5 recorded for their debut album, *DIANA ROSS PRESENTS THE JACKSON 5*, issued in December 1969 in the States and March 1970 in the UK.

First song the Jackson 5 recorded, on 17th May 1969, for Motown. Performed by the Jackson 5 during their first appearance on *The Ed Sullivan Show* in the States in 1969.

Live version recorded at the Jackson 5's homecoming concert in Gary, Indiana, on 29th May 1971, included on their album, *GOIN' BACK TO INDIANA*, issued in September 1971 in the States (no UK release). Footage screened on the group's *Goin' Back To Indiana* TV special, aired in the States on 19th September 1971.

Title given to a budget price reissue of *GOIN' BACK TO INDIANA*, minus *Maybe Tomorrow*, released in the States in 1974 (no UK issue).

Sly & The Family Stone took the song to no.14 on the R&B singles chart and no.22 on the Hot 100 in the States in 1969 – failed to chart in the UK.

STAND TALL

Song written by Michael in 1982, and registered with the United States Copyright Office in December 1985 – remains unreleased.

STANDING IN THE SHADOWS OF LOVE

Four Tops cover the Jackson 5 recorded on 17th May 1969, for their debut album, *DIANA ROSS PRESENTS THE JACKSON 5*, issued in December 1969 in the States and March 1970 in the UK.

The Four Tops version hit no.2 on the R&B singles chart and no.6 on the Hot 100 in the States in 1966, and no.6 in the UK the following year.

STAR SPANGLED BANNER

America's national anthem.

Performed by the Jackson 5 – accompanied by the Leman Monroe High School Band – at the opening game of the baseball World Series at the Riverfront Stadium in Cincinnati, Ohio, on 10th October 1970. In a later interview, Michael and his brothers admitted they didn't know the words, and had to quickly learn them on the way to the stadium.

Hit versions:
José Feliciano – no.50 on the Hot 100 in the States in 1968.
Whitney Houston – no.20 on the Hot 100 in 1991.

STARLIGHT / STARLIGHT SUN

Song Michael worked on during the *THRILLER* sessions, which turned into *Thriller* – referred to as 'Starlight Sun' by Michael, during his Mexican court deposition.

First heard by Michael when writer Rod Temperton brought a demo, with all the sounds programmed, to his Encino home for him to listen to.

Greg Phillinganes, Michael's keyboardist at the time, has confirmed he, Michael, Quincy Jones and Rod Temperton were in the studio, playing the song back, when Michael and Quincy started throwing ideas at each other – such as, changing certain chords to make the song sound darker, and adding the wolf howl. A day or so later, the song became *Thriller*.

Lyrics Michael sang during his court deposition: 'Starlight... Starlight sun... Gimme some starlight, for a new day has begun.'

Snippet of a demo version leaked on the internet in 2008.
Included on the second acetate version of the expanded, special edition of *THRILLER*, but later withdrawn – remains unreleased.

Also known by the title, *Give Me Some Starlight*.

STATE OF INDEPENDENCE

Jon & Vangelis song Donna Summer recorded, with Quincy Jones producing, for her eponymous 1982 album.

Backing vocals by an all-star chorus: Michael, Christopher Cross, James Ingram, Kenny Loggins, Lionel Richie, Dionne Warwick and Stevie Wonder.

Charted at no.14 in the UK, and no.31 on the R&B singles chart and no.41 on the Hot 100 in the States, in 1982.

No.1 in Holland.

Reissue peaked at no.45 in the UK in 1990, and a remixed version hit no.13 in the UK in 1996.

Official Versions:
Album Version.
Edit.
New Bass Mix.
Long Version/Quincy Mix.

N-R-G Mix.
No Drum Mix.
New Bass Mix Edit.
New Radio Millennium Mix.
Creation Mix.
DJ Dero Vocal Mix.
Murk Club Mix.
Jules & Skins Vocal.
Murk-A-Dub Dub.
Cuba-Libre Mix.
Jules & Skins Dub Mix.

Jon & Vangelis's original recording belatedly charted at no.67 in the UK in 1984.

STATE OF SHOCK

Song written by Michael with 14 year old Randy Hansen. Recorded by the Jacksons with Mick Jagger, for their *VICTORY* album, issued in July 1984.

Lead single from the album, credited 'Lead vocals by Michael Jackson & Mick Jagger'. Dance Mix featured additional vocals; instrumental version also released.

Achieved no.3 on the Hot 100 and no.4 on the R&B singles chart in the States, but stalled at no.14 in the UK (the only country where it was issued as a picture disc).

RIAA Gold Record (USA million seller).

Jagger, it was reported, would join the Jacksons on stage on 4th or 5th August 1984, at Madison Square Garden, to perform the song during the group's Victory Tour – from this, a promo video was to have been made. Despite confirmation from Chuck Sullivan, tour promoter, Jagger never appeared.

Official Versions:
Album Version.
7" Version.
Dance Mix.
Instrumental.

One of three songs Michael worked on with Queen's lead vocalist, Freddie Mercury, in 1983 – the others were *There Must Be More To Life Than This* and *Victory*.

'I was going to be on *THRILLER*,' confirmed Freddie, before his death from an AIDS-related illness in November 1991. 'We had three songs in the can but, unfortunately, they were never finished.'

Demo version by Michael and Freddie surfaced on the internet in 2002 – no official release.

STAY

Song written by Michael with Bryan Loren circa 1988, during the *DANGEROUS* sessions – remains unreleased.

STAY WITH LOVE

Love theme from the TV mini-series, *The Jacksons: An American Dream*, recorded by Jermaine Jackson and Syreeta Wright – featured on the accompanying soundtrack album, credited to the Jacksons, issued in October 1992 in the States and July 1993 in the UK.

STAYIN' ALIVE

Written and recorded by the Bee Gees for the 1977 film, *Saturday Night Fever* – hit no.1 on the Hot 100 in the States, and achieved no.4 in the UK.

Michael sang a few bars of the song – and got the words wrong – in his London hotel room in February 1979, when he was interviewed by Terry George.

STEAL AWAY

Song Kennis Jones has confirmed the Jackson 5 performed, with Michael singing lead, at a talent show at the Regal Theater, when they competed against his own first group, the Flairs.

'We tied for first place with a group that was not known at the time, called the Jackson 5,' confirmed Jones. 'A week later we came back to the Regal to break the tie with the Jackson 5, but they didn't show up for whatever reason.'

STEPPIN' OUT WITH MY BABY

Song the Jacksons performed on their TV series in 1976.

STILL IN LOVE WITH YOU

Written for the Jacksons album, *VICTORY* – lead vocal by Randy, but didn't make the album and remains unreleased.

STILL THE KING

Song will.i.am has confirmed he and Michael worked on in 2007 – remains unreleased.

'We probably did like three or four songs,' confirmed will.i.am, speaking in August 2007, 'two of them are finished. I don't know when he's gonna put them out, it's his project, ya know – I'd put them out tomorrow!'

STOP! IN THE NAME OF LOVE

Supremes hit the Jackson 5 sang as part of a 'Salute to the Vocal Groups' medley with *Opus One*, *Bei Mir Bist Du Schon*, *Yakety Yak*, an untitled Jackson 5 ditty and *Dancing Machine*, on *The Carol Burnett Show* in the States in January 1975 – clip included on the Vol.31 DVD of the show.

The Supremes took the song to no.1 on the Hot 100 and no.2 on the R&B singles chart in the States, and no.7 in the UK, in 1965.

STOP THE WAR

Song written by Michael with Carole Bayer Sager circa 1999 – remains unreleased.

STORMY MONDAY

Pre-Motown recording by the Jackson 5, first released in 1989 on the album, *BEGINNING YEARS 1967-1968*.

Remixed version featured on the albums, *BIG BOY*, released in Japan in 1993, and

THE JACKSON FIVE FEATURING MICHAEL JACKSON, issued later the same year in the UK (no USA release). Bonus tracks on the albums included the previously unreleased, original version of *Stormy Monday*, recorded between 1965-67.

STRANGER IN MOSCOW

Written and recorded by Michael for his album, HIS*TORY*, issued in June 1995.

Written in a Moscow hotel room in September 1993, soon after the allegations of child molestation broke – 'a strange, eerie, lonely time', according to Michael. 'The lyrics are totally autobiographical,' he confirmed. 'When you hear lines like "here abandoned in my fame, Armageddon of the brain" – at the time, on the last tour when we were in Moscow, that's really how I felt... just all alone in my hotel, and it was raining – and I just started writing it.'

Charted at no.4 in the UK, but wasn't released in the States until nearly a year later, when a remixed version struggled to no.50 on the R&B singles chart and no.91 on the Hot 100.

Official Versions:
Album Version.
Spensane Vocal Remix (R&B).
Basement Boys 12" Club Mix.
Tee's Capella A Cappella.
Basement Boys Bonus Dub Beats.
Tee's Bonus Beats.
Basement Boys Danger Dub.
Tee's Freeze Mix.
Basement Boys Radio Mix.
Tee's Freeze Radio.
Basement Boys Lonely Dub.
Tee's Bonus Beats Dub.
Hani's Dub Hop Mix.
Tee's In-House Club Mix.
Hani's Extended Chill Hop Mix.
Tee's Light AC Mix.
Hani's Num Club Mix.
Tee's Mission Mix Club.
Hani's Num Dub.
Tee's Radio Mix.

Hani's Num Radio Mix.
TNT Frozen Sun Mix-Club.
Radio Edit.
TNT Danger Dub.
Charles 'The Mixologist' Roanne's Full R&B Mix.
Charles 'The Mixologist' Roanne's Full Mix W/Mute Drop.

Promo short film, shot in black and white in an unused hanger in Van Nuys, California, directed by Nick Brandt – showed Michael walking in real time, while everything around him happened in slow motion.

Live performances screened in Germany and New Zealand, as part of televised concerts.

Nineteenth of Michael's 20 *'Visionary – The Video Singles'* reissues, with the music on one side of a Dual Disc and the accompanying short film on the other side. Issued in June 2006 in the UK – charted at no.22.

STRANGERS IN THE NIGHT

Song Frank Sinatra recorded for the 1996 album of the same title – achieved no.1 in both the UK and USA.

Michael, in amateur footage shot in black and white in 1975, and posted on YouTube in 2009, was heard singing a snippet of the song, including its title.

STREETWALKER

Written by Michael, song first mentioned in the British magazine *Revolution* in

1987, and cited by Michael in his court deposition in November 1993.

Described as a 'true orphan' by Bill Bottrell. 'I made that track,' he said, 'while MJ was on tour for *BAD*. Holed up in Smoketree for a couple of weeks, played all the stuff, and my friend Jason Martz came and played the blues harp solo. When I sent it in, Michael said, "Billy, that harmonica is ignorant!" – and not in a good way. I wrote the whole thing off, until noticing a week ago that they released it. As is!'

Remained unreleased until it was added to the expanded, special edition reissue of *BAD*, issued in October 2001. On the CD, Quincy Jones confirmed Michael wanted to include *Streetwalker* on the original release of *BAD*, while he favoured *Another Part Of Me* – which was finally chosen.

Included on the single release of *Cry* in the UK (no USA release).

Reputedly, Michael's song *Dangerous* evolved from *Streetwalker* – however, the similarities between the two songs are minimal.

STRENGTH OF ONE MAN

Song the Jacksons recorded for their self-titled debut album, issued in November 1976.

STYLE OF LIFE

Written by Michael with brother Tito, and recorded by the Jacksons for their self-titled debut album, issued in November 1976.

B-side of the Jacksons debut single, *Enjoy Yourself.*

Performed solo by Michael on *The Jacksons* TV series in 1977.

SUGAR BUM BUM

Calypso/Soco classic, best known version by Lord Kitchener, performed by Michael and his brothers during their concert dates in Trinidad's Port of Spain & San Fernando in February 1978.

SUGAR DADDY

Song the Jackson 5 released as a single in November 1971 in the States and March 1972 in the UK.

Achieved no.3 on the R&B singles chart and no.10 on the Hot 100 in the States, but failed to chart in the UK.

Featured on the 'Michael White' episode of the new Jackson 5 cartoon series in 1971.

Performed by the Jackson 5 on *Hellzapoppin'* in the States in 1972, and by the Jacksons on their TV series in 1977.

Originally planned as the lead single from a new Jackson 5 album, but instead included on the Jackson 5's *GREATEST HITS* compilation, issued in December 1971 in the States and August 1972 in the UK.

Original mono version included on the 2-for-1 CD, *THIRD ALBUM & MAYBE TOMORROW*, issued in the States in 2001.

SUNSET DRIVER

Written by Michael, and originally scheduled to appear on the expanded, special edition reissue of *OFF THE WALL* in 2001, but withdrawn.

Demo version, recorded in 1982, included on Michael's *THE ULTIMATE COLLECTION* box-set, issued in November 2004.

SUPERFLY SISTER

Written by Michael with Bryan Loren – one of 20-25 songs they worked on together, for a new album, but ultimately not one of them appeared on *DANGEROUS*.

'That song has always been one of my favourites,' said Loren, recalling *Superfly Sister*. 'Michael and I produced it fifty-fifty. Michael wrote the lyrics by himself but I came up with the title. I remember giving Michael a tape with the basic track, from there we wrote the melody together. A few days later, Michael came back with the lyrics to the song, and we basically recorded it right away.'

One of five previously unreleased songs included on Michael's album, *BLOOD ON THE DANCE FLOOR*, issued in April 1997.

SUPERSTAR

Female reply to Michael's *Billie Jean*, by Lydia Murdock – backing track based on *Billie Jean*, but changed sufficiently to deny Michael any song-writing credit.

'Michael was being provocative and ungentlemanly' said Murdoch. 'His record made good business sense, but mine came from the heart. For every man hurt in the '*Billie Jean*' syndrome, there are twelve girls left holding the baby.'

Charted at no.14 in the UK, and no.58 on the R&B singles chart in the States, in 1983.

SUPERSTITION

Stevie Wonder song the Jackson 5 often performed in concert in the early-to-mid 1970s.

Live recording featured on the Michael/Jackson 5's *LIVE!* album, issued in September 1988 in the UK (no USA release). All songs on the album were recorded at a concert on 30th April 1973, at the Osaka Koseinenkin Hall in Japan.

Included on the limited edition CD, *IN JAPAN!*, released by Hip-O Select in 2004 – only 5,000 copies pressed.

Stevie took the song to no.1 on both American charts in 1972, and to no.11 early the following year in the UK.

SURPRISE SONG

Single made available to members of The Jacksons World Club in 1984, as part of a fan package – featured Michael and his brothers ad-libbing, rather than singing an actual song.

SUSIE

Song written by Michael in 1978, and registered with the United States Copyright Office in November 1984 – remains unreleased.

Possibly the same song as *Little Susie* – unconfirmed.

SWEET MUSIC

One of three songs James Whitney has confirmed he wrote for Michael between 1976-79 – recorded by Michael but remains unreleased.

See also: *Disco Kids, Goodness Knows*.

TABLOID JUNKIE

Written by Michael with James Harris III and Terry Lewis, and recorded for his HIS*TORY* album, issued in June 1995.

Nearly titled 'Tabloid Jungle' – the song was a response to the gutter press's constant hounding of Michael.

Started as a Jam & Lewis demo, with no input by Michael early on.

TAKE IT FROM HERE

One of several songs written by Pharrell Williams and submitted for Michael's HIS*TORY* and *INVINCIBLE* albums, which were later recorded by Justin Timberlake, for his debut album *JUSTIFIED*, released in 2002.

TAKE ME BACK

Song Michael recorded for his album, *FOREVER, MICHAEL*, issued in January 1975 in the States and March 1975 in the UK.

B-side of the 1981 reissue of *One Day In Your Life* in the UK – this version is different to the album version.

TAKE MY HEART

One of two unreleased Jackson 5 songs featured on a 6.5" metal acetate, on Side 1, with *Jackson Man* on Side 2 – title credits hand-written in green wax crayon.

Acetate discovered by Adey Pierce in Indiana in 2000 – he purchased it from an ex-engineer, who had engineered the Jackson 5 recordings for Steel-Town.

Acetate value at £3,000 by *Record Collector* magazine, and sold on the internet auction site, eBay, for £4,200 in October 2006.

See also: *Jackson Man*.

TAKE THE 'A' TRAIN

Song performed by the Jacksons, with special guest Caroll O'Connor, on their TV series in 1976, as a medley with *Caravan* and *Don't Get Around Much Anymore*.

TEENAGE SYMPHONY

Previously unreleased Motown recording by the Jackson 5 featured on Michael's solo album, *LOOKING BACK TO YESTERDAY*, issued in February 1986 in the States and May 1986 in the UK.

Alternate version featured on the Jackson 5's 1986 compilation, *ANTHOLOGY*.

TELL ME I'M NOT DREAMIN'
(TOO GOOD TO BE TRUE)

Song recorded by Jermaine Jackson, as a duet with brother Michael, for his self-titled album, issued in May 1984 – the album was titled *DYNAMITE* in the UK and many other countries.

'I co-wrote it with Michael Omartian and Jake Ruska,' said Bruce Sudano. 'We were working on Jermaine's record. Michael Omartian was producing the album for Jermaine. Michael and I

became friends when he produced Donna (Summer)'s album, *SHE WORKS HARD FOR THE MONEY*, and we had co-written a couple of songs for that album. Michael had a track that Jermaine liked, and if I wanted to write something, it would probably get on the record.'

'Jermaine took the song and played it for his brother, Michael Jackson, who also liked it and it became a duet. Jermaine released it as his first single, radio went nuts about the song, and then Jermaine's record company got a call from Michael Jackson's record company, with a "Sist and Desist" from playing the song. Michael's *BAD* album was coming out and the company thought it would hinder Michael's new release.'

Jermaine concurred: 'A lack of communication between Clive Davis and CBS meant Arista were forbidden to issue the track as a single,' explained Jermaine. 'Basically, CBS were saying, why should we help you sell one of your albums?' As it happened, Michael's album *BAD* wasn't actually released until 1987.

White label promo copies released in the UK, backed with Jermaine's *Come To Me* and *Oh Mother*. Promo with picture sleeve issued in Japan.

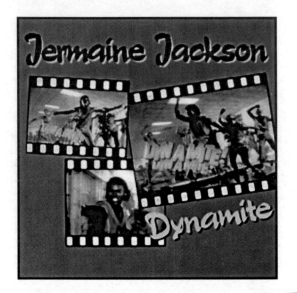

B-side of Jermaine's *Do What You Do* in the UK – instrumental version also released on some formats, including the 12" of Jermaine's single, *Dynamite*.

Grammy nomination: Best R&B Performance by a Duo or Group with Vocal.

Featured in a 1984 episode of the TV series *Fame*, titled 'The Heart Of Rock 'N' Roll' – an episode Michael's sister Janet appeared in, as herself.

Cover version recorded by Robert Palmer, for his 1988 album, *HEAVY NOVA*.

THANK HEAVEN

Song written by Michael in 1998, and registered with the United States Copyright Office in April of the same year – remains unreleased.

THANK U (FALETTINME BE MICE ELF AGIN)

Sly & The Family Stone classic the Jackson 5 often performed in concert during their early years at Motown.

Performance included on a promotional film sent to concert promoters in 1970, to let them know who the Jackson 5 were – filmed at the group's first Motown concert in Philadelphia. The promo also featured a performance of *ABC* from the same concert. Snippets later included in the *Goin' Back To Indiana* TV special.

Original version sampled by Michael & Janet on their *Scream Louder* remix of their duet, *Scream* (and by Janet on *Rhythm Nation*).

No.1 for Sly & The Family Stone on both American charts in 1970 – not a hit in the UK.

THANK YOU FOR LIFE

Song written by Michael circa 1976, but failed to make his album, *OFF THE WALL*.

Registered with the United States Copyright Office in November 1984. Also cited by Michael in his court deposition in 1984, and again in his court deposition in November 1993 – remains unreleased.

THAT

Song written by Michael, and registered with the United States Copyright Office in November 1998 – remains unreleased.

THAT GIRL

Song written by Michael with brothers Jackie, Marlon, Randy and Tito. Recorded circa 1978-80 by the Jacksons, but failed to make the albums, *DESTINY* or *TRIUMPH* – remains unreleased.

THAT KIND OF LOVER

Song written circa 2001 by Michael with Ray Ruffin, for consideration for Michael's album, *INVINCIBLE* – remains unreleased.

Ruffin was asked to submit songs for Michael to consider, and he in turn invited boyband A1 – with whom he had collaborated previously – to work with him. Members of A1, interviewed on the *Big Breakfast* TV show in the UK in February 2001, stated they had written three songs for Michael, and said they felt it was a great honour for them to do so.

If ever recorded by Michael, all three songs remain unreleased.

THAT'S HOW LOVE GOES

Song Jermaine recorded on 6th January 1972, with the Jackson 5 on backing vocals, for his solo debut album, titled simply, *JERMAINE.*

Jermaine's debut single, issued in August 1972 in the States and December 1972 in the UK – charted at no.23 on the R&B singles chart and no.46 on the Hot 100 in the States, but wasn't a hit in the UK.

Performed by Jermaine, backed by his brothers, on *Soul Train* and *The Flip Wilson Show* in the States in 1972.

Alternate version by the Jackson 5, with Jermaine and Michael sharing lead vocals, remains unreleased.

Live version featured on the Michael/Jackson 5's *LIVE!* album, issued in September 1988 in the UK (no USA release). All songs on the album were recorded at a concert on 30th April 1973, at the Osaka Koseinenkin Hall in Japan. Also included on the limited edition CD, *IN JAPAN!*, released by Hip-O Select in 2004 – only 5,000 copies pressed.

THAT'S HOW LOVE IS

Song Michael and his brothers recorded for Motown – remains unreleased.

THAT'S THE WAY (I LIKE IT)

Song the Jacksons performed on their TV series in 1976, as a medley with *Pick Up The Pieces*, with special guest, Dom DeLuise.

No.1 on both American charts, and no.4 in the UK, for KC & The Sunshine Band in 1975. A remixed version charted at no.59 in the UK in 1991.

THAT'S WHAT CHRISTMAS MEANS TO ME

Song the Jackson 5 recorded for their *CHRISTMAS ALBUM* circa 1970, but which failed to make the final track listing – remains unreleased.

Originally recorded by Stevie Wonder.

THAT'S WHAT LOVE IS MADE OF

Song recorded for Motown between 1970-73, but unreleased until it was included on Michael's album, *LOOKING BACK TO YESTERDAY*, issued in February 1986 in the States and May 1986 in the UK.

The Miracles took the song to no.35 on the Hot 100 in the States in 1964.

THAT'S WHAT YOU GET (FOR BEING POLITE)

Written by Michael with brother Randy, and recorded by the Jacksons for their album, *DESTINY*, issued in December 1978.

'*That's What You Get (For Being Polite)* was my way of letting on that I knew I wasn't living in an ivory tower,' said Michael, 'and that I had insecurities and doubts, just as all other teenagers do. I was worried that the world and all it had to offer could be passing me by, even as I tried to get on top of my field.'

'There's this person who's doing things for people,' said Marlon, 'and they back stab him, and that's what he gets for being polite. He's not happy with his life, and things don't turn out the way he wants them to.'

B-side of *Destiny* in the UK and of *Shake Your Body (Down To The Ground)* in the USA.

Mentioned by Michael at the beginning of his deposition hearing in Mexico in 1993 – he mentioned 'Jack Still', part of the song's lyric, separately, leading some fans to believe another song with this title existed.

THERE MUST BE MORE TO LIFE THAN THIS

One of three songs Michael worked on with Queen's Freddie Mercury, and recorded by Michael with Freddie on piano, in the summer of 1983 for the Jacksons album, *VICTORY* – Michael composed some of his own lyrics as the 5-6 hour session progressed.

Song first considered for release on Queen's 1982 album, *HOT SPACE* – it failed to make the group's 1984 album, *THE WORKS*, as well. Solo version by Freddie featured on his album, *MR BAD GUY*, issued in 1985.

Recording of Michael and Freddie working on the song in 1983 surfaced on the internet in 2002. This version featured Freddie talking about the song, and Michael singing solo, to piano accompaniment – no official release.

A second, longer version with vocals by Michael and Freddie also leaked on the internet – this is believed to be a fan-made version, that merged separate vocal recordings by Michael and Freddie.

Scheduled, along with *State Of Shock* by Jackson/Mercury, to be included on a Queen box-set to mark the 10th anniversary of Mercury's death – cancelled.

See also: *State Of Shock, Victory.*

THERE WAS A TIME

Song the Jackson 5 performed during their first national TV appearance, *The Hollywood Palace Special*, aired in the States on 18th October 1969.

Omitted from the accompanying soundtrack album, *MOTOWN AT THE HOLLYWOOD PALACE*, issued in March 1970 (no UK release).

Performed by the Jackson 5 on *American Bandstand* in February 1970, as part of a medley, with *Zip-A-Dee Doo-Dah* and *Shake That Money Maker*.

James Brown took the song to no.3 on the R&B singles chart and no.36 on the Hot 100 in the States in 1968 – not a hit in the UK.

THEY CAN'T TAKE THAT AWAY FROM ME

Snippet of a song Michael performed as part of a three song medley – also including *Gotta Dance* and *Putting On The Ritz* – on *The Jacksons* TV series in 1976.

THEY DON'T CARE ABOUT US

Written by Michael, and recorded for his *HISTORY* album, issued in June 1995.

'This was a song,' revealed Bryan Loren, 'that he'd started even before I joined him for *DANGEROUS*. One of the first things I heard was this song, but it got bumped at the time.'

Lyrics deemed 'anti-Semitic' by Jewish groups:

Jew me, sue me, everybody do me;
 Kick me, kike me,
don't you black or white me.

Michael, who insisted it was a public awareness song, responded by releasing a statement that read:

'The idea that these lyrics could be deemed objectionable is extremely hurtful to me, and misleading. The song in fact is about the pain of prejudice and hate, and is a way to draw attention to social and political problems. I very much regret and apologise from the bottom of my heart if I have hurt anyone's feelings in conveying my own.'

Michael further stated he would re-record the song, changing 'jew me' to 'do me' and 'kike me' to 'strike me', and that apology stickers would be affixed to all existing copies of *HISTORY*.

New pressings of *HISTORY* in 1996 saw 'jew me' changed to 'chew me', and 'kike me' changed to 'hike me'.

'I'm talking about myself as the victim,' Michael later explained. 'David Geffen, Jeffrey Katzenberg, Stephen Spielberg, Mike Milkin – these are my friends. They're all Jewish, so how does that make sense? I was raised in a Jewish community.'

Chosen for single release by Michael, ahead of Sony Music's preference, *Money*.

Charted at no.4 in the UK but, unsurprisingly given the controversy it had stirred up, struggled to no.10 on the R&B singles chart and no.30 on the Hot 100 in the States.

No.1 in the Czech Republic, Germany, Hungary and Italy.

Official Versions:
Album Version (original).
Radio Edit.
Album Version (revised/clean).
LP Edit.
A Cappella.
Single Edit.
Charles' Full Dirty Mix.
Track Masters Instrumental.
Charles' Full Joint Mix.
Track Masters Radio Edit.
Charles' Full Joint Mix – No Intro.
Track Masters Remix.
Charles' Full Joint Mix – No Rap.
Dallas Main Mix.
Love To Infinity's Anthem Of Love Dub.
Love To Infinity's Anthem Of Love Mix.
Love To Infinity's Anthem Of Love
   Radio Edit.
Love To Infinity's Classic Paradise Dub.
Love To Infinity's Classic Paradise Mix.
Love To Infinity's Classic Paradise Radio
   Mix.
Love To Infinity's Hacienda Mix.
Love To Infinity's Walk In The Park
   Mix.
Love To Infinity's Walk In The Park
   Radio Mix.

Two promo short films made, both directed by Spike Lee.

Shooting of the first short film delayed by 20 days, as the Governor of Rio was fearful filming the city's shanty town area of Doña Marta might adversely effect Brazil's chances of hosting the 2004 Olympic Games. Finished promo censored by MTV and VH1 as, although the offending words were muffled, Michael could still be seen mouthing 'jew me, sue me.' Premiered on 22nd March 1996.

Michael was reportedly unhappy with the first promo, and had Spike Lee put together a second, featuring prison footage shot in New York that wasn't used in the first version. This more accurately reflected the angry, defiant mood of the song, but was banned by MTV and several other TV stations, so was only rarely screened and still awaits an official release.

Live performances screened in Germany and New Zealand, as part of televised concerts.

Eighteenth of Michael's 20 *'Visionary – The Video Singles'* reissues, with the music on one side of a Dual Disc and the accompanying short film on the other side. Issued in June 2006 in the UK – charted at no.26.

Posthumous hit: no.4 in Switzerland, no.7 in Sweden, no.9 in Denmark, no.10 in Norway, no.12 in Austria & Germany, no.15 in New Zealand, no.19 in Finland, no.28 in UK and no.64 in USA (Hot Digital Songs).

THINGS I DO FOR YOU

Written by Michael with brothers Jackie, Marlon, Randy and Tito, and recorded by the Jacksons for their *DESTINY* album, issued in December 1978.

B-side of *Lovely One* in the UK.

B-side of *Heartbreak Hotel* in the USA.

Described by Marlon as 'a song about our Mum, because she always does a lot of things because she hates to say no. But no one ever returned the favours on her behalf. The message of the song is the things I do for you, in return do the same for me. If you want people to treat you in a certain way, you should treat them in the same way.'

Performed by the Jacksons on *American Bandstand*, *Soul Train* and their own *Midnight Special* TV show in 1979, and during a Destiny Tour concert screened on BBC2 in the UK.

Performed by Michael during his Bad World Tour – one such concert screened on Nippon TV in Japan.

Live version, recorded at a concert at Madison Square Garden in September 1981, featured on the Jacksons album, *LIVE*, issued in November 1981.

Live recording released as a single, some with a promo picture sleeve, in the UK (no USA release) – failed to chart. This version also issued as the B-side of Michael's *Thriller* in the UK.

THINK HAPPY

Song the Jacksons recorded for their self-titled debut album, issued in November 1976.

Promotional film clip (as very early music videos were called) filmed by the Jacksons.

Performed by the Jacksons on *Soul Train* in 1976 and their own TV series in 1977 – the *Soul Train* performance was included on the home video, *Soul Searching*, in 1984, along with *Shake Your Body (Down To The Ground)* and Jermaine's *Let's Get Serious*.

THIS HAD TO BE

Song written by Michael with George and Louis Johnson. Recorded by the Brothers Johnson, with Michael on backing vocals, for their 1978 album, *LIGHT UP THE NIGHT*.
The Brother's Johnson's *Strawberry Letter 23* was one of Michael's favourite songs of 1977.

THIS IS IT

Song written by Michael in 1980, and registered with the United States Copyright Office in November 1984 – remains unreleased.

THIS 'OLE MAN – ABC

Medley the Jackson 5 performed on the *Carol Burnett Show* in the States in March 1974. Host Carol played a class teacher who loosens up when her class – the Jackson 5 plus dancers – perform the medley.

THIS PLACE HOTEL

Alternative title for the Jacksons hit, *Heartbreak Hotel*, re-titled to avoid any confusion with Elvis Presley's classic – Michael, incredibly, maintains he wasn't aware of this when he wrote the song.

Live version with this title, recorded at a concert at Madison Square Garden in September 1981, featured on the Jacksons album, *LIVE*, issued in November 1981.

See also: *Heartbreak Hotel*.

THIS TIME AROUND

Written by Michael with Dallas Austin, Bruce Swedien and Rene, and recorded for his HIS*TORY* album, issued in June 1995.

Guest rapper: Notorious B.I.G.

'I got off the airplane somewhere in Texas, and answered my pager,' the late Notorious B.I.G. recalled in an interview in 1995. 'They were like, "Michael Jackson called – he wants to do a song with you!" I laughed 'cos I thought they were just frontin'… he wasn't in the studio when I did the song but when I was about to leave, he came through, listened to the joint, said he loved it and I jetted.'

B.I.G., apparently, tripped over hos words on meeting Michael, and kept telling him how much his music had meant to him in his life; he also, rather sheepishly, asked whether he could have his photograph taken with Michael, and Michael readily agreed.

Several promo remixes released, with *Earth Song*, in the States in 1995 but no commercial single release.

Charted at no.23 on the R&B airplay chart in the States.

"THIS TIME AROUND"
featuring remixes by:
Dallas Austin
Maurice Joshua
David Morales
"Earth Song"
featuring remix by
Hani
Don't miss the MICHAEL JACKSON HBO special DECEMBER 10!
K 7521 S1

Official Versions:
Album Version.
Instrumental.
Georgie's House'n'Around Mix.
Dallas Clean Album Remix.
Dallas Main Extended Mix.
Maurice's Club Around Mix.
Dallas Main Mix.
Maurice's Club Around Radio Mix.
Dallas Main Mix W/out Rap.
Maurice's Hip Hop Around Mix.
Dallas Radio Remix.
Dallas Radio Remix W/out Rap.
David Mitson Clean Edit.
D.M. AM Mix.
D.M. Bang Da Drums Mix.
D.M. Mad Club Mix.

D.M. Mad Club Mix – different.
The TimeLand Dub.
D.M. Mad Dub.
UBQ's Opera Vibe Dub.
D.M. Radio Mix.
Uno Clio Dub.
The Don's Control This Dub.
Uno Clio 12" Master Mix.
David Mitson Clean Album Mix.
The Neverland Dub (Aftermath).
Georgie's House'n'Around Edit.
Maurice's Hip Hop Around Mix W/Drop.
Maurice's Hip Hop Around Mix W/Biggie Drop W/out Rap.
Maurice's Hip Hop Around Mix W/Biggie Drop.

D.M. Radio Mix featured alternate vocals.

Sampled on *You've Really Got A Hold On Me*, with the late Notorious B.I.G., a track put together by DJ Vlad & Dirty Harry, on a tape titled *Rap Phenomenon*.

THREATENED

Written by Michael with Rodney Jerkins, Fred Jerkins III and LaShawn Daniels, and recorded for his album, *INVINCIBLE*, issued in October 2001.

Dedicated to 'The Guru of Special Effects', Rick Baker.

THREE STOOGES SONG, THE

Untitled song Michael wrote about *The Three Stooges*, as mentioned in his foreword to the book, *Curly: An Illustrated Biography Of The Superstooge*, written by Joan Howard Maurer and published in 1988. Joan's father was Moe Howard, one of *The Three Stooges* – of whom Michael is known to be a great fan.

THRILLER

Title track of the album that would go on to become the no.1 best selling record ever released, *THRILLER*, issued in December 1982.

Written by Rod Temperton; an inspiration was the Jacksons' hit, *Heartbreak Hotel*. Early titles include 'Starlight', 'Starlight Sun' and 'Give Me Some Starlight' – the title was changed after Michael told Temperton he wanted something that would appeal to kids.

Featured a rap by horror actor, Vincent Price – an unused, third verse of the rap was included on the expanded, special edition reissue of *THRILLER* in October 2001. On the morning of the recording, Temperton still hadn't completed writing the rap. 'I had one verse done,' he said. 'Then I started writing more in the back of the taxi to the studio. When we got there I saw a limousine and out stepped

Vincent Price, so I told my driver "go 'round the back". I gave the words to the secretary to photocopy. Vincent Price sat down with it and got it in two takes. Amazing!'

Speaking on Johnny Carson's *The Tonight Show* in 1983, Price revealed as payment he was given a choice, between taking a percentage of the album sales or $20,000 – and took the cash, so missing out on millions in royalties. Dispute over royalties meant Price's rap was removed from the 7" single edit.

'To me, the miraculous thing about the Vincent Price rap on *Thriller*,' said Bruce Swedien, 'is that Rod Temperton wrote a brilliant Edger Allan Poe style spiel in the taxi-cab on the way to the session! When the chips are down, that's when you find out what true genius is all about. Of course, speaking of genius, Vincent's performance was remarkable... timing, inflection – and he did it in two takes! Michael's vocals are more than wonderful, as well – what an experience!'

Debuted on the Hot 100 in the States at no.20 – the highest new entry for over 20 years (John Lennon's *Imagine* also debuted at no.20 in 1971). Rose to no.4, to give Michael his seventh Top 10 hit from *THRILLER* – a new record from one album.

Charted at no.3 on the R&B singles chart in the States, and achieved no.10 in the UK, where it logged 18 weeks on the Top 75.

No.1 in Belgium.

RIAA Platinum Record (USA million seller).

Official Versions:
Album Version.
Remixed Short Version.
Edit.
Instrumental.
Voice Over Session.
Video Soundtrack Version (13:30)

14 minute short film, directed by John Landis, cost in excess of $1 million. Premiered on MTV in the States on 2nd December 1983, and carried the following disclaimer:

Due to my strong personal convictions, I wish to stress that this film in no way endorses a belief in the occult.

UK premiere, on Channel 4's *The Tube*, at 1.00am on 3rd December 1983 – repeated late the following evening by public demand.

Cited by Michael as the 'most fun short film or video' he's ever made. 'I just

looooooved becoming a monster, because it gave me a chance to pretty much become someone else,' he said. 'It was just fun, hiding behind this mask and just really letting this part of you, your body, or your feelings out… it was just thrilling for me to do that. And the dance, and all the morphing, and all the fun things we did – it's so memorable!'

Michael's sister Janet reportedly appeared in the *Thriller* short film as a zombie.

Grammy Awards: Best Pop Vocal performance, Male and Best Video Album (for the home video, *Making Michael Jackson's Thriller*).

MTV Video Awards: Best Overall Performance, Viewer's Choice Award and Best Choreography.

American Music Video Awards: Best Home Video and Best Long Form Video (for *Making Michael Jackson's Thriller*). *Rolling Stone* magazine: Video of the Decade (1980s).

MTV & TV Guide: Best Music Video of the Millennium.

Inducted into the Music Video Producers Hall of Fame in 1991, and recognised by the 2006 edition of *Guinness World Records* as the 'Most Successful Music Video'.

Live performances screened in Germany, Japan and New Zealand, as part of televised concerts.

Live performance by Michael, at his Dangerous Tour concert in Bucharest, Romania, on 1st October 1992, featured on the DVD released as part of his box-set, *THE ULTIMATE COLLECTION*, issued in November 2004.

Part of a lawsuit heard in Mexico in 1993, when Robert Smith (*aka* Robert Austin), Reynard Jones and Clifford Rubin claimed it infringed the song, *Run On Manchild* – the judgement was in Rod Temperton's favour.

Voted no.20 Best Song of all time in early 2000, in Channel 4 and music retailer HMV's 'Music of the Millennium' poll.

Short film invariably ranked no.1 in polls of the best music videos ever made, by such organisations as *Rolling Stone*, CNN, *Entertainment Weekly*, MTV and VH1.

Lead cover version on the 1984 album, *THE HAPPY CHIPMUNKS SING MICHAEL JACKSON'S GREATEST HITS*. The album also featured versions of: *Rockin' Robin, Say Say Say, Rock With You, Beat It, Don't Stop 'Til You Get Enough, Wanna Be Startin' Somethin', Human Nature* and *Billie Jean*. Due to complaints from David Saville, who created the Chipmunks, the album was withdrawn, and re-issued the following year as *THE HAPPY HAMSTERS SING MICHAEL JACKSON'S GREATEST HITS*.

Cover version by Ian Brown featured on his single, *Golden Gaze*, issued in the UK in 2000.

Sampled in 2001 by Allstars on *Things That Go Bump In The Night* – charted at no.12 in the UK.

Recreated sample featured on *The Way It Is*, a track from Prodigy's 2004 album, *ALWAYS OUTNUMBERED, NEVER OUTGUNNED*. Writer Rod Temperton, when approached by Prodigy's Liam Howlett, suggested they recreate the original music. 'He gave me permission to use the publishing side of the sample, then we could actually recreate *Thriller*,' said Howlett. 'We spent over a week in the studio and it was very hard to recreate, but we recreated the actual sample ourselves. He certainly wouldn't let us use the original recording.'

Sampled on numerous other tracks, including:
Muddfoot by Biz Markie.
No Guest List by Def Squad.
Rhythm Trax – House Party Style by DJ Jazzy Jeff & The Fresh Prince.
Mad Scientist by Large Professor.
100 Miles And Runnin' by N.W.A.

911 Is A Joke by Public Enemy.
Make Love (a parody) by Chef (from *South Park*).

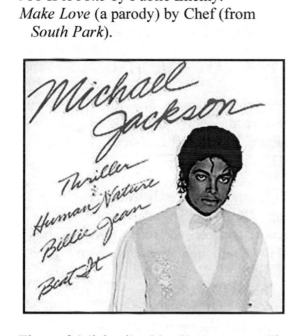

First of Michael's 20 *'Visionary – The Video Singles'* reissues, with the music on one side of a Dual Disc and the accompanying short film on the other side. Issued in February 2006 in most countries – hit no.1 in Spain, but ineligible to enter the UK as it came with a free *Visionary* box to house all 20 Dual Discs, and UK chart rules prohibit freebies of any kind. Box-set with all 20 discs released in the States in November 2006, where the discs were not issued individually.

Live version by Fall Out Boy, recorded at their concet at the Cricket Pavilion, Phoenix, in June 2007, featured on the home DVD, *LIVE IN PHOENIX*, released in 2008.

Posthumous hit: no.1 in Spain, no.2 in the USA (Hot Digital Songs), no.3 in Australia & Switzerland, no.5 in Austria, no.7 in Norway, no.8 in Ireland, no.9 in Germany & Holland, no.10 in Sweden, no.11 in Finland and no.12 in New Zealand & the UK.

THRILLER MEDLEY

Medley registered with the United States Copyright Office in June 1984, featured: *P.Y.T. (Pretty Young Thing)*, *Billie Jean*, *Human Nature* and *Beat It*.

THRILLER MEGAMIX

Megamix by Jason Nevins for the compilation, *KING OF POP*, released to coincide with Michael's 50th birthday in August 2008.

Featured tracks: *Billie Jean/Thriller/ Wanna Be Startin' Somethin'/P.Y.T. (Pretty Young Thing)/Beat/It*.

Released as a two track promo CD single in the UK with the title, *Jason Nevins King Of Pop Megamixes* – featured both the Extended Mix and Radio Edit.

Charted in the UK on the strength of downloads only, peaking at no.96.

THROUGH THICK AND THIN

Song the Jackson 5 originally recorded for their 1975 album, *MOVING VIOLATION*, but failed to make the final cut.

Featured on the first 'new' Jackson 5 album released by Motown after Michael and his brothers signed for CBS/Epic, *JOYFUL JUKEBOX MUSIC*, issued in October 1976 in the States and December 1976 in the UK.

THROWIN' YOUR LIFE AWAY

Song written by Michael in 1988, and registered with the United States Copyright Office in September of that year – remains unreleased.

TIME EXPLOSION

Song featured on the Jackson 5 album, *MOVING VIOLATION*, issued in May 1975 in the States and July 1975 in the UK.

TIME OUT FOR THE BURGLAR

Co-written by Jackie and Randy Jackson with six other writers, and recorded by the Jacksons as the theme song for the Whoopi Goldberg movie, *Burglar*.

Originally titled simply 'Time Out' – changed to tie-in with the movie.

First Jackson 5/Jacksons recording that didn't involve Michael (or Marlon, who had left the Jacksons to pursue a solo career).

Charted at no.88 on the R&B singles chart in the States, but failed to make the Hot 100, and wasn't a hit in the UK.

TIME WAITS FOR NO ONE

Written by Jackie and Randy Jackson, and recorded by the Jacksons for their album, *TRIUMPH*, issued in October 1980.

Fifth single released from the album in the UK (no USA release) – listed as a chart 'breaker' for one week, but didn't sell well enough to enter the Top 50.

TO KNOW

Song the Jackson 5 recorded for their album, *LOOKIN' THROUGH THE WINDOWS*, issued in May 1972 in the States and October 1972 in the UK.

B-side of *Corner Of The Sky* in the USA.

B-side of *Hallelujah Day* in the UK.

TO MAKE MY FATHER PROUD

Song recorded by Michael on 11th April 1973, and first released – with added overdubs – on his *FAREWELL MY SUMMER LOVE* album, issued in May 1984 in the States and June 1984 in the UK.

Original recording featured on *THE BEST OF...*, part of Motown's Anthology series, issued in the States in March 1995 (no UK release).

TO SATISFY YOU

Song written by Bryan Loren during the *DANGEROUS* sessions, but Michael didn't much like it, and let Loren record it for his 1992 album, *MUSIC FROM THE NEW WORLD* (released in Japan only) – Michael contributed backing vocals.

'When he decided he wasn't going to use it,' said Loren, 'I told him I wanted to keep his vocals and put it on my record. He said, "Of course".'

Also recorded – as *Satisfy You* – by Damion 'Crazy Legs' Hall, for his 1994 album, *STRAIGHT TO THE POINT*. The backing vocals, as done by Michael on Loren's version, were this time sung by Chanté Moore.

Solo version by Michael remains unreleased.

TO SIR WITH LOVE

Song Michael and his brothers recorded for Motown – remains unreleased.

Title song from the movie of the same name, starring Sidney Poitier – a no.1 on the Hot 100 in the States for Lulu in 1967.

TOBACCO ROAD

One of the songs the Jackson 5 performed at their Motown audition in 1968, and regularly sang in concert in the pre-Motown days.

Heard in *The Jacksons: An American Dream* TV series, but not performed by the Jackson 5.

TODO MI AMOR ERES TU

Spanish language version of Michael's *I Just Can't Stop Loving You*, recorded by Michael as a duet with Siedah Garrett.

Released as a single in some countries, including America (12" only), Spain and Columbia (7" blue vinyl, as well as black vinyl). Given away as a single with the first pressing of *BAD* in countries like Mexico and Colombia, before being added to the album as a bonus track on the second pressing.

Included on the mega-rare promo CD single, *Signature Series*, released in the States in 1993, and the expanded, special edition of *BAD* in 2001, as a bonus track. The former was scheduled to be given to buyers of a Sony Walkman, and included a message from Michael, in which he described his Heal The World Foundation and its aims – however, following the serious allegations made against Michael, the project was cancelled before the CD single made it past the pre-production stage. Promos were only given to Sony executives and people closely involved with the project – a maximum of 50 copies are believed to exist.

See also: *I Just Can't Stop Loving You*.

TODO PARA TI

Spanish language version of Michael's *What More Can I Give*, featuring contributions from Mariah Carey, Celine Dion, Gloria Estefan, Julio Iglasias, Ricky Martin and Jon Secada.

Recorded as a charity single, to aid the victims and their families of the 9/11 terrorist attack on the States, but Michael's record company refused to release it.

Made available as a download single in October 2003, but no commercial physical release.

See also: *What More Can I Give*.

TOMBOY

Song written by Michael in 1985, and registered with the United States Copyright Office in October that year. Considered by Michael for his album, *BAD*, but didn't make the final track listing.

Cited by Michael in his court deposition in November 1993 – remains unreleased.

Mistakenly believed by some fans to have been written by Quincy Jones.

TOO MUCH MONKEY BUSINESS

Original title of *Monkey Business*.

See also: *Monkey Business*.

TOO YOUNG

Song featured on Michael's album, *MUSIC & ME*, issued in April 1973 in the States and July 1973 in the UK.

Released as a single in a limited number of countries, including Italy and Mexico. Italian sleeve, on the reverse, strangely had the title *I Wasn't Born Yet* printed on it.

Hit versions:
Nat 'King' Cole – no.3 on the R&B singles chart in the States in 1951.
Bill Forbes – no.29 in the UK in 1960.
Donny Osmond – no.5 in the UK, and no.13 on the Hot 100 in the States, in 1972.

TORTURE

Written by Jackie Jackson with Kathy Wakefield, and originally planned as a duet between Jackie and Michael – Jermaine took on Jackie's vocals, as he wasn't sure he would be involved with the *VICTORY* album until the last minute, when he agreed to go on tour with his brothers. All six brothers sang backing vocals, and Randy played all the percussion.

Demo versions probably include one with Jackie and Michael singing lead, and maybe a solo version by Jackie.

Recorded by the Jacksons – with lead vocals credited to Michael and Jermaine – for the album, *VICTORY*, issued in July 1984.

Second single lifted from the album – charted at no.12 on the R&B singles chart and no.17 on the Hot 100 in the States, and no.26 in the UK.

Official Versions:
Album Version.

Extended 12" Dance Mix.
New Mix.
Instrumental.
7" Single Edit.
Video Version.

Promo short film directed by Jeff Stein. Michael and Jermaine refused to be involved with the promo, so their four brothers went ahead, and shot it without them.

TOUCH

Song featured on the Jackson 5's *SKYWRITER* album, issued in March 1973 in the States and July 1973 in the UK.

B-side of *Get It Together*.

Originally recorded by the Supremes, for their 1971 album of the same title – single achieved no.71 on the Hot 100 in the States.

TOUCH THE ONE YOU LOVE

Song recorded on 14th June 1973, and included in an up-dated mix on Michael's *FAREWELL MY SUMMER LOVE* album, issued in May 1984 in the States and June 1984 in the UK – demo version also known to exist.

Second and last single lifted from the album in the States, but failed to chart (no UK release).

B-side of *Girl You're So Together* in the UK.

Original mix included as a bonus track on Michael's posthumous *HELLO WORLD* compilation, issued in July 2009.

TOY, THE

Song Michael wrote for a Richard Prior movie in 1981, and registered with the United States Copyright Office in November 1983.

At his court deposition in December 1984, Michael explained how a lot of his unreleased songs are still very special to him, and cited *The Toy* as an example.

'Quincy wanted me to write a song for the movie with Richard Pryor, *The Toy*, and it got too close to my doing *THRILLER*, so I canned it. But I did write the song, and I did a demo of *The Toy*.'

TRACKS OF MY TEARS

Smokey Robinson song the Jackson 5 recorded in the pre-Motown days, first released in 1989 on the album, *BEGINNING YEARS 1967-1968*.

Song the Jackson 5 are believed to have performed at their Motown audition. It's always been thought the group only performed three songs at the audition, but new footage that has recently come to light suggests otherwise.

Title given to a pre-Motown compilation released in Holland in 2000.

The Miracles took the song to no.2 on the R&B singles chart and no.16 on the Hot 100 in the States in 1965, and to no.9 in the UK in 1969.

TRAGEDY OF A CHEER-LEADER

Song Michael cited he had written in his court deposition in November 1993 – remains unreleased.

TRUE LOVE CAN BE BEAUTIFUL

Song written by Jermaine Jackson with Bobby Taylor, and recorded by the Jackson 5 for their *ABC* album, issued in May 1970 in the States and August 1970 in the UK.

TRY A LITTLE TENDERNESS

Song the Jacksons performed on their TV series in 1976, with their special guest star, Sonny Bono (of Sonny & Cher), as part of a medley with *More Than I Know*, *Am I Blue* and *For Once In My Life*.

Hit versions:
Aretha Franklin – no.100 on the Hot 100 in the States in 1962.
Otis Redding – no.4 on the R&B singles chart and no.25 on the Hot 100 in the States, and no.46 in the UK, in 1967.

Three Dog Night – no.29 on the Hot 100 in 1969.
Ohio Players – no.40 on the R&B singles chart in 1981.
Commitments – no.67 on the Hot 100 in 1991.

TUBEWAY

Song written by Michael circa 1999, considered for but failed to make his album, *INVINCIBLE* – remains unreleased.

TURNING ME OFF

Song Michael cited he had written in his court deposition in November 1993 – remains unreleased.

TWENTY-FIVE MILES

Song Michael recorded in the early-to-mid 1970s for Motown, but remained unreleased until an overdubbed version appeared on his album, *THE ORIGINAL SOUL OF MICHAEL JACKSON*, issued in October 1987 in the States and February 1988 in the UK – demo version also known to exist.

Released as single, with the same picture sleeve as the album, in the States in October 1987 but failed to chart (no UK release).

Original mix included as a bonus track on Michael's posthumous *HELLO WORLD* compilation, issued in July 2009.

Edwin Starr took his original version to no.6 on both American charts, and to no.36 in the UK, in 1969.

TWINKLE, TWINKLE LITTLE ME

Song the Jackson 5 recorded for their *CHRISTMAS ALBUM* circa 1970, but which failed to make the final track listing – remains unreleased.

The Supremes took the song to no.5 on the Christmas Singles chart in the States in 1965.

TWIST & SHOUT

One of the first songs Michael recalled singing.

Heard in the TV mini-series, *The Jacksons: An American Dream* – it's probable the Jackson 5 performed the song in concert in the early days, but it's unlikely they recorded a version of it.

Hit versions:
Isley Brothers – no.2 on the R&B chart, and no.17 on the Hot 100, in the States

in 1962, and no.42 in the UK in 1963.
Beatles – no.2 on the Hot 100 in 1964,
and no.23 on the Hot 100 in 1986.
Salt-N-Pepa – no.4 in the UK in 1988,
and no.45 on the R&B chart in 1989.
Chaka Demus & Pliers – no.1 in the UK
in 1993.

U DON'T HAVE TO CALL

One of two songs written for Michael by
Pharrell Williams, but recorded by Usher
for his 2001 album, *8701*.

See also: *I Don't Know*.

UNBREAKABLE

Written by Michael with Rodney Jerkins,
Fred Jerkins III, LaShawn Daniels, Nora
Payne and Robert Smith, and recorded
for his album, *INVINCIBLE*, issued in
October 2001.

Backing vocals by Brandy, and featured a
rap by the Notorious B.I.G.. 'I was
actually with Biggie when he did that
rhyme,' said producer Rodney Jerkins.
'He was working with Shaq (Shaquille
O'Neal) on an album track called *You
Can't Stop The Reign*.'

Cited by Michael, during his on-line chat
with fans on 26th October 2001, as one of
his three personal favourite tracks on the
album. The same year, he explained the
message behind the song: 'That I'm
invincible, that I've been through it all.
You can't hurt me. Knock me down – I
get back up.'

Track Michael wanted to release as the
first of seven planned singles from

INVINCIBLE, accompanied by a 20
minute short film, set to co-star Mel
Gibson and Chris Tucker. A shorter
production schedule for the promo led to
Sony insisting on issuing *You Rock My
World* as the lead single instead.

Listed in *Music Week*, the UK's trade
music magazine, as a forthcoming new
release in early 2002, before Sony Music
made it known in March they had
officially discontinued promoting
INVINCIBLE, just six months after it
appeared – thus the international release
as singles of *Unbreakable*, *Butterflies*,
Cry, *Break Of Dawn*, *Speechless* and
Whatever Happens were all shelved.

Test pressings and promos only released
in the UK, included an instrumental
version.

UNDER THE BOARD WALK

One of the first songs Michael recalled
singing, and a song the Jackson 5 often
performed in the early days.

Recorded by the Jackson 5 in the pre-
Motown days, not released until 1989,
when an overdubbed version appeared on
the album, *BEGINNING YEARS 1967-
1968*.

Original, untouched recording made
available as one of the bonus tracks on
the albums, *BIG BOY*, issued in Japan in
1993, and *THE JACKSON FIVE
FEATURING MICHAEL JACKSON*,
released later the same year in the UK (no
USA release).

Hit versions:
Drifters – no.4 hit on the Hot 100 in the States, and no.45 in the UK, in 1964.
Billy Joe Royal – no.82 on the Hot 100 in 1978.
Tom Tom Club – no.22 in the UK in 1982.
Bruce Willis – no.2 in the UK, and no.59 on the Hot 100 and no.72 on the R&B singles chart in the States, in 1987.

UNDER YOUR SKIN

Song written by Michael in 1979, and registered with the United States Copyright Office in November 1984 – remains unreleased.

UNKNOWN / UNTITLED SONGS

Over the years a number of songs with a Michael Jackson connection have come to light, without the actual title being revealed. These include:

- Short, untitled ditty about themselves the Jackson 5 performed as part of a 'Salute to the Vocal Groups' medley with *Opus One*, *Yakety Yak*, *Bei Mir Bist Du Schon*, *Stop! In The Name Of Love* and *Dancing Machine*, on *The Carol Burnett Show* in the States in January 1975 – clip included on the Vol.31 DVD of the show.

- Untitled song Jermaine confirmed he was working on with Michael in 1973. 'I'm doing some producing on Michael now,' said Jermaine at the time. 'We have a studio at home now, my father did

it for us. Sid Fein, who is a big arranger for television shows and movies, is doing an arrangement of one of my songs for Michael – it's about a bird.'

- Untitled song – one of five hand-written by Michael circa 1979, to which the lyrics were included in a personal notebook, with young actor Mark Lester on the cover. Formed part of a 10,000+ piece collection of Jackson memorabilia purchased by Universal Express and some of its entertainment partners, in November 2006.

- Untitled song written by Michael with Jae-R and Omer Bhatti, with whom Michael recorded the song, as mentioned in a *Rolling Stone* article in 2003. Confirmed by Jae-R via his MySpace site – remains unreleased.

- Cancelled charity anthem in aid of the Indian Ocean tsunami on 26th December 2004, written by Michael, Randy Jackson and Brad Buxer. Mentioned by Michael in interviews with Jesse Jackson and Geraldo Rivera: 'I saw it the day after Christmas,' Michael told Rivera, 'and as the numbers kept escalating, it just became phenomenal, and not even I could believe that it was true. I was amazed. I said, I thought I should do something. That's what God gave us talent for – to give and to help people and give it back. So, my brothers and I decided to put a song together.'

- Song written by Michael and registered with the BMI in 2006; it's unclear whether the song is titled 'Unknown' or the song title is unknown – remains unreleased.

- Untitled song written by John Legend as a contender for Michael's follow-up to *INVINCIBLE* – mentioned in a *Rolling Stone* article in February 2007.

- Unfinished song Michael was working on just days before he died. 'He called me in an upbeat, excited mood,' said Michael's friend and self-help expert, Deepak Chopra. 'He was writing a song about the environment, and he wanted me to help informally with the lyrics.' Chopra confirmed Michael had cut a rough demo of the song.

UP AGAIN

Song featured on Michael's album, *MUSIC & ME*, issued in April 1973 in the States and July 1973 in the UK.

Scheduled to appear on the B-side of *Doggin' Around* in the States in February 1974 – release cancelled, although test pressings exist.

UP ON THE HOUSE TOP

Song the Jackson 5 recorded for their *CHRISTMAS ALBUM*, issued in October 1970 in the States and December 1970 in the UK – featured a line specially written for each member of the group.

One of four tracks from the album included on the *Merry Christmas From Michael Jackson With The Jackson 5 EP*, issued in the UK in 1987 (no USA release) – charted at no.91.

Also issued as a white label promo in October 1987, complete with picture sleeve, credited to Michael Jackson With The Jackson 5. Promo single also released in the States.

Tambourine cut from the intro on the version featured on *THE BEST OF – THE CHRISTMAS COLLECTION*, released in 2003.

UP THE LAZY RIVER

Song the Jackson 5 performed, along with *Opus One*, with the Mills Brothers, on the *One More Time* TV special in the States in January 1974.

UPPERMOST

Song featured on the Jackson 5's album, *SKYWRITER*, issued in March 1973 in the States and July 1973 in the UK.

UPSIDE DOWN

Diana Ross hit she performed at the Los Angeles Forum in 1981, when she called Michael up on stage, to sing the final chorus with her – later the same year featured in the *diana!* TV special, where Michael was Diana's special guest.

Diana took the song to no.1 on both American charts, and to no.2 in the UK, in 1980.

UPTIGHT (EVERYTHING'S ALRIGHT)

Stevie Wonder classic the Jackson 5 recorded a version of – remains unreleased.

Hit versions:
Stevie Wonder – no.1 on the R&B singles chart and no.3 on the Hot 100 in the States, and no.14 in the UK, in 1966.

Ramsey Lewis – no.30 on the R&B singles chart and no.49 on the Hot 100 in 1966.
Nancy Wilson – no.84 on the Hot 100 in 1966.
Jazz Crusaders – no.95 on the Hot 100 in 1966.

VIBRATIONIST

Song written by Michael with Teddy Riley circa 1999, but failed to make his album, *INVINCIBLE* – remains unreleased.

VICTORY

One of three songs Michael worked on with Queen's front-man, Freddie Mercury, when Michael invited him to Hayvenhurst in the summer of 1983 (the other two were *State Of Shock* and *There Must Be More To Life Than This*). Only Michael, Freddie and Freddie's personal assistant, Peter Freestone, were present during the 5-6 hour session – so, with no drummer and Michael not keen on using a drum machine, Freestone slammed a bedroom door in time with the rhythm.

Song began life as a Queen track, possibly intended for the group's *HOT SPACE* album. Michael and Freddie's version wasn't completed, so wasn't included on the Jacksons album of the same title, issued in July 1984.

Queen's Brian May told *Q* magazine in 1998 that he tried to finish the three Freddie/Michael songs, but didn't know how.

May and Roger Taylor are reported to have recorded backing vocals for the Freddie/Michael demo in 2002, for inclusion on a Queen box-set – however, copyright difficulties meant the track couldn't be released.

May's mother gave two Michael Jackson fans a cassette with *Victory* (and the two other Jackson/Mercury songs) on it, after they contacted her – no official release.

WABASH CANNONBALL

Song Michael and his siblings used to sing with their mother in Gary, Indiana, as confirmed in Katherine's autobiography, *My Family, The Jacksons*.

WAIT

Written by Jackie Jackson with David Paich, and recorded by the Jacksons for their album, *VICTORY*, issued in July 1984.

Fourth and last single taken from the album in the UK – failed to chart.

WALK ON – THE LOVE YOU SAVE

Live medley recorded at the Jackson 5's homecoming concert in Gary, Indiana, on 29th May 1971, included on their album, *GOIN' BACK TO INDIANA*, issued in September 1971 in the States (no UK release). Footage screened on the group's *Goin' Back To Indiana* TV special, aired in the States on 19th September 1971.

WALK ON – THE LOVE YOU SAVE – ABC

Medley performed live by Michael's nephews, 3T, during their *Brotherhood* concert tour.

WALK RIGHT NOW

Written by Michael with brothers Jackie and Randy, and recorded by the Jacksons for their *TRIUMPH* album, issued in October 1980.

Charted at no.7 in the UK, and no.50 on the R&B singles chart and no.73 on the Hot 100 in the States.
Limited edition picture disc released in the UK.

Official Versions:
Album Version.
7" Edit.
Extended Version.
Special Extended Remix (*aka* John Luongo Disco Mix).
Instrumental (*aka* John Luongo Instrumental Mix).

WALL, THE

Song the Jackson 5 recorded for their album, *MAYBE TOMORROW*, issued in April 1971 in the States and October 1971 in the UK.

Featured on 'The Tiny Five' episode of the Jackson 5 cartoon series in 1971.

WANNA BE STARTIN' SOMETHIN'

Written by Michael, and recorded for his *THRILLER* album, issued in December 1982. Believed by some fans to be a hidden criticism of the media pressure Michael faced at this time, and would continue to face long into the future.

First song written by Michael for *THRILLER*: '(It's a song) which I had written when we were doing *OFF THE WALL*,' he said, 'but had never given to Quincy for that album.'

Cited by Michael as a song that disappointed him: 'Song-writing is a very frustrating art form,' he said. 'You have to get on tape exactly what's playing in your head. When I hear it up here (his head), it's wonderful – I have to transcribe that on to tape.'

Fourth single released from the album – peaked at no.5 on both American charts and no.8 in the UK.

Official Versions:
Album Version.
Single Version.
Single Instrumental.
12" Extended Mix.
Brothers In Rhythm Mix.

Tommy D's Main Mix.

Edited instrumental version featured on the 7" single released in Japan, cut from 6:30 to 4:18 minutes.

Single Version recreated for inclusion on the 2005 compilation, *THE ESSENTIAL*, as the original either wasn't remastered or available for some reason. However, the original version, remastered, was included on various editions of the 2008 compilation, *KING OF POP*.

Inpromptu performance by Michael at New York's Peppermint Lounge on 25th March 1983 when, following a set by Grandmaster Flash & The Furious Five, he took to the stage and surprised everyone by lip-synching to *Don't Stop 'Til You Get Enough* and (10 minutes later) *Wanna Be Startin' Somethin'*.

Song chosen to open the Jacksons' Victory Tour and Michael's Bad World Tour concerts.

Live performance by Michael, at his Dangerous Tour concert in Bucharest, Romania, on 1st October 1992, featured on the DVD released as part of his box-set, *THE ULTIMATE COLLECTION*, issued in November 2004.

Live performances screened in Germany, Japan and New Zealand, as part of televised concerts.

Featured in 1990, along with *The Way You Make Me Feel*, in commercials for L.A. Gear – Michael was paid $10 million for his sponsorship of the brand.

Cover version by Jennifer Batten, while Whitney Houston performed a version live in concert, in Japan.

Sampled by:
Lord Tariq & Peter Gunz on *Startin' Somethin'*, from the 1998 album, *MAKE IT REIGN*.
Jamiroquai on the *Dinner With Greedo Mix* of *Love Foolosophy*, a track that featured on the 2001 album, *A FUNK ODYSSEY*.
Rihanna on *Don't Stop The Music*, from her 2007 album, *GOOD GIRL GONE BAD*.

Performed by Usher, Mya and Whitney Houston during the *Michael Jackson: 30th Anniversary Celebration, The Solo Years* concerts, staged at New York's Madison Square Garden on 7th and 10th September 2001.

Featured in the 2002 video game, *Grand Auto Theft: Vice City*, and its accompanying soundtrack.

Posthumous hit: no.20 in the USA (Hot Digital Songs), no.31 in Holland, no.57 in UK and no.75 in Germany.

WANNA BE STARTIN' SOMETHIN' 2008

Re-worked version, recorded in November 2007 with Akon – real name Alioune Badara Thiam – for *THRILLER 25*, with lead vocals by Akon and new vocals by Michael.

First, and most successful, single lifted from the album in many countries, including the USA where it did well to register at no.81 on the Hot 100. Also peaked at no.3 in Sweden, no.4 in New Zealand, no.8 in Australia and no.69 in the UK.

Official Versions:
Album Version.
Radio Edit.
Johnny Vicious Radio Mix.
Johnny Vicious Club Remix.
Johnny Vicious Club Radio Edit.
Johnny Vicious Warehouse Thrilla Dub.

Posthumous hit: no.52 in France.

WAY YOU LOVE ME, THE

Song written and recorded by Michael circa 2000, failed to make the *INVINCIBLE* album, but included on Michael's box-set, *THE ULTIMATE COLLECTION*, issued in November 2004.

WAY YOU MAKE ME FEEL, THE

Written by Michael, in response to his mother's request for a song with 'a shuffling kind of rhythm' – recorded for his album, *BAD*, issued in September 1987.
Originally titled *Hot Fever*.

Line 'Go on, girl!' inspired by Stevie Wonder's song, *Go Home* – revealed by Michael as he and Stevie were in an elevator, trading lines from *The Way You Make Me Feel*. Stevie said knowing he'd inspired Michael made him feel pretty good.

Third single from the album, and third single to top both American charts, a first for Michael.

No.1 in Ireland, and charted at no.3 in the UK.

Official Versions:
Album Version.
Dub.
A Cappella.
Dance Extended Mix.
Instrumental.
7" Mix.
Album Version incl. Vocal Fade.
Dance Remix Radio Edit.

7" Mix recreated for inclusion on the 2005 compilation, *THE ESSENTIAL*, as the original either wasn't remastered or available for some reason.

Remix with more prominent vocals and harmonies replaced the original version on later pressings of *BAD*.

Promoted with a nine minutes short film directed by Joe Pytka. Co-starred Tatiana Thumbtzen, and featured a cameo appearance by Michael's sister, La Toya. Premiered on 31st October 1987. Extended 25 minute version also made – exclusively screened by Michael at his Neverland home.

Performed, along with *Man In The Mirror*, by Michael at the Grammy Awards in March 1988 at Radio City Music Hall, New York – despite four nominations, Michael failed to win a single award.

Included, along with Raffaella Carra's *Tuca-Tuca*, in a medley titled *Tuca-Michael*, by Italian artist Charlie in 1988 – featured on his album, *PIRLA DANCE*.

Featured in 1990, along with *Wanna Be Start' Somethin'*, in commercials for L.A. Gear – Michael was paid $10 million for his sponsorship of the brand.

Performed by Michael – solo and as a duet with Britney Spears – during the *Michael Jackson: 30th Anniversary Celebration, The Solo Years* concerts, staged at New York's Madison Square Garden on 7th and 10th September 2001.

Cover version recorded by Paul Anka.

Seventh of Michael's 20 *'Visionary – The Video Singles'* reissues, with the music on one side of a Dual Disc and the accompanying short film on the other side. Issued in March 2006 in the UK – charted at no.17.

Posthumous Hit: no.6 in the USA (Hot Digital Songs), no.13 in Australia, no.17 in New Zealand, no.24 in Sweden, no.26 in Ireland, no.34 in UK and no.40 in Holland.

WE ARE HERE TO CHANGE THE WORLD

Written by Michael with John Barnes, and originally recorded in 1986 by Michael for *Captain EO*, the 3D-movie he filmed exclusively for Disney – premiered at the Epcot Centre on 12th September 1986.

Footage of Michael rehearsing the song in the studio has appeared on the internet – no official release.

Studio mix released for the first time on Michael's box-set, *THE ULTIMATE COLLECTION*, issued in November 2004.

Official Versions:
Movie Version.
Making Of Version.
George Lucas TV Special Version.
Studio Mix.

Cover version recorded by Deniece Williams, for her 1989 album, *AS GOOD AS IT GETS*.

WE ARE THE ONES

Song Michael wrote in 1978, and registered with the United States Copyright Office in November 1984 – remains unreleased.

WE ARE THE WORLD

Written by Michael with Lionel Richie, as America's answer to Band Aid's *Do They Know It's Christmas*, and recorded by USA For Africa to aid famine relief in Ethiopia – issued in March 1985.

USA For Africa: United Support of Artists For Africa.

Stevie Wonder was originally scheduled to write the song, but he was in New York, and unable to make it.

Lyrics to the song completed on 21st January 1985, and largely recorded – with some minor changes to the lyrics – immediately after the American Music Awards ceremony in Hollywood, on 28th January. The line 'we're taking our lives, in our own hands' was changed to 'we're saving our own lives', to avoid it being taken as a suicide line.

Cassette dub version sent out to participating artists on 24th January, with a request all cassettes be returned on the night of recording; the 'shalum sha-lingay' part wasn't used in the final recording.

Sir Bob Geldof, in his autobiography, spoke of Michael practising the song in various keys. 'Each one was perfect,' he wrote, 'and for anyone else would have been a take, rather than a practise.'

Several demo versions recorded by Michael, including a duet with Lionel Richie. Demo version, as included on the 2004 box-set, *THE ULTIMATE COLLECTION*, used as a guideline for other participating artists.

Soloists, in order of appearance on the record: Lionel Richie, Stevie Wonder, Paul Simon, Kenny Rogers, James Ingram, Tina Turner, Billy Joel, Michael Jackson, Diana Ross, Dionne Warwick, Willie Nelson, Al Jarreau, Bruce Springsteen, Kenny Loggins, Steve Perry, Daryl Hall, Huey Lewis, Cyndi Lauper, Kim Carnes, Bob Dylan and Ray Charles.

Chorus included La Toya, Randy, Marlon, Tito and Jackie Jackson (but not Jermaine or Janet – the latter was particularly upset at not getting an invite).

No.1 on both American charts, and in Australia, Belgium, Holland, Italy, New Zealand, Norway, South Africa, Sweden and the UK.

RIAA Platinum Record (x4).

No.1 best selling single of 1985, and no.5 best selling single of all time, in the States.

Estimated global sales: 7 million (about the same as Band Aid's *Do They Know It's Christmas*).

Grammy Awards: Record of the Year, Song of the Year, Best Pop Vocal Performance by a Duo or Group, Best Music Video – Short Form.

American Music Award: Song of the Year.

People's Choice Award: Favourite New Song.

Official Versions:
Album Version.
Single Version.
Demo – Solo Version.

Second version by Children Of The World (a group of children including Drew Barrymore, Kim Fields and Alfonso Ribeiro) – Michael is on record as saying he prefers this version. 'Since first writing it, I had thought that song should be sung by children,' he said. 'When I finally heard children singing it on producer George Duke's version, I almost cried – it's the best version I've heard.'

USA Foundation for Africa, by the end of 1985, had raised around $40 million to aid famine relief in Africa.

Part of a lawsuit heard in Mexico in 1993, when Robert Smith (*aka* Robert Austin), Reynard Jones and Clifford Rubin claimed it infringed the songs, *What Becomes Of The Children* and *If There Be You* – the judgement was in Michael and Lionel Richie's favour.

Special, limited edition animation cell issued in 1995 by Warner Brothers, to commerate the song's 10th anniversary – titled 'We Are The Toon'.

Performed at the Pavarotti & Friends concert in 1999, by Pavarotti with Boyzone, Mariah Carey and Lionel Richie – Michael was scheduled to appear, but cancelled as his son Prince was unwell.

Performed by Michael and his guests as the finale of the *Michael Jackson: 30th Anniversary Celebration, The Solo Years* concerts, staged at New York's Madison Square Garden on 7th and 10th September 2001 – omitted from the televised edit.

Performed by Michael and his guests at his 'Celebration Of Love' 45th birthday party, staged in Los Angeles on 30th August 2003.

Several demo versions recorded, including a duet by Michael and Lionel Richie – all unreleased, except a solo version by Michael included on his box-set, *THE ULTIMATE COLLECTION*, issued in November 2004.

Performed by invited guests and Michael's 'This Is It' dancers at the finale of the 'A Celebration of the Life of Michael Jackson 1958-2009' memorial concert at the Staples Center on 7th July 2009.

Posthumous hit: no.6 in Switzerland, no.14 in Norway, no.18 in Denmark, no.50 in USA (Hot Digital Songs) and no.77 in UK.

WE BE BALLIN'

Song originally co-written and produced by Rick 'Dutch' Cousin in 1997, and recorded by Ice Cube (*aka* O'Shea Jackson) as *We Be Clubbin'*, for the movie *The Player's Club* (which Ice Cube also directed).

Remixed in 1998 at the A&M studios in Hollywood, Los Angeles, by Cousin, with added vocals by Michael (who sang the chorus) and Shaquille O'Neal, and re-titled *We Be Ballin'*. Michael's involvement came about through O'Neal, who had guested on Michael's *2 Bad*.

'I produced and co-wrote the title track from *The Player's Club*, entitled *We Be Clubbin'*, in 1997,' confirmed Cousin. 'The song was an instant hit and the following year, we thought it to be a good idea to do a remix version of the song, entitled *We Be Ballin'*, featuring Michael Jackson and Shaquille O'Neal. The song was to be released on an NBA compilation album, set to be released that year, and was going to be featured in the infamous NBA 'I Love This Game' themed commercials. The NBA season was cut in half that year, due to the player

268

initiated strike against the league, and the entire project seemed to just disappear… the only folks I know to have copies of the record are Michael Jackson, Ice Cube and myself, and maybe less than a handful of other people.'

Promo CD featured two mixes: Master Mix and Street Mix (with a more edgy, urban feel) – both leaked on the internet in June 2008.

No official release.

No other genuine versions known, however, at least two unofficial fan-made versions do exist.

Cover version by Ricky Romance, dating from 2003, featured Michael's original 1997 vocals.

WE CAN CHANGE THE WORLD

Written by Tito Jackson with Wayne Arnold, and recorded by the Jacksons for their album, *VICTORY*, issued in July 1984.

Tito, so that he could record the drums, guitar and bass, moved all the furniture out of the living room – a move not appreciated by his late wife, Dee Dee. 'My wife was mad,' admitted Tito, 'because the carpet was in the hall and the sofas were in the entry way. The whole room was filled with my recording equipment.'

Described by Tito 'as holding a looking glass up to society, to get people to see things better'.

WE CAN HAVE FUN

One of 19 'Rare & Unreleased' tracks on the fourth CD of the Michael/ Jackson 5 box-set, *SOULSATION!*, issued in June 1995 in the States and July 1995 in the UK.

Recorded on 8th January and 11th February 1970.

WE CAN PUT IT BACK TOGETHER

Song Jermaine Jackson recorded for his 1980 album, *LET'S GET SERIOUS*, about getting back together with his brothers.

'*We Can Put It Back Together* is a very important song, very special to me,' said Jermaine. 'The song makes me cry sometimes, because it's about my brothers – I put in one word to tie-in a double meaning about a marriage that didn't make it, but basically, it's about my brothers.'

WE DON'T HAVE TO BE OVER 21 (TO FALL IN LOVE)

Jackson 5's second single, probably issued by Steel-Town Records in early-to-mid 1968 in the States (no UK release).

Reissued in March 1971, re-titled, *You Don't Have To Be Over Twenty One To Fall In Love*. Around the same time, an album titled *GETTING TOGETHER WITH THE JACKSON 5* appeared in the States (no UK release), but it only featured two songs by the group. The album sleeve featured amateur photographs taken at the Jackson 5's concert in Gary, Indiana, on 31st January 1971.

WE THANK YOU

Short song performed by the Jackson 5 at the close of their concerts.

Featured on the promo film Michael and his brothers shot, to be played at concert venues during their 1970 dates.

Performed live during the group's tour of Europe in 1972, at the Royal Command Performance in the UK, attended by HM The Queen Mother.

Snippet included at the end of Michael's *The Legend Continues…* home video.

WE WISH YOU A MERRY CHRISTMAS

Snippet by the Jackson 5, which they sang at the end of *Have Yourself A Merry Little Christmas*, on their 1970 album, *CHRISTMAS ALBUM*.

Appeared on its own on the Japanese compilation, *FREE SOUL*, released in 1999.

WE'RE ALL ALONE

One of seven demos Michael and his brothers are known to have recorded at their Encino home circa 1976, with Bobby Taylor, prior to signing with CBS/Epic.

Originally recorded by Boz Scaggs for his 1976 album, *SILK DEGREES*. The following year, a cover version by Rita Coolidge charted at no.6 in the UK and no.7 on the Hot 100 in the States.

See also: *People Got To Be Free*, *Piece Of The Pie*, *Rock In A Hard Place*.

WE'RE ALMOST THERE

Song Michael recorded for the album, *FOREVER, MICHAEL*, issued in January 1975 in the States and March 1975 in the UK.

Achieved no.7 on the R&B singles chart and no.54 on the Hot 100 in the States in 1975 (no UK release).

Performed by Michael on *American Bandstand* in January 1975.

Released as a single in the UK in 1981, as the follow-up to the chart topping *One Day In Your Life* – peaked at no.46.

B-side of *Happy (Love Theme From 'Lady Sings The Blues')* in the UK in 1983.

Alternate vocal can be found on a number of compilations, including: *18 GREATEST HITS* (1986), *MICHAEL JACKSON WITH THE JACKSON 5* (1992), *MOTOWN'S GREATEST HITS* (1992) and *THE BEST OF…* (2001),

DJ Spinna Remix, as included on the Japanese compilation, *SOUL SOURCE – JACKSON 5 REMIXES 2*, issued in 2001, featured alternate, extended vocals.

WE'RE COMING BACK

Song performed by the Jackson 5 on their second TV special on 5th November 1972, to the tune of *I Want You Back*, as they closed part one of their show for a commercial break.

WE'RE GONNA CHANGE OUR STYLE

Song featured on the Jackson 5 album, *JOYFUL JUKEBOX MUSIC*, issued in October 1976 in the States and December 1976 in the UK.

WE'RE GONNA HAVE A GOOD TIME

Song recorded at a Jackson 5 concert at Osaka Koseinenkin Hall in Japan on 30th April 1973, featured on the Michael/Jackson 5 album, *LIVE!*, issued in the UK in September 1988 (no USA release).

Included on the limited edition CD, *IN JAPAN!*, released by Hip-O Select in 2004 – only 5,000 copies pressed.

Originally recorded by Rare Earth, for their 1972 album, *WILLIE REMEMBERS* – single charted at no.93 on the Hot 100 in the States.

WE'RE HERE TO ENTERTAIN YOU

Song included on the Jackson 5's album, *JOYFUL JUKEBOX MUSIC*, issued in October 1976 in the States and December 1976 in the UK.

Issued as a single in the Philippines b/w *We're Gonna Change Our Style*.

Snippet featured on Michael's home video, *The Legend Continues...*, released in 1988 (1989 in the States).

WE'VE GOT A GOOD THING GOING

Song Michael recorded for his album, *BEN*, issued in August 1972 in the States and December 1972 in the UK.

B-side of *We're Almost There* in the UK in 1981.

DJ Bobi James remix featured on the album, *SOUL SOURCE – JACKSON 5 REMIXES 2*, released in Japan in 2001.

Hit covers versions (all titled *Good Thing Going*):
Sugar Minott – no.4 in the UK in 1981.
Yazz – no.53 in the UK in 1996.
Sid Owen – no.14 in the UK in 2000.

Alternate take, with slightly different lyrics, featured on the compilation, *THE STRIPPED MIXES*, issued in July 2009.

(WE'VE GOT) BLUE SKIES

Song featured on the Jackson 5's album, *MAYBE TOMORROW*, issued in April 1971 in the States and October 1971 in the UK.

Featured in the 'Ray And Charles Superstars' episode of the Jackson 5 cartoon series in 1971.

WE'VE GOT FOREVER

Song Michael recorded for his album, *FOREVER, MICHAEL*, issued in January 1975 in the States and March 1975 in the UK.

Performed by Michael in the States on *Soul Train* in 1975.

WE'VE HAD ENOUGH

Written by Michael with Rodney Jerkins, Fred Jerkins III, LaShawn Daniels and Carole Bayer Sager – written in 1999 and produced in 2000.

Failed to make the *INVINCIBLE* track listing, but featured on the box-set, *THE ULTIMATE COLLECTION*, issued in November 2004.

Originally rumoured to be a duet by Michael with sister Janet, about the way the media mistreated Michael and his family – unconfirmed.

WELCOME BACK, KOTTER

Short ditty Michael and his brothers performed on *The Rich Little Show* in the States, at the opening of a classroom skit that parodied the American sit-com of the same name.

Sit-com ran from 1975-1979, and starred Gabriel Kaplan as Gabe Kotter (a school teacher) and John Travolta as Vinnie Barbarino.

WHAT A FOOL BELIEVES

Song the Doobie Brothers recorded for their 1978, *MINUTE BY MINUTE*.

Home movie screened by Entertainment Tonight in July 2009 showed Michael singing a snippet of the song, while on the phone to Elizabeth Taylor – Michael stated he had sung backing vocals on this and another Dobbie Brothers track, *Minute By Minute*.

No independent confirmation.

The Doobie Brothers took the song to no.1 on the Hot 100 in the States, and to no.31 in the UK; the single was re-issued in the UK in 1987, and achieved no.57.

WHAT A LONELY WAY TO GO

Song written by Michael circa 1975, and cited by him in his court deposition in November 1993 – remains unreleased.

Jazz recording of the song surfaced on the internet in 2005 – reputedly a duet by Michael and brother Jermaine, however, this proved to be a fake.

(WHAT A) WONDERFUL WORLD

Song first recorded by Louis Armstrong in 1967, and released in January 1968 – hit no.1 in the UK (where a reissue charted at no.53 in 1988).

Michael sang the song, along with a couple of Beatles songs, for a handful of songs in The Dorchester hotel in London, during a visit to England in February 2008.

Cover versions recorded by numerous artists, including Diana Ross, Eva Cassidy, Anne Murray, Tony Bennett & k.d. lang, Rod Stewart & Stevie Wonder, Cliff Richard, Celine Dion and LeAnn Rimes.

WHAT ABOUT US

Song written by Michael, originally for his *DANGEROUS* album, demos of which evolved eventually into *Earth Song*. Demos, titled *What About Us*, leaked on the internet in 2003 – no official release.

WHAT BECOMES OF THE BROKENHEARTED

Jimmy Ruffin hit the Jackson 5 recorded a version of – remains unreleased.

Hit versions:
Jimmy Ruffin – no.6 on the R&B singles chart and no.7 on the Hot 100 in the States, and no.8 in the UK, in 1966.
Jimmy Ruffin (reissue) – no.4 in the UK in 1974.
Dave Stewart & Colin Blunstone – no.13 in the UK in 1981.
Paul Young – no.22 on the Hot 100 in 1992.
Robson & Jerome – no.1 in the UK in 1996.

WHAT DOES IT TAKE (TO WIN YOUR LOVE)

Song recorded by the Jackson 5 – remains unreleased.

Originally recorded by Jr. Walker & The All Stars, who took the song to no.1 on the R&B singles chart and no.4 on the Hot 100 in the States, and to no.13 in the UK, in 1969.

WHAT GOES AROUND COMES AROUND

Song included on Michael's album, *BEN*, issued in August 1972 in the States and December 1972 in the UK.

WHAT MORE CAN I GIVE

Written by Michael in 1998, and originally inspired by Nelson Mandela, a song he had planned to premiere at his 'Michael & Friends – What More Can I Give' concerts in June 1999, staged in the South Korean capital, Seoul, and in Munich, Germany.

'In an earlier conversation I had this year with President Mandela,' said Michael in 1999, 'we discussed the concept of giving, and the words 'what more can I give' kept coming into my mind… we all have to do what we can, to help end the needless suffering in the world.'

Re-written by Michael, following the '9/11' terrorists attacks in America on 11th September 2001 – recorded as a charity single with a host of stars, including Beyoncé, Mariah Carey, Celine Dion, Luis Miguel, Tom Petty, Carlos Santana, Usher and Luther Vandross.

Completed on 19th October 2001, premiered two days later at the 'United We Stand – What More Can I Give' concert at Washington DC's RFK Stadium, in front of 46,000 people.

Concert edited and aired on ABC TV on 1st November.

'I'm not one to sit back and say, "Oh, I feel bad for what happened to them",' said Michael. 'I want the whole world to sing (*What More Can You Give*), to bring us together as a world, because a song is a mantra, something you repeat over and over. And we need peace, we need giving, we need love, we need unity.'

Promo short film premiered at the Radio Music Awards in 2003.

Spanish language version, titled *Todo Para Ti*, also recorded – featured contributions from Michael, Mariah Carey, Celine Dion, Gloria Estefan, Julio Iglasias, Ricky Martin and Jon Secada. Serious disagreements between Michael and Sony Music meant both charity singles went unreleased – however, 200 promo copies were distributed to the artists involved and music industry representatives involved with the project.

Official Versions:
Long Version.
Radio Edit.

Made available as a download single in October 2003 – no other official release.

WHAT YOU DO TO ME

Song originally written by Michael in 1985, and registered with the United States Copyright Office in October the same year. Failed to make Michael's *BAD* album – remains unreleased.

Registered again in December 1998, possibly after being re-written, and considered for Michael's album, *INVINCIBLE* – remains unreleased.

WHAT YOU DON'T KNOW

Song featured on the Jackson 5's album, *DANCING MACHINE*, issued in September 1974 in the States and November 1974 in the UK.

Michael, in an interview with Don Cornelius in 1974, stated this song was originally recorded for one of his solo albums.

Performed solo by Michael on *Soul Train* in 1974, and by the Jacksons on their TV series in 1977.

Released as a single in France.

WHATEVER HAPPENS

Song written by Michael with Teddy Riley, Gilbert Cang, J. Quay and Geoffry Williams, and recorded for his

INVINCIBLE album, issued in October 2001.

Original demo version by composers Cang and Williams recorded in 1997 – posted on the internet site, youtube, in 2008.

Guest guitarist: Carlos Santana – his contribution was recorded in San Francisco in February 2001 (Michael couldn't attend due to other engagements). 'I was very honoured that he called on me to work with him and I love the song,' said Santana. 'He was really happy with it.'

Whistle solo by Carlos Santana and Stuart Brawley.

WHATEVER YOU GOT, I WANT

Song featured on the Jackson 5 album, *DANCING MACHINE*, issued in September 1974 in the States and November 1974 in the UK.

Michael, in an interview with Don Cornelius in 1974, stated this song was originally recorded for one of his solo albums.

Lead single from the album in the States (no UK release) – peaked at no.3 on the R&B singles chart and no.38 on the Hot 100.
B-side of *The Life Of The Party* in the UK.

Performed solo by Michael on *Soul Train* in 1974.

Sampled by K-Ci & JoJo on *Baby Come Back*, a song they recorded for their debut album, *LOVE ALWAYS*, released in 1997.

WHAT'S A GUY GOTTA DO

Song written by Pharrell Williams in 2000, for Michael's album, *INVINCIBLE*, but failed to make the final selection – remains unreleased.

'Meeting Michael Jackson has been the best moment of all this,' said Williams. 'He said that song I made for him, *What's A Guy Gotta Do*, was alright. He said he liked it, but in the end it wasn't right for him.'

WHAT'S IT GONNA BE

Song written by Michael, and registered with the BMI in 2006 – remains unreleased.

Not to be confused with song Michael's sister Janet recorded with Busta Rhymes.

WHAT'S YOUR GAME

Song written and produced by the Jackson 5, and recorded by four sisters managed by their father, M-D-L-T Willis – issued in November 1974 in the States (no UK released).

Charted at no.89 on the R&B singles chart.

WHAT'S YOUR LIFE

Song Michael cited he had written with brother Jermaine at his court deposition in November 1993 – remains unreleased.

WHATZUPWITU

Song recorded by Eddie Murphy, with Michael on backing vocals, for his 1993 album, *LOVE'S ALRIGHT* (no UK release) – recorded following Eddie's guest appearance in Michael's short film, *Remember The Time*.

Charted at no.74 on the R&B singles chart and listed at no.121 on the 'bubbling under' section of the Hot 100 in the States (no UK release).

Promo video, directed by Wayne Isham, featured Eddie and Michael dancing and singing on fluffy white clouds. No commercial release, except in Japan, where it was included on the DVD, *Music Video Clip! Dance 4*.

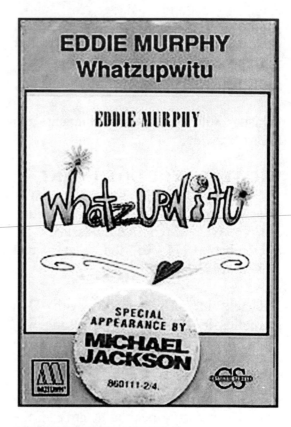

WHEN BABIES SMILE

Poem written by Michael – included in his book of poems and reflections, *Dancing The Dream*, published in 1992.

WHEN I COME OF AGE

Song written specially for Michael by Hal Davis, Don Fletcher and Weldon Dean Parkes, about a boy's wishes and what he would like to become when he grows up.

Recorded by Michael in the early-to-mid 1970s, released for the first time on his album, *LOOKING BACK TO YESTERDAY*, issued in February 1986 in the States and May 1986 in the UK.

Demo version, with alternate ending – different lyrics – known to exist.

WHEN I LOOK AT YOU

Song recorded by the Jacksons, and featured as a previously unreleased track on their single, *2300 Jackson Street*, issued in July 1989 in the States and August 1989 in the UK.

Michael wasn't one of the Jacksons who recorded this song.

WHEN THE SUN SHINES

Song Michael has confirmed he and his brothers used to sing as small boys growing up in Gary, Indiana.

'This is a true story. Nobody believes it – a lot of people say, " you jiving", but one day our television broke down at our house,' said Michael, 'and what we did to occupy the time, we would just sit around and look at one another. What we decided to do, we would wake up every morning singing songs – old folk songs like *Cotton Fields Back Home* and *When The Sun Shines* and all these kind of things.

We would start making harmonies, and the next thing you know that my father had a guitar in his closet and he would go to work. Tito would sneak and play it, and one day Tito got caught and he got a whippin', and after the whippin' my father said, "Now, let me see what you can play on that thing." And then Tito showed him what he can play and he was proud of him. He couldn't believe it!'

WHEN WE GROW UP (WE DON'T HAVE TO CHANGE AT ALL)

Song Michael performed as a duet with Roberta Flack, on a TV show titled *Free To Be...You And Me*, which aired on ABC TV on 11th March 1974 – the show went on to win an Emmy, for Best Children's Special. Michael and Roberta lip-synched their performance, therefore a recording of the song must exist – remains unreleased.

Accompanying soundtrack album featured a version of the song by Diana Ross.

TV show released on home video in the States in 2001 (no UK release).

WHEN YOU WISH UPON A STAR

Song Michael performed as part of a medley, with *Ease On Down The Road* and *Follow The Yellow Brick Road*, on the *Kraft Salutes Disneyland's 25th Anniversary Show* in 1980, accompanied by Mickey & Minnie Mouse, Donald Duck and Goofy – remains unreleased.

Snippet featured on Michael's home video, *The Legend Continues...*, as the credits rolled.

WHERE DID OUR LOVE GO

Supremes hit the Jackson 5 recorded a version of – remains unreleased.

Hit versions:
Supremes – no.1 on the Hot 100 and R&B singles charts, and no.3 in the UK, in 1964.
Donny Elbert – no.6 on the R&B singles chart and no.15 on the Hot 100 in 1971, and no.8 in the UK in 1972.
J. Geils Band – no.68 on the Hot 100 in 1976.
Manhatten Transfer – no.40 in the UK in 1978.
Tricia Penrose – no.71 in the UK in 1996.

WHERE DO I STAND

Written by Marlon Jackson for the Jacksons 1984 album, *VICTORY*, but failed to make the final track listing.

Recorded by Marlon for his debut solo album, *BABY TONIGHT*, issued in the States in 1987 (no UK release).

WHITE CHRISTMAS

Most successful Christmas song ever, which the Jackson 5 recorded a version of for their *CHRISTMAS ALBUM* circa 1970, but which failed to make the final track listing – remains unreleased.

Written by Irving Berlin for the film, *Holiday Inn*, and recorded by Bing Crosby in Los Angeles on 29th May 1942

– hit no.1 in the States and went on to become to the best selling single of all time.

Other hit versions:
Ravens – no.9 on the R&B singles chart in the States in 1948.
Mantovani – no.6 in the UK in 1952.
Drifters – no.2 on the R&B singles chart in 1954 (with several re-entries in later years).
Pat Boone – no.29 in the UK in 1957.
Andy Williams – no.1 on the Christmas Singles chart in the States in 1963.
Otis Redding – no.12 on the Christmas Singles chart in 1968.
Freddie Starr – no.41 in the UK in 1975.
Darts – no.48 in the UK in 1980.
Jim Davidson – no.52 in the UK in 1980.
Keith Harris & Orville – no.40 in the UK in 1985.
Max Bygraves – no.71 in the UK in 1989.

WHO DO YOU KNOW

Song Michael wrote circa 1981, but failed to make his album, *THRILLER*. Cited by Michael in his court deposition in November 1993 – remains unreleased.

WHO IS IT

Song written by Michael, and recorded for his album, *DANGEROUS*, issued in November 1991 – early versions were allegedly titled *Lying To Myself* and *It Doesn't Seem To Matter*. The latter was mentioned in *Revolution* magazine, in a list of supposed songs for the album.

Extended demo version featured different harmonies, some of which have been released on various remixes.

'This reminds me so much of *Dirty Diana*,' said producer Teddy Riley. 'I think he (Michael) recaptured that sound on this song… I think he went back to his roots of recording with this song to record an incredible track. I thought it would take someone like Quincy Jones to really put an incredible track like that together, I thought it would take someone like Quincy Jones to get that sound, but Michael came up with it.'

Charted at no.6 on the R&B singles chart and no.14 on the Hot 100 in the States, and no.10 in the UK – hit no.1 in Zimbabwe.

Released instead of *Give In To Me* in the States, following Michael's brief 'beat box' rendition during his televised interview with Oprah Winfrey – what Bruce Swedien, referring to Michael's vocal 'beat box' percussion, called his 'how now brown cow'.

Official Versions:
Album Version.
Patience Edit.
Most Patient Mix.
A Cappella.
Oprah Winfrey Special Intro.
Brotherly Dub.
P-Man Dub.
Brothers Cool Dub.
Patience Mix.
Patient Beats.
House 7".
Tribal Version.
IIIS Mix.
7" Edit.
Lakeside Dub.
7" Edit With Intro.
Moby's Raw Mercy Dub.

Brothers In Rhythm House Mix.

The Patience Mix, Most Patient Mix & Brothers In Rhythm House Mix all featured additional vocals not found on the album version of the song.

World premiere of promo short film, directed by David Fincher, on BBC2's *Def II* show in the UK on 13th July 1992. Michael was unhappy with the original edit of the short film, and had it re-edited – the first version was withdrawn, and the later version shown and included on his home video, *Dangerous – The Short Films*.

Promoted in the States with a montage of Michael's previous short films and in concert footage.

Remix included on the first acetate version of the expanded, special edition of Michael's *DANGEROUS* album in 2001 – bonus disc cancelled.

WHO IS THE GIRL WITH HER HAIR DOWN

Song Michael cited he had written in his court deposition in November 1993 – remains unreleased.

WHO'S BAD

Alternative title, possibly related to the ad-libs at the end of the short film, for Michael's hit, *Bad*, as registered with the United States Copyright Office on a number of occasions in the late 1980s.

See also: *Bad*.

WHO'S LOOKIN' FOR A LOVER

Song recorded for Motown, and included on Michael's album, *LOOKING BACK TO YESTERDAY*, issued in February 1986 in the States and May 1986 in the UK.

WHO'S LOVIN' YOU

Smokey Robinson song the Jackson 5 regularly performed live in the pre-Motown days, and one of the songs they performed at their Motown audition in 1968.

Originally recorded by the Miracles, and featured on their 1961 album, *HI, WE'RE THE MIRACLES*.

Recorded for their debut album, *DIANA ROSS PRESENTS THE JACKSON 5*, issued in December 1969 in the States and March 1970 in the UK.

Recorded on 19th, 20th and 24th July 1969.

B-side of the Jackson 5's debut single for Motown, *I Want You Back* – listed alongside the A-side on the Hot 100 in the States, hitting no.1.

One of three songs the Jackson 5 performed on their first appearance on the *Ed Sullivan Show* on 14th December 1969 in the States – this was a shortened version of the song.

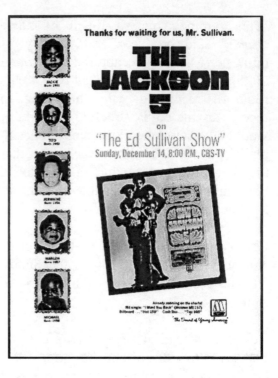

Live version, recorded in Indianapolis, Indiana on 29th May 1971, discovered in a North Hollywood vault by director Karen Arthur, just four days before the shooting of the TV mini-series *The Jacksons: An American Dream* finished shooting in 1992 – the script was hastily re-written so the song could be included.

Remixed live version included on the soundtrack album, *THE JACKSONS: AN AMERICAN DREAM*, issued in October 1992 in the States and July 1993 in the UK.

Cassette single and promo CD single issued in the States (no UK release), promoted by a 'new' video directed by Steve Barron, featuring the group's *Ed Sullivan Show* performance – charted at no.48 on the R&B singles chart but failed to make the Hot 100.

Original mono version (B-side of *I Want You Back*) included on the compilation, *THE BEST OF – THE MILLENNIUM COLLECTION*, issued in the States in 1999.

Original live recording added as a bonus track to the 'Two Classic Albums on One CD' reissue of *GOIN' BACK TO INDIANA & LOOKIN' THROUGH THE WINDOWS*, issued in the States in August 2001 (no UK release).

Single version with extended vocals, taken from the mono version and 'folded' into the stereo version, included on Michael's solo compilation, *LOVE SONGS*, issued in the UK in 2002 (no USA release).

Official Versions:
Album Version.
Mono Version.
Single Version.
Live Album Version
  (remixed/overdubbed).
Radio Edit.
Live Version.
Integral Mono Version.

Charted at no.54 in the UK in 2009, following the song's performance on the TV show *Britain's Got Talent* by 12 year old Shaheen Jafargholi.

Performed by Jafargholi at the 'A Celebration of the Life of Michael Jackson 1958-2009' memorial concert at the Staples Center on 7th July 2009. 'I just, when I first heard, I couldn't believe it,' said Jafargholi. 'I mean, I was – to be honest, honoured to be invited.'

Posthumous hit: no. 36 in the UK and no.55 in the USA (Hot Digital Songs).

WHO'S RIGHT, WHO'S WRONG

Song recorded by Kenny Loggins, with Michael and Richard Page on backing vocals, for his 1979 album, *KEEP THE FIRE*.

Interviewed in Japan in 1980, Michael revealed he had chosen the cover for Loggins's album, and that although Loggins had offered to pay him for his work on this song, he refused and said he had done it for friendship.

WHY

Song written by Kenneth 'Babyface' Edmonds, and originally scheduled to appear on Michael's album, HIS*TORY* – until his three nephews, 3T (Tito's sons Taj, Taryll and TJ) claimed it.

'The song was supposed to be on Michael's HIS*TORY* album, but we loved it so much that we kinda ended up stealing it from him,' confirmed TJ in early 1996. 'I mean, once he played it for us and saw our faces he was like, "You guys want this song?" – and that's exactly what happened, and working in the studio with him was such an experience.'

Recorded by 3T, as a duet with Michael (who also produced the track), for their debut album, *BROTHERHOOD*, released in 1996.

Hit no.2 in the UK, but struggled to no.71 on the R&B singles chart in the States, and only managed no.112 on the 'bubbling under' section of the Hot 100.

Promo short film featured Michael and his nephews – Michael, with Ralph Ziman, also directed.

Official Versions:
Album Version.
D.W. Bonus Mix.
Radio Edit.
Video Edit.

Completed solo version by Michael believed not to exist, as 3T's Taj has confirmed he and his brothers only ever heard Babyface's demo version, before recording the song.

WHY CAN'T I BE

Song written by Michael in 1980, and registered with the United States Copyright Office in November 1984. Also cited by Michael in his court deposition in December 1984 – remains unreleased.

WHY SHY

Song Michael cited he had written in his court deposition in November 1993 – remains unreleased.

WHY YOU WANNA TRIP ON ME

Song Michael recorded for his album, *DANGEROUS*, issued in November 1991.

Inspired by the things people say about Michael. 'We knew people were after him, people all talking about him,' said co-writer Teddy Riley. 'But we didn't get too direct, we didn't say anybody's name, 'cause when you're too direct it gets boring.'

'The element I'm most proud of in this song is my guitar playing,' said Riley. 'I thought he (Michael) was going to get another person to play on it but he wanted my good self playing. That was something special to me – I was using an acoustic Ovation guitar.'

Played over the closing credits on Michael's home video, *Dangerous – The Short Films*.

Master tapes from Teddy Riley's Future Records studio surfaced on eBay, featured unreleased mixes:

Why You Wanna Trip On Me Teddy's Human Beat Box
Why You Wanna Trip On Me Instrumental Only
Why You Wanna Trip On Me Rough Mix #46

Why You Wanna Trip On Me CD Guitar Riff Sample By Paul Jackson (Tracks 1-30: guitar riff samples varying in length from 14 seconds to 1:11)

WILL YOU BE THERE

Written by Michael, and recorded for his album, *DANGEROUS*, issued in November 1991.

Lyrics included in Michael's book of poems and reflections, *Dancing The Dream*, published in 1992 – the lyrics in the book are slightly different in places.

Featured the Andrae Crouch Singers on backing vocals, and opened with 67 seconds of Beethoven's *9th Symphony*, played by the Cleveland Orchestra – uncredited. $7 million copyright infringement lawsuit filed – settled in December 1992, and one outcome was all future copies of *DANGEROUS* must credit Ludwig Van Beethoven and the Cleveland Orchestra on *Will You Be There*.

'Bringing a vocal choir in on the track was a stroke of genius,' said Teddy Riley. 'It's something I'd consider doing since hearing him (Michael) do it. It's a long song as well, a lot of this album really clocks in. This nearly hits eigth minutes, I think – it's not a punchy radio edit! A lot of the songs on the album are long, that's what makes the album, I think.'

Theme to the movie, *Free Willy*, and included on the soundtrack album.

Subject of a lawsuit filed by Albano Carrisi, who claimed the melody of the song was stolen from his composition, *I Cigni Di Balaka*.

Achieved no.7 on the Hot 100 and no.53 on the R&B singles chart in the States, and no.9 in the UK – hit no.1 in Zimbabwe.

Two versions of the short film, directed by Vincent Paterson, released – with and without footage of the movie, *Free Willy*. The short films used footage of Michael performing the song at MTV's 10th anniversary show in 1991, and from his own Dangerous World Tour.

RIAA Gold Record (500,000 copies in USA).

MTV Movie Award: Best Song in a Movie.

Official Versions:
Album Version.
Instrumental.
Edit.
Radio Edit.

Performed by Michael as MTV's 10th anniversary celebration, *MTV 10*, in 1991; two years later, at the NAACP Image Awards, he joined Patti LaBelle and The Voices Of Faith Choir, to perform a version of the song.

Live performance by Michael, at his Dangerous Tour concert in Bucharest, Romania, on 1st October 1992, featured on the DVD released as part of his box-set, *THE ULTIMATE COLLECTION*, issued in November 2004.

Master tapes from Teddy Riley's Future Records studio surfaced on eBay, featured unreleased mixes:

Will You Be There With Poetry
Will You Be There Drum Ideas #26

Performed by Jennifer Hudson at the 'A Celebration of the Life of Michael Jackson 1958-2009' memorial concert at the Staples Center on 7th July 2009.

Posthumous hit: no.3 in Switzerland, no.10 in USA (Hot Digital Songs), no.14 in Denmark & Holland, no.22 in Sweden, no.26 in Germany, no.29 in New Zealand and no.51 in UK.

WINDOW SHOPPING

Song featured on the Jackson 5's album, *JOYFUL JUKEBOX MUSIC*, issued in October 1976 in the States and December 1976 in the UK.

Recorded on 15th December 1973 – a week before Jermaine married Berry Gordy's daughter, Hazel,.

Lead song on a four track Brazilian picture sleeve EP – also featured *You're My Best Friend, My Love, We're Here To Entertain You* and *Through Thick And Thin*.

Instrumental version appeared on the 1975 Motown album, *THE MAGIC DISCO MACHINE*, which featured unfinished/unreleased Motown tracks.

WINGS OF MY LOVE

Song Michael recorded for his debut solo album, *GOT TO BE THERE*, issued in January 1972 in the States and May 1972 in the UK.

Featured in the 'Who's Hoozis' episode of the new Jackson 5 cartoon series in 1971.

WITH A CHILD'S HEART

Stevie Wonder cover Michael recorded for his album, *MUSIC & ME*, issued in April 1973 in the States and July 1973 in the UK.

Peaked at no.14 on the R&B singles chart and no.50 on the Hot 100 in the States (no UK release).

Performed by Michael on *Soul Train* in the States in 1973.

B-side of *One Day In Your Life* in the UK in 1975.

Version with alternate ending featured on the 2009 compilation, *THE STRIPPED MIXES*.

Stevie Wonder's original, the flip-side of *Nothing's Too Good For My Baby*, was listed at no.8 on the R&B singles chart and no.131 on the 'bubbling under' section of the Hot 100 in 1966. Featured on Stevie's album, *UP-TIGHT EVERYTHING'S ALRIGHT*.

WITHOUT A SONG

Performed by the Jacksons on *The Tonight Show* in the States in 1977, as part of a medley with *You've Got A Friend, Make It With You, Behind Closed Doors, You've Made Me So Very Happy, You Are The Sunshine Of My Life, You And Me Against The World*.

Best known version by the Carpenters – short acappella version featured on the duo's 1994 compilation, *INTERPRETATIONS*, full length version included on their 2001 album, *AS TIME GOES BY*.

WITHOUT A SONG – YOU'VE GOT A FRIEND – MAKE IT WITH YOU – BEHIND CLOSED DOORS – YOU'VE MADE ME SO VERY HAPPY – YOU ARE THE SUNSHINE OF MY LIFE – YOU AND ME AGAINST THE WORLD

Medley performed by the Jacksons on *The Tonight Show* in the States in 1977, starring Johnny Carson and guest host Freddie Prinz.

Lead vocals by Michael on *You've Got A Friend* and *You And Me Against The World*, by Marlon on *Without A Song* and *You Are The Sunshine of My Life*, by Jackie on *Make It With You* and *You've Made Me So Very Happy*, and by Tito on *Behind Closed Doors*.

See also: *Without A Song, You've Got A Friend, Make It With You, Behind Closed Doors, You've Made Me So Very Happy, You Are The Sunshine Of My Life, You And Me Against The World*.

WONDERFUL WORLD OF CANDY

Song written and produced by Michael, and recorded at his private Neverland studio by Michael as a duet with Nisha Kataria in 2003 – confirmed by Dieter Wiesner, who was Michael's manager from 1996-2003, and introduced Michael and Nisha.

Originally intended for a children's charity project, but dropped following new accusations made against Michael – remains unreleased.

WONDERING WHO

Written by Jackie and Randy Jackson, and recorded by the Jacksons for their album, *TRIUMPH*, issued in October 1980.

B-side of *Can You Feel It*.

WORD TO THE BADD!!

Controversial song Jermaine recorded for his 1991 album, *YOU SAID, YOU SAID*, as a swipe at brother Michael, for not returning his calls.

Jermaine didn't originally plan to release the song, before it was leaked to American radio stations, around the time Michael's *Black Or White* made its debut.

Two versions: one, with lyrics directed at Michael; two, the album version with different lyrics not aimed at Michael. Promo 12" single released in the States featured a Jackson 5 introduction.

Media interest in the States helped the song to no.78 on the Hot 100 and no.88 on the R&B singles chart – not a hit in the UK.

WORDS WITHOUT MEANING

Song Michael co-produced with his nephews, 3T, for their debut album, *BROTHERHOOD*, released in 1995.

WORK THAT BODY

Song written by Michael with Bryan Loren.

Included on the first acetate version of the expanded, special edition of Michael's *DANGEROUS* album in 2001 – bonus disc cancelled.

A minute long snippet, along with *She Got It*, leaked on the internet in 2005 – no official release. Lyrics from the Jackson 5's *ABC*, as performed by an adult Michael, can be heard on this demo: 'Sit down, girl! I think I love you! No! Get up, girl! Show me what you can do!'

'*Work That Body* is complete,' confirmed Loren, 'with Michael repeating – at my behest – the rap from the Jackson 5's *ABC*. He did not want to do this, but realised the tongue-in-cheek fun contained in it.'

WORKING DAY AND NIGHT

Written by Michael, and recorded for his album, *OFF THE WALL*, issued in August 1979 – said by Michael to be very autobiographical in some ways, however, he wrote the song from a married man's viewpoint.

Michael's original demo recording featured as a bonus track on the expanded, special edition of *OFF THE WALL*, released in 2001.

B-side of *Rock With You* in the USA.

B-side of *Off The Wall* in the UK.

Live version, recorded at a concert at Madison Square Garden in September 1981, featured on the Jacksons album, *LIVE*, issued in November 1981.

Live performance by Michael, at his Dangerous Tour concert in Bucharest, Romania, on 1st October 1992, featured on the DVD released as part of his box-set, *THE ULTIMATE COLLECTION*, issued in November 2004.

Different live performance screened on Nippon TV in Japan.

Sampled by:
Will Smith on *Can You Feel Me*, a track he recorded for his 1991 album, *WILLENNIUM*.
Richie Rich on *Salsa House*, which appeared on at least two various artist compilations, namely *HOUSE SOUNDS OF LONDON* (1990) and *CLUB CLASSICS* (2003).

2008 Remix featured of the *P.Y.T. (Pretty Young Thing)* mini CD single, part of the *THRILLER 25: JAPANESE SINGLES COLLECTION* release in 2008.

WORLD IS A MESS, THE

Song performed by the Jackson 5, as part of a sketch, on Cher's TV show in the States on 11th March 1975 – the song introduced a segment in which Cher and two other guests portrayed the confused, first inhabitants in the Garden of Eden. The Jackson 5 also performed *I Am Love*.

Remains unreleased.

WORLD OF SUNSHINE

Song featured on the Jackson 5's album, *SKYWRITER*, issued in March 1973 in the States and July 1973 in the UK.

Performed by the Jacksons, accompanied by film footage of them on skates, on their TV series in 1976.

WOULD YA? WOULD YA?

Song recorded by the Jackson 5 for Motown, and registered with the United States Copyright Office in January 1973 – remains unreleased. Written by Freddie Perren and Christine Yarian.

Also known to fans by the title, *Wouldja*.

Instrumental disco mix, titled *Tryin' To Get Over*, featured on the 1975 promo album, *THE MAGIC DISCO MACHINE*.

WOULDN'T YOU LOVE TO LOVE ME

Song Prince demoed in 1976, then revamped in 1987 and submitted to Michael, for possible inclusion on *BAD*. But, just as Prince had turned down an approach to duet with Michael on *Bad*, so Michael rejected this song.

Song given to Taja Sevelle, who recorded it for her eponymous debut album, released in 1987 on Prince's Paisley Park record label.

YAKETY YAK

Coasters hit the Jackson 5 performed as part of a 'Salute to the Vocal Groups' medley with *Opus One*, *Bei Mir Bist Du Schon*, *Stop! In The Name Of Love*, an untitled Jackson 5 ditty and *Dancing Machine*, on *The Carol Burnett Show* in the States in January 1975 – clip included on the Vol.31 DVD of the show.

The Coasters took the song to no.1 on both American charts, and to no.12 in the UK, in 1958.

YEAH

Song Eddie Murphy recorded, backed by an all star choir, for his 1993 album, *LOVE'S ALRIGHT*.

All star choir: Michael and his sister Janet, with Paul McCartney, Luther Vandross, Julio Iglasias, Elton John, Garth Brooks, Jon Bon Jovi, Audrey Wheeler, Sandi Barber, Babyface, En Vogue, Johnny Gill, Amy grant, Aaron Hall, Hammer, Heavy D, Howard Hewett,Patti LaBelle, Emmanuel Lewis, Teddy Pendergrass, Richie Sambora, Barry White & Stevie Wonder.

1-track promo CD released in the States, as part of a limited edition box set (Motown W021582-4), issued to promote the formation of Murphy's Yeah Foundation charity – gold coloured wooden box with metal clasp also included 20 exclusive colour postcards, showing Murphy pictured with each of the guest artists, including Michael.

YESTERDAY

Beatles classic the Jackson 5 often performed in the early days, and during their Motown concerts in 1971, but never recorded.

'My favourite Beatles song is Paul's favourite Beatles song, *Yesterday*,' revealed Michael. 'It always touched me the most, it was always special to me. I think it's wonderful, the melody and the music and the whole feeling.'

Most covered song of all-time, according to *Guinness World Records*, with 2,500+ recorded versions by the year 2000.

Hit versions:
Beatles – no.1 on the Hot 100 in the States in 1965, no.8 in the UK in 1976.
Matt Monro – no.8 in the UK in 1965.
Marianne Faithful – no.36 in the UK in 1965.
Ray Charles – no.9 on the R&B singles chart and no.25 on the Hot 100 in the States, and no.44 in the UK, in 1967.
Wet Wet Wet – no.4 in the UK in 1997.

YESTER-ME, YESTER-YOU, YESTERDAY

Stevie Wonder song the Jackson 5 recorded a version of – remains unreleased.

Stevie took the song to no.2 in the UK, and no.5 on the R&B singles chart and no.7 on the Hot 100 in the States, in 1969.

YOU AIN'T GIVING ME WHAT I WANT (SO I'M TAKING IT ALL BACK)

One of 19 'Rare & Unreleased' tracks on the fourth CD of the Michael/ Jackson 5 box-set, *SOULSATION!*, issued in June 1995 in the States and July 1995 in the UK.

Recorded on 8th January 1970 – originally titled, *You're A, B, C's And D's*.

YOU AIN'T GONNA CHANGE NOTHIN'

Song written by Michael in 1975, and registered with the United States Copyright Office in November 1984. Also cited by Michael in his court deposition in November 1993 – remains unreleased.

YOU AND ME AGAINST THE WORLD

Performed by the Jacksons on *The Tonight Show* in the States in 1977, as part of a medley with *Without A Song*, *You've Got A Friend*, *Make It With You*, *Behind Closed Doors*, *You've Made Me So Very Happy*, *You Are The Sunshine Of My Life*.

Helen Reddy took the song to no.9 on the Hot 100 singles chart in the States in 1974.

YOU ARE A LIAR

Song Michael cited he had written in his court deposition in November 1993, and one of the many songs he considered recording for his album, *INVINCIBLE* – remains unreleased.

Also known by the title, *You're A Liar*.

YOU ARE MY LIFE

Written by Michael with Babyface, Carole Bayer Sager and John McClain, and recorded for his album, *INVINCIBLE*, issued in October 2001.

Included on the album at the expense of *Shout*.

YOU ARE MY SUNSHINE

One of numerous songs the Jackson family used to sing in Gary, Indiana, while they were growing up, as confirmed by mother Katherine in her autobiography, *My Family, The Jacksons*.

YOU ARE NOT ALONE

Written by R. Kelly in 1994, and recorded by Michael for his album, *HISTORY*, issued in June 1995.

'I was amazed when Michael called me because, for years, I just didn't expect to go to that level,' admitted R. Kelly. 'I was so nervous, I was afraid I wouldn't be able to finish the project. When I first got to the studio something weird came over me. Michael was on a different level, and it was a hell of a level to go to. But passion took me over, and it put a shield around me, and allowed me to be just a normal guy who felt like he worked with Michael all the time.'

Michael, after listening to the tape R. Kelly sent him, liked what he heard but felt the song needed a more prominent climax – which he wrote, with R. Kelly's approval.

Second single from the album – became the first single in the chart's 37 year history to enter Billboard's Hot 100 at no.1 in the States. Commemorated with a special award at the 6th annual Billboard Awards ceremony – Tina Turner collected the award on Michael's behalf, as he was in hospital, after he collapsed rehearsing for his planned HBO TV special, *Michael Jackson: One Night Only*. Feat recognised by *Guinness World Records* – Michael listed as the 'First Vocalist to enter the US Singles chart at Number One'.

Also hit no.1 on the R&B singles chart in the States, and in France, Ireland, New Zealand, Switzerland and the UK.

RIAA Platinum Record (USA million seller).

No.8 best selling single of 1995 in the UK.

25 years, seven months and one week between *I Want You Back* and *You Are Not Alone* hitting no.1 on the Hot 100 was a new record span between chart toppers (Cher beat this record in 1999, when her single *Believe* rose to no.1).

Short film, directed by Wayne Isham, premiered in the States on the MTV special, *Michael Jackson Changes History*, on 28th July 1995. Co-starred Michael's then wife, Lisa Marie Presley – both, controversially, were seen almost naked on the edge of a swimming pool. Pool sequences shot at Raleigh Stages, theatre sequences filmed at Pantages Theater in Hollywood. Version released on the home video, *History On Film*

Volume II, digitally altered to give Michael an 'angelic' look.

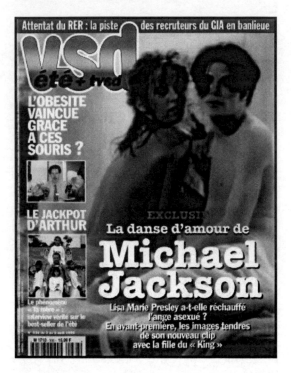

Grammy nomination: Song of the Year.

Official Versions:
Album Version.
Album Edit.
Album Version – different fade.
Jon B. Padappella.
Classic Club Edit.
Jon B. Remix Edit.
Radio Edit.
Knuckluv Dub Version.
R. Kelly Remix.
R. Kelly Remix Edit.
Jon B. Main Mix.
Frankie Knuckles – Classic Club Mix.
Frankie Knuckles – Franctified Club Mix.

Frankie Knuckles' Classic Club mix featured extended vocals.

Performed by Michael at a number of events, including:

- MTV Music Video Awards, staged in New York's Radio City Music Hall on 7th September 1995.

- 15th Anniversary celebrations of Black Entertainment Television, in Washington DC on 22nd September 1995 (aired 6th December) – Michael became the first inductee in BET's newly founded Walk of Fame.

- Soul Train 25th Anniversary Hall Of Fame TV Special, aired in the States on 22nd November 1995 – Michael performed both *Dangerous* & *You Are Not Alone* twice.

- The two Michael & Friends concerts, staged in Seoul, South Korea, on 25th June 1999, and in the Germany city of Munich two days later.

During Michael's *His*tory World Tour, a lucky girl was allowed on stage at each concert, to dance with Michael as he sang the song. Live performances from the tour screened in Germany and New Zealand.

Cover version recorded by Diana Ross, for her 1996 album, *VOICES OF LOVE*, as a prod – to see how Michael reacted to her version of the song. Interviewed on the UK's BBC Radio 1 in December 1996, Diana said, 'Just talking about him now makes my heart feel sad.'

Performed by Liza Minnelli during the *Michael Jackson: 30th Anniversary Celebration, The Solo Years* concerts, staged at New York's Madison Square Garden on 7th and 10th September 2001.

Sixteenth of Michael's 20 *'Visionary – The Video Singles'* reissues, with the music on one side of a Dual Disc and the accompanying short film on the other side. Issued in May 2006 in the UK – charted at no.30.

Law suit against R. Kelly filed in Belgium by brothers Eddy and Danny van Passel, who claimed the song sounded eerily similar to their song, *If We Can Start All Over*. 'It's identical,' said Danny, 'and I can't say more than that, except it's a protected copyright and you should ask permission first before you use it, and R. Kelly didn't ask for permission.'

Posthumous hit: no.12 in New Zealand, no.16 in Switzerland, no.17 in USA (Hot Digital Songs), no.22 in Australia, no.33 in Germany, no.35 in UK and no.37 in Sweden.

YOU ARE SO BEAUTIFUL

Song Michael began writing during his court trial in 2005, inspired by and as a thank you to his fans for their ongoing support – lyrics included in Michael's photobook, *My World – The Official Photobook Vol.1*, published in March 2006.

Song remains unreleased.

YOU ARE THE ONES (INTERLUDE)

Song recorded by Michael's nephews, 3T, as a tribute to the Jackson 5 – included on the Jacksons TV soundtrack album, *THE JACKSONS: AN AMERICAN DREAM*, issued in October 1992 in the States and July 1993 in the UK.

YOU ARE THE SUNSHINE OF MY LIFE

Performed by the Jacksons on *The Tonight Show* in the States in 1977, as part of a medley with *Without A Song, You've Got A Friend, Make It With You, Behind Closed Doors, You've Made Me So Very Happy, You And Me Against The World*.

No.1 on the Pop chart in the States in 1973; also peaked at no.3 on the R&B singles chart, and at no.7 in the UK.

YOU ARE THERE

Song featured on Michael's album, *FOREVER, MICHAEL*, issued in January 1975 in the States and March 1975 in the UK.

YOU CAN CRY ON MY SHOULDER

Song Michael recorded for his album, *BEN*, issued in August 1972 in the States and December 19772 in the UK.

B-side of *Ben*.

YOU CAN'T HURRY LOVE

Supremes cover recorded by the Jackson 5 – remains unreleased.

Hit versions:
Supremes – no.1 on both American charts, and no.3 in the UK, in 1966.
Phil Collins – no.1 in the UK in 1982, and no.10 on the Hot 100 in the States in 1983.

YOU CAN'T WIN

Song originally performed by Michael in the movie, *The Wiz* – premiered in Los Angeles in October 1978. Featured on the accompanying soundtrack double album, issued in September 1978 in the States and October 1978 in the UK.

Written by Charlie Smalls for the 1975 Broadway show, *The Wiz* – to be sung by the Winkies to Dorothy, when she was trapped in the lair of the Wicked Witch of the West. Dropped from the show, after its Boston try-out, but resurrected after Quincy Jones asked Smalls to write a new song for the film version, to replace the Scarecrow's solo, *I Was Born On The Day Before Yesterday*.

Title on the film credits: *You Can't Win, You Can't Break Even*.

First solo single by Michael released on CBS/Epic.

Charted at no.42 on the R&B singles chart and no.81 on the Hot 100 in the States – wasn't a hit in the UK.

Official Versions:
Album Version.
7" Part 1.
7" Part 2.
12" Extended Mix.

Snippet heard, on the radio when the children are in a car, in Michael's favourite film, *E.T. THE EXTRA-TERRESTRIAL.*

Included on the first acetate version of the expanded, special edition of Michael's *OFF THE WALL* album in 2001 – later withdrawn.

Performed by Jill Scott during the *Michael Jackson: 30th Anniversary Celebration, The Solo Years* concerts, staged at New York's Madison Square Garden on 7th and 10th September 2001.

YOU DON'T KNOW LIKE I KNOW

Sam & Dave song the Jackson 5 regularly performed live on the Chitli' Circuit circa 1965-67, and suggested by Shirley Cartman (Tito's music teacher) as a possible for the group's Motown audition in 1968 – rejected, as Sam & Dave were on a rival record label, Stax.

Hit for Sam & Dave in the States in 1966 – no.1 on the R&B singles chart and no.90 on the Hot 100 in the States (didn't chart in the UK).

YOU HAVEN'T DONE NOTHIN'

Musical assault on President Richard Nixon, written and recorded by Stevie Wonder for his Grammy Award winning 1974 album, *FULFILLINGNESS' FIRST FINALE.*

Credits 'Doo Doo Wopsssss by The Jackson 5', and Stevie could be heard singing, 'Jackson 5, sing along with me!'

Hit no.1 on both American charts and in Canada, and achieved no.30 in the UK.

YOU MADE ME WHAT I AM

Song included on the Jackson 5's album, *SKYWRITER*, issued in March 1973 in the States and July 1973 in the UK.

YOU NEED LOVE LIKE I DO (DON'T YOU?)

Song featured on the Jackson 5's album, *GET IT TOGETHER*, issued in September 1973 in the States and November 1973 in the UK.

B-side of *What You Don't Know* in France.

Originally recorded by Gladys Knight & The Pips – their version achieved no.3 on the R&B singles chart and no.25 on the Hot 100 in the States in 1970.

YOU NOT ME

Song Michael is known to have worked on – handwritten lyrics posted by Henry Vacroo on his 'j5secrets' website.

Some lyrics evolved into *This Had To Be*, which the Brothers Johnson recorded for their 1980 album, *LIGHT UP THE NIGHT*.

YOU ROCK MY WORLD

Written by Michael with Rodney Jerkins, Fred Jerkins III, LaShawn Daniels and Nora Payne, and recorded for his album, *INVINCIBLE*, issued in October 2001.

Originally titled *Rock My World*.

'My association with Michael came about after I was introduced to Carole Bayer Sager by Atlantic VP, Craig Kaman,' said Jerkins. 'She asked me if I would like to come to her house, and write with her and Michael – so I said, Cool! I flew to Los Angeles, and sure enough was there at her house… every time I see him, I tell him over and over – it's just incredible just to be here working with you, knowing how crazy I was about you when I was a kid.'

'We knew that it (*You Rock My World*) was going to be a corner-stone of the album, and it set the mood and the feel for the rest of the music,' said engineer Bruce Swedien. 'A lot of times, a real good piece of music will never get on the album, only because it just doesn't fit. You know Michael loves drama – if the music doesn't have drama, if it's just a derivative of a piece of music without drama, Michael's not going to go for it.'

Spoken intro by Michael and Chris Tucker – Tucker came into the studio to do a voice party for *INVINCIBLE*, but it wasn't until Rodney Jerkins heard it and thought it fitted the mood of the song, that it was agreed to use it for *You Rock My World*.

Lead single from the album – however, its release to radio stations had to be brought forward, after two New York stations broke the embargo Sony Music had placed on it.

Officially premiered on Michael's website on 24th August 2001.

Hit no.2 in the UK, and achieved no.10 on the Hot 100 and no.13 on the R&B singles chart in the States – on the strength of airplay alone, as no commercial single was released.

Fred Bronson, Billboard magazine's chart expert, felt it was 'a huge mistake' not to release the song as a single in the States: 'Certainly, if a commercial single had been available, it would have peaked higher – perhaps even at no.1.'

No.1 in France, Portugal and Spain.

Official Versions:
Album Version.
Instrumental.
A Cappella #1.
Radio Edit.
A Cappella #2.
Track Masters Remix (with Jay-Z).

Jay-Z chosen by Michael to remix the song because: 'he's hip, the new thing, and he's with the kids today. They like his work. He's tapped into the nerve of popular culture. It just made good business sense.'

Short film, directed by Paul Hunter, co-starred Chris Tucker, Michael Madson and Marlon Brando – three versions released, the longest almost 14 minutes long. Premiered on 21st September 2001 – based on a short story written by Michael with Paul Hunter.

NACCP Image Awards: Best Music Video.

Grammy nomination: Best Pop Vocal Performance, Male.

Performed by Michael and Usher during the *Michael Jackson: 30th Anniversary Celebration, The Solo Years* concerts, staged at New York's Madison Square Garden on 7th and 10th September 2001. Michael, unhappy with the first performance, told musical director Greg Phillinganes that the song's beat needed to be harder; he rehearsed the song four times after the first show, and added more dance steps to his second performance.

Originally scheduled to be the final release in Michael's *Visionary – The*

Video Singles project, and was illustrated on a scrapped version of the *Visionary* box. Replaced by *Heal The World*, allegedly because Sony didn't want to afford Michael's *INVINCIBLE* album any publicity at all.

Posthumous hit: no.60 in the UK and no.62 in USA (Hot Digital Songs).

YOU TOLD ME YOUR LOVIN'

Song written by Michael in 1979, and registered with the United States Copyright Office in November 1984.

A second version, with words and music by Michael's brother, Randy, also exists – both versions remain unreleased.

(YOU WERE MADE) ESPECIALLY FOR ME

Song featured on the Jackson 5 album, *MOVING VIOLATION*, released in May 1975 in the States and July 1975 in the UK.

Performed by the Jacksons on their TV series in 1976.

Live performance by the Jacksons, at a concert in Mexico in 1976, included on the home video, *The Jacksons In Concert*, released in 1981 in the UK (no USA release).

YOU WERE THERE

Written by Michael, with Alan 'Buz' Kohan, at the Shrine Auditorium – venue for Sammy Davis, Jr.'s 60th Anniversary Show, on 13th November 1989.

Performed by Michael – for the one and only time – at the show, after which he was heard saying he would never sing the song again, as it was 'Sammy's song.'

Registered with the United States Copyright Office in December 1989.

YOUNG FOLKS, THE

Song the Jackson 5 recorded for their second album, *ABC*, issued in May 1970 in the States and August 1970 in the UK.

B-side of *ABC* – featured a slightly different (mono), longer mix to the album version.

Unreleased mix featured in the 'Pinestock USA' episode of the Jackson 5 cartoon series in 1971.

Originally recorded by the Supremes, and included on their 1969 album, *CREAM OF THE CROP*. B-side of *No Matter What Sign You Are* – listed separately on the Hot 100, where it peaked at no.69.

YOUR LOVE IN MY LIFE

Song Michael produced for Colby O'Donis & Friends, for the album, *PARTY TIME*, released in 2004.

YOUR WAYS

Written by Jackie Jackson, and recorded by the Jacksons for their album, *TRIUMPH*, issued in October 1980.

B-side of *Walk Right Now* and *State Of Shock*.

YOU'RE A, B, C'S AND D'S

Original title of *You Ain't Giving Me What I Want (So I'm Taking It All Back)*, included on the Michael/Jackson 5 box-set, *SOULSATION!* in 1995.

YOU'RE GOOD FOR ME

Song recorded by the Jackson 5 circa 1973, but unreleased until it appeared on Michael's solo album, *LOOKING BACK TO YESTERDAY*, issued in February 1986 in the States and May 1986 in the UK.

YOU'RE IN GOOD HANDS

Song Jermaine Jackson recorded, with the Jackson 5 on backing vocals, for his 1973 album, *COME INTO MY LIFE*.

Achieved no.35 on the R&B singles chart and no.79 on the Hot 100 in the States, but wasn't a hit in the UK.

Performed by Jermaine on *Soul Train* in 1973.

YOU'RE MY BEST FRIEND, MY LOVE

Song featured on the Jackson 5 album, *JOYFUL JUKEBOX MUSIC*, issued in October 1976 in the States and December 1976 in the UK.

YOU'RE MY EVERYTHING

Temptations hit the Jackson 5 recorded a version of – remains unreleased.

The Temptations took the song to no.3 on the R&B singles chart and no.6 on the Hot 100 in the States, and no.26 in the UK, in 1967.

YOU'RE SUPPOSED TO KEEP YOUR LOVE FOR ME

Written by Stevie Wonder, and originally recorded in 1975 by Jermaine Jackson, with Stevie, Michael and Jackie Jackson on backing vocals.

'There's a song called *You're Supposed To Keep Your Love For Me*, which was recorded five years before it came out. Michael, Stevie, Jackie and myself sing backgrounds on it,' confirmed Jermaine. 'I'd been trying to get Stevie to put that song on one of my albums. He said, "I have to record this track 'cause it's kind of old now.". Just before, I had recorded four songs and so I said to Stevie, "Why don't you get this song ready for this album?" So he went into the studio to re-cut it, and he cut another two songs.'

Re-cut version, recorded solo by Jermaine, featured on his album, *LET'S GET SERIOUS*, issued in 1980.

Original recording, featuring Michael, remains unreleased.

YOU'RE THE ONE

Written by Michael with Alan 'Buz' Kohan.

Recorded by Jennifer Holiday, with Michael producing, for her 1985 album, *SAY YOU LOVE ME*. In her album notes, Holiday thanked Michael: 'To Michael

Jackson – I don't know why you chose me, but I'm deeply touched, very honored and mighty thankful to you for writing *You're The One* for me. Thank you so much for a beautiful experience.'

YOU'RE THE ONLY ONE

One of 19 'Rare & Unreleased' tracks listed as appearing on the Michael/Jackson 5 box-set, *SOULSATION!* in 1995 – however, the track that actually appeared on the fourth CD was *Ooh, I'd Love To Be With You* (from the Jackson 5's *SKYWRITER*).

Written by Deke Richards, Freddie Perren & Fonce Mizell – registered in December 1972.

Recorded by Jackie for his debut solo album – it's unlikely this is the same version supposed to feature on *SOULSATION!*

Titled *Are You The One* in pre-release notes.

YOU'VE CHANGED

Song the Jackson 5 originally recorded for Steel-Town Records, for the B-side of their debut single, *Big Boy*, issued in the States in January 1968 (no UK release).

Re-recorded on 19th and 29th July 1969 by the Jackson 5 for their debut album, *DIANA ROSS PRESENTS THE JACKSON 5*, issued in December 1969 in the States and March 1970 in the UK.

Mistakenly titled 'You've Changed Me' on early American pressings of the album sleeve, as Motown confused the song with another in their extensive back catalogue.

YOU'VE GOT A FRIEND

Song Michael recorded for his debut album, *GOT TO BE THERE*, issued in January 1972 in the States and May 1972 in the UK.

Lead song on a 4-track picture sleeve EP released in Mexico.

Performed by the Jacksons on *The Tonight Show* in the States in 1977, as part of a medley with *Without A Song*, *Make It With You*, *Behind Closed Doors*, *You've Made Me So Very Happy*, You *Are The Sunshine Of My Life*, *You And Me Against The World*.

Originally recorded by Carole King, for her Grammy winning album, *TAPESTRY*, released in 1971.

Hit versions:
James Taylor – no.1 on the Hot 100 in the States, and no.4 in the UK, in 1971.

Roberta Flack & Donny Hathaway – no.8 on the R&B singles chart and no.29 on the Hot 100 in the States in 1971.

Brand New Heavies – no.9 in the UK in 1997.

YOU'VE MADE ME SO VERY HAPPY

Snippet performed by Michael, along with Dionne Warwick and Smokey Robinson (with Stevie Wonder on piano), at the 1975 American Music Awards – dedicated to Berry Gordy, who won an Award of Merit.

Performed by the Jacksons on *The Tonight Show* in the States in 1977, as part of a medley with *Without A Song, You've Got A Friend, Make It With You, Behind Closed Doors, You've Made Me So Very Happy, You Are The Sunshine Of My Life, You And Me Against The World*.

Hit Versions:
Brenda Holloway – no.40 on the R&B singles chart in the States in 1967.
Blood, Sweat & Tears – no.2 on the Pop chart and no.46 on the R&B chart in the States, and no.35 in the UK, in 1969.
Lou Rawls – no.32 on the R&B chart and no.95 on the Pop chart in the States in 1970.

YOU'VE REALLY GOT A HOLD ON ME

Song recorded by Michael on 13th June 1973, and included in an up-dated mix on his album, *FAREWELL MY SUMMER LOVE*, issued in May 1984 in the States and June 1984 in the UK – demo version also known to exist.

Alternate version featured on the 1998 album, *MOTOWN SINGS MOTOWN TREASURES – THE ULTIMATE RARITIES COLLECTION*.

Original mix included as a bonus track on Michael's posthumous *HELLO WORLD* compilation, issued in July 2009.

Originally recorded by the Miracles, for their 1963 album, *THE FABULOUS MIRACLES*.

Hit versions:
Miracles – no.1 on the R&B singles chart and no.8 on the Hot 100 in the States in 1963.
Gayle McCormick – no.98 on the Hot 100 in 1972.
Eddie Rabbit – no.72 on the Hot 100 in 1979.

ZIP-A-DEE DOO-DAH

Song the Jackson 5 recorded for their debut album, *DIANA ROSS PRESENTS THE JACKSON 5*, issued in December 1969 in the States and March 1970 in the UK.

Performed live by the Jackson 5 at the *Daisy* club on 11th August 1969, for 300 specially invited guests – attended by Berry Gordy. The group's recorded version featured a snippet of Sly & The Family Stone's hit, *Sing A Simple Song*.

Rehearsal footage by the Jackson 5 featured on a promotional film, sent to concert promoters in 1970, to help to make them aware of the group.

Title given to a budget Jackson 5 compilation, released by Music for Pleasure in the UK in January 1979 (no USA issue).

Song originally featured in Disney's 1947 movie, *Song Of The South* – Grammy Award for Song of the Year.

Hit version:
Bob B. Soxx & The Blue Jeans – no.7 on the R&B singles chart and no.8 on the Hot 100 in 1962-63, and no.45 in the UK in 1963.

ZIP-A-DEE DOO-DAH – THERE WAS A TIME – SHAKE THAT MONEY MAKER

Medley – known as the 'Soul Medley' – the Jackson 5 performed on *American Bandstand* in the States in February 1970, with Michael strutting his stuff like James Brown – Michael and his brothers were also presented with Gold Discs.

RUMOUR HAS IT...

These songs may exist – but may not.

If they do exist, they may involve Michael – but they may not.

Some of the entries included in this section are BG (background) cues – not, as some fans believe, unreleased songs by Michael. BG cues are songs used as background music in a TV programme, and the title of the BG cue relates to the TV programme, not the song featured in the TV programme.

4 TRIBES

Remix version of *Wanna Be Startin' Somethin'* by Organ Donors, from the 2003 compilation, *BIG ROOM TUNES VOL.3* – mistakenly believed by many Jackson fans to be a new song.

1990

Song Michael is rumoured to have recorded for the shelved greatest hits package, *DECADE 1980-1990* – remains unconfirmed.

A SONG FOR YOU

ADDAMS'S GROOVE

Song Michael is rumoured to have written, and recorded in spring 1993, for the film *Addams Family Values* – Michael's involvement with the film was scrapped, following the serious allegations made against him at the time.

Alternate titles: *Family Affairs*, *Family Thing* and *Family Values*.

ALL OF MY CHILDREN

BG cue.

ALWAYS

AN ANGEL CAME TO ME

ASK HER IT

BENJAMIN

Song about a boy who aspires to join the circus, recorded by the Dan Priddy – Michael is known to like the song, but reports on some fan sites he is on the song are incorrect.

BREAKING

One of four songs recorded by Michael, reportedly leaked to CFM radio in the States – the station claimed the songs were recorded and mixed at Capital Studios in Hollywood. All four songs remain unconfirmed.

See also: *Dead Or Alive*, *Healing My Feelings*, *What About Me*.

BUBBLE

BYKER GROVE

CAN'T STOP ME NOW

Instrumental demo version exists as a bootleg, but is believed to be a fake.

CRUSH

Song Michael is rumoured to have planned to record as a duet with Lenny Kravitz, with a release date of early 2001 originally talked about – rumour may have arisen as Kravitz was working on the film *Blue Crush* around this time.

Instrumental demo surfaced on the internet in 2005.

DAWN OF A BRAND NEW DAY

Song rumoured to have been recorded by Michael and his brothers for Motown circa 1973 – remains unconfirmed.

DEAD OR ALIVE

One of four songs recorded by Michael, reportedly leaked to CFM radio in the States – the station claimed the songs were recorded and mixed at Capital Studios in Hollywood. All four songs remain unconfirmed.

See also: *Breaking*, *Healing My Feelings*, *What About Me*.

DEEP IN THE NIGHT

One of three titles – along with *Fever* and *Superfly Sister* – scribbled on a note, in a recording studio where Michael was working. May be a song title in its own right, or part of a song's lyrics, or just an idea.

DIRTY MINDS

Song Michael is rumoured to have recorded in 2003 – remains unconfirmed.

DO YOU EVEN CARE

Song Michael is rumoured to have recorded in 2003 – remains unconfirmed.

DON'T BE MESSIN'

DON'T LEAVE ME IN THE DARK

Song Michael is rumoured to have recorded in 2003 – remains unconfirmed.

DRAGON FLY

BG cue.

DUST IN THE WIND

Re-make of a Kansas song (which featured on their 1977 album, *POINT OF KNOW RETURN*), allegedly recorded by

Michael with Mariah Carey. Slated to appear on a six or seven track EP by Mariah titled *Don't Hesitate*, circa December 1996 – remains unconfirmed.

According to reports, the EP wasn't released, largely as a result of behind the scenes problems between Mariah and her husband, Tommy Mottola – president of her (and Michael's) record company, Sony Music Entertainment.

Kansas took the song to no.6 on the Hot 100 in the States.

EASY

BG cue.

ENTERTAINMENT TONIGHT

BG cue.

EVERYTHING ELSE IS A LIE

Song the Jacksons – minus Michael – are rumoured to have worked on circa 1996, for their shelved Humanity project.

FAINT

Song Michael is rumoured to have worked on circa 2003, claimed to feature Ashanti and Ja Rule on vocals – remains unconfirmed.

FAMILY AFFAIR

Touted as a song Michael planned to record for the film, *Addams Family Values* – unconfirmed.

FEVER

One of three titles – along with *Deep In The Night* and *Superfly Sister* – scribbled on a note, in a recording studio where Michael was working. May or may not be a song title.

Also rumoured to be the title of a song that failed to make the final track listing of Michael's album, *DANGEROUS* – however, it may have been confused with *Hot Fever*.

FORCE

Song Michael is rumoured to have written circa 2003, with Irv Gotti, Ashanti and Ja Rule, and recorded with Ashanti and Ja Rule.

FOREVER

Song Michael is rumoured to have worked on circa 2003 – remains unconfirmed.

GET IN TO THE GROOVE

Rumoured title of Michael's original demo versions of his hit, *Black Or White* – unconfirmed.

GET OUT OF MY MIND

Song written by the French composer, Nicolas Piedra, and recorded by the French artist, Ayhnik.

Recorded by Ashanti & Ja Rule – first surfaced on the internet in March 2003, with reported backing vocals from Michael. Ashanti's record management strongly denied Michael had been involved with the track, despite the vocals sounding suspiciously like his.

GET YOUR WEIGHT OFF ME

Instrumental demo rumoured to be from Michael's *INVINCIBLE* sessions. Surfaced on the internet in 2004 – no official release.

GIRL OF ANOTHER LOVE

Song Michael is rumoured to have considered for his album, *DANGEROUS* – remains unreleased.

Also known by the title, *Girl Of Another*.

GOT IT BACK LIKE THAT

Track Nas was rumoured to have recorded, featuring Michael, for his new album due September 2006 – not released.

HEALING MY FEELINGS

One of four songs recorded by Michael, reportedly leaked to CFM radio in the States – the station claimed the songs were recorded and mixed at Capital Studios in Hollywood. All four songs remain unconfirmed.

See also: *Breaking, Dead Or Alive, What About Me*.

HEARTLIGHT

Song Michael is rumoured to have recorded, before *Someone In The Dark*,

for the storybook album, *E.T. THE EXTRA-TERRESTRIAL*.

Recorded by Neil Diamond, for his album of the same title, in 1982.

HEAVEN IS HERE

HOT FUN IN THE SUMMERTIME

Sly & The Family Stone classic Michael is rumoured to have recorded circa 2003 – unconfirmed.

HOUSE OF STYLE

BG cue.

HUMANITY

Song the Jacksons – minus Michael – are rumoured to have worked on circa 1996, for the shelved project of the same title.

I DON'T KNOW

Song Neptune is rumoured to have written for Michael – unconfirmed.

I GOT HUSTLE

Song that gives Michael a co-writing credit – however, it's likely one of Michael's compositions is sampled, rather than it being a new track. Song sampled may be *Centipede* – unconfirmed.

I WANT TO EAT YOU UP

Allegedly the original title for Michael's hit, *Rock With You* – title supposedly changed, to better fit Michael's image.

I'LL GIVE YOU MY LIFE

Song Michael is rumoured to have recorded in 2003 – remains unconfirmed.

I'LL TRY ANYTHING ONCE

One of two songs Michael allegedly wrote for Kylie Minogue – slated to appear on her *FEVER* album in 2001, but remains unconfirmed.

See also: *Time Bomb*.

I'M NOT ALONE

A Cappella snippet – the opening lyrics of Michael's *P.Y.T. (Pretty Young Thing)*, heard on an unfinished demo by Michael. Michael also sang a few bars of the 'song' at the end of *The Way You Make Me Feel*, as seen on a bootleg DVD of the Dangerous Tour rehearsals.

Surfaced on the internet in 2003 – however, although some fans think differently, it's unlikely this is actually a new song.

INEVITABLE

Song Michael is rumoured to have recorded in 2003 – remains unconfirmed.

IT'S GONNA BE A BEAUTIFUL NIGHT

Rumoured collaboration between Michael and Prince – remains unconfirmed.

LIAR, LIAR

Song Michael is rumoured to have recorded in 2003 – remains unconfirmed.

LORE OF AGES

LOVE IN THE WRONG WAY

Song the Jacksons – minus Michael – are rumoured to have worked on circa 1996, for their shelved Humanity project.

MAMACITA

One of a number of tracks recorded by Jason Malachi, which have been incorrectly attributed to Michael by some sources. Other Malachi tracks claimed by some to be new/unreleased Michael recordings include:

- *Bigger Man*
- *Don't Walk Away* (different song to the similarly titled track

Michael recorded for *INVINCIBLE*).

- *Hydraulix*
- *If You Wanna Get With Me*
- *I've Got What You Want*
- *Let Me Let Go*
- *Tell It Like It Is*
- *You Don't Have To Do*

MAYBE TOMORROW

Different to the well known Jackson 5 recording.

MESSAGE IN OUR MUSIC

Song rumoured to have been recorded by the Jacksons – later appeared on the O'Jays album, *IN THE MUSIC*, released in 1976.

MONSTER

MY TENDER HEART

Song Michael is rumoured to have worked on in 2003 – remains unconfirmed.

NEVER STOP ME

Song Michael is rumoured to have worked on in 2003 – remains unconfirmed.

NO EXCUSE

Song Michael is rumoured to have worked on in 2003 – remains unconfirmed.

NOBODY ELSE

Song Michael is rumoured to have recorded in 2003 – remains unconfirmed.

NOW THAT I FOUND LOVE

Song reported in April 2006, claimed to be the first single from a new, as yet untitled Michael Jackson album, set for release in 'late 2007' – reportedly a collaboration between Michael, 50 Cent and Lucy Diamonds.

'It was kinda weird because I didn't even hear about it until after it hit *Rolling Stone*,' said writer Lucy Diamonds. 'It's not true, and I just wanted to say *Now That I Found Love* is my song. Not Michael Jackson's and not 50 Cent's, so if anybody on G-Unit is trying to do it, they can't.'

ON MY ANGER

Song rumoured to have been written by Michael with Teddy Riley circa 1999, and considered for Michael's album, *INVINCIBLE* – unconfirmed.

Alternate title: *Because Of Anger*.

OPEN MIND

Song Michael reportedly worked on in 2003 – remains unconfirmed.

PAPERBACK WRITER

Beatles hit a Dutch magazine alleged Michael had recorded in 1997, for a forthcoming album – remains unconfirmed.

PRAYER FOR PEACE

Song Michael reportedly worked on with Barry Gibb of the Bees Gees in 2003 – however, in October 2005, Barry confirmed the song's actual title was *All In Your Name*.

See also: *All In Your Name*.

PRESSURE I FEEL, THE

Song Michael is rumoured to have worked on in 2003 – remains unconfirmed.

RESPECT

Song Michael is rumoured to have worked on in 2003 – remains unconfirmed.

RESURRECTION

Rumoured title of a project shelved in late 2003, as a result of Michael's arrest and child molestation charges – it remains unconfirmed if there is a song with this title.

REVOLUTION

Song Michael is rumoured to have written circa 2001.

RUMORS

Song mistakenly believed by some fans to have been written by Michael, for Lindsay Lohan's album, *SPEAK*.

Actually written by Michael's nephews Taryll and TJ, with Corey Rooney – may have been written about Michael.

SATURDAY

SECRET PASSAGE

BG cue.

SEPTEMBER DAY

Song Michael is rumoured to have recorded in 2003 – remains unconfirmed.

STAND OUT

Track that surfaced on the internet and rumoured to be by Michael – actually by Tevin Campbell, and originally released on Disney's *A GOOFY SOUNDTRACK* album in 1995.

STILL GOT IT

Song Michael is rumoured to have written circa 2003.

STOP PLAYIN'

Leaked demo by Usher & T-Pain, which it is claimed also featured Michael – unconfirmed.

STRESSED OUT

Song the Neptunes are rumoured to have written for Michael – unconfirmed.

STRONG

Song Michael is rumoured to have worked on in 2003 – remains unconfirmed.

STUDIO 54 DISCO MIX

Disco mix that supposedly included a sample of Michael's voice – considered by most fans to be a fake. Michael did regularly visit the legendary Studio 54 club in the mid-1970s.

SUN IN THE NIGHT

Song Michael is rumoured to have worked on in 2003 – remains unconfirmed.

SUNFLOWER

TAKE MY HAND

Song Michael is rumoured to have worked on in 2003 – remains unconfirmed.

TAKIN' IT TO THE STREETS

Song the Doobie Brothers recorded for their 1976 album of the same name – Michael may have contributed backing vocals to the track, but this is unconfirmed.

The Doobie Brothers took the song to no.13 on the Hot 100 in the States, but it failed to chart in the UK.

TELL THEM WHY

Song about Michael, rumoured to have been recorded by Janet with Houston & Chingy, for her 2006 album, *20 Y.O.* – didn't appear on the album and remains unconfirmed.

THANK YOU

Song Michael is rumoured to have recorded in 2003 – remains unconfirmed.

THERE SHE GOES

Song Neptune is rumoured to have written for Michael – unconfirmed.

THIS IS OUR TIME

Written allegedly written by Michael with David Foster and Lauren Hill in 1999, and originally scheduled for Michael's album, *INVINCIBLE* – existence denied by Hill.

'I remember when my girlfriend called me up to congratulate me on the duet, and I was like – *whaaaat!*' said Hill. 'I mean, I think if I could choose one person in the industry I'd like to record with it'd be

Michael. He is so focused when it comes to what he wants, and who knows – maybe sometime in the future we will work together.'

THIS'LL MAKE YOU CRY

'TIL DEATH DO US PART

Song the Jacksons – minus Michael – are rumoured to have worked on circa 1996, for their shelved Humanity project.

TIME BOMB

One of two songs allegedly written by Michael for Kylie Minogue in 2001, for the American release of her album, *FEVER* – remains unconfirmed.

See also: *I'll Try Anything Once*.

TINGLE

In April 1984, *Breakaway* magazine's Richard Hack reported 'Tingle' would be the title of Michael's new album – he stated there would be three short films and a film. However, Hack quickly back-tracked, admitting he had been fooled by a spoof written about Michael's new album.

TO THE WORLD

Song Michael reportedly co-wrote with Carole Bayer Sager circa 2000 – remains unconfirmed.

TRASH

Song Michael is rumoured to have co-written with Irv Gotti, and worked on circa 2003 – remains unconfirmed.

TRIAL OF THE CENTURY

'New' song, reportedly by Michael with 50 Cent, Lucy Diamonds and DJ Whoo Kid, slated to hit the streets in May 2006 – quickly confirmed to be a hoax.

TRIPLE THREAT CABLE

BG cue.

TRUE LIFE

BG cue.

TRUST ABOUT YOUTH

Song Michael allegedly wrote circa 1991 and considered for his album, *DANGEROUS* – remains unconfirmed.

TRUST IN MY HEART

Song Michael is rumoured to have recorded in 2003, for an album he was working on at the time – unconfirmed.

ULTRASOUND

BG cue.

US TWO ARE IN LOVE

Song rumoured to have been considered, or recorded, for Michael's HIS*TORY* album – unconfirmed.

VERDICT

VISIONS

Song Michael is rumoured to have recorded in 2003 – remains unconfirmed.

WAY IT IS, THE

Song Michael is rumoured to have worked on in 2003 – remains unconfirmed.

WE WILL ALWAYS BE TOGETHER

Song the Jacksons – minus Michael – are rumoured to have worked on circa 1996, for their shelved Humanity project – remains unconfirmed.

WHAT ABOUT ME

One of four songs recorded by Michael, reportedly leaked to CFM radio in the States – the station claimed the songs were recorded and mixed at Capital Studios in Hollywood. All four songs remain unconfirmed.

See also: *Breaking*, *Dead Or Alive*, *Healing My Feelings*.

WHAT IS

WHIPLASH

Song rumoured to have been considered, or recorded, for Michael's HIS*TORY* album – unconfirmed.

WHO DO YOU KNOW

WOOP-T-WOO

Song that credits Michael as a co-writer, along with Khadejia Bass, Lamar Mitchell and Rufus Moore. Michael is also rumoured to sing backing vocals, but his involvement remains unconfirmed.

Recorded by Olivia for her eponymous debut album in 2001.

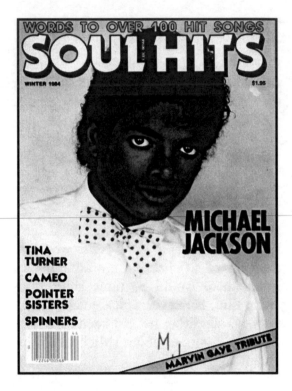

WORLD'S TOGETHER

Listed as a Michael Jackson song on at least one lyrics internet site – remains unconfirmed.

WOULDN'T U LOVE 2 LOVE ME

Song rumoured as a possible collaboration by Michael with Prince, supposedly passed on and *I Just Can't Stop Loving You* chosen instead – remains unconfirmed.

YOU CAN DO ANYTHING

Song reported to have been penned by Babyface, Carole Bayer Sager and Carole King, for Michael's *INVINCIBLE* album – remains unconfirmed.

Recorded by Carole King for her 2001 album, *LOVE MAKES THE WORLD*.

YOU CRY

Track slated to be a new song, and made available over the internet – proved to be *Be Not Always*, from the 1984 Jacksons album, *VICTORY*.

YOU DON'T HAVE TO CALL

Song Neptune is rumoured to have written for Michael – unconfirmed.

YOU-N-YOURS

Song that gives Michael a co-writing credit – however, it's likely one of Michael's compositions is sampled, rather than it being a new track. Song sampled may be *Centipede* – unconfirmed.

PART 2: THE ALBUMS

The albums released by the Jackson 5, Jacksons and Michael in the USA and/or UK are split into categories (studio albums, live albums, compilations, etc.), and are listed chronologically within each category.

Catalogue numbers, release dates, track listings and producer(s) are given for each album, together with other information, including:

- Chart positions achieved in the USA (Pop & R&B) and UK.
- USA sales awards by the RIAA (Recording Industry Association of America).
- UK sales awards by the BPI (British Phonographic Industry).
- American Music Awards, Grammy Awards & selected other awards.
- Hit singles lifted from the album (in the USA and/or UK).

JACKSON 5

Pre-Motown Compilations

GETTING TOGETHER WITH THE JACKSON 5

USA: Music-O MDS 1047 (1971).
UK: Not Released.

Jackson 5: *You Don't Have To Be Over Twenty-One To Fall In Love/Some Girls Want Me For Their Lover*

Despite the title, this album opened with two tracks from the Jackson 5 – but the remaining eight songs were by the Platters, Brooke Benton, Inez & Charlie Foxx, Jerry Butler, Frankie Lymon and Tommy Hunt.

Sleeve photographs taken at the group's last concert in Gary, Indiana – staged in the gym at West Side High School. The concert was widely reported locally and in the black press, and the Jackson 5 were given the keys to the city by Mayor Richard Hatcher.

BEGINNING YEARS 1967-1968

USA: S.D.E.G. SDE4018 (1989)
UK: Ichiban SDEMC 4018 (February 1990)

Monologue/We Don't Have To Be Over 21 (To Fall In Love)/You've Changed/Big Boy/Michael The Lover/Jam Session/My Girl/Soul Jerk/Under The Boardwalk/Saturday Nite At The Movies/Tracks Of My Tears/Lonely Heart/Stormy Monday

Belated compilation of pre-Motown recordings, included the group's first two singles, *Big Boy* and *We Don't Have To Be Over 21 (To Fall In Love)*, and their B-sides – all songs over-dubbed.

Re-packaged and reissued with numerous different titles, including:

IN THE BEGINNING (UK) Charly CDCD 1205.
HISTORIC EARLY RECORDINGS (UK) Charly CPCD 8122.
WE ARE THE JACKSON 5 (UK/Europe) Hallmark 311232/Razamataz RZ4027.
THE LEGEND BEGINS (UK) Hallmark 306572.
THE JACKSON FIVE (Holland) Experience EXPO 20.
STEELTOWN SESSIONS 1965-1967 (UK) Alfafame ALMACD 2.
TRACKS OF MY TEARS (Holland) GG034.
THE JACKSON 5 FEATURING JOHNNY JACKSON ON DRUMS! (Europe) Going for a Song GFS626
5 (Europe) Bellevue Entertainment 10278-2
BOYS & GIRLS – THE ORIGINAL SESSIONS (UK) Entertain Me 5060133744757

THE JACKSON FIVE FEATURING MICHAEL JACKSON

USA: Not Released.
UK: Stardust STACD 081 (September 1993).

Big Boy/You've Changed/We Don't Have To Be Over 21/Michael The Lover/ Stormy Monday/Saturday Night At The Movies/Tracks Of My Tears/A Change Is Gonna Come/Lonely Heart/Boys And Girls, We Are The Jackson Five (Jam Session)/My Girl/Soul Jerk/Under The Boardwalk

Bonus Tracks: Parts Of The Original Sessions From 1965 To 1967 – From The Rehearsals: The Introduction/Boys And Girls, We Are The Jackson Five/My Girl/Soul Jerk/Under The Boardwalk/ Saturday Night At The Movies/Stormy Monday/Tracks Of My Tears/Lonely Heart/A Change Is Gonna Come/Baby, You Don't Have To Go

Album of two halves; first half similar in content to *BEGINNING YEARS*, except songs had been remixed and extended, as well as overdubbed.

Second half featured original pre-Steel-Town recordings, most likely recorded by Joseph Jackson and/or Shirley Cartman in their living room(s).

First released in Japan, titled, *BIG BOY* (Jimco JICM 89317).

Released in various guises over the years, including:

THE FIRST RECORDINGS
   (Portugal/Europe) Goldies GLD 63301.
THE FIRST EVER RECORDING OF
   JACKSON 5: STORMY MONDAY
   (Switzerland/Europe) K Point Gold
   1612 1020-2
THE JACKSON FIVE FEATURING
   MICHAEL JACKSON (Europe)
   ACD CD 154.907

PRE-HISTORY

USA: Brunswick/Inverted BRV 81015-2
   (June 1996).
UK: Not Released.

*Let Me Carry Your Schoolbooks/I Never
Had A Girl/Monologue/MichaelThe
Lover/We Don't Have To Be Over 21 (To
Fall In Love)/Big Boy/You've Changed/
Jam Session (Part 1)/My Girl/Jam
Session (Part 2)/Under The Boardwalk/
Soul Jerk/Saturday Nite At The Movies/
Tracks Of My Tears*

Sub-titled '*The Lost Steeltown
Recordings*'.

First pre-Motown compilation to feature
Let Me Carry Your Schoolbooks and *I
Never Had A Girl*. Footnote confirmed
both songs were performed under the
name 'Ripples & Waves Plus Michael' –
implied they and the Jackson 5 were one
and the same group, which Steel-Town
founder Gordon Keith has always refuted.

Legal action brought by Gordon Keith,
who claimed he had not been recognised
for tracks that appeared on the album, and
that the Jackson 5 had infringed on the
name Ripples & Waves Plus Michael,
which was reportedly used by another
group from Gary, Indiana. Legal
representatives for the Jacksons argued
they did not authorise the release of the
album, so could not be held responsible.

In February 2004 a federal judge, Philip
Simon, ruled Michael had no
involvement in the album's release, and
as a result he was deleted as a defendant,
thus was cleared of any liability.
'(Michael) Jackson has testified that he
had no involvement in the production or
release of the album,' stated Simon in his
ruling, 'that he did not select or approve
of the songs on the album, and that he did
not receive any royalties from the album.'

SOUL MASTERS

Digital-only Release (2005).

*We Don't Have To Be Over 21/You've
Changed/Big Boy/Michael The Lover/
Baby You Don't Have To Go/Stormy
Monday/Boys & Girls, We Are The
Jackson 5/My Girl/Soul Jerk/Under The
Boardwalk/I Found A Love/Saturday
Night At The Movies/The Tracks Of My*

Tears/A Change Is Gonna Come/Lonely Heart

Compilation only available as a digital download – notable for the inclusion of *I Found A Love*, a 30 second previously unheard demo from the pre-Motown days.

Studio Albums

DIANA ROSS PRESENTS...

USA: Motown MS-700 (December 1969).
UK: Tamla Motown STML 11142 (March 1970).

Zip-A-Dee Doo-Dah/Nobody/I Want You Back/Can You Remember?/ Standing In The Shadows Of Love/You've Changed/ My Cherie Amour/Who's Lovin' You/ Chained/(I Know) I'm Losing You/Stand/ Born To Love You

Produced by Bobby Taylor & The Corporation (that is, Berry Gordy, Jr., Fonce Mizell, Freddie Perren & Deke Richards).

Originally going to be titled *INTRODUCING THE JACKSON 5.*

Spent nine weeks at no.1 on Billboard's R&B albums chart in the States, and achieved no.5 on the Pop chart and no.16 in the UK.

At this time, despite their success, it was revealed in Jet magazine that Michael and his brothers were allowed only $5 a week – and this was provided they completed all their chores. If they failed do do their chores, between studying and rehearsing, they were fined a dollar. 'That dollar fine,' said Michael, 'sometimes wrecks my allowance!'

Hit Singles:
I Want You Back.

ABC

USA: Motown MS-709 (May 1970).
UK: Tamla Motown STML 11153 (August 1970).

The Love You Save/One More Chance/ ABC/2-4-6-8/(Come Round Here) I'm The One You Need/Don't Know Why I Love You/Never Had A Dream Come True/True Love Can Be Beautiful/La-La Means I Love You/I'll Bet You/I Found That Girl/The Young Folks

Produced by The Corporation & Hal Davis.

Spent 12 weeks at no.1 on Billboard's R&B albums chart in the States, and peaked at no.4 on the Pop chart and no.22 in the UK.

Hit Singles:
ABC.
The Love You Save.

THIRD ALBUM

USA: Motown MS-718 (September 1970).
UK: Tamla Motown STML 11174 (February 1971).

I'll Be There/Ready Or Not Here I Come (Can't Hide From Love)/Oh How Happy/ Bridge Over Troubled Water/Can I See You In The Morning/Goin' Back To Indiana/How Funky Is Your Chicken/ Mama's Pearl/Reach In/The Love I Saw In You Was Just A Mirage/Darling Dear

Produced by The Corporation, Hal Davis, George Gordy & Lawrence Brown.

Spent 10 weeks at no.1 on Billboard's R&B albums chart in the States, and no.4 on the Pop chart – failed to chart in the UK.

Hit Singles:
I'll Be There.
Mama's Pearl.

CHRISTMAS ALBUM

USA: Motown MS-713 (October 1970).
UK: Tamla Motown STML 11168 (December 1970).

Have Yourself A Merry Little Christmas/ Santa Claus Is Comin' To Town/The Christmas Song/Up On The House Top/Frosty The Snowman/The Little Drummer Boy/Rudolph The Red-Nosed Reindeer/Christmas Won't Be The Same This Year/Give Love On Christmas Day/ Someday At Christmas/I Saw Mommy Kissing Santa Claus

Produced by Hal Davis & The Corporation.

Charted on Billboard's special Christmas albums chart, achieving no.1 in 1970, no.2 in 1971, and no.1 in both 1972 and 1973 (the chart was discontinued in 1974, and not resumed until 1983).

Hit Singles:
Santa Claus Is Coming To Town.
I Saw Mommy Kissing Santa Claus.

MAYBE TOMORROW

USA: Motown MS-735 (April 1971).
UK: Tamla Motown STML 11188 (October 1971).

Maybe Tomorrow/She's Good/Never Can Say Goodbye/The Wall/ Petals/Sixteen Candles/(We've Got) Blue Skies/My Little Baby/It's Great To Be Here/Honey Chile/I Will Find A Way

Produced by The Corporation, Hal Davis, Mel Larson & Jerry Marcellino.

First Jackson 5 album to be issued with a gatefold sleeve in the States.

Spent six weeks at no.1 on Billboard's R&B albums chart in the States, and peaked at no.11 on the Pop chart – failed to chart in the UK.

Hit Singles:
Never Can Say Goodbye.
Maybe Tomorrow.

LOOKIN' THROUGH THE WINDOWS

USA: Motown M750L (May 1972).
UK: Tamla Motown STML 11214 (October 1972).

Ain't Nothing Like The Real Thing/ Lookin' Through The Windows/Don't Let Your Baby Catch You/To Know/Doctor My Eyes/Little Bitty Pretty One/E-Ne-Me-Ne-Mi-Ne-Mo (The Choice Is Yours To Pull)/If I Have To Move A Mountain/ Don't Want To See Tomorrow/ Children Of The Light/I Can Only Give You Love

Produced by Jerry Marcellino & Mel Larson, Hal Davis, The Corporation & Willie Hutch.

Hit Singles:
Little Bitty Pretty One.

Lookin' Through The Windows.
Doctor My Eyes.

SKYWRITER

USA: Motown M761L (March 1973).
UK: Tamla Motown STML 11231 (July 1973).

Skywriter/Hallelujah Day/The Boogie Man/Touch/Corner Of The Sky/I Can't Quit Your Love/Uppermost/World Of Sunshine/Ooh, I'd Love To Be With You/You Made Me What I Am

Produced by Mel Larson & Jerry Marcellino, Freddie Perren & Fonce Mizell, Deke Richards, The Corporation, Hal Davis & Sherlie Matthews.

Originally the album was going to be titled after another track, *Hallelujah Day.*

Achieved no.15 on Billboard's R&B albums chart and no.44 on the Pop chart – failed to chart in the UK.

Hit Singles:
Corner Of The Sky.
Skywriter.
Hallelujah Day.
The Boogie Man.

Commercial for the album won 1st prize at the Atlanta Film Festival.

GET IT TOGETHER

USA: Motown M783V1 (September 1973).
UK: Tamla Motown STML 11243 (November 1973).

Get It Together/Don't Say Goodbye Again/ Reflections/Hum Along And Dance/Mama I Gotta Brand New Thing (Don't Say No)/It's Too Late To Change The Time/You Need Love Like I Do (Don't You?)/Dancing Machine

Produced by Hal Davis.

Alternate title: *GET IT TOGETHER, LEAVE IT ALONE.*

Charted at no.4 on Billboard's R&B albums chart and no.100 on the Pop chart – failed to chart in the UK.

Hit Singles:
Get It Together.
Dancing Machine.

DANCING MACHINE

USA: Motown M6-780S1 (September 1974).
UK: Tamla Motown STML 11275 (November 1974).

I Am Love/Whatever You Got, I Want/ She's A Rhythm Child/Dancing Machine/ The Life Of The Party/What You Don't Know/If I Don't Love You This Way/It All Begins And Ends With Love/The Mirrors Of My Mind

Produced by Mel Larson & Jerry Marcellino and Hal Davis.

Peaked at no.16 on Billboard's Pop albums chart, but didn't make the R&B chart and failed to chart in the UK.

Hit Singles:
Whatever You Got, I Want.
I Am Love

MOVING VIOLATION

USA: Motown M6-829S1 (May 1975).
UK: Tamla Motown STML 11290 (July 1975).

Forever Came Today/Moving Violation/
(You Were Made) Especially For Me/
Honey Love/Body Language (Do The
Love Dance)/All I Do Is Think Of
You/Breezy/Call Of The Wild/Time
Explosion

Produced by Brian Holland, Hal Davis, Mel Larson & Jerry Marcellino.

Last studio album the Jackson 5 recorded for Motown.

Achieved no.6 on Billboard's R&B albums chart in the States, and no.36 on the Pop chart – failed to chart in the UK.

Hit Singles:
Forever Came Today.
All I Do Is Think Of You
   (B-side of above).

JOYFUL JUKEBOX MUSIC

USA: Motown M6-865S1 (October 1976).
UK: Tamla Motown STML 12046 (December 1976).

Joyful Jukebox Music/Window Shopping/
You're My Best Friend, My Love/Love Is
The Thing You Need/The Eternal Light
/Pride And Joy/ Through Thick And
Thin/We're Here To Entertain You/Make
Tonight All Mine/We're Gonna Change
Our Style

Produced by Tom Bee & Michael Edward Campbell, Hal Davis, Sam Brown III, Freddie Perren & Fonce Mizell, Mel Larson & Jerry Marcellino.

First Jackson 5 release to single out Michael: it carried the credit 'featuring Michael Jackson'.

Released after the Jackson 5 had left Motown, and signed for CBS/Epic – hence included no newly recorded songs. The group's contract with Motown ran from 11th March 1969 to 10th March 1975, and they last recorded for the label on 28th May 1974 – most of the songs on this album were recorded in 1972-73.

No singles released and failed to chart in the States or UK.

Live Album

LIVE! / IN JAPAN!

USA: Hip-O Select/Motown B003070-02
   (December 2006 as *IN JAPAN!*).
UK: Motown WD 72641 (September
   1988 as *LIVE!*).

*Introduction/We're Gonna Have A Good
Time/Lookin' Through The Windows/Got
To Be There/Medley (I Want You Back/
ABC/The Love You Save)/Daddy's Home/
Superstition/Ben/ Papa Was A Rolling
Stone/That's How Love Goes/Never Can
Say Goodbye/Ain't That Peculiar/I
Wanna Be Where You Are*

Originally released in Japan in 1973,
titled *IN JAPAN!* (Motown SWX 6024).

Concert recorded at the Osaka
Koseinenkin Hall, Japan, on 30th April
1973.

Single vinyl album titled *IN CONCERT!*
(Tamla Motown STMA 15003)
discovered in the late 1990s, among a
batch of over 6,000 albums originally
owned by the Overseas Armed Forces
Radio Stations library in Singapore –
origins uncertain.

American release *IN JAPAN!* was
released as a limited edition of 5,000
copies – omitted to list *Medley (I Want
You Back/ABC/The Love You Save)* on
the sleeve.

TV Soundtrack Albums

GOIN' BACK TO INDIANA

USA: Motown M742L (September
   1971).
UK: Not Released.

*I Want You Back/Maybe Tomorrow/The
Day Basketball Was Saved/ Stand/I Want
To Take You Higher/Feelin' Alright/
Medley: Walk On – The Love You Save/
Goin' Back To Indiana*

Executive producer: Berry Gordy.

Accompanied the Jackson 5's first TV
special, filmed on 9-10th July 1971, and
aired in the States on ABC-TV on 19th
September 1971. Guest stars included
Bill Cosby (as roving news reported
'Scoop Newsworthy'), Tommy Smothers,
American footballer Roosevelt 'Rosey'
Grier and numerous pro-basketball stars,
with a short cameo appearance by Diana
Ross.

Included newly recorded versions of *I
Want You Back* and *Maybe Tomorrow*.
Side 2 showcased the quintet live in
concert – performance recorded in Gary,
Indiana on 29th May 1971.

Charted at no.5 on Billboard's R&B
albums chart, and no.15 in the Pop
albums chart, in the States.

Reissued in the States in 1974, minus
Maybe Tomorrow, titled *STAND*
(Pickwick SPC 3394).

THE JACKSONS: AN AMERICAN DREAM

USA: Motown 374636356-2 (October 1992).
UK: Motown 530119-2 (July 1993).

Who's Lovin' You (Live)/Kansas City (Jason Weaver)/*I'll Be There/In The Still Of The Nite (I'll Remember)* (Boyz II Men)/*Medley: Walk On/The Love You Save (Live)/I Wanna Be Where You Are* (Jason Weaver)/*Dancing Machine/The Dream Goes On* (Jermaine)/*Medley: I Want You Back/ABC (Live)/Stay With Love* (Jermaine & Syreeta Wright)/*Never Can Say Goodbye/You Are The Ones (Interlude)* (3T)/*Dancing Machine (Remix)*

Credited to the Jacksons, but mostly featured songs from the Motown era – some originals, some cover versions.

Executive producers: Suzanne de Passe & Steve McKeever.

Accompanied five hour TV mini-series based 'on the inspiring and true story of the Jackson family, from its humble origins in a Midwestern steel town to the centre stage of world entertainment'. Produced by Jermaine Jackson and his partner, Margaret Maldonado; cost $13.5 million to make and premiered in two parts on ABC-TV, on 15th and 18th November 1992.

Mini-series cast included: Lawrence-Hilton Jacobs (as Joseph Jackson), Angela Bassett (Katherine Jackson), Billy Dee William (Berry Gordy, Jr.), Vanessa Williams (Suzanne de Passe) and Holly Robinson (Diana Ross). Michael played by Alex Burrall (pre-Motown era), Jason Weaver (Jackson 5 era) and Wylie Draper (CBS/Epic era).

Estimated audience: 22 million – at the time, the highest ever ratings for such a mini-series.

Included a previously unreleased live version of *Who's Lovin' You*, recorded in Japan in 1973 (see *LIVE!/IN JAPAN!*) – discovered only days before filming of the mini-series finished.

Achieved no.41 on Billboard's R&B albums chart, and no.137 on the Pop albums chart, in the States.

Hit Singles:
Who's Lovin' You (Live).
In The Still Of The Nite (I'll Remember) (Boyz II Men).

Reissues with Bonus Tracks

DIANA ROSS PRESENTS... & ABC

USA: Motown 440 014 380-2 (August 2001).
UK: Not Released.

Bonus Track: *Oh, I've Been Bless'd*

THIRD ALBUM & MAYBE TOMORROW

USA: Motown 440 014 381-2 (August 2001).
UK: Not Released.

Bonus Tracks: *Sugar Daddy/I'm So Happy*

GOIN' BACK TO INDIANA & LOOKIN' THROUGH THE WINDOWS

USA: Motown: 440 014 382-2 (August 2001).
UK: Not Released.

Bonus Tracks: *Love Song/Who's Lovin' You (Live in Gary, Indiana)*

SKYWRITER & GET IT TOGETHER

USA: Motown 440 014 383-2 (August 2001).
UK: Not Released.

Bonus Tracks: *Pride And Joy/Love's Gone Bad/Love Is The Thing You Need*

DANCING MACHINE & MOVING VIOLATION

USA: Motown 440014 384-2 (August 2001).

UK: Not Released.

Bonus Tracks: *Through Thick And Thin/ Forever Came Today ('Disc-O-Tech #3' Version)*

THE CHRISTMAS COLLECTION

USA: Motown B0000707-02 (September 2003).
UK: Not Released.

Bonus Track: *Little Christmas Tree*

Achieved no.96 on Billboard's R&B albums chart, and no.7 on the R&B Catalog albums chart, in the States.

JOYFUL JUKEBOX MUSIC & BOOGIE

USA: Hip-O Select/Motown B0003016-02 (November 2004).
UK: Not released.

Bonus Track: *Hum Along And Dance (Uncut)*

Limited edition of 5,000 copies.

Compilations

GREATEST HITS

USA: Motown 741L (December 1971).
UK: Tamla Motown STML 11212
   (August 1972).

USA: *I Want You Back/ABC/Never Can Say Goodbye/Sugar Daddy/I'll Be There/ Maybe Tomorrow/The Love You Save/ Who's Lovin' You/ Mama's Pearl/Goin' Back To Indiana/I Found That Girl*

UK: *I Want You Back/ABC/Never Can Say Goodbye/I'll Be There/ Maybe Tomorrow/The Love You Save/Who's Lovin' You/Mama's Pearl/Goin' Back To Indiana/I Found That Girl/Got To Be There/ Rockin' Robin*

First greatest hits compilation by the Jackson 5 – and the only one released whilst they were still a Motown act.

American version included the non-album hit, *Sugar Daddy*.

Charted at no.2 on Billboard's R&B albums chart and no.12 on the Pop albums chart in the States, and no.26 in the UK.

Reissued on numerous occasions, not always with the original track listings.

USA SoundScan sales since 1991: around 500,000 – eligible for a RIAA Gold Record on this basis alone, and has probably sold well enough to merit a RIAA Platinum Record.

ANTHOLOGY

USA: Motown M7-868R3 (June 1976).
UK: Tamla Motown TMSP 6004
   (January 1977).

USA LP1: *I Want You Back/ABC/Don't Know Why I Love You/I'll Be There/The Love You Save/I Found That Girl/I Am Love/Body Language/Forever Came Today*

USA LP2: *Mama's Pearl/Got To Be There/ Goin' Back To Indiana/Never Can Say Goodbye/Sugar Daddy/Maybe Tomorrow/Get It Together/Dancing Machine/Whatever You Got, I Want/ We're Almost There/Just A Little Bit Of You/All I Do Is Think Of You*

US LP3: *Rockin' Robin/I Wanna Be Where You Are/Ben/That's How Love Goes* (Jermaine) */Love Don't Want To Leave* (Jackie)*/Daddy's Home* (Jermaine)*/Lookin' Through The Windows/Little Bitty Pretty One/Corner Of The Sky/Skywriter/Hallelujah Day/ The Boogie Man*

UK LP1: *I Want You Back/ABC/The Love You Save/I'll Be There/Mama's Pearl/ Never Can Say Goodbye/Got To Be There/Sugar Daddy/ Rockin' Robin/Little Bitty Pretty One/I Wanna Be Where You Are/Ain't No Sunshine/Lookin' Through The Windows/Ben/That's How Love Goes* (Jermaine)

UK LP2: *Doctor My Eyes/Daddy's Home* (Jermaine)*/Hallelujah Day/Morning Glow/Skywriter/Get It Together/The Boogie Man/Music And Me/Dancing Machine/The Life Of The Party/Whatever*

You Got, I Want/I Am Love/We're Almost There/Forever Came Today/Just A Little Bit Of You

Achieved no.32 on Billboard's R&B albums chart, and no.84 on the Pop albums chart, in the States – failed to chart in the UK.

MOTOWN SPECIAL

USA: Not Released.
UK: Tamla Motown STMX 6006 (March 1977).

Never Can Say Goodbye/ABC/My Cherie Amour/Standing In The Shadows Of Love/(Come Round Here) I'm The One You Need/(I Know) I'm Losing You/I'll Be There/Don't Know Why I Love You/Chained/Born To Love You/One More Chance/True Love Can Be Beautiful

BOOGIE

USA: Natural Resources NR-4013T1 (January 1979).
UK: Not Released.

Love's Gone Bad/I Ain't Gonna Eat Out My Heart Anymore/ABC/I Was Made To Love Her/One Day I'll Marry You/Never Can Say Goodbye/Oh, I've Been Bless'd/Penny Arcade/Just Because I Love You/Dancing Machine

Compilation including seven previously unreleased Michael/Jackson 5 recordings, originally issued in North America on a small, subsidiary Motown label – quickly withdrawn from sale. Also released in Australia, in what may the rarest pressing of the album.

Featured slightly different mixes of *ABC*, *The Love You Save* and *Dancing Machine*.

ZIP-A-DEE DOO-DAH

USA: Not Released.
UK: Music for Pleasure MfP 50418 (January 1979).

The Love You Save/Ain't Nothin' Like The Real Thing/Lookin' Through The Windows/Don't Let Your Baby Catch You/Doctor My Eyes/Zip-A-Dee Doo-Dah/My Cherie Amour/Little Bitty Pretty One/Ready Or Not, Here I Come/E-Ne-Me-Ne-Mi-Ne-Moe/If I Have To Move A Mountain/Don't Want To See Tomorrow/Children Of The Light

20 GOLDEN GREATS

USA: Not Released.
UK: Tamla Motown STML 12121 (September 1979).

I Want You Back/Lookin' Through The Windows/Skywriter/Ain't No Sunshine/

Doctor My Eyes/The Love You Save/I'll Be There/Rockin' Robin/Never Can Say Goodbye/Forever Came Today/Ben/Got To Be There/Dancing Machine/The Boogie Man/ABC/Little Bitty Pretty One/Hallelujah Day/Mama's Pearl/Get It Together/I Am Love

MOTOWN SUPERSTAR SERIES Vol.12

USA: Motown M5-112V1 (September 1980).
UK: Not Released.

Medley Of Hits (I Want You Back/ABC/ The Love You Save/I'll Be There/Never Can Say Goodbye/Dancing Machine/ Lookin' Through The Windows)/Mama's Pearl/Maybe Tomorrow/Get It Together/I Am Love

Featured a previously unreleased alternate take of *Get It Together*.

THE JACKSON 5 FEATURING MICHAEL JACKSON

USA: Not Released.
UK: Pickwick TMS 3503 (June 1982).

The Love You Save/Ain't Nothin' Like The Real Thing/Little Bitty Pretty One/ Lookin' Through The Windows/Don't Let Your Baby Catch You/Doctor My Eyes/ E-Ne-Me- Ne-Mi-Ne-Moe/Zip-A-Dee Doo-Dah/My Cherie Amour/If I Have To Move A Mountain/Children Of The Light/I Can Only Give You Love/Ready Or Not, Here I Come/Don't Want To See Tomorrow

THE GREAT LOVE SONGS OF...

USA: Motown 5346ML (June 1984).
UK: Tamla Motown WL 72290 (November 1984).

I'll Be There/Maybe Tomorrow/I Found That Girl/La-La Means I Love You/Ain't Nothing Like The Real Thing/One More Chance/Never Can Say Goodbye/Touch/ Don't Know Why I Love You/All I Do Is Think Of You/To Know/It All Begins And Ends With Love

MOTOWN LEGENDS

USA: Motown 5365 ML (June 1985).
UK: Not Released.

The Love You Save/Ain't Nothing Like The Real Thing/Lookin' Through The Windows/Don't Let Your Baby Catch You/Doctor My Eyes/Little Bitty Pretty One/Zip-A-Dee Doo-Dah/Ready Or Not, Here I Come (Can't Hide from Love)/

E-Ni-Me-Ni-Mi-Ni-Moe (The Choice Is Yours To Pull)/If I Have To Move A Mountain/Don't Want To See Tomorrow/Children Of The Light/I Can Only Give You Love/My Cherie Amour

ANTHOLOGY

USA: Motown MOTD2-6194 (August 1986).
UK: Tamla Motown WD 72529 (June 1987).

CD1: *I Want You Back/ABC/Don't Know Why I Love You/I'll Be There/The Love You Save/I Found That Girl/Mama's Pearl/Who's Lovin' You/Goin' Back To Indiana/Never Can Say Goodbye/Sugar Daddy/ Maybe Tomorrow/Lookin' Through The Windows/Little Bitty Pretty One/Teenage Symphony/Corner Of The Sky/Skywriter/Hallelujah Day/The Boogie Man/I Am Love*

CD2: *I Hear A Symphony/Get It Together/Dancing Machine/Whatever You Got, I Want/I Was Made To Love Her/All I Do Is Think Of You/Body Language/Forever Came Today/Got To Be There/Rockin' Robin/I Wanna Be Where You Are/Ben/We're Almost There/Just A Little Bit Of You/That's How Love Goes* (Jermaine)/*Love Don't Want To Leave* (Jackie)/*Daddy's Home* (Jermaine)/*Let's Get Serious* (Jermaine)/*You're Supposed To Keep Your Love For Me* (Jermaine)/*Let Me Tickle Your Fancy* (Jermaine)

Reissue of the similarly titled American triple album issued in 1976, with seven bonus tracks added – came with a deluxe 32 page booklet.

I'LL BE THERE

USA: Motown MOTC 3710 (1989).
UK: Not Released.

I'll Be There/I Want You Back/That's How Love Goes (Jermaine)/*We're Gonna Change Our Style/Body Language/I Can Only Give You Love/Call Of The Wild/Through Thick And Thin*

Released on cassette only.

THE LOVE YOU SAVE

USA: Motown MOTC 3031 (1989).
UK: Not Released.

The Love You Save/ABC/Darling Dear/The Wall/Don't Want To See Tomorrow/The Young Folks/I Am Love (Part 2)/Call Of The Wild

Released on cassette only.

MAMA'S PEARL

USA: Motown MOTC (1989).
UK: Not Released.

Mama's Pearl/Dancing Machine/Time Explosion/Breezy/The Eternal Light/Window Shopping/The Life Of The Party/Through Thick And Thin

Released on cassette only.

ORIGINAL MOTOWN CLASSICS

USA: Motown MSC 95000/PDK-2-1272 (1990).
UK: Not Released.

*I Want You Back/ABC/Never Can Say
Goodbye/The Love You Save/Oh How
Happy/La La (Means I Love You)/Doctor
My Eyes/Ain't Nothin' Like The Real
Thing/Stand/Bridge Over Troubled
Water/Petals/My Little Baby/Honey
Chile/Reach In/Darling Dear/Never
Had A Dream Come True*

Released on cassette only.

CHILDREN OF THE LIGHT

USA: Not Released.
UK: Spectrum 550076-2 (May 1993).

*The Love You Save/Ain't Nothing Like
The Real Thing/Lookin' Through The
Windows/Don't Let Your Baby Catch
You/I Can Only Give You Love/Little
Bitty Pretty One/Zip-A-Dee Doo-Dah/
Ready Or Not (Here I Come)/E-Ne-Me-
Ni-Mi-Ni-Moe (The Choice Is Yours To
Pull)/If I Have To Move A Mountain/
Don't Want To See Tomorrow/Children
Of The Light/Doctor My Eyes/My Cherie
Amour*

Re-issued in October 2000 with a
different sleeve.

MOTOWN LEGENDS

USA: Motown 374638506 2 (December
   1993).
UK: Not Released.

*Never Can Say Goodbye/I Can't Quit
Your Love/Get It Together/Standing In
The Shadows Of Love/Little Bitty Pretty
One/I Want You Back/Oh How Happy/
Sixteen Candles/Forever Came Today/
One More Chance/My Cherie Amour*

This compilation was re-packaged (with a
wrap-around card sleeve) and reissued in
October 2005, as *ROCK ON BREAKOUT
YEARS* (Madacy/Motown BOY2 51111).

THE ULTIMATE COLLECTION

USA: Motown 314530558-2 (February
   1996).
UK: Motown 530558-2 (August 1998).

*I Want You Back/ABC/The Love You
Save/I'll Be There/It's Your Thing/Who's
Lovin' You/Mama's Pearl/Never Can Say
Goodbye/ Maybe Tomorrow/Got To Be
There/Sugar Daddy/Rockin' Robin/
Daddy's Home* (Jermaine)/*Lookin'
Through The Windows/I Wanna Be
Where You Are/Get It Together/Dancing
Machine/The Life Of The Party/I Am
Love – Pts. I & II/Just A Little Bit Of
You/It's Your Thing (The J5 In '95
Extended Remix)*

Charted at no.141 on the UK albums
chart.

Posthumous hit: no.4 on the R&B catalog album chart and no.5 on the pop catalog albums charts in the USA, no.87 in Canada and no.95 in Ireland.

THE BEST OF – THE MILLENNIUM COLLECTION

USA: Motown 012153364-2 (October 1999).
UK: Not Released.

I Want You Back/ABC/The Love You Save/I'll Be There/Never Can Say Goodbye/Got To Be There/Sugar Daddy/Daddy's Home (Jermaine)/*I Wanna Be Where You Are/Maybe Tomorrow/Dancing Machine*

Achieved no. 17 on Billboard's R&B Catalog albums chart, and no.47 on the Pop Catalog albums chart, in the States.

RIAA Gold Record = 500,000 copies.

Posthumous hit: no.6 on the R&B catalog album chart and no.8 on the pop catalog

albums charts in the USA, and no.19 in Canada.

'RIPPLES AND WAVES' AN INTRODUCTION TO...

USA: Not Released.
UK: Motown 157170-2 (July 2000).

I Want You Back/Who's Lovin' You/Reach In/Honey Love/Got To Be There/Pride And Joy/The Eternal Light/Touch/Corner Of The Sky/The Boogie Man/Love Scenes/Money Honey/ Coming Home/Skywriter/Mama's Pearl/ She's Good/Maybe Tomorrow

ANTHOLOGY / GOLD / THE JACKSONS STORY / ICONS

USA: Motown 012159650-2 (October 2000 as *ANTHOLOGY*).
UK: Universal 9880152 (September 2005 as *GOLD*); Universal 9832422 (May 2006 as *THE JACKSONS STORY*); Spectrum 5316475 (May 2009 as *ICONS*).

CD1: *I Want You Back/Who's Lovin' You/ABC/The Young Folks/I Found That Girl/I'll Bet You/I'll Be There/Goin' Back To Indiana/ Mama's Pearl/Darling Dear/Never Can Say Goodbye/Maybe Tomorrow/It's Great To Be Here/Sugar Daddy/I'm So Happy/Medley (Sing A Simple Song/Can You Remember)/Doctor My Eyes/Little Bitty Pretty One/Lookin' Through The Windows/Love Song*

CD2: *Corner Of The Sky/Touch/ Hallelujah Day/Daddy's Home (live)/Get It Together/Hum Along And Dance/ Mama I Got A Brand New Thing (Don't Say No)/It's Too Late To Change The Time/Dancing Machine/Whatever You Got, I Want/The Life Of The Party/I Am Love/All I Do Is Think Of You/Forever Came Today/We're Here To Entertain You*

Third Jackson 5 compilation with the same title, but the first to not feature any solo recordings by Michael, Jermaine or Jackie.

SOUL LEGENDS

USA: Not Released.

UK: Motown 9841753 (August 2006).

Reach Out I'll Be There/It's Your Thing/Let's Have A Party/I Want You Back/My Girl/Whatever You Want, I Got/The Boogie Man/I'll Bet You/Mama I Gotta A Brand New Thing (Don't Say No)/Just A Little Misunderstanding/ Mama's Pearl/ABC/Dancing Machine/ Doctor My Eyes/Money Honey/A Fool For You/I'll Be There/Never Can Say Goodbye/You've Got A Friend

CLASSIC

USA: Not Released.
UK: Spectrum 5314941 (December 2008).

I Want You Back/Who's Lovin' You/ Reach In/Honey Love/Got To Be There/Pride And Joy/The Eternal Light/Touch/Corner Of The Sky/The Boogie Man/Love Scenes/Money Honey/ Coming Home/Skywriter/Mama's Pearl/She's Good/Maybe Tomorrow

Posthumous hit: no.4 in the UK (Budget Albums).

LOVE SONGS

USA: 001246402 (January 2009).
UK: Not Released.

*I'll Be There/Darling Dear/I Found That
Girl/Can You Remember/All I Do Is
Think Of You/Never Can Say Goodbye/
Breezy/To Know/Touch/ I'm So Happy/
Through Thick And Thin/It All Begins
And Ends With Love*

Posthumous hit: no.36 on the R&B
albums chart and no.186 on the Billboard
200 in the USA.

JACKSON 5 / MICHAEL JACKSON

Compilations

18 GREATEST HITS

USA: Not Released.
UK: Telstar STAR 2232 (July 1983).
  Motown ZL 72158 (re-issue, July
  1988).

*One Day In Your Life/Lookin' Through
The Windows/Got To Be There/Doctor
My Eyes/Ben/ABC/We're Almost There/
Skywriter/Rockin' Robin/Happy (Love
Theme From 'Lady Sings The Blues')/
Ain't No Sunshine/I'll Be There/I Want
You Back/The Love You Save/We've Got
A Good Thing Going/Mama's Pearl/
Never Can Say Goodbye/ Hallelujah Day*

No.1 in the UK for three weeks – helped
by TV advertising and the runaway
success of Michael's *THRILLER* album.

Happy (Love Theme From 'Lady Sings The Blues') lifted as a single – charted at no.52 in the UK.

No.10 best selling album of the year in the UK.

BPI Platinum Record = 300,000 copies.

GREAT SONGS & PERFORMANCES THAT INSPIRED THE MOTOWN 25th ANNIVERSARY T.V. SPECIAL

USA: Motown 5312ML (August 1983).
UK: Not Released.

I Want You Back/The Love You Save/I'll Be There/ABC/Rockin' Robin/Maybe Tomorrow/Got To Be There/I Wanna Be Where You Are/Ben/Dancing Machine

Compilation inspired by, but included no music recorded during, *Motown 25: Yesterday, Today, Forever* – a 25th anniversary celebration concert filmed at the Pasadena Civic Auditorium on 25th March 1983. At the concert, the original members of the Jackson 5 performed together for the first time since 1975, and were joined by Randy, to sing a medley of their Motown hits – after which, Michael stole the show with his rendition of *Billie Jean*.

Achieved no.7 on Billboard's Top Midline Albums chart (which was later re-vamped as the Catalog Albums chart), loggiong a creditable 50 weeks on the chart.

14 OF THEIR GREATEST HITS

USA: K-Tel NU 5510 (November 1983).
UK: Not Released.

Ben/Rockin' Robin/Never Can Say Goodbye/ Dancing Machine/We're Almost There/Just A Little Bit Of You/One Day In Your Life/Got To Be There/I'll Be There/ABC/The Love You Save/Oh How Happy/I Wanna Be Where You Are/I Want You Back

COMPACT COMMAND PERFORMANCES – 18 GREATEST HITS

USA: Motown MCD-06060MD1 (February 1984).
UK: Motown WD 72420 (May 1984).

Got To Be There/Rockin' Robin/I Wanna Be Where You Are/Ben/With A Child's Heart/One Day In Your Life/I Want You Back/Who's Lovin' You/ABC/The Love You Save/I'll Be There/Mama's Pearl/ Never Can Say Goodbye/Maybe Tomorrow/Sugar Daddy/Lookin'

*Through The Windows/Get It Together/
Dancing Machine*

14 GREATEST HITS

USA: Motown 6099ML (May 1984).
UK: Not Released.

*I Want You Back/ABC/The Love You
Save/I'll Be There/Mama's Pearl/Never
Can Say Goodbye/Maybe Tomorrow/
Lookin' Through The Windows/Dancing
Machine/Got To Be There/Rockin'
Robin/I Wanna Be Where You
Are/Ben/One Day In Your Life* [Cassette
Only: *Sugar Daddy/Little Bitty Pretty
One*]

Released as a picture disc album, and
came with a free poster and white glove,
printed all over with the old Jackson 5
logo.

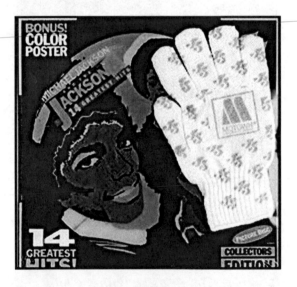

Cassette version titled *16 GREATEST
HITS* – came with the same white glove
and a stand-up photograph.

Peaked at no.168 on Billboard's Pop
albums chart – failed to register on the
R&B albums chart.

SOULSATION!

USA: Motown 31453-0489-2/4 (June
   1995).
UK: Motown 530 489-2 (July 1995).

CD1: *I Want You Back/Who's Lovin'
You/You've Changed/Stand!/Can You
Remember/ABC/The Love You Save/I
Found That Girl/La La (Means I Love
You)/I'll Bet You/(Come Round Here) I'm
The One You Need/The Young Folks/I'll
Be There/Goin' Back To Indiana/Can I
See You In The Morning/Mama's Pearl/
Reach In/Christmas Won't Be The Same
This Year/Santa Claus Is Coming To
Town/Never Can Say Goodbye/Maybe
Tomorrow/She's Good*

CD2: *Got To Be There/People Make The
World Go Round/Teenage Symphony/
Sugar Daddy/Ain't Nothing Like The
Real Thing/Lookin' Through The
Windows/Doctor My Eyes/Little Bitty
Pretty One/If I Had To Move A
Mountain/Rockin' Robin/I Wanna Be
Where You Are/Ben/ Skywriter/You Made
Me What I Am/Hallelujah Day/Touch/
Corner Of The Sky/The Boogie Man/Get
It Together/Dancing Machine/It's Too
Late To Change The Time/Whatever You
Got, I Want*

CD3: *The Life Of The Party/I Am Love –
Pts I & II/If I Don't Love You This
Way/Mama I Gotta Brand New Thing
(Don't Say No)/Forever Came Today/
Body Language (Do The Love Dance)/All
I Do Is Think Of You/It's A Moving*

Violation/(You Were Made) Especially For Me/ Honey Love/That's How Love Goes (Jermaine)/*Daddy's Home* (Jermaine)/*Just A Little Bit Of You/Love Is The Thing You Need/The Eternal Light/Pride And Joy/You're My Best Friend, My Love/Joyful Jukebox Music/Love Don't Wanna Leave* (Jackie)

CD4 Rare & Unreleased: *Can't Get Ready For Losing You/You Ain't Giving Me What I Want (So I'm Taking It All Back)/Reach Out I'll Be There/I'm Glad It Rained/A Fool For You/It's Your Thing/Everybody Is A Star/I Need You* (Jermaine)/*You're The Only One/Just A Little Misunderstanding/Jamie/Ask The Lonely/We Can Have Fun/I Hear A Symphony/Let's Have A Party/Love Scenes/LuLu/Money Honey/Coming Home*

Box-set credited to the Jackson Five in the States, and to Michael Jackson with the Jackson Five in the UK.

CD4 featured '19 Rare & Unreleased' recordings – but *Ask The Lonely* and *I Hear A Symphony* had actually been released before (in slightly different mixes), and *You're The Only One* was mistakenly replaced by *Ooh, I'd Love To Be With You* (from *SKYWRITER*), and remains unreleased.

Accompanied with a 68 pages booklet – featured many rare photographs and an in depth essay by Davis Ritz.

EARLY CLASSICS

USA: Not Released.
UK: Spectrum/Motown 552224-2 (July 1996).

I Want You Back/Can You Remember/ Who's Lovin' You/True Love Can Be Beautiful/In Our Small Way/Goin' Back To Indiana/Can I See You In The Morning/I'll Bet You/Rockin' Robin/

*People Make The World Go Round/
Doggin' Around/Never Can Say
Goodbye/Lookin' Through The
Windows/We've Got A Good Thing
Going/The Young Folks/My Little
Baby/(We've Got) Blue Skies/With A
Child's Heart*

THE BEST OF – THE MOTOWN YEARS

USA: Not Released.
UK: PolyGram TV 530804-2 (July 1997).

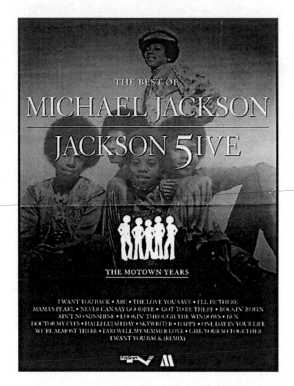

*I Want You Back/ABC/The Love You
Save/I'll Be There/Mama's Pearl/Never
Can Say Goodbye/Got To Be There/
Rockin' Robin/Ain't No Sunshine/Lookin'
Through The Windows/Ben/Doctor My
Eyes/Hallelujah Day/Skywriter/Happy/
One Day In Your Life/We're Almost
There/Farewell My Summer Love/Girl*

*You're So Together/I Want You Back
(Remix)*

TV advertised compilation released to
tie-in with Michael's *BAD* album and
Bad World Tour.

Achieved no.5 on the UK albums chart.

Re-promoted in October 2001, prior to
the release of Michael's *INVINCIBLE*
album – charted at no.33.

BPI Gold Record = 100,000 copies.

THE SILVER COLLECTION

USA: Not Released.
UK: Spectrum 9846942 (June 2007).

*I Want You Back/Rockin' Robin/Goin'
Back To Indiana/(We've Got) Blue Skies/
Don't Let Your Baby Catch You/
Skywriter/Can You Remember/Morning
Glow/Children Of The Light/Zip-A-Dee
Doo-Dah*

Posthumous hit: no.5 in the UK (Budget Albums).

THE VERY BEST OF...

USA: Not Released.
UK: Motown 98489970 (September 2007)

I Want You Back/ABC/The Love You Save/I'll Be There/Mama's Pearl/Never Can Say Goodbye/Got To Be There/ Rockin' Robin/Ain't No Sunshine/Lookin' Through The Windows/Ben/Doctor My Eyes/ Hallelujah Day/Skywriter/Happy (Love Theme From 'Lady Sings The Blues')/We're Almost There/One Day In Your Life/Girl You're So Together/ Farewell My Summer Love/I Want You Back (PWL Remix '88)/It's Your Thing (The J5 In '95 House Remix)

Compilation originally released in continental Europe in December 2005 – cover design borrowed from the UK/Europe edition of the *SOULSATION!* box-set.

Posthumous hit: no.12 in Ireland, no.15 in UK, no.18 in new Zealand, no.41 in Australia and no.50 in France.

THE MOTOWN YEARS

USA: Not Released.
UK: UMTV 5311546 (September 2008).

CD1: *ABC/Never Can Say Goodbye/ Ready Or Not (Here I Come)/Love Song/Forever Came Today/The Life Of The Party/Doctor My Eyes/All I Do Is Think Of You/I Am Love (Parts 1 & 2)/Darling Dear/Maybe Tomorrow/I*

Found That Girl/It's Too Late To Change The Time/ Lookin' Through The Windows/Who's Loving You/Whatever You Got, I Want/I'll Be There

CD2: *I Want You Back/Dancing Machine/Sugar Daddy/Little Bitty Pretty One/Hum Along And Dance/Corner Of The Sky/I'm So Happy/Get It Together/ Goin' Back To Indiana/Skywriter/The Love You Save/ Mama's Pearl/Touch/La La (Means I Love You)/It's Great To Be Here/Hallelujah Day/Santa Claus Is Coming To Town*

CD3: *Farewell My Summer Love/You've Got A Friend/My Girl/One Day In Your Life/Just A Little Bit Of You/Got To Be There/We've Got A Good Thing Going/ Rockin' Robin/Ben/I Wanna Be Where You Are/Girl You're So Together/We're Almost There/Wings Of My Love/Girl Don't Take Your Love From Me/Music And Me/Ain't No Sunshine*

Charted at no.34 in the UK.

Posthumous hit: no.1 in Norway, no.4 in in Holland & UK, no.7 in Spain, no.10 in

France, no.12 in New Zealand, no.14 in Australia, no.18 in Denmark, no.19 in Switzerland, no.21 in Mexico, no.36 in Germany and no.38 in Ireland.

JACKSONS

Studio Albums

THE JACKSONS

USA: Epic 34229 (November 1976).
UK: Epic EPC 86009 (November 1976).

Enjoy Yourself/Think Happy/Good Times/ Keep On Dancing/Blues Away/Show You The Way To Go/Living Together/Strength Of One Man/Dreamer/Style Of Life

Executive producers: Kenneth Gamble & Leon Huff.

Included, for the first time on a Jackson release, two songs composed by Michael: *Blues Away* and *Style Of Life* (written with Tito). Michael and his brothers also co-produced the songs.

Charted at no.6 on Billboard's R&B albums chart and no.36 on the Pop albums chart in the States, and at no.54 in the UK.

RIAA Gold Record = 500,000 copies.

Hit Singles:
Enjoy Yourself.
Show You The Way To Go.
Dreamer.

GOIN' PLACES

USA: Epic 34835 (October 1977).
UK: Epic EPC 86035 (October 1977).

Music's Takin' Over/Goin' Places/ Different Kind Of Lady/Even Though You're Gone/Jump For Joy/Heaven Knows I Love You, Girl/Man Of War/Do What You Wanna/Find Me A Girl

Executive producers: Kenneth Gamble & Leon Huff.

Two songs credited all five Jackson brothers as co-writers: *Different Kind Of Lady* and *Do What You Wanna*.

Achieved no.11 on Billboard's R&B albums chart, and no.63 on the Pop albums chart, in the States, and no.45 in the UK.

Hit Singles:
Goin' Places.
Find Me A Girl.
Even Though Your Gone.

DESTINY

USA: Epic 35552 (December 1978).
UK: Epic EPC 83200 (December 1978).

Blame It On The Boogie/Push Me Away/
Things I Do For You/Shake Your Body
(Down To The Ground)/Destiny/Bless His
Soul/All Night Dancin'/That's What You
Get (For Being Polite)

Executive producers: Bobby Colomby &
Mike Atkinson.

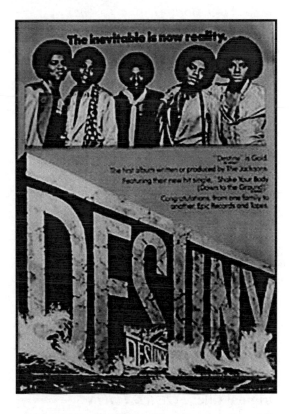

All songs, except *Blame It On The Boogie*, written and produced by the Jacksons. Marlon, in a Billboard interview, gave an insight into the way he and his brothers worked. 'We'd send maybe Tito and Michael in to mix it down,' he revealed, 'then fresh ears would come in and listen to it, because if you keep hearing the song over and over, you lose something.'

Peaked at no.3 on Billboard's R&B albums chart, and no.11 on the Pop albums chart, in the States, and at no.33 in the UK.

RIAA Platinum Record (USA million seller).

Hit Singles:
Blame It On The Boogie.
Shake Your Body (Down To The Ground).
Destiny.

Posthumous hit: no.20 on the R&B catalog album chart in the USA.

TRIUMPH

USA: Epic 36424 (October 1980).
UK: Epic EPC 86112 (October 1980).

Can You Feel It/Lovely One/Your Ways/ Everybody/Heartbreak Hotel/Time Waits For No One/Walk Right Now/Give It Up/Wonderin' Who

Written & produced by the Jacksons – Michael wrote or co-wrote six of the nine songs.

Original title: *FOUNDATION.*

First release under the Jacksons' Peacock Productions company – so-named after Michael came across an article about the peacock, which inspired him and Jackie to write 'Peacock History', which featured on the album's sleeve:

Through the ages, the peacock has been honoured and praised for its attractive, illustrious beauty. In all the bird family, the peacock is the only species that integrates all colours into one, and displays this radiance of fire only when in love. We, like the peacock, try to integrate all races into one, through the love and power of music.

Early songs published by Peacock Music Publishing Company: *Day Dreams* (written by Regina L. Brown & William D. Jolly), *Do The Fonz* (Ray Jessel, Arnie Kogen, Bill Davis & R.N. Wilkins) and *On The Wall* (Ray Jessel).

In a world that needs to rock together... a new album that'll light the way.

The Jacksons. "Triumph." Featuring the single, "Lovely One." On Epic Records and Tapes.

Produced and Written by The Jacksons. Management Weisner/De Mann Entertainment, Inc & Joe Jackson. Photography Francesco Scavullo. "Epic" is a trademark of CBS Inc © 1980 CBS Inc.

Heartbreak Hotel re-titled *This Place Hotel* on later pressings, to avoid confusion with the Elvis Presley classic of the same title.

Hit no.1 for two weeks on Billboard's R&B albums chart, and achieved no.10 on the Pop albums chart, in the States, and charted at no.13 in the UK.

Grammy nomination: Best Rhythm & Blues Vocal By A Duo, Group Or Chorus (the Jacksons lost out to the Manhattans, who took the award for *Shining Star*).

RIAA Platinum Record (USA million seller).
BPI Gold Record = 100,000 copies.

Hit Singles:
Lovely One.
Heartbreak Hotel.
Can You Feel It.
Walk Right Now.

VICTORY

USA: Epic 38946 (July 1984).
UK: Epic EPC 86303 (July 1984).

Torture/Wait/One More Chance/Be Not Always/State Of Shock/We Can Change The World/The Hurt/Body

Produced by the Jacksons, David Paich & Steve Porcaro.

First and to date only Jacksons album recorded by all six Jackson brothers – also the first Jackson album released, following the mega-success of Michael's *THRILLER*.

Different picture discs released in the USA & UK. The UK picture disc featured a live shot from the Victory Tour, and included a competition leaflet (the prize was a trip to the States, to see the Jacksons in concert). The American picture disc reproduced the album cover, with one significant difference: artist Michael Whelan, at the request of the Jacksons, added a white dove on Randy's left shoulder, after it was agreed to release white doves at each of the concerts.

Victory Tour opened in Kansas City on 6th July 1984 – yet featured none of the songs on the album of the same name; Jermaine later confirmed he and his brothers weren't happy with the album. 'The whole fiasco happened,' he stated, because it was decided that we had to have product to sell while we were on the road. As a result, a sub-standard Jacksons album was released, which damaged our reputation.'

Achieved no.3 on Billboard's R&B albums chart, and no.4 on the Pop albums chart, in the States, and no.3 in the UK.

RIAA 2 x Platinum = 2 million copies.
BPI Gold Record = 100,000 copies.

Hit Singles:
State Of Shock.
Torture.
Body.

2300 JACKSON STREET

USA: Epic 40911 (June 1989).
UK: Epic 463352 1 (June 1989).

Art Of Madness/Nothin (That Compares 2 U)/Maria/Private Affair/2300 Jackson Street/Harley/She/Alright With Me/Play It Up/Midnight Rendezvous/If You'd Only Believe

Produced by the Jacksons, Michael Omartian, L.A. Reid & Kenneth 'Babyface' Edmonds, Teddy Riley & Gene Griffin.

First Jacksons album not to involve Michael (or Marlon, who had officially quit the Jacksons to pursue a solo career), other than him adding guest vocals to the title track.

Michael went on record as saying he loved the album but, perhaps significantly, it was the last album the Jacksons were contracted to record for CBS/Epic. 'I have to say I really put a lot of time, effort and creativity into the Jacksons album,' Jermaine complained, 'but the reason it's not happening as it should be, is because CBS are sitting on their fat butts and not promoting it.'

Peaked at no.14 on Billboard's R&B singles chart, and no.59 on the Pop chart, in the States, and at no.39 in the UK.

Hit Singles:
Nothin (That Compares 2 U).
2300 Jackson Street.

Live Album

LIVE

USA: Epic 37545 (November 1981).
UK: Epic EPC 88562 (November 1981).

LP1: *Opening – Can You Feel It/Things I Do For You/Off The Wall/Ben/This Place Hotel/She's Out Of My Life/Movie And Rap (Excerpts: I Want You Back/Never Can Say Goodbye/Got To Be There)*

LP2: *Medley (I Want You Back/ABC/The Love You Save)/I'll Be There/Rock With You/Lovely One/Working Day And Night/Don't Stop 'Til You Get Enough/ Shake Your Body (Down To The Ground)*

Produced by the Jacksons.

Recorded during the group's Triumph Tour in September 1981, at a concert at Madison Square Garden – concert attended by Quincy Jones, Steven Speilberg, Cher, Katharine Hepburn, Jane Fonda, Dan Aykroyd, Andy Warhol, Jamie Lee Curtis and Tatum O'Neal.

Achieved no.10 on Billboard's R&B albums chart, and no.30 on the Pop albums chart, in the States, and no.53 in the UK.

RIAA Gold Record = 250,000 copies (double album – each disc counted separately).

Things I Do For You (Live) issued as a single in the UK – failed to chart.

Posthumous hit: no.15 on the R&B catalog albums chart and no.17 on the pop catalog albums chart in the USA.

Reissues with Bonus Tracks

DESTINY

USA: Epic/Legacy 88697308692 (September 2008).
UK: Sony 88697308692 (September 2008).

Bonus Tracks: *Blame It On The Boogie (John Luongo Disco Mix)/ Shake Your Body (Down To The Ground) (John Luongo Disco Mix)*

TRIUMPH

USA: Epic/Legacy 88697335582 (September 2008).
UK: Sony 88697335582 (September 2008).

Bonus Tracks: *This Place Hotel (Single Version)/Walk Right Now (John Luongo Disco Mix)/Walk Right Now (John Luongo Instrumental Mix)*

Compilations

THE ESSENTIAL

USA: Legacy/Epic EK 86455 (March 2004).
UK: Not Released.

Enjoy Yourself (Extended Version)/Show You The Way To Go/Goin' Places/Find Me A Girl/Blame It On The Boogie/Shake Your Body (Down To The Ground)/ Lovely One/This Place Hotel/Can You Feel It/ Walk Right Now/State Of Shock/ 2300 Jackson Street/Nothin (That Compares 2 U)/Don't Stop 'Til You Get Enough (Live)

Spent a solitary week at no.99 on Billboard's R&B albums chart – failed to register on the Pop chart.

Posthumous hit: no.16 on the R&B catalog album chart in the USA.

THE VERY BEST OF...

USA: Not Released.
UK: Epic 5163669 (June 2004).

CD1: *I Want You Back/ABC/The Love You Save/I'll Be There/Mama's Pearl/Never Can Say Goodbye (Single Version)/Sugar Daddy (Single Version)/Dancing Machine (Single Version)/Lookin' Through The Windows/Doctor My Eyes/Ain't No Sunshine/Got To Be There (Single Version)/Rockin' Robin/Ben (Single Version)/One Day In Your Life/Farewell My Summer Love*

CD2: *Can You Feel It (Single Edit)/Blame It On The Boogie/Enjoy Yourself/Show You The Way To Go (Single Version)/Even Though You're Gone/Goin' Places/Torture/Shake Your Body (Down To The Ground) (Single Version)/Lovely One/This Place Hotel/Walk Right Now (Single Version)/State Of Shock/2300 Jackson Street/Nothin (That Compares 2 U)/Don't Stop 'Til You Get Enough (Live)*

Charted at no.7 in the UK.

BPI Gold Record = 100,000 copies.

THE JACKSONS STORY

USA: Hip-O Records/Motown
  B000305802 (July 2004).
UK: Not Released.

*I Want You Back/ABC/The Love You Save/I'll Be There/Mama's Pearl/Never Can Say Goodbye/Got To Be There/Rockin' Robin/Ben/Dancing Machine/*Let's Get *Serious (Jermaine)/Enjoy Yourself/ Show You The Way To Go/ Blame It On The Boogie/Shake Your Body (Down To The Ground)/Lovely One/This Place Hotel/Can You Feel It/Don't Stop 'Til You Get Enough/Billie Jean*

Spent one week at no.74 on Billboard's R&B albums chart – failed to make the Pop albums chart.

Re-titled and reissued with eco-friendly packaging in August 2007 (Hip-O Records/Motown B0009599-D2), as *THE JACKSONS STORY: NUMBER 1'S* – spent a week at no.86 on Billboard's R&B albums chart.

Posthumous hit: no.10 on the R&B catalog album chart and no.19 on the pop catalog album charts in the USA.

SUPER HITS

USA: Sony BMG A 721343 (November 2007).
UK: Not Released.

Enjoy Yourself/Show You The Way To Go/Do What You Wanna/Goin' Places/Shake Your Body (Down To The Ground)/Lovely One/Walk Right Now/Torture/Body/Nothin (That Compares 2 U)

Posthumous hit: no.48 on the pop catalog albums chart in the USA.

THE VERY BEST OF

USA: Epic/Legacy 88697335592 (January 2009).
UK: Not Released.

Music's Takin' Over/Goin' Places/Enjoy Yourself/Blame It On The Boogie/Shake Your Body (Down To The Ground)/All Night Dancin'/Things I Do For You/Lovely One/State Of Shock/Torture/Live Medley (I Want You Back/ABC/The Love You Save)/This Place Hotel/2300 Jackson Street/Man Of War

Posthumous hit: no.35 on the R&B album chart in the USA.

CAN YOU FEEL IT – COLLECTION

USA: Not Released.
UK: Sony 88697473382 (March 2009).

Can You Feel It/Blame It On The Boogie/Shake Your Body (Down To The Ground)/2300 Jackson Street/Enjoy Yourself/State Of Shock/One More Chance/Walk Right Now/Private Affair/Nothin (That Compares 2 U)/Dreamer/Goin' Places/Torture/Show You The Way To Go

Posthumous hit: no.7 in the UK (Budget Albums) and no.66 in Australia.

MICHAEL JACKSON

Studio Albums

GOT TO BE THERE

USA: Motown M747L (January 1972).
UK: Tamla Motown STML 11205 (May 1972).

Ain't No Sunshine/I Wanna Be Where You Are/Girl Don't You Take You Love From Me/In Our Small Way/Got To Be There/Rockin' Robin/ Wings Of My Love/Maria (You Were The Only One)/Love Is Here And Now You're Gone/You've Got A Friend

Produced by The Corporation, Hal Davis, Willie Hutch, Mel Larson & Jerry Marcellino.

Release meant Michael became the first Motown to launch a solo career, while at the same time remaining a member of a group: both Diana Ross and Smokey Robinson had to leave the Supremes and Miracles, respectively, before they were allowed to go solo.

Charted at no.3 on Billboard's R&B albums chart, and no.14 on the Pop chart, in the States, and at no.37 in the UK.

Hit Singles:
Got To Be There.
Rockin' Robin.
I Wanna Be Where You Are.
Ain't No Sunshine.

Posthumous hit: no.32 in the UK (Budget Albums).

BEN

USA: Motown M755L (August 1972).
UK: Tamla Motown STML 11220
  (December 1972).

Ben/The Greatest Show On Earth/People Make The World Go Round/We've Got A Good Thing Going/Everybody's Some- body's Fool/My Girl/What Goes Around Comes Around/In Our Small Way/Shoo- Be-Doo-Be-Doo-Da-Day/You Can Cry On My Shoulder

Produced by The Corporation, Hal Davis, Mel Larson, Jerry Marcellino & Bobby Taylor.

Original American sleeve depicted Michael rising above one large and a pack of smaller rats – however, feeling rats would literally scare off prospective buyers, Motown hurriedly withdrew the cover, and reissued the album without any rats on the sleeve.

Achieved no.4 on Billboard's R&B albums chart, and no.5 on the Pop albums chart, in the States, and no.17 in the UK.

Hit Singles:
Ben.

MUSIC & ME

USA: Motown M767L (April 1973).
UK: Tamla Motown STML 11235
  (July 1973).

With A Child's Heart/Johnny Raven/Up Again/All The Things You Are/Happy (Love Theme From 'Lady Sings The Blues')/Too Young/Doggin' Around/ Euphoria/Morning Glow/Music And Me

Produced by Hal Davis, Freddie Perren, Fonce Mizell, Mel Larson, Jerry Marcellino & Bob Gaudio.

Charted at no.24 on Billboard's R&B albums chart and no.92 on the Pop albums chart in the States – didn't chart in the UK.

Hit Singles:
With A Child's Heart.
Happy (Love Theme From 'Lady Sings The Blues').

FOREVER, MICHAEL

USA: Motown M6-825S1 (January 1975).
UK: Tamla Motown STMA 8022 (March 1975).

We're Almost There/Take Me Back/One Day In Your Life/Cinderella Stay Awhile/We've Got Forever/Just A Little Bit Of You/You Are There/Dapper-Dan/

Dear Michael/I'll Come Home To You

Produced by Brian Holland, San Brown III, Hal Davis, Freddie Perren & Fonce Mizell.

Peaked at no.10 on Billboard's R&B albums chart and no.101 on the Pop albums chart in the States – failed to chart in the UK.

Joseph Jackson cited Motown's lack of promotion, and lack of faith in his sons' writing/producing abilities, for poor sales – the latter, ultimately, led to Michael and his brothers (Jermaine apart) leaving Motown, and signing with CBS/Epic.

Hit Singles:
We're Almost There.
Just A Little Bit Of You.
One Day In Your Life.

OFF THE WALL

USA: Epic 35745 (August 1979).
UK: Epic EPC 4500861 (August 1979).

Don't Stop 'Til You Get Enough/Rock With You/Working Day And Night/Get On The Floor/Off The Wall/Girlfriend/ She's Out Of My Life/I Can't Help It/It's The Falling In Love/Burn This Disco Out

Produced by Quincy Jones; three songs co-produced by Michael, which he also wrote: *Don't Stop 'Til You Get Enough*, *Working Day And Night* and *Get On The Floor*. Michael, having worked with him on The Wiz, approached Quincy for advice, when he'd decided he wanted to do a solo album but didn't know any great producers. 'I'll tell you what,' said Quincy, 'why don't you let me do it?'

Heatwave's Rod Temperton also penned three songs for the album, and in so doing he tried to find out about Michael's character. 'I knew he loved Charlie Chaplin,' he said, 'and I thought *Off The Wall* was a nice thing for Michael… *Rock With You* was a rhythm section idea I'd had – I thought I'd go with this one, too, because he's good at handling very melodic things.'

Mike Salisbury, the man behind the concept of the sleeve design, has revealed before he was brought in, 'they had him (Michael) seated on a bale of straw, wearing cowboy clothes'. Salisbury wasn't convinced this would work, so he 'designed a person and created an identity for him… it's a metaphor. He's just a kid out from under his Dad, so I think the album cover should make a statement that

his solo debut is as big as Sinatra coming on stage in Vegas.'

Album cover photo shoot took place at the Griffith Observatory at the Hollywood Planetarium. Michael liked Salisbury's idea of a tuxedo (found in Yves St. Laurent), but insisted he wanted to wear white socks (custom made for him by top Hollywood designer Bob Mackie) and glove. But… the socks didn't work, until Salisbury remembered Fred Astaire, Gene Kelly and Cary Grant. 'They put their hands in their pockets to raise the trousers so you could see the socks,' said Salisbury. 'Michael! Put your hands in your pockets. Raise your thumbs and raise your trousers!' And so a memorable album sleeve was created.

Achieved 16 weeks at no.1 on Billboard's R&B albums chart, and peaked at no.3 on the Pop albums chart, in the States, and charted at no.5 in the UK.

RIAA 7 x Platinum = 7 million copies.
BPI 6 x Platinum = 1.8 million copies.

Hit Singles:
Don't Stop 'Til You Get Enough.
Rock With You.
Off The Wall.
She's Out Of My Life.
Girlfriend.

First solo album to produce four Top 10 hits on both side of the Atlantic, and to produce five hits in the UK.

American Music Awards:
Favourite Male Soul Singer.
Favourite Soul Album.
Favourite Soul Single: *Don't Stop 'Til You Get Enough.*

Grammy Award:
Best R&B Vocal Performance, Male:
   Don't Stop 'Til You Get Enough.

Inducted into the Grammy Hall of Fame in 2008.

Posthumous hit: no.3 on the R&B catalog album chart and no.4 on the pop catalog album chart in the USA, no.3 in the UK (a new peak), no.7 in France, no.9 in Italy, no.10 in Canada, no.11 in Ireland & Spain, no.17 in Australia, no.20 in Poland, no.27 in Switzerland, no.37 in Germany and no.39 in the Czech Republic.

THRILLER

USA: Epic 38112 (December 1982).
UK: Epic EPC 85930 (December 1982).

Wanna Be Startin' Somethin'/Baby Be Mine/The Girl Is Mine/Thriller/Beat It/Billie Jean/Human Nature/P.Y.T. (Pretty Young Thing)/The Lady In My Life

Produced by Quincy Jones; three songs co-produced by Michael, which he also wrote: *Wanna Be Startin' Somethin'*, *Beat It* and *Billie Jean*.

'Before we started on *Thriller*, I was working on Donna Summer's second Geffen album,' said Quincy Jones. 'I thought it would take four months, but it went seven... By the time I finished Summer's record, we only had eight weeks to do *Thriller*. Sometimes that's better. You don't have time to sit there and get paralysis from analysis – you just go with your best instincts.'

'When we started *Thriller*, the first day at Westlake (Studio),' said engineer Bruce Swedien, 'we were all there and Quincy walked in followed by me and Michael and Rod Temperton and some other people. Quincy turned to us and he said, "OK, guys – we're here to save the recording industry." Now that's a pretty big responsibility – but he meant it. And that's why those albums, and especially *Thriller*, sound so incredible.'

Swedien has confirmed, when they first finished mixing the album, they had too much playing time for the two sides of a vinyl LP (over 25 minutes), and that this would effect the sound quality – something he was quick to point out, but no-one listened to him. 'I played the reference LP in the control room,' said Swedien. 'We listened, and the sound on the LP is dog doo-doo – it was horrible… Quincy remembers that we had 28 minutes on each side. I felt like shouting, *I told you so!* The Epic dudes were

popping corks, but out of the corner of my eye I saw Michael sneak out of the control room, and go to the other studio, across the hall. Quincy saw him, too, and followed him. I was next… I remember that Michael was crying, he was heartbroken. Again, I felt like shouting, *I told you so!*'

Quincy suggested they take two days off, before coming back in, to edit and remix one song a day. 'We had nine songs on the album,' said Swedien. '*The Girl Is Mine* was already out, so we needed eight more days. To quote Quincy Jones… "And we put those babies – put 'em in the pocket, man – that was it, it was over! Over!" We edited the songs down, we remixed and over-dubbed… the rest is history… I think that *THRILLER* was such a phenomenal success because the music that was on it, reached everyone! Great songs! Killer songs! *THRILLER* went everywhere, it appeals to people from eight to eighty – everywhere in the world… just think, a young black kid, being the idol of so many millions of kids all over the world. That never happened before.'

Remixing of the album was concluded on 8th November 1982 – the last thing to be recorded for the original album sessions were the overdubs for *Beat It*.

Early track listing, which included four songs that failed to make the final cut, was:

Wanna Be Startin' Somethin'/Hot Street/ The Girl Is Mine/Thriller/Billie Jean/ She's Trouble/Nightline/Carousel/The Lady In My Life (full length version)

Three different picture discs released – in Japan, the UK and the USA.

Spent 37 weeks at no.1 on both Billboard's R&B and Pop albums charts, and eight weeks at no.1 in the UK.

RIAA 27 x Platinum = 27 million copies – only *THEIR GREATEST HITS 1971-1975* by the Eagles has a higher certification in the States (28 x Platinum).

BPI 11 x Platinum = 3.3 million copies.

No.1 best selling album of 1983 in both the UK and USA; no.4 best selling album of 1984 in the States and no.6 best selling album of 1984 in the UK.

No.1 best selling album of all-time.

Reported in *The Guinness Book Of (World) Records* to have gained 67 Gold and 58 Platinum awards in 28 countries on six continents.

Hit Singles:
The Girl Is Mine.
Billie Jean.
Beat It.
Wanna Be Startin' Somethin'.
Human Nature.
P.Y.T. (Pretty Young Thing).
Thriller.

First album to generate seven Top 10 hits in the States; and to generate six hits – five of them Top 10 – in the UK.

American Music Awards:
Favourite Pop/Rock Male Artist.
Favourite Pop Album.
Favourite Pop Single: *Billie Jean.*
Favourite Pop Video: *Beat It.*
Favourite Soul Male Vocalist.
Favourite Soul Album.
Favourite Soul Video: *Beat It.*
Award Of Merit.

Michael was the youngest ever recipient of the special Award Of Merit.

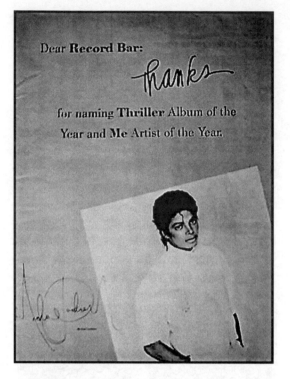

Voted no.2 Best Album of All-Time in the UK's Music of the Millennium poll, organised by Channel 4 and HMV (the Beatles topped the poll with *SGT. PEPPER'S LONELY HEARTS CLUB BAND*).

Inducted into the Grammy Hall of Fame in 2008.

Grammy Awards:
Album Of The Year.
Record Of The Year: *Beat It*.
Best New R&B Song: *Billie Jean*.
Best Pop Vocal Performance, Male:
   Thriller.
Best Rock Vocal Performance, Male:
   Beat It.
Best R&B Vocal Performance, Male:
   Billie Jean.
Producer Of The Year (with Quincy
   Jones).

Michael was the third youngest recipient of the prestigious Album Of The Year award (only Stevie Wonder and Barbra Streisand were younger). Michael dedicated the award to one of his idols, Jackie Wilson, who had just passed away.

The Brit Awards:
Best Album.
Best International Solo Artist.

Among 25 recordings added to the Library of Congress's National Recording Registry in 2008, which preserves recorded works that are considered culturally or historically important. Also added, Joni Mitchell's *FOR THE ROSES*, the original cast recording of *MY FAIR LADY*, Roy Orbison's *Oh Pretty Woman* and *The Tracks Of My Tears* by Smokey Robinson & The Miracles.

Posthumous hit: no.1 on the R&B catalog album chart and no.2 on the pop catalog album chart in the USA, no.1 in France, Italy & New Zealand, no.2 in Germany, no.3 in Australia, Ireland & UK, and no.6 in Canada.

BAD

USA: Epic 40600 (September 1987).
UK: Epic EPC 4502901 (September 1987).

Bad/The Way You Make Me Feel/Speed Demon/Liberian Girl/Just Good Friends/ Another Part Of Me/Man In The Mirror/I Just Can't Stop Loving You/Dirty Diana/ Smooth Criminal [CD bonus track: *Leave Me Alone*]

Produced by Quincy Jones; co-produced by Michael Jackson, who wrote nine of the eleven tracks on the album.

Project started with Michael and Quincy sifting through the 60 or songs Michael had written himself. 'Fifty percent of the battle,' said Quincy, 'is trying to figure out which songs to record – it's total instinct.'

Rumours – nearly all proved incorrect – abounded, in the build-up prior to the album's release, including:

- It's an album of Beatles songs.
- It's called *MEISTERWERK*.
- It's produced by Quincy Jones.
- It includes an anti-crack song with Run-DMC.
- It includes a ballad with Barbra Streisand.
- It's produced by Thomas Dolby.

- It's called *BAD*.
- It includes a version of *Free Nelson Mandela* with George Michael.
- It includes duets with Freddie Mercury and Stevie Wonder.

Original sleeve photograph, showing Michael wearing a black patterned veil over his face, rejected by Walter Yetnikoff, President of CBS Records. Instead, an impromptu photo shoot was staged during the filming of a short film for the title cut, and one of the resultant photographs used.

Shipped over two million copies in the States, and shifted 350,000 copies in its first week in the UK – out-selling the no.2 album by a record margin of 10:1.

Spent 18 weeks at no.1 on Billboard's R&B albums chart, and six weeks at no.1 on the Pop albums chart, in the States, and five weeks at no.1 in the UK.

No.1 in more than 20 countries, including: Argentina, Australia, Belgium, Brazil, Canada, Denmark, Finland, France, Germany, Greece, Holland, Hong Kong, Israel, Italy, Japan, New Zealand, Norway, South Africa, Spain, Sweden, Switzerland, Turkey and Zimbabwe.

RIAA 8 x Platinum = 8 million copies.
BPI 13 x Platinum = 3.9 million copies.

No.1 best selling album of 1987 and no.4 best selling album of 1988 in the UK, and no.6 best selling album of 1987 in the States.

Hit Singles:
I Just Can't Stop Loving You.
Bad.
The Way You Make Me Feel.
Man In The Mirror.
Dirty Diana.
Another Part Of Me.
Smooth Criminal.
Leave Me Alone.
Liberian Girl.

First five singles all topped Billboard's Hot 100 – a record.

Generated a record breaking nine Top 30 singles in the UK.

Grammy Awards:
Video Pioneer Award.
American Music Award of Achievement.
Best Video, Short Form: *Leave Me Alone.*

American Music Award:
Favourite Soul/R&B Single, Male: *Bad.*

Soul Train Awards:
Best R&B/Urban Contemporary Single, Male: *Man In The Mirror.*
Best R&B/Urban Contemporary Music Video: *Man In The Mirror.*
Heritage Award – recognising career achievements.
Sammy Davis, Jr. Award – recognising outstanding stage performances.

The Brit Awards:
Best International Artist, Male.
Best Music Video: *Smooth Criminal.*

World Music Award:
Number One Video in the World: *Dirty Diana.*

In early 1988, five tracks replaced with alternate mixes on all new pressing (excluding some special releases in Japan), namely:

- *Bad*
- *The Way You Make Me Feel*
- *I Just Can't Stop Loving You* (whispered introduction edited, as Michael found it embarrassing)
- *Dirty Diana*
- *Smooth Criminal*

Posthumous hit: no.1 in the UK (Budget Albums), no.2 on the R&B catalog album chart in the USA, no.3 in the Czech Republic & Italy, no.4 in France, Poland & on the pop catalog album chart in the USA, no.6 in Germany, no.8 in Canada, no.9 in Ireland & UK, no.13 in Australia & Spain, no.20 in Switzerland and no.26 in Mexico.

DANGEROUS

USA: Epic 45400 (November 1991).
UK: Epic 4658021 (November 1991).

Jam/Why You Wanna Trip On Me/In The Closet/She Drives Me Wild/Remember The Time/Can't Let Her Get Away/Heal The World/Black Or White/Who Is It/ Give In To Me/Will You Be There/Keep The Faith/Gone Too Soon/Dangerous

Produced by Michael Jackson, Teddy Riley, Bruce Swedien & Bill Bottrell – Michael wrote or co-wrote 12 of the 14 songs on the album.

Michael originally planned to follow *BAD* with a double compilation album, *DECADE 1980-1990*, which would have featured:

- Four songs from *OFF THE WALL* (*Don't Stop 'Til You Get Enough, Rock With You, Off The Wall & She's Out Of My Life*).
- Seven songs from *THRILLER* (*The Girl Is Mine, Billie Jean, Beat It, Wanna Be Startin' Somethin', Human Nature, P.Y.T. (Pretty Young Thing) & Thriller*).
- Six songs from *BAD* (from *I Just Can't Stop Loving You, Bad, The Way You Make Me Feel, Man In The Mirror, Dirty Diana, Another Part Of Me & Smooth Criminal*).
- *Someone In The Dark* (from the E.T. storybook album).
- *Come Together* (from *Moonwalker*).
- Two songs by the Jacksons (*State Of Shock & This Place Hotel*).
- Two vintage Motown songs rematsered by Michael (*I'll Be There & Never Can Say Goodbye*).
- Up to five new songs (possibly including *Heal The World* (early version), *Who Is It* (alternative version), *Gone Too Soon* (alternative version) & *Men In Black*.

DECADE 1980-1990 project scrapped a year after planned release date, in favour of a new studio album – which Michael decided to record without Quincy Jones.

'Michael was growing, and wanted to experiment free of the restrictions of the Westlake scene,' said Bill Bottrell. 'That's why he got me and John Barnes to work at his home studio for, like, a year and a half. On and off. We would program, twiddle, and build the tracks for much of that album, send the results on two inch down to Westlake, and they would, at their discretion, re-record, and add things like strings and brass. This is how MJ started to express his creative independence, like a teenager leaving the nest. I eventually got fired from *BAD* and Frank DiLeo took me to luch and said, "Don't worry, next album you will be a producer", and everybody kcpt their word.'

20-25 songs written by or with Bryan Loren all failcd to make the album. '*DANGEROUS* was a rough period for me,' admitted Loren. 'As we'd recorded so much music and none of it was used for that project... there are some songs that even in their unfinished format, you can hear their potential.'

'I got the call to produce some tracks on Michael Jackson's *DANGEROUS* around 1991,' said Teddy Riley, who admitted he fclt under pressure. 'I didn't want to be the one to fail Michael, and I'm so grateful it didn't... I brought R&B back to Michael in its barest form; R&B and funk. We recorded it in California, at Record One, and then we ended up in Larrabee Studios. I was using a lot of vintage stuff to get the sound we needed. Reeds and SSL XLs were mainly the boards we used – I always loved vintage better than digital. It's way better, much warmer.'

Album headed in a very different direction, prior to Riley's involvement. '*Dangerous* had already been recorded by Bill Bottrell, but the music didn't move Michael,' said Riley. 'I told Michael: I like Billy. I like his producing, and everything about him. But this is your album, Michael. If this is the right tune, I can utilise what you have in your singing. He said, "Try it. I guess we gotta use what we love." And we did. I'm quite sure that if anyone else had come up with a better *Dangerous*, he would have used that – so it's not actually about me or Billy, it's about the music. I always say the music is the star.'

'He was an inspiration to work with,' said Riley.'I kinda learned his way of working and stuck with that formula – so he changed the way I worked on production with artists… it's difficult to pick out the strongest elements on the album. Is it my music or his lyrics? In the end, I'd say it's both. There was nothing weaker than the other. That's why it was such a perfect album and such a big seller.'

Distinctive sleeve design by Mark Ryden, with ongoing input from Michael and Sony's senior art director, Nancy Donald, took six months to complete.

Vinyl picture disc planned, but cancelled when it was realised the album was a double vinyl album. Test pressings, which played Christmas songs by pianist Richard Clayderman, made in limited

numbers – many more bootleg pressings exist.

Several early acetates have surfaced over the years, including a DAT tape with the following track listing:

Jam/Monkey Business/In The Closet/Who Is It/Give In To Me/For All Time/If You Don't Love Me/Keep The Faith/Gone Too Soon/Dangerous/Serious Effect/What About Me.

Album released on a Thursday, instead of the usual Monday, in the UK to reduce the threat of parallel imports – sold 200,000+ copies in just three days, good enough to outsell U2's new album, *ACHTUNG BABY*, and claim the no.1 spot.

Achieved 12 weeks at no.1 on Billboard's R&B albums chart, and four weeks at no. on the Pop albums chart, in the States, and one week at no.1 in the UK.

No.5 best selling album of 1991 and 1992 in the UK, and no.6 best selling album of 1992 in the States.

Also hit no.1 in: Australia, Austria, Canada, Cuba, Denmark, Finland, France, Germany, Israel, Italy, Mexico, New Zealand, Norway, Spain, Sweden, Switzerland, Turkey & Zimbabwe.

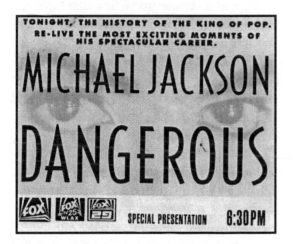

RIAA 7 x Platinum = 7 million copies.
BPI 6 x Platinum = 1.8 million copies.

Hit Singles:
Black Or White.
Black Or White (C&C Remixes).
Remember The Time.
In The Closet.
Jam.
Who Is It.
Heal The World.
Give In To Me.
Will You Be There.
Gone Too Soon.

Nine Top 30 singles in the UK equalled the record Michael had set with *BAD* – and *Gone Too Soon* made it a record ten Top 40 hits lifted from one album.

Grammy Award:
Grammy Legend Award.

American Music Awards:
Favourite Soul/R&B Album, Male.
Favourite Soul/R&B Single, Male:
  Remember The Time.

World Music Awards:
Best Selling American Artist Of The
  Year.
World's Best Selling Recording Artist Of
  The Year.
World's Best Selling Recording Artist Of
  The Era.

Voted no.42 Best Album of All-Time in the UK's Music of the Millennium poll, organised by Channel 4 and HMV.

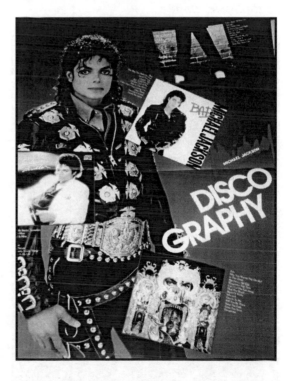

Posthumous hit: no.1 in the UK (Budget Albums), no.2 in the Czech Republic, no.4 in Italy, no.5 on the R&B catalog and pop catalog album charts in the USA, no.5 in Germany, no.6 in France & Poland, no.12 in Mexico, no.13 in Canada, no.14 in Australia, no.21 in Ireland & Spain, and no.28 in Switzerland.

HISTORY PAST, PRESENT AND FUTURE BOOK 1

USA: Epic 59000 (June 1995).
UK: Epic 4747094 (June 1995).

CD2 *History Continues: Scream/They Don't Care About Us/Stranger In Moscow/This Time Around/Earth Song/ D.S./Money/Come Together/You Are Not Alone/Childhood (Theme From 'Free Willy 2')/Tabloid Junkie/2 Bad/History/ Little Susie/Smile*

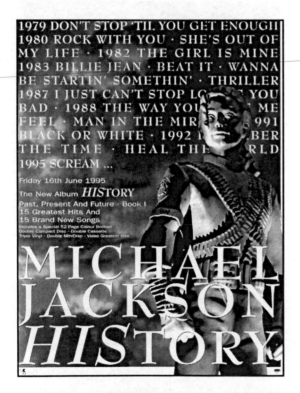

Double CD: one CD of greatest hits and one CD of new songs.

Produced by Michael Jackson, Jimmy Jam, Terry Lewis & Janet Jackson, Dallas Austin, David Foster, Bill Bottrell, R. Kelly & Bruce Swedien.

*HIS*TORY = His Story.

Title suggested by Dan Beck, after he was told by Sandy Gallin they (Michael's team) had to come up with a name for the album by the next day. Beck thought about the play on words re Madonna's *THE IMMACULATE COLLECTION* compil-ation, and came up with *HIS*TORY – which Michael loved, and he thanked Beck for his 'historical thinking' in the album's booklet.

'In truth,' confessed Michael, 'I really didn't want the album to be about old songs. It's a greatest hits album, but to me greatest hits albums are boring. And I wanted to keep creating. The new songs are very different – they are very autobiographical. I mean, they come from the heart – they are about myself.'

David Glew, Epic's Chairman, agreed: 'This is an intensely personal record. Michael's lyrics can be taken as a response to the situations that have overtaken his life in the past couple of years.'

New songs recorded between January 1994 and April 1995, except *Come Together* and *Earth Song*, which were pulled from the vaults and finished for *HIS*TORY.

$30 million promotional campaign launched on MTV on 22nd May 1995, with a four minute 'History Teaser' –

filmed in Budapest, Hungary, in August 1994. Later, in mid-June, nine huge 10m statues of Michael – made of fiberglass and steel, and weighing over 2,000kg each – were floated down major rivers in Europe, including the River Thames in London.

Sold 391,000 copies in its first week in the States – smashing the previous record of 360,00 (held by the Beatles for *LIVE AT THE BBC*), to become the biggest selling multi-disc debutant of the SoundScan era. Spent two weeks at no.1 on Billboard's R&B and Pop album charts.

Released on a Friday in the UK – sold 100,000+ copies in just two days, more than the week's no.2 and no.3 albums – by Pink Floyd and Bjork – put together.

Sold 7.5 million copies worldwide in six weeks.

RIAA 7 x Platinum = 3.5 million copies (each disc counted separately).
BPI 4 x Platinum = 1.2 million copies.

Also hit no.1 in: Australia, Austria, Belgium, Canada, Chile, Denmark, France, Germany, Holland, Hong Kong, Indonesia, Ireland, Israel, Italy, Japan, Korea, Malaysia, Mexico, New Zealand, Norway, Singapore, Spain, Switzerland, Taiwan, Thailand, Turkey & Zimbabwe.

Hit Singles:
Come Together
   (B-side of *Remember The Time*).
Scream.
Scream (7" & 12" Mixes).

Childhood (Theme From 'Free Willy 2')
   (B-side of *Scream*).
You Are Not Alone.
Earth Song.
They Don't Care About Us.
Stranger In Moscow.
History (double A-side with *Ghosts*).
Smile (posthumous hit).

Grammy Award:
Best Music Video, Short Form: *Scream*.

Grammy Nominations:
Album of the Year.
Song of the Year: *You Are Not Alone*.

American Music Award:
Favourite Pop/Rock Artist, Male.

MTV Music Video Awards:
Best Dance Video: *Scream*.
Best Choreography: *Scream*.
Best Art Direction: *Scream*.

Voted no.16 Best Album of All-Time in the UK's Music of the Millennium poll, organised by Channel 4 and HMV.

Posthumous hit: no.4 in Germany, no.7 in France and Ireland, no.10 in Switzerland, no.10 on the R&B catalog album and pop catalog album charts in the USA, no.13 in the Czech Republic, no.14 in Australia & Poland, no.15 in Italy, no.16 in Denmark & Norway, no.17 in New Zealand & UK, no.35 in Sweden, and no.36 in Mexico.

INVINCIBLE

USA: Epic 69400 (October 2001).
UK: Epic 495174 2 (October 2001).

Unbreakable/Heartbreaker/Invincible/
Break Of Dawn/Heaven Can Wait/You
Rock My World/Butterflies/Speechless/
2000 Watts/You Are My Life/Privacy/
Don't Walk Away/Cry/The Lost Children/
Whatever Happens/Threatened

Produced by Michael Jackson, Rodney Jerkins, Dr. Freeze, Teddy Riley, Andre Harris, Babyface & R. Kelly.

Released with four limited edition sleeves, red, green, blue and yellow, as well as the standard silver-grey.

Dedicated by Michael to his parents, grandmother and Benjamin 'Benny' Hermansen, a 15 year old Afro-Norwegian boy stabbed to death on 26th January 2001 by a group of neo-Nazis, in the Norwegian capital, Oslo.

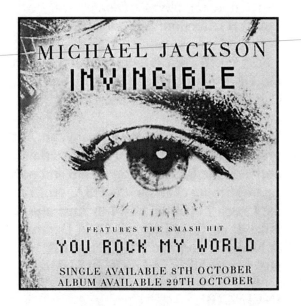

Song written by Christian Ingebritsen of A1, for possible inclusion, failed to make the album. 'I couldn't believe it when I found out Michael Jackson was listening to the song,' said Ingebritsen. 'He's been

my hero since I was a kid. It's a dream come true… these things don't happen in real life!'

Cost around $30 million to make – reportedly the most ever spent on an album. However, this was the last studio album Michael was contracted to record for Sony, and prior to its release he informed Tommy Mottola, Sony's Chairman, he would not be renewing his contract.

Sold 366,000 copies in its first week in the States, and 110,000 copies in the UK. Achieved no.1 for four weeks on Billboard's R&B albums chart, and no.1 for one week on the Pop albums chart, in the States, and no.1 for one week in the UK.

Michael didn't take his success for granted. 'It's a great honour,' he said, speaking at his first in-store record signing at the Virgin Megastore in New York's Times Square. 'I'm very happy. We worked very hard on it, and I'm blessed that the fans accepted it the way they did… every time there's a no.1 album, or song, it's as if this is the first one.'

Shipped 5.4 million copies by the end of 2001 – good enough to make it the no.11 best seller of the year globally.

RIAA 2 x Platinum = 2 million copies.
BPI Platinum Record = 300,000 copies.

Also hit no.1 in: Australia, Belgium, Denmark, France, Germany, Holland, Hungary, Lithuania, Malaysia, Norway, Sweden, Switzerland & Turkey.

Grammy Nomination:
Best Male Pop Vocal Performance:
  You Rock My World.

NAACP Award:
Best Music Video: *You Rock My World.*

Hit Singles:
You Rock My World.
Cry.
Butterflies.
Heaven Can Wait.

Further singles planned, but early in 2002 Sony cancelled the physical release of *Butterflies* in the States and the release of *Unbreakable* in the UK and elsewhere, along with all further promotion of the album – much to the dismay of Michael and his fans, who organised numerous protests and petitions against the decision, and launched a 'Make *INVINCIBLE* visible' campaign. Michael himself finally spoke out in May 2002, when he launched a scathing attack on Mottola, accusing him of:

- Sabotaging his career by refusing to release any singles from *INVINCIBLE.*

- Failing to advertise and promote the album during a record breaking American TV special (that is, Michael's 30th Anniversary Celebration).

- Wrecking possible plans to sign a lucrative record contract with another record label.

- Refusing to release the *What More Can I Give* and *Todo Para Ti* charity singles.

Michael confirmed, during a visit to the UK in June, he was only contracted to deliver one more album to Sony, and stated that would be a greatest hits box-set with two new songs. 'I can give them any old songs,' he said. 'I'm a free agent now, but I walk away with fifty percent of Sony Music Publishing – they're very angry with me!'

Posthumous hit: no.3 in the UK (Budget Albums), no.8 on the R&B catalog album chart and no.9 on the pop catalog album chart in the USA, no.18 in France & Italy, no.26 in Germany, no.28 in the Czech Republic, no.32 in Poland and no.37 in Australia.

Live Album

30TH ANNIVERSARY T.V. SPECIAL

USA: CBS EMIT 2505-ADD / EMIT 2515-ADD (October 2001 / promo).
UK: Not Released.

CD1: *Wanna Be Startin' Sometin'* (Usher, Mya & Whitney Houston)/*Ben* (Billy Gilman)/*It Wasn't Me/Angel* (Shaggy & Ricardo Rikrock)/*Heal The World* (Monica, Deborah Cox, Mya, Rah Digga & Tamia)/*My Baby* (Lil' Romeo & Master P)/*She's Out Of My Life* (Marc Anthony)/*Bootylicious/Billie Jean* (Destiny's Child)/*You Are Not Alone* (Liza Minnelli)/*I Just Can't Stop Loving You* (James Ingram & Gloria Estefan)/ *Man In The Mirror* (98 Degrees, Usher &

Luther Vandross)/*Can You Feel It/ Medley (ABC/The Love You Save)/I'll Be There/I Want You Back/Dancing Machine* (& 'N Sync)/*Shake Your Body (Down To The Ground)/The Way You Make Me Feel* (& Britney Spears)/*Black Or White* (& Slash)/*Beat It* (& Slash)/*Billie Jean/You Rock My World* (& Usher)

CD2: *I Want Candy* (Aaron Carter)/*One Day In Your Life (Incidental)/Get Your Freak On* (Nelly Furtado & Missy 'Misdemeanor' Elliot)/*Home* (Monica)/ *You Can't Win* (Jill Scott)/*Ease On Down The Road* (Al Jarreau, Jill Scott, Monica & Deborah Cox)/*I'll Never Love This Way Again* (Dionne Warwick)/*I Will Survive* (Gloria Gaynor)/*The Way You Make Me Feel/What More Can I Give* (& Billy Gilman, Usher, Mariah Carey, etc.)/ *We Are Here To Change The World (from 'Captain EO')*

Recorded at Michael's '30th Anniversary Celebration: The Solo Years' concerts, staged at Madison Square Garden, New York, on 7th and 10th September 2001.

Promo only release – distributed to radio stations across the States, to promote the accompanying two hour TV special, aired by CBS-TV on 13th November.

CD2 much rarer – featured two bonus tracks not recorded at the concert, the previously unreleased *What More Can I Give*, and from Michael's short film *Captain EO*, *We Are Here To Change The World*.

Storybook Album

E.T. THE EXTRA-TERRESTRIAL

USA: MCA 70000 (November 1982).
UK: MCA 70000 (January 1983).

Someone In The Dark/Landing/ Discovery/Home/Intrusion/Chase/ Goodbye

Narrated by Michael with music by John Williams.

Produced by Quincy Jones.

Based on one of Michael's all-time favourite films, *E.T. The Extra-Terrestrial*.

Featured one new song by Michael, *Someone In The Dark*.

Legal action by Michael's record company forced the withdrawal of the album in the States, after MCA broke its agreement with CBS/Epic, by releasing the album before the end of 1982 and by releasing *Someone In The Dark* as a promo single.

Charted at no.82 in the UK, and at no.201 on the 'bubbling under' section of Billboard's Pop albums chart in the States.

Grammy Award:
Best Recording for Children.

Original Soundtrack Album

THE WIZ

USA: MCA MCA2-14000 (September 1978).
UK: MCA MCA-MCSP 287 (October 1978).

LP1: *Main Title (Overture, Part One)/ Overture (Part Two)/The Feeling That We Have/Can I Go On?/Glinda's Theme/He's The Wizard/Soon As I Get Home/Home/You Can't Win/Ease On Down The Road/What Would I Do If I Could Feel?/Slide Some Oil To Me/(I'm A) Mean Ole Lion/Poppy Girls*

LP2: *Be A Lion/End Of The Yellow Brick Road/Emerald City Sequence/So You*

Wanted To See The Wizard/Is This What Feeling Gets? (Dorothy's Theme)/Don't Nobody Bring Me No Bad News/A Brand New Day (Everybody Rejoice)/Liberation Ballet/Believe In Yourself/Home

Music & Lyrics by Charlie Smalls.
Musical Director: Quincy Jones.

Included one solo song by Michael, *You Can't Win*, and one duet by Michael and Diana Ross: *Ease On Down The Road*. Michael also contributed vocally to *Be A Lion* and *A Brand New Day*.

Achieved no.33 on Billboard's R&B albums chart, and no.40 on the Pop albums chart, in the States – failed to chart in the UK.

RIAA Gold Record = 250,000 copies (each disc counted separately).

Reissues & Remix Albums with Bonus Tracks

BLOOD ON THE DANCE FLOOR

USA: Epic 68000 (April 1997).
UK: Epic 487500 1 (April 1997).

Blood On The Dance Floor/Morphine/ Superfly Sister/Ghosts/Is It Scary/Scream Louder (Flyte Tyme Mix)/Money (Fire Island Radio Edit)/2 Bad (Refugee Camp Mix)/Stranger In Moscow (Tee's In-House Club Mix)/This Time Around (D.M. Radio Mix)/Earth Song (Hani's Club Experience)/You Are Not Alone (Classic Club Mix)/History (Tony Moran's History Lesson)

Sub-titled 'HIS*TORY IN THE MIX*'.

Featured five previously unreleased songs – the first five tracks; two, *Ghosts* and *Is It Scary*, were first heard in Michael's mini-movie, *Ghosts*. Originally scheduled to feature *In The Back*, *On The Line* and an unreleased remix of *Tabloid Junkie* as well.

Spent two weeks at no. on the UK's albums chart, and peaked at no.12 on the R&B albums charts and no.24 on the Pop albums chart in the States.

RIAA Platinum Record (USA million seller).
BPI Gold Record = 100,000 copies.

Also achieved no.1 in: Belgium, France, Greece, Holland, New Zealand, Spain & Turkey.

Hit Singles:
Blood On The Dance Floor.
Ghosts (double A-side with *History*).

Posthumous hit: no.4 in the UK (Budget Albums), no.8 on the R&B catalog album chart and no.11 on the pop catalog album chart in the USA, no.17 in Spain, no.21 in the Czech Republic & Italy, and no.47 in Germany.

OFF THE WALL (Special Edition)

USA: Epic EK 66070 (October 2001).
UK: Epic EPC 504421 2 (October 2001).

Bonus Tracks: *Don't Stop 'Til You Get Enough* (original demo recording)/ *Workin' Day And Night* (original demo recording).

Plus interviews with producer Quincy Jones and songwriter Rod Temperton.

Charted at no.6 on Billboard's R&B Catalog albums chart, and no.7 on the Pop Catalog albums chart, in the States, and rose as high as no.13 on the UK's albums chart.

THRILLER (Special Edition)

USA: Epic EK 66073 (October 2001).
UK: Epic EPC 504422 2 (October 2001).

Bonus Tracks: *Someone In The Dark/ Billie Jean* (original demo recording)/ *Carousel*

Plus interviews with Quincy Jones and Rod Temperton, and featured Vincent Price.

Spent three weeks at no.1 on Billboard's R&B Catalog albums chart, and peaked at no.3 on the Pop Catalog albums chart, in the States, and charted at no.26 in the UK.

BAD (Special Edition)

USA: Epic EK 66072 (October 2001).
UK: Epic EPC 504423 2 (October 2001).

Bonus Tracks: *Streetwalker/I Just Can't Stop Loving You* (Spanish Lyric Version)/ *Fly Away*

Plus interview with Quincy Jones.

Pcaked at no.3 on Billboard's R&B Catalog albums chart, and no.8 on the Pop Catalog albums chart, in the States, and achieved no.38 in the UK.

Note: there was also a Special Edition of *DANGEROUS* but, despite a test acetate of 'bonus cuts' being pressed, the original CD was reissued with no bonus tracks.

Track listing of the test acetate: *Bumper Snippet (Kid Part)/Monkey Business/ Work That Body/If You Don't Love Me (Edited Version)/Serious Effect (Short Version)/Happy Birthday, Lisa/Black Or White (Clivilles & Cole Radio Mix)/ Dangerous (Early Version)/Who Is It (IHS Mix).*

THRILLER 25
(25th Anniversary Edition)

USA: Epic/Legacy 88697179862
(February 2008).
UK: Epic/Legacy 88697179862
(February 2008).

Bonus Tracks: *The Girl Is Mine 2008/ P.Y.T. (Pretty Young Thing) 2008/Wanna Be Startin' Somethin' 2008/Beat It 2008/ Billie Jean 2008/For All Time*

Bonus Track in Japan only: *Got The Hots* – previously unreleased.

Bonus DVD: short films for *Thriller, Billie Jean & Beat It*, plus Michael's legendary Motown 25 performance of *Billie Jean.*

Also featured a short Vincent Price voice-over.

Executive Producer: Michael Jackson.

Slightly belated 25th anniversary re-issue of 'the world's best selling album of all-time' (the original appeared in December 1982). Four different editions released:

- Classic Edition (with original sleeve).
- Zombie Edition (with zombie sleeve).
- Deluxe Edition (with gatefold sleeve – limited to 20,000 copies).
- Double Vinyl Edition with gatefold sleeve.

Bonus remixes were actually re-workings of the songs, with contempory artists will.i.am, Akon, Kanye West and Fergie.

On *The Girl Is Mine 2008*, for example, Paul McCartney's vocals were completely removed and vocals by will.i.am added.

In the States, some stores stocked exclusive editions of the Classic Edition, with a bonus track 17 (listed on a sticker, but not the CD sleeve):

- Best Buy: *Thriller (1982 Def Remix)*.
- Circuit City: *Wanna Be Startin' Somethin' (1982 Dance Mix)*.
- Independent Music Stores: *Billie Jean (1982 Radio Edit Remix)*.
- Target: *Billie Jean (1982 Club Remix)*.

Additionally, also in the States only, *Billie Jean (Underground Mix)* and *Thriller (Instrumental)* were made available from amazon.com and iTunes. DJ Georgie Porgie was responsible for the exclusive *Billie Jean* remixes.

Deluxe Fan Pack stocked by Walmart in the States, comprising the *THRILLER 25* CD and *NUMBER ONES* DVD.

Shipped one million copies in its first week: sold 166,000 copies in the States alone, where – as an old album – it was ineligible to enter the Billboard 200 albums chart. It debuted at no.2 on Billboard's Top Comprehensive Albums chart, which lists catalog albums as well as current releases, just 14,000 copies behind Jack Johnson's *SLEEP THROUGH THE STATIC* – this made it the highest ever charting catalog album on Top Comprehensive Albums chart (which began in 1994).

Hit no.1 on Billboard's Pop and R&B/Hip Hop Catalog albums charts, for 11 and 16 weeks respectively, and peaked no.3 in the UK.

Also achieved no.1 in Belgium, Colombia, France, Greece, India and Norway, no.2 in Australia, Denmark, Germany, Holland, Ireland, Mexico, Portugal, Spain, Sweden and Switzerland, no.3 in Brazil, Canada and New Zealand, no.4 in Poland and no.5 in Austria.

BPI Platinum Record = 300,000 copies.

Hit Singles:
The Girl Is Mine 2008.
Wanna Be Startin' Somethin' 2008.
Beat It 2008.
Billie Jean 2008.

Released as a picture disc vinyl album (Sony 88697353391), with the album's original track listing restored, in continental Europe in September 2008 – limited edition of 6,000. The two sides of the album depicted the new, Classic and Zombie edition, sleeves.

No.1 best selling Catalog album of 2008 in the States.

Posthumous hit: no.1 in the Czech Republic, Mexico, Portugal & Switzerland, no.2 in Canada, no.5 in Austria & Finland, no.6 in Holland & Spain, no.8 in Denmark, no.9 in UK, no.10 in Sweden and no.28 in Portugal.

Compilations

THE BEST OF...

USA: Motown M6-851S1 (August 1975).
UK: Tamla Motown STML 12005 (September 1975); Tamla Motown STMA 9009 (re-issue, June 1981).

USA: *Got To Be There/Ben/With A Child's Heart/Happy (Love Theme From 'Lady Sings The Blues')/One Day In Your Life/I Wanna Be Where You Are/Rockin' Robin/We're Almost There/Morning Glow/Music And Me*

UK: *Got To Be There/Ain't No Sunshine/ My Girl/Ben/Greatest Show On Earth/I Wanna Be Where You Are/Happy (Love Theme From 'Lady Sings The Blues')/ Rockin' Robin/Just A Little Bit Of You/One Day In Your Life/Music And Me/In Our Small Way/We're Almost There/Morning Glow*

Achieved no.44 on Billboard's R&B albums chart and no.156 on the Pop albums chart in the States – failed to chart in the UK first time around.

1981 reissue, thanks to the success of the reactivated *One Day In Your Life*, rose to no.11 on the UK's album chart.

BPI Silver Record = 60,000 copies.

MOTOWN SUPERSTAR SERIES Vol.7

USA: Motown M5-107V1 (August 1980).
UK: Not Released.

One Day In Your Life/Ben/Take Me Back/ Just A Little Bit Of You/I Wanna Be Where You Are/We're Almost There/ Cinderella Stay Awhile/Got To Be There/Rockin' Robin/With A Child's Heart

ONE DAY IN YOUR LIFE

USA: Motown M8-956M1 (March 1981).
UK: Motown STML 12158 (July 1981).

USA: *One Day In Your Life/Don't Say Goodbye Again/You're My Best Friend,*

My Love/Take Me Back/We've Got Forever/It's Too Late To Change The Time/You Are There/Dear Michael/I'll Come Home To You/Make Tonight All Mine

UK: *One Day In Your Life/We're Almost There/You're My Best Friend, My Love/ Don't Say Goodbye Again/Take Me Back/ It's Too Late To Change The Time/We've Got A Good Thing Going/You Are There/ Doggin' Around/Dear Michael/Girl Don't Take Your Love From Me/I'll Come Home To You*

Compilation issued to cash-in on the success of the reactivated title track. In addition to songs from Michael's solo Motown albums, also featured songs from the Jackson 5 albums, *GET IT TOGETHER* and *JOYFUL JUKEBOX MUSIC.*

Charted at no.29 in the UK, and achieved no.41 on Billboard's R&B albums chart and no.144 on the Pop albums chart in the States.

AIN'T NO SUNSHINE

USA: Not Released.
UK: Pickwick TMS 3511 (June 1982).

Rockin' Robin/Johnny Raven/Shoo-Be-Doo-Be-Doo-Dah-Day/Happy (Love Theme From 'Lady Sings The Blues')/ Too Young/Up Again/With A Child's Heart/Ain't No Sunshine/Euphoria/ Morning Glow/Music And Me/All The Things You Are/Cinderella Stay Awhile/We've Got Forever

FAREWELL MY SUMMER LOVE

USA: Motown 6101ML (May 1984).
UK: Motown ZL 72227 (June 1984).

Don't Let It Get You Down/You've Really Got A Hold On Me/Melodie/Touch The One You Love/Girl You're So Together/ Farewell My Summer Love/Call On Me/Here I Am (Come And Take Me)/To Make My Father Proud

Originally titled *FAREWELL MY SUMMER LOVE 1984.*

Compilation of nine – from 40 – previously unreleased songs found in Motown's vaults; all nine songs were updated with modern overdubs, prior to release.

Charted at no.9 in the UK, and achieved no.31 on Billboard's R&B albums chart and no.46 on the Pop albums chart in the States.

Hit Singles:
Farewell My Summer Love.
Girl You're So Together.

THE GREAT LOVE SONGS OF...

USA: Motown 5345ML (June 1984).
UK: Tamla Motown WL 72289
   (November 1984).

Got To Be There/I Wanna Be Where You Are/In Our Small Way/Girl Don't Take Your Love From Me/Maria (You Were The Only One)/Love Is Here And Now You're Gone/Happy (Love Theme From 'Lady Sings The Blues')/I'll Come Home To You/You Are There/One Day In Your Life

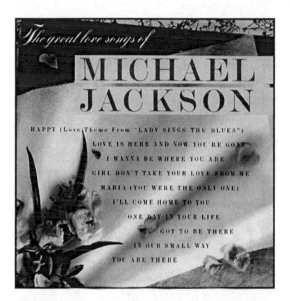

MOTOWN LEGENDS

USA: Motown 5369ML (June 1985).
UK: Not Released.

Rockin' Robin/Johnny Raven/Shoo-Be-Doo-Be-Doo-Da-Day/Happy (Love Theme From 'Lady Sings The Blues')/

Too Young/Up Again/With A Child's Heart/Ain't No Sunshine/Euphoria/Morning Glow/Music And Me/All The Things You Are, Are Mine/Cinderella Stay Awhile/We've Got Forever

LOOKING BACK TO YESTERDAY

USA: Motown 5384ML (February 1986).
UK: Tamla Motown WL 72424 (May
   1986).

When I Come Of Age/Teenage Symphony/I Hear A Symphony/Give Me Half A Chance /Love's Gone Bad/Lonely Teardrops/You're Good For Me/That's What Love Is Made Of/I Like You The Way You Are (Don't Change Your Love On Me)/Who's Lookin' For A Lover/I Was Made To Love Her/If'n I Was God

Another Motown compilation of previously unreleased songs, or 'Never Before Released Masters,' as the album sleeve proclaimed.

Credited to Michael, although six of the twelve songs were actually recorded by the Jackson 5.

Two songs – *Love's Gone Bad* and *I Was Made To Love Her* – previously featured on the hastily withdrawn Jackson 5 compilation, *BOOGIE*.

ANTHOLOGY

USA: Motown MOTD2-6195 (August 1986).
UK: Tamla Motown WD 72530 (April 1987).

CD1: *Got To Be There/Rockin' Robin/ Ain't No Sunshine/Maria (You Were The Only One)/I Wanna Be Where You Are/ Girl Don't Take Your Love From Me/ Love Is Here And Now You're Gone/ Ben/People Make The World Go Round/Shoo-Be-Doo-Be-Doo-Dah-Day/With A Child's Heart/Everybody's Somebody's Fool/In Our Small Way/All The Things You Are/You Can Cry On My Shoulder/Maybe Tomorrow/I'll Be There/ Never Can Say Goodbye/It's Too Late To Change The Time/Dancing Machine*

CD2: *When I Come Of Age/Dear Michael/Music And Me/You Are There/ One Day In Your Life/Love's Gone Bad/ That's What Love Is Made Of/Who's Lookin' For A Lover/Lonely Teardrops/ We're Almost There/Take Me Back/Just A Little Bit Of You/Melodie/I'll Come Home To You/If'n I Was God/Happy (Love Theme From 'Lady Sings The Blues')/Don't Let It Get You Down/Call On Me/To Make My Father Proud/ Farewell My Summer Love*

THEIR VERY BEST – BACK TO BACK

USA: Not Released.
UK: PrioriTyV PTVR 2 (November 1986).

Michael: *Billie Jean/Thriller/Beat It/ She's Out Of My Life/Farewell My Summer Love/One Day In Your Life*

TV advertised double album, featured one side of solo recordings by four artists: Diana Ross, Michael Jackson, Gladys Knight & Stevie Wonder.

Peaked at no.21 in the UK.

LOVE SONGS

USA: Not Released.
UK: Telstar STAR 2298 (October 1987).

Michael: *Got To Be There/Ain't No Sunshine/Farewell My Summer Love/ Ben/One Day In Your Life/I'll Be There/Never Can Say Goodbye/Girl You're So Together*

TV advertised album credited to Michael Jackson & Diana Ross – included solo Motown recordings by both but no collaborations.

Charted at no.12 in the UK.

BPI Platinum Record = 300,000 copies.

THE ORIGINAL SOUL OF...

USA: Motown 6250 (October 1987).
UK: Motown ZL 72622 (February 1988).

Twenty-Five Miles/Dancing Machine (Remix)/It's Too Late To Change The Time (Remix)/Melodie (Remix)/Ain't No Sunshine (Remix)/Got To Be There/ Doggin' Around/Rockin' Robin/If You Don't Love Me This Way (Remix)/You've Got A Friend (Remix)/Forever Came Today

Compilation including one previously unheard recording – a cover of Edwin Starr's *Twenty-Five Miles* – and remixes of well know songs by Michael and his brothers.

THE MICHAEL JACKSON MIX

USA: Not Released.
UK: Stylus SMR 745 (December 1987).

CD1 Love Mix: *Ben/Ain't No Sunshine/ One Day In Your Life/Never Can Say Goodbye/Got To Be There/Happy (Love Theme From 'Lady Sings The Blues')/I'll Be There/We're Almost There/People Make The World Go Round/Who's Lovin' You/I Was Made To Love Her/You've Really Got A Hold On Me/Music And Me/Call On Me/Lonely Teardrops/You've Got A Friend/Girl Don't Take Your Love From Me/We've Got A Good Thing Going/I'll Come Home To You*

CD2 Dance Mix: *ABC/I Want You Back/ Get It Together/The Boogie Man/Just A Little Bit Of You/The Love You Save/ Farewell My Summer Love/Love Is Here And Now You're Gone/Hallelujah Day/ Skywriter/ Lookin' Through The Windows/Sugar Daddy/Don't Let It Get You Down/Girl You're So Together/ Mama's Pearl/My Girl/Dancing*

Machine/Shoo-Be-Doo-Be-Doo-Dah-Day/Doctor My Eyes/Rockin' Robin/Little Bitty Pretty One

TV advertised double album featuring '40 specially sequenced hits by the world superstar' – that is, two extra-long remixes of Motown hits by Dakeyne for DMC.

Two promo CD EPs released, one for the Love Mix and the second for the Dance Mix.

Achieved no.27 in the UK.

BPI Platinum Record = 300,000 copies.

THE BAD MIXES

USA: Epic ESK 1215MC (May 1988 / promo).
UK: Not Released.

Another Part Of Me (7" Version)/ (Extended Dance Mix)/Dirty Diana/Man In The Mirror/The Way You Make Me Feel (7" Version)/(Dance Extended Mix)/Bad (7" Version)/(Dance Extended Mix)/I Just Can't Stop Loving You (7" Version)/Smooth Criminal (7" Version)/ (Annie Mix)/(Dance Mix Dub Version)/(A Cappella Mix)

Limited edition promo only CD distributed to radio stations and record stores, as a test disc for Monster Cable products – numbered from 1 to 6,000.

Promo nine track version also released (Epic ESK 1215).

MY GIRL

USA: Motown MOTC 3711 (1989).
UK: Not Released.

Ben/I Wanna Be Where You Are/My Girl/ We've Got Forever/Dapper-Dan/What Goes Around Comes Around/Cinderella Stay Awhile/Happy (Love Theme From 'Lady Sings The Blues')

Released on cassette only.

GOT TO BE THERE

USA: Motown MOTC 3732 (1989).
UK: Not Released.

Rockin' Robin/Got To Be There/Maria (You Were The Only One)/Girl Don't Take Your Love From Me/I Like You The Way You Are (Don't Change Your Love On Me)/Don't Let It Get You Down/We've Got Forever/Cinderella Stay Awhile

Released on cassette only.

MOTOWN'S GREATEST HITS

USA: Not Released.
UK: Motown 53001142 (February 1992).

I Want You Back (PWL Mix)/Doctor My Eyes/One Day In Your Life/Lookin' Through The Windows/Got To Be There/I'll Be There/The Love You Save/ABC/Rockin' Robin/Ben/Never Can Say Goodbye/Farewell My Summer Love/I Want You Back/Mama's Pearl/Ain't No Sunshine/Girl You're So Together/Hallelujah Day/Skywriter

Charted at no.53 in the UK.

MUSIC AND ME

USA: Not Released.
UK: Spectrum 550078-2 (May 1993).

Rockin' Robin/Johnny Raven/Shoo-Be-Doo-Be-Doo-Dah-Day/Happy (Love Theme From 'Lady Sings The Blues')/Too Young/Up Again/With A Child's Heart/Ain't No Sunshine/Euphoria/Morning Glow/Music And Me/All The

Things You Are, Are Mine/Cinderella Stay Awhile/We've Got Forever

Re-issued in October 2000 with a different sleeve.

MOTOWN LEGENDS

USA: Motown 374638505 2 (December 1993).
UK: Not Released.

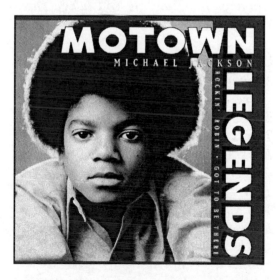

Rockin' Robin/Got To Be There/Maria (You Were The Only One)/You've Got A

Friend/Girl Don't Take Your Love From Me/I Wanna Be Where You Are/Don't Let It Get You Down/We've Got Forever/My Girl/Cinderella Stay Awhile/I Like You The Way You Are (Don't Change Your Love On Me)

THE BEST OF... (Anthology Series)

USA: Motown 31453-0480-2 (March 1995).
UK: Not Released.

CD1: *Got To Be There/Rockin' Robin/ Ain't No Sunshine/Maria (You Were The Only One)/I Wanna Be Where You Are/Girl Don't Take Your Love From Me/Love Is Here And Now You're Gone/Ben/People Make The World Go Round/Shoo-Be-Doo-Be-Doo-Da-Day/With A Child's Heart/Everybody's Somebody's Fool/Greatest Show On Earth/We've Got A Good Thing Going/In Our Small Way/All The Things You Are/ You Can Cry On My Shoulder/Maybe Tomorrow/I'll Be There/Never Can Say Goodbye/It's Too Late To Change The Time/Dancing Machine*

CD2: *When I Come Of Age/Dear Michael/Music And Me/You Are There/One Day In Your Life/Make Tonight All Mine/Love's Gone Bad/ That's What Love Is Made Of/ Who's Looking For A Lover/Lonely Teardrops/ Cinderella Stay Awhile/We're Almost There/Take Me Back/ Just A Little Bit Of You/Melodie/I'll Come Home To You/If'n I Was God/Happy (Love Theme From 'Lady Sings The Blues')/Don't Let It Get You Down/Call On Me/To Make My Father Proud/ Farewell My Summer Love*

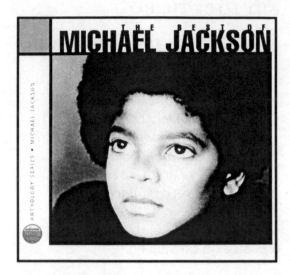

HISTORY PAST, PRESENT AND FUTURE BOOK 1

USA: Epic 59000 (June 1995).
UK: Epic 4747094 (June 1995).

CD1 *History Begins: Billie Jean/The Way You Make Me Feel/Black Or White/Rock With You/She's Out Of My Life/Bad/I Just Can't Stop Loving You/Man In The Mirror/Thriller/Beat It/The Girl Is Mine/ Remember The Time/Don't Stop 'Til You Get Enough/Wanna Be Startin' Somethin'/Heal The World*

Double CD: one CD of greatest hits and one CD of new songs – see CD2 *History Continues.*

Reissued as a single CD titled, *GREATEST HITS* HISTORY *VOLUME 1* – see below.

THE BEST OF – THE MILLENNIUM COLLECTION

USA: Motown 012159917-2 (November 2000).
UK: Not Released.

Got To Be There/I Wanna Be Where You Are/Rockin' Robin/People Make The World Go Round/With A Child's Heart/Happy (Love Theme From 'Lady Sings The Blues')/Ben/We're Almost There/Just A Little Bit Of You/One Day In Your Life/Music And Me

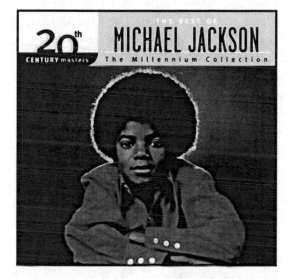

Posthumous hit: no.18 on the R&B catalog album chart and no.46 on the pop catalog album chart in the USA, and no.27 in Canada.

THE UNIVERSAL MASTERS COLLECTION

USA: Not Released.
UK: Spectrum 134912 (May 2001).

One Day In Your Life/Rockin' Robin/People Make The World Go 'Round/

Happy (Love Theme From 'Lady Sings The Blues')/With A Child's Heart/Music And Me/Got To Be There/Ben/We're Almost There/Just A Little Bit Of You/I Wanna Be Where You Are/In Our Small Way/My Girl/Dapper-Dan/We've Got A Good Thing Going

Released in France with the title *LES TALENTS DU SIECLE* ('Talents Of The Century') (Motown 013 491-2).

Reissued in December 2008, re-titled *CLASSIC* (Spectrum 5314948).

Posthumous hit (as *CLASSIC*): no.2 in the UK (Budget Albums).

GREATEST HITS *HISTORY* VOLUME 1

USA: Epic 85250 (November 2001).
UK: Epic 501869 2 (November 2001).

Billie Jean/The Way You Make Me Feel/Black Or White/Rock With You/She's Out Of My Life/Bad/I Just Can't Stop Loving You/Man In The Mirror/Thriller/Beat It/The Girl Is Mine/Remember The Time/Don't Stop 'Til You Get Enough/Wanna Be Startin' Somethin'/Heal The World

CD1 *History* Begins, from *HISTORY PAST PRESENT AND FUTURE BOOK 1*, repackaged and reissued – see above.

Charted at no.15 in the UK, and achieved no.45 on Billboard's R&B albums chart and no.85 on the Pop albums chart in the States.

RIAA Gold Record = 500,000 copies.

Posthumous hits: no.8 on the R&B catalog album chart and no.8 on the pop catalog album chart in the USA, no.8 in Canada, no.9 in Mexico, no.30 in the Czech Republic and no.59 in Switzerland.

LOVE SONGS

USA: Not Released.
UK: Motown 440 016 819-2 (January 2002).

Who's Lovin' You/A Fool For You/ Everybody's Somebody's Fool/Got To Be There/We're Almost There/We've Got A Good Thing Going/Maybe Tomorrow/ Call On Me/You Are There/One Day In Your Life/If I Don't Love You This Way/Wings Of My Love/I'll Come Home To You/I'll Be There

TWELVES

USA: Not Released.
UK: Epic XPR3744 (2003 / promo).

Don't Stop 'Til You Get Enough (12" Version)/Rock With You/Human Nature/ Billie Jean (12 Version)/Thriller (12" Version)/Bad (Dance Extended Mix Includes False Fade)/The Way You Make Me Feel (Dance Extended Mix)/Smooth Criminal (Extended Dance Mix)/Black Or White (Clivilles & Cole House/Club Mix)/You Are Not Alone (Frankie Knuckles Classic Song Version)/Earth Song (Hani's Club Experience)/Blood On The Dance Floor (Fire Island Vocal Mix)/ You Rock My World/One More Chance (Paul Oakenfold Mix)/MJ Megamix/Michael Jackson Anthology Mix

Box set of seven 12" singles released to promote Michael's forthcomg greatest hits collection, *NUMBER ONES*. Placed together, the seven singles formed a large *Off The Wall* era picture of Michael.

NUMBER ONES

USA: Epic EK 88998 (November 2003).
UK: Epic 513800 0 (November 2003).

USA: *Don't Stop 'Til You Get Enough/ Rock With You/Billie Jean/Beat It/ Thriller/I Just Can't Stop Loving You/Bad/Smooth Criminal/The Way You Make Me Feel/Man In The Mirror/Dirty Diana/Black Or White/You Are Not Alone/Earth Song/You Rock My World/ Break Of Dawn/ One More Chance/Ben (live).*

UK: *Don't Stop 'Til You Get Enough/ Rock With You/Billie Jean/Beat It/ Thriller/Human Nature/I Just Can't Stop Loving You/Bad/The Way You Make Me Feel/Dirty Diana/Smooth Criminal/Black Or White/You Are Not Alone/Earth Song/ Blood On The Dance Floor/You Rock My*

World/Break Of Dawn/One More Chance

Released with four different sleeves, featuring poses of Michael from four different eras.

Included one new song: *One More Chance*.

Single Mix of *Man In The Mirror* (USA edition only) had to be recreated, as the original either wasn't remastered or available for some reason.

Spent one week at no.1 in the UK, and achieved no.6 on Billboard's R&B albums chart and no.13 on the Pop albums chart in the States.

Hit Single:
One More Chance.

RIAA Platinum Record = 1 million copies.
BPI 6 x Platinum = 1.8 million copies.

Posthumous hit: no.1 in Canada, New Zealand, UK, and on the R&B catalog and pop catalog album charts in the USA, no.2 in Australia, Germany & Poland, no.9 in Switzerland, no.14 in the Czech Republic, no.16 in Mexico, no.17 in Sweden, no.31 in Denmark and no.39 in Italy.

THE ULTIMATE COLLECTION

USA: Epic E5K 92600 (November 2004).
UK: Epic ESK 92600 (November 2004).

CD1: *I Want You Back/ABC/I'll Be There/Got To Be There/I Wanna Be Where You Are/Ben/Dancing Machine (Single Version)Enjoy Yourself/Ease On Down The Road/You Can't Win/Shake A Body (Early Demo)/Shake Your Body (Down To The Ground ((Single Edit)/ Don't Stop 'Til You Get Enough/Rock With You/Off The Wall/She's Out Of My Life/Sunset Driver (Demo)/Lovely One/This Place Hotel*

CD2: *Wanna Be Startin' Somethin'/The Girl Is Mine/Thriller/Beat It/ Billie Jean/P.Y.T. (Pretty Young Thing) (Demo)/Someone In The Dark/State Of Shock/Scared Of The Moon (Demo)/We Are The World (Demo)/We Are Here To Change The World*

CD3: *Bad/The Way You Make Me Feel/Man In The Mirror/I Just Can't Stop Loving You/Dirty Diana/Smooth Criminal/Cheater (Demo)/Dangerous (Early Version)/Monkey Business/Jam/ Remember The Time/Black Or White/ Who Is It (IHS Mix)/Someone Put Your Hand Out*

CD4: *You Are Not Alone/Stranger In Moscow/Childhood (Theme From 'Free Willy 2')/On The Line/Blood On The Dance Floor/Fall Again (Demo)/In The Back/Unbreakable/You Rock My World/Butterflies/Beautiful Girl (Demo)/The Way You Love Me/We've Had Enough*

DVD: *Jam/Wanna Be Startin' Somethin'/Human Nature/Smooth Criminal/I Just Can't Stop Loving You/She's Out Of My Life/I Want You Back – The Love You Save/I'll Be There/ Thriller/Billie Jean/Working Day & Night/Beat It/Will You Be There/Black Or*

White/Heal The World/Man In The Mirror

Box-set comprising four CDs and one DVD, including previously released recordings and demo versions of well known songs.

Japanese limited edition release featured five additional songs:

- *Blame It On The Boogie*
- *Human Nature*
- *Another Part Of Me*
- *Heal The World*
- *One More Chance*

Charted at no.48 on Billboard's R&B albums chart, and no.154 on the Pop albums chart, in the States, and peaked at no.75 in the UK.

Posthumous hit: no.8 on the pop catalog album chart and no.12 on the R&B catalog album chart in the USA, no.29 in Spain, no.33 in Switzerland and no. 40 in Norway.

THE ESSENTIAL

USA: Legacy/Epic E2K 94287 (July 2005); Legacy/Epic 88697309852 (August 2008 – 3.0 Limited Edition Reissue).
UK: Legacy/Epic 520422 2 (July 2005).

USA CD1: *I Want You Back/ABC/The Love You Save/Got To Be There/Rockin' Robin/Ben/Enjoy Yourself/Blame It On The Boogie/ Shake Your Body (Down To The Ground)/Don't Stop 'Til You Get Enough/Rock With You/Off The Wall/ She's Out Of My Life/The Girl Is Mine/ Billie Jean/Beat It/Wanna Be Startin' Somethin'/Human Nature/P.Y.T. (Pretty Young Thing)/Thriller*

USA CD2: *Bad/I Just Can't Stop Loving You/Leave Me Alone/The Way You Make Me Feel/Man In The Mirror/Dirty Diana/ Another Part Of Me/Smooth Criminal/ Black Or White/Heal The World/ Remember The Time/In The Closet/Who Is It/Will You Be There/Dangerous/You Are Not Alone/You Rock My World*

USA CD3 (3.0 Reissue only): *Can't Get Outta The Rain/Say Say Say/Jam/They Don't Care About Us/Blood On The*

Dance Floor/Stranger In Moscow/ Butterflies

UK CD1: *I Want You Back/ABC/The Love You Save/Got To Be There/Rockin' Robin/Ben/Blame It On The Boogie/ Shake Your Body (Down To The Ground)/Don't Stop 'Til You Get Enough/Off The Wall/She's Out Of My Life/Can You Feel It/The Girl Is Mine/ Billie Jean/Beat It/Wanna Be Startin' Somethin'/Human Nature/P.Y.T. (Pretty Young Thing)/I Just Can't Stop Loving You/Thriller*

UK CD2: *Bad//The Way You Make Me Feel/Man In The Mirror/Dirty Diana/ Another Part Of Me/Smooth Criminal/ Leave Me Alone/Black Or White/ Remember The Time/In The Closet/Who Is It/Heal The World/Will You Be There/You Are Not Alone/Earth Song/ They Don't Care About Us/You Rock My World*

7"/Single mixes of several tracks had to be recreated, as the original either wasn't remastered or available for some reason:

- *Human Nature*
- *Off The Wall*
- *Rock With You*
- *The Way You Make Me Feel*
- *Wanna Be Startin' Somethin'*

Achieved no.2 in the UK, and peaked at no.50 on Billboard's R&B albums chart and no.96 on the Pop albums chart in the States.

BPI 2 x Platinum = 600,000 copies.

Reissued in the States, to coincide with Michael's 50th birthday, in August 2008 with a bonus third CD – originally, this was due to include the full length version of *The Lady In My Life*, but it didn't appear.

Plans to re-packaged and reissued as *THE HITS* in the UK in July 2009, to coincide with Michael's opening O2 dates, shelved following Michael's death on 25th June 2009 – original release re-promoted instead.

Posthumous hit: no.1 in Australia, Finland, Ireland, Mexico & UK, no.2 France, New Zealand, Switzerland & on the R&B catalog and pop catalog album charts in the USA, no.3 in Norway, Portugal & Sweden, no.4 in the Czech Republic & Canada, no.5 in Poland, no.6 in Denmark & Italy, no.8 in Austria, no.18 in Germany and no.23 in Spain.

VISIONARY – THE VIDEO SINGLES

USA: Sony 700406 (November 2006).
UK: Sony 82876725202 to 82876773482 (February to June 2006).

Thriller (US Single Edit)/(Album Version)/ (Video)
Don't Stop 'Til You Get Enough (7" Single Edit)/(Original 12" Edit)/ (Video)
Rock With You/(Masters At Work Remix)/ (Video)
Billie Jean/(Original 12" Edit)/(Video)
Beat It/(Moby's Sub Mix)/(Video)
Bad/(Extended Dance Mix Incl. False Fade)/(Video)
The Way You Make Me Feel (7" Edit)/ (Extended Dance Mix)/(Video)
Dirty Diana/(Instrumental)/(Video)
Smooth Criminal/(Extended Dance Mix)/ (Video)
Leave Me Alone/Another Part Of Me (Extended Dance Mix)/Leave Me Alone (Video)
Black Or White (7" Edit)/(C&C House With Guitar Radio Mix)/(Video)
Remember The Time/(New Jack Jazz Mix)/ (Video)
In The Closet (7" Edit)/(Club Mix)/(Video)
Jam (7" Edit)/(Silky 12" Mix)/(Video)
Heal The World (7" Edit)/Will You Be There/Heal The World (Video)
You Are Not Alone (Radio Edit)/(Classic Club Mix)/(Video)
Earth Song (Radio Edit)/(Hani's Extended Radio Experience)/(Video)
They Don't Care About Us (LP Edit)/ (Love To Infinity's Walk In The Park Mix)/(Video/Brazil Version)
Stranger In Moscow (Album Version)/ (Tee's In-House Club Mix)/(Video)
Blood On The Dance Floor (Single Edit)/ (Fire Island Vocal Mix)/(Video)

Box-set of 20 'DualDisc' CDs, with music on one side of the CD and a music video on the other.

CDs released individually in the UK (and other countries outside the USA), starting with *Thriller*, which came with with free limited edition *Visionary* box.

Thriller ineligible to chart in the UK due to the free *Visionary* box, but the other 19 singles all charted; *Billie Jean* fared best, peaking at no.11, while *Earth Song* stalled at no.34.

15 of the singles hit no.1 in Spain, with the other five – *Don't Stop 'Til You Get Enough, Black Or White, Remember The Time, In The Closet* and *They Don't Care About Us* – peaking at no.2.

THE ESSENTIAL COLLECTION

USA: Not Released.
UK: Spectrum WITUN107 (2008)

One Day In Your Life/Rockin' Robin/ People Make The World Go 'Round/ Happy (Love Theme From 'Lady Sings The Blues')/With A Child's Heart/Music And Me/Got To Be There/Ben/We're Almost There/Just A Little Bit Of You/I Wanna Be Where You Are/In Our Small Way/My Girl/Dapper-Dan/We've Got A Good Thing Going

Compilation sold exclusively by Woolworth, as part of their 'WorthIt!' series of budget price releases – first released in continental Europe in May 2005, with a different CD sleeve.

Michael Jackson "The Essential Collection"

GOLD

USA: Motown B0011431-02 (August 2008).
UK: Universal 1773967 (July 2009).

CD1: *Got To Be There/Maria (You Were The Only One)/Rockin' Robin/Ain't No Sunshine/I Wanna Be Where You Are/ Girl Don't Take Your Love From Me/ Ben/People Make The World Go 'Round/ Shoo-Be-Doo-Be-Doo-Da-Day/We've Got A Good Thing Going/When I Come Of Age/I Want You Back (Single Version)/Who's Lovin' You (Single Version)/Darling Dear (Single Version)/ Never Can Say Goodbuy (Single Version)/Maybe Tomorrow (Single Version)*

CD2: *With A Child's Heart/Happy (Love Theme From 'Lady Sings The Blues')/ Morning Glow/Music And Me/We're Almost There/Just A Little Bit Of You/ Dear Michael/I'll Come Home To You/*

If'n I Was God/Who's Looking For A Lover/One Day In Your Life/You're My Best Friend, My Love/It's Too Late To Change The Time/Call On Me/Melodie/ Farewell My Summer Love

Posthumous hit: no.22 on the R&B album chart and no.139 on the Billboard 200 in the USA, and no.59 in Canada.

KING OF POP

USA: Not Released.
UK: Sony 88697356512 (August 2008); 88697356532 (September 2008 – Deluxe Edition).

CD1: *Billie Jean/Bad/Smooth Criminal/ Thriller/Black Or White/Beat It/Wanna Be Startin' Somethin'/Don't Stop 'Til You Get Enough/The Way You Make Me Feel/Rock With You/You Are Not Alone/ Man In The Mirror/Remember The Time/Scream/You Rock My World/They Don't Care About Us/Earth Song*

CD2 (Deluxe Edition only): *Dirty Diana/ Say Say Say/Off The Wall/Human Nature/*

I Just Can't Stop Loving You/Heal The World/Will You Be There/Stranger In Moscow/Speechless/She's Out Of My Life/ The Girl Is Mine/Butterflies/Who Is It/Ghosts/Blood On The Dance Floor/ Workin' Day And Night/History/Give In To Me

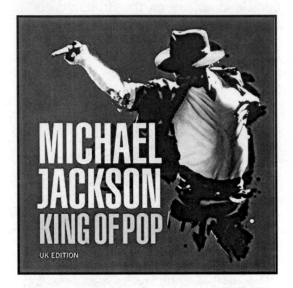

CD3 (Deluxe Edition only): *Can't Get Outta The Rain (Single Version)/On The Line/Someone Put Your Hand Out/Is It Scary (Single Radio Edit)/Smile (Short Version)/Billie Jean (Original 12" Version)/Wanna Be Startin' Somethin' (Extended 12" Mix)/Bad (Dance Extended Mix Includes False Fade)/The Way You Make Me Feel (Dance Extended Mix)/Another Part Of Me (Extended Dance Mix)/Smooth Criminal (Extended Dance Mix)/Black Or White (Clivilles & Cole House/Club Mix)/Thriller Megamix (Radio Edit)*

Released to celebrate Michael's 50th birthday in August 2008.

Fans in each country where the album was issued were given the chance to vote on songs they wanted to be included on the compilation – hence 12 songs that appeared on *NUMBER ONES* were repeated on the standard, one CD edition (and a further four were repeated on CD2 of the Deluxe Edition).

Entered the UK chart at no.5, and rose two places the following week, to equal the no.3 peak achieved by *THRILLER 25* earlier the same year.

BPI Platinum Record = 300,000 copies.

Hit Single:
Thriller Megamix.

Posthumous hit: no.5 in the UK.

HELLO WORLD: THE COMPLETE MOTOWN SOLO COLLECTION

USA: Hip-O-Select/Motown B0012421-02 (July 2009).
UK: Universal 1792469 (August 2009).

CD1: *Ain't No Sunshine/I Wanna Be Where You Are/Girl Don't Take Your Love From Me/In Our Small Way/Got To Be There/Rockin' Robin/Wings Of My Love/Maria (You Were The Only One)/ Love Is Here And Now You're Gone/ You've Got A Friend/Ben/Greatest Show On Earth/People Make The World Go 'Round/We've Got A Good Thing Going/ Everybody's Somebody's Fool/My Girl/ What Goes Around Comes Around/In Our Small Way/Shoo-Be-Doo-Be-Doo-Da-Day/You Can Cry On My Shoulder/ Don't Let It Get You Down (Original Mix)/You've Really Got A Hold On Me (Original Mix)/Melodie (Original Mix)/ Touch The One You Love (Original Mix)*

CD2: *With A Child's Heart/Up Again/All The Things You Are/Happy (Love Theme From 'Lady Sings The Blues')/Too Young/Doggin' Around/Euphoria/Morning Glow/Johnny Raven/Music And Me/We're Almost There/Take Me Back/One Day In Your Life/Cinderella Stay Awhile/We've Got Forever/Just A Little Bit Of You/You Are There/Dapper-Dan/Dear Michael/I'll Come Home To You/Girl You're So Together (Original Mix)/Farewell My Summer Love (Original Mix)/Call On Me (Original Mix)*

CD3: *When I Come Of Age/Teenage Symphony/I Hear A Symphony/Give Me Half A Chance/Love's Gone Bad/Lonely Teardrops/You're Good For Me/That's What Love Is Made Of/I Like The Way You Are (Don't Change Your Love On Me)/Who's Lookin' For A Lover/I Was Made To Love Her/If 'N I Was God/To Make My Father Proud (Original Mix)/Here I Am (Come And Take Me) (Original Mix)/Twenty-Five Miles (Original Mix)/Don't Let It Get You Down/You've Really Got A Hold On Me/Melodie/Touch The One You Love/Girl You're So Together/Farewell My Summer Love/Call On Me/Here I Am (Come And Take Me)/To Make My Father Proud*

3CD box-set was originally scheduled to be released in mid July, to coincide with the opening dates of Michael's 'This Is It' dates – scheduled to be a USA-only limited edition of 7,000 copies, prior to Michael's passing.

As indicated by the title, the set brought together – for the first time – the solo recordings Michael made while he was at Motown. The first CD featured his first two solo albums, *GOT TO BE THERE* and *BEN*, the second CD featured his third and fourth solo albums, *MUSIC & ME* and *FOREVER, MICHAEL*, and the third CD featured the two albums of 'new' songs released in the mid 1980s, *LOOKING BACK TO YESTERDAY* and *FAREWELL MY SUMMER LOVE*.

Previously unheard original mixes of the songs from *FAREWELL MY SUMMER LOVE* also included, spread over the three CDs, along with the original mix of *Twenty-Five Miles*.

In Our Small Way and *Johnny Raven* both featured previously unreleased introductions, with studio noise and a '1, 2, 3' count-in heard on the former.

The original mix of *Touch The One You Love* was an alternate vocal take, and numerous lines were missing from the original mix of *Don't Let It Get You Down* featured.

Posthumous hit: no.85 on the R&B albums chart in the USA.

THE COLLECTION

USA: Not Released.
UK: Sony 88697536212 (July 2009).

Box-set of five albums on CD in card sleeves:

- *OFF THE WALL* (Special Edition)
- *THRILLER*
- *BAD* (Special Edition)

- *DANGEROUS* (Special Edition)
- *INVINCIBLE*

Although Sony deliberately chose to focus on full original studio albums for this release, many fans queried the omission of HIS*TORY* (CD1) and *BLOOD ON THE DANCE FLOOR*.

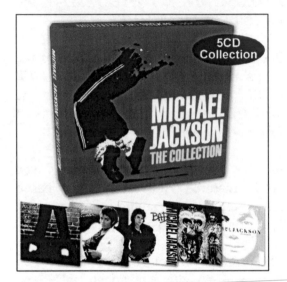

Posthumous hit: no.1 in Denmark, no.2 in Finland, Holland, Italy & Poland, no.3 in Portugal, no.4 in Germany, no.5 in Norway & Sweden, no.6 in France & Switzerland, no.7 in the Czech Republic, no.13 in Austria, no.14 in UK, and no.28 in Ireland.

THE STRIPPED MIXES / THE MOTOWN 50 MIXES

USA: Motown B0013303-02 (July 2009 as *THE STRIPPED MIXES*).
UK: Universal 2714978 (July 2009 as *THE MOTOWN 50 MIXES*).

I'll Be There (Minus Mix)/Ben (Stripped Mix)/Who's Loving You (Stripped Mix)/ Ain't No Sunshine (Stripped Mix)/I Want You Back (Stripped Mix)/ABC (Stripped Mix)/We've Got A Good Thing Going (Stripped Mix)/With A Child's Heart (Stripped Mix)/Darling Dear (Stripped Mix)/Got To Be There (Stripped Mix)/ Never Can Say Goodbuy (Stripped Mix)

Album of new 'stripped' mixes, utilized the original Motown session tapes, with certain instruments and studio frills stripped away – aimed at showcasing Michael's vocals and the harmonies provided by his brothers.

Several songs featured extended vocals: *ABC, Darling Dear, I Want You Back* (and a cute little giggle by Michael at the end as well), *I'll Be There, Never Can Say Goodbye, Who's Lovin' You & With A Child's Heart*.

Got To Be There featured extra and different background vocals, while *We've Got A Good Thing Going* featured a previously unreleased alternate vocal with slightly different lyrics.

I'll be There made available on iTunes in June, and the compilation was made available digitally two weeks before the CD version was released.

Posthumous hit: no.57 on the Billboard 200 in the USA and no.76 in the UK.

THE DEFINITIVE COLLECTION

USA: Motown 2714783 (September 2009).
UK: Not Released.

I Want You Back/ABC/The Love You Save/I'll Be There/Never Can Say Goodbye/Maybe Tomorrow/Ain't No Sunshine/Got To Be There/Rockin' Robin/I Wanna Be Where You Are/Ben/With A Child's Heart/One Day In Your Life/Dancing Machine/We're Almost There/Just A Little Bit Of You/Farewell My Summer Love/Who's Lovin' You/I'll Be There (Minus Mix)

Credited to Michael alone, despite the inclusion of numerous Jackson 5 hits.

Debuted on the R&B albums chart at no.17, and on the Billboard 200 at no.46, in the States.

Selected Compilations released outside the USA & UK

Here is a round-up of some of the albums that have been released outside the USA and UK over the years.

SUPER DELUXE
Jackson Five

Japan: Victor / Motown SWX 10107 (1972 / promo).

Little Bitty Pretty One/The Love You Save/ABC/Maybe Tomorrow/Honey Chile/Bridge Over Troubled Water/Sugar Daddy/I Want You Back/Lookin' Through The Windows/I'll Be There/Mama's Pearl/Never Can Say Goodbye/La La (Means I Love You)/Goin' Back To Indiana

BOTH SIDES
Jackson Five

Japan: Victor/Motown SJET 7540 (1972).

ABC/The Love You Save/I Want You Back/Goin' Back To Indiana/Honey Chile/Mama's Pearl/I'll Be There/La La (Means I Love You)/Maybe Tomorrow/Never Can Say Goodbye/Bridge Over Troubled Water

PORTRAIT OF...
Michael Jackson / Jackson 5

Europe: C 06294121 (1972).
*Ben/Ain't No Sunshine/Rockin' Robin/
Got To Be There/In Our Small Way/
Everybody's Somebody's Fool/I Wanna
Be Where You Are/Little Bitty Pretty
One/Goin' Back To Indiana/Children Of
The Light/I'll Be There/To Know/Lookin'
Through The Windows/Corner Of The
Sky*

THE MICHAEL JACKSON ALBUM
Michael Jackson

Germany: Electrola SHZE 385 (1973 /
  promo).

*Ain't No Sunshine/Wings Of My Love/
With A Child's Heart/Maria (You Were
The Only One)/All The Things You Are/
My Girl/Shoo-Be-Doo-Be-Doo-Dah-
Day/Greatest Show On Earth/What Goes
Around Comes Around/Happy (Love
Theme From 'Lady Sings The Blues')/
Love Is Here And Now You're Gone/Ben*

Full release of album cancelled –
however, vinyl copies are know to exist.

TWIN DELUXE
Jackson 5

Japan: Motown SJET 94343 (1973).

LP1: *ABC/I Want You Back/With A
Child's Heart/Sugar Daddy/Maybe
Tomorrow/La-La Means I Love You/
Daddy's Home* (Jermaine)/*The Love You
Save/I Wanna Be Where You Are/Honey
Chile/Goin' Back To Indiana*

LP2: *Ben/Corner Of The Sky/Hallelujah
Day/That's How Love Goes* (Jermaine)/
*Rockin' Robin/Little Bitty Pretty One/
Come Into My Life* (Jermaine)/*Got To Be
There/Never Can Say Goodbye/Mama's
Pearl/Happy (Love Theme From 'Lady
Sings The Blues')/Lookin' Through The
Windows*

GREATEST HITS
Jackson 5

Japan: Victor/Motown SWX 9013-14
  (1975).

LP1: *Dancing Machine/Get It Together/
Hallelujah Day/We're Almost There/I Am
Love (Part 1)/Forever Came Today/
Daddy's Home* (Jermaine)/*Lookin'
Through The Windows/I'll Be There/
Never Can Say Goodbye/Maybe
Tomorrow/Got To Be There*

LP2: *Ben/Corner Of The Sky/Sugar
Daddy/I Wanna Be Where You Are/
Mama's Pearl/Little Bitty Pretty
One/ABC/I Want You Back/Rockin'
Robin/That's How Love Goes*
(Jermaine)/*The Love You Save/Goin'
Back To Indiana*

NEW SOUL – 14 GREATEST HITS
Jackson 5

Japan: Victor/Motown VIP 10125 (1976).

*ABC/Hallelujah Day/Dancing Machine/
The Love You Save/Little Bitty Pretty
One/Get It Together/We're Almost
There/I Am Love (Part 1)/Lookin'
Through The Windows/I'll Be There/
Daddy's Home* (Jermaine)/*Ben/I Want
You Back/Goin' Back To Indiana*

OS GRANDES SUCESSOS (THE BEST OF…) VOL.2
Michael Jackson

Brazil: Motown 5047149 A (1980).
My Girl/Johnny Raven/Take Me Back/ Euphoria/Cinderella Stay Awhile/Shoo-Be-Doo-Be-Doo-Dah-Day/Too Young/All The Things You Are/Up Again/Doggin' Around/Just A Little Bit Of You/You Can Cry On My Shoulder

Volume 1 was as released in the States in 1975.

EXITOS (HITS)
Michael Jackson & The Jacksons

Ecuador: CBS 933-0003 (1984).

Don't Stop 'Til You Get Enough/Rock With You/Off The Wall/Billie Jean/ Thriller/Beat It/P.Y.T. (Pretty Young Thing)/Wanna Be Startin' Somethin'/ Shake Your Body (Down To The Ground)/Working Day And Night

INSTRUMENTAL VERSION COLLECTION
Michael Jackson

Japan: Epic 20-8P-5158 (1988).

Billie Jean (Instrumental)/Thriller (Instrumental)/Bad (Dub Version)/The Way You Make Me Feel (Dub Version)/ Man In The Mirror (Instrumental)/Dirty Diana (Instrumental)/Another Part Of Me (Instrumental)

Re-issued in 1996 (Epic ESCA 6615).

THE HISTORY OF…
Michael Jackson

Japan: Epic QY-8P-90094 (1991 / promo).

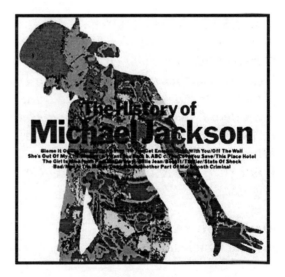

Blame It On The Boogie/Don't Stop 'Til You Get Enough/Rock With You/Off The Wall/She's Out Of My Life/Medley: (I Want You Back/ABC/The Love You Save)/This Place Hotel/The Girl Is Mine/Billie Jean/Beat It/Thriller/State Of Shock/Bad/Man In The Mirror/Dirty

Diana/Another Part Of Me/Smooth Criminal

DANGEROUS – THE REMIX COLLECTION
Michael Jackson

Japan: Epic ESCA 5801 (1992).

Black Or White (C&C House/Club Mix)/Remember The Time (New Jack Main Mix)/Remember The Time (Acapella)/In The Closet (The Reprise)/In The Closet (The Underground Mix)/Who Is It (Lakeside)/Who Is It (Moby's Raw Mercy Dub)/Jam (Silky 7")/Jam (Roger's Jeep Mix)/Give In To Me (Vocal Version)

DANGEROUS TOUR SOUVENIR
Michael Jackson

Malaysia: Epic/Sony (1992).

Off The Wall/She's Out Of My Life/Don't Stop 'Til You Get Enough/ Rock With You (Masters At Work Remix)/Thriller/Billie Jean/Beat It (Moby's Sub Mix)/Bad/Man In The Mirror/Smooth Criminal (Annie Mix)/Dangerous/Who Is It/Black Or White (Clivilles & Cole Radio Mix)/Come Together

MICHAEL JACKSON II
Michael Jackson

South Korea: Music Design Records MDRC-1083 (1992).

The Girl Is Mine/Thriller/Beat It/P.Y.T. (Pretty Young Thing)/Man In The Mirror/ Another Part Of Me/Bad/Billie Jean/The Way You Make Me Feel/Human Nature/I Just Can't Stop Loving You/Dirty Diana

DANGEROUS TOUR SOUVENIR
Michael Jackson

Malaysia: Epic ESCA 5703 2 (1993 / promo).

Off The Wall/She's Out Of My Life/Don't Stop 'Til You Get Enough/ Rock With You (Masters At Work Remix)/Thriller/Billie Jean/Beat It (Moby's Sub Mix)/Bad/Man In The Mirror/Smooth Criminal (Annie Mix)/Dangerous/Who Is It/Black Or White (Clivilles & Cole Radio Mix)/Come Together

LUCKY SOUNDS
Jackson 5

France: Motown 530406 2 (1995).

I Want You Back/ABC/The Love You Save/One More Chance/Mama's Pearl/ Goin' Back To Indiana/Never Can Say Goodbye/Maybe Tomorrow/Sugar Daddy/Little Bitty Pretty One/Lookin' Through The Windows/Skywriter/Get It Together/Dancing Machine/Whatever You Got, I Want/I Am Love/Body Language (Do The Love Dance)/2-4-6-8/ The Young Folks/(Come 'Round Here) You're The One I Need

WE LOVE YOU!
Michael Jackson & The Jackson Five

Germany: Motor/Motown 530801 2 (1997).

Rockin' Robin/Ain't No Sunshine/I Want You Back/People Make The World Go 'Round/Got To Be There/Dapper-Dan/ Stand!/My Girl/We've Got A Good Thing Going/Doctor My Eyes/Shoo-Be-Doo-Be-

Doo-Dah-Day/Euphoria/ABC/You've Got A Friend/Love Is Here And Now You're Gone/Doggin' Around/Ain't Nothing Like The Real Thing/Take Me Back/We're Almost There/I'll Be There

MASTER SERIE (MASTER SERIES)
Michael Jackson With The Jackson 5

France: Podis/Motown 530771 2 (1997).

Lookin' Through The Windows/Doctor My Eyes/Skywriter/Happy (Love Theme From 'Lady Sings The Blues')/The Boogie Man/ Reflections/I Am Love/It's Too Late To Change The Time/Get It Together/Dancing Machine/Whatever You Got, I Want/The Life Of The Party/ We're Almost There/Just A Little Bit Of You/One Day In Your Life/You Are There/Take Me Back/Forever Came Today

THE REAL THING
Jackson Five

Germany: Motown (1998).

I Want You Back/ABC/Never Can Say Goodbye/I'll Be There/Dancing Machine/Rockin' Robin/Ain't No Sunshine/Ben/People Make The World Go 'Round/Got To Be There/Dapper-Dan/Stand!/My Girl/We've Got A Good Thing Going/Doctor My Eyes/Shoo-Be-Doo-Be-Doo-Dah-Day/Euphoria/You've Got A Friend/Love Is Here And Now You're Gone/Doggin' Around/Ain't Nothing Like The Real Thing/Bridge Over Troubled Water/Take Me Back/ We're Almost There

FREE SOUL
Jackson Five

Japan: Polydor POCT 1612 (1999).

Christmas Won't Be The Same This Year/We Wish You A Merry Christmas/ E-Ne-Me-Ne-Mi-Ni-Moe (The Choice Is Yours To Pull)/It's Great To Be Here/I Want You Back/ABC/I Will Find A Way/Live It Up (Jermaine)*/Sugar Daddy/ Mama's Pearl/Darling Dear/I'll Be There/Never Can Say Goodbye/What Goes Around Comes Around/Don't Let Your Baby Catch You/The Love You Save/Petals/Got To Get To You Girl* (Jermaine)*/Don't Want To See Tomorrow/I Wanna Be Where You Are/We're Almost There/That's How Love Goes* (Jermaine)

SOUL SOURCE JACKSON 5 REMIXES
Jackson 5

Japan: Motown UPCH 1034 (2000).

I Want You Back (Readymade 524 Mix)/Darling Dear (Rejuvenated By MURO Mix)/It's Great To Be Here (Kenny Dope Mix)/I Wanna Be Where You Are (Monday Michiru)/ABC (Love Stream Mix)/Hum Along And Dance (United Future Organisation Mix)/I'll Be There (SCOF Remix)/ABC (Kubotam Takeshi Remix)/I Want You Back (Kei's Routine Jazz Party Mix)/Never Can Say Goodbye (OSWA 3000 Remix)

MILLENNIUM EDITION
Jackson Five With Michael Jackson

Germany: Universal 157294 2 (2000).
*I Want You Back/Who's Lovin' You/
Reach In/Honey Love/Got To Be
There/Pride And Joy/The Eternal
Light/Touch/Corner Of The Sky/The
Boogie Man/Love Scenes/Money
Honey/Coming Home/Skywriter/Mama's
Pearl/She's Good/Maybe Tomorrow*

JACKSON FIVE
Jackson Five

France: Universal 157170 2 (2000).

Track listing same as the German release,
MILLENNIUM EDITION.

SOUL SOURCE JACKSON 5
 REMIXES 2
Jackson 5

Japan: Motown UPCH 1090 (2001).

*The Love You Save (Asakusa S.C. '01
Mix)/ABC (Readymade Super 524 Mix)/
Dancing Machine (Topless In Action
Remixxx)/We're Almost There (DJ Spina
Remix)Ain't No Sunshine (SSY Remix)/
Good Thing Goin' (DJ Bobi James)/ABC
(Justa Roots Rock Mix)/Ben (HF Remix
#2)/Get It Together (4Hero Remix)/Can I
See You In The Morning (Electric Sheep
Remix)*

***ORO* (GOLD)**
Michael Jackson

Argentina: Universal 013491-2 (2002).

*One Day In Your Life/Rockin' Robin/
People Make The World Go 'Round/
Happy (Love Theme From 'Lady Sings
The Blues')/With A Child's Heart/Music
And Me/Got To Be There/Ben/We're
Almost There/Just A Little Bit Of You/I
Wanna Be Where You Are/In Our Small
Way/My Girl/Dapper-Dan/We've Got A
Good Thing Going*

NUMBER ONES
Michael Jackson

Japan: Epic EICP-333 & China: Epic HL
 1734 (2003).

*Don't Stop 'Til You Get Enough/Rock
With You/Billie Jean/Beat It/Thriller/
Human Nature/I Just Can't Stop Loving
You/Bad/The Way You Make Me Feel/
Man In The Mirror/Dirty Diana/Smooth
Criminal/Black Or White/You Are Not
Alone/Earth Song/Blood On The Dance
Floor/You Rock My World/One More
Chance*

THE VERY BEST OF –
 ANTHOLOGY 1969-1987
Jackson 5 / Jacksons

Japan: Universal UICY 1269/70 (2004 /
 promo).

CD1: *I Want You Back/ABC/The Love
You Save/I'll Be There/Mama's Pearl/
Never Can Say Goodbye/Sugar Daddy
(Single Version)/Dancing Machine
(Single Version)/Lookin' Through The
Windows/Doctor My Eyes/Ain't No
Sunshine/Got To Be There (Single
Version)/Rockin' Robin/Ben (Single
Version)One Day In Your Life/Farewell
My Summer Love*

CD2: *Can You Feel It (Single Edit)/ Blame It On The Boogie/Enjoy Yourself/ Show You The Way To Go (Single Version)/Dreamer/Even Though You're Gone/Goin' Places/Torture/Shake Your Body (Down To The Ground)/Lovely One/This Place Hotel/Walk Right Now (Single Version)/State Of Shock/2300 Jackson Street/Nothin (That Compares 2 U)/Don't Stop 'Til You Get Enough (Live From 1981 US Tour)*

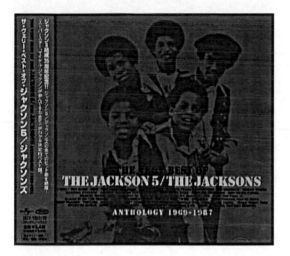

LEGENDS
Michael Jackson

Far East: Universal 07314013491-2 (2005 / Phillipines).

One Day In Your Life/Rockin' Robin/ People Make The World Go 'Round/ Happy (Love Theme From 'Lady Sings The Blues')/With A Child's Heart/Music And Me/Got To Be There/Ben/We're Almost There/Just A Little Bit Of You/I Wanna Be Where You Are/In Our Small Way/My Girl/Dapper-Dan/We've Got A Good Thing Going

THE ESSENTIAL COLLECTION
Michael Jackson

Europe: Universal 982 027-2 (2005).

One Day In Your Life/Rockin' Robin/ People Make The World Go 'Round/ Happy (Love Theme From 'Lady Sings The Blues')/With A Child's Heart/Music And Me/Got To Be There/Ben/We're Almost There/Just A Little Bit Of You/I Wanna Be Where You Are/In Our Small Way/My Girl/Dapper Dan/We've Got A Good Thing Going

Released in the UK in 2008 as a Woolworths exclusive, with a different CD sleeve.

COLOUR COLLECTION
Jackson 5

Europe: Motown 060249849192 (2007).

I Want You Back/ABC/The Love You Save/I'll Be There/Never Can Say Goodbye/Got To Be There/Sugar Daddy/ Daddy's Home (Jermaine)/I Wanna Be Where You Are/Maybe Tomorrow/ Dancing Machine

COLOUR COLLECTION
Michael Jackson

Europe/Australia/Taiwan: Motown
    98436332 (2007 / Holland).

*One Day In Your Life/Rockin' Robin/
People Make The World Go Round/
Happy/With A Child's Heart/Music And
Me/Got To Be There/Ben/We're Almost
There/Just A Little Bit Of You/I Wanna
Be Where You Are/In Our Small Way/My
Girl/Dapper-Dan/We've Got A Good
Thing Going*

Both *COLOUR COLLECTION*
compilations (along with a host of others
similarly titled releases by one-time
Motown artists) were issued with a cut-
out gatefold sleeve, which permitted the
CD to be seen.

CDs were pressed in a number of 'vinyl
look' colours, in different countries,
including green and purple (Michael) and
pale yellow (Jackson 5).

KING OF POP
Michael Jackson

Compilation released from late August
2008 onwards, to celebrate Michael's
50th birthday – track listing voted on by
fans in each individual country, hence the
track listing in each country was
different.

Here's a round-up of track listings from
around the world:

Argentina: Sony 88697356232
    (November 2008).

*Billie Jean/Beat It/Black Or White/
Bad/Heal The World/Human Nature/
Don't Stop 'Til You Get Enough/Smooth
Criminal/Man In The Mirror/I Just Can't
Stop Loving You/Come Together/Thriller
Megamix*

Australia: Sony 88697356252 (White
    Sleeve, August 2008).

CD1: *Billie Jean/Man In The Mirror/
Smooth Criminal)/Beat It/Thriller/They
Don't Care About Us/Who Is It/Black Or
White/You Rock My World/Wanna Be
Startin' Somethin'/The Way You Make
Me Feel)/Don't Stop 'Til You Get
Enough/Dirty Diana/Blood On The
Dance Floor/Rock With You/Stranger In
Moscow/Remember The Time*

CD2: *Will You Be There/Give In To Me/
You Are Not Alone/Say Say Say/Scream/
State Of Shock/Got The Hots/You Can't
Win/Fall Again (Demo)/Sunset Driver
(Demo)/Someone Put Your Hand Out/In
The Back/We Are The World (Demo)/One
More Chance/Thriller Megamix*

Australia: Sony 88697356242 (Red Sleeve, August 2008).

CD1: *Billie Jean/Man In The Mirror/ Smooth Criminal)/Beat It/Thriller/They Don't Care About Us/Who Is It/Black Or White/You Rock My World/Wanna Be Startin' Somethin'/The Way You Make Me Feel)/Don't Stop 'Til You Get Enough/Dirty Diana/Blood On The Dance Floor/Rock With You/Stranger In Moscow/Remember The Time*

CD2: *Will You Be There/Give In To Me/You Are Not Alone/Bad/Earth Song/ Speechless/Human Nature/Heal The World/Dangerous/Blame It On The Boogie/Ghosts/Off The Wall/Butterflies/ Say Say Say/Scream/Thriller Megamix*

Austria: Sony 88697356262 (August 2008).

CD1: *Man In The Mirror/Smooth Criminal/Billie Jean/The Way You Make Me Feel/Black Or White/Remember The Time/You Are Not Alone/Human Nature/ Wanna Be Startin' Somethin'/They Don't Care About Us/Dirty Diana/We've Had Enough/Give In To Me/Will You Be There/Heal The World/Got The Hots*

CD2: *ABC/Can You Feel It/Say Say Say/Thriller/Bad/Who Is It/Earth Song/Beat It/Rock With You/I Just Can't Stop Loving You/We Are The World (Demo)/Stranger In Moscow/You Rock My World/Scream/Ghosts/Thriller Megamix*

Belgium: Sony 88697356272 (*Het Nieuwsblas* Edition, August 2008).

CD1: *Thriller/Beat It/Billie Jean/Bad/ Black Or White/Smooth Criminal/Dirty Diana/Can You Feel It/Heal The World/ Don't Stop 'Til You Get Enough/Wanna Be Startin' Somethin'/Blame It On The Boogie/I Just Can't Stop Loving You/ Earth Song/Childhood (Theme From 'Free Willy 2')/The Girl Is Mine/Rock With You*

CD2: *Man In The Mirror/Liberian Girl/ Blood On The Dance Floor/The Way You Make Me Feel/We Are The World (Demo)/Baby Be Mine/ Dangerous/They Don't Care About Us/Billie Jean 2008/ Human Nature/History/Say Say Say/ Remember The Time/You Rock My World/Beautiful Girl/Another Part Of Me*

Belgium: Sony 88697356282 (*Bel.RTL* Edition, August 2008).

CD1: *Billie Jean/Beat It/Bad/Blood On The Dance Floor/Say Say Say/Blame It On The Boogie/Can You Feel It/Heal The World/Don't Stop 'Til You Get Enough/ Earth Song/Thriller/Dirty Diana/Human Nature/ Smooth Criminal/I Just Can't Stop Loving You/Rock With You/Man In The Mirror*

CD2: *Wanna Be Startin' Somethin'/ Smile/Remember The Time/Come Together/The Girl Is Mine/Stranger In Moscow/P.Y.T. (Pretty Young Thing)/Off The Wall/Liberian Girl/Ghosts/The Way You Make Me Feel/Scream/Childhood (Theme From 'Free Willy 2')/Jam/They Don't Care About Us/Leave Me Alone/ We Are Here To Change The World*

Brazil: Sony 1269-2 (October 2008).

Thriller/Don't Stop 'Til You Get Enough/ Billie Jean/Black Or White/Heal The World/Say Say Say/Beat It/Rock With You/Human Nature/Bad/You Are Not Alone/Will You Be There/The Way You Make Me Feel/Man In The Mirror/ Wanna Be Startin' Somethin' 2008/The Girl Is Mine 2008

Finland: Sony 88697379024 (October 2008).

Billie Jean/Thriller/Beat It/Smooth Criminal/Bad/Earth Song/Black Or White/Dirty Diana/You Are Not Alone/I Just Can't Stop Loving You/Heal The World/They Don't Care About Us/ Scream/Man In The Mirror/Liberian Girl/Say Say Say/Don't Stop 'Til You Get Enough/Wanna Be Startin' Somethin'

France: Sony 88697356312 / 88697356332 (Collector's Edition) (December 2008).

CD1: *Billie Jean/Black Or White/Beat It/Off The Wall/Thriller/Smooth Criminal/Man In The Mirror/Remember*

The Time/Human Nature/ Ghosts/Who Is It/Blood On The Dance Floor/One More Chance/Earth Song/Heal The World/Say Say Say/Thriller Megamix

CD2: *Don't Stop 'Til You Get Enough/ Bad/Wanna Be Startin' Somethin'/Rock With You/The Way You Make Me Feel/They Don't Care About Us/Dirty Diana/P.Y.T. (Pretty Young Thing)/You Are Not Alone/Whatever Happens/Cry/ Will You Be There/Working Day And Night/You Rock My World/Dangerous/ Got The Hots*

CD3 (Collector's Edition only): *Carousel/Rock With You (Original LP Version)/Stranger In Moscow (Tee's In House Club Remix)/The Girl Is Mine/The Way You Love Me/Is It Scary/Childhood (Theme From 'Free Willy 2')/Bad (Dance Extended Mix Includes False Fade)/ Wanna Be Startin' Somethin' (Extended 12" Mix)/Billie Jean (Original 12" Version)/Another Part Of Me (Extended Dance Mix)/The Way You Make Me Feel (Dance Extended Mix)/Black Or White (Clivilles & Cole House/Club Mix)*

Germany: Sony 88697356342 (August 2008).

CD1: *Billie Jean/Beat It/Thriller/Smooth Criminal/Bad/Dirty Diana/Black Or White/Man In The Mirror/Earth Song/ Heal The World/They Don't Care About Us/Who Is It/Speechless/The Way You Make Me Feel/We've Had Enough/ Remember The Time*

CD2: *Whatever Happens/You Are Not Alone/Say Say Say/Liberian Girl/Wanna Be Startin' Somethin'/Don't Stop 'Til You*

Get Enough/I Just Can't Stop Loving You/Give In To Me/Dangerous/Will You Be There/Scream/You Rock My World/Stranger In Moscow/Rock With You/Got The Hots/Thriller Megamix

The German edition was also released in Switzerland.

Greece: Sony 88697356352 (November 2008).

CD1: *Billie Jean/Beat It/Smooth Criminal/Bad/Jam/Rock With You/Dirty Diana/Black Or White/Scream/Wanna Be Startin' Somethin'/Don't Stop 'Til You Get Enough/In The Closet/Liberian Girl/The Girl Is Mine/Stranger In Moscow/Blood On The Dance Floor/Dangerous*

CD2: *Thriller/Off The Wall/Wanna Be Startin' Somethin' 2008/Can You Feel It/They Don't Care About Us/Come Together/Human Nature/Earth Song/You Are Not Alone/The Way You Make Me Feel/Remember The Time/Man In The Mirror/Ghosts/Invincible/Thriller Megamix*

Holland: Sony 88697356402 (August 2008).

Billie Jean/Thriller/Beat It/Smooth Criminal/Dirty Diana/Don't Stop 'Til You Get Enough/Man In The Mirror/They Don't Care About Us/Black Or White/Wanna Be Startin' Somethin'/Bad/Ben/Can You Feel It/She's Out Of My Life/Remember The Time/Will You Be There/Who Is It/I'll Be There

Holland: Sony 88697356412 (August 2008).

CD1: *Billie Jean/Thriller/Beat It/Smooth Criminal/Dirty Diana/Don't Stop 'Til You Get Enough/Man In The Mirror/They Don't Care About Us/Black Or White/Wanna Be Startin' Somethin'/The Way You Make Me Feel/Bad/Earth Song/Ben)/Heal The World/Liberian Girl/Rock With You*

CD2: *Can You Feel It/She's Out Of My Life/You Are Not Alone/Stranger In Moscow/The Girl Is Mine/Remember The Time/You Rock My World/Human Nature/Give In To Me/Will You Be There/Off The Wall/I'll Be There/Who Is It/Blood On The Dance Floor/Say Say Say/Blame It On The Boogie/Ghosts/Got The Hots*

Hong Kong: Sony 88697356362 (August 2008).

CD1: *Billie Jean/Bad/Say Say Say/Thriller/Ghosts/Will You Be There/Heal The World/Smooth Criminal/Jam/Scream/I Just Can't Stop Loving You/Black Or White/They Don't Care About Us/Come Together/We Are The World (Demo)*

CD2: *Don't Stop 'Til You Get Enough/Beat It/Dangerous/Dirty Diana/You Are Not Alone/Remember The Time/The Way You Make Me Feel/Man In The Mirror/Earth Song/She's Out Of My Life/The Girl Is Mine/You Rock My World/Blood On The Dance Floor/Wanna Be Startin' Somethin'/Billie Jean 2008/Thriller Megamix*

Hungary: Sony 88697356372 (August 2008).

Billie Jean/Black Or White/Thriller/ Smooth Criminal/Earth Song/Bad/Beat It/Dirty Diana/They Don't Care About Us/Heal The World/Remember The Time/Say Say Say/Dangerous/Give In To Me/You Are Not Alone/Thriller Megamix

India: Sony 88697433472 (February 2009).

CD1: *Billie Jean/Bad/Thriller/Black Or White/Heal The World/Smooth Criminal/ Jam/The Way You Make Me Feel/I Just Can't Stop Loving You/They Don't Care About Us/In The Closet/Baby Be Mine/ Stranger In Moscow/Come Together/Will You Be There*

CD2: *Don't Stop 'Til You Get Enough/ Beat It/Dangerous/Dirty Diana/You Are Not Alone/Remember The Time/Earth Song/Off The Wall/You Rock My World/ Man In The Mirror/Break Of Dawn/ Butterflies/Blood On The Dance Floor/ Wanna Be Startin' Somethin'/Billie Jean 2008*

Italy: Sony 88697356382 (September 2008).

CD1: *Billie Jean/Black Or White/Man In The Mirror/Whatever Happens/Smooth Criminal/Beat It/Off The Wall/We've Had Enough/ Dangerous/They Don't Care About Us/Human Nature/Wanna Be Startin' Somethin'/Ghosts/You Rock My World/Earth Song*

CD2: *Thriller/Tabloid Junkie/Liberian Girl/Remember The Time/We Are The World (Demo)/Who Is It/Speechless/ Morphine/The Way You Make Me Feel/ Bad/Blood On The Dance Floor/Rock With You/Don't Stop 'Til You Get Enough/You Are Not Alone/Heal The World/Got The Hots/Carousel*

Japan: Epic EICP-1055 (September 2008).

Billie Jean/Man In The Mirror/Smooth Criminal/Thriller/Beat It/Bad/ Black Or White/Heal The World/Rock With You/ Human Nature/We Are The World (Demo)/Say Say Say/ Scream/Remember

The Time/Off The Wall/Ben/Thriller Megamix

Mexico: Sony 886974043720 (November 2008).

CD1: *Beat It/Rock With You/Don't Stop 'Til You Get Enough/Human Nature/ Thriller/I Just Can't Stop Loving You/ Bad/Dirty Diana/The Way You Make Me Feel/Smooth Criminal/Black Or White/ You Are Not Alone/You Rock My World/ Earth Song/Blame It On The Boogie*

CD2: *Say Say Say/Billie Jean/Off The Wall/Shake Your Body (Down To The Ground)/Can You Feel It/P.Y.T. (Pretty Young Thing)/Wanna Be Startin' Somethin'/Man In The Mirror/Another Part Of Me/Who Is It/Leave Me Alone/ Remember The Time/In The Closet/Will You Be There/They Don't Care About Us*

New Zealand: Sony 88697356432 (August 2008).

Billie Jean/Thriller/Don't Stop 'Til You Get Enough/Man In The Mirror/Black Or White/Blame It On The Boogie/Beat It/Smooth Criminal/Bad/Rock With You/ The Way You Make Feel/Heal The World/ Scream/Dirty Diana/Remember The Time/ They Don't Care About Us/ Stranger In Moscow

Philippines: Sony 88697356442 (August 2008).

CD1: *Blame It On The Boogie/Don't Stop 'Til You Get Enough/Rock With You/Off The Wall/She's Out Of My Life/The Girl Is Mine/Thriller/ Beat It/Billie Jean/ Human Nature/P.Y.T. (Pretty Young*

Thing)/The Way You Make Me Feel/Man In The Mirror/I Just Can't Stop Loving You/Smooth Criminal/In The Closet

CD2: *Remember The Time/Heal The World/Black Or White/Gone Too Soon/Dangerous/Scream/They Don't Care About Us/Earth Song/You Are Not Alone/Childhood (Theme From 'Free Willy 2')/Blood On The Dance Floor/ Invincible/We Are The World (Demo)/ Wanna Be Startin' Somethin' 2008/Say Say Say/Got The Hots/Thriller Megamix*

Poland: Sony 88697356452 (October 2008).

CD1: *Billie Jean/Black Or White/ Thriller/Earth Song/Remember The Time/Say Say Say/Blood On The Dance Floor/Scream/Who Is It/Blame It On The Boogie/Ghosts/Rock With You/Heal The World/Human Nature/Liberian Girl/ Dangerous*

CD2: *Smooth Criminal/Give In To Me/Beat It/Man In The Mirror/They Don't Care About Us/Can You Feel It/Dirty Diana/You Are Not Alone/ Wanna Be Startin' Somethin'/You Rock My World/The Way You Make Me Feel/ Stranger In Moscow/Bad/Don't Stop 'Til You Get Enough/We Are The World (Demo)*

Portugal: Sony 88697370832 (December 2008).

Billie Jean/Black Or White/Beat It/Bad/ Smooth Criminal/You Are Not Alone/ Thriller/Earth Song/Man In The Mirror/ You Rock My World/The Way You Make Me Feel/Heal The World/Don't Stop 'Til

You Get Enough/Rock With You/Dirty Diana/Remember The Time

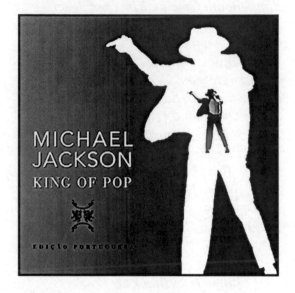

Russia: Sony 88697356462 (October 2008).

Billie Jean/Wanna Be Startin' Somethin'/ We Are The World (Demo)/Dirty Diana/Smooth Criminal/Black Or White/Who Is It/Earth Song/On The Line/They Don't Care About Us/Stranger In Moscow/Blood In The Dance Floor/ Fall Again/Break Of Dawn/Whatever Happens/We've Had Enough

South Korea: Sony S30500C (December 2008).

CD1: *Billie Jean/Beat It/Black Or White/ Heal The World/You Are Not Alone/ Thriller/Dangerous/Bad/We Are The World (Demo)/Jam/Man In The Mirror/ The Girl Is Mine/Remember The Time/ Smooth Criminal/The Way You Make Me Feel/History*

CD2: *Will You Be There/I Just Can't Stop Loving You/Rock With You/Don't Stop*

'Til You Get Enough/Come Together/ Scream/Human Nature/Earth Song/ Wanna Be Startin' Somethin'/You Rock My World/ Off The Wall/Keep The Faith /Smile/Who Is It/Childhood (Theme From 'Free Willy 2')

Spain: 88697433512 (January 2009).

Thriller/Billie Jean/Bad/Beat It/Smooth Criminal/Black Or White/Man In The Mirror/The Way You Make Me Feel/ Remember The Time/Don't Stop 'Til You Get Enough/They Don't Care About Us/ Rock With You/Blood On The Dance Floor/Heal The World/Wanna Be Startin' Somethin'/Unbreakable/We Are The World (Demo)

Sweden: Sony 88697356472 (October 2008).

CD1: *Billie Jean/Thriller/Beat It/Bad/ Black Or White/Smooth Criminal/The Way You Make Me Feel/Man In The Mirror/Don't Stop 'Til You Get Enough/ Blame It On The Boogie/Dirty Diana/ They Don't Care About Us/The Girl Is*

Mine/Heal The World/We Are The World
(Demo)/ Liberian Girl

CD2: *Earth Song/Can You Feel It/I Just
Can't Stop Loving You/I'll Be There/Say
Say Say/Ben/Shake Your Body (Down To
The Ground)/Got The Hots/Someone Put
Your Hand Out/On The Line/State Of
Shock/We Are Here To Change The
World/One More Chance/We've Had
Enough/Wanna Be Startin' Somethin'
2008/Thriller Megamix*

Thailand: Sony 88697356492
(December 2008).

CD1: *Black Or White/Smooth Criminal/
Bad/Beat It/Billie Jean/Thriller/Don't
Stop 'Til You Get Enough/Wanna Be
Startin' Somethin'/The Way You Make
Me Feel/Off The Wall/Remember The
Time/You Rock My World/Give In To
Me/Jam/Scream/Blood On The Dance
Floor/They Don't Care About Us*

CD2: *We Are The World (Demo)/Heal
The World/You Are Not Alone/ Childhood
(Theme From 'Free Willy 2')/Will You Be
There/The Girl Is Mine/Human Nature/I
Just Can't Stop Loving You/She's Out Of
My Life/Man In The Mirror/Rock With
You/Blame It On The Boogie/Say Say
Say/Earth Song/Stranger In Moscow/I
Just Can't Stop Loving You (Spanish
Version)/One More Chance*

Turkey: Sony 88697356502 (November
2008).

*Thriller/Smooth Criminal/Billie Jean/
Black Or White/They Don't Care About
Us/Bad/Remember The Time/Wanna Be
Startin' Somethin'/In The Closet/Beat*

It/Don't Stop 'Til You Get Enough/
Scream/Who Is It/The Way You Make Me
Feel/You Rock My World/You Are Not
Alone/ Liberian Girl/Off The Wall

Few true rarities featured on any of the
KING OF POP editions, but worth
mentioning are:

- *Thriller Megamix* – previously
  unreleased.
- *Carousel* – supposedly full length
  version included on the French
  and Italian editions – however,
  this version had a shorter
  instrumental bridge section than
  the full version found on Michael
  Sembello's website.
- *Rock With You* – original album
  mix included on the French
  Collector's Edition.
- *Wanna Be Startin' Somethin'
  (Single Version)*.
- *Can't Get Outta The Rain.*
- *Is It Scary (Single Radio Edit).*
- *Smile (Short Version).*
- *On The Line.*
- *Someone Put Your Hand Out.*

The compilation hit no.1 in Austria, and
achieved no.4 in Belgium (Flanders),
Holland and Hungary, no.5 in Australia,
no.6 in Germany, no.7 in Poland, no.9 in
Sweden, and no.10 in Japan.

European editions gave fans exclusive
access to Michael's Opendisc site, via
inserting the CD into their computer, with
10 additional classic tracks in the
Jukebox, and more.

Posthumous hit: no.1 in Austria, Germany, Holland, Italy, Poland, Spain & Switzerland, no.2 in France, no.3 in Ireland, Mexico & Sweden, no.5 in Portugal, no.6 in Australia & New Zealand, no.15 in Finland, no.35 in Denmark & no.37 in the Czech Republic.

MELLOW
Michael Jackson

Japan: Motown UICZ-1327 (2009).

I Wanna Be Where You Are/Ben/I'll Be There (Minus Mix)/You've Got A Friend/ My Girl/Rockin' Robin/Never Can Say Goodbye/We're Almost There/Farewell My Summer Love/Darling Dear/Coming Home/ Maybe Tomorrow/Music And Me/Ain't No Sunshine/Everybody's Somebody's Fool/People Make The World Go 'Round/Wings Of My Love/Got To Be There/Maria (You Were The Only One)/One Day In Your Life/Greatest Show On Earth/Morning Glow/Happy (Love Theme From 'Lady Sings The Blues')

SOUL SOURCE BEST OF JACKSON 5 REMIXES
Jackson 5

Japan: Motown UICZ-1328 (2009).

Ben (HF Remix #4)/Darling Dear (Rejuvenated By Muro Mix)/I'll Be There (Scof Remix)/ABC (Justa Roots Rock Mix)/I Want You Back (Readymade 524 Mix)/The Love You Save (Asakusa S.C. '01 Mix)/We're Almost There (DJ Spinna Remix)/It's Great To Be Here (Kenny Dope Remix)/I Want You Back (Kei's Routine Jazz Pati Mix)/ABC (Love Stream Mix)/Get It Together (4 Hero Remix)/Never Can Say Goodbye (Osawa 3000 Remix)/Dancing Machine (Topless In Action Remixxx)/Ain't No Sunshine (SSY Remix)/I Want You Back '86

THE VERY BEST OF
Michael Jackson With The
Jackson Five

Japan: Motown UICY-1448 (2009).

*I Want You Back/ABC/The Love You
Save/I'll Be There/Mama's Pearl/Never
Can Say Goodbye/Got To Be There/
Rockin' Robin/Ain't No Sunshine/Lookin'
Through The Windows/Ben/Doctor My
Eyes/Hallelujah Day/Skywriter/Happy
(Love Theme From 'Lady Sings The
Blues')/We're Almost There/One Day In
Your Life/Girl You're So Together/
Farewell My Summer Love/I Want You
Back ('88 PWL Remix)/It's Your Thing
(The J5 In '95 House Remix)/I'll Be
There (Minus Mix: Acoustic Version)*

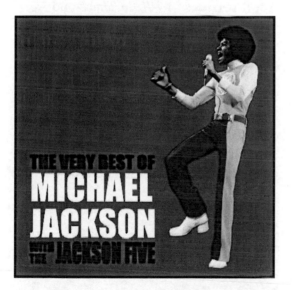

Japanese Mini Singles & LPs

Reissues on CD of 7" singles and vinyl
albums, with the original sleeve artwork
accurately reproduced in miniature on the
card sleeve (with obi-strip).

THRILLER 25: JAPANESE
SINGLES COLLECTION

Japan: Sony EICP 945-951 (2008).

The Girl Is Mine
  b/w *Can't Get Outta The Rain*
Billie Jean
  b/w *It's The Falling In Love*
Beat It
  b/w *Get On The Floor*
Wanna Be Startin' Somethin'
  b/w *(Instrumental)*
Human Nature
  b/w *Baby Be Mine*
P.Y.T. (Pretty Young Thing)
  b/w *Working Day And Night (2008
  Remix)*
Thriller
  b/w *Things I Do For You (Live)*

Included a new remix of *Working Day
And Night*.

Achieved no.119 on the Japanese albums
chart.

MICHAEL JACKSON ALBUMS

Japan: Sony EICP 1194-1199 (2009).

OFF THE WALL (bonus tracks as per the
  2001 Special Edition)
THRILLER (bonus tracks as per the 2001
  Special Edition)
BAD (bonus tracks as per the 2001
  Special Edition)
DANGEROUS
*HISTORY PAST PRESENT AND
  FUTURE BOOK 1* (2 discs)

JACKSONS ALBUMS

Japan: Sony EICP 1200-1206 (2009).

THE JACKSONS
GOIN' PLACES
DESTINY
TRIUMPH
BEST LIVE (2 discs)
VICTORY

MOTOWN ALBUMS

Japan: Sony EICY 94292-94302 (2009).

DIANA ROSS PRESENTS... / ABC
THIRD ALBUM / MAYBE TOMORROW
GOIN' BACK TO INDIANA /
   LOOKIN' THROUGH THE WINDOWS
SKYWRITER / GET IT TOGETHER
DANCING MACHINE /
   MOVING VIOLATION
JOYFUL JUKEBOX MUSIC / BOOGIE
CHRISTMAS ALBUM
IN JAPAN
HELLO WORLD: THE MOTOWN
   SOLO COLLECTION (3 discs)

All mini CD singles and LPs were issued as limited editions, and quickly sold out.

Cancelled Releases

DECADE 1980-1990

CD1: *Don't Stop 'Til You Get Enough/ Rock With You/Off The Wall/She's Out Of My Life/Heartbreak Hotel/Someone In The Dark/Wanna Be Startin' Somethin'/ The Girl Is Mine/Thriller/Beat It/Billie Jean/ Human Nature/P.Y.T. (Pretty Young Thing)/State Of Shock*

CD2: *Bad/The Way You Make Me Feel/ Man In The Mirror/I Just Can't Stop Loving You/Dirty Diana/Smooth Criminal/Come Together/I'll Be There (Adult Version)/Never Can Say Goodbye (Adult Version)/Black Or White/Heal The World/Who Is It*

Also known by the title, *DECADE 1979-1989*.

More than a year after the planned release date, compilation cancelled, in favour of a brand new studio album – *DANGEROUS*, which featured the three wholly new tracks on *DECADE 1980-1990*: *Black Or White*, *Heal The World* and *Who Is It*.

Adult versions of *I'll Be There* and *Never Can Say Goodbye*, recorded in conjunction with the Pepsi commercials, remain unreleased.

Test pressings reputed to have been circulated with a 40 page booklet, and early graphic designs for the compilation's sleeve are known to have been acquired by Jackson collectors.

First test pressing featured Michael's eyes on the sleeve; the second test pressing was plain, printed text.

CHRISTMAS ALBUM (untitled)

Michael's 1991 deal with Sony included a wide range of projects – including a remix album and, intriguingly, a Christmas album. Following the 1993 child molestation allegations, the delayed remix album finally – *BLOOD ON THE DANCE FLOOR* – finally hit the shelves in 1997, but no festive offering has ever appeared.

It's possible Michael worked on, or recorded, a few songs for the proposed Christmas album, but anything he did record remains unreleased.

One Christmas song was recorded during the summer of 1994, with a children's choir. Michael insisted that the entire studio be decorated with Christmas lights, a tree, fake snow and a sled, to set the right atmosphere to their recording. Michael also bought a gift for everyone.

SERIES OF REMIXES

Planned for 1992, but cancelled, was a series of previously unheard remixes including:

- *Don't Stop 'Til You Get Enough* remixed by Little Louie & Kenny Dope.
- *Beat It* remixed by Maurice Joshua & E.Smoove.
- *Off The Wall* remixed by Frankie Knuckles & David Morales.

- *Shake Your Body (Down To The Ground)* remixed by Tommy Musto.

HUMANITY

Jacksons project Michael and his brother Jermaine signed a contract for on 16th June 1995, with a view to releasing a 15 track album the following year – only two of the tracks were scheduled to feature Michael.

Alternative title: *GENERATION*.

THE BEST OF...

Jacksons compilation, comprising hits and a few bonuses, Sony planned to release in October 1995, but shelved.

THRILLER – THE SINGLES

Series of seven maxi-singles from *THRILLER*, planned for released by Sony Australia in 2003, but ultimately shelved.

Original track listings:

The Girl Is Mine: *The Girl Is Mine/ Can't Get Outta The Rain/Someone In The Dark/Rock With You (Classic Radio Edit)/Remember The Time (Silky Soul 12" Mix)/Don't Stop 'Til You Get Enough (Enough Mix)/Billie Jean (Moran's Lucious Vocal)/Wanna Be Startin' Somethin' (Brothers In Rhythm House Mix)/Black Or White (Clivilles & Cole House/Dub Mix)/Thriller (Def Thrill Mix)*

Billie Jean: *Billie Jean/(Long Version) /(Instrumental)/Can't Get Outta The Rain/Billie Jean (Tony Moran Mix)/(Four On The Floor Remix – Radio Edit)*

Beat It: *Beat It/Get On The Floor/Beat It (Instrumental)/(Moby's Sub Mix)/Burn This Disco Out*

Wanna Be Startin' Somethin': *Wanna Be Startin' Somethin'/(Instrumental)/ (12" Mix)/(Brothers In Rhythm Mix)/ (Brothers In Rhythm House Mix)/(Tommy D's Main Mix)*

Thriller: *Thriller/(Instrumental)/Things I Do For You/Thriller (Frankie Knuckles & David Morales Remix)/(Danny Tenaglia Mix)*

P.Y.T. (Pretty Young Thing): *P.Y.T. (Pretty Young Thing)/Heartbreak Hotel/Working Day And Night (Live)/Childhood/Off The Wall/Billie Jean/Wanna Be Startin' Somethin'/Black Or White/Jam/Beat It/They Don't Care About Us/Scream/Ease On Down The Road*

Human Nature: *Human Nature/Baby Be Mine/Human Nature (Instrumental)/Rock With You/Billie Jean/Don't Stop 'Til You Get Enough/Remember The Time/The Way You Make Me Feel/Wanna Be Startin' Somethin'/P.Y.T. (Pretty Young Thing)*

Revised track listings:

The Girl Is Mine: *The Girl Is Mine/ Can't Get Outta The Rain/Someone In The Dark/Billie Jean (Moran's Luscious Vocal)*

Billie Jean: as original listing.

Beat It: as original listing.

Wanna Be Startin' Somethin': as original listing.

Thriller: as original listing.

P.Y.T. (Pretty Young Thing): *P.Y.T. (Pretty Young Thing)/Heartbreak Hotel/ Working Day And Night (Live)/Ease On Down The Road*

Human Nature: *Human Nature/Baby Be Mine/Remember The Time/Wanna Be Startin' Somethin'*

THE HITS

Re-packaged and re-titled edition of Michael's *THE ESSENTIAL* compilation, with an identical track listing, scheduled for release in the UK and other countries outside North America in July 2009.

Release shelved, following Michael's passing on 25th June 2009 – *THE ESSENTIAL* re-promoted instead.

At the time of his death, Michael was working on three projects:

- The 'This Is It' Concerts.
- Album of pop songs.
- Album of classical music.

The latter project was confirmed by David Michael Frank, a film/TV composer and conductor, who Michael contacted in early 2009. Frank met Michael at his Holmby Hills home at the end of April.

'He said he listened to classical music all the time, it was his absolute favourite,' said Frank. 'I was impressed with the pieces he mentioned: Aaron Copland's *Rodeo*, *Fanfare For The Common Man* and *Lincoln Portrait*, Leonard Bernstein's *West Side Story*... Michael mentioned that he loved Elmer Bernstein's film music, too, and he specifically mentioned *To Kill A Mockingbird*.'

Michael revealed he was making a CD of classical music, and he was anxious to get the pieces he had written orchestrated, and recorded with a big orchestra.

'My guess is that each piece would be seven to ten minutes long... it's very pretty music,' said Frank. 'One piece had an Irish quality about it. I suggested that we could use a Celtic harp. The pieces sound like pretty film score music, with very traditional harmony, and definitely very strong melodies.'

David Frank, just a week before Michael died, was contacted by Michael's manager, Frank DiLeo, who wanted a budget for the project, including the costs of orchestration.

'Now I have no idea what's going to happen with this,' said Frank. 'I'm hoping the family will do something to get this done. I will not bring it up until after what I think is an appropriate time.'

Michael was working, among others, on a pop album with Akon and Claude Kelly – according to Akon, Michael was motivated by the ticket sales for his O2 dates.

'He said, "My fans are still there, they still love me – they're alive",' said Akon. 'His kids are like his first priority, and they had never seen him perform live. He was trying to create the most incredible show for his kids.'

'He (Michael) still had a good voice and never had a problem singing,' said Greg Phillinganes. 'There were questions about him being able to pull off the tour on the choreography side, but sources working with him told me he was dancing all the time, every day, and was very focused, excited and committed to making the tour the best it could be... it was the biggest comeback of his career, arguably the biggest comeback in pop music – even bigger than Elvis. So obviously he'd want to do the best he could. He never did anything half-assed – which is originally got him to the stature he had.'

Forthcoming Albums

Here are three projects slated to appear soon after the cut-off date for this book.

CHRISTMAS ALBUM
Jackson 5

Reissue of the group's 1970 album, scheduled to feature 10 bonus tracks:

Seasons Greetings From Michael Jackson/Little Christmas Tree/Seasons Greetings From Tito Jackson/Up On The House Top (DJ Re-Edit)/Seasons Greetings From Jackie Jackson/Rudolph The Red Nosed Reindeer (Stripped Mix)/ Seasons Greetings From Jermaine Jackson/Someday At Christmas (Stripped Mix)/Give Love On Christmas Day (Group Acappella Version)/J5 Christmas Medley

Release date announced as 13th October 2009.

THE REMIX SUITES: I-V
Michael Jackson

Motown/Universal project – will feature 20+ songs by Michael and the Jackson 5, remixed by some of the biggest producers in urban music.

First batch of five remixed tracks released digitally in August 2009:

- *Never Can Say Goodbye* by the Neptunes.
- *I Wanna Be Where You Are* by Dallas Austin.
- *ABC* by Salaam Remi.
- *Dancing Machine* by Polow Da Don.
- *Skywriter* by Stargate.

I Wanna Be Where You Are also featured alternate vocals.

'That song (*ABC*) was one of the first songs I remember hearing on my own,' said Remi. 'I think it came out around the time I was coming up as a kid. A remix, it isn't just changing the music – to me, it's about re-imagining the vibe. I wanted to do something that, when it pops up, it makes you say, "Wow!" And to feel like it could be performed that way, not like it was just glued together.'

Complete set of remixes scheduled for release at the end of October 2009.

THIS IS IT
Michael Jackson

Live album recorded at the rehearsals for the planned O2 dates, likely to be released to coincide with the film of the same name, which is due to premier at the end of October 2009.

Reportedly, the album will also feature one previously unreleased song by Michael – this is unconfirmed.

PART 3: THE FILMS

This section is split into two parts:

- Films: full length films & short films that featured more than one song.

- Short Films / Music Videos that featured only one song.

Films

Michael was linked with numerous film projects over the years, and often stated his desire to become more involved in making movies. His first film, *The Wiz*, premiered in 1978 – before which, at least three film projects are known to have been shelved:

- *Isomin Cross & Son* – based on a screenplay by Raymond St. Jacques. Set in the 1860s, the film would have cast Michael and his brothers in the role of slaves fighting to win their freedom, but Berry Gordy's opposition effectively killed off the project.

- *The Boxcar Children* – according to Billboard magazine, in December 1973 Motown were planning to make a film based on the book of the same title (by Gertrude Chandler Warner), with Michael in a starring role.

- *Twenty-Four Robbers* – working title for a film Michael would have starred in. A contract for the film, dated 21st July 1976 and signed by Michael and a representative of Jackson-Arons Enterprises, appeared on the internet auction eBay in early 2009.

THE WIZ

Started life as a musical with an all-black cast, loosely based on *The Wizard Of Oz* – opened on Broadway on 5th January 1975, with Stephanie Mills as Dorothy, the role made famous in the original film version by Judy Garland.

Broadway musical won seven Tony Awards, including Best Musical and Best Score, and ran for 1,672 performances.

Motown acquired the film rights in 1977, with the intention of producing a low budget film, possibly starring Stephanie Mills in her Broadway role. Diana Ross, keen to follow-up her films *Lady Sings The Blues* and *Mahogany*, had other ideas. The opposition of Berry Gordy, her mentor for the best part of two decades, only increased Diana's resolve – and Diana it was who won the lead role.

Michael felt the film script for *The Wiz* was truer to L. Frank Baum's book than the Broadway version or the MGM musical, *The Wizard Of Oz*. 'I think that the stage and the MGM version kind of missed the point,' he stated. 'The message is that these people are looking for something they already have. It's inside them already, but they don't know it because they don't have that belief in themselves to realise it.'

Michael accepted the part of the scarecrow against the wishes of his father and brothers, who all felt he wasn't yet ready to make his film debut. Other parts went to Ted Ross (the cowardly lion; Ross also appeared in the Broadway show in the same role) and Nipsey Russell (the tin man), with funny-man Richard Pryor playing the Wiz and Lena Horne making a cameo appearance as the good witch, Glinda.

Sidney Lumet directed, and he it was who unwittingly influenced Michael's future direction, by twisting the arm of a good friend he recruited as Musical Director for the project: Quincy Jones.

Filming, at Astoria Studios and on location in New York, ran from October to December 1977 and cost $24 million, making *The Wiz* the most expensive musical ever at the time.

During the making of the film, Michael stayed at Manhatten's Sutton Place with his sister LaToya – the first time he had spent time away from his brothers. While in New York, he got to know Liza Minnelli (daughter of Judy Garland), and spent countless hours with his good friend and co-star Diana Ross.

Each morning, it took Michael four hours to transform into the scarecrow, and he readily confessed to being inspired by Ray Bolger's performance as the same character in *The Wizard Of Oz*. Some days, so wrapped up in the part was he, Michael returned to his hotel still dressed as the scarecrow.

Film premiered at Pitts Century Plaza Theatre in Century City, Los Angeles, in October 1978, but failed to live up to its potential at the box office.

Although it went on to receive an Academy Award nomination, for the film's cinematography, *The Wiz* wasn't a success. Critics slated Diana Ross in particular, claiming she was too old to play Dorothy (she was 33 at the time). Diana defended herself, quick to point out that nowhere in his novel *The Wonderful World Of Oz*, does author L. Frank Baum reveal Dorothy's age. She cited endless reading of the script, resulting in a lack of spontaneity, as the main reason for the film's lack of success. In her words: 'Some of the magic that is so necessary to pull off such a story was sacrificed in the name of preparedness.'

Michael's film debut was more positively reviewed and *You Can't Win*, his one solo performance in *The Wiz* – which he sings hanging from a pole, surrounded by four mocking crows – was released as a single. *You Can't Win*, unlike *Ease On*

Down The Road, didn't feature in the stage show, but was specially written for the film version.

Michael's favourite song from *The Wiz*: 'It's the one that Diana and Lena Horne do,' he revealed at the time, 'It's called *Believe In Yourself*, and it's my favourite because of what it says. I like what it says.'

Following *The Wiz*, Michael was offered lead roles in a number of films, among them *A Chorus Line*, *Summer Stock* (with a plot centered on two boys making their way in show business) and *The Story of Bill Robinson – Mr Bojangles*. The part of Paul, a transvestite, in *A Chorus Line* particularly attracted him.

'I love the part!' he enthused. 'It's dramatic, emotional … ' But Michael was also conscious of his public image. 'If I do it, people will link me with the part,' he feared. 'Because of my voice, some people already think I'm that way – homo. Though actually I'm not at all. It's just a lot of gossip.'

Ultimately, Michael declined not only *A Chorus Line*, but all the other film offers he received, too.

30th anniversary digitally remastered DVD, released in the States in February 2008, came with a bonus eight track CD.

CD track listing: *He's The Wizard/You Can't Win/Ease On Down The Road/ Slide Some Oil To Me/(I'm A) Mean Old Lion/Emerald City Sequence/A Brand New Day/Home*.

CAPTAIN EO

17 minute 3D Disney space fantasy directed by Francis Ford Coppola and produced by George Lucas, best known for *The Godfather* and *Star Wars*, respectively – originally titled 'The Intergalactic Man'. George Lucas first suggested the mini-movie be re-titled 'Captain EO' ('EO' is from the Greek goddess *Eos* – the Goddess of Dawn).

Began filming in July 1985 and cost an estimated $30 million; the 3D spectacular was – minute for minute – the most expensive film yet made. At the same time, work started on two specially built cinemas, at Disneyland in Anaheim, California, and at the Epcot Center in Orlando, Florida. More than a year in the making, premiered at the Epcot Center on

12th September 1986, and six days later at Disneyland.

Michael starred as the officer-in-charge of a spaceship crewed by an odd assortment of animated characters named Geex, Hooter, Fuzzball, Minor Domo and Major Domo. Their mission was to rescue the Supreme Leader, played by Anjelica Huston, from dark forces that have turned her into an evil witch queen.

Billed as 'a celebration of triumph over evil', included two songs written and performed by Michael, *Another Part Of Me* (later featured on Michael's album *BAD*) and *We Are Here To Change The World*.

In the States, finally replaced in March 1997, by a new feature, *Honey, I Shrunk The Kids*.

Premiered At Tokyo Disneyland, Japan, on 20th March 1987, with the final screening in September 1996.

Premiered at Disneyland Paris, France, on 12th April 1992, where it closed on 17th August 1998.

No commercial release on video or DVD.

MOONWALKER

Billed as 'A Movie Like No Other'.

Cost Michael an estimated $27 million to make, and premiered at the Cannes Film Festival in France on 18th May 1988.

Numerous disagreements in the States led to Frank DiLeo's decision not to release the film to cinemas – a decision it has been claimed cost Michael many millions of dollars in lost box office receipts. Instead, in January 1989, *Moonwalker* was immediately released on home video.

Opened with clips of Michael performing *Man In The Mirror* live, followed by a 'retrospective' that included songs from both the Motown and Epic eras, ending with *Bad*.

Bad turned into *Badder*, with nine year old Brandon Adams playing Michael and lip-synching *Bad*, as he leads a bunch of kids through an entertaining re-make of the *Bad* promo. Among the *Badder* dancers, Michael's nephew Jermaine Jackson, Jr..

Next up *Speed Demon*, the first of two highly innovative short films, to promote songs from Michael's album *BAD*. Mixing claymation with real life footage, *Speed Demon* saw Michael fleeing eager fans and paparazzi alike, and included an amusing shot of Michael hiding behind a Statue Of Liberty that comes alive just long enough to comment, 'Land of the free, home of the weird!'

More than half an hour into *Moonwalker*, after the amusing and innovative *Leave Me Alone* promo, the film segment *Smooth Criminal* finally starts.

Three children, Brandon Adams (as Zeke), 11 year old Kellie Parker (Katie) and 13 year old Sean Lennon (son of John and Yoko, as Sean), plus Skipper the Old English Sheepdog, co-star as Michael is pitted against the evil drugs baron Mr Big, played by Joe Pesci.

Colin Chilvers, who picked up an Oscar for Best Special Effects for his work on the *Superman* films, directed the whole of *Smooth Criminal*. Michael's man-to-robot, flesh-to-metal, transformation has

to be seen to be believed, and it is easy to believe claims that the *Smooth Criminal* segment alone contains 200+ special effects shots – more than in the whole of a full length movie like *Close Encounters Of The Third Kind*.

After Zeke, Katie and Sean have been saved and Mr Big destroyed, Michael's manager Frank DiLeo makes a brief cameo appearance, to re-unite Michael and the children with Skipper. An excellent live performance of the Beatles' *Come Together* – a song Michael had originally recorded with *BAD* in mind – is a fitting climax to what truly is 'A Movie Like No Other'.

In the UK, as in most other countries, *Moonwalker* was first released to cinemas, opening on 26th December 1988.

Moonwalker – The Storybook and a Sega/Genesis computer game testify to *Moonwalker*'s popularity, and industry recognition came in the form of two Grammy nominations.

Moonwalker itself lost out in the category Best Video, Long Form – to Janet Jackson's *Rhythm Nation 1814*! But, deservedly, the Grammy for Best Video, Short Form went to Michael for *Leave Me Alone*.

GHOSTS

Started life as a promo for *2 Bad*, one of the songs on Michael's HIS*TORY* album, but the project grew and grew – to nearly 40 minutes long!

Inspired in part by the 1964 film, *The Seven Faces of Dr. Lao*, Michael added two brand new songs to *Ghosts*, the title song and *Is It Scary* (a song Michael had originally written for the film *Addams Family Values*).

Based on an original concept by Michael and Stephen King, the original screenplay was written by King in 1993 – however, following the allegations made against Michael, the project was shelved for a while.

Screenplay re-worked by Stan Winston and Mick Garris, who centered it on the song *2 Bad*. 'It started out being twelve to fifteen minutes long,' said Winston, 'but as we were shooting it grew in power and length.'

Winston – the multi-award winner behind the spectacular special effects in *Jurassic*

Park, *Aliens* and *Terminator 2* – also directed the short film.

Ghosts was produced over an eight week period, and cost Michael an estimated $7-9 million. He played several roles, including a maestro who is targeted by angry parents determined to drive him from his haunted Normal Valley home, because he is different.

'You're weird,' a fat, grey-haired Mayor sneers, 'You're strange… you're scaring these kids.' Brave words to commit to film, considering recent events and the media's warped portrayal of Michael!

Michael challenges the Mayor: first one to get scared leaves town. So begins a wonderfully ghoulish display of singing and dancing, with breath-taking special effects.

'Is this scary?' one of Michael's characters asks, and the answer is yes – *Ghosts* is delightfully scary. And, as the credits roll, make-up artists are shown

410

turning Michael into – the fat, grey-haired Mayor!

Songs *2 Bad*, *Ghosts* and *Is It Scary* all slightly remixed for the short film, at Michael's request, with the first chords of *Bad* sampled for *2 Bad* – this came from Brad Buxer's sample set that he used during Michael's tour.

In the States, *Ghosts* premiered on 24th October 1996 at the Motion Picture Academy Of Arts in Beverly Hills, California, alongside Stephen King's full length horror movie *Thinner*. Elsewhere, Michael made his fans wait: the Australian premiere, at Sydney, coincided with Michael's concerts in November. Japanese fans had to wait until Michael played Tokyo on 20th December.

European fans had to be even more patient, with *Ghosts* not getting a premiere until midnight on 8th May 1997, at the 50th Cannes Film Festival in France, which Michael attended. The UK premiere followed a week later, at London's The Odeon.

MEN IN BLACK II

Sequel directed by Barry Sonnenfield – once again, co-starred Will Smith and Tommy Lee Jones as Agent Jay and Agent Kay, respectively.

Executive producer: Steven Speilberg.

Estimated budget: $140 million.

Premiered in July 2002 – featured a brief cameo appearance by Michael, as Agent M.

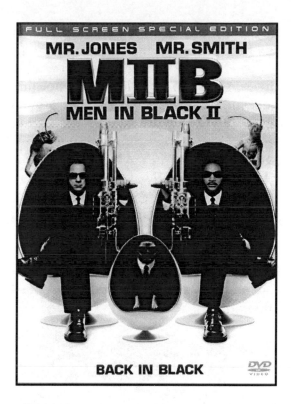

Will Smith, when asked if Michael played an alien in the film, said: 'Listen, Michael Jackson is really funny! To have time to spend with him, and actually be around him – he's not what people think he is… he's like, a black belt, too – so he will kick your @#%$ if you say somethin' about him.'

'You know, when he comes on the screen, people are really happy,' said Smith, once the film was completed. 'It's as if Michael is saying to the world, "OK, all right. I'm human just like everyone else. I appreciate a good joke just like everyone else does." But the thing that I loved so much is he kept wanting to play it serious. You know, he was like, "You know, I'm a man in black, I just want it to be really serious." I think people are going to be really shocked and really surprised, and enjoy seeing Michael in this film and in this light.'

Grossed over $52 million on its opening weekend, and went on to gross around $442 million globally.

MISS CAST AWAY AND THE ISLAND GIRLS

Directed, produced and written by Bryan Michael Stoller.

Largely filmed in the summer of 2003, and released straight to DVD in August 2004.

Spoof of films like *Airplane!*, *Jurassic Park* and *Planet Of The Apes* – plot revolved around a group of Miss Galaxy beauty contestants, whose plane crashes on a deserted island, where they discover

Noah's Ark that is guarded by a huge prehistoric pig.

Michael made a 10 minute cameo appearance as Agent MJ, a shadowy figure collaborating with the Vatican to manipulate the shipwrecked crew – this parodied his role in *Men In Black II*.

'Michael was excited about it,' said director Stoller, 'because, as most people know, he did a 30 second cameo in *Men In Black II* where he wanted to be an agent, and they wouldn't let him, so that was the joke.' Stoller described Michael's role as an 'Obi-Wan Kenobi character'.

Michael's scenes were filmed at his Neverland Ranch, as seen on the DVD's bonus features – and at times Stoller found filming quite challenging.

'It's his home,' said Stoller. 'It's all normal to him that there's a train running around the property tooting its horn.' Stoller and Michael were enjoying some soup and talking, when two elephants walked by. 'Michael's continuing to sip his soup like a fly flew by,' said Stoller, 'and I turn to Michael and look at him, and he's not even acknowledging the elephants – he looked at me and laughed. I didn't think of it until we were actually shooting. I didn't anticipate that we were going to shoot somewhere, and there was going to be trains and elephants!'

THIS IS IT

Before his passing on 25th June 2009, more than 100 hours of Michael's preparations and rehearsals for his 'This Is It' concerts at the O2 Arena in London were filmed by concert promoter AEG Live.

Columbia Pictures paid $60 million for rights to the footage, and on 10th August – after Michael's mother Katherine raised no objections – LA Superior Court Jundge Mitchell Beckloff approved a major deal between Michael's estate, AEG Live and Columbia Pictures, to produce a full length film based around footage from Michael's final rehearsals.

It is expected the film will premiere at the end of October 2009, for a short two week run – it's likely a 'live' album will also be released.

Short Films / Music Videos

Don't Stop 'Til You Get Enough (1979).
Rock With You (1979).
She's Out Of My Life (1980).
Billie Jean (1983).
Beat It (1983).
Say Say Say (1983) & Paul McCartney.
Thriller (1983).
We Are The World (1985) USA For Africa.
Bad (1987).
The Way You Make Me Feel (1987).
Man In The Mirror (1988).
Dirty Diana (1988).
Another Part Of Me (1988).
Smooth Criminal (1988).
Leave Me Alone (1988).
Speed Demon (1988).
Come Together (1988).
Liberian Girl (1989).
Black Or White (1991).
Remember The Time (1992).
In The Closet (1992).

Who Is It (1992).
Jam (1992).
Heal The World (1992).
Give In To Me (1993).
Will You Be There (1993).
Will You Be There – *Free Willy* Version (1993).
Gone Too Soon (1993).
Right Here (1993) SWV feat. Michael.
Whatsupwitzu (1993) Eddie Murphy feat.Michael.
Scream (1995) & Janet Jackson.
Childhood (Theme From 'Free Willy 2') (1995).
You Are Not Alone (1995).
Earth Song (1995).
They Don't Care About Us – Brazil Version (1996).
They Don't Care About Us – Prison Version (1996).
Why (1996) 3T feat. Michael.
Stranger In Moscow (1996).
Blood On The Dance Floor – Original Version (1997).
Blood On The Dance Floor – Refugee Camp Mix (1997).
Blood On The Dance Floor – Version Sony refused to release (1997).
Ghosts (1997).
History (1997).
What More Can I Give (2001/unreleased) MJ & Friends
You Rock My World (2001).
Cry (2001).
One More Chance (2003/unreleased).

PART 4: THE HOME VIDEOS

The first two Jackson home videos, released in 1979 in Japan, and in the UK, were credited to the Jacksons, but all subsequent releases have been credited to Michael.

For each home video USA and/or UK catalogue numbers, release dates and track listings (where applicable) are given, together with other information. Only official releases are listed, including home videos released in Japan and South Korea only, respectively.

THE JACKSONS

Japan: TOEI (1979).

Dancing Machine/Things I Do For You/ Ben/Keep On Dancing/Medley (I Want You Back/ABC/The Love You Save)/I'll Be There/Enjoy Yourself/Destiny/Show You The Way To Go/All Night Dancin'/ Blame It On The Boogie

Concert recorded in February 1979 during the 1st leg of the group's Destiny Tour, in London, England.

Concert televised by BBC2 in the UK.

THE JACKSONS IN CONCERT

USA: Not Released.
UK: VCL V1588 (1981).

(You Were Made) Especially For Me/ Never Can Say Goodbye/Papa Was A Rolling Stone/I Am Love/Rockin' Robin/ The Life Of The Party/Forever Came Today/Ben/I'll Be There/Medley (I Want YouBack/ABC/ The Love You Save)/ Dancing Machine/Body Language (Do The Love Dance)

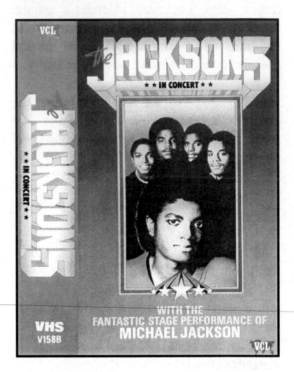

Sleeve depicted Michael and his brothers around the time of the Triumph Tour, however, this 43 minute edited was actually recorded at a concert in Mexico City in December 1975, at one of the first performances the Jacksons gave following their split with Motown – hence Jermaine is absent.

Sleeve also printed with a '5' replacing the last letter in Jacksons, to give 'Jackson 5'.

Dressed in white – white rhinestone jackets, white flared trousers, white shoes

– the Jacksons also, cheekily, appeared wearing broad belts with large heart-shaped buckles, in the centre of which there was a dazzling 'J5' logo.

Reminiscent of *The Jacksons* TV shows – more cabaret than anything else. Better, much better, was to come but even so, it sold well enough to register at no.2 on the UK's fledgling Music Video chart, as published in *Record Mirror*.

Also released in France in 1984.

MAKING MICHAEL JACKSON'S THRILLER

USA: Vestron 11000 (December 1983).
UK: Vestron MA 11000 (March 1984).

Directed by John Landis, who Michael contacted after seeing the film *An American Werewolf In London*, which Landis had directed. 'He contacted me and asked me if I would make a video with him,' said Landis. 'And I said no, actually... but he persisted and said, "No, no, no – I really wanna make it." So when I returned to LA I called Rick Baker, who had done the make-up effects for *American Werewolf* and said, Rick, Michael Jackson wants to become a monster!'

'John told me about the idea but I was reluctant,' said Baker. 'At first I didn't want to do it. It's not the most popular job – it's like being a dentist in a way: they have to sit in a chair for hours while you work on them, it's uncomfortable – it's not something actors look forward to.'

Landis's intention was to make a 14 minute theatrical short film and, with his producer/editor, George Folsey, Jr., he worked on a budget – and costed the project at almost half a million dollars. But, given *THRILLER* had already been the year's best selling album and was still selling respectively well, Michael's record company refused to provide the necessary funds.

'George's idea,' said Landis, 'was: why don't we film us filming it, and then we can make a 45 minute documentary called 'The Making Of Thriller', then in total that's an hour. And then sell that to get the money to make *Thriller*.' Bidding war between cable companies ensued, with MTV and Showtime each putting up $250,000, toward the cost of making the short film.

Final footage only 26 minutes long – prompting Landis to visit Michael's Encino home, to search for any footage he could make use of. 'And I found a box of home movies,' he said, 'and now everyone's seen it, that amazing 8mm footage of Mike dancing at five years old. I found that in a closet so I said, OK, we own this, too... we called it 'The Making Of Filler'.

Premiere staged because Michael wanted a premiere. 'It was incredible,' said Landis. 'There was everyone from Diana Ross and Warren Beatty to Prince. It was nuts! Amazing... got a standing ovation and all that stuff and they're shouting, "Encore! Encore!"... then Eddie Murphy got up and shouted, "Show the goddamn thing again!" So they sat and watched

Thriller again. Why not? It was just amazing…'

An hour long, *Making Thriller* opened with the full length *Thriller* short film. Following this, there was a rare and fascinating behind the scenes peek at a genius at work.

Metamorphosis, focusing on his amazing transformation into a werewolf, showed just how far Michael is prepared to go, in his quest to break new ground – to be the best. 'I actually tried to talk him out of it,' monster maker Rick Baker confesses on camera. 'I told him how horrible an experience it's going to be, and that he's going to have to do this every day.'

But changing into a werewolf was an essential ingredient, one that excited Michael, and he refused to allow thoughts of personal discomfort to dissuade him from going ahead.

Also featured: *Who's Lovin' You* (from a 1969 *Ed Sullivan Show*), the *Beat It* and *Can You Feel It* promos, the Home Movies clip and Michael's stunning *Billie Jean* routine from *Motown 25*.

No plans to release *Making Thriller* on home video until Walter Furst, from Vestron Video, contacted John Landis. Released in the States just a few weeks after the *Thriller* short film premiered on MTV, sales of the home video impressive. At the time, the RIAA didn't certify sales of music videos, but had it done so Gold and Platinum awards would have been virtually instant.

In the UK, the home video shifted over 100,000 copies within the first week of issue, and *Making Thriller* soon became the runaway no.1 best selling music video to date.

Grammy Award:
Best Video Album.

American Music Video Awards:
Best Home Video.
Best Long Form Video.

No official DVD release.

THE LEGEND CONTINUES

USA: Vestron 5358 (May 1989).
UK: Video Collection MJ 1000 (June 1988).

Two years in the making, started life as a one hour special for the American cable network *Showtime*, titled *Motown On Showtime: Michael Jackson*.

Michael, although he co-operated fully with the project and was an Executive Producer with Suzanne de Passe, persistently refused to be interviewed for the special. Instead, a host of celebrities were drafted in, to help to tell Michael's rags to riches story and generally sing his praises.

Quincy Jones, Tommy Chong (of Bobby Taylor & the Vancouvers), Marlon Jackson, Smokey Robinson, Sammy Davis, Jr., Dick Clark, Hermes Pan (choreographer to Fred Astaire), Katharine Hepburn, Elizabeth Taylor, Gene Kelly, Sophia Loren, Yoko Ono and Sean Lennon all contributed.

More interesting were the numerous clips of performances and promos Michael and his brothers had made over the years. The focus was on the Motown era, however, several later clips were also included. Prominent among them, Michael's show stealing performance of *Billie Jean* on *Motown 25: Yesterday, Today, Forever*, plus: *Ease On Down The Road, Rock With You, Don't Stop 'Til You Get Enough, Thriller, Say Say Say, Beat It* and *We Are The World*. And, to finish, there was a rousing live in concert performance of *Heartbreak Hotel*, filmed during Michael's tour of Australia.

Motown On Showtime: Michael Jackson first aired on *Showtime* on 12th March 1988. Three months later, nearly a year ahead of the States, it appeared on home video in the UK as *The Legend Continues...*. It proved an instant smash,

topping the Music Video chart for an awesome 20 weeks; and, for 12 of those weeks, Michael had the UK's no.2 best selling music video as well, as *Making Michael Jackson's Thriller* enjoyed a new lease of life.

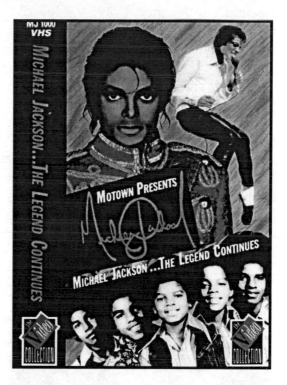

Success in the States was on a similarly spectacular scale. Six weeks at no.1 on the Top Videocassettes Sales chart was complimented by two week at no.1 on the Top Music Videocassettes chart – where Michael achieved the rare distinction of replacing himself at no.1. The previous best seller: *Moonwalker*.

Not available on DVD.

MOONWALKER

USA: CMV 49009 (January 1989).
UK: Guild Home Video GH 8580 (April 1990).

*Man In The Mirror/Retrospective/
Badder/Speed Demon/Leave Me Alone/
Smooth Criminal* (film)/*Come Together*

Released immediately on home video in
the States, without being screened in
cinemas, in January 1989 – shipped a
record 300,000 units, and sold twice that
amount in just six weeks.

Achieved no.1 on Billboard's Top
Videocassettes Sales chart; toppled one
of Michael's all time favourite film, *E.T.*,
from top spot and reigned for 14 weeks.

No.1 for an uninterrupted 22 weeks on
Billboard's Top Music Videocassettes
chart, before another of Michael's home
videos finally dethroned it: *The Legend
Continues*....

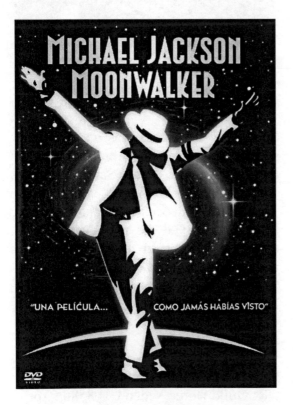

In the UK, as in most other countries,
Moonwalker was first released to
cinemas, and when it was released on
home video, strangely, it was deemed
ineligible for the Music Videos chart.
Nevertheless, it stormed into the overall
Video chart at no.1, where it spent a
single week.

Available on DVD.

RIAA 8 x Platinum = 800,000 copies.

Posthumous hit: no.1 in the UK.

DANGEROUS – THE SHORT FILMS

USA: Epic 49164 (December 1993).
UK: SMV 49164 2 (December 1993).

Black Or White/Heal The World
(Superbowl Performance)/*Remember The
Time/Will You Be There* (MTV 10 TV
Special Performance)/*In The Closet/Gone
Too Soon/Jam/Heal The World/Give In
To Me/Who Is It/Dangerous* (Tour
Montage)

Also featured behind the scenes footage
of the making of *Black Or White*,
Remember The Time, *Jam* and *In The
Closet*, two Pepsi-Cola advertisements,
footage of the 1993 NAACP Image
Awards and the 35th Grammy Awards,
where Michael joyously accepted the
Grammy Legend Award from his sister,
Janet.

Achieved no.4 on Billboard's Top Music
Videocassettes chart, and spent four
weeks at no.2 on the UK's Music Video
chart (held off the top spot by the latest
teen sensations, Take That).

RIAA 2 x Platinum = 200,000 copies.

Posthumous hit: no.2 in France, no.3 in Denmark & Ireland, no.4 in UK, no.5 in Australia, Austria & USA, and no.9 in Italy.

VIDEO GREATEST HITS –
HISTORY

USA: Epic 50123 (June 1995).
UK: SMV 50123 2 (June 1995).

Brace Yourself/'Kaleidoscope Of Michael Jackson – *Carmina Burana*'/*Billie Jean/The Way You Make Me Feel/Black Or White/Rock With You/Bad/Thriller/Beat It/Remember The Time/Don't Stop 'Til You Get Enough/Heal The World*

Billed '10 Of The Greatest Short Films Of All Time By The King Of Pop!'

Lengthy opening and much briefer climax to *Bad*, both filmed in black & white, edited – as was the scene-setting beginning of *The Way You Make Me Feel*. Full length versions did feature on the DVD, released in 2001.

Achieved five weeks at no.1 on Billboard's Top Music Video Cassettes chart; re-entered the Top 10 in 2001, thanks to the release of the DVD version – spent more than three years on the chart in total.

Also enjoyed a lengthy chart run in the UK, but stalled at no.2 for nine weeks on Music Week's Music Videos chart, behind Bill Whelan's hugely successful *Riverdance*.

RIAA 5 x Platinum = 500,000 copies.

Posthumous hit: no.1 in Denmark, no.2 in France & Italy, no.3 in Australia, Austria & USA, no.4 in Ireland & Portugal, and no.5 in UK.

HISTORY TOUR IN SEOUL

South Korea: Sony (1996).

Scream/They Don't Care About Us/In The Closet/Wanna Be Startin' Somethin'/Stranger In Moscow/Smooth Criminal/You Are Not Alone/The Way You Make Me Feel/I Want You Back/The Love You Save/I'll Be There/Billie Jean/Thriller/Beat It/Come Together~D.S./Dangerous/Black Or White/Earth Song/Heal The World

Concert recorded at Seoul's Chamsil Olympic Stadium on 11th October 1996, and released in South Korea only as a VHS (NTSC format) home video.

HISTORY ON FILM VOLUME II

USA: Epic 50138 (May 1997).
UK: SMV 50138 2 (May 1997).

Teaser/Billie Jean (Motown 25 Performance)/*Beat It/Liberian Girl/Smooth Criminal/Medley* (MTV Video Music Awards Performance)/*Dangerous* (MTV VMA Performance)/*You Are Not Alone* (MTV VMA Performance)/*Thriller/Scream/Childhood (Theme From 'Free Willy 2')/You Are Not Alone/Earth Song/They Don't Care About Us (Brazil Version)/Stranger In Moscow/ Blood On The Dance Floor (Refugee Camp Mix)/Brace Yourself*

Michael, at a special meeting with Sony representatives on 22nd October 1996, rejected the original version as, in his opinion, it didn't included enough new and exciting material – thus forcing Sony to go away, and eventually come back with the version that was released.

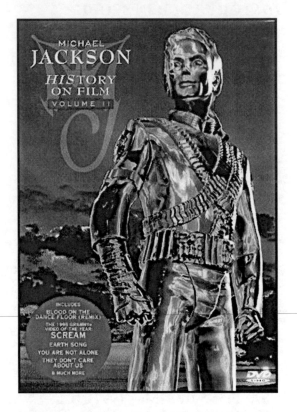

Debuted on Billboard's Top Music Videos chart at no.1, a position it held for two weeks.

In the UK, on Music Week's Music Videos chart, Michael had to settle for a lengthy 12 week stint in the runner-up spot, behind *Spice: Official Video Volume I* by the Spice Girls.

RIAA 3 x Platinum = 300,000 copies.

Posthumous hit: no.3 in Denmark, no.4 in Austria & USA, no.5 in France, no.6 in Australia, no.9 in UK, no.10 in Ireland and no.11 in italy.

GHOSTS

USA: Not Released.
UK: Epic EPC 489155 2 (December 1997).

First issued as a limited edition 'Deluxe Collector Box Set', timed to catch the Christmas market – comprised four items:

- *Ghosts* home video.
- *Ghosts* program (as printed for the Cannes Film Festival).
- *BLOOD ON THE DANCE FLOOR* album on CD.
- Exclusive 3 track 'minimax' single.

Classed as a video for chart purposes, performed remarkably well, in reaching no.8 on Music Week's Music Videos chart.

Issued as a standard home video in the UK in early February 1998 (SMV 200788 2) – broke Michael's run of no.2 music videos, when it made its debut at no.1, ahead of *Girl Power! Live In Istanbul* by the Spice Girls. Held the top spot for two weeks.

Not available on DVD, but released as a Video-CD (playable on PCs and most DVD players) in several Asian countries, including Singapore, South Korea and Taiwan.

MUSIC VIDEO – SPECIAL EDITION

South Korea: Epic CPK-2514 (2002 / promo).

Two disc set comprising Michael's *INVINCIBLE* album on CD, plus an exclusive bonus, 10 track Video-CD , with a 20 pages booklet.

Video-CD: *Unbreakable/Cry/Dirty Diana/Smooth Crimunal/Billie Jean/Beat It/Scream/Black Or White/Jam/You Rock My World*

Michael didn't shoot a short film for *Unbreakable* (though one was planned, before the promotion of his *INVINCIBLE* album prematurely ended), hence a montage of clips was used on this release.

NUMBER ONES

USA: Epic EVD 56999 (November 2003).
UK: Epic EVD 202250 9 (November 2003).

Don't Stop 'Til You Get Enough/Rock With You/Billie Jean/Beat It/ Thriller/Bad (Short Version)/The Way You Make Me Feel (Edit)/Man In The Mirror/Smooth Criminal (Fast/Blurry Version)/Dirty Diana/ Black Or White (Edit)/You Are Not Alone/Earth Song/Blood On The Dance Floor (Re-Edited Version)/You Rock My World (10:26 Edit)

Like the album of the same name, released with four different sleeves, showing Michael in poses from different eras.

Achieved no.1 on Billboard's Music Videos chart in the States, where it spent nearly four years on the chart – also no.1 in Australia.

Posthumous hit: no.1 in Australia, Denmark, New Zealand & USA, no.2 in Austria, France, Ireland, Italy & UK, and no.5 in Portugal.

THE ONE

USA: Epic EVD 58511 (March 2004).
UK: Epic EPC 202019 9 (March 2004).

Relatively short, 39 minute home DVD which originally aired on CBS TV in the States on 2nd January 2004, as 'The Michael Jackson Special'. Featured a brief overview of Michael's career highlights, with guests including Quincy Jones, Dick Clerk, Isaac Hayes, Beyonce Knowles, Wyclef Jean, Shaggy and Missy Elliot.

Highlights included Michael's Motown 25 performance of *Billie Jean*, and live clips of *Ben* (from the Academy Awards ceremony), *Don't Stop 'Til You Get Enough* (from the Jacksons Triumph Tour) and *Bad* (from the world tour of the same name).

Achieved no.2 in the UK, but spent two weeks on the Music Video chart; in the States, it spent a solitary week at no.28 on Billboard's Music Video chart.

RIAA Gold = 50,000 copies.

THE ONE

Posthumous hit: no.2 in France, no.4 in Denmark & Italy, no.6 in Ireland & UK, no.8 in USA, no.9 in Australia and no.10 in Austria.

LIVE IN BUCHAREST: THE DANGEROUS TOUR

USA: Legacy/Epic/MJJ EVD 53497 (July 2005).
UK: Epic EPC 204003 9 (July 2005).

Jam/Wanna Be Startin' Somethin'/ Human Nature/Smooth Criminal/I Just Can't Stop Loving You/She's Out Of My Life/I Want You Back – The Love You Save/I'll Be There/Thriller/Billie Jean/ Working Day & Night/Beat It/Will You Be There/Black Or White/Heal The World/Man In The Mirror

Concert recorded on 1st October 1992, in front of 70,000 fans, in Bucharest,

Romania – however, the DVD actually featured footage filmed in London and Madrid as well.

Film rights to the concert originally bought by HBO (Home Box Office), an American cable station, for a reported $20 million – the highest sum ever paid for a pop concert. First aired on 10th October, and screened in more than 60 countries.

First released on DVD as part of Michael's *THE ULTIMATE COLLECTION* box-set, released in November 2004.

Charted at no.2 for five weeks in the UK, and no.6 in the States – went all the way to no.1 in France, Greece and Italy.

RIAA Gold = 50,000 copies.

Posthumous hit: no.1 in Austria, Czech Republic, Denmark, France, Italy, New Zealand, Portugal & USA, and no.2 in Australia & UK.

HISTORY I + II

USA: Not Released.
UK: Sony 88697360639 (August 2008).

Limited edition 2-disc set, comprising the DVDs originally released as *VIDEO GREATEST HITS – HISTORY* and *HISTORY ON FILM VOLUME II*.

Debuted at no.6 in the UK, but rose no higher during a short, four week chart run.

Posthumous hit: no.1 in New Zealand, no.3 in Ireland, no.4 in UK, no.5 in Australia, no.7 in Denmark and no.8 in France.

PART 5: THE CONCERTS

Michael made his first public singing appearance at the age of five years, when he sang an *a cappella* version of *Climb Ev'ry Mountain* (from *The Sound Of Music*) during assembly at his school, Garnett Elementary.

Shortly afterwards, Michael joined the family group comprising his four older brothers, and the Jackson Brothers became the Jackson Five. Joined initially by neighbours Reynaud Jones (on lead guitar) and Milford Hite (on drums), the group made their competition debut in 1965, at the annual Roosevelt High Talent Show. They performed *My Girl* and *Barefootin'*, and were awarded first place.

Other competitions followed and, with Johnny Jackson (no relation) now added as the group's drummer, father Joseph booked his sons to appear at numerous local bars and clubs. Some of the venues Michael and his brothers played in the early days include:

- Mister Lucky's Lounge, Gary, Indiana

- Guys & Gals Cocktail Lounge & Restaurant, Chicago
- Traveler's Lounge, Racine, Wisconsin
- Regal Theatre, Chicago
- Apollo, Harlem, New York.

Michael was still two months away from his ninth birthday when he and his brothers played at the Traveler's Lounge – from 9.00pm to 1.00am – in July 1967, and at Guys & Gals Cocktail Lounge & Restaurant the Jackson 5 often opened for the Dollettes: a group of female strippers.

The Jackson 5's first major concert took place at the Los Angeles Forum on 20th June 1970. Later the same year, Michael and his brothers hit the road for a series of short, North American tours – the tours lasted an amazing two years, and between dates the Jackson brothers somehow found time to record, release and promote several albums and singles as well.

Of course, Michael's more recent world tours are far better documented than the early Jackson 5 shows – however, we have detailed all known concert dates, and listed other tours we are aware of. We accept the listing is incomplete, and we would welcome any and all extra information, to help us to fill the gaps in any future editions of this book.

JACKSON 5

1970-72: North America

The Jackson 5 played a series of one nighters during the first eight months of 1970, including:

2 May	Philadelphia, Pennsylvania
19 June	San Francisco, California
20 June	Los Angeles, California
12 August	Detroit, Michigan

A typical Summer set list ran as follows:

Stand/Don't Know Why I Love You/Zip-A-Dee Doo-Dah/It's Your Thing/There Was A Time/I Found That Girl/Thank You (Falettin Be Mice Elf Again)/Brand New Thing

Brand New Thing was used to introduce young Randy on stage, but was never recorded and released by the Jackson 5. Later shows saw *Zip-A-Dee Doo-Dah* dropped, and replaced with *How Funky Is Your Chicken* and *Bridge Over Troubled Water*.

The Jackson 5's first national tour kicked off in October 1970.

9 October	Boston, Massachusetts
10 October	Cincinnati, Ohio
11 October	Memphis, Tennessee
16 October	New York City, New York
17 October	Detroit, Michigan
18 October	Chicago, Illinois
28 November	Rochester, Michigan
27 December	Charlotte, North Carolina
28 December	Greensboro, North Carolina
29 December	Nashville, Tennessee
30 December	Jacksonville, Florida

Concert scheduled for Buffalo, New York, cancelled when threats were made against Michael's life. Three Texas dates were also scrapped, following the Southern Christian Leadership Council Operation's objections that Motown hadn't hired a black promoter for the tour.

1971

2 January	Miami Beach, Miami
3 January	Mobile, Alabama

29 January	Dayton, Ohio	8 August	Miami Beach, Florida
30 January	Columbus, Georgia	10 August	Tampa, Florida
31 January	Gary, Indiana	11 August	Birmingham, Alabama
		13 August	Kansas City, Missouri

At the end of January, Michael and his brothers returned to their home town, Gary, for the first time since their move to California – they played two benefit concerts at the West Side High School, for Mayor Richard Hatcher's re-election campaign. A sign erected outside them family's old home, at 2300 Jackson Street, read: 'Welcome Home Jackson Five ~ Keepers Of The Dream'. The homecoming was filmed and screened as part of the *Goin' Back To Indiana* TV special, aired on ABC-TV in the States on 19th September 1971.

14 August	St Louis, Missouri
15 August	Memphis, Tennessee
17 August	Montgomery, Alabama
18 August	Tulsa, Oklahoma
20 August	Denver, Colorado
22 August	Los Angeles, California
28 August	Columbus, Ohio
29 August	Des Moines, Iowa
31 August	Toronto, Canada

9 September	Detroit, Michigan
12 September	Honolulu, Hawaii

15 October	Chicago, Illinois

26 September	Baltimore, Maryland (2 shows)

27 March	Shreveport, Louisiana
28 March	New Orleans, Louisiana

1 April	Memphis, Tennessee
2 April	Tampa, Florida
4 April	Jackson, Mississippi

25 December	Los Angeles, California
27 December	Houston, Texas
28 December	Dallas, Texas
29 December	Norfolk, Nebraska
30 December	Richmond, Vermont

28 May	Philadelphia, Pennsylvania
29 May	Gary, Indiana
30 May	Oklahoma City, Oklahoma

On Christmas Day, Michael and his brothers – including eight year old Randy, who played conga drums – played a 45 minute concert for 400 blind children from the Foundation for the Junior Blind. The concert included, for the first time, some of the group's festive songs. 'You know, really,' said Michael after the concert, 'this is what Christmas is all about: giving,' A second festive date, for underpriviledged children, took place on 5th January, and Michael and his brothers dressed as Santa Claus and gave out gifts to the children who attended.

16 July	New York City, New York
17 July	Charleston, Virginia
18 July	Hampton, Virginia
20 July	Charlotte, North Carolina
21 July	Toledo, Ohio
23 July	Chicago, Illinois
24 July	Cincinnati, Ohio
25 July	Detroit, Michigan
27 July	Flint, Michigan
28 July	Fort Wayne, Indiana
30 July	Pittsburgh, Pennsylvania
31 July	Baltimore, Maryland

1 August	Raleigh, North Carolina
2 August	Macon, Georgia
7 August	Columbia, South Carolina

1972

1 January	Nashville, Tennessee
2 January	Greenville, South Carolina

5 January	Los Angeles, California
12 January	Atlanta, Georgia
29 January	Baltimore, Maryland
	(2 shows)

On 12th January, the Jackson 5 topped the bill at the Metropolitan Auditorium in Atlanta, at the first annual concert to commemorate the birthday of the late civil rights campaigner, Martin Luther King. Support acts included the Supremes (now minus Diana Ross).

| 12 February | St Louis, Missouri |

26 March	Shreveport, Louisiana
27 March	New Orleans, Louisiana
29 March	Tampa, Florida
31 March	Jackson, Mississippi

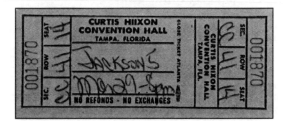

| 1 April | Memphis, Tennessee |

| 30 June | New York City, New York |

1 July	Baltimore, Maryland
2 July	Norfolk, Nebraska
7 July	Richmond, Vermont
8 July	Charlotte, North Carolina
9 July	Greensboro, North Carolina
14 July	Cincinnati, Ohio
15 July	Pittsburgh, Pennsylvania
16 July	Cleveland, Ohio
18 July	Chicago, Illinois
21 July	Tulsa, Oklahoma
22 July	Dallas, Texas
23 July	Houston, Texas
24 July	New Orleans, Louisiana
29 & 30 July	Chicago, Illinois

Typical set list for Summer 1972:

Stand/I Want You Back/ABC/Mama's Pearl/Sugar Daddy/I'll Be There/Goin' Back To Indiana/Brand New Thing/ Bridge Over Troubled Water/I Found That Girl/I Saved My Love For You/ Lookin' Through The Windows/Got To Be There/You've Got A Friend/Rockin' Robin/I Wanna Be Where You Are/That's How Love Goes/Never Can Say Goodbye

I Saved My Love For You was a song Jermaine recorded for, but which was left off, his debut solo album.

4 August	Columbus, Ohio
5 August	Atlanta, Georgia
6 August	Nashville, Tennessee
11 August	Savannah, Georgia
12 August	Washington, D.C.
13 August	Charleston, Virginia
17 August	Louisville, Kentucky
18 August	Kansas City, Missouri
19 August	St Louis, Missouri
20 August	Indianapolis, Indiana
22 August	Sedalia, Missouri
25 August	San Francisco, California
26 August	Los Angeles, California
27 August	San Diego, California
29 August	Honolulu, Hawaii

| 5 October | Chicago, Illinois |

In September, Michael and his brothers participated in a five day event in Chicago, part of an annual Black Expo event, which was behind the Operation PUSH (People Unite to Save Humanity) project. A double album *SAVE THE CHILDREN*, released in 1974, included the Jackson 5's live rendition of *I Wanna Be Where You Are*.

1972: Europe

The Jackson 5's first tour outside North America saw them flying to Europe – scenes at London's Heathrow Airport, when the group landed, were described as being akin to Beatlemania.

Prior to the tour starting, on 30th October, Michael and his brothers appeared on the bill of the Royal Command Performance, staged at the London Palladium in the presence of HM Queen Elizabeth, The Queen Mother.

2 November	Amsterdam, Holland
3 November	Brussels, Belgium
4 November	Munich, Germany
5 November	Frankfurt, Germany
6 November	Paris, France
9 November	Birmingham, England (2 shows)
10 November	Manchester, England
11 November	Liverpool, England (2 shows)
12 November	London, England

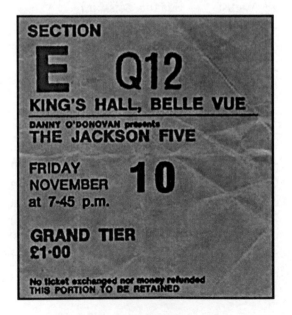

First UK dates unable to take place any earlier, thanks to stringent British laws re child performers: special dispensation would have been required for young Michael to appear on stage or TV after 8.00pm (unless the given TV appearance was pre-recorded).

'We shall continue trying to bring the Jacksons over,' said a Motown spokesman in 1971, 'but frankly we are not very optimistic. The British laws are far too complicated and restrictive.'

When they played at the Liverpool Empire, the Jackson 5 smashed the previous attendance record – held by the Beatles! The group's support act for the UK dates was Elton John.

18 November   Hollywood, California

The Hollywood concert was a fundraiser for the NAACP (National Association for the Advancement of Coloured People).

The Jackson 5 played a series of short tours in 1973-74, starting with three dates on home soil.

1973: USA & Japan

2 March	Oklahoma City, Oklahoma
3 March	Monroe, Louisiana
4 March	Houston, Texas
27 April	Tokyo, Japan
28 April	Hiroshima, Japan
30 April	Osaka, Japan
1 May	Osaka, Japan
2 May	Tokyo, Japan

The Jackson 5 made a special guest appearance at the 2nd Tokyo Music Festival on 27th April.

The first concert staged at Osaka's Koseinenkin Hall was recorded and released as an album, titled *IN JAPAN!*, in Japan only. The album was subsequently released as *LIVE!* in the UK in 1988, and finally appeared in the States – as *IN JAPAN!* – on CD in 2006.

Japanese 24 page glossy tour programmed titled 'Jackson 5 + 1', in recognition of young Randy's participation.

5 May	Portland, Oregon
6 May	Scattle, Washington
18 May	Philadelphia, Pennsylvania
19 May	Dayton, Ohio
20 May	Columbus, Ohio

1973: Australia & New Zealand

The Jackson 5 were the first black group ever to tour Australia.

23 June	Brisbane, Australia
26 June	Melbourne, Australia
29 June	Perth, Australia
30 June	Adelaide, Australia

1 July	Adeleide, Australia
2 July	Sydney, Australia
4 July	Christchurch, New Zealand
5 July	Wellington, New Zealand

1973: North America

13 July	Boston, Massachusetts
14 July	New Haven, Connecticut
15 July	Providence, Rhode Island
17 July	San Juan, Puerto Rica
20 July	Pittsburgh, Pennsylvania
21 July	Long Pond, New Jersey
22 July	New York City, New York
24 & 25 July	Chicago, Illinois
27 July	Cleveland, Ohio
28 July	Detroit, Michigan
29 July	Saratoga, California
3 August	Richmond, Virginia
4 August	Hampton, Virginia
5 August	Baltimore, Maryland
7 August	Greensboro, North Carolina
8 August	Nashville, Tennessee
10 August	Columbia, South Carolina
11 August	Atlanta, Georgia
12 August	Miami, Florida
17 August	Memphis, Tennessee
18 August	St Louis, Missouri
19 August	Indianapolis, Indiana
21 August	New Orleans, Louisiana
22 August	Dallas, Texas
24 August	San Francisco, California
25 August	Fresno, California
26 August	Los Angeles, California
28 August	Boston, Massachusetts
29 August	Montreal, Canada
31 August	Columbus, Ohio
2 September	Honolulu, Hawaii
21 October	San Antonio, Texas

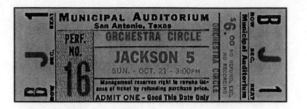

1974: Senegal

1 February	Dakar (Demba Diop Stadium), Senegal
2 & 3 February	Dakar (Daniel Sorano National Theatre), Senegal

During the visit, plans were announced for the Jackson 5's film debut, *Isomin Cross & Son*. Based on a screenplay by Raymond St. Jacques, and set in the 1860s, the film would have cast Michael and his brothers as slaves fighting to win their freedom – but Berry Gordy strongly opposed the project, so it never went ahead.

Footage shot for a proposed film, *The Jackson 5 In Africa*, starting the group's arrival at Dakar Airport, where they were greeted by costumed dancers and musicians. The film would have included concert footage, but was cut short when investors ran out of funding. Footage filmed re-discovered following Michael's passing, and screened at the Downtown Film Festival in New York in July 2009.

Visit to Senegal ended prematurely as Michael, his brothers and their father had difficulties in adapting to the local cuisine.

1974: USA & Europe

In April, the Jackson 5 – joined by sisters Janet, La Toya and Rebbie – played their first series of shows at the prestigious MGM Grand Hotel in Las Vegas, Nevada – this time, against the advice of Berry Gordy, who nevertheless put out a press statement following the success of the record breaking shows. It read: 'We were always certain that the boys had what it took. This is just the tip of the iceberg where the Jackson 5's talent is concerned...'.

UK dates prematurely announced for 30 & 31 May and 1 June – dates re-scheduled for mid-June.

22 February	Houston, Texas
9, 10, 11, 12, 13, 14, 15, 16, 17, 18,19, 20, 21, 22 & 23 April	Las Vegas, Nevada

Set list for the Las Vegas shows:

Skywriter/Killing Me Softly With His Song/Danny Boy/By The Time I Get To Phoenix/Bi Min Bist Da Schon/The Love You Save/I'll Be There/ABC/I Want You Back/Love Is Strange (Janet & Randy)/*Indian Love Call* (Janet & Randy)/*I Got You Babe* (Janet & Randy)/*The Beat Goes On* (Janet & Randy)

26, 27 & 28 April	Lake Tahoe, Nevada
13 May	Washington, D.C.
14 & 15 June	London, England
16 June	Manchester, England
18 June	Birmingham, England
19 June	Glasgow, Scotland (2 shows)
22 June	Los Angeles, California

24, 25, 26, 27,
28, 29 &
  30 June   Chicago, Illinois

8, 9, 10, 11, 12,
  13 & 14 July San Carlos, California
15 July   Pittsburgh, Pennsylvania
16 July   Trenton, New Jersey
21 July   Richmond, Virginia
26 July   Buffalo, New York
27 July   New York City, New York
29, 30 &
  31 July   Cleveland, Ohio

1, 2, 3 &
  4 August   Cleveland, Ohio
6 August   Huntsville, Alabama
7 August   New Orleans, Louisiana
10 August   St Louis, Missouri
11 August   Kansas City, Missouri
16 August   St Paul, Minnesota
17 August   Spokane, Washington
21, 22, 23, 24,
  25, 26, 27,
  28, 29, 30
  & 31 August,
  1, 2 &
  3 September Las Vegas, Nevada

1974: South America

5 September – Tour of Panama, Venuzuela
  1 October   & Brazil – most dates and
               venues not known.

19 & 20
  September   Rio de Janeiro, Brazil

1974: USA Dates

4, 5 &
  6 October   Lake Tahoe, Nevada

1974: Far East & Australasia

7 October – 1 November	Tour of Japan, Hong Kong, Australia, New Zealand & Philippines – dates and venues unknown.

1974: USA

3 November	Oakland, California
20, 21, 22, 23, 24, 25, 26, 27, 28, 29, 30 November, 1, 2 & 3 December	Las Vegas, Nevada

1975: West Indies & USA

January	Short tour of the West Indies – dates and venues unknown.
7, 8, 9, 10, 11, 12 & 13 February	New York City, New York
8 March	Kingston, Jamaica

Michael and his brothers shared the stage with Bob Marley & The Wailers in Kingston, Jamaica.

The Jackson 5's Motown contract expired in March 1976, and Michael and his brothers – minus Jermaine (who elected to stay with Motown), but with young Randy – signed with CBS/Epic Records, and changed their name to the Jacksons.

JACKSONS

1975: USA & Mexico

1975

11 June	Chicago, Illinois
6 July	Long Island, New York
1 September	Mount Vernon, New York

Mount Vernon 'Forever Came Today' date billed as 'The Labor Day Concert', with special guest stars Tavares.

December	Mexico City, Mexico – date unknown.

Mexican concert filmed and televised in Latin America – seen by around 35 million people, and released in 1981 in the UK as a home video titled, *THE JACKSON 5 IN CONCERT*.

18 December	San Carlos, California

1976: Philippines

13, 14 & 15 February	Manila (Folk Arts Theatre), Philippines
17, 18 & 19 February	Manila (Araneta Coliseum), Philippines

1977: Europe

May	Two and a half week tour, including dates in Glasgow, Amsterdam, Paris, Bremen & London – most dates unknown.
19 May	Glasgow, Scotland

At Glasgow's King's Hall, the Jacksons appeared before (and met) HM Queen Elizabeth II and The Duke of Edinburgh at the Royal Command Performance, as part of the Queen's Silver Jubilee celebrations.

1978: Goin' Places Tour

Tour started on 22 January, taking in North & Central America and Europe – most dates and venues unknown.

24 &
25 February   Port of Spain, Trinidad
26 February   San Fernando, Trinidad

Typical set-list: *Intro~Think Happy/Get It Together/Forever Came Today/I Am Love/Keep On Dancing/Ben/Show You The Way To Go/Goin' Places/Never Can Say Goodbye/Got To Be There/Sugar Daddy/I Wanna Be Where You Are/I'll Be There/I Want You Back/ABC/The Love You Save/Find Me A Girl/Dancing Machine/Enjoy Yourself*

1979: Destiny Tour

Year long tour split into two legs: the 1st leg saw Michael and his brothers visit Europe and Africa, before returning to the States – which is where all concerts during the 2nd leg of the tour, bar one (in Canada), were staged.

1st Leg
22, 24
& 26 January   Bremen, Germany
27 January   Frankfurt, Germany
28, 29 &
30 January   Madrid, Spain

1 & 2 February Amsterdam, Holland

6, 7, 8 &
9 February   London, England
10 February   Brighton, England
11 February   Preston, England
12 February   Wakefield, England
13 February   Sheffield, England

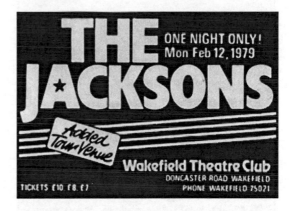

The Jacksons spent 14th and 15th February in Geneva, Switzerland, filming their guest spot on the *The ABBA Special*, which was screened later the same year – they performed *Blame It On The Boogie* and *Shake Your Body (Down To The Ground)*.

16 February   Glasgow, Scotland
17 February   Manchester, England
18 February   Birmingham, England

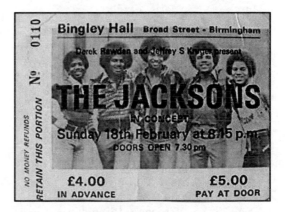

19 February   Halifax, England
20 February   Leicester, England
21 February   Cardiff, Wales

23 & 24 February	London, England
25 February	Poole, England
26 February	Amsterdam, Holland
29 February	Avignon, France

One of the London dates was filmed for a BBC TV special. In early 1982, the Jacksons took court action, to stop the syndication of the TV special. Cumulative damages of $600,000 were sought, and Michael and his brothers demanded the destruction of all copies of the unauthorised *Jacksons Live At The Rainbow* videotape.

2 March	Paris, France
6, 7, 8, 9 & 10 March	Johannesburg, South Africa
12, 13, 14 & 15 March	Dakar, Senegal
19, 20 & 21 March	Johannesburg, South Africa
14 & 15 April	Cleveland, Ohio, USA
19 & 22 April	Valley Forge, Pennsylvania, USA
25, 26, 27 & 29 April	Chicago, Illinois
3 May	St Petersburg, Florida
4 May	Fort Pierce, Florida

6 May	Jacksonville, Florida
10 & 12 May	Houston, Texas
13 May	Baton Rouge, Louisiana
16 May	Birmingham, Alabama
17 May	Columbus, Georgia
18 May	Nashville, Tennessee
19 May	Atlanta, Georgia
20 May	Memphis, Tennessee
24 May	Pine Bluff, Arkansas
26 May	Kansas City, Missouri
27 May	Oklahoma City, Oklahoma
30 May	Shreveport, Louisiana
1 June	Norfolk, Virginia
3 June	Columbia, South Carolina
8 June	Charlotte, North Carolina
9 June	Washington, D.C.
10 June	Greensboro, North Carolina

Set list for the 1st leg of the tour:

Dancing Machine/Things I Do For You/Ben/Keep On Dancing/Medley (I Want You Back/ABC/The Love You Save)/I'll Be There/Enjoy Yourself/ Destiny/Show You The Way To Go/All Night Dancin'/Blame It On The Boogie

2nd Leg:

2 & 3 October	New Orleans, Louisiana
4 October	Shreveport, Louisiana
5 October	Mobile, Alabama
6 October	Huntsville, Alabama
7 October	Louisville, Kentucky
12 October	Philadelphia, Pennsylvania
13 October	Rochester, New York
14 October	Pittsburgh, Pennsylvania
15 October	Saginaw, Michigan
19 October	Indianapolis, Indiana
20 October	St Louis, Missouri
21 October	Dayton, Ohio
25 October	Columbus, Ohio
26 October	Syracuse, New York
27 October	Buffalo, New York
28 October	Springfield, Massachusetts

1 November	Kalamazoo, Michigan
2 November	Chicago, Illinois
3 November	Cleveland, Ohio
4 & 5 November	Detroit, Michigan
7 November	Baltimore, Maryland
8 November	Uniondale, New York
9 November	Richmond, Virginia
10 November	Hampton, Virginia
11 November	Fayetteville, North Carolina
14 November	Fort Worth, Texas
15 November	Baton Rouge, Louisiana
16 November	Jackson, Mississippi
17 November	Lake Charles, Louisiana
18 November	Houston, Texas
20 November	Columbus, Georgia
21 November	Greenville, South Carolina
22 November	Savannah, Georgia
23 November	Macon, Georgia
24 November	Nashville, Tennessee
25 November	Atlanta, Georgia
29 November	Albuquerque, Colorado
30 November	Denver, Colorado
2 December	Honolulu, Hawaii
6 December	Portland, Oregon
8 December	Seattle, Washington
9 December	Vancouver, Canada
13 December	San Bernardino, California
14 December	Phoenix, Arizona
15 December	San Diego, California
16 December	Oakland, California
18 December	Los Angeles, California
19 December	Washington, D.C.

Set list for the 2nd leg of the tour:

Dancing Machine/Things I Do For You/ Off The Wall/Ben/Medley (I Want You Back/ABC/The Love You Save)/I'll Be There/Rock With You/ Enjoy Yourself/ Don't Stop 'Til You Get Enough/Shake Your Body (Down To The Ground)

Stage costumes for the tour, created by Jackie's wife Enid, were auctioned off at the end of the tour, with the proceeds going to the Black Linkage for Adoptive Children. Highest price: $575 for Michael's costume, purchased by a Michael impersonator.

1980:

5 February	Honolulu, Hawaii
17, 18, 19, 25 & 26 September	Los Angeles, California

1981: Triumph Tour

Three month tour of North America – all but one of the concerts were staged in the United States.

Start of tour delayed, after Randy's Mercedes was involved in a horrific accident in Hollywood, in March 1980 – initially, doctors feared his legs would have to be amputated, or that he would never walk again. Randy spent six months in hospital, and it was another ten months before he was well enough to join his brothers for the tour.

9 July	Memphis, Tennessee
13 July	Buffalo, New York
22 July	Atlanta, Georgia
25 July	Charlotte, North Carolina
26 July	Hampton, Virginia
31 July & 1 August	Washington, D.C.
2 August	Buffalo, New York
5 August	Toronto, Canada
12 August	Atlanta, Georgia
15 August	Philadelphia, Pennsylvania
18 & 19 August	New York City, New York

26 August   Milwaukee, Wisconsin
29 August   Detroit, Michigan

8 September   Kansas City, Missouri
10 September   Denver, Colorado
16 September   San Francisco, California
17 September   San Diego, California
18, 19, 25 &
  26 September Los Angeles, California

Set list for the tour:

Intro~Can You Feel It/Things I Do For You/Off The Wall/Ben/Heartbreak Hotel/ She's Out Of My Life/Movie & Rap (Including Excerpts Of I Want You Back/Never Can Say Goodbye/Got To Be There)/Medley (I Want You Back/ABC/ The Love You Save)/I'll Be There/Rock With You/Lovely One/Working Day And

Night/Don't Stop 'Til You Get Enough/ Shake Your Body (Down To The Ground)

Space-age set, inspired by the film *Close Encounters Of The Third Kind*, designed by Michael – he also brought in magician Doug Henning, to work on the show's special effects.

Concert staged at Atlanta's Omni Auditorium on 22nd July raised $100,000 for the Atlanta Children's Fund, set up to benefit families who had been victims of a series of recent, horrific kidnappings and murders.

Tour grossed around $5.5 million.

1984: Victory Tour

Tour of North America by all six Jackson brothers, with Jermaine rejoining his brothers on stage for the first time since the Jackson 5 days – Michael was opposed to the tour from the start, not least because he didn't like or trust the tour's promoter, Don King.

6, 7 & 8 July	Kansas City, Missouri
13, 14 & 15 July	Dallas, Texas
21, 22 & 23 July	Jacksonville, Florida
29, 30 & 31 July	East Rutherford, New Jersey
4 & 5 August	New York City, New York
7, 8 & 9 August	Knoxville, Tennessee
17, 18 & 19 August	Detroit, Michigan
25 & 26 August	Buffalo, New York

1 & 2
  September   Philadelphia, Pennsylvania
7 & 8
  September   Denver, Colorado
17 & 18
  September   Montreal, Canada
21 & 22
  September   Washington, D.C.
28 & 29
  September   Philadelphia, Pennsylvania

5, 6 &
  7 October   Toronto, Canada

12, 13 &
  14 October   Chicago, Illinois
19 & 20
  October   Cleveland, Ohio
26 & 27
  October   Atlanta, Georgia

2 & 3
  November   Miami, Florida
9 & 10
  November   Houston, Texas
16, 17 &
  18 November   Vancouver, Canada
30 November,
  1, 2, 7, 8 &
  9 December   Los Angeles, California

Set list didn't feature a single track from the album after which the tour was named:

Wanna Be Startin' Somethin'/Things I Do For You/Off The Wall/Human Nature (With Ben Intro)/Heartbreak Hotel/She's Out Of My Life/Let's Get Serious/You Like Me, Don't You/Tell Me I'm Not Dreaming (Too Good To Be True)/ Medley (I Want You Back/ABC/The Love You Save)/Rock With You/Lovely One/ Working Day And Night/Beat It/Billie Jean/Shake Your Body (Down To The Ground)

A number of scheduled concerts were either cancelled or re-scheduled:

- 17 & 18 August – Indianapolis, Indiana.
- 2, 4, 7, 9, 11 & 12 September – Los Angeles (The Forum), California; replaced by November/December dates at LA's Dodger Stadium.

- 3 September – Philadelphia, Pennsylvania; concert rained out and re-scheduled on 28 September.
- 13 & 14 October – Pittsburgh, Pennsylvania.
- 7 & 8 November – Anaheim, California.
- 23 November – Phoenix, Arizona.

Controversy over ticketing arrangements – initially, fans were obliged to pay up-front for four tickets (no more, no less) with no guarantee they would receive a single ticket – angered Michael, who became the main focus of protests. He resolved this would be his last tour with his brothers, and announced he had decided to donate all the money he received from the tour to charity.

Three charities benefitted by nearly $2 million each: The TJ Martell Foundation for Leukaemia & Cancer Research, the United Negro College Fund and the Ronald McDonald Camp For Good Times (a Los Angeles based charity for terminally ill patients).

Michael's father, Joseph, and promoter Don King planned to take the tour to Europe in early 1985, but Michael's refusal to participate meant no further dates could be scheduled.

Tour referred to by Michael as 'the final curtain' and 'the last hurrah'.

Tour attended by over 2 million people, and grossed an estimated $75 million – smashed record of $30 million achieved in 1981 by the Rolling Stones.

MICHAEL JACKSON

1987-89: Bad World Tour

Hugely successful first solo tour by Michael – 123 dates kicked off in September 1987 and the tour didn't finish until January 1989.

Tour sponsored by Pepsi.

1st Leg:

1987

12, 13 & 14 September	Tokyo, Japan
19, 20 & 21 September	Osaka, Japan
25, 26 & 27 September	Yokohama, Japan

3 & 4 October	Yokohama, Japan
10, 11 & 12 October	Osaka, Japan
13 November	Melbourne, Australia

438

20 & 21	
November	Sydney, Australia
25 & 28	
November	Brisbane, Australia

Japanese dates, and each performance of *I Just Can't Stop Loving You*, dedicated to a five year old boy, Yoshioka Hagiwara, who had recently been kidnapped and murdered. Michael earned $63 million from the 14 Japanese concerts alone.

Yokohoma concert on 26th September filmed and televised in Japan by Nippon TV.

Special guest appearance by Stevie Wonder at Brisbane concert on 28th November – he joined Michael on stage to perform *Bad* (not, as is often cited, *Just Good Friends*).

Set list for the 1st leg of the tour:

Wanna Be Startin' Somethin'/Things I Do For You/Off The Wall/Human Nature/ Heartbreak Hotel/She's Out Of My

Life/Medley (I Want You Back/The Love You Save/I'll Be There)/Rock With You/Lovely One/ Working Day And Night/Beat It/Billie Jean/Shake Your Body (Down To The Ground)/Thriller/I Just Can't Stop Loving You (with Sheryl Crow)/*Bad*

2nd Leg:

1988

23 & 24	
February	Kansas City, Missouri
3, 4 & 5 March	New York City, New York
12 & 13 March	St Louis, Missouri
18 & 19 March	Indianapolis, Indiana
20 March	Louisville, Kentucky
23 & 24 March	Denver, Colorado
30, 31 March	
& 1 April	Hartford, Connecticut
8, 9 &	
10 April	Houston, Texas
13, 14 &	
15 April	Atlanta, Georgia
19, 20 &	
21 April	Chicago, Illinois
25, 26 &	
27 April	Dallas, Texas
4, 5 & 6 May	Minneapolis, Minnesota
23 & 24 May	Rome, Italy
29 May	Turin, Italy
2 June	Vienna, Austria
5, 6 & 7 June	Rotterdam, Holland
11 & 12 June	Gothenburg, Sweden
16 June	Basel, Switzerland
19 June	Berlin, Germany
27 & 28 June	Paris, France
1 July	Hamburg, Germany
3 July	Cologne, Germany
8 July	Munich, Germany
10 July	Hockenheim, Germany

14, 15, 16, 22	
& 23 July	London, England
26 July	Cardiff, Wales
30 & 31 July	Cork, Ireland
5 August	Marbella, Spain
7 August	Madrid, Spain
9 August	Barcelona, Spain
11 August	Nice, France
14 August	Montpellier, France
19 August	Lausanne, Switzerland
21 August	Wurzburg, Germany
23 August	Werchter, Belgium
26 & 27	
August	London, England
29 August	Leeds, England

2 September	Hannover, Germany
4 September	Gelsenkirchen, Germany
6 September	Linz, Austria
10 September	Milton Keynes, England
11 September	Liverpool, England
26, 27 &	
28 September	Pittsburgh, Pennsylvania

3, 4 &	
5 October	East Rutherford, New Jersey
10 & 11	
October	Cleveland, Ohio
13, 17, 18 &	
19 October	Washington, D.C.
24, 25 &	
26 October	Detroit, Michigan
7, 8 &	
9 November	Irvine, California
13 November	Los Angeles, California,
USA	
9, 10, 11, 17, 18,	
19, 24, 25 &	
26 December	Tokyo, Japan

1989:
| 16, 17, 18, 26 & | |
| 27 January | Los Angeles, California |

440

Set list for the 2nd leg of the tour:

Wanna Be Startin' Somethin'/Heartbreak Hotel/Another Part Of Me/I Just Can't Stop Loving You (with Sheryl Crow)/ *She's Out Of My Life/Medley (I Want You Back/The Love You Save/I'll Be There)/ Rock With You/Human Nature/Smooth Criminal/Dirty Diana/Thriller/Working Day And Night/Beat It/Billie Jean/Bad/ The Way You Make Me Feel/Man In The Mirror*

A number of concerts were either cancelled or re-scheduled:

- 2 December 1987 – Wellington, New Zealand.
- 6 December – Auckland, New Zealand.
- 30 May 1988 – Lyon, France.
- 30 & 31 October, 1 & 2 November – Tacoma, Washington.
- 14, 15, 20, 21 & 22 November – Los Angeles, California; re-scheduled in January 1989.

Biggest concert of the tour was staged at Liverpool's Aintree Racecourse (home of the famous Grand National steeplechase) on 11th September 1988 – 125,000 fans attended. 'I have always considered Liverpool the home of contemporary pop music,' Michael told the press, 'by virtue of its being the birth place of the incomparable Beatles.'

Seven sold out concerts at London's Wembley Stadium, attended by 504,000 fans, set a record not broken before the stadium was demolished in 2003. The UK dates earned Michael around £16 million (£700,000 per hour).

Wembley concert on 16th July 1988 attended by HRH Prince Charles and Princess Diana – prior to the concert, Michael presented the Royal couple with a cheque for $450,00, for The Prince's Trust and re-development of Great Ormond Street Children's Hospital. As a mark of respect to his Royal guests, Michael offered to drop *Dirty Diana* from the set list, but Princess Diana insisted he must perform it.

90,000 fans at the Leeds concert on 29th August, before *Another Part Of Me*, sang *Happy Birthday* to Michael on his 30th birthday.

Proceeds from LA's Sports Arena concert on 27th January 1989 donated to Childhelp USA, the largest child abuse prevention charity in the States.

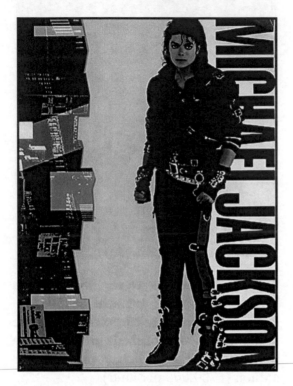

Around 4.4 million people attended the tour's 123 concerts, which grossed $125 – easily a world record at the time.

Nominated, at the Inaugural International Rock awards in April 1989, for Tour Of The Year 1988 – award went to the human rights organisation Amnesty International's multi-artist tour (supported by Tracey Chapman, Peter Gabriel, Bruce Springsteen and Sting).

1992-93: Dangerous World Tour

Michael's second solo tour, like his first, was sponsored by Pepsi – started on 27th June 1992 and ended prematurely on 11th November 1993.

Prior to the tour, Michael announced all profits would be donated to various charities, most notably his own Heal The World Foundation.

1st Leg:

1992

27 June	Munich, Germany
30 June & 1 July	Rotterdam, Holland
4 July	Rome, Italy
6 & 7 July	Monza, Italy
11 July	Cologne, Germany
15 July	Oslo, Norway
17 & 18 July	Stockholm, Sweden
20 July	Copenhagen, Denmark
22 July	Werchter, Belgium
25 July	Dublin, Ireland
30 & 31 July	London, England
5 August	Cardiff, Wales
8 August	Bremen, Germany
10 August	Hamburg, Germany
13 August	Hamelin, Germany
16 August	Leeds, England
18 August	Glasgow, Scotland
20, 22 & 23 August	London, England
26 August	Vienna, Austria
28 August	Frankfurt, Germany
30 August	Ludwigshafen, Germany

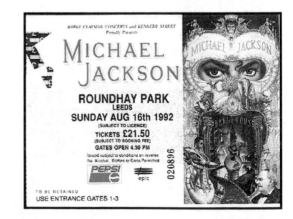

2 September	Bayreauth, Germany
4 September	Berlin, Germany
8 September	Lausanne, Switzerland
13 September	Paris, France
16 September	Toulouse, France
18 September	Barcelona, Spain
21 September	Oviedo, Spain
22 September	Madrid, Spain
26 September	Lisbon, Portugal

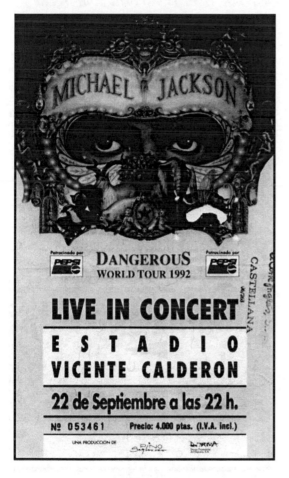

1 October   Bucharest, Romania

12, 14, 17, 19,
  22, 24, 30 &
  31 December Tokyo, Japan

Film rights to Bucharest concert, Michael's first behind the Iron Curtain, sold to the American cable station, HBO (Home Box Office) for around $20 million – the most ever paid for a pop concert. Concert first screened in the States on 10th October, giving HBO their highest ever ratings – also screened in at least 60 other countries. Released on DVD, as part of *THE ULTIMATE COLLECTION* box-set, in 2004, and as a stand alone DVD titled *Live In Bucharest: The Dangerous Tour*, the following year – however, as well as Bucharest, the DVD also featured footage shot at concerts in London and Madrid.

At 30th and 31st December concerts at Japan's Tokyo Dome, Michael was joined on stage by Slash, for *Black Or White*.

Set list for the 1st leg of the tour:

Carmina Burana~Brace Yourself (Video Introduction)/*Jam/Wanna Be Startin'*

443

Somethin'/Human Nature/Smooth Criminal/I Just Can't Stop Loving You (with Siedah Garrett)/She's Out Of My Life/Medley (I Want You Back/The Love You Save/I'll Be There)/Thriller/Billie Jean/ Working Day And Night/Beat It/ Will You Be There/The Way You Make Me Feel/Bad/Black Or White/Heal The World/Man In The Mirror

The Way You Make Me Feel and *Bad* were dropped from the set list after the 15th July concert in the Norwegian capital, Oslo.

2nd Leg:

1993

24 & 27 August	Bangkok, Thailand
29 August & 1 September	Singapore, Singapore
4 & 6 September	Taipei, Taiwan
10 & 11 September	Fukuoka, Japan
15 September	Moscow, Russia
19 & 21 September	Tel Aviv, Israel
23 September	Istanbul, Turkey
26 September	Tenerife, Canary Islands, Spain
8, 10 & 12 October	Buenos Aires, Argentina
15 & 17 October	Sao Paulo, Brazil
23 October	Santiago, Chile
29, 31 October, 7, 9 & 11 November	Mexico City, Mexico

Set list for the 2nd leg of the tour:

Carmina Burana~Brace Yourself (Video Introduction)/*Jam/Wanna Be Startin' Somethin'/Human Nature/Smooth Criminal/I Just Can't Stop Loving You (with Siedah Garrett)/She's Out Of My Life/Medley (I Want You Back/The Love You Save/I'll Be There)/Thriller/Billie Jean/Will You Be There/Dangerous/Black Or White/Heal The World/Man In The Mirror*

Dangerous was only added to the set list for the last few dates.

Michael cancelled and re-scheduled a number of concerts, mainly due to illness:

- 1 August 1992 – London, England; re-scheduled for 23 August.
- 21 August – London, England; re-scheduled for 20 August.

- 6 September – Gelsenkirchen, Germany.
- 11 September – Basel, Switzerland.
- 2 October – Izmir, Turkey.
- 4 October – Istanbul, Turkey.
- 8 October – Athens, Greece.
- 25 August 1993 – Bangkok, Thailand; re-scheduled for 26 August but cancelled again – finally went ahead on 27 August.
- 30 August – Singapore, Singapore.
- 21 October – Santiago, Chile
- 2 November – Mexico City, Mexico

Start of 2nd leg of tour coincided with false accusations of child molestation against Michael – stress caused by this led to his dependency on prescription pain killers, which ultimately resulted in a decision to end the tour early, after the Mexico City dates, so that Michael could seek treatment.

Concerts on the tour enjoyed by around 3.5 million fans.

1996-97: *History* World Tour

Michael launched his third solo tour in spectacular fashion – in front of a sell-out crowd of 123,000, a mini-spaceship crashed through the 210 foot stage and the spaceship's door blew open to reveal Michael, wearing a dazzling silver and gold futuristic outfit, complete with helmet.

1st Leg:

1996

7 September	Prague, Czech Republic
10 September	Budapest, Hungary
14 September	Bucharest, Romania
17 September	Moscow, Russia
20 September	Warsaw, Poland
24 September	Zaragoza, Spain
28, 30 September & 2 October	Amsterdam, Holland

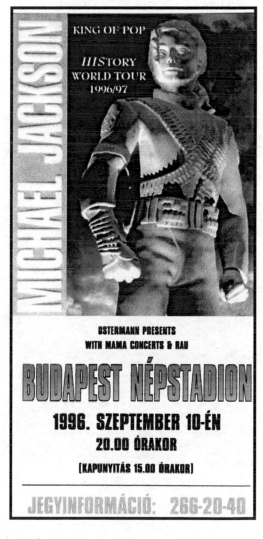

7 October	Tunis, Tunisia
11 & 13 October	Seoul, South Korea
18 October	Taipei, Taiwan

445

20 October	Kaoshung, Taiwan
22 October	Taipei, Taiwan
25 October	Singapore, Singapore
27 & 29 October	Kuala Lumpur, Malaysia

Seoul concert at Chamsil Olympic Stadium filmed, and released locally only on VHS (NTSC format) home video.

1 November	Bombay, India
5 November	Bangkok, Thailand
9 & 11 November	Auckland, New Zealand
14 & 16 November	Sydney, Australia
19 November	Brisbane, Australia

| 22 & 24 November | Melbourne, Australia |
| 26 November | Adelaide, Australia |

30 November, 2 & 4 December	Perth, Australia
8 & 10 December	Manila, Philippines
12, 15, 17 & 20 December	Tokyo, Japan
26 & 28 December	Fukuoka, Japan
31 December	Bandar Seri Begawan, Brunei

1997

| 3 & 4 January | Honolulu, Hawaii, USA |

2nd Leg:

31 May	Bremen, Germany
3 June	Cologne, Germany
6 June	Bremen, Germany
8 & 10 June	Amsterdam, Holland
13 June	Kiel, Germany
15 June	Gelsenkirchen, Germany
18 June	Milan, Italy
20 June	Lausanne, Switzerland
22 June	Bettembourg, Luxembourg
25 June	Lyon, France
27 & 29 June	Paris, France
2 July	Vienna, Austria
4 & 6 July	Munich, Germany
9 July	Sheffield, England
12, 15 & 17 July	London, England
19 July	Dublin, Ireland
25 July	Basel, Switzerland

27 July	Nice, France
1 August	Berlin, Germany
3 August	Leipzig, Germany
10 August	Hockenheim, Germany
14 August	Copenhagen, Denmark
16 August	Gothenburg, Sweden
19 August	Oslo, Norway
22 August	Tallinn, Estonia
24 & 26 August	Helsinki, Finland
29 August	Copenhagen, Denmark

3 September	Ostend, Belgium
6 September	Valladolid, Spain
4 & 6 October	Cape Town, South Africa
10 & 12 October	Johannesburg, South Africa
15 October	Durban, South Africa

Set list for the tour:

Medley (Scream/They Don't Care About Us/In The Closet)/Wanna Be Startin' Somethin'/Stranger In Moscow/You Are Not Alone/The Way You Make Me Feel/Medley (I Want You Back/The Love You Save/I'll Be There)/Medley (Rock With You/Off The Wall/Don't Stop 'Til You Get Enough)/Billie Jean/Thriller/Beat It/Come Together~D.S./Blood On The Dance Floor/Dangerous/Black Or

White/Earth Song/Heal The World/History

Come Together~D.S. was dropped from the set list after the end of December 1996, the *Off The Wall* medley was dropped after the concert on 10th June 1997, and *The Way You Make Me Feel* was dropped after 15th June 1997

Blood On The Dance Floor was added to the set list for the 2nd leg of the tour, but dropped after 19th August 1997.

Interludes for the show included a *Remember The Time* video montage after the Jackson 5 medley, a Panther interlude after *Blood On The Dance Floor*, and a *We Are The World* video after *Earth Song*.

Michael cancelled and re-scheduled several concerts:

- Casablanca, Morocco – two concerts planned for early October 1996 cancelled after authorities refused permission for the concerts to go ahead; no official explanation why was given.

- South African cities of Cape Town, Durban and Johannesburg – planned January 1997 dates all cancelled, and re-scheduled for October the same year.

- Ostend, Belgium – concert scheduled for 31 August 1997 cancelled, following tragic death of Princess Diana in Paris, France (where Michael was staying, prior to his concert); concert went ahead three days later, when Michael dedicated it to the memory of the 'Queen of Hearts.'

Concerts attended by 4.5 million fans – topping the number achieved by the Bad World Tour.

2009-10: *'This Is It'* UK Dates

After months of speculation, at a press conference on 5th March 2009, Michael confirmed he would play 10 dates at London's O2 Arena in July. He stated: 'This is it. I just want to say these, these will be my final show performances in London. This is it, this is it and when I say "this is it" it really means this is it, because… I'll be performing the songs my fans want to hear. This is it, I mean, this is – this is the final curtain call.'

Pre-sale tickets, available only to people who registered for a pre-sales code, went on sale on a few days later – the unprecedented demand for tickets led to further dates being announced, with a total of 50 dates selling out on 13th March – the first day tickets went on general sale. All dates sold out within four hours of tickets going on general sale.

Tour originally scheduled to launch on 8th July, but the first four dates were put back to allow more time for reheasals:

- 8 July 2009 put back to 13 July.
- 10 July 2009 changed to 1 March 2010.
- 12 July 2009 changed to 3 March 2010.
- 14 July 2009 changed to 6 March 2010.

2009:
13, 16, 18, 22, 24, 26, 28 & 30 July

1, 3, 10, 12, 17, 19, 24, 26, 28 & 30 August

1, 3, 6, 8, 10, 21, 23, 27 & 29 September
2010:
7, 9, 12, 14, 16, 18, 23, 25, 27 & 29 January

1, 8, 10, 12, 16, 18, 20, 22 & 24 February

1, 3 & 6 March

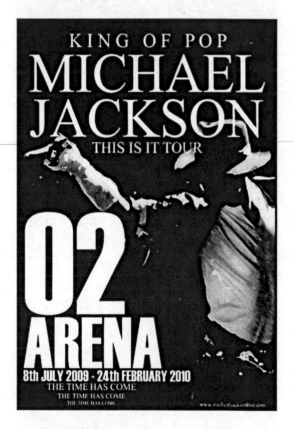

Tragically, Michael's sudden and premature death on 25th June 2009, meant all the *This Is It* dates were cancelled.

ONE-OFF CONCERTS

Michael has made a number of high profile, one-off concert appearances in recent years, solo and as part of much larger concerts, most prominent among them:

16 July 1996 – The Royal 50th Birthday Concert

Free concert at the Jerudong Park Amusement Park in Bandar Seri Begawan, Brunei, to celebrate the 50th birthday of one of the world's richest men, Hassanal Bolkiah Mu'izzaddin Waddaulah, the 29th Sultan of Brunei – attended by around 60,000 people.

Michael was paid an estimated $15-20 million by the Sultan of Brunei for the concert.

Set list: *Intro~Carmina Burana/Jam/ Wanna Be Startin' Somethin'/ Human Nature/Smooth Criminal/I Just Can't Stop Loving You/She's Out Of My Life/ Jackson 5 Medley/Thriller/Billie Jean/ The Way You Make Me Feel/Beat It/You Are Not Alone/Dangerous/Black Or White/Man In The Mirror/Earth Song*

25 & 27 June 1999 – Michael & Friends 'What More Can I Give?'

Two charity concerts staged to raise fund for the Nelson Mandela Children's Fund, the International Federation of Red Cross & Red Crescent Societies and UNESCO – raised $3.3 million.

First concert staged at the Chamsil Olympic Stadium, South Korea.

Controversy caused by high ticket prices and the date of the concert, which was on the 49th anniversary of the Korean War – a date deliberately chosen to highlight the conflict. Michael, at the close of *Earth Song*, spoke in favour of the reunification of South & North Korea, and promised to be there if it happened. Other performers included: All Saints, Barenaked Ladies, Andrea Bocelli, Boyzone, Mariah Carey, A.R. Rahman, the Scorpions, Ringo Starr, Status Quo, Luther Vandross and Zucchero.

Second concert staged at the Olympic Stadium in Munich, Germany – Michael suffered bruising and minor burns, when during his *Earth Song* performance, the bridge platform separated too soon, causing the middle section to fall to the stage, where it narrowly missed hitting Michael. Other performers included: BLACKstreet, Boyz II Men, Vanessa Mae, the Scorpions, Slash, Status Quo and Luther Vandross.

Michael closed both concerts with a half hour set, opening with a medley of hits: *Don't Stop 'Til You Get Enough/The Way You Make Me Feel/Jam/Scream/Black Or White/Billie Jean*. Michael closed the shows with *Dangerous*, *Earth Song* and *You Are Not Alone*.

Concerts attended by 115,000 people, and both televised; the second was broadcast globally over the internet and registered a world record 10 million 'hits' in one day.

7 & 10 September 2001 – 30th Anniversary Celebration

Both concerts, sub-titled 'The Solo Years', staged at Madison Square Garden, New York, and celebrated Michael's 30th anniversary as a solo performer.

Michael's first concerts on the American mainland for over a decade; tickets cost from $45 to $2,500 – the most expensive ever. The shows had a combined audience of 35,000 and grossed over $10 million.

Michael, flanked by his parents, Elizabeth Taylor and Macauley Culkin, watched the first half of the first show, which opened with Mya, Whitney

Houston & Usher performing *Wanna Be Startin' Somethin'*.

Michael performed with his brothers for the first time since 1984's Victory Tour: *Can You Feel It, Medley (I Want You Back/ABC/The Love You Save)/I'll Be There/Dancing Machine* (with 'N Sync)/*Shake Your Body (down To The Ground)*.

Without his brothers, Michael performed: *The Way You Make Me Feel* (with Britney Spears)/*Black Or White* (with Slash)/*Beat It* (with Slash)/*Billie Jean/You Rock My World* (with Usher).

Other guests and performers at the first concert included: Marlon Brando, Ray Charles, Destiny's Child, Gloria Estefan, James Ingram, Liza Minnelli and Shaggy.

Second concert featured a slightly different, though equally impressive, line-up.

Highlights of the two concerts were edited together for a two hour TV special – aired on CBS-TV in the States on 13th November. Prior to the special, CBS pressed a limited number of two promotional CDs, for distribution to radio stations across the country; the much rarer CD2 also featured two bonus tracks: *What More Can I Give* and *We Are Here To Change The World (from Captain EO)*.

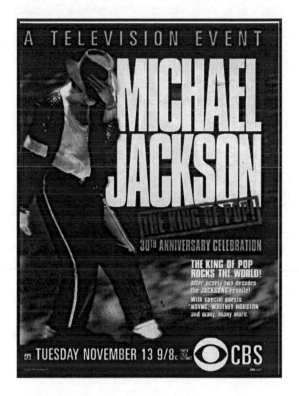

21 October 2001 – United We Stand 'What More Can I Give?'

11 hour charity concert at the RFK Stadium in Washington, D.C. – raised over $3 million for the American Red Cross Liberty Relief Fund, the Pentagon Relief Fund and the Salvation Army Relief Fund, in response to the 9/11 terrorist attacks.

Headlined by Michael, with numerous other acts also appearing, including Aerosmith, America, Backstreet Boys, James Brown, Mariah Carey, Destiny's Child, P. Diddy, Goo Goo Dolls, Al Green, Carole King, Huey Lewis, Ricky Martin, Bette Midler, 'N Sync, Pink, Rod Stewart & Usher.

Show opened by the Backstreet Boys, who sang America's national anthem, and closed by Michael with *Man In The Mirror* – following which, Michael was joined on stage by other artists present, to perform *What More Can I Give*, which he dedicated to the families of the victims of 9/11. 'You are not alone,' said Michael. 'You are in our hearts, in our thoughts and in our prayers.'

Concert attended by over 46,000 people.

Two hour TV special aired in the States on 1st November.

24 April 2002 – A Night At The Apollo

Concert to raise funds for the Democrat Party's 'Every Vote Counts' campaign, staged at the Apollo Theater in Harlem, New York – attended by 1,500 guests and raised around $2.5 million.

Co-hosted by Chris Tucker and actress Cicely Tyson, with other speakers and performers including former President Bill Clinton, Tony Bennett and k.d. lang – Michael performed a medley featuring *Dangerous*, *Black Or White* and *Heal The World*, and during *Black Or White* he was joined on stage by guitarist Dave Navarro, formerly of Jane's Addiction and the Red Hot Chili Peppers.

Four days earlier, Michael treated fans at the American Bandstand 50th Anniversary Celebration, to two electrifying performances of *Dangerous*. Staged at the Pasadena Civic Auditorium in Pasadena, Califormnia, Michael was introduced by the host of the longest running musical show in US TV history, Dick Clark – then, following Michael's first performance, Clark returned to the stage to announce that Michael, always the perfectionist, wasn't pleased with his performance, and wanted to the song over – which sent the crowd wild with delight.

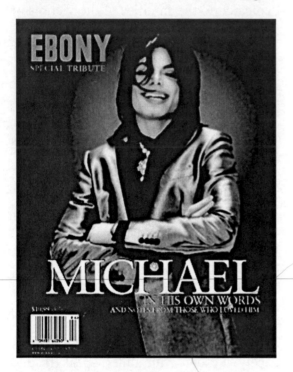

TRIBUTE CONCERT

In early August 2009, it was formally announced that Michael's brother Jermaine was playing a leading role in organising a star-studded farewell concert, to pay tribute to Michael.

Venue announced as the Schoenbrunn Palace (once home to Emperor Franz Joseph) in Vienna, Austria – chosen following Jermaine's visit a month earlier, to accept a posthumous award on behalf of Michael at the Save the World Awards, organised by World Awards Media.

Date confirmed as 26th September – Jermaine will be one of around 10 acts who will perform 15-20 of Michael's hits, in a show expected to run for around three hours.

No further details were available at our cut-off date.

PART 6: THE BOOKS

Five books have been written by, or attributed to, Michael – his autobiography, a storybook, an illustrated books of poems and reflections, a photobook and a book celebrating the biggest selling album of all time.

Michael, at the time of his passing, had approved and endorsed a sixth book.

MOONWALK

Published in April 1988, by Doubleday in the States and William Heinmann Ltd in the UK. 283 pages – illustrated with black/white photographs and colour plates.

Written by Michael, in collaboration with Doubleday editor, Shaye Areheart and Jacqueline Kennedy Onassis, who also penned the Foreword – dedicated to Fred Astaire.

Stormed to no.1 on the best seller lists published in both the Los Angeles Times and the New York Times. Sold nearly half a million copies in the States alone, in the space of just six months.

Also topped best seller lists in the UK, where an initial print run of 70,000 copies sold out within days; two further print runs, totalling 43,000, also quickly sold out.

In the book, Michael admitted, in the early days, he had 'a turbulent relationship' with his father, and stated: 'I'm one of the loneliest people in the world.'

Generally slated by critics, who felt the book didn't tell Michael's whole story – not by a long way. Michael's sister La Toya agreed, and dismissed the book as 'cold and impersonal', while brother Marlon went on record as saying, 'eighty percent of it is false.'

Published in English, Dutch, German, Italian, Japanese and Spanish.

Scheduled to be re-published in October 2009.

MOONWALKER – THE STORYBOOK

Published in November 1988 by Doubleday in the States and William Heinemann in the UK. 74 glossy, full colour pages (80 in the UK).

Tells the story of Michael's 'movie like no other', *Moonwalker* – primarily aimed at children aged 8-12 years.

Published in English and Japanese.

DANCING THE DREAM

Published in June 1992 by Doubleday. 150 glossy, full colour pages.

Collection of 'poems and reflections', illustrated with over 100 photographs, drawings and paintings from Michael's personal collection – dedicated 'to Mother with love'.

Introduction by Elizabeth Taylor; 'I think he is one of the finest people to hit this planet,' she wrote, summing up, 'and, in my estimation, he is the true King of Pop, Rock and Soul.'

Published in English, Chinese and German.

Re-published, with a new front cover, at the end of July 2009.

MY WORLD – THE OFFICIAL PHOTOBOOK VOL.1

Published in March 2006 by MJ Licensing LLC. 56 full colour pages.

Photobook featuring rare photographs from the period 1980-2006, from Michael's personal archive – also included personal thoughts and the hand-written lyrics to four of Michael's biggest hits, *Bad*, *Billie Jean*, *Black Or White* and *Smooth Criminal*.

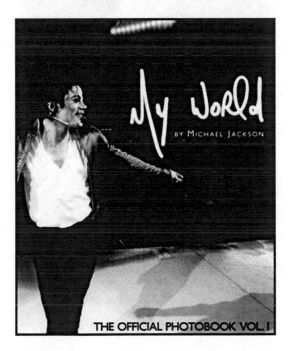

Published in English only.

THRILLER 25 – THE BOOK

Punlished in October 2008 by the ML Publishing Group, to coincide with Michael's 50th birthday. 146 glossy, full colour pages.

Originally scheduled to be published in August 2008 (September 2008 in the States) – released put back due to a request from the licensor for changes and corrections. Sales of the original edition did surface in continental Europe – these were unauthorised and were stopped, but not before an unknown number of books were sold.

Sub-titled 'Celebrating the biggest selling album of all time', featured 180+ exclusive photographs, and a wealth of information about the *THRILLER* album, including:

- Behind the scenes in the studio recording the album;
- Michael's revolutionary short films for the album;
- The Jacksons' Victory Tour;
- Grammy's most glorious night;

- The stories behind the songs on the album;
- Hand written lyrics by Michael;
- Unreleased songs from the *THRILLER* sessions;
- Exclusive interviews with Quincy Jones, Rod Temperton, Bruce Swedien, John Landis, Tamara Conniff (Editorial Editor of *Billboard* magazine), and many others.

OFFICIAL MICHAEL JACKSON OPUS, THE

Approved and endorsed by Michael, and more recently his estate, this 400 page book is due to be published in December 2009. It will include drawings, notes and hand written lyrics by Michael, as well as rare photographs of Michael, plus essays by people who knew and worked with Michael, and contributions by Michael's fans.

The book will be leather bound, and will come with a silk covered clamshell black case. It will come with a pair of white gloves, to be worn when viewing the book, to help to keep it in pristine condition.

The book will weigh a hefty 12kg (26lb), and the price will also be high: £109/$165 for the pre-ordered standard edition, with a special edition expected to cost between £400-500/$600-750.

Five copies, signed by celebrities, will be auctioned off, with the proceeds going to some of the charities Michael supported.

PART 7: CHARTOGRAPHY

This chartography focuses on Michael's chart successes, solo and with his brothers, in five countries: USA (Pop & RnB charts), Canada, UK, Germany & Australia.

Charts:

The following charts are covered:

- USA: Hot 100 Singles/Tracks, Billboard 200 Albums, Top 100 R&B Singles/Tracks & Top 100 R&B Albums.
- Canada: Hot 100 Singles/Tracks & Top 100 Albums.
- UK: Top 100 Singles & Top 100 Albums.
- Germany: Top 100 Singles & Top 100 Albums.
- Australia: Top 100 Singles & Top 100 Albums.

As older 'catalog' singles/tracks and albums (and in the early 1970s festive singles and albums) are excluded from mainstream American charts and the Canadian singles/tracks chart, and low priced albums are excluded from the UK albums chart, information from the following charts is also detailed:

- USA: Top 75 Digital Songs, Top 50 Catalog Albums, Top 25 R&B Catalog Albums, Christmas Albums & Singles.
- Canada: Top 75 Digital Songs.
- UK: Top 50 Budget Albums.

Information from these charts is denoted with an asterisk '*'.

Key:

Date = earliest date of chart entry in the USA or UK (or any of the other countries, for titles that didn't chart in the USA or UK).

USA = Pop charts in USA, RnB = R&B chart in USA, Can = Canada, UK = United Kingdom, Ger = Germany, Aus = Australia.

Throughout the chartography, singles are listed in lower case and ALBUMS in capitals.

JACKSON 5 / JACKSONS: 1969 ~ 1977

Date	USA	RnB	Can	UK	Ger	Aus	Title
Nov 69	1(1)	1(1)	2	2		77	I Want You Back
Jan 70	5	1(9)	10	16		17	DIANA ROSS PRESENTS…
Mar 70	1(2)	1(4)	3	8		14	ABC (single)
May 70	1(2)	1(6)	8	7		59	The Love You Save
Jun 70	4	1(12)	25	22		14	ABC (album)
Sep 70	1(5)	1(6)	10	4	45	31	I'll Be There
Sep 70	4	1(10)	9				THIRD ALBUM
Dec 70	1(6)*		45				CHRISTMAS ALBUM
Dec 70	1(2)						Santa Claus Is Comin' To Town
Jan 71	2	2	3	25			Mama's Pearl
Apr 71	2	1(3)	14	33		77	Never Can Say Goodbye
May 71	11	1(6)	16				MAYBE TOMORROW
Jul 71	20	3	22				Maybe Tomorrow
Oct 71	16	5	24				GOIN' BACK TO INDIANA
Dec 71	10	3	11				Sugar Daddy
Jan 72	12	2	40	26			GREATEST HITS
Apr 72	13	8	24			47	Little Bitty Pretty One
Jun 72	7	3	47	18			LOOKIN' THROUGH THE WINDOWS
Jul 72	16	5	69	9			Lookin' Through The Windows
Oct 72	18	9	35				Corner Of The Sky
Dec 72				43			Santa Claus Is Comin' To Town
Feb 73				9			Doctor My Eyes
Mar 73	28	10		20		41	Hallelujah Day
Apr 73	44	15	60			41	SKYWRITER
Aug 73	28	2	88				Get It Together
Sep 73				23		87	Skywriter
Sep 73	100	4					GET IT TOGETHER
Mar 74	2	1(1)	2	53			Dancing Machine
Apr 74				58			The Boogie Man
Oct 74	16		12				DANCING MACHINE
Oct 74	38	3	25				Whatever You Got, I Want
Jan 75	15	3	45				I Am Love
Jun 75	36	6					MOVING VIOLATION
Jun 75	60	6	79				Forever Came Today
Nov 75		50					All I Do Is Think Of You
Jul 76	84	32					ANTHOLOGY
Oct 76	6	2	5	42			Enjoy Yourself
Dec 76	36	6	42	54			THE JACKSONS
Apr 77	28	6	52	1(1)			Show You The Way To Go
Aug 77				22			Dreamer
Oct 77	52	8	62	26			Goin' Places
Oct 77	63	11		45			GOIN' PLACES

JACKSON 5 / JACKSONS: 1978 ~ 2009

Date	USA	RnB	Can	UK	Ger	Aus	Title
Feb 78		38					Find Me A Girl
Feb 78			31				Even Though You're Gone
Sep 78	54	3		8		4	Blame It On The Boogie
Dec 78	11	3	30	33		5	DESTINY
Jan 79	7	3	13	4		59	Shake Your Body (Down To The Ground)
Feb 79				39			Destiny
Sep 80	12	2	40	29			Lovely One
Oct 80	10	1(2)	37	13		13	TRIUMPH
Dec 80	22	2		44			Heartbreak Hotel
Feb 81	77	30		6		10	Can You Feel It
Jun 81	73	50		7			Walk Right Now
Nov 81	30	10		53		2	LIVE
Mar 83	7*						GREAT SONGS & PERFORMANCES...
Jul 83				1(3)		53	18 GREATEST HITS
Jun 84	168						14 GREATEST HITS
Jun 84	3	4	6	14	23	10	State Of Shock
Jul 84	4	3	10	3	5	9	VICTORY
Aug 84	17	12	7	26	31	32	Torture
Oct 84	47	39		94			Body
Feb 87		88					Time Out For The Burglar
Dec 87				91			I Saw Mommy Kissing Santa Claus
Apr 88				8			I Want You Back ('88 Remix)
May 89	77	4		33	26	89	Nothin (That Compares 2 U)
Jun 89	59	14		39		81	2300 JACKSON STREET
Jul 89		9		76			2300 Jackson Street
Oct 92		48				96	Who's Lovin' You (Live)
Nov 92	137	41					AN AMERICAN DREAM
Jul 97				5			THE BEST OF (J5 & Michael)
Aug 98				141			THE ULTIMATE COLLECTION
Mar 02	47*	17*					THE MILLENNIUM COLLECTION
Dec 03		96					THE CHRISTMAS COLLECTION
Mar 04		99					THE ESSENTIAL JACKSONS
Jul 04				7		15	THE VERY BEST OF (Jacksons)
Aug 04		74					THE JACKSONS STORY
Jan 07				53			I Want You Back
Sep 07		86					THE JACKSONS STORY: No.1's
Sep 08				34			THE MOTOWN YEARS
May 09				54			Who's Lovin' You
							Posthumous Hits
Jul 09	29*			49		84	I'll Be There
Jul 09	31*		39*	43	76	52	I Want You Back
Jul 09	34*		42*	50		43	ABC (single)

JACKSON 5 / JACKSONS: 2009

Date	USA	RnB	Can	UK	Ger	Aus	Title
Jul 09	50*						Shake Your Body (Down To The Ground)
Jul 09	72*						Never Can Say Goodbye
Jul 09	55*			36			Who's Lovin' You
Jul 09	5*	4*	87				THE ULTIMATE COLLECTION
Jul 09	8*	6*	19				THE MILLENNIUM COLLECTION
Jul 09	19*	10*					THE JACKSONS STORY: No.1's
Jul 09		35				71	THE VERY BEST OF (Jacksons)
Jul 09		16*				78	THE ESSENTIAL JACKSONS
Jul 09	186	36					LOVE SONGS
Jul 09		12*					TRIUMPH / DESTINY
Jul 09		20*					DESTINY
Jul 09		17*	59			99	GOLD
Jul 09			55			44	Blame It On The Boogie
Jul 09			59			41	Can You Feel It
Jul 09				4	61	43	THE MOTOWN YEARS
Jul 09				15		46	THE VERY BEST OF (J5 & Michael)
Jul 09				7*		66	CAN YOU FEEL IT - COLLECTION
Jul 09				4*			CLASSIC
Jul 09				5*			THE SILVER COLLECTION
Aug 09	17*	15*					LIVE
Aug 09	48*	21*					SUPER HITS

460

MICHAEL JACKSON: 1971 ~ 1984

Date	USA	RnB	Can	UK	Ger	Aus	Title
Oct 71	4	4	3	5		83	Got To Be There
Feb 72	14	3		37			GOT TO BE THERE
Mar 72	2	2	13	3		16	Rockin' Robin
May 72	16	2	57				I Wanna Be Where You Are
Aug 72				8			Ain't No Sunshine
Aug 72	1(1)	5	6	7		1(8)	Ben
Aug 72	5	4	12	17		65	BEN
May 73	50	14	60				With A Child's Heart
May 73	92	24				27	MUSIC & ME
Aug 73						98	Morning Glow
Sep 73						31	Happy
Feb 75	101	10					FOREVER, MICHAEL
May 75	54	7	79				We're Almost There
May 75	23	4	43				Just A Little Bit Of You
Sep 75	156	44					THE BEST OF
Sep 78	41	17	35	45			Ease On Down The Road
Jan 79	81	42					You Can't Win
Jul 79	1(1)	1(5)	3	3	13	1(3)	Don't Stop 'Til You Get Enough
Sep 79	3	1(16)	4	5	25	1(2)	OFF THE WALL
Nov 79	1(4)	1(6)	3	7	58	4	Rock With You
Nov 79	10	5	11	7		94	Off The Wall
Apr 80	10	43	15	3		17	She's Out Of My Life
Jul 80				41			Girlfriend
Apr 81	55	42		1(2)		9	One Day In Your Life
Apr 81	144	41		29			ONE DAY IN YOUR LIFE
Jun 81				11		76	THE BEST OF
Aug 81				46			We're Almost There
Nov 82	2	1(3)	8	8	53	4	The Girl Is Mine
Dec 82	1(37)	1(37)	1(13)	1(8)	1(11)	1(11)	THRILLER
Jan 83	1(7)	1(9)	1(7)	1(1)	2	1(5)	Billie Jean
Feb 83	1(3)	1(1)	1(2)	3	2	2	Beat It
Feb 83	201			82			E.T. THE EXTRA-TERRESTRIAL
May 83	5	5	11	8	16	25	Wanna Be Startin' Somethin'
Jul 83				1(3)		53	18 GREATEST HITS
Jul 83	7	27	17		64	64	Human Nature
Jul 83				52			Happy
Oct 83	10	46	24	11	51	40	P.Y.T. (Pretty Young Thing)
Oct 83	1(6)	2	1(1)	2	12	4	Say Say Say
Nov 83	4	3	4	10	21	4	Thriller
Dec 83				66			9 SINGLES PACK
Jan 84	2	1(5)	2	6	2	12	Somebody's Watching Me
May 84	38	37		7	51	68	Farewell My Summer Love

MICHAEL JACKSON: 1984 ~ 1996

Date	USA	RnB	Can	UK	Ger	Aus	Title
Jun 84	46	31		9	40	90	FAREWELL MY SUMMER LOVE
Jun 84	168						14 GREATEST HITS
Aug 84				33			Girl You're So Together
Mar 85	1(4)	1(2)	3	1(1)	2	1(9)	We Are The World
Nov 86				21			THEIR VERY BEST BACK TO BACK
Aug 87	1(1)	1(1)	2	1(2)	2	10	I Just Can't Stop Loving You
Sep 87	1(6)	1(18)	1(1)	1(5)	1(11)	2	BAD
Sep 87	1(2)	1(3)	1(1)	3	4	4	Bad
Oct 87				12		86	LOVE SONGS
Nov 87	1(1)	1(4)	3	3	12	5	The Way You Make Me Feel
Dec 87				27			THE MICHAEL JACKSON MIX
Feb 88	1(2)	1(1)	6	21	23	39	Man In The Mirror
Apr 88	80	4		37			Get It
Apr 88	1(1)	5	15	4	3	27	Dirty Diana
Jul 88				91			SOUVENIR SINGLES PACK
Jul 88	11	1(1)	46	15	10	49	Another Part Of Me
Nov 88	7	2	41	8	9	31	Smooth Criminal
Feb 89				2	16	37	Leave Me Alone
Jul 89				13	23	50	Liberian Girl
Nov 91	1(7)	3	1(8)	1(2)	2	1(8)	Black Or White
Nov91	1(4)	1(12)	2	1(1)	1(1)	1(6)	DANGEROUS
Jan 92				14		18	Black Or White (C&C Remixes)
Jan 92	3	1(2)	5	3	8	6	Remember The Time
Feb 92				53		27	MOTOWN'S GREATEST HITS
Apr 92	6	1(1)	13	8	15	5	In The Closet
Jul 92	26	3	21	13	18	11	Jam
Jul 92	14	6	20	10	9	34	Who Is It
Aug 92				32			TOUR SOUVENIR PACK
Oct 92						83	BOX SET
Dec 92	27	62	17	2	3	20	Heal The World
Feb 93				2	10	4	Give In To Me
May 93	121	74					Whatzupwitu
Jul 93	7	53	3	9	12	58	Will You Be There
Dec 93				33	45	76	Gone Too Soon
Jun 95	5	2	5	3	8	2	Scream
Jun 95				43			Scream (7"/12" Mixes)
Jun 95	1(2)	1(2)	1(5)	1(2)	1(2)	1(3)	*HIS*TORY
Sep 95	1(1)	1(4)	2	1(2)	4	7	You Are Not Alone
Dec 95				1(6)	1(6)	15	Earth Song
Apr 96	30	10		4	1(3)	16	They Don't Care About Us
Aug 96	112	71		2	29	46	Why
Nov 96	91	50		4	21	14	Stranger In Moscow

MICHAEL JACKSON: 1997 ~ 2008

Date	USA	RnB	Can	UK	Ger	Aus	Title
May 97	42	19	4	1(1)	5	5	Blood On The Dance Floor
May 97	24	12	16	1(2)	2	2	BLOOD ON THE DANCE FLOOR
Jul 97				5	14	43	History / Ghosts
Jul 97				5			BEST OF: THE MOTOWN YEARS
Sep 01	10	13	2	2	6	4	You Rock My World
Nov 01	14	2					Butterflies
Nov 01	1(1)	1(4)	3	1(1)	1(1)	1(1)	INVINCIBLE
Dec 01				25	76	43	Cry
Nov 01	85	45	20	15		52	GREATEST HITS *HISTORY* VOL.1
Mar 02		72					Heaven Can Wait
Oct 03	83	40	41	5	29		One More Chance
Nov 03	13	6	26	1(1)	16	6	NUMBER ONES
Dec 04	154	48		75			THE ULTIMATE COLLECTION
Jul 05	96	50	24	2	10	12	THE ESSENTIAL
Sep 05					70		LIVE IN BUCHAREST (DVD)
Feb 06					70	55	Thriller
Mar 06				17	77	66	Don't Stop 'Til You Get Enough
Mar 06				15		55	Rock With You
Mar 06				11	74	58	Billie Jean
Mar 06				15	76	66	Beat It
Apr 06				16	86	91	Bad
Apr 06				17		79	The Way You Make Me Feel
Apr 06				17	86	60	Dirty Diana
Apr 06				19	94	88	Smooth Criminal
Apr 06				15	89	68	Leave Me Alone
May 06				18	81	56	Black Or White
May 06				22	97	72	Remember The Time
May 06				20		68	In The Closet
May 06				22	98	60	Jam
Jun 06				27	90	63	Heal The World
Jun 06				30	100	65	You Are Not Alone
Jun 06				34	89	67	Earth Song
Jun 06				26	96	75	They Don't Care About Us
Jul 06				22		65	Stranger In Moscow
Jul 06				19			Blood On The Dance Floor
Jan 08			76	32	21	60	The Girl Is Mine 2008
Feb 08	81		32	69		8	Wanna Be Startin' Somethin' 2008
Feb 08	1(11)*	1(16)*	2	3	2	2	THRILLER 25
Mar 08			77				Beat It 2008
Sep 08				3	6	5	KING OF POP
Sep 08				96			Thriller Megamix
Sep 08				34			THE MOTOWN YEARS

CHESTERTON/VALPARAISO

Post-Tribune

FRIDAY
June 26, 2009

Good day to our readers,
including valued subscriber
Dona Dalka of Portage.

© 2009 VOLUME 99, ISSUE 208   NORTHWEST INDIANA'S LEADING NEWSPAPER   WWW.POST-TRIB.COM

KING OF POP DEAD AT 50

GARY'S FAVORITE SON **MICHAEL JACKSON** SUFFERS HEART ATTACK

FULL REPORT, **A14**

Michael Jackson, at age 13 in 1972, was the youngest member of the Jackson Five.
AP FILE PHOTO

MICHAEL JACKSON: 2009 ~ Posthumous Hits

Date	USA	RnB	Can	UK	Ger	Aus	Title
Jul 09	2*		7*	12	9	3	Thriller
Jul 09	2*		7*	2		8	Man In The Mirror
Jul 09	4*		6*	10	18	7	Billie Jean
Jul 09	6*		13*	34	61	13	The Way You Make Me Feel
Jul 09	7*		11*	19	14	17	Beat It
Jul 09	9*		19*	38	69	21	Don't Stop 'Til You Get Enough
Jul 09	12*		22*	13	38	16	Smooth Criminal
Jul 09	13*		8*	25	31	6	Black Or White
Jul 09	14*		48*	98		98	P.Y.T. (Pretty Young Thing)
Jul 09	17*		33*	54	98	36	Rock With You
Jul 09	20*		52*	57	75	53	Wanna Be Startin' Somethin'
Jul 09	23*		30*	40	44	27	Bad
Jul 09	17*		23*	35	33	22	You Are Not Alone
Jul 09	32*		60*	26	22	64	Dirty Diana
Jul 09	35*			81	67	40	Remember The Time
Jul 09	21*		28*	62		63	Human Nature
Jul 09	10*		11*	51	26	42	Will You Be There
Jul 09	51*			73			Off The Wall
Jul 09	62*			60	94	50	You Rock My World
Jul 09	70*			70		71	Scream
Jul 09	75*			46		14	Ben
Jul 09	139	22	46				GOLD
Jul 09	1(10)*	1(7)*	1(1)	1(1)	2	2	NUMBER ONES
Jul 09	2*	2*	4	1(7)	18	1(7)	THE ESSENTIAL
Jul 09	2*	1(3)*	6	3	2	3	THRILLER
Jul 09	4*	3*	10	3	37	17	OFF THE WALL
Jul 09	4*	2*	8	1(5)*	6	13	BAD
Jul 09	5*	5*	13	1(1)*	5	14	DANGEROUS
Jul 09	8*	8*	8				GREATEST HITS *HISTORY* V.1
Jul 09	5*	12*	29		37		THE ULTIMATE COLLECTION
Jul 09	10*	10*		17	4	14	*HISTORY*
Jul 09	9*	8*		3*	26	37	INVINCIBLE
Jul 09	11*	8*		4*	47	78	BLOOD ON THE DANCE FLOOR
Jul 09				33	12	77	Earth Song
Jul 09	64*		49*	28	12	18	They Don't Care About Us
Jul 09	39*			44	18	26	Heal The World
Jul 09				78		88	I Just Can't Stop Loving You
Jul 09				88		97	She's Out Of My Life
Jul 09				92			Ain't No Sunshine
Jul 09				94			One Day In Your Life
Jul 09				5	1(7)	6	KING OF POP
Jul 09			2	9			THRILLER 25

MICHAEL JACKSON: 2009 ~ Posthumous Hits

Date	USA	RnB	Can	UK	Ger	Aus	Title
Jul 09				4	36	43	THE MOTOWN YEARS
Jul 09				15		46	THE VERY BEST OF (& J5)
Jul 09		19*					OFF THE WALL / INVINCIBLE
Jul 09				74		63	Give In To Me
Jul 09				86			Liberian Girl
Jul 09				66	95		Leave Me Alone
Jul 09				91	80	95	Stranger In Moscow
Jul 09	50*		46*	77			We Are The World (USA For Africa)
Jul 09	56*			74	71	56	Smile
Jul 09	67*						Gone Too Soon
Jul 09				2*			CLASSIC
Jul 09				5*			THE SILVER COLLECTION
Jul 09	57	21		76			THE STRIPPED MIXES / THE MOTOWN 50 MIXES
Jul 09	46*	18*	27				THE MILLENNIUM COLLECTION
Jul 09					89	93	The Girl Is Mine
Jul 09					92	90	Blood On The Dance Floor
Jul 09					99		Dangerous
Jul 09				14	2	16	THE COLLECTION
Jul 09					8		LIVE IN BUCHAREST (DVD)
Jul 09					28		HISTORY ON FILM VOL. II (DVD)
Jul 09						80	Thriller Megamix
Jul 09						27	BAD / DANGEROUS
Jul 09			88			25	OFF THE WALL / THRILLER
Aug 09		20*					LOVE SONGS
Aug 09				32*			GOT TO BE THERE
Aug 09		85					HELLO WORLD
Sep 09	46	17					THE DEFINITIVE COLLECTION

Note: At the time we went to press, Michael's *NUMBER ONES* compilation was still at no.1 in the States, on both the Pop Catalog & R&B Catalog album charts, and *THE DEFINITIVE COLLECTION* had just made its chart debut.

PART 8: USA DISCOGRAPHY

This discography includes known promo/test pressings of singles, which for whatever reason were never released commercially in any format. All 7"/12" singles before 1980 were issued without a picture sleeve (p/s), and all singles from 1980 onwards with a p/s, unless otherwise stated. Significant re-issues only are listed.

THE JACKSON 5

All releases on Motown / Universal unless otherwise stated.

Albums

DIANA ROSS PRESENT THE JACKSON 5 (December 1969) MS-700; CD: 3746351292
ABC (May 1970) MS-709; CD: 3746351522
THIRD ALBUM (September 1970) MS-718; CD: 3746351572
CHRISTMAS ALBUM (October 1970) MS-713; CD: 3746352502
MAYBE TOMORROW (April 1971) MS-735; CD: 3746352282
GOIN' BACK TO INDIANA (September 1971) M742L
GREATEST HITS (December 1971) M741L; CD: 3746352012
LOOKIN' THROUGH THE WINDOWS (May 1972) M750L
SKYWRITER (March 1973) M761L; CD: 3746354692
GET IT TOGETHER (September 1973) M783V1
MAYBE TOMORROW (1974) Pickwick SPC 3394 – re-issue minus She's Good/16 Candles
STAND (1974) Pickwick SPC 3503 – re-issue of GOIN' BACK TO INDIANA minus Maybe Tomorrow
DANCING MACHINE (September 1974) M6-780S1
MOVING VIOLATION (May 1975) M6-829S1
ANTHOLOGY (June 1976) M7-868R3; 2CD: MOTD2-868
JOYFUL JUKEBOX MUSIC (October 1976) M6-865S1
BOOGIE (January 1979) Natural Resources NR-4013T1
SUPERSTAR SERIES VOL.12 (September 1980) M5-112V1
GREAT SONGS AND PERFORMANCES THAT INSPIRED THE MOTOWN 25th ANNIVERSARY T.V. SHOW (August 1983) 5312ML; CD: 3746353122
14 OF THEIR GREATEST HITS (November 1983) K-Tel NU 5510
COMPACT COMMAND PERFORMANCES – 18 GREATEST HITS (February 1984) CD: MCD-6070MD1
14 GREATEST HITS (May 1984) 6099ML – picture disc with glitter glove and poster
THE GREAT LOVE SONGS OF (June 1984) 5346ML

MOTOWN LEGENDS (June 1985) 5365ML
ANTHOLOGY (August 1986) 2CD: MOTD2-6194
THIRD ALBUM/MAYBE TOMORROW (August 1986) CD: MOTD 8011
DIANA ROSS PRESENTS/ABC (August 1986) CD: MOTD 8019
BEGINNING YEARS 1967-1968 (1989) S.D.E.G. SDE4018; CD: SDE 4018
AN AMERICAN DREAM (October 1992) CD: 374636356-2
MOTOWN LEGENDS (NEVER CAN SAY GOODBYE) (December 1993) CD:
  344638506-2
SOULSATION! (June 1995) 4CD Box Set: 3145304892/4
THE ULTIMATE COLLECTION (February 1996) CD: 314530558-2
PRE-HISTORY – THE LOST STEELTOWN RECORDINGS (June 1996)
  Brunswick/Inverted CD: BRV 81015-2

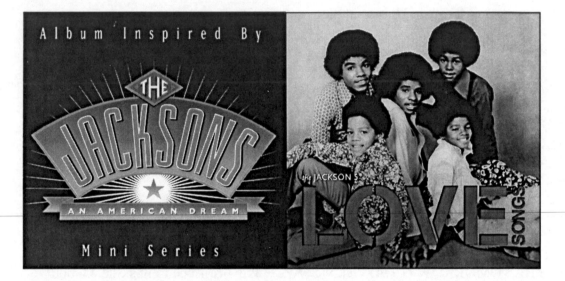

THE BEST OF – THE MILLENIUM COLLECTION (October 1999) CD: 012153364-2
ANTHOLOGY (October 2000) 2CD: 012159650-2
DIANA ROSS PRESENTS THE JACKSON 5 & ABC (August 2001) CD: 440 014 380-2
THIRD ALBUM & MAYBE TOMORROW (August 2001) CD: 440 014 381-2
GOIN' BACK TO INDIANA & LOOKIN' THROUGH THE WINDOWS (August 2001)
  CD: 440 014 382-2
SKYWRITER & GET IT TOGETHER (August 2001) CD: 440 014 383-2
DANCING MACHINE & MOVING VIOLATION (August 2001) CD: 440 014 384-2
THE BEST OF – THE CHRISTMAS COLLECTION (September 2003) CD:
  B0000707-02
JOYFUL JUKEBOX MUSIC & BOOGIE (November 2004) CD: Hip-O Select
  B0003016-02
ROCK ON BREAKOUT YEARS (October 2005) BOY2 51111
IN JAPAN! (December 2006) CD: Hip-O Select B003070-02
LOVE SONGS (January 2009) CD: 001246402

Cassette Only Albums

16 GREATEST HITS (May 1984) 6100MC
I'LL BE THERE (1989) MOTC 3710
THE LOVE YOU SAVE (1989) MOTC 3031
MAMA'S PEARL (1989) MOTC 3733
ORIGINAL MOTOWN CLASSICS (1990) MSC 95000/PDK-2-1272

Albums With A Connection

MOTOWN AT THE HOLLYWOOD PALACE (March 1970) MS-703 – includes live
performances of Sing A Simple Song (Intro)/Can You Remember, I Want You Back and
brief dialogue between Michael & Diana Ross
GETTING TOGETHER WITH THE JACKSON 5 (March 1971) Music-O MDS 1047 –
various artist album which includes You Don't Have To Be Over Twenty-One To Fall In
Love/Some Girls Want Me For Their Lover
DIANA! (March 1971) MS-719; CD: 3746351552 – includes two live medleys Mama's
Pearl/Walk On/The Love You Save and I'll Be There/Feelin' Alright (with Diana Ross)
THE MOTOWN STORY (March 1971) MS-5-726 – includes I Want You Back, with 22
second introduction by Michael
SAVE THE CHILDREN (April 1974) M-800-R2 – includes a live version of Michael's I
Wanna Be Where You Are performed by the Jackson 5
MOTOWN SUPERSTARS SING MOTOWN SUPERSTARS (May 1983) 5310ML –
includes the previously unreleased Ask The Lonely, recorded in 1970

7" Singles

Big Boy/You've Changed (January 1968) Steeltown 681

We Don't Have To Be Over 21 (To Fall In Love)/Jam Session (1968) Steeltown 682

I Want You Back/Who's Lovin' You (October 1969) M1157

ABC/The Young Folks (February 1970) M1163

The Love You Save/I Found That Girl (May 1970) M1166

I'll Be There/One More Chance (August 1970) M1171

Santa Claus Is Comin' To Town/Christmas Won't Be The Same This Year (November 1970) M1174

Mama's Pearl/Darling Dear (January 1971) M1177 – with p/s

Never Can Say Goodbye/She's Good (March 1971) M1179

You Don't Have To Be Over Twenty One To Fall In Love/Some Girls Want Me For Their Lover (March 1971) Dynamo D146

Feelin' Alright (& Diana Ross)/Love Story (Diana Ross & Bill Cosby) (May 1971) DJ 719 – promo only with p/s

Maybe Tomorrow/I Will Find A Way (June 1971) M1186F

Sugar Daddy/I'm So Happy (November 1971) M1194F

Little Bitty Pretty One/If I Have To Move A Mountain (April 1972) M1199F

Lookin' Through The Windows/Love Song (June 1972) M1205F

Corner Of The Sky/To Know (October 1972) M1214F

I Want You Back/ABC (November 1972) Y443F

The Love You Save/I'll Be There (November 1972) Y446F

Hallelujah Day/You Made Me What I Am (February 1973) M1224F

The Boogie Man/Don't Let You Baby Catch You (March 1973) M1230F – promo only with p/s

Mama's Pearl/Never Can Say Goodbye (June 1973) Y499F

Maybe Tomorrow/Sugar Daddy (June 1973) Y501F

Get It Together/Touch (August 1973) M1277F

Dancing Machine/It's Too Late To Change The Time (February 1974) M1286F

Little Bitty Pretty One/Lookin' Through The Windows (April 1974) Y552F

Corner Of The Sky/Hallelujah Day (April 1974) Y553F

Whatever You Got, I Want/I Can't Quit Your Love (October 1974) M1308F

I Am Love (Part 1)/(Part 2) (December 1974) M1310F

Dancing Machine/Get It Together (April 1975) Y576F

Forever Came Today/All I Do Is Think Of You (June 1975) M1356F

Body Language (Do The Love Dance)/Call Of The Wild (October 1975) M1375F – promo only

Up On The Housetop/Up On The House Top (1987) 1914MF – promo only

12" Singles

Four Tops/Temptations: Medley Of Hits/Jackson 5: Medley Of Hits: I Want You Back/
  ABC/The Love You Save/I'll Be There/Never Can Say Goodbye/Dancing Machine/
  Lookin' Through The Windows (June 1983) 4510MG – no p/s
Dancing Machine (Original Version)/(Radio Remix)/(Extended Dance Mix)/(Dub Mix)/
  I Want You Back/ABC/The Love You Save (1992) 374631080-1 – promo only with
  no p/s
It's Your Thing (The J5 In '95 Extended Remix)/(Instrumental)/(A Cappella)/(Original
  1969 Mix)/I Wanna Be Where You Are/Dancing Machine/Never Can Say Goodbye
  (1995) 374631294-1 – promo only with no p/s
I Want You Back '98 (Club Mix)/(T.V. Track)/(Radio Edit W/out Rap)/(Clean Radio Edit
  (W/Rap)/A Cappella)/(Instrumental) (1998) 374633004 – promo only

CD Singles

Give Love On Christmas Day (1986) PCD-1020 – promo only
I Want You Back/ABC/I'll Be There/Little Bitty Pretty One (1989) MOTD 70004
Who's Lovin' You (Live Radio Edit)/(Live Album Version)/(Original Version) (October
  1992) 374631066-2
Big Boy/You've Changed (June 1995) Inverted 705245-1228-2
I Want You Back '98 (Clean Radio Edit W/rap)/(Radio Edit W/out Rap)/(Club Mix)
  (1998) 374633004-2 – promo only

Cassette Singles

Who's Lovin' You (Live Version)/(Original Version) (October 1992) 374632182-4

MICHAEL JACKSON – The Motown Era

All releases on Motown unless otherwise stated.

Albums

GOT TO BE THERE (January 1972) M747L; CD: 3746354162
BEN (August 1972) M755L; CD: 3746351532
MUSIC & ME (April 1973) M767L
FOREVER, MICHAEL (January 1975) M6-825S1
THE BEST OF (August 1975) M6-851S1; CD: 3746351942
SUPERSTAR SERIES VOL.7 (August 1980) M5-107V1
ONE DAY IN YOUR LIFE (March 1981) M8-956M1; CD: 3746353522
FAREWELL MY SUMMER LOVE (May 1984) 6101ML

THE GREAT LOVE SONGS OF (June 1984) M345ML
MOTOWN LEGENDS (June 1985) 5369ML
LOOKING BACK TO YESTERDAY (February 1986) 5384ML; CD: MOTD 5384
ANTHOLOGY (August 1986) 2CD: MOTD2-6195
GOT TO BE THERE/BEN (August 1986) CD: MOTD 8000
THE ORIGINAL SOUL OF (October 1987) 6250M; CD: MOTD 6250
MOTOWN LEGENDS (ROCKIN' ROBIN) (December 1993) CD: 374638505-2
THE BEST OF (ANTHOLOGY SERIES) (March 1995) 2CD: 314530480-2

THE BEST OF – THE MILLENNIUM COLLECTION (November 2000) CD:
   012159917-2
GOLD (August 2008) 2CD: B0011431-02
HELLO WORLD: THE COMPLETE MOTOWN SOLO COLLECTION (July 2009)
   3CD: Hip-O Select B0012421-02
THE STRIPPED MIXES (July 2009) CD: B001330302
THE DEFINITIVE COLLECTION (September 2009) CD: 2714783

Cassette Only Albums

MY GIRL (1989) MOTC 3711
GOT TO BE THERE (1989) MOTC 3732

Albums With A Connection

A MOTOWN CHRISTMAS (September 1973) M795V2; CD: 3746352562 – includes the
   previously unreleased Little Christmas Tree

MOTOWN CELEBRATES SINATRA (October 1998) CD: 314530975-2 – includes Michael's version of All The Things You Are, and features a still of Michael taken from the 1971 TV special Diana! on the sleeve

7" Singles

Got To Be There/Maria (You Were The Only One) (October1971) M1191F
Rockin' Robin/Love Is Here And Now You're Gone (February 1972) M1197F
I Wanna Be Where You Are/We've Got A Good Thing Going (May 1972) M1202F – with p/s
Ben/You Can Cry On My Shoulder (July 1972) M1207F
Everybody's Somebody's Fool/Shoo-Be-Doo-Be-Doo-Dah-Day (1972) M1218F – promo only
With A Child's Heart/Morning Glow (April 1973) M1218F
Got To Be There/Rockin' Robin (June 1973) Y503F
Ben/I Wanna Be Where You Are (April 1974) Y555F
Doggin' Around/Up Again (October 1973) M1270F – test pressing only
We're Almost There/Take Me Back (February 1975) M1341F
Just A Little Bit Of You/Dear Michael (April 1975) M1349F
We're Almost There/Just A Little Bit Of You (April 1977) Y597F
One Day In Your Life/Take Me Back (March 1981) M1512F – no p/s
Farewell My Summer Love/Call On Me (May 1984) M1739F
Touch The One You Love/Girl You're So Together (August 1984) M1757F
Melodie/Up On The House Top (1987) 1914MF – promo only
Twenty-Five Miles/Up On The Housetop (October 1987) 1914MF

CD Singles

Got To Be There/Rockin' Robin/I Wanna Be Where You Are/Just A Little Bit Of You (1989) MOTD 70006

THE JACKSONS

All releases on CBS/Epic or Sony unless otherwise stated.

Albums

THE JACKSONS (November 1976) 34229; CD: EK 34229; PAT 3687769 – picture disc
GOIN' PLACES (October 1977) 34835; CD: EK 34835; PIC VEU REC – picture disc
DESTINY (December 1978) 35552; CD: EK 35552; 88697308692 (September 2008) – with two bonus tracks

TRIUMPH (October 1980) 36424; CD: EK 36424; 88697335582 (September 2008) – with three bonus tracks
LIVE (November 1981) 37545; CD: EGK 37545
VICTORY (July 1984) 38946; CD: EK 38946; 8E8 3957651 – picture disc
2300 JACKSON STREET (June 1989) 40911; CD: EK 40911
THE ESSENTIAL (March 2004) CD: EK 86455
THE JACKSONS STORY (July 2004) CD: Hip-O Records B0003058-02
THE JACKSONS STORY: NUMBER 1'S (August 2007) CD: Hip-O Records B0009599-D2
SUPER HITS (November 2007) CD: BMG A 721343
THE VERY BEST OF (January 2009) CD: 88697335592

7" Singles

Enjoy Yourself/Style Of Life (October 1976) 50289
Show You The Way To Go/Blues Away (March 1977) 50350
Enjoy Yourself/Show You The Way To Go (October 1977) 15 2354
Goin' Places/Do What You Wanna (October 1977) 50454
Find Me A Girl/Different Kind Of Lady (January 1978) 50496
Blame It On The Boogie/Do What You Wanna (August 1978) 50595
Shake Your Body (Down To The Ground)/That's What You Get (For Being Polite) (January 1979) 50656 – with p/s
Lovely One/Bless His Soul (September 1980) 50938 – no p/s
Heartbreak Hotel/Things I Do For You (November 1980) 50959
Can You Feel It/Wonderin' Who (April 1981) 01032 – no p/s
Walk Right Now/Your Ways (June 1981) 02132
Lovely One/Michael: She's Out Of My Life (June 1981) 15 02157 – no p/s
Things I Do For You (Live)/Working Day And Night (Live) (1981) 14 02720 – promo only with no p/s
State Of Shock/Your Ways (June 1984) 34 04503
Torture/(Instrumental) (August 1984) 34 04575
Body/(Instrumental) (October 1984) 34 04673
State Of Shock/Torture (July 1985) 15 05536
Time Out For The Burglar/The Distance: News At 11 (January 1987) MCA 53032
Nothin (That Compares 2 U)/Alright With Me (May 1989) 34 68688
2300 Jackson Street/When I Look At You (July 1989) 34 69022

12" Singles

Shake Your Body (Down To The Ground)/That's What You Get For Being Polite (January 1979) 28 50721
Walk Right Now (Part 1)/(Part 2) (June 1981) 49 02403

Things I Do For You (Live)/Working Day And Night (Live) (1981) AS1387 – promo only with no p/s
State Of Shock (Dance Mix)/(Instrumental) (June 1984) 49 05022
Torture/(Instrumental) (August 1984) 49 05075
Time Out For The Burglar (Extended Version)/(Instrumental)/(Bonus Beats) (January 1987) MCA 23729
Shake Your Body (Down To The Ground)/Walk Right Now (1987) 49H 06910
Lovely One/Can You Feel It (1989) 49H 07548
Heartbreak Hotel/Blame It On The Boogie (1989) 49H 08142
Nothin (That Compares 2 U) (Extended)/(Sensitive Vocal)/(Bass World Dub)/(The Mix)/(Choice Dub) (May 1989) 49 6823381
Enjoy Yourself/Blame It On The Boogie (Remix)/Walk Right Now (1997) 49 78583
Shake Your Body (Down To The Ground)/Can You Feel It (1997) 49 78584

Cassette Singles

Nothin (That Compares 2 U)/Alright With Me (May 1989) 34T 68688
2300 Jackson Street (Short Version)/When I Look At Her (July 1989) 34T 69022

CD Singles

Nothin (That Compares 2 U)/Alright With Me (May 1989) 34K 68688
Nothin (That Compares 2 U) (7" Edited Version)/(Album Version)/(The Mix)/(Choice Dub)/(Extended Version)/(Sensitive Vocal Mix)/(Bass World Dub) (May 1989) 49K 68688
2300 Jackson Street/Keep Her/When I Look At Her (July 1989) 34K 69022
Private Affair (1989) ESK 1869 – promo only

MICHAEL JACKSON – The Epic Era

All releases on CBS/Epic or Sony unless otherwise stated.

Albums

OFF THE WALL (August 1979) FE 35745; CD: EK 35745
E.T. THE EXTRA-TERRESTRIAL (November 1982) MCA 70000
THRILLER (December 1982) QE 38112; CD: EK 38112; 8E8 38867 – picture disc
BAD (September 1987) 40600; CD: EK 40600; 9E9 44043 – picture disc
THE BAD MIXES (May 1988) CD: ESK 1215/ESK 1215MC – limited edition 'Monster Cable' promo
DANGEROUS (November 1991) E2 45400; CD: EK 45400; EK 48900 – limited edition 'pop-up'; 7464 45400-2 – CD with elongated packaging

HISTORY PAST, PRESENT AND FUTURE BOOK 1 (June 1995) E3 59000 – 3LP Box Set; 2CD: E3K 59000

BLOOD ON THE DANCE FLOOR – HISTORY IN THE MIX (May 1997) E2 68000; CD: EK 68000

OFF THE WALL (SPECIAL EDITION) (October 2001) CD: EK 66070

THRILLER (SPECIAL EDITION) (October 2001) CD: EK 66073

BAD (SPECIAL EDITION) (October 2001) CD: EK 66072

DANGEROUS (SPECIAL EDITION) (October 2001) CD: EK 66071

30TH ANNIVERSARY T.V. SPECIAL (October 2001) 2CD: CBS EMIT 2505-ADD / EMIT 2515-ADD – promo only

INVINCIBLE (October 2001) E2 69400 – 2LP; CD: EK 69400

GREATEST HITS HISTORY VOLUME 1 (November 2001) CD: 85250

NUMBER ONES (November 2003) CD: EK 88998

THE ULTIMATE COLLECTION (November 2004) 4CD/DVD: E5K 92600

THE ESSENTIAL (July 2005) 2CD: E2K 94287; (August 2008) 3CD:88697309852 – limited edition 3.0 version

THRILLER 25 (February 2008) 2LP: 88697233441; CD (standard sleeve): 88697233422; CD (zombie sleeve): 88697179872; Deluxe CD (gatefold zombie sleeve): 88697220962 – CD versions with bonus DVD

Original Soundtrack Album

THE WIZ (Original Motion Picture Soundtrack) (September 1978) MCA MCA2-14000; CD: MCAD2-11649

Singles Box-Set

VISIONARY – THE VIDEO SINGLES (November 2006) 700406 – box-set of 20 DualDisc singles (as per UK release, but not issued individually)

Home Videos & DVDs

MAKING MICHAEL JACKSON'S THRILLER (December 1983) Vestron 11000

MOONWALKER (January 1989) CMV 49009

THE LEGEND CONTINUES… (May 1989) Vestron 5358

DANGEROUS – THE SHORT FILMS (December 1993) 49164

VIDEO GREATEST HITS – *HIS*TORY (June 1995) 50123

*HIS*TORY ON FILM VOLUME II (May 1997) 50138

NUMBER ONES (November 2003) EVD 56999

THE ONE (March 2004) EVD 58511

LIVE IN BURCHAREST: THE DANGEROUS TOUR (July 2005) EVD 53497

7 " Singles

Ease On Down The Road/The Wiz: Poppy Girls (September 1978) MCA 40947 – with p/s

You Can't Win (Part 1)/(Part 2) (January 1979) 50654

Don't Stop 'Til You Get Enough/I Can't Help It (July 1979) 50742

Rock With You/Working Day And Night (October 1979) 50797

Off The Wall/Get On The Floor (February 1980) 50838

She's Out Of My Life/Get On The Floor (April 1980) 50871

Don't Stop 'Til You Get Enough/Jacksons: Shake Your Body (Down To The Ground) (December 1980) 15 02388

Off The Wall/Rock With You (June 1981) 15 02156

The Girl Is Mine/Can't Get Outta The Rain (October 1982) 34 03288; 55 03288 – Instant Classics re-issue (February 1984)

Someone In The Dark (Long Version)/(Short Version) (November 1982) S45 1786 – promo only

Billie Jean/Can't Get Outta The Rain (January 1983) 34 03509; 55 03509 – Instant Classics re-issue (April 1983)

Beat It/Get On The Floor (March 1983) 34 03759; 55 03759 – Instant Classics re-issue (August 1983)

Wanna Be Startin' Somethin'/(Instrumental) (May 1983) 34 03914; 55 03914 – Instant Classics re-issue (February 1984)

Human Nature/Baby Be Mine (July 1983) 34 04026

Say Say Say/Paul McCartney: Ode To A Koala Bear (October 1983) Columbia 04168

P.Y.T. (Pretty Young Thing)/Working Day And Night (October 1983) 34 04165; 55 04165 – Instant Classics re-issue (February 1984)

Thriller/Can't Get Outta The Rain (February 1984) 34 04364

I Just Can't Stop Loving You/Baby Be Mine (July 1987) 34 07253

Bad/I Can't Help It (September 1987) 34 07418

477

The Way You Make Me Feel/(Instrumental) (November 1987) 34 07645
Man In The Mirror/(Instrumental) (January 1988) 34 07668et It/(Istrumental) (April 1988)
Motown 1930
Dirty Diana/(Instrumental) (April 1988) 34 07739
Another Part Of Me/(Instrumental) (July 1988) 34 07962
Smooth Criminal/(Instrumental) October 1988) 34 08044
Black Or White/(Instrumental) (November 1991) 34 74100
Remember The Time/Black Or White (Underground Club Mix) (January 1992) 34 74200
In The Closet (7" Edit)/(The Mission Radio Edit) (April 1992) 34 74266
Jam (7" Edit)/Rock With You (Masters At Work Remix) June 1992) 34 74333
Heal The World/She Drives Me Wild (November 1992) 34 74708
Who Is It/Wanna Be Startin' Somethin' (Brothers In Rhythm Mix) (March 1993) 34 74406
Will You Be There/(Instrumental) (July 1993) 34 77060
Gone Too Soon/(Instrumental) (November 1993) 34 78007 – no p/s
Scream (Single Edit)/Childhood (Theme From 'Free Willy 2') (May 1995) 34 78000
You Are Not Alone (Album Edit)/Scream Louder (Flyte Tyme Remix) (August 1995)
   34 78002
They Don't Care About Us (Single Version)/Rock With You (Frankie Knuckles Radio
   Mix) (May 1996) 34 78264
Blood On The Dance Floor/Dangerous (Roger's Dangerous Edit) (April 1997) 34 78007
Stranger In Moscow (Tee's Radio Mix) (July 1997) 34 78012
You Rock My World (September 2001) 79656 – promo only with no p/s
Cry/Cry (October 2001) ZSS 79960 – promo only with no p/s

12" Singles

Ease On Down The Road (September 1978) MCA 1669
You Can't Win (Part 1)/(Part 2) (January 1979) 28 50658
Billie Jean (Long Version)/(Instrumental) (January 1983) 49 03557
Wanna Be Startin' Somethin' (Long Version)/(Instrumental) (May 1983) 49 03915
Thriller/(Instrumental) (July 1983) 49 04961
Say Say Say (Long Version)/(Instrumental)/Paul McCartney: Ode To A Koala Bear
   (October 1983) Columbia 44 04169
I Just Can't Stop Loving You/Todo Mi Amor Eres Tu (Spanish Version) (July 1987) EPSL
   69007
Bad (Extended Dance Mix With False Fade)/(7" Remix)/(7" Edit)/(Dub)/(A Cappella)
   (September 1987) 49 07462
The Way You Make Me Feel (4 Mixes) (November 1987) 49 07487
Dirty Diana/(Instrumental) (April 1988) 49 07583
Another Part Of Me (Extended Dance Mix)/(Radio Edit)/(Dub Mix)/(A Cappella) (July
   1988) 49 07855

Smooth Criminal (Extended Dance Mix)/(Extended Dance Mix Radio Edit)/('Annie' Mix)/(Dub Mix)/(A Cappella) (October 1988) 49 07895

Don't Stop 'Til You Get Enough/Wanna Be Startin' Somethin' (1989) 49H 06911

Beat It/Working Day And Night (1989) 49H 06971

Billie Jean/You Can't Win (Part 1) (1989) 49H 07549

Off The Wall/Thriller (1989) 49H 08144

Black Or White (Clivilles & Cole House/Club Mix)/(Clivilles & Cole House/Dub Mix)/(House With Guitar Radio Mix)/(Single Mix)/(Instrumental)/(Tribal Beats) (January 1992) 49 74099

Remember The Time (Silky Soul 12" Mix)/(E-Smoove's Late Nite Mix)/(Silky Soul Dub)/(12" Main Mix)/Black Or White (Underground Club Mix) (January 1992) 49 74201

In The Closet – Mixes Behind Door #1 (Club Mix)/(Underground Mix)/(Touch Me Dub)/(KI's 12") (April 1992) 49 74267

In The Closet – Mixes Behind Door #2 (The Mission)/(Freestyle Mix)/(Mix Of Life)/(Underground Dub) (April 1992) 49 74304

Jam (Roger's Club Mix)/(Atlanta Techo Mix)/(Teddy's Jam)/(Roger's Jeep Mix)/E-Smoove's Jazzy Jam)/Don't Stop 'Til You Get Enough (Roger's Underground Solution) (June 1992) 49 74334

Who Is It (Brothers In Rhythm House Mix)/(Tribal Version)/(Brothers In Rhythm Cool Dub)/(Lakeside Dub)/Beat It (Moby's Sub Mix) (March 1993) 49 74420

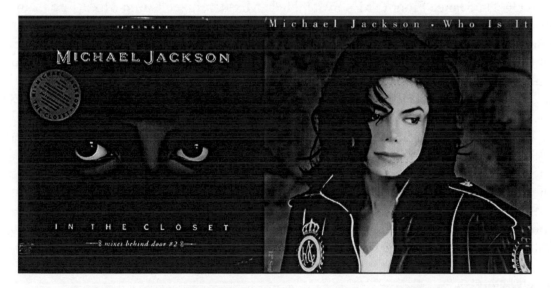

Scream (Classic Club Mix)/(Pressurized Dub Pt.1)/(Naughty Main Mix)/(Dave 'Jam' Hall's Extended Urban Remix)/(Single Edit #2)/Childhood (Theme from 'Free Willy 2') (May 1995) 49 78001

You Are Not Alone (Frankie Knuckles Franctified Club Mix)/(Album Version)/Michael Jackson Megaremix/Scream Louder (Flyte Tyme Remix) (August 1995) 49 78003

Earth Song (Hani's Around The World Experience)/(Hani's Club Experience)/(Album Version)/(Hani's Radio Experience) (November 1995) EAS 7605 – promo only with no p/s

This Time Around (D.M. Mad Club Mix)/(D.M. Radio Mix)/(Maurice's Club Around Mix)/(Georgie's House'n'Around Mix)/(The Timeland Dub)/(The Neverland Dub – Aftermath)/(The Don't Control This Dub)/(UBQ's Opera Vibe Dub)/(D.M. Bang Da Drums Mix) (November 1995) EAS 7603 – promo only double pack with no p/s

This Time Around (Dallas Main Extended Mix)/(Maurice's Hip Hop)/(Maurice's Hip Hop Around Mix w/o Rap)/(Dallas Main Mix)/(Dallas Main Mix w/o Rap)/(Album Instrumental) (November 1995) EAS 7606 – promo only with no p/s

This Time Around (Uno Clio 12" Master Mix)/(D.M. AM Mix)/(D.M. Mad Dub)/(Uno Clio Dub) (November 1995) EAS 7607 – promo only with no p/s

They Don't Care About Us (Single Version)/(Charles' Full Joint Mix)/(Dallas Main Mix)/(Love To Infinity's Walk In The Park Radio Mix)/(Love To Infinity's Classic Paradise Radio Mix)/(Track Masters Radio Edit)/Rock With You (Frankie's Favorite Club Mix)/Earth Song (Hani's Club Experience) (May 1996) 49K 78212

They Don't Care About Us (Love To Infinity's Classic Paradise Mix)/(Love To Infinity's Anthem Of Love Mix)/(Love To Infinity's Hacienda Mix)/This Time Around (D.M. Mad Club Mix) – They Don't Care About Us (Dallas Main Mix)/(Charles' Full Joint Mix)/(Track Masters Remix)/(A Cappella)/Earth Song (Hani's Club Experience)/Rock With You (Frankie's Favorite Club Mix) (May 1996) 49X 78212 – two 12" singles pack

Blood On The Dance Floor/(TM's Switchblade Mix)/(Refugee Camp Mix)/(Fire Island Vocal)/ Dangerous (Roger's Rough Dub) (April 1997) 49 78008

Stranger In Moscow (Tee's In House Club Mix)/(Hani's Num Club Mix)/(TNT Danger Dub)/(Basement Boys 12" Club Mix)/Blood On The Dance Floor (T&G Pool Of Blood Dub) (July 1997) 49 78013

Intro/You Rock My World (Album Version)/(Instrumental)(A Cappella) (September 2001) EAS 24918 – promo only with no p/s

You Rock My World (Masters At Work Remix Featuring Jay-Z) (November 2001) EAS 54911 – promo only with no p/s

Butterflies/Butterflies (November 2001) EAS 54863 – promo only with no p/s

Butterflies (I Like Mike Mixes) (December 2001) BOTU 001 – promo only orange vinyl with no p/s

Butterflies (Master Mix)/(Michael A Cappella)/((Eve A Cappella)/(Instrumental) (January 2002) EAS 56719 – promo only with no p/s

Cassette Singles

Bad (Dance Extended Mix With False Fade)/(7" Single Mix)/(Dance Remix Radio Edit)/(Dub Version)/(A Cappella) (September 1987) 4ET 07462

The Way You Make Me Feel (Dance Extended Mix)/(Dance Remix Radio Edit)/(Dub Version)/(A Cappella) (November 1987) 4ET 07487

Man In The Mirror/(Instrumental) (January 1988) 34T 07668

Get It/(Instrumental) (April 1988) Motown 4607

Dirty Diana/(Instrumental) (April 1988) 34T 07739

Another Part Of Me/(Instrumental) (July 1988) 34T 07962

Smooth Criminal/(Instrumental) (October 1988) 34T 08044

Black Or White/(Instrumental) (January 1992) 34T 74100

Remember The Time/Black Or White (Clivilles & Cole Radio Mix) (January 1992) 34T 74200

Remember The Time (Silky Soul)/(New Jack Main Mix)/(New Jack Jazz)/(E-Smoove's Late Nite Mix)Black Or White (The Clivilles & Cole Radio Mix)/(The Clivilles & Cole House/Club Mix)/(The Underground Club Mix) (January 1992) 49T 74201

In The Closet (Radio Edit)/(Club Edit)/(KI's 12")/(Freestyle Mix)/(The New Mark Mix) (April 1992) 49T 74267

Jam (Radio Mix)/Rock With You (Masters At Work Remix) (June 1992) 34T 74333

Jam (Roger's Jeep Mix)/(Teddy's Jam)/(Video Mix)/(More Than Enuff Mix)/Don't Stop 'Til You Get Enough (Roger's Underground Solution) (June 1992) 49T 74334

Heal The World/She Drives Me Wild (November 1992) 34T 74708

Heal The World/(7" Edit With Intro) (November 1992) 34T 74790 – with lyrics

Who Is It (7" Edit)/(The Oprah Winfrey Special Intro) (March 1993) 34T 74406

Who Is It (The Oprah Winfrey Special Intro)/(Patience Edit)/(The Brothers Patience Mix)/(Brothers In Rhythm House Mix)/Wanna Be Startin' Somethin' (Brothers In Rhythm House Mix) (March 1993) 49T 74420

Will You Be There (Radio Edit)/(Instrumental) (July 1993) 34T 77060

Gone Too Soon/(Instrumental) (November 1993) 34T 77312

Scream/Childhood (Theme From 'Free Willy 2') (May 1995) 34T 78001

Scream (Naughty Radio Edit With Rap)/(Dave 'Jam' Hall's Urban Remix Edit)/(D.M. R&B Radio Mix)/(Single Edit)/(Naughty Main Mix)/(Dave 'Jam' Hall's Extended Urban Remix)/(D.M. R&B Extended Mix)/Childhood (Theme From 'Free Willy 2') (May 1995) 49T 78001

You Are Not Alone (Album Edit)/Scream Louder (Flyte Tyme Remix) (August 1995) 34T 78002

You Are Not Alone (R Kelly Remix Edit)/(Classic Club Edit)/(Jon B Remix Edit)/Scream Louder (Flyte Tyme Remix)/You Are Not Alone (R Kelly Remix)/(Classic Club Mix)/(Jon B Remix) (August 1995) 49T 78003

They Don't Care About Us (Single Version)/(Charles Full Joint Mix – No Intro)/Rock With You (Frankie Knuckles Radio Mix)/Earth Song (Hani's Radio Experience) (May 1996) 34T 78264

Why (Radio Edit)/3T: Didn't Mean To Hurt You ('96) (August 1996) MJJ 36T 78366

Billie Jean (Remix)/Off The Wall (1997) 49 78582

Blood On The Dance Floor/(Refugee Camp Edit)/Dangerous (Roger's Dangerous Edit) (April 1997) 34T 78007

Stranger In Moscow (3 Mixes) (July 1997) 34T 78012

CD Singles

Beat It/Billie Jean (1987) 34K 06453

I Just Can't Stop Loving You/Baby Be Mine (July 1987) 34K 07253

The Way You Make Me Feel/(Instrumental) (November 1987) 34K 07645

Man In The Mirror/(Instrumental) (January 1988) 34K 07668

Dirty Diana/(Instrmental) (April 1988) 34K 07739

Another Part Of Me (Dance Mix)/(Dub Mix)/(A Cappella) (July 1988) 34K 07855

Thriller/(Instrumental) (1988) 49K 04961

Black Or White/(Instrumental) (November 1991) 34K 74100

Remember The Time (Silky Soul 7")/(New Jack Radio Mix)/(12" Main Mix)/(E-Smoove's Late Nite Mix)/(Maurice's Underground)/Black Or White (The Clivilles & Cole Radio Mix)/(House With Guitar Radio Mix)/(The Clivillies & Cole House/Club Mix)/ (Underground Club Mix) (January 1992) 49K 74201

In The Closet (Club Edit)/(Underground Mix)/(The Promise)/(The Vow)/Remember The Time (New Jack Jazz) (April 1992) 49K 74267

Jam (Roger's Jeep Radio Mix)/(Silky 7")/(Roger's Club Mix)/(Atlanta Techno Mix)/Rock With You (Masters At Work Remix) (June 1982) 49K 74334

Give In To Me (Edit)/(Instrumental) (1992) XPCD 258 – promo only

Who Is It (Oprah Winfrey Special Intro)/(Patience Edit)/(House 7")/(Brothers In Rhythm House Mix)/Beat It (Moby's Sub Mix) (March 1993) 49K 74420

Signature Series: Heal The World/Todo Mi Amor Eres Tu/Billie Jean (Four On The Floor Remix – Radio Edit)/Wanna Be Startin' Somethin' (Tommy D's Main Mix) (1993) ESK 5400 – promo only, included a message from Michael about his Heal The World Foundation; released cancelled – a maximum of 50 copies exist

Gone Too Soon (November 1993) ESK 5562 – promo only

Scream (Single Edit)/Childhood (Theme From 'Free Willy 2') (May 1995) 34K 78000

Scream (Single Edit #2)/(Def Radio Mix)/(Naughty Radio Edit With Rap)/(Dave 'Jam' Hall's Extended Urban Remix)/(Classic Club Mix)/Childhood (Theme From 'Free Willy 2') (May 1995) 49K 78001

You Are Not Alone (Radio Edit)/Scream Louder (Flyte Tyme Remix) (August 1995) 34K 78002

You Are Not Alone (Album Edit)/(Radio Edit)/(Frankie Knuckles Franctified Club Mix)/Scream Louder (Flyte Tyme Remix)/MJ Megaremix (August 1995) 49K 78003

Earth Song (Hani's Radio Experience)/(Radio Edit)/(Album Version) (November 1995) ESK 7605 – promo only with no p/s

This Time Around (Dallas Clean Album Remix)/(David Mitson Clean Album Mix)/(Dallas Radio Mix)/(Dallas Radio Mix W/out Rap)/(Maurice's Hip Hop Around Mix W/drop)/ (Maurice's Hip Hop Around Mix W/out Rap)/(Maurice's Club Around Radio Mix)/ (D.M. Radio Mix)/Earth Song (Radio Edit)/(Album Version)/(Hani's Radio Experience) (November 1995) ESK 7521 – promo only with no p/s

They Don't Care About Us (Single Version)/Rock With You (Frankie Knuckles' Radio Mix)/Earth Song (Hani's Radio Experience)/Wanna Be Startin' Somethin' (Brothers In Rhythm Mix) (May 1996) 34K 78264

They Don't Care About Us (Single Version)/(Charles' Full Joint Mix)/(Dallas Main Mix)/(Love To Infinity's Walk In The Park Radio Mix)/(Love To Infinity's Classic Paradise Radio Mix)/(Track Masters Radio Edit)/Rock With You (Frankie's Favorite Club Mix)/Earth Song (Hani's Club Experience) (May 1996) 49K 78212

Why (Radio Edit)/3T: Didn't Mean To Hurt You ('96) (August 1996) 36K 78366

Blood On The Dance Floor/(TM's Switchblade Edit)/(Refugee Camp Edit)/Dangerous (Roger's Dangerous Edit) (April 1997) 34K 78007

Blood On The Dance Floor (7" Mix)/(TM's Switchblade Edit)/(Refugee Camp Edit)/(Fire Island Radio Edit)/(TM's Switchblade Mix)/Dangerous (Roger's Dangerous Club Mix) (April 1997) 49K 78008

Stranger In Moscow (Tee's Radio Mix)/(Charles Roane's Full R&B Mix)/(Hani's Num Radio Mix)/Off The Wall (Junior Vasquez Remix) (July 1997) 34K 78012

Stranger In Moscow (Tee's Radio Mix)/(Charles Roane's Full R&B Mix)/(Hani's Num Radio Mix)/(Tee's In-House Club Mix)/(Basement Boys 12" Club Mix)/(Hani's Extended Chill Hop Mix)/Off The Wall (Junior Vasquez Remix) (July 1997) 49K 78013

Intro/You Rock My World (Album Version)/(Radio Edit) (September 2001) ESK 24918 – promo only

Butterflies (November 2001) ESK 54863 – promo only with no p/s

Thriller (Single Version)/Can't Get Outta The Rain (October 2007) 18009 2 – 'ringle' with bonus ringtone and wallpaper; quickly withdrawn from sale as found to be defective

Wanna Be Startin' Somethin' 2008 (January 2008) – promo only with no p/s

Wanna Be Startin' Somethin' 2008 – Johnny Vicious Remixes (Radio Mix)/(Club Remix)/(Warehouse Thrilla Dub)/(Radio Edit) (January 2008) – promo only with no p/s

PART 9: UK DISCOGRAPHY

This discography includes known promo/test pressings of singles which, for whatever reason, were never released commercially in any format. All 7"/12" singles before 1980 were issued without a picture sleeve (p/s), and all singles from 1980 onwards with a p/s, unless otherwise stated. Significant re-issues only are listed.

THE JACKSON 5

All releases on (Tamla) Motown / Universal unless stated.

Albums

DIANA ROSS PRESENTS THE JACKSON 5 (March 1970) STML 11142
ABC (August 1970) STML 11156
CHRISTMAS ALBUM (December 1970) STML 11168; CD: Spectrum 550 141-2
THIRD ALBUM (February 1971) STML 11174; CD: 530 160-2
MAYBE TOMORROW (October 1971) STML 11188; CD: 530 163-2
GREATEST HITS (August 1972) STML 11212; WL 72087 – re-issue (1984); CD: WD 72087
LOOKIN THROUGH THE WINDOWS (October 1972) STML 11214
SKYWRITER (July 1973) STML 11231; CD: 530 209-2
GET IT TOGETHER (November 1973) STML 11243
DANCING MACHINE (November 1974) STML 11275
MOVING VIOLATION (July 1975) STML 11290; CD: 530 446-2
JOYFUL JUKEBOX MUSIC (December 1976) STML 12046
ANTHOLOGY (January 1977) TMSP 6004
MOTOWN SPECIAL (March 1977) STMX 6006
ZIP-A-DEE DOO-DAH (January 1979) Music for Pleasure MfP 50418
20 GOLDEN GREATS (September 1979) STML 12121
THE JACKSON 5 FEATURING MICHAEL JACKSON (June 1982) Pickwick 3503
COMPACT COMMAND PERFORMANCES – 18 GREATEST HITS (May 1984) CD: WD 72420
THE GREAT LOVE SONGS OF (November 1984) WL 72290; CD: WD 72290
DIANA ROSS PRESENTS/ABC (November 1986) CD: ZD 72483
ANTHOLOGY (June 1987) 2CD: WD 72529
LIVE! (September 1988) WL 72641; CD: WD 72641
BEGINNING YEARS 1965-1967 (February 1990) Ichiban/SDEG CD: SDECD 4018
CHILDREN OF THE LIGHT (May 1993) CD: Spectrum 550076-2; re-issued (October 2000) with different sleeve
AN AMERICAN DREAM (July 1993) CD: 530119-2

THE JACKSON FIVE FEATURING MICHAEL JACKSON (September 1993) CD:
Stardust STACD 081
SOULSATION! (July 1995) 4CD Box Set: 530489-2
THIRD ALBUM/MAYBE TOMORROW/SKYWRITER (November 1995) 3CD Box Set:
530438-2
EARLY CLASSICS (July 1996) CD: Spectrum 552224-2
THE BEST OF (& Michael) (July 1997) CD: PolyGram TV 530804-2
THE LEGEND BEGINS (August 1997) CD: Hallmark 306572
THE ULTIMATE COLLECTION (August 1998) CD: 530558-2
STEELTOWN SESSIONS 1965-1967 (December 1998) CD: Alfafame ALMACD 2
WE ARE THE JACKSON 5 (August 1999) CD: Hallmark 31123
'RIPPLES AND WAVES' AN INTRODUCTION TO THE JACKSON FIVE (July 2000)
157170-2
CHILDREN OF THE LIGHT/EARLY CLASSICS/MUSIC AND ME (Michael)
(November 2001) 3CD Box Set: Spectrum 544696-2
GOLD (September 2005) 2CD: 9880152

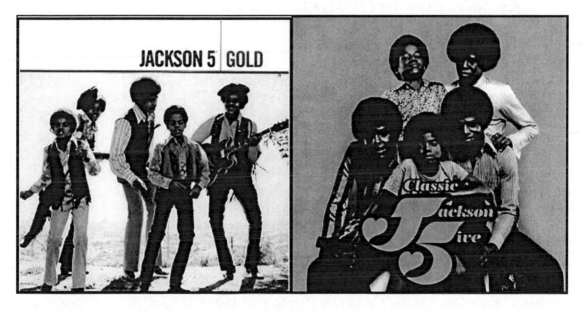

THE JACKSONS STORY (May 2006) 2CD: 9832422
SOUL LEGENDS (August 2006) CD: 9841753
THE SILVER COLLECTION (& Michael) (June 2007) CD: Spectrum 9846942
THE VERY BEST OF (& Michael) (September 2007) CD: 98489970
THE MOTOWN YEARS (& Michael) (September 2008) 3CD: UMTV 5311546
BOYS & GIRLS – THE ORIGINAL SESSIONS (November 2008)Entertain Me
5060133744757
CLASSIC (December 2008) CD: Spectrum 5314941
ICONS (May 2009) Spectrum 5316475

Albums With A Connection

DIANA! (October 1971) STMA 8001 – includes two live medleys Mama's Pearl/Walk On/The Love You Save and I'll Be There/Feelin' Alright (with Diana Ross)

THE MOTOWN STORY (March 1972) TMSP 1130 – includes I Want You Back, with 22 second introduction by Michael

SAVE THE CHILDREN (July 1974) TMSP 1133 – includes a live version of Michael's I Wanna Be Where You Are performed by the Jackson 5

A MOTOWN CHRISTMAS (November 1976) STML 12037 – includes Frosty The Snowman/Santa Claus Is Comin' To Town/Up On The House Top/Christmas Won't Be The Same This Year

MOTOWN SUPERSTARS SING MOTOWN SUPERSTARS (August 1983) STMS 5100 – includes the previously unreleased Ask The Lonely, recorded in 1970

Home Video

THE JACKSONS IN CONCERT (1981) VCL V1588

Singles Box Set With A Connection

The Motown 20th Anniversary Singles Box Set (October 1980) SPTMG 2 – box set of 15 Motown singles including TMG 963, 969 & 973

7" Singles

I Want You Back/Who's Lovin' You (January 1970) TMG 724
ABC/The Young Folks (May 1970) TMG 738
The Love You Save/I Found That Girl (July 1970) TMG 746
I'll Be There/One More Chance (November 1970) TMG 758
Mama's Pearl/Darling Dear (April 1971) TMG 769
Never Can Say Goodbye/She's Good (July 1971) TMG 778
Sugar Daddy/I'm So Happy (March 1972) TMG 809
Little Bitty Pretty One/Maybe Tomorrow (September 1972) TMG 825
Lookin' Through The Windows/Love Song (October 1972) TMG 833 – with p/s
Santa Claus Is Comin' To Town/Someday At Christmas/Christmas Won't Be The Same This Year (December 1972) TMG 837
Doctor My Eyes/My Little Baby (February 1973) TMG 842
Hallelujah Day/To Know (May 1973) TMG 856
Skywriter/Ain't Nothin' Like The Real Thing (August 1973) TMG 865 – with p/s
Get It Together/Touch (November 1973) TMG 878
The Boogie Man/Don't Let Your Baby Catch You (April 1974) TMG 895
Dancing Machine/It's Too Late To Change The Time (June 1974) TMG 904
The Life Of The Party/Whatever You Got, I Want (November 1974) TMG 927

I Am Love (Part 1)/(Part 2) (March 1975) TMG 942
Forever Came Today/I Can't Quit Your Love (September 1975) TMG 1001
Jukebox Gems: Skywriter/I Want You Back/The Love You Save (August 1977) TMG
    1081 – with p/s
I Want You Back/The Love You Save (October 1980) TMG 963 – no p/s
I'll Be There/ABC (October 1980) TMG 969 – no p/s
Lookin' Through The Windows/Doctor My Eyes (October 1980) TMG 975 – no p/s
I Saw Mommy Kissing Santa Claus/Frosty The Snowman/Santa Claus Is Comin' To
    Town/Up On The Housetop (November 1987) ZB 41655
I Want You Back ('88 Remix)/Never Can Say Goodbye (April 1988) ZB 41913
ABC/The Love You Save (May 1988) ZB 41941 – no p/s

Cassette Singles

Motown Flip Hits EP: I Want You Back/I'll Be There/Lookin' Through The
    Windows/ABC (July 1983) CTME 2034

12" Singles

I Saw Mommy Kissing Santa Claus/Frosty The Snowman/Santa Claus Is Comin' To
    Town/Up On The Housetop (November 1987) ZT 41656
I Want You Back ('88 Remix)/(Original Mix)/(Dub Mix)/Never Can Say Goodbye (April
    1988) ZT 41914

CD Singles

Vintage Gold EP: I Want You Back/ABC/I'll Be There/Little Bitty Pretty One (June 1989)
    ZD 41949
Boyz II Men: In The Still Of The Nite (I'll Remember)/Snippets From 'The Jacksons: An
    American Dream' [Who's Lovin' You (live)/Kansas City/I'll Be There/I Wanna Be
    Where You Arc/Dancing Machine (Remix)]/The Jackson 5 Medley [I Want You Back
    (live)/ABC (live)] (February 1993) TMGCD 1415

MICHAEL JACKSON – The Motown Era

All releases on (Tamla) Motown unless stated.

Albums

GOT TO BE THERE (May 1972) STML 11205; CD: WD 72068
BEN (December 1972) STML 11220; CD: WD 72069
MUSIC & ME (July 1973) STML 11235

FOREVER, MICHAEL (March 1975) STMA 8022; CD: WD 72121

THE BEST OF (September 1975) STML 12005; CD: WD 72063

ONE DAY IN YOUR LIFE (July 1981) STML 12158

AIN'T NO SUNSHINE (June 1982) Pickwick TMS 3511

18 GREATEST HITS (July 1983) Telstar STAR 2232; CD: TCD 2232; WD 72629 – re-issue (1988)

FAREWELL MY SUMMER LOVE (June 1984) ZL 72227; WL 72630 – re-issue (1988) with different sleeve; CD: ZD 72630

THE GREAT LOVE SONGS OF (November 1984) WL 72289; CD: WD 72289

LOOKING BACK TO YESTERDAY (May 1986) WL 72424; CD: WD 72424

GOT TO BE THERE/BEN (November 1986) CD: ZD 72468

ANTHOLOGY (April 1987) 2CD: ZD 72530

LOVE SONGS (& Diana Ross) (October 1987) Telstar STAR 2298; CD: TCD 2298

THE MICHAEL JACKSON MIX (December 1987) Stylus SMR 745; CD: SMD 745

THE ORIGINAL SOUL OF (February 1988) ZL 72622; CD: ZD 72622

MOTOWN'S GREATEST HITS (February 1992) 5300141; CD: 530014-2

MUSIC AND ME (May 1993) CD: Spectrum 550078-2; re-issued (October 2000) with different sleeve

BEN/FOREVER, MICHAEL/MUSIC & ME (November 1995) 3CD Box Set: Spectrum 530439-2

THE BEST OF (& Jackson 5ive) (July 1997) CD: Polygram TV 530804-2

THE UNIVERSAL MASTER COLLECTION (May 2001) Spectrum 134912; reissued as CLASSIC (December 2008) CD: Spectrum 5314948

CHILDREN OF THE LIGHT (Jackson 5)/EARLY CLASSICS (with the Jackson 5)/
  MUSIC AND ME (November 2001) 3CD Box Set: Spectrum 544696-2
LOVE SONGS (January 2002) CD: 440 016 819-2
THE SILVER COLLECTION (& Jackson 5) (June 2007) CD: Spectrum 9846942
THE VERY BEST OF (& Jackson 5) (September 2007) CD: 98489970

THE ESSENTIAL COLLECTION (2008) CD: Spectrum WITUN107
THE MOTOWN YEARS (& Jackson 5) (September 2008) 3CD: UMTV 5311546
GOLD (July 2009) 2CD: 1773967
THE MOTOWN 50 MIXES (July 2009) CD: I2714978
HELLO WORLD: THE MOTOWN SOLO COLLECTION (August 2009) 3CD box-set:
  1792469

Albums With A Connection

A MOTOWN CHRISTMAS (November 1976) STML 12037 – includes the previously
   unreleased Little Christmas Tree
A MOTOWN CHRISTMAS CAROL (October 1995) CD: 530433-2 – includes Christmas
   greetings from several Motown artists including Michael
MOTOWN CELEBRATES SINATRA (October 1998) CD: 530975-2 – includes
   Michael's version of All The Things You Are, and features a still of Michael taken from
   the 1971 TV special Diana! on the sleeve

7" Singles

Got To Be There/Maria (You Were The Only One) (January 1972) TMG 797
Rockin' Robin/Love Is Here And Now You're Gone (May 1972) TMG 816
Ain't No Sunshine/I Wanna Be Where You Are (July 1972) TMG 826
Ben/You Can Cry On My Shoulder (November 1972) TMG 834
Morning Glow/My Girl (July 1973) TMG 863
Music And Me/Johnny Raven (May 1974) TMG 900
One Day In Your Life/With A Child's Heart (April 1975) TMG 946
Just A Little Bit Of You/Dear Michael (October 1975) TMG 1006
Ben/Marvin Gaye: Abraham, Martin And John (April 1980) TMG 1165
Got To Be There/Marv Johnson: I Miss You Baby (October 1980) TMG 973 – no p/s
One Day In Your Life/Take Me Back (April 1981) TMG 976 – no p/s
We're Almost There/We've Got A Good Thing Going (July 1981) TMG 997
Happy (Love Theme From 'Lady Sings The Blues')/We're Almost There (July 1983)
   TMG 986 – some with poster sleeve; TMGP 986 – picture disc
Farewell My Summer Love/Call On Me (May 1984) TMG 1342
Girl You're So Together/Touch The One You Love (August 1984) TMG 1355
Got To Be There/Rockin' Robin (April 1985) TMG 994 – no p/s

12" Singles

We're Almost There/We've Got A Good Thing Going (July 1981) TMGT 997
Happy (Love Theme From 'Lady Sings The Blues')/We're Almost There (July 1983)
   TMGT 986 – no p/s
Farewell My Summer Love (Extended Version)/Call On Me (May 1984) TMGT 1342
Girl You're So Together/Touch The One You Love/Ben/Ain't No Sunshine (August 1984)
   TMGT 1355
Got To Be There/Rockin' Robin (April 1985) TMGT 994 – no p/s

Cassette Singles

Motown Flip Hits EP: One Day In Your Life/Got To Be There/Ben/Ain't No Sunshine (July 1983) CTE 2035

CD Singles

Vintage Gold EP: Got To Be There/Rockin' Robin/1 Wanna Be Where You Are/Just A Little Bit Of You (June 1989) ZD 41951

THE JACKSONS

All releases on CBS/Epic or Sony unless stated.

Albums

THE JACKSONS (November 1976) EPC 86009; CD: CDEPC 32101
GOIN' PLACES (October 1977) EPC 86035; CD 46583 2
DESTINY (December 1978) EPC 83200; CD: CDEPC 32365; 88697308692 (September 2008) – with two bonus tracks
TRIUMPH (October 1980) EPC 86112; CD: CDEPC 86112; 88697335582 (September 2008) – with three bous tracks
LIVE (November 1981) EPC 88562; CD: CDEPC 88562
VICTORY (July 1984) EPC 86303; CD: CDEPC 450450 2; EPC 86303 – picture disc
2300 JACKSON STREET (June 1989) EPC 463352 1; CD: EPC 463352 2
DESTINY/TRIUMPH/VICTORY (October 1996) 3CD Box Set: 485319 2
THE VERY BEST OF (June 2004) 2CD: 5163669

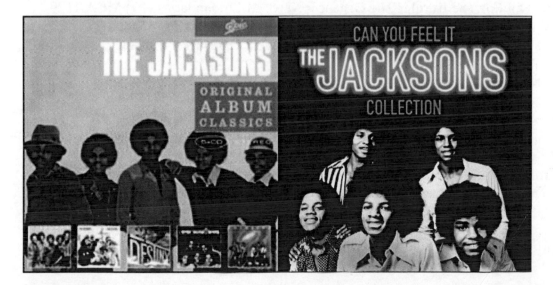

ORIGINAL ALBUM CLASSICS (June 2008) 5CD Box Set comprising THE JACKSONS, GOIN' PLACES, DESTINY, TRIUMPH & VICTORY – 88697304722
CAN YOU FEEL IT COLLECTION (March 2009) CD: 88697473382

7" Singles

Enjoy Yourself/Style Of Life (October 1976) EPC 4708

Enjoy Yourself/Style Of Life (March 1977) EPC 5063
Show You The Way To Go/Blues Away (May 1977) EPC 5266
Dreamer/Good Times (July 1977) EPC 5458
Goin' Places/Do What You Wanna (October 1977) EPC 5732
Even Though You're Gone/Different Kind Of Lady (January 1978) EPC 5919
Music's Taking Over/Man Of War (March 1978) EPC 6263
Blame It On The Boogie/Do What You Wanna (September 1978) EPC 6683
Destiny/That's What You Get (For Being Polite) (December 1978) EPC 6983
Shake Your Body (Down To The Ground)/All Night Dancin' (March 1979) EPC 7181
Lovely One/Things I Do For You (October 1980) EPC 9302 – no p/s
Heartbreak Hotel/Different Kind Of Lady (December 1980) EPC 9391
Can You Feel It/Wonderin' Who (February 1981) EPC 9554 – no p/s
Walk Right Now/Your Ways (June 1981) EPC A1294; EPC A11 1294 – picture disc
Time Waits For No One/Give It Up (September 1981) EPC A1579 – no p/s
Things I Do For You (live)/Don't Stop 'Til You Get Enough (live) (November 1981) EPC A1902 – some with promo p/s
State Of Shock/Your Ways (June 1984) EPC A4431; WA 4431 – picture disc
Show You The Way To Go/Blame It On The Boogie (July 1984) A4582 – no p/s
Torture/(Instrumental) (August 1984) A4675
Body/(Instrumental) (November 1984) A4883
Wait/She's Out Of My Life (live) (February 1985) A6105
Time Out For The Burglar/The Distance: News At 11 (January 1987) MCA 1129
Nothin (That Compares 2 U)/Alright With Me (May 1989) EPC 654808 7
2300 Jackson Street/When I Look At You (August 1989) EPC 655206 7

12" Singles

Enjoy Yourself/Style Of Life (March 1977) EPC 12-5063 – with p/s
Blame It On The Boogie (Album Version)/Do What You Wanna (September 1978) EPC 12-6683
Destiny (Album Version)/Blame It On The Boogie (Special 7 Minute Extended Disco Remix)/That's What You Get (For Being Polite) (December 1978) EPC 12-6983 – with p/s
Shake Your Body (Down To The Ground) (Special Disco Remix)/All Night Dancin' (March 1979) EPC 12-7181 – with p/s

Can You Feel It (Album Version)/Wonderin' Who/Shake Your Body (Down To The Ground) (February 1981) EPC 12-9554 – no p/s

Walk Right Now (Album Version)/Your Ways (June 1981) EPC A12-1294 – no p/s

State Of Shock (Dance Mix)/(Instrumental)/Your Ways (June 1984) EPC TA4431

Torture/(Instrumental)/Show You The Way To Go/Blame It On The Boogie (August 1984) TA4675

Torture (New Mix)/(Instrumental) (August 1984) QTA4675 – with wrap around tour poster

Body (Extended Remix)/(Instrumental) (November 1984) TA4883

Wait/She's Out Of My Life (live) (February 1985) TA6105

Time Out For The Burglar/The Distance: News At 11 (January 1987) MCA S1129

Nothin (That Compares 2 U) (The Mix)/(Choice Dub)/(Sensitive Vocal Mix) (May 1989) 654808 1

Nothin (That Compares 2 U) (Extended Version)/(Bass World Dub)/Heartbreak Hotel (May 1989) 654909 8

2300 Jackson Street/When I Look At You/Keep Her (August 1989) 655206 6

2300 Jackson Street/When I Look At You/Please Come Back To Me (August 1989) 655206 8

Shake Your Body (Down To The Ground)/Blame It On The Boogie (1990) Old Gold OG 4142 – no p/s

Can You Feel It/Walk Right Now (September 1990) Old Gold OG 4192 – no p/s

Cassette Singles

Greatest Original Hits EP: Can You Feel It/Shake Your Body (Down To The Ground)/Show You The Way To Go/Blame It On The Boogie (August 1981) EPC A40 2627

Nothin (That Compares 2 U) (Edit)/Alright With Me (May 1989) 654808 4

2300 Jackson Street/When I Look At You (August 1989) 655206 4

CD Singles

Solid Gold EP: Show You The Way To Go/Blame It On The Boogie/Can You Feel It (May 1989) 654570 3

Nothin (That Compares 2 U)/(The Mix)/(Extended) (May 1989) 654808 2

Art Of Madness/Keep Her (Larrabee Mix) (July 1989) 654844 1

2300 Jackson Street (Album Version)/Keep Her/When I Look At You (August 1989) 655206 2

MICHAEL JACKSON – The Epic Era

All releases on CBS/Epic or Sony unless otherwise stated.

Albums & Box Sets

OFF THE WALL (August 1979) EPC 83468; CD: CDEPC 83468; 481578 2 – Essential Album Collection CD re-issue (1995) in red box

THRILLER (December 1982) EPC 85930; CD: CDEPC 85930; EPC 11 85930 – picture disc; MILLEN4 – Millennium Limited Edition (2000) in digipack

E.T. THE EXTRA-TERRESTRIAL (January 1983) MCA 70000

THEIR VERY BEST – BACK TO BACK (& Diana Ross, Gladys Knight, Stevie Wonder) (November 1986) PrioriTyV PTVR 2

BAD (September 1987) EPC 450290 1; CD: EPC 450290 2; 450290 8 – cassette gift pack; 450290 0 – picture disc; 450290 9 – picture disc CD

DANGEROUS (November 1991) 465802 1; CD: 465802 2; 465802 9 – CD gold disc with 10x10" pop-up 'Collectors Edition First Printing'

OFF THE WALL/DANGEROUS (February 1993) 2CD Set: 465802 2D

HISTORY PAST, PRESENT AND FUTURE BOOK 1 (June 1995) EPC 474709 4; 2CD: EPC 474709 2

BLOOD ON THE DANCE FLOOR – HISTORY IN THE MIX (May 1997) 487500 1; CD: 487500 2

GHOSTS (December 1997) EPC 489155 2 – limited edition box set including Ghosts home video, BLOOD ON THE DANCE FLOOR album on CD, exclusive minimax CD single and Ghosts premiere programme

OFF THE WALL (SPECIAL EDITION) (October 2001) CD: EPC 504421 2

THRILLER (SPECIAL EDITION) (October 2001) CD: EPC 504422 2

BAD (SPECIAL EDITION) (October 2001) CD: EPC 504423 2

DANGEROUS (SPECIAL EDITION) (October 2001) CD: 504424 2

INVINCIBLE (October 2001) CD: 495174 2

GREATEST HITS HISTORY VOLUME 1 (November 2001) CD: 501869 2

NUMBER ONES (November 2003) CD: 513800 0

THE ULTIMATE COLLECTION (November 2004) 4CD/DVD ESK 92600

OFF THE WALL/THRILLER (November 2004) 2CD Set: 517554 2

BAD/DANGEROUS (November 2004) 2CD Set: 517555 2

THE ESSENTIAL (July 2005) 2CD: 520422 2

BLOOD ON THE DANCE FLOOR/INVINCIBLE (March 2006) 2CD Set: 8287682494 2

THRILLER 25 (February 2008) 2LP: 88697233441 – limited edition 2,000 copies; CD (standard sleeve): 88697179862; CD (zombie sleeve): 88697179872; deluxe CD (gatefold zombie sleeve): 88697220962 – CD versions with bonus DVD

KING OF POP (August 2008) CD: 88697356512; (September 2008) 3CD: 88697356532 – deluxe edition

THE COLLECTION (July 2009) 5CD box-set (OFF THE WALL/THRILLER/BAD/ DANGEROUS/INVINCIBLE): 88697536212

Original Soundtrack Album

THE WIZ (Original Motion Picture Soundtrack) (October 1978) MCA MCSP 287

Home Videos & DVDs

MAKING MICHAEL JACKSON'S THRILLER (March 1984) Vestron MA 11000
THE LEGEND CONTINUES… (June 1988) Video Collection MJ 1000
MOONWALKER (April 1990) Guild Home Video GH 8580
DANGEROUS – THE SHORT FILMS (December 1993) SMV 49164 2
VIDEO GREATEST HITS – *HIS*TORY (June 1995) SMV 50123 2
*HIS*TORY ON FILM VOLUME II (May 1997) SMV 50138 2
GHOSTS (February 1998) SMV 200788 2
NUMBER ONES (November 2003) EVD 202250 9
THE ONE (March 2004) EPC 202019 9
LIVE IN BUCHAREST: THE DANGEROUS TOUR (July 2005) EPC 204003 9
HISTORY I + II (August 2008) 2DVD: 88697360639

Singles Packs

9 Singles Pack (November 1983) MJ 1 – nine red vinyl singles with p/s
Souvenir Singles Pack (July 1988) MJ 5 – five square (uncut) picture discs
Tour Souvenir Pack (August 1992) MJ 4 – four picture disc CD singles

7" Singles

Ease On Down The Road/The Wiz: Poppy Girls (October 1978) MCA 396
You Can't Win (Part 1)/(Part 2) (May 1979) EPC 7135; S EPC 12-7135 – picture disc
Don't Stop 'Til You Get Enough/I Can't Help It (August 1979) EPC 7763
Off The Wall/Working Day And Night (November 1979) EPC 8045
Rock With You/Get On The Floor (February 1980) EPC 8206 – no p/s
She's Out Of My Life/Jacksons: Push Me Away (April 1980) EPC 8384
Girlfriend/Jacksons: Bless His Soul (July 1980) EPC 8782 – no p/s
Off The Wall/Don't Stop 'Til You Get Enough (April 1982) EPC 8856 – no p/s
Greatest Original Hits EP: Don't Stop 'Til You Get Enough/Rock With You/She's Out Of My Life/Off The Wall (November 1982) EPC A2906

The Girl Is Mine/Can't Get Outta The Rain (November 1982) EPC A2729; EPC A11 2729
– picture disc

Billie Jean/It's The Falling In Love (January 1983) EPC A3084

Beat It/Burn This Disc Out (March 1983) EPC A3258

Wanna Be Startin' Somethin'/Jacksons: Rock With You (live) (June 1983) A3427

Say Say Say/Paul McCartney: Ode To A Koala Bear (October 1983) Parlophone R6062

Thriller/Jacksons: Things I Do For You (live) (November 1983) A3643 – limited edition
with calendar poster bag

The Man (& Paul McCartney) (December 1983) Parlophone R-6606 – promo only with
no p/s

P.Y.T. (Pretty Young Thing)/Jacksons: This Place Hotel (live) (March 1984) A4136

Ease On Down The Road/The Wiz: Poppy Girls (May 1984) MCA 898

Tell Me I'm Not Dreaming (Too Good To Be True) (& Jermaine Jackson)/Jermaine
Jackson: Come To Me (One Way Or Another)/Oh Mother (1984) Arista JMJDJ 1 –
promo only with no p/s

I Just Can't Stop Loving You/Baby Be Mine (July 1987) 650202 7; 650202 0 – with
poster sleeve

Bad/(Dance Remix Radio Edit) (September 1987) 651155 7

The Way You Make Me Feel/(Instrumental) (November 1987) 651275 7 – some with
competition leaflet

Man In The Mirror (Single Mix)/(Instrumental) (February 1988) 651388 7; 651388 9 –
square picture disc

Get It/(Instrumental) (May 1988) Motown ZB 41883

Dirty Diana/(Instrumental) (July 1988) 651546 0; 651546 7 – with cardboard figure of
Michael

Another Part Of Me/(Instrumental) (September 1988) 652844 7; 652844 0 – with poster
sleeve; 652844 9 – with Bad Tour backstage pass

Smooth Criminal/(Instrumental) (November 1988) 653026 7; 653026 0 – with four souvenir postcards

Leave Me Alone/Human Nature (February 1989) 654672 7; 654672 0 – with pop-up sleeve

Liberian Girl/Girlfriend (July 1989) 654947 0; 654947 9 – with star mobile pack

Black Or White/(Instrumental) (November 1991) 657598 7

Remember The Time/Come Together (February 1992) 657774 7

In The Closet (7" Edit)/(The Mission Radio Edit) (April 1992) 658018 7 – with poster sleeve

Who Is It (Edit)/Rock With You (Masters At Work Remix) (July 1992) 658179 7 – limited number with die-cut portrait stand

Jam (7" Edit)/Beat It (Moby's Sub Mix) (September 1992) 658360 7 – with two prints

Heal The World (7" Edit)/She Drives Me Wild (November 1992) 658488 7 – with poster sleeve

Give In To Me/Dirty Diana (February 1993) 659069 7 – with poster sleeve

Will You Be There (Edit)/Girlfriend (May 1993) 659222 7 – with poster sleeve

Gone Too Soon/(Instrumental) (November 1993) 659976 7

Scream (Def Radio Mix)/(Single Edit) (June 1995) 662127 7 – with poster sleeve

12" Singles

Ease On Down The Road (US Version)/The Wiz: Poppy Girls (October 1978) MCA 12 396

You Can't Win (Part 1)/(Part 2) (May 1979) 12EPC 7135

Don't Stop 'Til You Get Enough (Extended)/I Can't Help It (August 1979) 12EPC 7763

Rock With You/Get On The Floor/You Can't Win (Extended) (February 1980) 12EPC 8206 – no p/s

Billie Jean (Extended Remix)/(Instrumental)/It's The Falling In Love (January 1983) A13 3084

Beat It/Burn This Disco Out/Jacksons: Don't Stop 'Til You Get Enough (live) (March 1983) TA3258

Wanna Be Startin' Somethin'/(Instrumental)/Jacksons: Rock With You (live) (June 1983) TA3427

Say Say Say (Jellybean Remix)/(Instrumental)/Paul McCartney: Ode To A Koala Bear (October 1983) Parlophone 12 R6062

Thriller (Remix 7")/(Album Version)/Jacksons: Things I Do For You (live) (November 1983) EPC TA3643 – some with different picture sleeve & calendar

P.Y.T. (Pretty Young Thing)/Thriller (Instrumental)/Jacksons: This Place Hotel (live) (March 1984) EPC TA4136

Ease On Down The Road/The Wiz: Poppy Girls (May 1984) MCA MCAT 898

I Just Can't Stop Loving You/Baby Be Mine (July 1987) 650202 6 – with poster

Bad (Extended Dance Mix With False Fade)/(Dub Mix)/(A Cappella) (September 1987) 651155 6

Bad (Dance Extended Mix With False Fade)/(7" Mix)/(Dance Radio Edit)/(Dub)/(A Cappella) (September 1987) 651100 6 – red vinyl

The Way You Make Me Feel (7" Mix)/(A Cappella)/(Dance Radio Edit)/(Dub – Get Into The Groove) (November 1987) 651275 3 – double groove vinyl

The Way You Make Me Feel (Extended Mix)/(Dub)/(A Cappella) (November 1987) 651275 8

Man In The Mirror (Single Mix)/(Album Mix) (February 1988) 651388 6

Get It (Extended Mix)/(Instrumental) (May 1988) Motown ZT 41884

Dirty Diana/(Instrumental)/Bad (Extended Dance Mix With False Fade) (July 1988) 651546 8; 652864 6 – with wrap-around tour poster

Another Part Of Me (Extended Mix)/(Radio Edit)/(Dub)/(A Cappella) (September 1988) 652844 6

Smooth Criminal (Extended Dance Mix)/(Dub)/(A Cappella) (November 1988) 653026 8; 653170 6 – with Moonwalker advent calendar

Smooth Criminal (Extended Dance Mix)/('Annie' Mix)/(Radio Edit) (November 1988) 653026 1

Leave Me Alone/Don't Stop 'Til You Get Enough/Human Nature (February 1989) 654672 6

Liberian Girl/Get On The Floor/Girlfriend (July 1989) 654947 8

Liberian Girl/Girlfriend/You Can't Win (Extended Mix) (July 1989) 654947 1

Black Or White/Bad/Black Or White (Instrumental)/Thriller (November 1991) 657598 6

Black Or White (Clivilles & Cole House/Club Mix)/(Clivilles & Cole House/Dub Mix)/(Underground Club Mix)/(House With Guitar Radio Mix)/(Tribal Beats) (January 1992) 657731 6

Remember The Time (12" Main Mix)/(New Jack Mix)/(Silky Soul 12" Mix)/(Silky Soul Dub)/(E-Smoove's Late Nite Mix) (February 1992) 657774 6

In The Closet (The Mission)/(Freestyle Mix)/(Mix Of Life)/(Underground Dub) (April 1992) 658018 6

Who Is It (Patience Mix)/(Most Patient Mix)/(IHS Mix)/(P-Man Dub) (July 1992) 658179 6

Jam (Roger's Club Mix)/(More Than Enuff Mix)/(E-Smoove's Jazzy Jam)/(Teddy's 12" Mix)/(Roger's Underground Mix)/(Silky 12") (September 1992) 658360 6

Heal The World/Wanna Be Startin' Somethin' (Brothers In Rhythm House Mix)/Don't Stop 'Til You Get Enough (Roger's Underground Solution)/Rock With You (Masters At Work Remix) (November 1992) EPC 658488 8 – with poster

Gone Too Soon/Human Nature/She's Out Of My Life/Thriller (December 1993) 659976 6

Scream (Classic Club Mix)/(D.M. R&B Extended Mix)/(Def Radio Mix)/(Naughty Main Mix)/(Naughty Main Mix No Rap)/(Dave 'Jam' Hall's Extended Urban Remix) (June 1995) 662127 6

Scream (Pressurized Dub Pt.1)/(Pressurized Dub Pt.2)/(Album Version)/(Single Edit #2)/(Naughty Pretty-Pella)/(Naughty A Cappella) (June 1995) 662127 8

Blood On The Dance Floor (TM's O-Positive Dub)/(Fire Island Dub)/Dangerous (Roger's Dangerous Club Mix)/(Roger's Rough Dub) (May 1997) 664462 0 – with blue sleeve

Blood On The Dance Floor/Dangerous (Roger's Dangerous Edit)/Blood On The Dance Floor (Refugee Camp Mix)/(Refugee Camp Edit) (May 1997) 664462 6 – with lime green sleeve

Blood On The Dance Floor (Fire Island Vocal Mix)/(Fire Island Radio Mix)/(TM's Switchblade Mix)/(TM's Switchblade Edit) (May 1997) 664462 8 – with red sleeve

Is It Scary (Eddie's Love Mix)/(Eddie's Rub-A-Dub)/(Eddie's Love Mix Radio Edit) (September 1997) XPR 3168 – promo only with no p/s

Is It Scary (Deep Dish Dark & Scary Remix)/(Deep Dish Double-O-Jazz-Dub)/Deep Dish Dark & Scary Remix Radio Edit) (September 1997) XPR 3195 – promo only with no p/s

Smile/Is It Scary (Deep Dish Dark & Scary Remix)/(Eddi'es Rub-A-Dub Mix)/(Eddie's Love Mix)/Off The Wall (Junior Vasquez Remix) (November 1997) 665130 6 – withdrawn

Off The Wall/Don't Stop 'Til You Get Enough (March 2000) VJAY1 – vinyl junkie limited edition re-issue

Intro/You Rock My World/(Instrumental)/(A Cappella) (October 2001) 672029 2

Shout/Streetwalker/Cry (December 2001) 672182 6

Unbreakable/You Rock My World (Featuring Jay-Z)/Smooth Criminal (The Autopsy Featuring Wix Tang Clan & Mobb Deep) (February 2002) – promo only with no p/s

One More Chance/Billie Jean (November 2003) 674480 8 – picture disc

One More Chance (Brian Rawling Metro Mix)/(Paul Oakenfold Urban Mix)/(Paul Oakenfold Mix)/(Ron G Club Mix)/(Album Version) (December 2003) 674480 6

Cassette Singles

Greatest Original Hits EP: Don't Stop 'Til You Get Enough/She's Out Of My Life/Off The Wall/Rock With You (March 1983) EPC A40 2906

The 12" Tape: Billie Jean/Beat It/Wanna Be Startin' Somethin'/Thriller/P.Y.T. (Pretty Young Thing) (1986) EPC 450127 4

Bad (Dance Extended Mix Including False Fade)/(Dub Version)/(A Capella) (September 1987) 651155 4

Leave Me Alone/Don't Stop 'Til You Get Enough/Human Nature (February 1989) 654672 4

Liberian Girl (Edit)/Girlfriend (July 1989) 654947 4

Black Or White/(Instrumental) (November 1991) 657598 4

Remember The Time/Come Together (February 1992) 657774 4

In The Closet (7" Edit)/(The Mission Radio Edit) (April 1992) 658018 4 – with competition leaflet

Who Is It (Edit)/Rock With You (Masters At Work Remix) (July 1992) 658179 4

Jam (7" Edit)/Beat It (Moby's Sub Mix) (September 1992) 658360 4

Heal The World/She Drives Me Wild (November 1992) 658488 4

Give In To Me/Dirty Diana (February 1993) 659069 4

Will You Be There (Edit)/Girlfriend (June 1993) 659222 4

Gone Too Soon/(Instrumental) (December 1993) 659976 4

Scream (Single Edit)/Childhood (Theme From 'Free Willy 2') (May 1995) 662022 4

You Are Not Alone (Radio Edit)/Scream Louder (Flyte Tyme Mix) (August 1995) 662310 4

Earth Song (Radio Edit)/(Hani's Extended Radio Experience) (November 1995) 662695 4

They Don't Care About Us (LP Edit)/(Love To Infinity's Walk In The Park Radio Mix) (April 1996) 662950 4

Why (Radio Edit)/3T: Tease Me (Single Edit) (August 1996) MJJ 663648 4

Stranger In Moscow (Album Version)/(Tee's Radio Mix) (November 1996) 663787 4

With 3T: I Need You (Album Version)/3T: Brotherhood (November 1996) MJJ 663991 4

Blood On The Dance Floor/(Refugee Camp Edit)/Dangerous (Roger's Dangerous Edit) (April 1997) 664462 4

History (Tony Moran's History Lesson Edit)/(Radio Edit)/Ghosts (Radio Edit) (July 1997) 664796 4

Intro/You Rock My World/(Radio Edit) (October 2001) 672029 4

Cry/Shout/Streetwalker (December 2001) 672182 4

CD Singles

The Way You Make Me Feel (Dance Extended Mix)/(Dub Version)/(A Cappella) (November 1987) 651275 9

Man In The Mirror/(Album Mix)/(Instrumental) (February 1988) 651388 2

Dirty Diana/(Instrumental)/Bad (Dance Extended Mix Includes 'False Fade') (July 1988) 651546 9

Another Part Of Me (Extended Dance Mix)/(Radio Edit)/(Dub Mix)/(A Cappella) (September 1988) 652844 2; 653004 2 – picture disc

Smooth Criminal (Extended Dance Mix)/('Annie' Mix)/(A Cappella) (November 1988) 653026 2

Leave Me Alone/Don't Stop 'Til You Get Enough/Human Nature/Wanna Be Startin' Somethin' (Extended) (February 1989) 654672 2

Solid Gold EP: Billie Jean/Don't Stop 'Til You Get Enough/Wanna Be Startin' Somethin' (May 1989) 655572 3

Liberian Girl (Edit)/Girlfriend/The Lady In My Life/Get On The Floor (July 1989) 654947 2

Black Or White/(Instrumental)/Smooth Criminal (November 1991) 657598 2

Black Or White (Clivilles & Cole House/Club Mix)/(Clivilles & Cole House/Dub Mix)/ Underground Club Mix)/(House With Guitar Radio Mix)/(Tribal Beats) (January 1992) 657731 2

Remember The Time (Original Version)/(Silky Soul 7")/(New Jack Main Mix)/Come Together (February 1992) 657774 2

In The Closet (7" Edit)/(Club Mix)/(Undeground Mix)/(Touch Me Dub)/(KI's 12")/(The Promise) (April 1992) 658018 2

Who Is It (Most Patient Mix)/(IHS Mix)/Don't Stop 'Til You Get Enough (Roger's Underground Club Solution) (July 1992) 658179 5

Jam (7" Edit)/(Roger's Jeep Mix)/(Atlanta Techo Mix)/Wanna Be Startin' Somethin' (Brothers In Rhythm House Mix) (September 1992) 658360 2

Heal The World (7" Edit)/(Album Version)/She Drives Me Wild/Man In The Mirror (November 1992) 658488 5 – some as picture disc

Give In To Me/Dirty Diana/Beat It (February 1993) 659069 2

Will You Be There (Edit)/Man In The Mirror/Girlfriend/Will You Be There (Album Version) (June 1993) 659222 2

Gone Too Soon/Human Nature/She's Out Of My Life/Thriller (December 1993) 659976 2

Scream (Single Edit)/(Def Radio Mix)/(Dave 'Jam' Hall's Urban Remix Edit)/Childhood (Theme from 'Free Willy 2') (May 1995) 662022 2

Scream (Classic Club Mix)/(D.M. R&B Extended Mix)/(Pressurized Dub Pt.1)/(Dave 'Jam' Hall's Extended Urban Mix)/(Naughty Main Mix)/(Single Edit #2) (June 1995) 662022 5

You Are Not Alone (Radio Edit)/(Frankie Knuckles – Franctified Club Mix)/(Frankie Knuckles – Classic Song Version)/(Jon B. Main Mix)/(Jon B. Padappella) (August 1995) 662310 2

You Are Not Alone/(R.Kelly Remix)/Rock With You (Masters At Work Remix)/ (Frankie's Favorite Club Mix) (August 1995) 662310 8

Earth Song (Radio Edit)/(Hani's Club Experience)/DMC Megamix: Billie Jean/Rock With You/Bad/Thriller/Don't Stop 'Til You Get Enough/Black Or White/Scream/Wanna Be Startin' Somethin' (November 1995) 662695 2

Earth Song (Radio Edit)/(Hani's Radio Experience)/Wanna Be Startin' Somethin' (Brothers In Rhythm Mix)/(Tommy D's Main Mix) (December 1995) 662695 5

They Don't Care About Us (LP Edit)/(Love To Infinity's Walk In The Park Mix)/(Love To Infinity's Classic Paradise Mix)/(Love To Infinity's Anthem Of Love Mix)/(Love To Infinity's Hacienda Mix)/(Dallas Austin Main Mix) (April 1996) 662950 2

They Don't Care About Us (Single Edit)/(Track Masters Remix)/(Charles' Full Joint Remix)/Beat It (Moby's Sub Mix) (April 1996) 662950 7

Why (Radio Edit)/3T: Tease Me (Single Edit)/Didn't Mean To Hurt You/What Will It Take (August 1996) MJJ 663648 2

Why (Album Version)/3T: Tease Me (Todd Terry's Tease Club Mix)/(Todd Terry's TNT Tease Dub)/(Acapella) (August 1996) MJJ 663648 5

Stranger In Moscow (Album Version)/(Charles 'The Mixologist' Roane Full Mix w/mute Drop)/(Tee's Light AC Mix)/(Tee's Freeze Radio)/(Tee's In-House Club Mix)/(TNT Frozen Sun Mix-Club) (November 1996) 663787 2

Stranger In Moscow (Album Version)/(Hani's Extended Chill Hop Mix)/(Hani's Num Club Mix)/(Basement Boys Radio Mix)/(Spensane Vocal Remix (R&B))/(12" Dance Club Mix) (November 1996) 663787 5

With 3T: I Need You (Album Version)/(Linslee Campbell Remix)/(Linslee Campbell Breakdown Remix)/3T (Featuring Prince Markie Dee): Brotherhood (Single Edit) (November 1996) MJJ 663991 2

With 3T: I Need You (Christmas Mix)/(Singalong Version)/3T: Anything (Acoustic Version) (November 1996) MJJ 663991 5 – gatefold cartoon sleeve with special Christmas messages

Blood On The Dance Floor/(TM's Switchblade Mix)/(Refugee Camp Mix)/(Fire Island Vocal Mix)/(Fire Island Dub) (April 1997) 664462 2

Blood On The Dance Floor/(TM's Switchblade Edit)/(Fire Island Radio Edit)/Dangerous (Roger's Dangerous Club Mix) (April 1997) 664462 5 – transluscent red disc with black MJ silhouette

History (7" History Lesson Edit)/(Radio Edit)/Ghosts (Radio Edit)/(Mousse T's Club Mix) (July 1997) 664796 2

History (Tony Moran's History Lesson)/(Tony Moran's Historical Dub)/(MARK!'s Vocal Club Mix)/(The Ummah Radio Mix)/(The Ummah Urban Mix) (July 1997) 664796 5

Is It Scary (Radio Edit) (September 1997) SAPMCS 4562 – promo only

Smile (Short Version) (November 1997) SAMPCS 4673 – promo only with no p/s

On The Line/Ghosts (Mousse T's Radio Rock Singalong Remix)/Is It Scary (DJ Greek's Scary Mix) (December 1997) EPC 665268 2 – issued as part of Ghosts Box Set only

Intro/You Rock My World/(Radio Edit)/(Instrumental)/(A Cappella) (October 2001) 672029 2

Cry/Shout/Streetwalker/Cry (Short Film) (December 2001) 672182 2

One More Chance/(Paul Oakenfold Urban Mix) (November 2003) 674480 2

One More Chance/(Paul Oakenfold Mix)/(Brian Rawling Metro Mix)/(Ron G Club Mix) (November 2003) 674480 5

The Girl Is Mine 2008/(Club Mix)/The Girl Is Mine (Original Demo Recording) (February 2008) 88697 22620 2

Wanna Be Startin' Somethin' 2008 (Radio Edit)/(Album Version) (March 2008) – promo only with no p/s

Jason Nevins King Of Pop Megamixes (Extended Mix)/(Radio Edit) (August 2008) – promo only with no p/s; featured on most editions of KING OF POP as 'Thriller Megamix'

DualDisc Video Singles

Thriller (US Single Edit)/(Album Version)/(Video) (February 2006) 82876725202 – with free limited edition Visionary box.

Don't Stop 'Til You Get Enough (7" Single Edit)/(Original 12" Edit)/(Video) (February 2006) 82876725112

Rock With You/(Masters At Work Remix)/(Video) (February 2006) 82876725132

Billie Jean/(Original 12" Edit)/(Video) (March 2006) 82876725172

Beat It/(Moby's Sub Mix)/(Video) (March 2006) 82876725182

Bad/(Extended Dance Mix Incl. False Fade)/(Video) (March 2006) 82876725242

The Way You Make Me Feel (7" Edit)/(Extended Dance Mix)/(Video) (March 2006) 82876725252

Dirty Diana/(Instrumental)/(Video) (April 2006) 82876725272

Smooth Criminal/(Extended Dance Mix)/(Video) (April 2006) 82876725292

Leave Me Alone/Another Part Of Me (Extended Dance Mix)/Leave Me Alone (Video) (April 2006) 82876725302

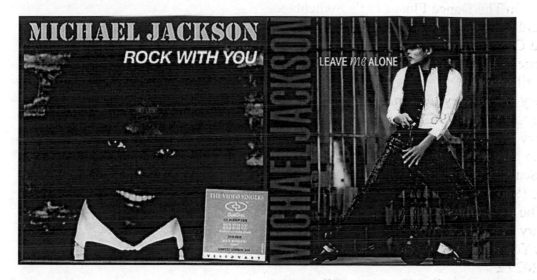

Black Or White (7" Edit)/(C&C House With Guitar Radio Mix)/(Video) (April 2006) 82876773302

Remember The Time/(New Jack Jazz Mix)/(Video) (May 2006) 82876773322

In The Closet (7" Edit)/(Club Mix)/(Video) (May 2006) 82876773342

Jam (7" Edit)/(Silky 12" Mix)/(Video) (May 2006) 82876773362

Heal The World (7" Edit)/Will You Be There/Heal The World (Video) (May 2006) 82876773382

You Are Not Alone (Radio Edit)/(Classic Club Mix)/(Video) (May 2006) 82876773402

Earth Song (Radio Edit)/(Hani's Extended Radio Experience)/(Video) (June 2006) 82876773422

They Don't Care About Us (LP Edit)/(Love To Infinity's Walk In The Park Mix)/(Video/Brazil Version) (June 2006) 82876773442

Stranger In Moscow (Album Version)/(Tee's In-House Club Mix)/(Video) (June 2006) 82876773462

Blood On The Dance Floor (Single Edit)/(Fire Island Vocal Mix)/(Video) (June 2006) 82876773482

9 780755 204786